W9-BEE-437

COMPARATIVE POLITICS 94/95

Twelfth Edition

Editor

Christian Søe
California State University, Long Beach

Christian Søe was born in Denmark, studied in Canada and the United States, and received his doctoral degree in political science from the Free University in Berlin. He is a political science professor at California State University, Long Beach. Dr. Søe teaches a wide range of courses in comparative politics and contemporary political theory, and actively participates in professional symposiums in the United States and abroad. His research deals primarily with developments in contemporary German politics, and he has been a regular observer of elections and party politics in that country. At present Dr. Søe is observing the shifts in the balance of power within the German party system, with particular attention to its implications for the formation of new government coalitions and changes in policy directions.

His most recent publications are chapters on the Free Democratic Party in *The New Germany Votes,* and on the Danish-German relationship in *The Germans and Their Neighbors.* He served as co-editor of the latter book, an eighteen-country study of the German question from different external perspectives.

Annual Editions
A Library of Information from the Public Press

Cover illustration by Mike Eagle

The Dushkin Publishing Group, Inc.
Sluice Dock, Guilford, Connecticut 06437

This map has been developed to give you a graphic picture of where the countries of the world are located, the relationship they have with their region and neighbors, and their positions relative to the superpowers and power blocs. We have focused on certain areas to more clearly illustrate these crowded regions.

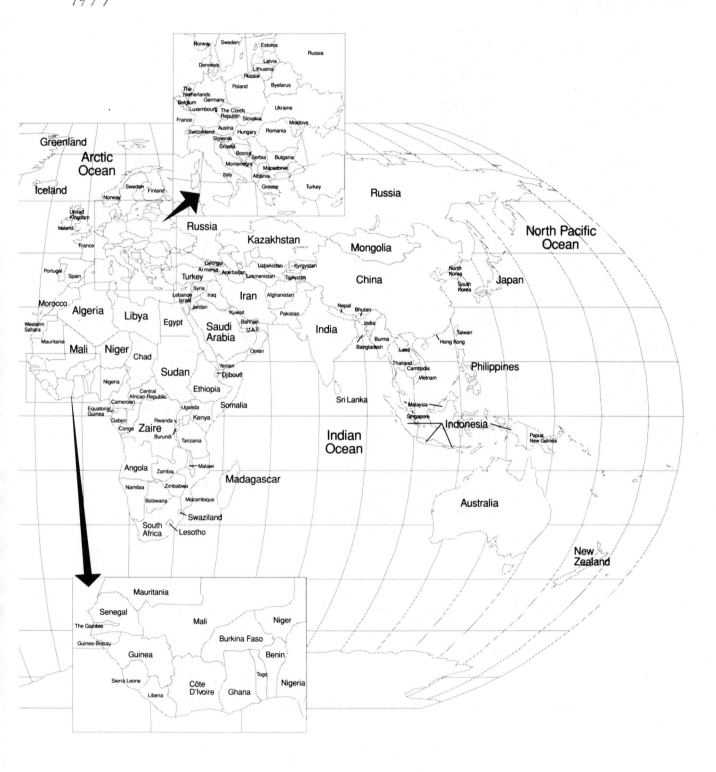

The Annual Editions Series

Annual Editions is a series of over 60 volumes designed to provide the reader with convenient, low-cost access to a wide range of current, carefully selected articles from some of the most important magazines, newspapers, and journals published today. Annual Editions are updated on an annual basis through a continuous monitoring of over 300 periodical sources. All Annual Editions have a number of features designed to make them particularly useful, including topic guides, annotated tables of contents, unit overviews, and indexes. For the teacher using Annual Editions in the classroom, an Instructor's Resource Guide with test questions is available for each volume.

VOLUMES AVAILABLE

Africa
Aging
American Foreign Policy
American Government
American History, Pre-Civil War
American History, Post-Civil War
Anthropology
Biology
Business Ethics
Canadian Politics
Child Growth and Development
China
Comparative Politics
Computers in Education
Computers in Business
Computers in Society
Criminal Justice
Drugs, Society, and Behavior
Dying, Death, and Bereavement
Early Childhood Education
Economics
Educating Exceptional Children
Education
Educational Psychology
Environment
Geography
Global Issues
Health
Human Development
Human Resources
Human Sexuality
India and South Asia
International Business
Japan and the Pacific Rim

Latin America
Life Management
Macroeconomics
Management
Marketing
Marriage and Family
Mass Media
Microeconomics
Middle East and the Islamic World
Money and Banking
Multicultural Education
Nutrition
Personal Growth and Behavior
Physical Anthropology
Psychology
Public Administration
Race and Ethnic Relations
Russia, Eurasia, and Central/Eastern Europe
Social Problems
Sociology
State and Local Government
Third World
Urban Society
Violence and Terrorism
Western Civilization, Pre-Reformation
Western Civilization, Post-Reformation
Western Europe
World History, Pre-Modern
World History, Modern
World Politics

Library of Congress Cataloging in Publication Data
Main entry under title: Annual Editions: Comparative Politics. 1994/95.
    1. World politics—Periodicals. 2. Politics, Practical—Periodicals. I. Søe, Christian, comp.
II. Title: Comparative Politics.
ISBN 1-56134-267-X   909′.05   83-647654

© 1994 by The Dushkin Publishing Group, Inc., Guilford, CT 06437

Twelfth Edition

Printed in the United States of America

Editors/ Advisory Board

EDITOR

Christian Søe
California State University
Long Beach

ADVISORY BOARD

Mark Bartholomew
University of Maine
Farmington

Louis Cantori
University of Maryland
Baltimore

Leonard Cardenas
Southwest Texas State University

Parris Chang
Pennsylvania State University
University Park

Maureen A. Covell
Simon Frasier University

Jane Curry
Santa Clara University

Robert L. Delorme
California State University
Long Beach

John Echeverri-Gent
University of Virginia

Richard S. Flickinger
Wittenberg University

E. Gene Frankland
Ball State University

Ronald Inglehart
University of Michigan

Karl H. Kahrs
California State University
Fullerton

Aline Kuntz
University of New Hampshire

Frank A. Kunz
McGill University

Gregory Mahler
University of Mississippi

Anthony M. Messina
Tufts University

Joyce Marie Mushaben
University of Missouri
St. Louis

Helen Purkitt
United States Naval Academy

Martin Slann
Clemson University

Frederick Swan
Livingstone College

Joel D. Wolfe
University of Cincinnati

Rodger Yeager
West Virginia University

Eleanor E. Zeff
Drake University

Charles Ziegler
University of Louisville

STAFF

To the Reader

In publishing ANNUAL EDITIONS we recognize the enormous role played by the magazines, newspapers, and journals of the *public press* in providing current, first-rate educational information in a broad spectrum of interest areas. Within the articles, the best scientists, practitioners, researchers, and commentators draw issues into new perspective as accepted theories and viewpoints are called into account by new events, recent discoveries change old facts, and fresh debate breaks out over important controversies. Many of the articles resulting from this enormous editorial effort are appropriate for students, researchers, and professionals seeking accurate, current material to help bridge the gap between principles and theories and the real world. These articles, however, become more useful for study when those of lasting value are carefully *collected, organized, indexed,* and *reproduced* in a *low-cost format,* which provides easy and permanent access when the material is needed. That is the role played by *Annual Editions.* Under the direction of each volume's *Editor,* who is an expert in the subject area, and with the guidance of an *Advisory Board,* we seek each year to provide in each *ANNUAL EDITION* a current, well-balanced, carefully selected collection of the best of the public press for your study and enjoyment. We think you'll find this volume useful, and we hope you'll take a moment to let us know what you think.

This collection of readings brings together articles that will help you understand the governments and politics of a number of foreign countries from a comparative perspective. You will soon discover that such a study not only opens up a fascinating world beyond our borders, but also leads to greater insights into the American political process.

The articles in unit one cover Great Britain, Germany, France, Italy, and Japan in a serial manner. Each of these modern societies has developed its own political framework and agenda, and each has sought to find its own appropriate dynamic balance of continuity and change. Nevertheless, as the readings of unit two show, it is possible to point to some common denominators and make useful cross-national comparisons among these and other representative democracies. Unit three goes one step further by discussing the impact of two major changes that are rapidly transforming the political map of Europe—the irregular but impressive growth of the European Union (EU), and the political and economic reconstruction of Central and Eastern Europe after the collapse of the Communist regimes in that part of the world. The continuing political importance of Europe has been underscored by these two developments.

Unit four looks at developments in some of the so-called Third World countries, with articles on Mexico, sub-Saharan Africa, South Africa, China, and India. A careful reader will come away with a better understanding of the diversity of social and political conditions in these countries. Additional readings cover the newly industrialized countries of Eastern and Southeastern Asia—the so-called "tigers" or "dragons," which have managed to generate a self-sustaining process of industrial modernization.

Unit five considers three major trends in contemporary politics from a comparative perspective. The "third wave" of democratization may already have crested, but it is nevertheless important in having changed the politics of many countries. The widespread shifts toward a greater reliance on markets to perform the task of economic allocation, in place of centralized planning and heavy governmental regulation, is also of great significance. The move is frequently toward a "mixed economy," and it should not be misunderstood for a victory of doctrinaire laissez-faire. Finally, the surge of what has been called "identity politics," with particular emphasis on exclusive cultural or ethnic group assertion, is a development that bears careful watching.

There has rarely been so interesting and important a time for the study of comparative politics as now. We can already see that the political earthquake of 1989–1991 has altered the political landscape with consequences that will be felt for many years to come. The aftershocks continue to remind us that we are unlikely to ever experience a condition of political equilibrium. But even in a time of political transformation, there are important patterns of continuity as well. We must be careful to look for both as we seek to gain a comparative understanding of the politics of other countries and peoples as well as of our own condition.

This is the twelfth edition of *Annual Editions: Comparative Politics* and it is a sobering reminder that the first edition appeared just as the Brezhnev era had come to a close in what was then the Soviet Union. Over the years, the new editions have tried to reflect the developments that eventually brought about the post–cold war world of today. In a similar way, the present edition tries to present information and analysis that will be useful in understanding today's political world and its importance in shaping tomorrow's developments.

A special word of thanks goes to my past and present students at Long Beach State, who keep me posted on the concerns and needs that this anthology must address. Susan B. Mason, who received her master's degree in political science at my university, continues to be a superb research assistant. Special recognition also goes to another graduate of our M.A. program, Deborah Lancaster, as well as to two of our current graduate students, Linda Wohlman and Raid Khoury. They have all worked hard and reliably in helping me to locate suitable materials for this year's edition.

I am very grateful to members of the advisory board and The Dushkin Publishing Group as well as to many readers who have made useful comments on past selections and suggested new ones. I ask you all to help me improve future editions by keeping me informed of your reactions and suggestions for change. Please complete and return the article rating form in the back of the book.

Christian Søe
Editor

Contents

Unit 1

Pluralist Democracies: Country Overviews

Twenty-two selections examine the current state of
politics in Western Europe, Great Britain, Germany,
France, Italy, and Japan.

The concepts in bold italics are developed in the article. For further expansion please refer to the Topic Guide and the Index.

The concepts in bold italics are developed in the article. For further expansion please refer to the Topic Guide and the Index.

Unit 2

Modern Pluralist Democracies: Factors in the Political Process

Eleven selections examine the functioning of Western European democracies with regard to political ideas and participation, ethnic politics, the role of women in politics, and the institutional framework of representative government.

Unit 3

Europe—West, Center, and East: The Politics of Integration, Transformation, and Disintegration

Twelve selections examine the European continent: the European Community, Western European society, post-communist Central and Eastern Europe, and Russia and the other post-Soviet Republics.

Unit 4

The Third World: Diversity in Development

Ten selections review Third World economic and political development in Latin America, Africa, China, India, and newly industrialized countries.

The concepts in bold italics are developed in the article. For further expansion please refer to the Topic Guide and the Index.

Unit 5

Comparative Politics: Some Major Trends, Issues, and Prospects

Six selections discuss the rise of democracy, how capitalism impacts on political development, and the political assertion of group identity in contemporary politics.

The concepts in bold italics are developed in the article. For further expansion please refer to the Topic Guide and the Index.

Topic Guide

This topic guide suggests how the selections in this book relate to topics of traditional concern to students and professionals involved with the study of comparative politics. It is useful for locating articles that relate to each other for reading and research. The guide is arranged alphabetically according to topic. Articles may, of course, treat topics that do not appear in the topic guide. In turn, entries in the topic guide do not necessarily constitute a comprehensive listing of all the contents of each selection.

TOPIC AREA	TREATED IN:	TOPIC AREA	TREATED IN:
Africa	49. Africa: Falling Off the Map? 50. South African Parliament Adopts New Constitution	**Economics and Politics (cont.)**	36. Goodbye to a United Europe? 39. Europe's Recession Prompts New Look at Welfare Costs 40. And Now the Hard Part 43. Hangover 45. Road to Ruin 47. Mexico's Efforts at 'Salinastroika' 49. Africa: Falling Off the Map? 51. In China, Communist Ideology Is Dead 52. Long March from Mao 53. India: Charting a New Course? 54. Miracles Beyond the Free Market 55. Visible Hand 58. Capitalism and Democracy 61. Jihad vs. McWorld
British Government and Politics	1. Europeans Fear 2. Has the Sun Set on Britain? 3. Britain's Constitutional Question 4. Should John Major Go? 5. Parties in Question 6. Ireland Undivided? 30. Parliament and Congress 31. Electoral Reform 32. Presidents and Prime Ministers 35. European Union: Now What? 36. Goodbye to a United Europe? 38. Diagnosis: Healthier in Europe 39. Europe's Recession Prompts New Look at Welfare Costs 56. New Era in Democracy		
		Elections	1. Europeans Fear 5. Parties in Question 10. Germans Turn Their Backs on Politics 11. Long Year in German Politics 14. France: The Right Triumphs 17. Political Renewal Italian Style 19. Political Revenge in Italy 20. Old Sake in New Bottles 22. Japan: The End of One-Party Dominance 29. What Democracy Is . . . and Is Not 31. Electoral Reform 44. Russian Elections
Central and Eastern Europe	33. As the World Turns Democratic 40. And Now the Hard Part 56. A New Era in Democracy 57. 'Missing Middle' of Democracy 59. New Tribalism 60. Debate on Cultural Conflicts		
Chinese Government and Politics	51. In China, Communist Ideology Is Dead 52. Long March from Mao 56. New Era in Democracy	**Ethnicity and Politics**	1. Europeans Fear 7. Invisible Wall 8. Dark Winter of Helmut Kohl 13. French Funk 16. Thoughts on the French Nation Today 25. Western Europe Is Ending Its Welcome to Immigrants 41. Nationalism Redux 42. Looking at the Past 43. Hangover 53. India: Charting a New Course? 56. New Era in Democracy 59. New Tribalism 61. Jihad vs. McWorld
Conservative Party in Britain	4. Should John Major Go? 5. Parties in Question 31. Electoral Reform		
Democracy	1. Europeans Fear 11. Long Year in German Politics 14. France: The Right Triumphs 17. Political Renewal Italian Style 20. Old Sake in New Bottles 23. End of Politics 24. Identity Crisis on the Left 26. Frenchwomen Say It's Time to Be 'a Bit Utopian' 27. Women, Power, and Politics: The Norwegian Experience 28. We the Peoples 29. What Democracy Is . . . and Is Not 31. Electoral Reform 33. As the World Turns Democratic 34. Maths of Post-Maastricht Europe 36. Goodbye to a United Europe? 43. Hangover 44. Russian Elections 56. New Era in Democracy 57. 'Missing Middle' of Democracy 58. Capitalism and Democracy 61. Jihad vs. McWorld	**European Community**	See European Union
		European Union	1. Europeans Fear 4. Should John Major Go? 8. Dark Winter of Helmut Kohl 13. French Funk 16. Thoughts on the French Nation Today 34. Maths of Post-Maastricht Europe 35. European Union: Now What? 36. Goodbye to a United Europe? 38. Diagnosis: Healthier in Europe 39. Europe's Recession Prompts New Look at Welfare Costs
Eastern Europe	See Central and Eastern Europe		
Economics and Politics	1. Europeans Fear 2. Has the Sun Set on Britain? 4. Should John Major Go? 5. Parties in Question 7. Invisible Wall 8. Dark Winter of Helmut Kohl 13. French Funk 22. Japan: The End of One-Party Dominance 25. Western Europe Is Ending Its Welcome to Immigrants 35. European Union: Now What?	**Federal and Unitary Systems**	3. Britain's Constitutional Question 6. Ireland Undivided? 12. "Old" and the "New" Federalism in Germany 13. French Funk 16. Thoughts on the French Nation Today 17. Political Renewal Italian Style 33. As the World Turns Democratic 34. Maths of Post-Maastricht Europe 35. European Union: Now What? 36. Goodbye to a United Europe? 42. Looking at the Past 53. India: Charting a New Course?

TOPIC AREA	TREATED IN:	TOPIC AREA	TREATED IN:
French Government and Politics	1. Europeans Fear 13. French Funk 14. France: The Right Triumphs 15. Mr. French 16. Thoughts on the French Nation Today 23. End of Politics 24. Identity Crisis on the Left 25. Western Europe Is Ending Its Welcome to Immigrants 26. Frenchwomen Say It's Time to Be 'a Bit Utopian' 31. Electoral Reform 32. Presidents and Prime Ministers 34. Maths of Post-Maastricht Europe 35. European Union: Now What? 36. Goodbye to a United Europe? 38. Diagnosis: Healthier in Europe 39. Europe's Recession Prompts a New Look at Welfare Costs	**Mexican Government and Politics** **Parliamentary Politics and Parliamentary Systems**	47. Mexico's Efforts at 'Salinastroika' 48. Revolution Continues 3. Britain's Constitutional Question 4. Should John Major Go? 17. Political Renewal Italian Style 18. Godmother 22. Japan: The End of One-Party Dominance 26. Frenchwomen Say It's Time to Be 'a Bit Utopian' 27. Women, Power, and Politics: The Norwegian Experience 28. We the Peoples: A Checklist for New Constitution Writers 29. What Democracy Is . . . and Is Not 30. Parliament and Congress 32. Presidents and Prime Ministers 34. Maths of Post-Maastricht Europe 36. Goodbye to a United Europe? 43. Hangover 45. Road to Ruin
German Government and Politics	1. Europeans Fear 7. Invisible Wall 8. Dark Winter of Helmut Kohl 10. Germans Turn Their Backs on Politics 11. Long Year in German Politics 12. "Old" and the "New" Federalism in Germany 24. Identity Crisis on the Left 25. Western Europe Is Ending Its Welcome to Immigrants 31. Electoral Reform 34. Maths of Post-Maastricht Europe 35. European Union: Now What? 36. Goodbye to a United Europe? 38. Diagnosis: Healthier in Europe 39. Europe's Recession Prompts New Look at Welfare Costs	**Presidential Politics and Presidential Systems**	13. French Funk 14. France: The Right Triumphs 15. Mr. French 28. We the Peoples 29. What Democracy Is . . . and Is Not 30. Parliament and Congress 32. Presidents and Prime Ministers 43. Hangover 44. Russian Elections 45. Road to Ruin 47. Mexico's Efforts at 'Salinastroika' 48. Revolution Continues
India's Government and Politics	53. India: Charting a New Course? 56. New Era in Democracy 59. New Tribalism 60. Debate on Cultural Conflicts	**Russia and Other Post-Soviet Republics**	42. Looking at the Past 43. Hangover 44. Russian Elections 45. Road to Ruin 59. New Tribalism
Italy's Government and Politics	1. Europeans Fear 17. Political Renewal Italian Style 18. Godmother 19. Political Revenge in Italy 35. European Union: Now What?	**Social Democrats and Democratic Socialists**	1. Europeans Fear 5. Parties in Question 8. Dark Winter of Helmut Kohl 11. Long Year in German Politics 13. French Funk 14. France: The Right Triumphs 16. Thoughts on the French Nation Today 17. Politial Renewal Italian Style 18. Godmother 19. Political Revenge in Italy 20. Old Sake in New Bottles 22. Japan: The End of One-Party Dominance 23. End of Politics 24. Identity Crisis on the Left 27. Women, Power, and Politics: The Norwegian Experience 58. Capitalism and Democracy
Japan's Government and Politics	20. Old Sake in New Bottles 21. Prince of Politics Ascends 22. Japan: The End of One-Party Dominance		
Less Developed Countries (LDCs)	46. Let's Abolish the Third World 47. Mexico's Efforts at 'Salinastroika' 48. Revolution Continues 49. Africa: Falling Off the Map? 50. South African Parliament Adopts New Constitution 51. In China, Communist Ideology Is Dead 52. Long March from Mao 53. India: Charting a New Course? 54. Miracles Beyond the Free Market 55. Invisible Hand 56. New Era in Democracy 59. New Tribalism 60. Debate on Cultural Conflicts 61. Jihad vs. McWorld	**Women in Politics**	7. Invisible Wall 26. Frenchwomen Say It's Time to Be 'a Bit Utopian' 27. Women, Power, and Politics: The Norwegian Experience

Pluralist Democracies: Country Overviews

Great Britain, Germany, France, and Italy rank among the most prominent industrial societies in Western Europe. Although their modern political histories vary considerably, they have all become pluralist democracies with diversified and active citizenries, well-developed and competitive party systems, and representative forms of governments. Japan is less pluralist in sociocultural terms, but it occupies a similar position of primacy among the few industrial democracies in Asia. A study of comparative government can usefully begin by examining the politics of these countries more closely through the articles in this and the following two units.

The articles in the first unit cover the political systems of Britain, France, Germany, Italy, and Japan. Each of these modern societies has developed its own set of governmental institutions, defined its own political agenda and found its own dynamic balance of continuity and change. Nevertheless, as later readings will show more fully, it is possible to find some common denominators and make useful cross-national comparisons among these and other representative democracies. Moreover, the West European countries all show the impact of two major developments that are transforming the political map of the continent: (1) the growth of the European Community (EC), which in November 1993 became the European Union (EU), and (2) the efforts of socioeconomic and political reconstruction in the countries of Central and Eastern Europe after their recent exit from communist rule.

The continuing political importance of Europe has been underscored by both of these developments. The integration of the European Community, which led to the European Union, has been a process of several decades, but it accelerated markedly in the last half of the 1980s as a result of the passage and stepwise implementation of the Single European Act, which set as a goal the completion of a free market among the twelve EC-member countries by the end of 1992. The Maastricht Treaty of 1991 outlined a further advance toward supranational integration by setting up the goal of achieving a common European monetary system and foreign policy toward the end of the decade.

The first article gives a country-by-country overview of the political developments in Western Europe during 1992. It reports that the "Europhoria," which a few years ago greeted the end of the cold war and the seemingly inexorable onset of European unification, has given way to a new malaise in much of the Continent. The revival of "Europessimism" has been fed by a combination of economic setbacks, sociocultural tensions, political scandals, and a revival of right-wing populist parties and movements. While each country has its own peculiar mix of such problems, the article also points to a common pattern beneath the differences.

Great Britain has long been regarded as a model of parliamentary government and majoritarian party politics. In the 1960s and 1970s, however, the country became better known for its chronic governing problems. Serious observers spoke about the British sickness or "Englanditis," a condition characterized by such problems as economic stagnation, social malaise, political polarization, and a general incapacity of the elected government to deal effectively with such a situation of relative deterioration.

As if to defy such pessimistic analyses, if only temporarily, Britain by the mid-1980s began to pull far ahead of other West European countries in its annual economic growth. This apparent economic turnabout could be linked in part to the policies of Prime Minister Margaret Thatcher, who came to power in May of 1979 and introduced a drastic change in economic and social direction for the country. She portrayed herself as a conviction politician, determined to introduce a strong dose of economic discipline by encouraging private enterprise and reducing the role of government, in marked contrast to what she dismissed as the consensus politics of her Labour and Conservative predecessors. Her radical rhetoric and somewhat less drastic policy changes spawned yet another debate about what came to be called the Thatcher Revolution and its social and political consequences.

The concern about ungovernability, which had dominated earlier discussions about British politics, has not ceased, but it has broadened to include questions about the consequences of Thatcher's economic and social policies. During the last decade, the British debate also extended to some new concerns about the government's efforts to tighten central controls over education at all levels, its introduction of cost controls into the popular National Health Service, its privatization of electricity and water industries as well as its inroads upon what had long been considered established rights in such areas as local government powers and civil liberties.

For the mass electorate, however, nothing seems to have been so upsetting as the introduction of the community charge, or poll tax, a tax on each adult resident that would replace the local property tax or rates as a means of financing local public services. Although the poll tax was very unpopular, Thatcher resisted all pressure to abandon the project before its full national implementation in early 1990. Not only did such a tax appear inequitable or regressive, as compared to one based on property values, it also turned out to be set much higher by local governments than the national government originally had estimated. The politically disastrous result was that the revenue measure was anything but neutral in its impact. It created an unexpectedly large proportion of immediate losers, that is, people who had to pay considerably more in local taxes than previously, while the immediate winners were people who had previously paid high property taxes. Not surprisingly, the national and local governments disagreed about who was responsible for the high poll tax bills, but the voters seemed to have little difficulty in assigning blame to Margaret Thatcher and the Conservative Party as originators of the unpopular reform. Many voters were up in arms, and some observers correctly anticipated that the tax rebellion would undermine Thatcher's position in her own party and become her political Waterloo.

John Major, who was chosen by his fellow Conservative Members of Parliament to be Thatcher's successor as prime minister and leader of the Conservative Party, had long been regarded as one of her closest cabinet supporters. He was thought to support her tough economic strategy, which she often described as dry, but he preferred a more compassionate or wet social policy without indulging in the Tory tradition of welfare paternalism against which Margaret Thatcher had also railed. Not surprisingly, he made early plans for abandoning the hated poll tax. His undramatic governing style was far less confrontational than that of his predecessor, and some nostalgic critics were quick to call him dull. In the Gulf War of 1991, Major continued Thatcher's policy of giving strong British support for firm and ultimately military measures against the government of Iraq, which had invaded and occupied oil-rich Kuwait. Unlike his predecessor after the Falkland Battle, however, he did not follow up on a quick and popular military victory by calling for general elections.

By the time of Thatcher's resignation, Labour appeared to be in a relatively good position to capitalize on the growing disenchantment with the Conservative government. The big political question had become whether Prime Minister Major could recapture some of the lost ground. Under its leader, Neil Kinnock, Labour had begun to move back toward its traditional center-left position, presenting itself as a politically moderate and socially caring reform party. Labour had a leading position in some opinion polls, and it won some impressive victories in by-elections to the House of Commons. In the shadow of the Gulf War, Labour was overtaken by the Conservatives in the polls, but its position improved again a few months later.

As the main opposition party, however, Labour was now troubled by a new version of the Social Democratic and Liberal alternatives that had fragmented the non-Conservative camp in the elections of 1983 and 1987. The two smaller parties, which had operated as an electoral coalition or "Alliance" in those years, had drawn the conclusion that their organizational separation was a hindrance to the political breakthrough they hoped for. After the defeat of 1987, they joined together as the Social and Liberal Democrats (SLD) but soon became known simply as Liberal Democrats. Under the leadership of Paddy Ashdown, they attempted to overcome the electoral system's bias against third parties by promoting themselves as a reasonable centrist alternative to the Conservatives on the right and the Labour Party on the left. Their strategic goal was to win the balance of power in a tightly fought election and then, as parliamentary majority-makers, enter a government coalition with one of the two big parties. One of their main demands would then be that the existing winner-takes-all, or plurality electoral system, based on single-member districts, be replaced by some form of proportional representation (PR) in multimember districts. Such a system, which is used widely in Western Europe, would almost surely guarantee the Liberal Democrats not only a relatively solid base in the House of Commons but also a pivotal role in a future process of coalition politics in Britain. Given their considerable electoral support, the Liberal Democrats would then enjoy a position comparable to or even better than that of their counterparts in Germany, the Free Democrats (FDP), which have been a junior member of governments in Bonn for decades.

The rise of this centrist "third force" in British electoral politics during the 1980s had been made possible by a temporary leftward trend of Labour and the rightward movement of the Conservatives. The challenge from the middle had the predictable result of the two main parties seeking to "recenter" themselves, as became evident in the general election called by Prime Minister Major for April 9, 1992. The timing seemed highly unattractive for the governing party, for Britain was still suffering from its worst recession in years. Normally, a British government chooses not to stay in office for a full five-year term. Instead, it prefers to dissolve the House of Commons at an earlier and politically convenient time. It will procrastinate, however, when the electoral outlook appears to be dismal. By the spring of 1992 there was hardly any time left for further delay, since an election

had to come before the end of June under Britain's five-year limit. The polls did not look good for the Conservatives, and many observers suggested the likelihood of either a slim Labour victory or, as seemed far more likely, a "hung" Parliament, in which no party would end up with a working majority. The latter result would have led either to a minority government, which could be expected to solve the impasse by calling an early new election, or a coalition government including the Liberal Democrats as the majority-making junior partner.

The outcome of the 1992 general election confounded many observers who had expected a change in government. Instead, the Conservatives were enabled to continue into an unprecedented fourth consecutive term of office. Despite the recession, they garnered the same overall percentage of the vote (about 43 percent) as in 1987, while Labour increased its total share only slightly, from 32 to 35 percent. The Liberal Democrats received only 18 percent, about 6 percent less than the share the Alliance had won in its two unsuccessful attempts to "break the mold" of the party system in 1983 and 1987. In the House of Commons, the electoral system's bias in favor of the front-runners showed up once again. The Conservatives lost 36 seats but ended up with 336 of the 651 members—a small but sufficient working majority, unless a major issue should fragment the party. Labour increased its number of seats from 229 to 271—a net gain of 42, but far short of an opportunity to threaten the majority party. The Liberal Democrats ended up with 20 seats, down from 22. Additional parliamentary seats went to representatives of the small regional parties from Northern Ireland, Scotland, and Wales.

In the aftermath of the election, John Major has run into considerable difficulties with a wing of his own party that follows Thatcher in opposing his European policy. It was only by threatening to dissolve Parliament and call a new election that Major brought the dissidents into line during a crucial vote on the Maastricht Treaty in the summer of 1993. The Labour Party has elected a new leader, John Smith, but it is also torn by factional disputes. Here the major ideological and strategic cleavage runs between traditional socialists and more pragmatic reformers or modernizers, who wish to continue the centrist policies of Kinnock and Smith.

Germany was united in 1990, when the eastern German Democratic Republic, or GDR, was merged into the western Federal Republic of Germany. The two German states had been established in 1949, four years after the total defeat of the German Reich in World War II. During the next 40 years, rival elites subscribed to the conflicting ideologies and interests of East and West in the cold war. East Germany comprised the territory of the former Soviet Occupation Zone of Germany, where the Communists exercised a power monopoly and established an economy based on central planning. In contrast, West Germany, which emerged from the former American, British, and French zones of postwar occupation, developed a pluralist democracy and a flourishing market economy. When the two states were getting ready to celebrate their fortieth anniversaries in 1989, no leading politician was on record as having foreseen that the German division would come to end during the course of the following year.

Mass demonstrations in several East German cities and the westward flight of thousands of citizens brought the GDR government to make an increasing number of concessions in late 1989 and early 1990. The Berlin Wall ceased to be a hermetical seal after November 9, 1989, when East Germans began to stream over into West Berlin. Collectors and entrepreneurs soon broke pieces from the Wall to keep or sell as souvenirs, before public workers set about to remove the rest of this symbol of the cold war and Germany's division. Under new leadership, the ruling Communists of East Germany introduced a form of power sharing with noncommunist groups and parties. It was agreed to seek democratic legitimation through a free election in March 1990, also in the hope of reducing the westward flight of thousands of East Germans with its devastating consequences for the economy.

The East German Communists slowly abandoned their claim to an exclusive control of power and positions, but by the time of the March 1990 election it was clear even to them that the pressure for national unification could no longer be stemmed. The issue was no longer whether the two German states would be joined together, but how and when. These questions were settled when an alliance of Christian Democrats, largely identified with and supported by Chancellor Helmut Kohl's party in West Germany, won a surprisingly decisive victory with 48 percent of the vote throughout East Germany. It advocated a short, quick route to unification, beginning with an early monetary union in the summer and a political union by the fall of 1990. This also meant that the new noncommunist government in East Germany, headed by Lothar de Maiziere of the Christian Democratic Union (CDU), followed the short route to merger with the Federal Republic under Article 23 of the West German Basic Law. The Social Democrats (SPD) won only 22 percent of the East German vote in March 1990. That amounted to a defeat for its alternative strategy for unification that would have involved the protracted negotiation of a new German constitution, as envisaged by Article 146 of the Basic Law.

During the summer and fall of 1990, the governments of the two German states and the four former occupying powers completed their so-called two-plus-four negotiations that resulted in mutual agreement on the German unification process. A monetary union in July was followed by a political merger in October 1990. In advance of unification, Bonn was able to negotiate an agreement with Moscow in which the latter accepted the gradual withdrawal of Soviet troops from eastern Germany and the membership of the larger, united Germany in NATO, in return for considerable German economic support for the Soviet Union. The result was a major shift in both the domestic and international balance of power.

The election results of 1990 raised but did not answer the question of how national unification will eventually reshape the German party system. One certainty is that the special electoral arrangement, intended to protect new political groupings in eastern Germany, will have been lifted by the next Bundestag election—October 1994. Anyone interested in political development will want to keep a close eye on the difficult transition period in Germany. State and local elections suggest that the Greens have become stronger and that they will return as a viable political force to the Bundestag in 1994. But there is also a possibility that a far-right party, which uses xenophobic slogans against foreign immigrants and asylum-seekers, could play the role of a spoiler or even get enough votes to enter the Bundestag for the first time since 1949. One such party, the German People's Union (DVU). was elected to the state parliaments in Bremen and Schleswig-Holstein in the fall of 1991 and the spring of 1992 respectively. Another ultraright party, the Republikaner, won representation in West Berlin in 1989 and entered the state parliament of Baden-Wüerttemberg by winning over 10 percent of the vote in April 1992. It has also been strong in some local elections since then.

The articles on Germany include economic and political balance sheets on the challenges and accomplishments of national unification. Of particular interest for students of political institutions is the extension of the West German federal system to the new states in the East, as Arthur Gunlicks points out in his insightful analysis. However, the task of postcommunist recon-struction in Germany goes far beyond the transfer of institutions and capital from West to East. The transition to pluralist democracy and a market economy in eastern Germany also requires a social and cultural transformation, as several authors suggest. Moreover, there are new problems facing the larger and more powerful Germany on the international scene, as it seeks to deal with a mixture of expectations and anxieties that it arouses abroad. No wonder some western Germans have developed a kind of nostalgia for the less complicated and demanding existence before reunification!

France must also cope with major political challenges within a rapidly changing Europe. The bicentennial of the French Revolution was duly celebrated in 1989. It served as an occasion for public ceremonies and a revival of historical-political debates about the costs and benefits of that great exercise in the radical transformation of a society. Ironically, however, for some years before there had been mounting evidence that the sharp ideological cleavages, which marked French politics for so much of the past two centuries, were losing significance. Instead, there was emerging a more pragmatic, pluralist form of accommodation in French public life.

To be sure, this deradicalization and depolarization of political discourse is by no means complete in France. If the Communists have become weakened and ideologically confused, Le Pen's National Front on the extreme right has had some populist success with a xenophobic rhetoric directed primarily against the many residents of Arab origins in the country. The apparent electoral appeal of his invective has led some leaders of the establishment parties to voice more carefully formulated reservations about the presence of so many immigrants. An entirely new and different political phenomenon for France is the appearance of two Green parties, one more conservative and the other more socialist in orientation. In the regional elections of March 1992, the environmentalists together received about 15 percent of the vote, slightly more than the share received by the National Front.

As widely expected, the Socialists suffered a major setback in the parliamentary elections of 1993. After the second round, held a week after the first, it was clear that the conservative alliance of the center-right Giscardists (the Union pour la Démocratie Française, or UDF) and the neo-Gaullists (the Rassemblement pour la République, or RPR) had garnered about 40 percent of the popular vote.

The Socialists and their close allies were among the losers in this largest electoral landslide in French democratic history. Receiving less than 20 percent of the popular vote, or about one-half as much as five years earlier, they plummeted from their previous share of 282 seats in 1988 to only 70 seats. The Communists, with about half as many votes, were able to win 23 seats, because much of their electoral support is concentrated in some urban districts. With a similar share of the vote, the National Front won no seats at all. The environmental alliance was doubly disappointed, winning a smaller share of the vote than expected and capturing no seats either.

Mitterrand's seven-year presidential term does not expire until 1995. However, after the parliamentary rout of the Socialists in March 1993, he was faced with the question of whether to resign early from the presidency or, as under similar political circumstances in 1986, to enter a period of "cohabitation" with a conservative prime minister. Mitterrand opted for the latter solution, but he made sure to appoint a moderate Gaullist, Edouard Balladur, as the new prime minister. Balladur in turn appointed a new, compact government that included members from all main factions of the conservative alliance. During his first few months in office, Balladur retained an unusual popularity, but his government's attempt to introduce austerity policies became the target of a series of political demonstrations by various affected groups, including trade unionists, students, and young people. By the beginning of 1994 Balladur had begun to slip in the polls, but he was still considered a possible alternative to Jacques Chirac as Gaullist candidate for the presidency in 1995. The most frequently named Socialist candidates were Jacques Delors and Michel Rocard.

The articles in this section provide a perspective on what some observers call "the new France." In fact, contemporary French politics and society combine some traits that reflect continuity with the past and some that suggest considerable innovation. One recurrent theme among observers is the decline of the previously sharp ideological struggle between the Left and the Right. There may well be a sense of loss among some French intellectuals who still prefer the political battle to have apocalyptic implications.

The loss of the great ideological alternatives may help account for the mood of political *malaise* that many observers claim to discover in contemporary France. But the French search for political direction and identity in a changing Europe has another major origin as well. The sudden emergence of a larger and potentially more powerful Germany next door cannot but have a disquieting effect upon France, even though opinion polls in 1990 showed a strong support for the right of the Germans to choose national unification. French elites now face the troubling question of redefining their country's role in a post–cold war world, in which the Soviet Union has lost in power and influence while Germany has gained in both.

In this new European setting, some observers have even suggested that we may expect a major new cleavage in French politics between those who favor a reassertion of the traditional French nation-state ideal—a kind of "neo-Gaullism" that can be found on both the Left and Right—and those who want the country to accept a new European order, in which the sovereignty of both the French and German nation-states would be diluted or contained by a network of international obligations within the larger European framework.

Italy is roughly comparable to France and Britain in population and economic output, but it has a different political tradition that includes a long period of fascist rule and a far more persistent element of north-south regionalism. Italy became a republic after World War II and, using a system of proportional representation, developed a multiparty system in which the center-right Christian Democrats played a central role as the major coalition party. The Communists, as the second major party, were persistently excluded from government at the national level. They played a considerable role in local politics, however, and embarked relatively early on a nonrevolutionary path of seeking socialist reforms in a pluralist society. Under their recently adopted new name, Democratic Party of the Left (PDS), the former Communists essentially adopted social democratic reform positions. In 1993 and 1994, they experienced a political revival, as Italian voters abruptly turned away from the Christian Democrats and other corrupt establishment parties.

The corruption issue came to the fore as the cold war ended. As middle class fears of Communism declined, many Italians were no longer willing to tolerate the self-serving manner in which the establishment parties and their leaders had prospered from all manners of side-payments for political services and government contracts. Some vigorous prosecutors and judges played a major role in exposing the extent of what became known popularly as *tangentopoli* (kickback city) in public affairs.

In late March 1994, Italy finally held what has been regarded as the most important parliamentary elections in over four decades. Once again Italian voters demonstrated their disgust with the old government parties. Using a new electoral system, in which three-quarters of the members of parliament are elected on a winner-takes-all basis and the rest by proportional representation, they decimated the centrist alliance that included the former Christian Democrats. On the left, an alliance led by the PDS won 213 of the 630 seats in the Chamber of Deputies, compared to the 46 seats for the main centrist group. But it was the Freedom Alliance of the right that triumphed by winning 366 seats.

Japan, the fifth country in this study of representative governments of industrial societies, has long fascinated students of comparative politics and society. After World War II, a representative democracy was installed in Japan under American supervision. This political system soon acquired indigenous Japanese characteristics that set it off from the other major democracies examined here.

For almost four decades the Japanese parliamentary system was dominated by the Liberal Democratic Party that, as the saying goes, is "neither liberal, nor democratic, nor a party." It is essentially a conservative political force, comprising several delicately balanced factions. At periodic intervals the LDP's parliamentary hegemony has been threatened, but it was always able to recover and retain power until 1993. In that year, it lost several important politicians who objected to the LDP's reluctance to introduce political reforms. As a result of these defections, the government lost its parliamentary majority. A vote of no confidence was followed by early elections in July 1993, in which the LDP failed to recover its parliamentary majority for the first time in almost four decades. Seven different parties, which span the spectrum from conservative to socialist, thereupon formed a coalition government headed by Morihiro Hosokawa, one of the politicians who had earlier left the LDP and formed a reform party of his own.

Observers differed about the significance of the political change in Japan. Some argued that the continued power wielded by Japan's entrenched bureaucratic elites would guarantee that the political changes remained more apparent than real. Others placed more importance on the end of one-party hegemony in the country, stressing that, although the coalition government itself was internally weak, it was obligated to introduce electoral reforms that would result in a long-term shift in the balance of power in Japanese politics.

Looking Ahead: Challenge Questions

What were the main features of "Thatcherism," and why was it so controversial? Explain the basic outcome of the British general election of 1992.

How and why did Bonn underestimate the problems of reconstruction in eastern Germany? How does federalism represent an example of the institutional transfer from the western to eastern part of united Germany?

What are the signs that French politics have become more centrist or middle-of-the-road for the main political parties?

Why has Italy been called the "sick man" of Western Europe? What is *tangentopoli*?

Explain the political outcome and significance of the 1993 parliamentary elections in Japan.

Europeans Fear That Leaders Are Not Equal to Their Task

Alan Cowell

Special to The New York Times

ROME, Aug. 9—Confronted by political scandal, recession and the erosion of familiar comforts, Western Europeans have come to sense that the very people they chose to solve their problems have been in power too long to steer a dejected Continent through the shifting shoals that mark the close of the 20th century.

This year alone, France's Socialists have been ignominiously ousted from power, their counterparts in Spain have lost absolute control of Parliament for the first time in a decade, and an entire political elite has been decapitated by scandal in Italy. In Britain, Prime Minister John Major holds the dubious distinction of becoming his country's least-loved Prime Minister since polling began. And in Germany, Chancellor Helmut Kohl's popularity is at an all-time low.

To judge from conversations in London, Paris, Bonn and Rome, a malaise has settled into a region unnerved by joblessness, a decline in social services and the apparent failure of a tired old guard of politicians to produce a vision of the future.

'Mental Exhaustion' Seen

In Bonn, "there is real mental exhaustion" among leaders, said a se-nior official of the Free Democrats, the junior party in Germany's govern-ing coalition, speaking on condition of anonymity. "Crisis management pervades all the issues, and improvi-sation only fuels the discontent."

"For the first time, parents are say-ing that things are going to be worse for their children," said Martine Au-bry, a Socialist who served as Labor Minister in France's previous Gov-ernment. "Before, they saw society as constantly improving."

The bleakness is compounded by predictions in all four capitals of a surge in nationalism that has mu-tated into violence against foreigners, adoption of stricter immigration poli-cies in France and in Germany and a rise in support for the chauvinistic Northern League in Italy.

Even as Europe's old guard strug-gles in vain to freshen its image—Italy's Christian Democrats want to change their name to the Popular Party, and governing parties rou-tinely recruit people in their '40s as junior ministers—a new generation of leaders seems far from asserting itself.

In Britain, there's "a feeling that the Government can't cope and no other set of politicians could cope either," said Lord Rees-Mogg, for-mer editor of The Times and a Con-servative member of the House of Lords. He said that Britons' attitude toward their politicians—be they Con-servatives, Labor Party members or Liberal Democrats—"is one of psycho-logical, almost clinical depression."

Since the fall of Communism changed the Continent's perception of itself as an increasingly cohesive and ever more prosperous bloc con-fronting other great blocs—the So-viet Union, the United States and Asia—the old calculations, and the politicians who based their careers on them, are faltering.

"Europe's politicians are generally stuck in a time warp," said Anatole Kaletsky, an economic commentator in London. "They are preoccupied with the problems of the 70's and 80's, but the challenges ahead are going to be quite different from the past 20 years."

Some common strands are evident in the challenges facing Europe's po-litical systems. Of all the nations of Western Europe, Germany and Italy seem to have been most unsettled by the fall of Communism. After the euphoria of German reunification faded, politicians in Bonn were con-fronted with the unexpectedly high social, political and economic costs of integrating the Communist east and the affluent west; with no East bloc specter to warn against, Rome's leaders have largely been stripped of their role as a cold-war bastion against Western Europe's strongest Communist Party.

Politicians are also drained by the battle with high unemployment—2.95 million are out of work in Britain and more than 3 million in France and in Spain—at a time when global competition threatens to consign the welfare state to the history books.

In Spain, France and Italy, Socialist parties have all come under pressure and been tainted in varying degrees by corruption allegations.

Prime Minister Felipe González was returned to office in June for the fourth time, but only after apologizing for his Government's economic "errors" and warning that a rightist victory would mean deep cuts in social benefits. Corruption charges have brought the virtual demise of Italy's Socialists this year, and France's Socialists were trounced in parliamentary elections in March.

"The Socialist alternative has disappeared," said Tony Benn, a Labor Party lawmaker in London, reflecting an impression across the Continent that tough capitalist policies have won the day.

Even center-right parties are in retreat in Germany, Britain and Italy. And the ideological void is such that "the variables between left and right are much narrower," said Alain Duhamel, a conservative commentator in Paris.

Though it has taken a far tougher stand than the Socialists on limiting immigration, for example, France's three-month-old conservative Government has generally pursued economic policies that seem little different from those of his predecessors, resisting a devaluation of the franc even when lower interest rates offered a hope of reviving economic growth.

In countries whose politics were long viewed as a contest between moderate left and right, commentators now tend to focus on the danger of allowing any party to govern too long. In a recent commentary on Conservative Party financing, a British Catholic weekly in London remarked that "being in power too long" produces a certain "whiff" of corruption. Nowhere is that more evident than in Italy, where a vast corruption scandal seems inextricable from the struggle between old and new.

ITALY
Scandal Brings Calls for Renewal

Possibly the most quoted comment about the nation's politics came from the Sicilian writer Giuseppe Tomasi di Lampedusa, who posited that, in Italy, everything has to change so that nothing will change.

That strain of cynicism suffuses what is without doubt Western Europe's most dramatic break with a discredited past. A corruption scandal that began in February 1992 has wrapped its tentacles around the entire business and political elite that has run the country since World War II.

Overwhelmed by evidence of graft, the Socialist Party of former Prime Minister Bettino Craxi has shriveled. The most senior echelons of the Christian Democrats are decimated. Giulio Andreotti, seven times prime minister and a symbol of postwar Italy, faces charges of corruption and association with the Mafia—allegations that he denies—and most of his senior lieutenants are under investigation for fiscal wrongdoing.

So pervasive was the system of kickbacks that a former Health Minister has been accused of taking bribes from a private television station in return for publicly financed advertising on the dangers of AIDS. The biggest private and state companies have been implicated in the network of bribery.

As the standing of the old guard has plummeted, recent municipal elections have shown a rise in support for forces previously barred from the corridors of power—the insurgent Northern League, particularly in Italy's wealthy northern region, and the former Communists, now known as the Democratic Party of the Left, in Italy's center.

The shift in voting patterns has begun to set off alarms—in part because of the Northern League's embrace of xenophobia and in part because the decline of established parties has removed Italy's political center of gravity.

"The will to change is accompanied by a new form of intolerance and bitter local patriotism, which are dangerous because they tend to divide rather than unify," said Dacia Maraini, a prominent Florentine novelist and poet.

Warning that racist appeals could splinter this culturally diverse nation, one politician, Giuseppe Ayala, is seeking to promote a new centrist alliance to challenge the Northern League's leader, Umberto Bossi. "The greater the number of votes obtained by the League, the greater the threat to national unity," Mr. Ayala said.

There is little doubt that the people want profound political change. A referendum last April showed Italians overwhelmingly in favor of political reform. Municipal elections in June left the Socialists in complete collapse, and the once-powerful Christian Democrats with only a rump of support in their traditional southern domain.

The recent suicides of the Italian industrialists Raul Gardini and Gabriele Cagliari—both fleeing the ramifications of the country's corruption scandal—briefly gave the nation pause as it was confronted with the emotional toll of Italy's sudden moral rectitude. But in a land where corruption remains endemic—from tax evasion to the $50 "tip" for a bureaucrat's smallest favor—the public has overwhelmingly supported the corruption inquiry.

While Italy has a new Government led by Carlo Azeglio Ciampi, a former central bank governor who has no political affiliation, the prospects for change are uncertain. The Italian Parliament, elected in April 1992, before the vast scope of Government corruption had become known, still reflects the old order. Dominated by a coalition led by Christian Democrats, it has little interest in calling new elections.

Only huge public pressure for change led the lawmakers to enact reforms last week changing the old system of pure proportional representation in Parliament, a system that had produced 52 unstable coalition governments since World War II.

The new rules, under which most lawmakers are to be elected by direct ballot, are expected to reduce the number of parties in Parliament and make for more durable governments. But both Parliament and the Government seem reluctant to call a new election before next spring.

"They want to postpone early elections as much as possible, or they hope they won't be held until it is possible to dampen the winds of change," said Gianni Vattimo, a philosophy professor at the University of Turin.

Many political analysts say a parliamentary election next spring would probably help the Northern League translate its powerful support in the north into a strong parliamentary bloc in Rome. But it is unclear what else could emerge as politicians jostle to re-invent themselves. The only issue uniting new forces like the centrist alliance sought by Mr. Ayala and Mario Segni, a maverick Christian Democrat, seems to be a rejection of the past.

"We must say it frankly: We have produced a political class which we can only be ashamed of," Mr. Ayala said recently.

GERMANY

Indecision At Europe's Heart

In a recent opinion survey in Germany, 72 percent of the respondents thought it "scandalous" that former Labor Minister Günther Krause used public money to pay his domestic help and cover the costs of a household move.

The amount involved, and the nature of the crime, may seem minuscule in comparison with what passes for corruption in Italy. Nonetheless, Mr. Krause resigned in May, just as Economics Minister Jürgen Mollemann had stepped down in January after acknowledging that he had written letters promoting a relative's business interests—a common practice among German politicians.

Ebbing Confidence in the Old Guard

BRITAIN

Percentage of people saying they were . . .

Satisfied with Mr. Major's leadership: 55%, 19%

Satisfied with the Government: 40%, 12%

April 1992* *Post-election.

July 1993

Source: Market and Opinion Research International

FRANCE

Percentage of people saying they had confidence in . . .

July 1988 / July 1993

President Mitterrand: 63%, 37%

Prime Minister Michel Rocard: 61%

Prime Minister Edouard Balladur*: 68%

*Took office as Prime Minister in March.

Source: Le Figaro Magazine-Sofres

GERMANY

Source: Emnid Institute

Percentage of people supporting Germany's governing coalition.

1990† — 44%, 11%

1993* — 37%, 9%

Chancellor Kohl's Christian Democratic Alliance

Free Democrats

†Election results. *Poll taken in late June; respondents were asked, "If elections took place on Aug. 1, which party would you vote for?"

ITALY

How two parties that long dominated Italy have fared in municipal elections.

1988 / 1993

Christian Democrats: 29%, 19%

Socialists: 18%, 4%

*Took office in April; no party affiliation.

Source: La Repubblica

In July, Interior Minister Rudolf Seiters resigned unexpectedly after a man described as a member of the Red Army Faction guerrilla group was killed at extremely close range in a shootout with an anti-terrorist squad in the eastern town of Bad Kleinen. The man was shot at close range by a special anti-terrorist squad, setting off accusations that it was an execution-style killing.

The impression created by the scandals, the resignations and the Government's frequent indecisiveness is that, after almost 12 years of rule sustained by the prosperity of the 1980's, the resolve of the Christian Democrats and their coalition partners, the Free Democrats, has slackened just as the country is facing up to the staggering financial costs of reunification.

"The population has the feeling that the basic problems are not being solved," said Meinhard Miegel, head of an independent research institute in Bonn. And on a European level, he said, "I think we have a common problem regardless of heads of state being in power for a long time.

"No Government is coming to grips with the problems," he said. "There's no exception."

In Germany, the challenges are immense. The cost of absorbing the wrecked economy of the former East Germany since October 1990 has been far greater than politicians or many ordinary Germans had expected. Millions of refugees from Eastern Europe poured into the country until tighter restrictions were imposed on July 1 eliminating the automatic right to political asylum. Inflation, unemployment and the unabated right-wing violence against foreigners haunt a Government that seems fearful of acknowledging the very weight of the problems.

"The violence happens, they get together to deal with it and then put it on the back burner," said an official of the Free Democratic Party, speaking on condition of anonymity. He lamented the absence of long-term strategies to cope with what many see as an alarming rise in neo-Nazism.

With elections looming next year—and talk of a subsequent grand coalition of Christian Democrats, Free Democrats and Social Democrats—opinion surveys show Mr. Kohl trailing behind his most likely challenger,

the newly chosen leader of the Social Democrats, Rudolf Scharping.

Perhaps tellingly, neither man drew overwhelming support in the survey. The poll by the Allensbach Institute showed Mr. Scharping with 32 percent of the vote and Mr. Kohl with 24 percent. Equally worrisome, Government officials said, are predictions that far fewer Germans will bother to go to the polls next time than in previous elections.

Across Europe, people "are not particularly interested in selecting the most able people to be in charge of politics," Mr. Miegel said. Developments in France and Britain are putting that assertion to the test.

BRITAIN

Tory Leader Sinks In the Polls

Whenever Prime Minister John Major peers across the Channel these days, it must be with a sense of envy. Even though the British leader says he has brought down inflation and sees the beginning of the end to his country's recession, poll experts estimate that only 19 percent of the British are satisfied with his performance as leader.

In Paris, by contrast, Edouard Balladur, another conservative Prime Minister facing similar economic and fiscal problems, is enjoying such overwhelming support after three months in office that one commentator calls him "the Balladur phenomenon."

Yet Mr. Major's problems are also strikingly different from those faced by Mr. Balladur. Personally he cannot shake off the impression that he is a "wimp," as he puts it. His Conservative Party has been in office for 14 years, a period overwhelmingly dominated by the tenure of his strong-willed predecessor, Margaret Thatcher. Even some of the party's senior members believe a spell in opposition would help the Conservatives regenerate.

In a reflection of its deep unpopularity, the Conservatives lost an important by-election in Christchurch, a middle-class stronghold for the

party in southern England for the last 83 years. Many attributed the Conservatives' loss to Mr. Major's low standing and to what The Economist of London recently described as "the whiff of a party that is arrogant, out of touch and bloated by power."

Lord Rees-Mogg, a Conservative adversary of Mr. Major, said the Prime Minister is "a very depressing chap. He takes a decision, often gets it wrong, goes through with it with great obstinacy, and then panicks and abandons his position. That's the A-B-C of John Major."

When a left-wing British magazine, The New Statesman, asserted recently that Mr. Major had had an extramarital relationship, he sued the publication for libel. But when the dispute drew widening public attention, he retreated and settled out of court for token damages of £1,001—the equivalent at the time of about $1,500—without securing an apology from the magazine.

Mr. Major's own party is riven with dissent over the Government's policy on fuller integration of the European Community, so much so that Mr. Major resorted to a high-stakes gamble by calling a confidence vote in Parliament—where his party has a narrow, 17-seat majority—to complete the debate on ratifying the Maastricht Treaty on European union.

"We've been through a difficult period," he acknowledged. "There have been difficult decisions that have had to be taken. Some difficult decisions lie ahead. I'm not going to be deflected from those difficult decisions."

Mr. Major's Government can also point to some economic progress, including signals that Britain's recession may be ending. The inflation rate is down to 2.8 percent, and unemployment has been gradually declining. But none of that seems to shake off the feeling that if general elections were held right now, the Conservatives would lose badly.

Deepening the mood of malaise, some commentators say, is a sense that the Labor Party opposition under John Smith has not seized the opportunity to present itself as a credible alternative the way the conservatives did in France in the parliamentary elections last spring.

Part of the problem is generational. Mr. Major himself is only 50, but to many Britons, his Government represents the tail end of 14 years of Conservative rule that set off the Thatcherite boom of the 1980's only to dump them into recession when the bubble of privatization burst.

Mr. Major, said Dottie Riley, a literary agent in London, "just does not inspire confidence."

Across the Channel, Mr. Balladur, 64, is doing the opposite, though no one is certain how long his appeal will last.

FRANCE

Voters in Search Of New Leaders

Mr. Balladur offers the French a "reassuring," patrician image of competence, says the journalist Pierre Hasky, even though his Government has been buffeted by Europe's currency turmoil and strong downward pressure on the French franc.

"He made fewer promises and gave no false hopes, so people take him seriously," said Mr. Duhamel, the conservative commentator. Such an approach caught the national mood at a time when, according to Ms. Aubry, the former Socialist Cabinet member, "the French don't want to be told stories anymore."

The new conservative Government got off to a somewhat bumpy start. In May, France's previous Prime Minister, Pierre Bérégovoy, took his life, apparently humiliated by allegations in the press and by

conservative politicians about an interest-free loan he had accepted from a man who was later indicted on insider-trading charges.

His death stunned France and set off national soul-searching over the mud slinging that had dominated the parliamentary campaign. But the tragedy did not prevent public support from coalescing for his successor.

Mr. Duhamel remarked that Mr. Balladur was "politically still very young," having served in government only once, as Finance Minister from 1986 to 1988—the last time parliamentary elections forced President François Mitterrand to "cohabit" with a conservative government.

None of that obscures the dilemma that Mr. Balladur runs the Government in loose consultation with Mr. Mitterrand, a 76-year-old Socialist who is as much a symbol of political longevity in France as Chancellor Kohl is in Germany or as Giulio Andreotti once seemed to be in Italy.

Parliamentary and presidential elections run on different schedules in France, and the next presidential vote is set for 1995. That vote looms over French politics and reinforces the impression that the French, too, are living through an uneasy period of transition.

A slightly "younger" generation—those who were high-school or college students during the street protests of 1968—has not made a significant mark, though Socialist governments have sought to appoint members of that age group to Cabinet posts. Some activists who were briefly viewed as potential challengers to the old elite, like Brice Lalonde, a former student leader who now directs a political alliance of environmentalist groups, fared

badly in the parliamentary elections.

Once again, the politicians mentioned as likely candidates for the 1995 presidential elections have a familiar ring.

In theory, Mr. Balladur became Prime Minister so that the leader of his neo-Gaullist party, former Prime Minister Jacques Chirac, could remain above the fray of day-to-day politics yet capitalize on any Government successes in making his presidential bid in 1995. The only problem with that calculation is that, after four months in office, Mr. Balladur is now running ahead of both Mr. Chirac and his conservative coalition partner, former President Valéry Giscard d'Estaing, in opinion surveys.

None of the poll ratings mask what is viewed in Britain, France, Germany and Italy as a fundamental gulf between people and politicians.

What the politicians offer, in varying degrees and with varying effectiveness, is management; what they do not offer is the broader vision that inspired the French under de Gaulle or the Germans under Adenauer. "French politics were too ideological, and now it's gone too far the other way; there's no ideology, no ideas," Ms. Aubry said.

After decades of certainty, even complacency, about its security and prosperity, it is difficult to tell what force could energize Western Europe again.

"The most important problem," said Mr. Miegel, the analyst in Bonn, "is a problem afflicting all our societies: All these states got too wealthy. They are very cushioned, very comfortable—and generally have a lack of stimulus."

[This is the fourth in a 5-part series entitled *A Continent Adrift*. Ed.]

Has the Sun Set on Britain?

The island nation is coming to terms with its diminished role in the new world order

Eugene Robinson

Washington Post Foreign Service

LONDON

Britain is a relatively rich country with industrial might, nuclear weapons and a permanent seat on the U.N. Security Council. It has international commitments and first-class diplomats, and is one of the few nations that consistently takes a global view of events.

But is Britain still important?

Politically, economically and culturally, Britain has long seen itself as one of the world's true heavyweights. But in the estimation of many observers—and in the nightmares of British policy-makers—middleweight status is an increasingly accurate description.

Those who see Britain's role as in decline say the two relationships from which Britain has derived its importance in the postwar era are both being reexamined. The United States, with a new generation of leaders in charge, may no longer put the "special relationship" with Britain above all others. Britain's stature in Europe, meanwhile, is diminished by the emergence of a unified Germany as the region's powerhouse.

"My feeling is that Britain, like some other European countries is clinging to a set of myths that no longer can be maintained," says Jonathan Eyal of the Royal United Services Institute, a London think tank. "Here, they talk as though all the important issues still have to be decided in London. I don't think that's the case anymore."

British intellectuals and politicians have been debating since World War II whether Britain has entered into a permanent decline as a world power and the country's place on the world stage has diminished dramatically over the past half century. But the current debate is new in the sense that it reflects developments since the end of the Cold War.

The British government is determined that Britain continue to "box above its weight" on the world stage, in Foreign Secretary Douglas Hurd's phrase. But ordinary Britons may be losing their enthusiasm for the fight.

In a poll taken in December, only 34 percent of those surveyed said Britain should continue trying to be "a power in the world"—while 49 percent said Britain should be more "like Sweden or Switzerland."

Before World War II, Britain had its far-flung empire to confer status and power. Throughout the Cold War, Britain derived outsized importance from its strategic geographical position as an island off the European coast and from its diplomatic position with a foot in both the American and European camps.

As Europe took steps toward union, Britain participated but remained somewhat aloof. Economically and politically, Britain was at least coequal with France and Germany, the other big European powers. And whenever Europe looked like an unattractive option, there was always Britain's alliance with the United States to fall back on.

Now, the world is a different place. The Cold War has ended, and with it the Soviet threat that made Britain's geography so important. It no longer counts for much that Britain is perfectly situated to keep Russian submarines from breaking out into the North Atlantic, or to serve as an offshore platform from which to battle Communist hordes overrunning the continent.

Economic strength is much more important in determining a nation's position in the world—and the figures show that Britain now has just the fourth-largest economy in Europe, behind Germany, France and Italy.

A reunited Germany is now clearly the dominant economic power in the region, partnered with France in a strong push toward closer European union. Britain's leaders continue to agonize over how closely to link up with what they fear will become a European superstate. The United States, meanwhile, is preoccupied with its own problems and appears determined to take more of a multilateral approach to world affairs.

"I think Britain is at a rather important juncture in its national life," says U.S. Ambassador Raymond G. H. Seitz. "For years, for generations, they enjoyed this semi-detachment from a world where, more or less, they felt that if they could not control events, at least they could control their own fate. . . . Now, I think the sense of having options is what has slipped away."

Not everyone believes Britain's days as a major player are growing short. Prime Minister John Major, for one, insists that Britain can put itself "at the heart of Europe," influencing the shape of the union as it develops, while still maintaining the special relationship with the United States.

"I'm very much a believer in the potentially significant role of Britain [as] a country of Europe, but not exclusively of Europe, with the United States as its most important ally," says Charles Powell, who was a top adviser to former prime minister Margaret Thatcher.

"One has to say with some regret that our ability to back up our positions with force has been diminished," Powell says. "That fact could, over time, make us less attractive to the United States. . . . But I still believe we have a significant role to play."

Britain still has global military commitments and is able to project its power like few other nations. British forces played a major role in the Persian Gulf War, for example, and have pulled some of the toughest and most dangerous duty in the humanitarian relief effort in Bosnia.

But maintaining those commitments is expensive, and Britain's economy has been ailing. With nearly 3 million Britons unemployed and collecting benefits, the government's budget deficit is running at about $75 billion a year. The government would like to cut defense expenditures to bring them more in line with other European countries, but officials here worry that if strength is cut too close to the bone, Britain will weaken its argument for keeping its Security Council seat—coveted by both Germany and Japan.

"The aspiration that the political establishment has had in positioning Britain as one of the leading geopolitical players is increasingly untenable," says David Kern, chief economist and head of market intelligence for National Westminster Bank. "We have to devote resources in the defense area that are increasingly out of line with our economic base."

In the short and even the medium term, Kern says, Britain's economic prospects are somewhat brighter than those of other European countries.

Last September, when the British pound crashed, Britain was forced to make a humiliating exit from the European system of fixed currency values known as the Exchange Rate Mechanism. But that withdrawal allowed Britain to cut interest rates sharply, stimulating the economy. Unemployment is falling slightly, business confidence is up, industrial output has risen sharply and inflation is below 2 percent, its lowest level in nearly three decades.

Britain's leaders believe that in their effort to hold down labor costs and boost productivity, they are the vanguard of what will be a European rush toward greater competitiveness.

But the encouraging recent economic performance is relative, since the starting point for these gains was a deep recessionary trough. The economy is still not functioning anywhere near capacity, and since Britain has to export in order to grow, continuing economic trouble in important markets such as Germany may slow the recovery.

In addition, Britain faces a potential deficit in infrastructure. Spending on big capital projects has been repeatedly postponed. For example, when the long-awaited Channel Tunnel finally opens next year, travelers will board a high-speed train in Paris, zoom to the coast and under the English Channel, emerge in southeastern England—and then chug ever so slowly toward London, over twisting track laid down decades ago. France's high-speed rail link to and from the tunnel is built; Britain's is on the drawing board.

On the plus side, London remains the region's preeminent financial center. No other city in Europe even approaches its concentration of banks, investment houses and insurance companies.

More than $200 billion passes each day through London's foreign exchange market, the largest in the world. Banks in London account for about one-fifth of all international bank lending. Insurance companies in London account for one-fifth of the total international insurance market—although Lloyd's of London has suffered record losses.

In the long term, though, Kern says, Britain's economic prospects may depend on events largely outside its control—the success or failure of the attempt by Germany, France and the "inner core" of European Community nations to move toward economic and monetary union. Britain has opted out of the EC goal of a single European currency, but Germany and France continue to move in that direction. If they fail, Britain will look prescient. If they succeed, Kern says, Britain could regret being left out.

Britain's Hamlet-like indecision over European union is not likely to be resolved anytime soon, even though the fight over the Maastricht Treaty is finally settled. While the British business community, particularly in the industrial north, has been quick to embrace the advantages of the European single market, bartenders, cab drivers, tabloid newspapers and even some government officials still refer to "Europe" as if it were a strange and distant place—rather than a larger whole to which Britain belongs.

Eyal, among others, says the United States has already decided that Germany should be considered its key European ally. "The problem is that Britain cannot offer what the United States needs most—to guide Europe into a kind of unity that doesn't transform it into a trade fortress," he says. "The British have not been good at guiding the integration process. The Germans are."

Although traditionalist proponents of the special relationship consider this view nonsense, British officials were nonetheless confused and crestfallen when, during an EC summit in Copenhagen several weeks ago, German Chancellor Helmut Kohl appeared to be acting as President Clinton's junior partner.

Brandishing a letter from Clinton, Kohl asked his fellow heads of state to consider lifting the arms embargo for the Bosnian Muslims—a proposal that Britain vehemently opposes. The EC did not budge, and the White House failed to press the matter. Still, the episode unnerved British officials who are used to having private communications from Washington come through London, not Bonn.

British leaders are generally uncertain about Clinton's team, especially the advisers who are not drawn from the familiar Anglophile U.S. foreign policy establishment.

When a State Department official, in unguarded remarks, recently sketched for reporters a policy of U.S. disengagement from its unchallenged leading role in world affairs, the Clinton administration quickly issued firm denials that any such withdrawal was taking place. Leaders here, however, wondered if they had glimpsed the administration's true colors.

Some believe that Britons are just in a mood to feel weak and unloved. Polls have shown a sharp drop in respondents' confidence in almost all major institutions, from the justice system to the royal family. Politicians, especially, have suffered. Major is now the most unpopular prime minister since opinion polling began.

"The great thing we have to avoid is a sort of crippling loss of self-confidence," Powell says. "I think it is connected with the general loss of political confidence here, in the system, in the way things are going for the country."

Major and his aides respond that the government is unpopular, and people are unsettled, because the country is now beginning to tackle the tough problems. As economic recovery builds, they say, the mood will shift.

Says a spokesman for the prime minister: "You can't suppress good news forever."

Britain's Constitutional Question

Politicians and others urge adoption of a written charter and a bill of rights

By Alexander MacLeod

Special to The Christian Science Monitor

LONDON

BRITAIN has long taken pride in the fact that its constitution, unlike those of most other democracies, is unwritten. But pride is giving way to doubt, and pressure is building for a fresh look at ways of securing the rights of British citizens.

Anthony Barnett, an advocate of a written constitution and a bill of rights, says he thinks that relying on Magna Carta, signed by England's King John at Runnymede in 1215, is an insufficient basis for ensuring that the rule of law prevails.

Mr. Barnett is coordinator of Charter 88, a nonpartisan group of lawyers and intellectuals modeled on Charter 77, the human-rights group that played a major part in destroying communism in Czechoslovakia.

He notes that Britain is the only member of the 12-nation European Community and its 25-nation sister body, the Council of Europe, without a written constitution.

"The result is that Britain is now regularly facing constitutional issues it is ill-equipped to handle," Barnett says.

King John's "great charter" was imposed on him by rebel barons who saw it as a barrier against the monarch's arbitrary actions. It remains the basis of Britain's common-law system and such institutions as the right of trial by jury and habeas corpus.

But growing numbers of British political observers and groups say its rambling provisions do not fit with modern times. The Liberal Democrat party will enter the coming general election with calls for a written constitution guaranteeing civil liberties at the center of its policies.

The opposition Labour Party also is proposing constitutional reforms, including a separate parliament for Scotland, a British bill of rights, and the abolition of the House of Lords.

The ruling Conservatives will fight the election on the "Magna Carta principle" – a defense of the status quo – but Douglas Hurd,

> **'Britain is ... facing constitutional issues it is ill-equipped to handle.'**
>
> *– Anthony Barnett, constitutional advocate*

the foreign secretary, whose work brings him into regular contact with European governments, is on record as saying that his party should give "serious thought" to constitutional change.

Prominent members of Britain's political and legal establishment are now counted among those who demand that the country should have a bill of rights.

Lord Scarman, a former judge of the Court of Appeal, has been campaigning for a written constitution for decades, arguing that allowing Parliament to pass laws without regard to a framework of citizens' rights is a recipe for unfairness.

Since Britain entered the European Community (EC) 19 years ago and began rubbing shoulders with countries where human rights are enshrined in written constitutions, Mr. Scarman's campaign has been taken up by a younger generation.

Last November, Charter 88 organized its own convention in Manchester at which four draft constitutions were considered. All the drafts indicated that across the political spectrum there is a demand for fundamental change.

Tony Benn, the left-wing Labour Member of Parliament (MP), proposed an elected upper chamber to replace the House of Lords. He also argued that women should have 50 percent of the seats in the lower and upper houses, and that the government should appoint a human-rights commissioner with the power to refer to Parliament abuses of human rights by the courts.

Frank Vibert, deputy director of the Institute for Economic Affairs, a right-wing think tank that former prime minister Margaret Thatcher favors, presented a draft that called for taking away the queen's right to give final approval to new laws.

Mr. Vibert also proposed that a Parliament-elected official should give formal assent to legislation and that the European Convention on Human Rights should be made part of British law. An elected upper house, he argued, should act as a constitutional court to monitor observance of a written constitution.

Barnett is convinced that the Charter 88 constitutional convention has already had a major impact on the thinking of the main political parties.

"The European Court of Human Rights in Strasbourg continues to have cases referred to it by British citizens unhappy with the way the law of their own country is administered," he says. "More often than not the court finds in favor of the citizen. The reason is that it is applying a code of human rights that is absent in the British system."

Britain and the European Court are deadlocked on the question of lengthy detention before trial. The Strasbourg court has ruled that such detention is wrong. Britain argues that it is lawful under the Prevention of Terrorism Act used to cope with sectarian violence in Northern Ireland.

Roy Hattersley, Labour's deputy leader who will probably become home secretary if his party comes to power at the general election, is a dedicated supporter of constitutional reform. "For socialists," he says, "reform of the constitution is one of the ways by which a more equal, and therefore more free, society can be created."

The Labour Party has adopted a determined approach to the way members of Parliament are elected. Last year Neil Kinnock, the party leader, appointed a 20-member task force of political and constitutional experts, headed by Raymond Plant, a professor of politics at the University of Southampton, to examine this aspect of Britain's political system.

MPs are elected under the "first past the post" system, whereby a person who gains only one more vote than an opponent receives is automatically elected.

Mr. Plant and his committee are examining several forms of proportional representation (PR), in which voters are asked to rank candidates in order of preference.

Second preferences are distributed to reflect the numerical support gained by candidates of smaller parties. Supporters say that distributing the votes of individual electors among candidates ensures a more representative Parliament and gives smaller parties stronger representation. Most EC parliaments operate under a PR system.

Significantly, Labour says that if it wins the next general election, members of its promised Scottish Parliament will be chosen by a PR system.

Official Conservative policy, however, remains unchanged on either a bill of rights or a new electoral system. John Patten, a Home Office minister, dismisses the former as unwise and the latter as unnecessary. "The reformers want to sweep away the existing constitutional edifice and replace it with grandiose, ill-thought-out schemes," he says. "I think we should call the repairman only when it is necessary."

Should John Major go?

**This newspaper has endorsed many of the British government's policies.
Yet it has become hard to endorse Mr Major's leadership**

THE British Cabinet, like governments and politicians everywhere and almost always, is a tempting target for jokes, titillation and sneers. Usually this is mere entertainment, with little impact on the effectiveness or otherwise of government. Not now. Taken on their individual merits, the "scandals" that are dogging John Major's Conservative Party are trivial, some so trivial they do not even deserve the word scandal. Yet together they are endangering the government's ability to do its job—to govern. And they are doing so because the party has destroyed its own credibility. Responsibility for that has to end up behind the door of 10 Downing Street.

It was from there that what is now the defining phrase of this government—Back to Basics—emerged last autumn. As a slogan it is absurdly banal. Both those alliterative words were poorly chosen: "back" is a direction rightly absent from most political lexicons, while "basics" invited unflattering reflection on the 14 previous, supposedly fundamentalist, years of Conservative administration. Never mind that behind it may have lain well-meaning intentions in social policy and some valid points about links between private behaviour and public spending. Never mind that Mr Major himself has never raised the vexed question of unwed mothers. The slogan was so broad and so redolent of nostalgia-laden "family values" that it almost guaranteed what has now come about: a search for scandal and hypocrisy, and a disarray and inconsistency in the government itself that would be comic if it did not risk becoming so tragic.

For until now the surprising thing about John Major was how much he and his government had achieved, and against what odds. Winning the 1992 general election in mid-recession was a remarkable coup. Despite his tiny majority, Mr Major has pushed through a lot of tough policies, some radical, many of them endorsed by this newspaper: ratification of the Maastricht treaty, reform of education and health, rail privatisation. On crime, things look more doubtful. It is questionable whether, in three years' time, the studious populism of Michael Howard, the home secretary, will have begun to reduce crime. That civil liberties may be eroded by the bye is worrisome. But the government has shown a commendable readiness to tackle vested interests, such as the police and prison officers.

Most importantly, the economy is on the mend. The government was severely embarrassed by Britain's enforced departure from Europe's exchange-rate mechanism in September 1992. It was negligent in allowing public borrowing to balloon. But since then its macroeconomic measures have been broadly correct. The November budget was as tough as it had to be. Britain is in better shape than its main European competitors, and not only because, having been first into recession it is first out of it. Mr Major must take a slice of the credit.

Mr Major's welfare

It is on what is probably the most important issue facing Britain and many other countries—the reshaping of the welfare state—that this government has run into most trouble. Admittedly its attitude in this area is still evolving. That is not a cause for shame. To effect a shift from the universal welfare state to a system that is both cheap enough that taxpayers are willing to finance it and effective enough to offer a real safety net to the poor and vulnerable cannot be done in a single leap. On this politically dangerous territory, Mr Major travels warily. He has at least put the issue on the agenda.

Yet if anything is actually to be achieved, something more is required. That something is a mixture of an increasing clarity about where the government is heading, with a belief that the government means what it says and says what it means. Which brings things back, as it were, to basics. Assuming that it was intended to live beyond the party conference, the slogan must have been meant to provide this clarity and credibility: to welfare policy itself, but also, then, to the rest of the government's programme. However, horrified by the controversy and moralistic breast-beating that some welfare issues provoked, Mr Major now gives the impression that he regrets they were ever mentioned. The very opposite of clarity has been achieved.

The Tim Yeo affair should never have been allowed to rock the government. Mr Major should have roundly acknowledged that, yes, he expects high standards of morality from his ministers but that, no, adultery is not automatically a sacking offence. Instead, snared by his own slogan, he obtusely disclaimed the moral content of his message. He has tried (and failed) to flick off the problems of this junior environment min-

From *The Economist*, January 15, 1994, pp. 17-18. © 1994 by The Economist, Ltd. Distributed by The New York Times Special Features. Reprinted by permission.

ister (the fathering of one and, it was more recently revealed, a second illegitimate child) as a "silly indiscretion".

Mr Major has fine qualities. But his handling of the Yeo affair epitomises virtually everything that is wrong with his leadership. His failure to defend what the public rightly saw as the all-encompassing nature of back-to-basics illustrates his inability to crystallise complex policies and communicate them. Too often he vacillates: witness his unconvincing disavowal of the moral aspects of the slogan. Too often he hesitates or swims with the tide: witness his willingness, at the party conference, to embrace that fateful populism which seemed to unify the Tories in October—only to disembowel them in January. Underlying too much of Mr Major's decision-making is a concern more for popularity than principle and policy. The irony is that this makes him less popular, not more. Once, his evident sincerity gave him some protection; even that no longer seems to hold true.

In politics, it may be argued, it is never too late. A coup—most notably a breakthrough in Northern Ireland, though this looks less likely by the day—could rescue Mr Major and restore his credibility. Yet this cannot be relied upon. If he is to carry on in Downing Street, Mr Major and his ministers will have to hope that steady actions make up for what words have lost. He is defended by the poverty of alternatives: a feeble, divided Labour Party, and Liberal Democrats who still appear to have no chance of governing alone. Tory rivals are already proving subversive, but none seems keen to take Mr Major's place before the summer when local and European elections have passed. This is scant comfort. The plain fact is that time, and patience, are running out.

The Parties in Question

British Political Parties Fail to Set Clear Course

Three Key Groups Tired, Wavering, Adrift at Annual Seaside Conferences

Eugene Robinson

Washington Post Foreign Service

LONDON—The Conservative Party hoped to stage this year's annual general conference as a show of unity, a "turning point" for embattled Prime Minister John Major. But instead, the Tories spent their week in Blackpool struggling with Margaret Thatcher's legacy, trying to refute reports that Thatcher considers her successor an intellectual lightweight.

The Labor Party hoped to use its conference to score big points against Major, the most unpopular prime minister in British history. But instead, Labor delegates spent their week in Brighton fighting a bitter internecine battle over the influence of the big labor unions on party policy, and bemoaning their leadership's lack of charisma.

The Liberal Democrats hoped to use their conference to establish themselves as the future of British politics. But they spent their week in Torquay trying, and failing, to persuade themselves and others that they will someday be ready to govern.

If British politics once brought to mind a stirring horse race, now the image is more of a slow plod around a beaten track. Fourteen years of uninterrupted Conservative government have left the Tories exhausted, Labor at sea and the Liberal Democrats still not quite ready for the big leagues.

"I think the Tories are in a very considerable mess, although they could win the next elections," said David Butler, an Oxford University professor and an expert on British politics. "Whether the Labor Party can look like a competent alternative government is an open question. . . . I wish, wish, wish I could have more faith in any of the parties."

The result is that at a time when Britain is at pains to define a new role for itself in the post-Cold War world, both politically and economically, none of the parties is developing a compelling vision of the future or a map for getting there.

Unless Major falters, he is not required to call elections until early 1997. That means the Tories have more than three years to find themselves, and the other parties have the period to mount a credible challenge. At the moment, however, the parties seem to be stalled or headed in reverse.

The party in the deepest trouble is the one still enjoying a run of unparalleled electoral success. The Conservatives have been in power since Thatcher took office in 1979. Although she has been gone for nearly three years now, the party is still grappling with her ghost. And last week, without uttering more than a few innocuous sentences, Thatcher dominated the party conference.

But at issue was not what Thatcher said, but what she wrote. On Tuesday, as the Tories opened their meeting, the Daily Mirror—a London tabloid that supports the Labor Party—reported that Thatcher's memoirs, set for publication this week, contain disparaging references to Major.

Thatcher, who was ousted as prime minister and party leader in a 1990 palace coup, wrote that Major gave her only lukewarm support as she battled to keep her job, according to the Mirror.

More damagingly, the Mirror said, she reportedly wrote that he had "a tendency to be defeated by platitudes, which I find disturbing," and that "intellectually, he drifted with the tide."

"It seemed strange to me that he did not feel more at home with tackling the difficult issues he faced at the Treasury," Thatcher was said to have written about Major's tenure as chancellor of the exchequer. We "had to bring others who were more at ease with large ideas and strategies into the discussion."

After the leaks appeared in the Mirror, Thatcher issued a statement of support for Major, but did not deny the alleged quotes from her book.

In opinion pools, the Conservative trail not only Labor, but the Liberal Democrats as well. Numerous missteps by Major and his cabinet, along with a British economy that is struggling to get out of recession, have sent approval ratings plunging to new lows. Newspapers that normally support the Tories by reflex have been baying for Major's head.

At the Blackpool conference, the Conservatives tried a new approach to defining a guiding philosophy to replace Thatcherism, this time settling on a theme that could be called "family values."

Speaker after speaker thundered against coddled criminals, sponging immigrants, welfare mothers and politically correct

From *Washington Post*, October 10, 1993, pp. A33, A48. © 1993 by The Washington Post. Reprinted with permission.

civil servants. Major's minister promised to get tough with crime, tough with foreigners, tough with everybody; and they wrapped themselves in the Union Jack.

"I wish, wish, wish I could have more faith in any of the parties."

—David Butler

Given the Tories' disarray, the Labor Party should be making great gains. But Labor is having an identity crisis of its own, as commentators ask whether the party is electable.

Labor was leading in all polls before the April 1992 general election, but Major and the Tories came from behind as voters became nervous about what a Labor government would mean. Would it be the blow-dried, reasonable party leadership that kept appearing in the television ads? Or would it be a crew of wide-eyed socialists, dominated by militant union leaders?

A Gallup poll last month showed that voters believe the party is more moderate than in the past, when at times it took radical positions, and that it would pay more attention to social services than the Tories. But voters also believed that Labor was unlikely to improve the economy, that it seemed a party of the past and that it was "too much under the unions' thumb."

Since the election, party leader John Smith has been trying to reform Labor's image to make it more palatable. He staked his authority, and perhaps his position as leader, on a proposal to curtail the bloc vote that the unions exercise in party matters such as the selection of candidates. That system, in which union leaders were allowed to cast millions of votes for their members, smacked of smoke-filled rooms.

But union leaders fought the proposal. Although Smith eventually got most of what he wanted, the bitter debate served mainly to remind voters of how much influence over the party the unions still retain.

A consultant's review, ordered by Smith's office, found that the party was unfocused and badly managed and had too many second-raters at the top who worried more about their positions inside the party than about winning elections.

That leaves the Liberal Democrats, the only party that seems to be gaining ground. They have creamed both the Tories and Labor in special elections to replace two members of Parliament who died, and in local government balloting. Their leader, Paddy Ashdown, is generally considered more forceful and charismatic than either Major or Smith.

The party's strength is also its weakness: being perceived as having many policies, but no real ideology.

For all their gains, the Liberals have only 22 seats in the 650-member House of Commons. Party leaders keep proposing a system of proportional representation that would give them more clout, but so far the Tories, with more than 300 seats, and Labor, with almost that many, have not been willing to consider any changes.

Seaside beggars every one

All three of Britain's political parties are in a sad way—and the saddest of all is the Tory party

THIS is the time of year that political-party hacks live for, when Westminster grandees and constituency activists decamp to the seaside, for a week of speech-making and bar-hopping. The parties emerge from these ancient rituals hung over but re-invigorated, the grandees inspired by the rank-and-file, the rank-and-file flattered by the grandees.

That is the official version, anyway. In reality, the political classes are dreading the next few weeks—the grandees because they are terrified of embittered backwoodsmen, the managers because they fear that the truth will out. The truth is that the political parties are in a worrying state, distrusted by the public, unpopular with many of their own members, poorly organised, struggling to recruit the talent and cash they need even to keep going.

The rot has gone furthest in the Conservative Party. The Tories' Central Office has accumulated overdrafts and loans of £19.2m ($29m). Corporate and individual donations are drying up. Membership has plunged from a high-point of about 2.5m in the mid-1950s to about 700,000 today. (All these figures are approximate: Central Office has never bothered to keep proper records.) The party is ageing as well as impecunious. According to Patrick Seyd, an academic at Sheffield University who has studied the membership of both of the big parties, the average Tory member is 63 years old.

As a mass organisation, the party has been losing ground rapidly to Labour. In the mid-1970s, there were five members of the Conservative Party for every member of the Labour Party; now there are only two-and-a-half. If you exclude the "inactive", party membership is almost equal, at 200,000. Three-quarters of the Tory members contribute nothing to their party other than their membership fees, which they presumably regard as a sort of insurance premium against socialism.

Relationships between the national party and its local branches have also reached an all-time low, with many Conservative associations, disgusted by government bungling, withholding their party contributions. Activists worry that, on everything from Europe to police reform, party leaders are hopelessly out of touch with their own supporters. The decision to put value-added tax on fuel has infuriated the faithful, not least because so many of them are cash-strapped and thin-blooded old-age pensioners.

From *The Economist*, September 25, 1993, pp. 65, 68. © 1993 by The Economist, Ltd. Distributed by The New York Times Special Features. Reprinted by permission.

Much of the blame for this lies with Margaret (now Lady) Thatcher and her acolytes. Michael Pinto-Duschinsky, a political scientist at Brunel University, points to the contrast between the two great post-war revivals of the Tory party, the one that began in the late 1940s and the one that began in the late 1970s. In the first revival, the party concentrated on building constituency organisations as well as winning parliamentary seats. Membership soared from 266,000 in 1944 to 2.5m a decade later, and most constituencies were graced with their own full-time, paid agent.

In the second revival, the party devoted too little attention to its local roots. Instead, Mrs Thatcher relied on direct communication with the voters, through her dominance of the House of Commons. Party membership halved between the mid-1970s and the late 1980s. In several parts of the country, the constituency parties all but died out. This neglect is doubly puzzling. First, Mrs Thatcher was closer to most members, ideologically and personally, than any of her predecessors. Second, her soulmates across the Atlantic, in the Republican Party, engineered an impressive organisational revival in the late 1970s.

The Labour Party is in a rather better state, thanks largely to Neil Kinnock, its former leader. As well as adding 20,000 new members in the past couple of years, the party is now solvent, not least because it charges an annual membership fee of £18. The party has been much more innovative than its rivals, pioneering party credit cards (the party takes a cut from every transaction) and inventing imaginative and often lavish social events. The average Labour Party member is much younger (48 against 63) and better educated than the average Tory.

For all that, Labour is prey to a host of dangerous diseases. Its membership is still only about 260,000, less than a third of the number in the early 1950s, and those members are deeply divided by class and ideology. Middle-class Labourites (three-quarters of the total) are generally "right-wing" on economic issues and "left-wing" on social issues. The reverse is true of its working-class stalwarts. The party is poorly organised, stuffed with time-servers and, after four Conservative election victories, hard-pressed to recruit ambitious young politicians. It is still failing to make headway in the populous south. Above all, the party runs the risk of reforming itself into oblivion. To make itself electable, it needs to muzzle its mostly left-wing activists and cut its trade-union links. Yet the party relies on the activists for enthusiasm and the unions for money.

What about the Liberal Democrats? Surely they are bucking the trend of party decline? Not quite. True, the party is not the joke it was when it was formed from the fragments of the Liberal Party and the SDP

Local grievances

THE scene: Blackburn, Lancashire, on September 16th. The local Labour Party branch is holding an open meeting in the town's central library to discuss "law 'n' order". The meeting is part of "Labour week", featuring events that range from a heritage walk round landmarks of Blackburn's industrial past to a blues night. The "law 'n' order" meeting features a leading criminologist and a senior policeman. It is held to show that Labour really cares about crime. But do the people of Blackburn care that Labour cares? The audience of eight (some of whom may be looking for another event) seems no more than mildly intrigued.

By today's standards, Blackburn's is a thriving Labour Party. It has an active member of parliament, Jack Straw, the shadow environment secretary, and 600 members, one for every 44 Labour voters. Some local parties now have fewer than 100 members. Yet Blackburn's comrades are unhappy. "The word is demoralisation," says Phil Riley, the party secretary. "We don't know what it is that we are supposed to do."

The complaints flow freely. The party's national membership scheme calls for an £18 ($27) annual subscription: fine down south, but enough to deter tighter-fisted Blackburnians. In the national party's tiff with the unions over one member, one vote, Blackburn sides with the unions. The local party relies on their help and their money.

Politically, Blackburn thinks the party leadership has gone from bad (Neil Kinnock) to worse (John Smith). Their complaint is not the common one heard in the south that Mr Smith is too conservative, failing to appeal to the newly-prosperous classes. It is that he is aping the Tories in a rush to the centre ground. On council estates—still numerous in Blackburn—"they're saying, 'I don't bother voting', " according to Mr Riley. Or local Labourites are turning to the more populist Liberal Democrats.

Blackburn is touchy about betrayal. One former local MP was Philip Snowden, the firebrand socialist of the 1920s, who became the "Iron Chancellor"—famous for betraying his class, cutting unemployment benefit and quitting Labour. As Labour abandons more and more of the baggage of traditional socialism, the activists of Blackburn feel that, yet again, they are being betrayed.

Just now "betrayal" is a word some Tory activists use of John Major. One of the MPs for Southend-on-Sea, in Essex, is Teddy Taylor; he and his supporters are fanatically anti-*communautaire*. By origin, Mr Taylor is a Glaswegian. By instinct, however, he is pure Essex. In the 1980s he and his supporters were in their pomp, enthralled by Mrs Thatcher's populism and enriched by her economics. Since then, times have been tougher. Sir Teddy's anti-EC stand has made him unpopular with the leadership, but the locals love it.

Nevertheless, membership of the local Tory party has been falling. One loyalist explains: "The government doesn't seem to be doing Conservative things." Putting VAT on fuel and making belligerent noises about the police have gone down badly. So has the chancellor of the exchequer, Kenneth Clarke, who is dubbed a "bully boy". A certain lack of enthusiasm is apparent. The young wives' group had to be abandoned when it was discovered that the chairwoman-elect was 65. Have they considered a blues night?

in 1988. It has won spectacular by-election victories, especially in the south-west, and is terribly modern: it knows all about credit cards, direct mailing, and so on.

But, with 100,000 members, the party is smaller than the Alliance of the mid-1980s, and a fraction of the size of the Liberal Party of Asquith and Lloyd George. It is recruiting most new members from the other two parties rather than from the ranks of the uncommitted. More worrying still, the members it poaches are less active now than they used to be. Despite its recent origins, the party is suffering from organisational prob-

lems, most notably tensions between the leadership and members over goals (the leadership is far more pro-European than the average member) and methods (the party has begun an inquiry into the Tower Hamlets branch's "racist" campaigning.)

Psephologists cite a bewilderingly wide range of reasons for the decline of the parties: the spread of television (the parties had their heyday in the pre-television 1940s and early 1950s); the breakdown of communities (political loyalty is at its fiercest in class-based constituencies); the development of nightclubs and discotheques (the local parties used to be excellent dating agencies); the rise of pressure groups and, most plausibly, the emergence of a new sort of politics, based on shopping for policies rather than tribal loyalties. Whatever the reason, parties are clearly becoming marginal: in 1990 only 7.4% of the electorate were party members and only 2.2% were activists, according to a survey cited by Sheffield University's Patrick Seyd.

Does this matter? According to one argument, mass parties must go the way of vinyl records. If politicians want to communicate with the voters, they can appear on televi-

sion. If they want to raise funds, they can tap friendly foreign businessmen. If they want to sound out popular opinion, they can call in pollsters. If they want to devise a policy, they can turn to the think-tanks. Who needs amateur party activists when you can employ professionals?

John Major, for one. Leaving aside the question of whether politics ought to be reduced to just another consumer choice, and an infrequently exercised one at that, mass members clearly serve valuable practical functions: they recruit talent, raise funds, invent policies and reduce political volatil-

ity. Under Margaret Thatcher, with her huge majorities and loyal cheerleaders in the press, anti-government swings in by-elections, local elections and Euro-elections proved to be merely embarrassing. Under John Major, with a tiny majority and an increasingly critical press, such swings could prove fatal, wiping out his majority and provoking unceasing challenges to his leadership—or that of any likely successor.

To Mr Major's growing list of grudges against Lady Thatcher, he might add the fact that she let the grass roots of his party wither.

Britain's Tiny Liberal Democrat Party Gains Clout at Expense of Tories, Labor

Kevin Helliker

Staff Reporter of The Wall Street Journal

TORQUAY, England—Britain's most charismatic politician is the leader of a party that many people outside the United Kingdom have never heard of, and that few people inside the country heretofore have taken seriously.

But why should they? Of the 651 seats in the House of Commons, Paddy Ashdown and his Liberal Democrats hold 22.

Yet, meeting for their annual party conference—followed next week by the Labor conference in Brighton and the week after that by the Conservative conference in Blackpool—the Liberal Democrats suddenly find themselves the hottest party in British politics: winner of the last two national by-elections, and a steady gainer in party membership, local government seats and public approval ratings.

BUBBLE WON'T BURST

"This is not a bubble in danger of bursting, but a step by step expansion of our influence," says MP Robert Maclennan, home affairs spokesman for the Liberal Democrats.

No one expects the Liberal Democrats to win a national election. But the plummeting popularity of Tory conservatism and lingering nervousness about Labor socialism could combine to keep both parties from winning a majority of seats in the next election. In that case, the middle-of-the-road Liberal Democrats could force one of the two major parties to include it in a coalition government.

Although skeptics note that the Liberal Democrats have surged previously only to collapse before national elections, many political analysts believe it's different this time. "The Liberal Democrats are in a stronger position today than they've ever

been before, and it shows every sign of lasting," says Patrick Seyd, a lecturer in politics at Sheffield University.

Bolstering this belief, polls show that 25% of Britons would vote Liberal Democrat in a national election, up from 18% in the latest election in April of last year. Moreover, since 1983, the party has nearly doubled the number of its members serving as local government councilors.

Supporters say the Liberal Democrats combine Tory managerial expertise with Labor compassion for the underprivileged, while eschewing what is perceived as the worst traits of those parties: Tory patronage and elitism, Labor lack of initiative.

The Liberal Democrats, proclaims Mr. Ashdown, are "on the verge of a break-through into the big time." Showing some hubris, he adds that his goal in politics is to be prime minister.

Even if the current popularity surge

continues, in national elections many votes secured by Liberal Democrats fail to translate into seats in the Commons. That is because Britain has a winner-take-all constituency system. The Liberal Democrats won only 3% of the seats in 1992, for example, even though they got 18% of the vote.

In the first major speech of the gathering, party president Charles Kennedy outlined the major challenge facing the party: "Is it really going to be oh so different this time?" Or, he asked, are the Liberal Democrats again going to settle for "the cheers today, tears tomorrow school of politics?"

Even the most optimistic Liberal Democrats foresee the party winning no more than 60 seats in the next national election. But that would probably be sufficient to force one of the other parties to include it in a coalition government, and the Liberal Democrats are sure to make electoral reform a key condition of any such alliance. A change in the system might enable the Liberal Democrats to increase their presence in Parliament and perhaps even gain control of it, although that eventuality is too remote for most political analysts even to contemplate.

"A very big question in the public's mind is 'Can the Liberal Democrats lead the country?' " says Robert Worcester, chairman of MORI, a polling and market research agency. "The answer is, 'not today.' "

WINNING POLLS

Mr. Ashdown is determined to change that. He is scoring markedly higher in the polls these days than either Labor Party leader John Smith or Prime Minister John Major of the ruling Tory party.

Mr. Ashdown is a former officer of the Royal Marines who obtained a degree in Mandarin Chinese at the University of Hong Kong. He has lived in Belfast, India, Geneva and the jungles of Borneo, which bolsters his image here as an intellectual adventurer. He's 52 years old and a fitness fanatic.

Mr. Ashdown portrays himself as an outsider. This is crucial at a time when Britons, weary of recession, growing crime and uninspired leadership from Mr. Major, are feeling hostile toward politicians. "What helps Mr. Ashdown and the Liberal Democrats is that while people here have always had a certain amount of contempt for politicians, now they hate them," says Lord Stoddard of Swindon, a former MP and now a Labor member of the House of Lords. "That's a problem for the Tory and Labor parties."

The Tory government's problems—a sluggish economy and utter lack of party unity—are splashed daily across the front page here. But Labor has failed to exploit the Tory party's troubles. For instance, although Tory support is weakening in its biggest stronghold—the south of England—Labor has been unsuccessful in picking up many votes there, with the swing votes mainly going to the Liberal Democrats.

TORY WOES HELP LABOR

Nationwide, Tory troubles have helped Labor in the polls. Now, 45% of Britons say they would vote Labor, compared with the 35% who actually did in the last election. But there is a reluctance among Labor leaders to take much heart from polls, because only days before that election they had a narrow lead in the polls.

That the problems of the two major parties represent an opportunity for the Liberal Democrats was illustrated in a by-election in late July in the constituency of Christchurch. Only 12 months after these voters elected a Conservative by a margin of 23,000—continuing a string of Tory victories there that dated back to 1906—the death of that MP prompted a by-election that the Liberal Democrats won by 16,000 votes, representing the largest swing against a sitting British government since 1945.

An Ireland Undivided?

Stands of London and Dublin Differ

James F. Clarity

Special to The New York Times

DUBLIN, Dec. 7—While hopes for the new Northern Ireland peace initiative persist, the Governments of Ireland and Britain remain deeply divided over whether there can ever be a united Ireland free of British rule, the ultimate goal of the Irish Republican Army, but the ultimate abomination to the leaders of Ulster's Protestant majority.

In their meeting last week, Prime Ministers John Major of Britain and Albert Reynolds of Ireland sought to work out a statement of principles that would lead first to a prolonged cessation of violence in the British province and then to a place at a peace talks table for Sinn Fein, the political arm of the I.R.A.

After a heated discussion last week in Dublin over the wording of such a statement, the Prime Ministers, who will discuss it again this weekend in Brussels, must produce words that are acceptable to both the I.R.A. and the Protestant Unionists.

Two Referendums

And what they produce must give Gerry Adams, the president of Sinn Fein, an indication of new British flexibility that he can take to the I.R.A. as a political victory, a rationale for laying down its arms with honor and talking.

But the formula cannot appear to be an appeasement to the I.R.A. because this would enrage many people, south and north, particularly the leaders of the Protestant majority in the province who want to remain part of Britain.

The basic difference is that Mr. Reynolds wants the formula to state that Irish self-determination will be decided in two separate referendums in the North and in his Irish Republic. He has insisted that if the Protestant majority in the north vetoed union, the Republic would accept the decision.

But the Protestants, most of whom see themselves as British, not Irish, oppose the referendum, seeing it as an Irish trick, with London's connivance, to put pressure on them to unite. Mr. Major has insisted that he would never support British abandonment of the north without the consent of the majority, which is indeed the policy of Ireland and Britain, written formally in the 1985 Anglo-Irish agreement. So he wants the statement somehow to be reassuring to the Protestants.

Politics and Predicaments

The other side is the British desire to get Ireland to assert in a convincing way that it is prepared to revise its 1937 Constitution, in which it claims sovereignty over the north. Mr. Reynolds had promised that the Irish would put the constitutional claim to a referendum only as part of an overall solution, but on Sunday he indicated he would put such a guarantee in writing.

The political predicaments of the two Prime Ministers also have some bearing. While Mr. Reynolds, with a 37-vote majority in Parliament, has more freedom to negotiate, Mr. Major has a slim majority in his Parliament and must be careful not to estrange the nine Ulster Unionist Party members.

If the talks between the two Prime Ministers succeed, officials say, there could be an end of violence before Christmas. If the peace lasted two or three months, it could lead to an invitation to Sinn Fein to join peace talks. Most years, the I.R.A. has voluntarily enacted a cease-fire for several days around Christmas.

An interim solution has been suggested by John Hume, a Social Democratic and Labor Party Member of Parliament and the most influential Roman Catholic leader in Ulster: a new relationship, possibly a federation between north and south, encouraged by the movement in the European Community toward political union.

Benefits of a Settlement

For Britain, a peaceful settlement of the struggle that has killed more than 3,000 people since 1969 would be a relief, with troops leaving and an end to the threat of I.R.A. bombs in Britain. For London, relinquishing power in the province of Ulster, even gradually, is a matter of cutting losses, of extricating Britain in a way that might enhance John Major's stature in British history.

Nor is there any certainty about how many Irish really want drastic change in the political relationship between north and south. In the south, which is 95 percent Catholic, most people try to push the northern violence out of their minds. Some fear that a united Ireland would mean trying to absorb nearly a million Protestants, and the possibility of a new civil war without benefit of the 17,000 British soldiers.

A recent survey published in The Irish Times surprised many officials and analysts with the news that only 32 percent of Northern Ireland's 650,000 Catholics favored a united Ireland as their first-choice political solution. Slightly more respondents favored joint authority by Britain and Ireland.

Population Shifts Assessed

There is also the prospect that the Catholic minority in the north might grow to become a majority that could vote to join Ireland.

But if that should happen, it won't be soon, according to Garret Fitz-Gerald, former Prime Minister.

"Even if it were a fact that within 20 years there would be an equal number of Catholics and Protestants in the Northern Ireland population, this would not be true of the voting population until 18 years later," he wrote.

"And in any event public opinion polls have shown that even as a distant proposal, one-fifth of the Catholic population do not want a united Ireland. It would be helpful if this fact were better known among Unionists, whose unrealistic fear of being forced into a united Ireland one way or the other are in danger of inhibiting the restoration of peace and stability in the north."

The Invisible Wall

The separate minds of two Germanys defy reunification

Marc Fisher

Washington Post Foreign Service

ROHRLACK, Germany

Nearly four years after they began their adventure in the new world, Elke and Ekkehard Hotz look up from their satellite-delivered TV picture and find themselves in the wrong century. In their small corner of reunited Germany, they live with no car and no phone. The roving physician who used to serve their village of 160 people in what was formerly East Germany no longer makes his rounds. Factories near Rohrlack, a 90-minute drive north of Berlin, have shut their gates permanently. Shops are shuttered, bus lines canceled, youth clubs closed. Their children must fight off teenage bullies wearing swastikas and steel-tipped boots.

"The people here say, 'Build the Wall again, bring back East Germany,' " Elke Hotz says. "People in the village live without sewers, without bathrooms, without clean water. They live like they did at the end of the war, when we were all bottomed out."

In the heady days after Communist East Germany was wiped off the roster of nations, the chancellor of German unity, Helmut Kohl, promised to turn the east into a "flourishing landscape" in three to five years.

In some places, Germany has achieved exactly that. Cranes line the autobahns as western investors create an auto culture, erecting chain stores, car lots and even Germany's first U.S.-style suburban shopping mall, near Leipzig. Everywhere in the east, work crews lay track for high-speed trains.

Berlin's new center—where Communist bureaucrats once worked in hulking, pollution-darkened, war-damaged buildings—now features pricey leatherware and exotic Cajun cooking. The French department store Galeries Lafayette is building a new complex next to a Hilton hotel.

At Berlin's trendy Borchardt's restaurant, those who can afford a $25 plate of venison enjoy a fantasy that would have been dismissed as preposterous only four years ago: a fine meal in a marble-clad east German restaurant, with South African wine, paid for with an American Express card.

Nevertheless, despite the veneer of western affluence nearly four years after the revolution of 1989, Germans east and west are growing apart as much as they are coming together. Even young eastern Germans are proving resistant to the natural blending process that most on both sides of the former divide had expected.

Only 22 percent of western Germans and 11 percent of easterners say they feel a common German identity—a sharp drop from previous surveys, according to a new poll by the Allensbach Institute. For the first time since reunification, a majority of easterners now tell pollsters they consider themselves "former citizens of East Germany" rather than part of a united Germany.

"As far as inner unity goes," Kohl said recently, "the economic and social challenges will admittedly take longer and cost more than most, including myself, had originally assumed. . . . What I hoped to achieve in three to five years will perhaps need twice that time."

Even that timetable appears optimistic. Although eastern Germany will soon be more advanced than the west in some ways—spanking new highways, a digital telephone system, new universities, a more varied retail sector—easterners have developed a second-class mentality that will not easily vanish.

The collapse of industry in the east and the declining confidence and performance of major manufacturers in the west, combined with political paralysis, are inflating the ranks of the disaffected, the nostalgic and the political extremes—and helping to convince many in the east that they have no place in western society.

"There is a collective pathology at work," says Hans-Joachim Maaz, an eastern psychotherapist who specializes in the transition to post-Communist life. "The Ossis [eastern Germans] have a deep need to subordinate themselves, while the Wessis [westerners] have a similar need to dominate. The huge costs of reunification have made it easier for the west to believe that easterners are responsible for their own problems."

To a surprising degree, the fallen Wall continues to divide the Germans—the 64 million in the west from the 16 million in the east—even physically. Two in five western Germans have not yet met an easterner, according to a new survey by the Infas Institute. A poll by Bonn's Ministry for Women and Youth reveals that young western Germans are even less adventurous: 55 percent of 14- to 27-year-olds have not yet been to the east, while all but 6 percent of eastern youths have visited the west.

Many western Germans have soured on their eastern brethren, concluding that they are either uninterested in or incapable of adjusting to western ways. "We have no unity of purpose," says Kurt Biedenkopf, premier of the eastern state of Saxony but himself a westerner. "We lack comparable living conditions. Western Germans see the east as a burden they need to unload as fast as possible."

An internal paper of the Free Democratic Party, the junior partner in Kohl's ruling coalition, concluded that "western Germans are increasingly unwilling to make further sacrifices for German unity. The mental divide will deepen. This issue will likely become a taboo topic that politicians will avoid, but it will play a decisive role in the election booths."

Even sympathetic westerners find their contacts with the east frustrating.

"I have relatives in the east with whom we had had hardly any contact until two years ago," says J. C. Liesecke, a military officer in the west. "We had a few meetings, and it was very difficult. We even speak a different language. We had to explain to them what insurance was. And you think, are they stupid? No, not stupid. We just have so little in common."

The Bonn government's decision to pump more than $65 billion a year into the east—most of it in unemployment and welfare payments and make-work and retraining programs—has clamped a lid on social unrest in a region with a 40 percent jobless rate, but it also has fostered a culture of dependency.

"A lot of people in eastern Germany are readily and easily moving into roles as permanent welfare recipients because that most resembles the lives they led in the previous system, where the state took care of everything," Biedenkopf says.

Slowly, Bonn politicians and western executives have begun to accept Biedenkopf's argument that economic transition is the easy part of introducing a market economy; the tough part is the cultural shift.

"The call for west Germans to take part in and sacrifice for German unity obviously was too late and too weak," President Richard von Weizsaecker said recently.

Several major German institutions recently have begun to reach out to drifting easterners. The Federal Center for Political Education has issued a booklet called "What to Do"—the title is lifted from Lenin—offering easterners tips on dealing with western bureaucracy. A private group of advertising and media companies has launched an ad campaign with the slogan, "We're more alike than we think."

Two weeks ago Kohl said Germany's next president—a largely ceremonial post that nonetheless carries considerable moral weight—should be an easterner. An impressive roster of intellectuals and politicians proposed physicist Jens Reich, an early dissident in East Germany and a leader of the 1989 revolution, for the presidency.

"I am no candidate for the struggling Ossis," Reich says, but rather a role model for all Germans. "We can only succeed if we overcome the civil war within us, the Wall in the mind between east and west."

Few eastern Germans regret the demise of the Communist regime that snooped into their private lives, sapped individual creativity and force-fed a mind-numbing political and social conformism. Most eastern Germans became instant aficionados of the consumer society.

But the insecurity and fears surrounding a transition that has included the systematic dismantling of everything from day-care centers to state-provided burials have had a devastating social impact: Since 1989, the eastern birth rate has dropped by half. The number of marriages is down 38 percent. Together, the numbers indicate that young eastern Germans increasingly face the new society alone.

In a society in which women formerly made up half of the work force, 7 in 10 are jobless, most of them against their will.

"There's a terrible lethargy here now," says Baerbel Bohley, an artist and political activist who played a prominent role in the 1989 revolt. "People sit back and say, 'Do it for us.' We have freedom now, and that is worth something. But we look at the Wessis and they seem so tall. They rule us, and we take it."

East and west seem so far apart now that newspapers print separate bestseller lists for the two regions. Eastern readers put three of their own novelists atop their list; no easterner appears on the western list. While easterners snap up English dictionaries, westerners read novelists Gabriel Garcia Marquez and John Grisham and historian Paul Kennedy.

The unexpected social divide, along with neo-Nazi violence that plagues both east and west, has contributed to businesses' skepticism about investing in the east. Mainstream politicians find themselves ignoring the east because they cannot hope to win votes there. In universities and schools, a generation of eastern scholars and teachers has become embittered as they lose jobs to westerners selected solely because they are not "politically tainted."

Kohl's unity policy was based in large part on a 1991 consultant's report on the eastern economy that recommended allowing the Communist industrial base to collapse and replacing it with "islands of creativity"—new, high-tech industries supported by massive, Japanese-style government investment.

But Kohl took only part of the advice. "They thought the market would solve everything," says Matthias Greffreth, editor of the eastern Berlin-based weekly Wochenpost. "It didn't."

Instead of making enormous public investments to create jobs in the east over the long term, the Bonn government put hundreds of billions of dollars into easing the plight of millions of jobless easterners with make-work and retraining programs.

"There are tiny villages now in the east where 60 people have been retrained to cut your hair," Greffreth says.

"It was one or the other: Pay the Ossis individually, or take over the market function and invest in jobs that wouldn't materialize for 10 or 20 years," a Kohl adviser says. "We had to buy social peace."

Critics of the government's approach point to two mistakes: By deciding to return property nationalized by the Communists to the original owners rather than compensating them for their loss, Germany has allowed millions of property claims to stall potential investors from forging ahead with projects. And by promising easterners rapid progress toward western wages, the government eliminated what could have been a key lure for investors—the prospect of a cheaper labor market.

Bonn leaders had reckoned with what they call a "lost generation"—the 40-and-older easterners who will likely never again find work. But their loss and bitterness seeped unchecked into the younger generation, as children lost respect for parents drifting through life without purpose or pride.

The Federal Labor Office estimates that of the 155,000 eastern teenagers who will seek apprenticeships this fall, at least 35,000 will end up empty-handed.

One result has been a growing nostalgia for the old East Germany, a historical revisionism that Bohley calls a "dangerous force. It's meant as a defense against the west, but it only hurts and paralyzes ourselves."

"We had national pride," says Klaus-Dieter Gerlach, an industrial engineer who works for the Deutsche Reichsbahn, the eastern railroad, one of the few German enterprises that has retained a separate identity in the post-unity era. "We were the world's 10th-largest industrial power. Our statesmen were warmly received in Bonn. In East Germany, if you were a railroad man, you had an identity. No more."

Although East Germany's industrial might turned out to be wildly exaggerated, many in the east still defend their former country's strengths. Paramount among them, the defenders say, was the niche society, the close private relationships that people developed as an escape from the conformist repression of the totalitarian state.

"I had a circle of 10 friends," Gerlach says. "We did everything together—drinking Thursday nights, being with the families Fridays, going out to [nightclub shows] on Saturdays. There's nothing anymore, no activities.

"Our circle has slowly broken up. Two are unemployed, three went west to get jobs. The rest of us, maybe we talk on the phone once in a while, but there's this jealousy now. One will say, 'Why do he and his wife have jobs and I don't?' Money is everything now. Previously, you didn't need it; now, it's necessary to be educated, to find work, to travel, to spend an evening with friends."

Like many easterners, jobless or employed, Gerlach spends endless hours reciting the woes of reunification and waxing nostalgic about the Communist state he was thrilled to see fall.

Yet in some ways, eastern Germans are more optimistic than westerners, whose comfortable, affluent lives have been rocked by the multiple traumas of reunification. Polls show that while a large majority of westerners say Germany's economic woes will grow worse, the eastern prognostication is evenly split.

Biedenkopf, Saxony state's premier, is trying to bridge the east-west divide by building Saxon pride, focusing on the most successful organizing concept of German political history, the regional identities that have a more successful past than German nationalism. Old "tribal" regional differences in dialects and slang, cooking and humor survived the Communists' attempts to create a single East German identity.

And many in the east welcome the freedom to rediscover their Prussian or Thuringian roots. An industrial park in Ziesen, 60 miles west of Berlin, is being built with the name Prussia Park—an impossibility only four years ago.

But the larger problem remains: adjusting to western ways. "We can't understand the system, because we didn't grow up with it," says Elke Hotz. "I was at the village shop, and I found some women standing there with a package of frozen potato puffs and they hadn't a clue. I had to explain the whole idea to them."

Much of what ails the east will be cured by time and the continuing infusion of aid from the west. But some do not want to wait.

What both sides of the German divide need, psychotherapist Maaz says, is a "1968, a protest against authoritarian structures." But instead of seeking social change, he says, Germans are turning on themselves, producing striking increases in street crime, anti-foreigner attacks, political scandal and business failures.

To the surprise of many in the west, the most dramatic evidence of the country's troubles has arisen in their own, presumably more stably, part of the country. Western Germans found the euphoria of reunification replaced by a panorama of problems: economic decline, crime, rising taxes, xenophobia, large-scale illegal immigration.

"We knew our system was sick," easterner Maaz says. "The westerners thought theirs was healthy. Now, when so many problems emerge, some people react not in democratic ways but by looking to authority to give them the security they crave."

Bohley, the artist turned political activist, has not painted since before the Wall fell. "Painting is a matter of looking, taking time, and everything was moving so quickly," she says. "Now, I don't know, I'm exploring what we have in common with the westerners. And I think maybe we're not so far from each other.

"Previously, we always lived for the socialism that was supposed to come in 50 years. Now we are free to live in the present. Maybe we and the westerners can discover the present together."

(Continued)

Searching for identity, Germany struggles with its history

Marc Fisher

Washington Post Foreign Service

BERLIN

Sometime before the century's end, most likely after he wins a fourth term next year, Chancellor Helmut Kohl will leave office, and the vital connection between a confused, insecure new Germany and the confident generation that rebuilt the country after World War II will slip into history.

Kohl's generation of Germans born toward the start of Nazi rule was "blessed by the mercy of late birth," as the 63-year-old chancellor often says. Scarred by fascism but too young to bear responsibility for its crimes, these people built a new society and will carry their pride to their graves.

Now, however, a new generation of politicians is taking over, people born toward the end of the war, people who know their parents started from nil but who never had to face hardship themselves. They include what many derisively tag the Tuscany Faction of the opposition Social Democratic Party—stylish, richly tanned politicians who spend their leisure months in Italy and have deeply ambivalent attitudes toward power and leadership.

"We lack the strong personalities with the will of leadership and the readiness to run a personal risk," says Norbert Gansel, 52, a senior Social Democratic legislator. "My party and my generation are not prepared to fight things through. The problem is, German politics cannot appeal to a national dream as [Americans] can. There is no German dream. There is only German nightmare. People talk about returning to normalcy now that the Wall is down. What does normalcy mean in German history? And what does return mean?

"The German capacity to adapt is a problem. Two world wars brought not only enormous territorial losses but millions of Germans who lost everything to bomb raids, like my family. The little pieces of jewelry, the china, all blown away by a bomb. And then, the terrible inflation at the end of the war. It all changed German society enormously. There is a German desire for security now. And we live in a time of insecurity. Insecurity never helps people live with insecurity. It only makes them more determined to maintain their security."

"There's a certain hedonism to my generation," says Claus Leggewie, 43, a political scientist. "We've had no terribly difficult challenges. The politicians of this generation act as if being German is unpleasant. The idea that Germany now has to take on new responsibilities is very uncomfortable for them because it means they must decide what Germany's interests are."

Almost four years after the fall of the Berlin Wall, reunified Germany finds itself in a tangle of questions about its identity and its capacity to change. A powerful country that has defined itself for a half century by economic success and political consensus now stands troubled and pessimistic at the edge of a generational transition.

The country Kohl has shepherded from the cocoon of U.S. and NATO protection into a new vulnerability as the major power in the continent's center is once again where it hoped never to be—at the heart of a volatile and struggling Central Europe.

The Wall's demise and the swift reunification—all accomplished in a historic instant of extraordinary happenstance and well-timed spurts of international leadership—forced a new beginning upon the Germans.

It is a painful time for a country unaccustomed to difficulty. Economists say Germany suffers structural woes that will produce long recession, high unemployment and continuing temptations for major companies to export jobs. "I see no light at the end of the tunnel," says Willi Liebfritz, director of the Ifo research institute in Munich.

A national poll by ZDF television in May found 96 percent of Germans surveyed unhappy with their country's plight. Although 4 percent said Germany was "all right," 46 percent saw "big problems," 38 percent worried about a "difficult crisis" and 12 percent were so morose as to say Germany "faces catastrophe."

Politicians and business leaders of all ideological stripes speak of a battle for resources pitting rich against poor, east against west, and even generation against generation.

Kohl has told aides he feels obliged to stay in office for several more years in part because of the ahistorical drift he sees in the postwar generation of politicians. The chancellor spelled out his fears in a recent television interview, saying that if Germany fails to complete its own unification and European integration in the next few years, "we will experience the same evil spirits that have reemerged in Yugoslavia and Central Europe. We are not invulnerable to nationalism, chauvinism and xenophobia, to all the evils that have found their way here often enough."

In a preview of one of his main campaign themes for next year's reelection effort, Kohl presented himself as a historical bridge to the "immeasurable suffering" of World War II and warned that Germany and Europe could once again "stand before the question of war or peace" next century.

"Kohl may recognize the problems, but what has he done about nationalism and its violent impact here?" asks Margarita Mathiopoulos, a Greek-German banker, political scientist and author of "The End of the Bonn Republic."

"What Germany needs," she says, "is leadership that does not succumb to the romantic, racially based nationalism" that raises the specter of fascist ideology. Without strong mainstream leadership and a healthy sense of nationhood, she says, Germany risks a dangerous vacuum filled by extremists offering simple solutions. "We must ask how much of our famous democratic stability is based on real democratic consciousness, and how much is a product only of economic prosperity?" she says.

Foreign Minister Klaus Kinkel's calls for "healthy patriotism" would be unremarkable almost anywhere else. But for many in Germany's postwar generation, the very ideas of patriotism and leadership are tainted, primitive reminders of Adolf Hitler and Joseph Goebbels and their manipulation of the populace. The word for leader, *Fuehrer,* was poisoned by Hitler. Even a casual use of the word in conversation causes many Germans to gulp.

Neither is suspicion of patriotism purely a reaction to the Nazis: German history is a long series of struggles within the nation. "I have no mind at all for the German nationality," Bismarck, a Prussian, wrote in 1862. "To me, a war against the king of Bavaria or Hanover is the same as a war against France."

"We Germans have a broken relationship with our nation," says Ben Grewing of the Federal Center for Political Education, a government agency charged with spreading the gospel of democracy. "In Germany, we are proud of what we have, not of who we are."

Since the 1950s, Germany has measured its stability and its adoption of democratic ideals largely through the success of its auto and machine tool industries and the solidity of the German mark. Now many are asking if the national foundation does not need something more.

A few weeks ago, 500 billboards with the slogan "Germany Is Becoming More German" sprouted around Berlin. The words are imposed over a masked or bandaged face of a woman staring through a half-dozen daggers that pierce the wall behind her.

FACING A TROUBLED FUTURE?

DIVIDED NATION

Despite a common language and many shared traditions, eastern and western Germans remain far apart in attitudes and interests. Surveys indicate that, compared with their western counterparts, easterners are:

- more pacifistic;
- more optimistic about their own lives;
- more wary of international alliances;
- and more dependent on government.

ECONOMY

A recession and high unemployment created when East Germany's industrial base collapsed have been exacerbated by the strength of the German mark . . .

. . . which has made German exports more expensive and led to their decline in many foreign markets.

Officially, eastern Germany's jobless rate—including the unemployed and those on make-work projects and retraining programs—stands at 35 percent; unofficial estimates top 40 percent.

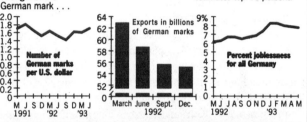

COMPETITIVENESS

The World Competitiveness Report, released by the Geneva World Economic Forum, shows Germany slipping to fifth from second overall among 38 industrial nations, and to ninth from second in the quality of its business management. The report cited Germany's falling per capita income–a result of absorbing the poor east, rising inflation and struggle for national identity.

IMMIGRATION

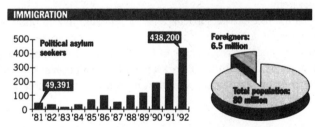

More than a million foreigners have moved to Germany since the country was reunited in 1990. In 1992, 440,000 entrants applied for political asylum, the only legal route for most foreigners. This year, 193,000 asylum-seekers arrived in the first five months. Germany has decided to turn away illegal migrants at its borders and deport asylum-seekers whose applications have been rejected.

Germany last year accepted 79 percent of all refugees seeking political asylum in the 12-country European Community. And Germany has accepted more than 300,000 refugees from the war in the Balkans, more than any other country.

RIGHT-WING VIOLENCE

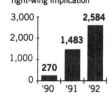

Violent incidents with proven or suspected right-wing implication

In 1992, neo-Nazis and other right-wing radicals committed more than 2,500 violent incidents against foreigners in Germany. Seventeen people died in the violence. Anti-foreigner crimes have continued at a similar rate this year.

SOURCES: Bloomberg Business News, German Embassy in Washington.

Compiled by The Washington Post's Berlin Bureau, Jeannette Belliveau, William Hifner.

The billboards are artist Katharina Sievering's attempt to confront Germans with their self-image. "The poster assumes Germans have a bad conscience and that Germans are feared," says Peter Herbstreuth, art critic of Berlin's Tagesspiegel newspaper. If Germans themselves associate Germanness with guilt and nativism, then Kinkel's appeals for a "healthy patriotism" will remain little more than rhetoric.

For the past 50 years, Germans have pursued a different ideal: the successful manager who aims for compromise and consensus, disdaining personal vision or charismatic appeal.

"The whole of modern Germany society is built on cooperation and continuity," says Leggewie, the political scientist. "Parties, newspapers, industry—none of them is used to competition or confrontation. Neither is the government: We spent half a century as the object of other countries' foreign policies. Even the '60s were not the national crisis for us that it was for the French."

But in an era of confrontation both within German society and in a Europe roiling with ethnic and economic conflict, that model may no longer suffice.

"Our society's greatest weakness is an engagement gap," says Werner Hoyer, 41, parliamentary leader of the Free Democrats, the junior partners in Kohl's coalition. "You don't get involved unless it immediately helps your business or family. We have no tradition of volunteerism as you [Americans] do. The generation of Kohl and [former longtime foreign minister Hans-Dietrich] Genscher had the will, the burning desire to build something new. They were historically minded and willing to forgo material things for a political career. My generation doesn't have that sense of mission that produces leadership. In my generation, politics is not very high-ranking in the social hierarchy."

In the face of rising social tensions and an influx of political and economic refugees, accompanied by a violent scapegoating of foreigners, Germans look toward their political leaders for a vision of the future. They come away empty-handed and frustrated. The country suffers from a deep disaffection with politics.

Many of Germany's troubles are similar to problems facing most major industrial nations. The need for structural economic change, the dangers of ethnic strife and the failure of politicians to provide answers have been dominant themes in the United States, Britain and France.

But as in so many of this century's most important issues, what sets Germany apart today is its struggle with history. Germans from all major parties watched Bill Clinton's presidential campaign with palpable jealousy, marveling at Americans' ability to generate hope in hard times. Kohl himself deeply admired Margaret Thatcher's knack for combining tough policies in Britain with hopeful, optimistic politics.

In Germany, however, pessimism reigns, a cultural tradition with deep roots and often unhappy consequences. "There is Goetterdaemmerung everywhere in Germany," Hoyer says. Finance Minister Theo Waigel speaks of "a national identity crisis" and the "sharpest economic crisis" since the Great Depression.

Germans have reacted to the strains of reunification and the collapse of its direct neighbor, the Communist East Bloc, with an endless reexamination of what it means to be German. We Germans, says Malte Lehming in a commentary in the Tagesspiegel, "find ourselves in a permanent condition of self-searching, a kind of eternal puberty."

An exasperated Kohl recently complained about "all this moaning and whining. No other country would have responded to its unification, a gift of history, with so much public brooding." Despite "unprecedented prosperity," Kohl said, Germans "react with excessive nervousness or even hysteria to the slightest fluctuations and changes."

Indeed, despite its problems, Germany has managed to use Europe's system of linked currencies to spread the cost of German reunification around the continent, and Germans continue to enjoy one of the highest standards of living—and the most generous vacation benefits and work conditions—in the world.

The chancellor has taken to regularly scolding his countrymen for taking their leisure as a birthright and for "spreading cultural pessimism," attitudes he says would have prevented West Germans of the 1950s from creating their economic miracle out of the ruins of World War II.

That admonition is one that Kohl's successors, whichever party they may represent, will not be able to make, if only because the miracle of the '50s was another generation's achievement.

A string of scandals resulting in the disgraced departure of four nationally known politicians so far this year has only reinforced the public impression that the new generation of politicians lacks the moral fiber of, for example, former chancellor Willy Brandt, who fled Nazi Germany and returned as an underground resistance fighter. The impact is considerable: Although 90 percent of Germans voted in 1990, one-third of Germans now tell pollsters they plan to boycott next year's elections.

Even as politician Hoyer and his colleagues warn that they must provide a vision of the new Germany or risk opening the door to nationalist extremists, many of these same Germans cannot bring themselves to champion Kinkel's "healthy patriotism." Among 14- to 27-year-old Germans, according to a new poll commissioned by the Ministry for Women and Youth, 47 percent of those polled in the west say they are proud to be German, while 68 percent of eastern youths express such pride.

"Why must I be a patriot?" says Egon Zeidler, a shopkeeper in east Berlin. "Somewhere in my head, I still think if we Germans aren't going to be a great military power, we should at least be a great economic power. And then comes national pride that someone smart can reawaken. And what's the next step? Kicking the next guy. And that's how it starts."

"It," of course, is the terrifying memory that lurks in the minds of older Germans and their children, if not in the youngest Germans. Even a generation removed, the memory is enough to render patriotism a soiled, suspicious concept.

"I always called myself a European," says Torsten Schramm, the son of an SS officer who responded to his father's life by becoming a director of Action Reconciliation, an organization that sends young Germans to perform public service work in Jewish institutions in Israel, the United States and elsewhere.

"This new 'I'm proud to be German' that you hear more and more now sounds macho to me," he says. "But I see that we need self-confidence to protect ourselves from the right-wing radicals. It's very hard for those of us who came up through the peace movement. We really don't know what to think."

Since the Persian Gulf War, Germany has struggled over its future military role, debating endlessly the clash between the country's postwar pacifism and its new, post-unification responsibility to share defense burdens with the United States and the United Nations. "Obviously, we need to show more solidarity to our friends who showed solidarity to us for all these years," Hoyer says. "But we should not simply give up this culture of reticence we have developed for very good historical reasons."

President Richard von Weizaecker—an elder statesman who has asked Germany's allies to be patient as the country seeks a middle ground between its historic extremes of pacifism and militarism—nonetheless has grown impatient with politicians who shy from recognizing that united Germany now has its own interests.

Weizsaecker says he dismisses the often-heard view that Germany "should hide itself in European integration to relieve foreign fears of a greater Germany. This is neither morally necessary nor a reasonable definition of our interests."

The dilemma Germany will face in the coming years is a choice between the extremes—whether right-wing nationalism or left-wing denial of nationhood—and the middle—Weizsaecker's honest balancing act of national interests with the postwar pledge to avoid going it alone.

Answers will be a long time coming, and they will be hard fought, but for politicians of the postwar generation—and for young Germans of the post-Wall generation—the only alternative to a dangerous flirtation with extremism is a rigorous attempt to find their own answer to the identity question.

THE DARK WINTER OF HELMUT KOHL

HIS STAR TARNISHED, GERMANY'S HERO OF REUNIFICATION FACES A WALL OF PROBLEMS

Tyler Marshall

Tyler Marshall is The Times' *Berlin Bureau chief.*

The little east German farming village of Trantow has been scrubbed from one end to the other for its big day. Mayor Uta Kruger, who was shifting hay in the nearby fields when the advance team descended on her a week ago, now stands nervously in her Sunday best outside the village inn, listening for the sounds of the helicopter. Up the hill at the agricultural station, tough-speaking farmhands, high-heeled television reporters and blue-suited bureaucrats tiptoe through the cattle droppings, positioning themselves.

Suddenly, he's here, the chancellor, Helmut Kohl, his 6-foot-4, 287-pound frame towering over Mayor Kruger, his formidable presence keeping the crowd around him at bay as a farm director machine-guns him with statistics and other details about the station. Kohl is pleased. The good citizens of Trantow are his kind of people—rural, hard-working, doggedly determined. Buoyed by the success of their station's transition from communist collective to free-enterprise producer, they still believe that a united Germany will bring the good life. Of the 550 souls who live in and around the village, about 50 are without work, but Kohl has come to accentuate the positive. He lunches with farmers, listening more than talking, then walks through the village toward the open wheat field where his helicopter waits.

This is CDU country, territory where Kohl's conservative Christian Democratic Union holds sway despite the region's crippling unemployment, its shattered industry and its bleak outlook. Here in the remote rolling hills of Mecklenburg-Western Pomerania, the poorest of Germany's 16 states, the euphoria of German unity may have faded, but hostility has not yet set

in. He meets brave smiles and polite applause. We all knew it would take longer to reach the rainbow, they say. It's not his fault.

"Sure it's tough for some, but not everything can happen overnight," says Kruger with a shrug after the visit. "People have to keep their nerve and somehow make their way through it."

Trantow is one of three stops on the day's journey to the east, a region that received Kohl as a demigod in 1990, the year of reunification—the man who delivered them from communism, gave them the mighty deutsche mark, negotiated nearly half a million Russian soldiers out of their land, rejoined them with the West and, above all, promised them the Western-style prosperity they had for years seen only on television screens.

"No one will be worse off; for many, life will be better," he had promised. But with one of three working-age east Germans out of a job, Kohl's words now haunt him, and a sullen sense of betrayal festers in many parts of the east.

The chancellor, celebrated at home and abroad three years ago as "King Kohl," the father of German reunification and Europe's new great statesman, the man Harvard Magazine introduced in the summer of 1990 as "A New Hercules," has tumbled from grace at a speed hardly thought possible.

Opinion polls today put Kohl and his party at near-record lows. With elections looming in October for the federal Parliament, and hence for the chancellorship, the burly leader finds himself back where he was before the wall fell: in a fight for political survival. Even within the ranks of his own Christian Democrats, whispers of frustration grow more intense.

His insistence in nominating an obscure eastern politician, Steffen Heitmann, as his party's candidate for next May's presidential election, followed by Heitmann's political self-destruction and eventual withdrawal in November, amounted to a serious personal setback for Kohl and raised questions about his judgment. And local elections last month in the eastern state of Brandenburg that left his Christian Democrats struggling to keep even with the political resurgence of former Communists was a further embarrassment for the chancellor.

Kohl, as he begins his 12th year in power, may be doing poorly in the polls, but the main-opposition Social Democrats aren't doing much better. Racked by their own internal divisions and led by Rudolf Scharping, an inexperienced national chairman, the Socialists face an uphill struggle if they are to be considered a credible alternative to the Christian Democratic Union.

So at the start of the biggest election year in the country's post–World War II era, all four German mainstream parties face the ominous threat of the growing strength of the far left and extreme right. Collectively, these parties add up to about 30% of the voters, a figure that could conceivably leave Kohl and his Social Democrat opponents with two unpleasant options after the parliamentary elections: joining together in a so-called "grand coalition," or seeking an alliance with a party from the political fringe.

As Kohl begins his campaign, he struggles with a series of ever-deepening problems. Germany's economy sputters as do those of its key trading partners, while reunification has brought a series of unexpected nightmares, including the resurrected ghost of the country's Nazi past. The dream of deeper European integration—an idea Kohl considers essential for Germany's long-term stability—is losing its luster, and his attempts to nudge Germany toward accepting a greater global role are meeting stiff domestic resistance, a fact that has tarred his country with the image of being an uncertain partner. As the world watches Boris N. Yeltsin's hair-raising ride with Russian democracy, the leader of Europe's other great power struggles in the shadows to control problems that are more subtle and complex, but whose outcome is equally important to the continent's future.

In a leisurely conversation in his spacious wood-paneled office at the Federal Chancellory in Bonn, the 63-year-old chancellor appeared unruffled by events around him. He dismissed international concern about the wave of right-wing extremism in Germany as "absolutely unjustified," sketched out his dream of Germany taking its place in a united Europe and gave no hint of quitting.

As Kohl prepares to embark on what many believe will be his last reelection campaign, one overriding question hangs in the air: Can he recapture the fire that propelled him to short-term greatness? Or is he in truth a mundane figure who rose briefly above himself and whose only real strength is endurance?

Helmut Kohl has made a career out of being underestimated, ever since The Times of London introduced the new German chancellor to its readers in October, 1982, as a "colourless man from the sticks." His big, ungainly form, legendary appetite, flat, uninspiring speech delivery, distaste for formality, inability to master languages and suspicion of intellectuals have combined to present an impression of uncultured mediocrity. His thickly accented *Pfalzer* German (which sounds like someone trying to speak with a mouth full) completes the image. Some carp that he's not only the first postwar German chancellor unable to converse in a foreign language, he's also the first unable to speak his own.

In her memoirs, former British Prime Minister Margaret Thatcher dismisses Kohl as a man with "the sure touch of a German provincial politician." The collective result of these characterizations is a sitting-duck target for political cabaret artists and jokesters.

The picture is deceptive. In fact, few political figures labor under a public image so radically at odds with reality. Certainly Kohl is a man of simple pleasures and basic values—a man raised in a lower-middle-class neighborhood of a company town who remains committed to the lessons learned there. His office ornaments include a fish tank, a rock collection and a plastic statue of Mother Teresa. For him, what matters most is loyalty, not excellence; character, not intelligence; people, not ideas.

But there is more to Kohl, much more. He holds a Ph.D. in history; he is a student of art and music, a connoisseur of good wines and arguably the best-read man ever to hold the office of German chancellor. His former spokesman, Hans Klein, recalls Kohl being ambushed by a French television reporter at the Frankfurt Book Fair, demanding to know what French literature he had read during the previous year. After reeling off a series of titles, the chancellor ended up debating the reporter on the pros and cons of a recently published biography of Jean-Paul Sartre. Kohl's personal friendship with François Mitterrand—the French president's portrait hangs in Kohl's office—is said to stem in part from their common interest in literature.

But while the chancellor counts many conservative philosophers and intellectuals among his friends, his respect for deep thinkers stops at politics. "I belong to the generation that hasn't forgotten that it was tough-fisted men like Harry Truman and George Marshall, not the professors from Princeton or wherever, who said we can't repeat the mistakes of 1918 or 1919," Kohl declared in our conversation. That comment says much about Kohl's origins and the extent to which they remain embedded in his thinking.

The last of three children born into a staunchly Roman Catholic family in Ludwigshafen, he remains very much a product of his home and of his time. The secluded bungalow in suburban Oggersheim with the name "H. Kohl" painted in black on the mailbox outside is only a few miles from the smokestacks of the giant BASF chemical works and from his own parents' home downtown. It was here, as a young teen-ager in a city substantially flattened by Allied bombing, that he endured most of World War II.

It was here that he helped rescue people and their belongings from burning buildings and pulled bodies from the rubble. It is also where Kohl met his wife, Hannelore, and where he learned the value of hard work, loyalty and a kind of street-style leadership that so often falls to big, crafty men.

From the beginning, Kohl was a *macher*—a doer—and an organizer. He joined the new Christian Democrats at 16, and in a party that today counts three quarters of a million members, Kohl holds membership No. 246.

Although Kohl left for the state legislature at age 28 and has been in Bonn for nearly 20 years, his ties remain in Ludwigshafen, deep in the Palatinate. For many years, he'd gather a few friends in his spare time and go to the local sauna—a habit that relaxed him and provided him with an effective way to get honest opinions. Today, his friends are world leaders and he treats them little differently, holding informal talks with Russian President Boris N. Yeltsin in a sauna and taking state visitors back to his home for weekends, the way college students bring home a roommate. He takes them through the surrounding wine country, and subjects them to the dubious pleasure of his favorite dish, *saumagen,* a mix of meat, potatoes and vegetables stuffed into a pig's belly and then boiled.

During his summer vacations in Austria, he spends a day with famed Nazi-hunter Simon Wiesenthal, a man he has known for 20 years. "We walk in the woods or in the hills, and talk and talk," Wiesenthal told me. "For me, it's good to know how he really feels. For him, it's important to hear the views of someone who isn't one of his advisers."

For a people whose hearts danced atop the Berlin Wall in the incredible autumn of 1989 and whose eyes watched the fireworks over the Brandenburg Gate on Unification Day a year later, disappointment has followed disappointment on an unexpected downhill ride that today heads toward a German future filled with troubling question marks.

Europe's bellwether economy, the core of the continent's counterweight to the United States and Japan, is in crisis. Instead of the anticipated second *Wirtschaftswunder,* unity has transformed eastern Germany into an industrial desert that survives mainly on hope and subsidies from the west that total nearly $100 billion annually. Frequently, hope runs out—a fact underscored by the flow of east-to-west migration that last year averaged more than 16,000 persons a month.

In western Germany, a people accustomed to steadily increased wealth and affluence over the past four decades now wallow in the worst recession of the postwar era. Unemployment stands at a postwar high of nearly 3.5 million. Pillars of German industry such as Daimler-Benz are actively shedding workers for the first time since West Germany's famed Economic Miracle began in the 1950s. Volkswagen has scaled production back so much that it recently decided to implement a four-day work week instead of laying off 31,000 workers.

Western Germans see a Europe with no Iron Curtain, watch the influx of easterners and foreigners and begin to realize that their lives have permanently and materially changed for the worse. For them, change means declining living standards, an end to their enviable annual wage hikes, six weeks of vacation, and painfully, a dimming dream of the 35-hour workweek with full pay. "We live in an industrial park, not in an amusement park," Kohl reminds his people.

It is not a message they like to hear. As resentment builds on both sides of Germany's old political divide, support erodes for the nation's traditional custodians of power—the Christian Democratic Union and other mainline parties that have been the keys to stability throughout the postwar era.

As Germany struggles, the world outside has suddenly become a tougher place. The ominous shadow of the Soviet threat may be gone, but so is the allied commitment that sheltered Germans from foreign evils for four decades.

Meanwhile, the very cornerstones of Germany's foreign policy have begun to wobble. The Atlantic Alliance is in the depths of a major crisis, while the dream of European unity—a dream to which Germans have long hooked much of their patriotism and a good chunk of their identity—is under growing strain. If that dream should end, so too would Germany's path to the future.

The country's main allies are demanding a greater global role of Germany, including active participation in United Nations peacekeeping missions and taking part as an equal in any new system of collective security. Half-pushed, half-dragged by their allies—and frequently by the chancellor himself—the Germans move toward this responsibility with a mixture of fear, foreboding and a common realization that they are psychologically unprepared for the task.

The big man enters the room full of reporters, his eyes darting around nervously like an animal on uncertain turf. Not photogenic, rarely eloquent, and quick to argue when challenged, Kohl frequently gets a rough ride from the national media, and his guard is up when he is around the press. But on this occasion, the reporters are American, more interested in probing his foreign-policy views on the eve of a

Washington visit than attacking him on domestic policy. Sensing the lack of threat, Kohl's mood changes immediately. He smiles, pushes back and begins to reel off a string of anecdotes, most of which involve a larger message gained from encounters with ordinary people. The questions end and the hour draws late, but Kohl, now at full throttle, talks on, embellishing his stories amid the warmth of the occasion.

If there is a comparable figure to Helmut Kohl in recent times, it is not another European but the late U.S. President Lyndon B. Johnson, whose physical bulk, coarse manner and thick accent masked unseen strengths. Like Johnson, Kohl understands power and how to use it and combines a ruthless streak for political survival and tough power-brokering skills with a rare sense of duty to country that borders on a calling. "The last dinosaur," commented the weekly magazine Der Spiegel, in an article on Kohl's 10th anniversary in office.

Like Johnson's image, Kohl's also suffers in part because of the enormity of the problems he confronts.

"Actually, I live quite well from being underestimated," he told me with a hint of a smile. "My predecessor [Helmut Schmidt] believed I was a village idiot, and so-called German intellectuals, they say that on even-numbered days I can read and on odd-numbered days I can write—that doesn't bother me at all."

But only a part of Kohl's political strength stems from his deceptive image. His real strengths lie elsewhere: an uncanny instinct for power and how to use it, an ability to smell the public mood, and a natural curiosity about people that ranges from presidents to potato farmers. "I study people the way others study books," he once said. There is no grand idea or *ism* attached to Kohl. Indeed, after watching Kohl in power for 11 years, political observers still find it hard to define his ideology—a task one pundit has likened to nailing pudding to a wall.

Franz-Josef Strauss, Bavaria's great postwar figure and a fellow conservative, once dismissed Kohl as "a successful state governor who needs to recognize his limits." But as Kohl consistently got the better of him, the Bavarian's contempt turned into a quiet rage. "There were Strauss confidants who were certain he hated Kohl," comments columnist and onetime Kohl spokesman Peter Boenish. "It was worse."

The axioms that underpin Kohl's vision of Germany's place in the world have been largely unchanged since he sat at the knee of West Germany's first postwar chancellor, Konrad Adenauer, four decades ago: German reunification in peace and freedom, reconciliation with France, compensation for Israel and support for the Atlantic Alliance and European unity.

Much of what anchors the chancellor's political compass comes from his own personal experience. His commitment to the trans-Atlantic Alliance, for example, is laced with teen-age memories of American CARE packages and his close friendships with American Presidents (photos of former Presidents Reagan and Bush are the only two non-family photographs on his desk). His careful attention to Germany's relationship with France is that of a man born less than an hour's drive from the present French frontier in a region swept by war with depressing regularity over the centuries.

"The towns and villages around my home have been destroyed, at least in part, by every generation [over the past 250 years]," he told a television interviewer last year.

Kohl's gut relationship to policies is matched by his strong sense of the public mood. It is an instinct he works hard to keep honed. His circle of friends back in Ludwigshafen are not big-shot industrialists but very ordinary people—a priest, a farmer, an innkeeper. On Saturday mornings, Kohl occasionally shops by himself in a large open market in the town square.

"He stands there and talks with people," says Erich Ramstetter, a friend and the deacon at the Ludwigshafen church where Kohl was baptized, married and still attends Mass. "He wants to know what the farmer is getting for potatoes. He really wants to know."

Despite this common touch, Kohl has never been a popular chancellor, with his personal ratings invariably trailing those of the party as a whole. His non-intellectual image and poor television presence work to dampen his appeal.

More than any other factor, Kohl's longevity stems from the vise-like grip he holds on his party. Kohl watched, and learned from the demise of great leaders like Ludwig Erhard and Helmut Schmidt, who fell because they neglected their political base. And in the parliamentary democracies of Europe, Kohl understands, power still resides in the smoke-filled rooms and party caucuses, not the photo-ops and primaries that drive American politics.

But Kohl's strengths are also his great weaknesses. His commitment to character values has left him virtually bereft of strategic thinking and goals for a nation desperately searching to redefine itself in the wake of unification and great social change. "He has no great vision for a justly organized society," says Martin Suesskind, Bonn bureau chief for the Süddeutsche Zeitung for the last 14 years. "I believe that under Kohl's chancellorship we've become a less cohesive people than we once were."

When he does err, the mistakes can reach a grand scale. His conviction, for example, that East Germans were simply West Germans deprived of opportunity led the chancellor to badly misjudge the cleft between the two peoples and reject the idea of any special government authorities to deal with eastern affairs. "I just didn't believe how deep the human divide is after 40 years," he told me.

His repeated failure to lead a vigorous counterattack against the neo-Nazi threat has cost his country dearly in terms of image. To this day, Kohl has never visited the site of any right-wing extremist attacks or been seen publicly consoling the families of their victims. Last June, he pointedly refused to attend the funeral of five Turkish nationals who died in an arson attack allegedly carried out by a group of German youths. Those who know the chancellor well believe that his failure to deal more effectively with the problem of attacks on foreigners lies partly in his lack of personal experience with the country's ethnic minorities. Because few in these groups can vote, he has no compelling political need to do so.

The war cemetery in the small western town of Bitburg contained no surprises, Kohl's staff had assured members of President Ronald Reagan's advance team preparing the 1985 state visit. During two excursions there by U.S. officials, there was nothing to hint otherwise.

Snow had covered the grave markers on the first trip, and rain had quickly driven officials away on the second. So it was only after Reagan's visit to Bitburg was announced officially that the truth became known: Not only German soldiers were buried there but several members of Hitler's elite Waffen SS combat divisions as well.

For Reagan and his horrified advisers, the revelation meant that the cemetery visit had to be canceled. It meant no such thing for Helmut Kohl. For him, the wreath laying was much more than one more symbol of reconciliation between America and Germany 40 years after the final shots of Europe's bloodiest war. The meaning went deeper. The presidential wreath was a reaffirmation of a Kohl axiom: that modern Germany is a country like any other. Just as visiting dignitaries honor war dead on visits to Washington, Moscow, Paris and London, so, too, should they do it in Germany.

The degree to which Kohl insisted that Reagan go through with the ceremony is an indicator of how strongly the chancellor insists that Germany be treated like a normal country. Arguments mounted from the intellectual left—such as author Günter Grass' contention that Germany can never get beyond Auschwitz and should not even try—are dismissed by Kohl with a single word: absurd. For him, democratic Germany should never deny Auschwitz, but must move beyond it.

Much of Kohl's years as a politician have been devoted to building the accoutrements of normalcy for his country, including a rekindling of patriotism. As governor of Rhineland Palatinate, the brought a black, red and gold flag used during a 19th-Century democratic protest not far from his home into the state legislature. Under his chancellorship, German flags have returned to ministerial offices, the national soccer team learned to sing the national anthem once again, and words like *Vaterland, Heimat* and *Volk*—words so debauched by Nazi propaganda that they rankled when spoken—began reappearing.

Despite protests from abroad and the German political left, Kohl has never wavered. He simply bulls ahead, convinced that such symbols are essential ingredients for pride and stability. He also knew Germany's silent majority was pleased.

In November, in the face of protests, he dedicated a memorial in Berlin "to the victims of war and tyranny," which political critics claimed lumped Nazism's victims together with its perpetrators.

The criticism that came with Bitburg was repeated six years later when he upgraded the reburial of Frederick the Great—the personification of Prussian militarism—first with his own presence (albeit as a private person) and then by insisting that an eight-member Bundeswehr honor guard also take part as the king's remains were returned to his Sans Souci Palace in Potsdam.

For Kohl, none of this had to do with reviving German militarism or justifying the past. It had to do with building a normal future.

This conviction of normalcy is one additional factor that helps explain Kohl's curious inaction in the face of rising xenophobia in Germany. For him, the skinheaded thugs involved in the attacks against foreigners have little to do with German society. They are part of a broader European phenomenon with no connection to the Third Reich, let alone to the postwar democratic successor state, he insists, declaring: "That is not Germany."

For Kohl, the main lesson of history is not that Germans must be on the watch for a second Holocaust but that they must avoid a third national catastrophe. For him, the two World Wars stand together as proof that Germany's abnormality lies in the undeniable reality of its size and strength, not any congenital evil.

For Helmut Kohl, reunification three years ago wasn't a political goal. It was a conviction, as fundamental and indisputable as a Christian's belief in the second coming. It would happen; the only question was when. Through his wife, who spent her youth in Leipzig, he had a personal link to the east; and during the Cold War, he was a rarity among West German politicians for his habit of crossing into the East for private visits there. Once the Berlin Wall fell in November, 1989, Kohl wasted little time.

Gathering his closest advisers in the chancellory on the night of Nov. 23, Kohl approved a daring but risky idea put forward by his chief foreign-affairs adviser, Horst Teltschik. The chancellor would brush aside the hand-wringing that had already begun among Germany's neighbors and broach the unthinkable: He would outline a plan for West German reunification with the country's Communist half.

The outcome of that evening—a 10-point plan outlining a gradual, phased move toward a reunited Germany—looks almost timid in the light of subsequent events. But with revolution spreading uncertainty throughout Eastern Europe and fears growing in Western Europe of a resurgent Germany, the very idea of unity was considered too explosive to discuss openly.

The chancellor's speech unveiling the plan was nothing less than a bombshell. Not even his own foreign minister, Hans-Dietrich Genscher, knew it was coming. Suddenly, the issue of German unity was out of the closet. And Kohl had given it shape and form. Thus began what would become a perfect political year for the chancellor, as he boldly brought the east out of the Soviet orbit and fixed his stature as a European statesman.

After his initial reunification plan was announced, it would take another three weeks and his first-ever official trip to East Germany—to Dresden—before the chancellor realized that events were moving much faster than he anticipated.

The euphoric reception Kohl received that night was televised around the globe. For those who watched, it was the latest in a series of remarkable reunions between Germans east and west. For Kohl the scene carried a far deeper message, and he read it immediately.

Descending from his official aircraft at the Dresden airport, the chancellor took one look at the crowd that had come to meet him—the cheering workers, well-wishers who had climbed onto the terminal roof for a glimpse of him—and he knew that unity would come fast. He turned to chancellory minister Rudolf Seiters, descending the steps behind him, and shared his revelation. "Seiters," he said, "it's over."

He was right. Germany would soon be one again. But for Kohl, unity would also end a political highpoint, since dimmed by the troubles that he and his country face today.

Germany and Its European Environment

Elizabeth Pond

Elizabeth Pond is a freelance journalist and author based in Bonn. Her most recent book is *Beyond the Wall: Germany's Road to Unification* (Washington, D.C.: Brookings, 1993).

THERE ARE TWO ways to look at Germany and its European environment. The first is short term, journalistic, the glass dramatically half empty at a time of social turmoil and economic and political drift—in a word, the orthodox view. The second is long term, set in a different perspective, the glass half full, against all the odds of history.

The two opposing viewpoints no longer represent a dichotomy between dominant conservative and embattled liberal, even though throughout the 1980s and in 1990 the fears (in the United States) of potential German disasters were more pronounced on the right and confidence in the sturdiness of German democracy more common on the left. In particular, the Reagan right (and, to be sure, the Polish-influenced National Security Council of Jimmy Carter) feared "self-Finlandization" of the Federal Republic of Germany. Weaknesses of an open society might be exploited by the clever Russians, it was argued. Moscow might play the "German card"—that is, offer the unification the West Germans were assumed to be panting after at the price of German neutrality.

As it turned out, history did not take that turn. The bloodless revolution on the streets of Dresden and Leipzig not only forced unification on the indifferent or reluctant West Germans, but also triggered the breakaway of the Russians' external and even internal empires. This example then persuaded a few tens of thousands of Muscovites to abandon their accustomed passivity and protest the hardline coup attempt against Mikhail Gorbachev of August 1991. By that December the Soviet Union had imploded. It was not Germany but Russia that was neutralized as the Cold War ended.

Yet some of the old suspicions of Germany linger on and are reactivated whenever drunken German youths firebomb a Turkish home, or economic forecasts predict a 2 percent drop in German gross domestic product (GDP), or Germans quarrel among themselves about sending the Bundeswehr on allied expeditions outside the territory of the North Atlantic Treaty Organization (NATO). There was a spasm of alarm about an assertive Germany when Bonn forced the European Community (EC) to recognize Croatia at the end of 1991. This was swiftly supplanted by alarm about just the opposite phenomenon: Germany's economic weakness and domestic preoccupation as the task of reconstructing eastern Germany proved to be so exhausting. Would democracy falter as prosperity faltered? Would neo-Nazis benefit? Would the end of Germany's need for U.S. security also end the close transatlantic relationship? Would European integration and its explicit and implicit constraints on a dynamic Germany prove to be no more than an evanescent reaction to the Soviet threat of 45 years as European populations rebelled against the overweening Maastricht treaty?

The thesis of this essay, in exploring such questions in the long term, is that even in the midst of seismic change Germany remains a stable, conservative democracy capable of solving its multiple crises; that Germany's Western identity is finally assured; that the country's traditional creeping consensus is being rebuilt, slowly but surely; that Germany is condemned to leadership willy-nilly, both in western and eastern Europe; and that the EC, having rejuvenated itself before German unification, provides a sufficient channel for the energies loosed by Germany's third rise in a century.

The European Context

Any examination of unified Germany's internal and external health must necessarily start with the European context. It was fortunate indeed that prior to German union a somnolent EC had already rejuvenated itself in projecting

From *The Washington Quarterly*, Vol. 16, No. 4, Autumn 1993, pp. 131-140. © 1993 by The Center for Strategic and International Studies and the Massachusetts Institute of Technology. Reprinted by permission of The MIT Press, Cambridge, MA.

a single European market by the year 1992. This political as well as economic quickening provided a benign framework in which German union became, as Chancellor Helmut Kohl said time and again, a catalyst for further European integration rather than a booby trap for it. Mindful of the catastrophic course of events in the twentieth century, the non-Germans strove to bind the new German Gulliver to the pan-European institution of the EC. And the Germans themselves, as Kohl also said time and again, agreed that they needed to be so bound, for the peace of Europe. Even though they did not realize it, the French were knocking on an open door when they insisted after the Berlin Wall opened in November 1989 that Germany endorse European monetary union and a European central bank, and in early 1990 (however ambivalent the French themselves were about the prospect) that Germany endorse political union.

The ambitious Maastricht treaty was the result—as is the current backlash to that treaty. The Danes cherish their favorite small apples that fail to meet the EC minimum size. The French want to protect their ripe cheeses from the horrors of Eurohomogenization. Eighty percent of Germans, the most earnest Europeans of all, still wish to hang on to their "lovely deutsche mark" and not merge it into a common European currency. Yet ratification of the treaty has squeaked through in all member states, and although leaders are now toning down their EC rhetoric under the sheer workload of admitting Austria, Sweden, Finland, and Norway, they fully expect to resume forward motion at the intergovernmental conference of 1996.

Conventional wisdom in the United States interprets the present pause as a pullback in response to voter rebellion against Maastricht targets set by political elites who had lost touch with the man and woman on the street. Such a gloss misses the vigorous dynamics of post–cold war Europe, however. The EC has always advanced by messy lurches, with two steps forward, one step back. The basic urge of Europeans—an impressive 60 to 70 percent in all EC member countries except for Britain and Denmark, according to opinion surveys—is to want more integration. They may de-

mur at the specific terms of Maastricht but they do not oppose its direction. This, at least, is the firm conviction of German policymakers.

Moreover, the Western cooperative system is rapidly spreading eastward. It acts as a magnet: Poland, the Czech and Slovak republics, and Hungary, plus the Baltic states, Slovenia, and even Bulgaria and Romania are all lining up to join the premier institutions of the EC and NATO as fast as possible. Far from reverting to the "renationalization" that so many American commentators feared with the dissolution of the pax Sovietica, countries in both western and eastern Europe are adjusting to the new uncertainties and loss of Russian threat by pressing for even more pan-European cooperation.

Not even the tragedy in the former Yugoslavia contradicts this analysis. The photogenic carnage there has diverted media attention from the slow, prosaic growth of voluntary institutions in Central Europe. But the sensation of the emerging European order is not atavistic reversion to tribal passions (or, more accurately perhaps, the deliberate power play of resort to criminality) among the southern Slavs and the Caucasian and Central Asian fringes of the decayed Russian empire. The real innovation is that the new habits of a heartland western Europe that emerged from its own centuries of civil wars only two generations ago already radiate such attraction to Central Europe, despite all the agonies of systemic transformation. By joining the Western community, Estonia seeks to emulate the relaxed wealth of a Finland that 45 years ago shared Estonia's low standard of living. Saxony and Bohemia similarly seek to emulate Bavaria—and Bohemia hopes to recapture some of the entrepreneurial and democratic spirit it manifested in the 1920s. Hungary, the one nation with sizable minorities abroad after the terrible exterminations and forced population resettlements of World War II, today sees far less profit in old-fashioned irredentism than in becoming a new Austria. Poland has no wish to perpetuate its old hostility with Ukraine and makes a point of nurturing good relations with Kiev. Eastern Europe is determined to end its backwardness and perennial lag behind western Europe.

In this atmosphere the degeneration

in the former Yugoslavia is seen in the neighborhood as a dangerous exception, but not as the wave of the future. Yugoslavia to the south and the Russian periphery to the east define the new psychological and soon, perhaps, economic West–East faultline. They do not define European destiny.

In this respect, too, it is the Germans more than any other West Europeans who understand the need to incorporate the new Central European democracies into the Western system swiftly. Germany and the EC, whatever their own internal problems, are the pivots in the spread of the Western system. Even in terms of security, even well before realization of the EC's wish for a common foreign and security policy, the Community will increasingly be the most important institution on a continent in which military power is a coin of decreasing value. Whatever the outcome in ex-Yugoslavia, at the end of the day the belligerents there will have to respond to the economic and political incentives and disincentives of the EC if they want a decent standard of living. Ostracism will be a powerful tool. Geographically, economically, and politically Germany will play the central role both in the "deepening" of EC institutions in the west and in the Community's "widening" to the east.

This special German commitment should continue. Kohl fears that his successors will not be as pro-Europe as the generation that itself experienced the trauma of World War II. Hence his goal of locking the Germans into Europe irrevocably by means of the Maastricht agreement. Yet the pro-Maastricht consensus of all the major German parties remains firm. And Bundesbank opponents of monetary union will not wag the government tail on this political decision when it comes due toward the end of the century (except in setting the specific terms of union). Nor should popular German unease about future loss of the deutsche mark (or appeals to the constitutional court to declare unconstitutional increasing surrender of German sovereignty to the EC) be regarded as fundamental public opposition to deepening the EC. Every chancellery or foreign ministry official dealing with the issue in Bonn fully expects that the Germans and French will press ahead with new initiatives for greater economic, political, and foreign policy coordination in the EC at the 1996 summit.

Furthermore, on the issue of bringing Central Europe into the club, the Germans are alone in knowing viscerally that Central Europe must become an organic part of Western Europe. The only Western advocate of Central European membership in NATO is German defense minister Volker Rühe. Similarly, Germany has been the only EC country actively in favor of going beyond the EC association treaties with Central European countries to give them a commitment that they will be members by the turn of the century. The poor Mediterranean members fear diversion of EC development funds they would otherwise receive to the even poorer countries to the east. The British are pushing Central European membership, but with the ulterior motive of making the EC too unwieldy to strengthen its political institutions further. And France—despite the fact that the single most effective aid to the struggling Central European democracies would be to open West European markets to them—still wants to keep Community markets closed to the few product categories in which Central Europe enjoys a comparative advantage: agriculture, steel, and textiles.

Given the parsimonious opening of West European markets so far to the new EC associates, Poles and Czechs (and Americans) might judge that Germany is hiding behind France and is doing precious little to help the Central Europeans. Yet in internal EC maneuvering, the Germans are the only EC members who are addressing this question at all. They know that Central Europe cannot remain a backwater as in past centuries. They know that a new economic iron curtain must not spring up, if only because the emigration pressure into Germany and Western Europe would then become intolerable. It is in this context that the Germans insist—counterfactually, according to most other EC members—that there is no inherent conflict between widening and deepening.

Can Germany Do It?

The question then arises: What capability does Germany have to fulfill its good intentions? In the narrower domestic context, what kind of partner will Germany be in this Europe of the

1990s? How well is Germany coping with the economic, political, and other tribulations of unification?

First, economics. The difficulties of building a modern economy in eastern Germany in the midst of European and world recession—and even of correcting the structural maladjustments in western Germany that business executives have suddenly discovered—are well known. A laundry list would have to include the 2 percent decline in GDP in Germany in 1993; enough inflation and budget deficit for the Bundesbank to continue high short-term interest rates that cast a pall on all of Europe; an eastern German black hole that is soaking up $100 billion in transfers from western Germany annually; productivity in eastern Germany that is only a third of that in western Germany versus wages in eastern Germany that are two-thirds those in western Germany; a shortfall of investment when three-quarters of that $100 billion goes for consumption and only one-quarter for investment; the endless snarls from giving preference to restitution of expropriated property over compensation; and threatened bankruptcy in far too many of western Germany's workhorse medium- and small-size companies.

Some Germans talk of crisis. Maybe so. But Americans who are not economists may perhaps be excused for failing to take all the crisis talk seriously so long as the dollar continues to fall rather than rise. All the tales of economic woe about how badly off the German economy has been in the past three years have failed to lift the dollar from its undervaluation. The paltry $25 billion that does go into investment in eastern Germany each year is still more than double total Western investment in Poland, Hungary, and the Czech and Slovak republics in the past three years. And the current economic miracle is that although production in eastern Germany dropped by an incredible two-thirds following unification, and unemployment is now pushing a real 40 percent, family income there has still risen by 10 percent. Some 75 percent of homes in eastern Germany now have freezers; 50 percent have videorecorders; almost 20 percent have computers.

Granted, the politics of this magnitude of economic adjustment is crabby. The Saarländer who considered himself poor in 1989 and was

happy to take his handout from Baden-Württemberg in equalization payments was not overjoyed to be told in 1990 that he really was rich and had to dig into his own pocket to help his cousin in Mecklenburg. It is very hard to shift from the West German politics of the past 35 years, which distributed a steady increase in wealth, to the new politics of distributing the belt tightening.

Yet this adjustment is going forward in the old spirit of German consensus. It is slow; it is acrimonious. The "solidarity pact" that the government is jawboning employers and various blocs of employees into accepting may increase costs and prolong high interest rates. The courts may be increasing rigidities by rulings such as the recent one that said an unemployed person could not be forced to take a job 30 or 35 kilometers away, even in the same region, because the cultural differences between the two communities might cause intolerable strain. Government and opposition may be unable to muster the will to slash old West German subsidies to obsolescent industries or trim social welfare payments in any way that would help cut the soaring budget deficit. Yet the trade unions are practicing restraint, by and large. The major parties and politicians are perforce cooperating in hammering out the division of the enormous costs of unification between the Länder and setting up that solidarity pact. And it would be surprising if by the turn of the century eastern Germany did not have the most modern telecommunications and some of the most modern just-in-time production in Europe.

Ossis and Wessis

Joined with economics is the problem of irritations between easterners and westerners—"Ossis" and "Wessis." The difficulties here are also well known. Both sides were surprised to discover after 40 years under different systems that they had grown in such different directions. West German bureaucrats were by and large reluctant to serve in the East. They had to be ordered by their parent western Länder to do so on a temporary basis—and because they could not get decent housing and schooling for their families they put down no roots and flew home almost every weekend during their two-year loan. Wessis complained that Ossis did not know how to work; Ossis complained that Wessis bossed them around. East German workers held that economic and social justice required equal pay for equal jobs. West German executives considered economic justice to require pay according to productivity. East Germans, unlike their next-door Czechs and Poles, expected to achieve the West German standard of living within a few years—and many now feel cheated because this has not occurred.

Yet the curious fact has to be noted that opinion polls show strikingly similar attitudes among eastern and western Germans on a wide range of issues. (The one exception, beyond the question of whether the Wessis are giving the Ossis enough money, shows up in responses to queries about sending German soldiers on United Nations [UN] or NATO missions abroad.) Some "Wossis" like former foreign minister Hans-Dietrich Genscher (a Wossi is a West German who has ties to the east and is perceived as sympathetic by the East Germans) believe that rapprochement between the two will in fact proceed very fast and be basically achieved by the end of the century. Others, noting the virtually indistinguishable views of young eastern and western Germans in in-depth opinion surveys, maintain that it will take a full generation. But hardly anyone worries nowadays that a Mezzogiorno of permanently disaffected poor or second-class citizens might develop in eastern Germany.

Certainly the tasks are great in eastern Germany. Apartment buildings that have not been repaired for half a century need reconstructing. Railroad beds need to be laid—and are being laid at a prodigious rate, as anyone who trundles along on the old Reichsbahn trains to Berlin sees. Indigenous entrepreneurs and politicians need to learn the ropes of an unfamiliar new system. Eastern jurists need to be educated in the complex West German legal system that was thrust upon them in what West German officials now call the second great mistake, after treatment of property ownership, in the hasty unification treaty. Police need to be retrained away from internal spying to crowd control. Local administrators need to work their way through the bureaucratic maze and

learn the new game of politeness to customers, as thousands of posters from the *Zentrale für politische Bildung* remind them. Education needs to be modernized (in western as well as eastern Germany), and the time cut for obtaining a degree if Germany is to remain competitive in a single-market Europe.

Violence and the Right

Then there is the most serious problem: stemming violence against foreigners in both eastern and western Germany and instituting a reasonable immigration policy in the country as a whole. At present, Germany takes in two-thirds of all the immigrants to Western Europe, many of them in the guise of seekers of political asylum who get rejected but are not then expelled from the country (or, of course, granted citizenship or any political voice). Given their low birthrate, Germans will need to continue to take in and regularize immigration of a young work force in order to pay their own pensions—but Germany still protests loudly that it is not an immigration country, and it makes naturalization difficult, even for Turks who have lived in Berlin for a decade. After 15 years of dispute the major parties did come together in 1993 on first-step negative legislation to limit the influx, they hoped, of the poor who flock to Germany for a better life and utter the magic word *Asyl* at the border. The parties have not yet faced the issues of immigration and naturalization as such, however. Some politicians expect legislation in these areas after the 1994 election, but that is far from clear.

After the 17 deaths in 1992 in far-right attacks on foreigners (or, in one case, a German who was thought to be Jewish), serious control measures were instituted that had not been taken before. The turning point was the murder by gasoline bombing in the town of Mölln in November 1992, not of newcomers to Germany, but of three Turkish residents of many years, including two children. Some small neo-Nazi groups were outlawed. The federal prosecutor stepped in, for the first time, and two youths were arrested almost immediately. Significantly, too, for Germans who have historically avoided getting involved in defending others' rights—and in sharp

contrast to the Germans who stood by and cheered in Rostock in summer 1992 as the wave of violence against foreigners started—hundreds of thousands of Germans in Berlin, Munich, Hamburg, and elsewhere began a series of candlelight marches to protest racism. For six months it looked as if the tide might have turned. The two young Germans charged with the Mölln murders went on trial in mid-1993. The 19-year-old, the younger of the two, recanted any attachment to far right causes. The hope was that the wide publicity about this trial for sordid murder—and the trial's deglorification of getting drunk with one's buddies and throwing bombs—might break the contagious allure of this kind of criminal activity to peer groups. But in May long-term resident Turks, including children, were murdered—again by arson—in Solingen. Turk-skinhead clashes and some street fights between Turkish groups of competing political orientation erupted.

To restore civility, major efforts will be needed, not only in police protection but also in general police training and investigation, in neglected housing policy, and in activities for youth. Following the Solingen murders the formerly taboo subject of dual citizenship for Turks who would otherwise lose inheritance and other rights in Turkey is also on the German agenda.

In passing it should be noted that the term "neo-Nazi" is not generally an accurate description of the drunken youth gangs that are out there being nasty. Some are neo-Nazi. But many more adopt Nazi symbols simply as the most effective way to rebel and offend their elders. Any neo-Nazi manifestation in Germany understandably gets much more publicity than far-right activity elsewhere. On balance, however, there is probably less far-right activity in Germany than in France, and in party politics there is certainly less far-right sentiment.

Beyond Malaise

Lack of strong political leadership in solving these pressing problems—Kohl is widely perceived as a passive and tired chancellor after 13 years in office, and the opposition Social Democrats are in utter disarray—has led to a feeling of drift and the alienation of many voters from the government and the mainstream parties. There is a sense that the way the remote party bureaucrats decide legislation and trade-offs is far removed from a democracy responsive to its citizens. Disaffection is indicated by loosening loyalty to the traditional parties, and by low voter turnouts; 30 percent are nonvoters in western Germany, 40 percent in eastern Germany (after the incredible 93 percent participation in the German Democratic Republic's first free election in 1990). The argument that this is a kind of normalization and depoliticization common to all of Europe—and that the United States would be overjoyed to have a comparable 60 to 70 percent of its electorate vote—is small comfort to the Germans. Nor was there much reassurance in the jump of far-right parties to double-digit percentages of support in local elections in spring 1993 or in the subsequent move by the Bavarian Christian Social Union to poach back far-right votes.

Yet despite all the malaise and lack of strong leadership, those mills of consensus continue to grind away. The parties are slowly putting together the two-thirds parliamentary majority for the first major overhaul of the constitution since it was written—an overhaul made necessary both by unification and by the increasing transfer of powers from Bonn to Brussels under the Maastricht treaty. The Länder are defending their rights under German federalism and clawing back some of the powers they say the central government took from them over the past 40 years. In particular, the Länder have won agreement on a new article 23 to the constitution, giving the upper house, the Bundesrat, some right of refusal over any new cession of national authority to the EC.

In foreign policy the most burning issue concerns sending Bundeswehr troops abroad in UN- or NATO-approved peacekeeping, peacemaking, or crisis-control operations. Pending political and legal clarification, the government did decide to let air force officers serve in NATO AWACS (airborne warning and control system) surveillance flights over former Yugoslavia. Without going into the peculiarities of the decision—by the convoluted means of a failed appeal by the coalition junior partner, the Liberals, for a constitutional court injunction banning such participation—suffice it to say that the trend in public

opinion is in fact moving in the direction of such participation. Although it was almost unnoticed abroad, this trend began during the Persian Gulf War, at the moment when the Iraqi Scuds began landing on Israel.

What got the headlines in the United States at the time were the initial renewed antiwar demonstrations in Germany and the Bonn government's conspicuous public silence on the issue over two long weeks. What was actually going on in the population as a whole, however, was a sea change in German postwar thinking. For 40 years—not surprisingly, given the nuclear balance of terror and Hitler's discrediting of military power—the common assumption was that peace is always more moral than war. When those Scuds threatened to kill Jews, whom Germans have a special historical responsibility to protect, however—especially if those Scuds might have been tipped with chemical warheads provided by renegade German chemical manufacturers—this axiom was fundamentally challenged. Suddenly, in an imperfect world of sinners as well as saints, peace in the face of a bully looked like appeasement. More Germans actually approved than disapproved the American-led war on Iraq. And all the wars on the fringes of Russia and in former Yugoslavia have only reinforced the new popular respect for potential military protection in a still unstable Europe.

It is still a long way from that gathering consensus to accepting routine *German* participation in UN or ad hoc alliance military operations outside NATO territory. The memory of Hitler is still too fresh for that. And the Social Democrats, although they are feeling pressed by changing public opinion, still insist on rigid confinement of any Bundeswehr participation abroad to peace*keeping* and not peace*making* or crisis-control efforts. But the government has already dispatched military doctors to Cambodia and other Bundeswehr units to join UN peacekeepers in Somalia and aid multinational assistance to the Kurds in Iraq. It would not approve Bundeswehr action in Yugoslavia under any circumstances because of Hitler's occupation of that country, but it has clearly signaled its intent to send troops abroad in the future to less sensitive regions like any other European

country. To this end it will seek constitutional amendments or else formalize a majority Bundestag revision of the contrary restrictive interpretation of the constitution of the past 20 years. Significantly, the more negative eastern German attitudes on this issue are increasingly converging with the western.

In broader foreign policy, Kohl has already had the first summit with new French prime minister, Edouard Balladur, and has apparently begun the same kind of close working relationship with him that the chancellor has had with President François Mitterrand. There is some initial progress in the subsequent French acceptance of the earlier U.S.–European oilseed deal that is a precondition for a final settlement of the General Agreement on Tariffs and Trade. And French–German initiatives to correct the EC's "democratic deficit," design monetary union, and promote a common EC foreign policy may be expected once the dust settles after admission of Austria and the three Scandinavian countries to the club. Although German officials vehemently deny it, these initiatives will probably go in the direction of a two-speed Europe, increasing the area of majority rather than unanimous decisions and permitting the core nations that want faster integration to go ahead of the foot-draggers in various areas.

The December 1994 general election will no doubt stimulate allied worry about German stability, but it should not alter the prognosis outlined in this essay. If exhausted voters are still going to the polls by then—there will be a dozen and a half local, state, and European elections in 1994 before the general election rolls around—the center-right coalition between conservatives (the Christian Democratic Union and the Christian Social Union) and Liberals will probably be reelected, and Kohl will probably continue as chancellor. If the far-right Republikaner party fails to enter the Bundestag—and if the Greens get back in, as they probably will—there would be no way for the Liberals to switch back to alliance with the Social Democrats to form a majority. The present center-right coalition would carry on.

The one potential spoiler to this scenario would be a win by the Republikaner party of the 5 percent minimum needed to get into the Bundestag. That could produce a distribution of some 36 or 37 percent each for the Union and Social Democratic parties and some 8 percent each for Liberals and Greens.

In such a case the present majority coalition of conservatives and Liberals would be reduced to a minority of about 44 percent. Yet if the kingmakers of the past quarter century, the Liberals, switched back to the Social Democrats—their allies from 1969 to 1982—this would also yield only a 44 percent minority. The Liberals (and the mainstream conservatives) would under no conditions include the Republikaner in a center-right coalition to gain a majority. Nor would the Liberals (or the mainstream Social Democrats) include the Greens in a center-left coalition at the federal level to gain a majority.

The universal assumption therefore is that another grand coalition—without Kohl—would be formed between the conservatives and the Social Democrats, as from 1966 to 1969. Such an outcome would be viewed with some foreboding, because the lack of a mainstream "parliamentary opposition" in the late 1960s strengthened the extreme left in the "out-of-parliament opposition" that later degenerated into left-anarchist violence.

Certainly there is cause for concern in the far-right gains last spring in local and state elections. Much of this shift, however, reflects the usual phenomenon of protest votes (and a low voter turnout that exaggerates them) in off-elections. Current opinion surveys show Republikaner sentiment back down, hovering at just about the 5 percent threshold. The hopeful interpretation of these figures is that the scare about the Republikaner may well dissipate as did the earlier scare about the far-right National Democratic party, which soared in local elections in the late 1960s but was ultimately rejected by West Germany's overwhelmingly moderate voters with a share of under 5 percent in the 1969 federal election.

Conclusion

This essay is far more optimistic than most German commentary. But that is to be expected. German pessimism is the functional equivalent of American optimism—an excellent tool for solving intractable problems. Germans worry their problems to death—and then discover that in the course of fretting about them and tinkering with them they have actually made them manageable. Unless the Germans somehow cease to be German, an American can afford to be at least provisionally optimistic.

Germans turn their backs on politics

Disenchanted electors are deserting mainstream parties in droves. Tony Paterson reports from Berlin at the start of a gruelling election year

Tony Paterson

The Germans have coined a new word to describe the phenomenon. They call it *Parteiverdrossenheit* or PV: weariness with political parties. Hardly a day passes without the term appearing in print or on television.

For despite Bonn's frantic efforts to reverse the exodus, voters are deserting mainstream parties in droves, either by not voting at all or by switching their support to fringe parties and new political groups.

The development could not have come at a worse time for Chancellor Kohl's ruling Christian Democrats (CDU) and the main opposition Social Democrats (SPD). Both face a gruelling 1994 with no less than 18 local and regional elections culminating in a full general election at the end of October.

The blame for PV's unstoppable rise is down to the fact that Germany's politicians have lost touch with ordinary people. Potential voters complain that politicians have failed them on key issues.

For the east Germans, this means the CDU has failed to keep its 1990 post-unification promises. It has also introduced tax increases and brought about a drop in living standards, record unemployment and the worst economic recession since the Second World War. Nor does it show any signs of ending.

Added to this is the state of Kohl's CDU. After 11 years in office, the party is looking tired and incapable of providing solutions. "This is no year for political softies," warned finance minister Theo Waigel. Kohl refuses to be drawn, concentrating instead on economic issues. The only poll he cares about, he says, is the election itself.

Pundits are divided over whether PV affects 40 or 50 per cent of the electorate. But they all agree on one thing: that disaffection felt towards Germany's political establishment has never been so great. Opinion polls suggest that only one out of 11 west Germans and one in 20 east Germans are "convinced voters". "With such voter-flexibility, every election can turn into a landslide," said the country's Emnid political research institute.

At the other end of the spectrum, Germans who do vote are opting for parties which were once considered fringe political elements—Greens, far-right Republicans, the reformed communist party of east Germany PDS, or others.

Last month, the PDS humiliated Kohl's CDU by driving it into third place in elections in the east German state of Brandenburg. In Hamburg city state elections, a newly-formed Statt (Instead of) party inflicted a devastating blow to the SPD by depriving it of its ruling majority.

Significantly, Statt campaigned with virtually no political programme and insisted that it wanted "ordinary people to be allowed to have a say".

"Voters simply do not feel they are adequately represented under the current political set-up," said Hamburg Professor, Hans Eichler, who recently conducted a survey on PV in the city and discovered the existence of 550 alternative political groups.

The latest to cash in on PV is Germany's anti-Maastricht campaigner Manfred Brunner, who plans to launch his DM (Democracy and Market Economy) party or Citizens' Movement for a Europe of Nations in Weimar at the end of January. He is hopeful of getting 35 per cent of the vote in the general election.

His forecast may seem ludicrously optimistic. It looks less exaggerated when seen against the results of a poll of 2,015 Germans published in *Stern* magazine last week. One of the questions was: "What would be your ideal government after this year's general election?"

Only 11 per cent of those asked said that they wanted to see Germany's coalition of GDU, the Bavarian Christian Social Union (CSU) and the liberal Free Democrats (FDP) continue to hold office. The most popular choice with 26 per cent was a coalition comprising the SPD and Greens. Only 16 per cent wanted a grand coalition involving both CDU and SPD.

Kohl has crushed all challengers to his position inside his party. As a result the CDU is frequently written off as a party of Kohl's "yes-men".

The SPD, which has managed to put up three challengers to Kohl in 11 years without winning a general election, has finally settled on Rudolf Scharping as its candidate for this year's contest. But like Kohl, he too is saddled with problems. The main one being that he is an unknown who has never held office in national politics. "It would almost be a miracle if Scharping managed to make the SPD the strongest party in parliament," said *Die Zeit*.

Around this political vacuum now tread Germany's established political parties— the CDU, CSU, SPD and FDP. All have governed Germany. For the first time they see their hold on German politics under threat. Both CDU and SPD realise that their only chance of keeping the mainstream alive after the election may be as a grand coalition government. And the FDP is likely to be the victim.

From *European*, January 14–20, 1994. The *European* is published by The European Limited, Orbit House, 5 New Fetter Lane, London, England EC4A 1AP. Reprinted by permission.

CHOOSING THE PRESIDENT

All political parties with representation in parliament are entitled to nominate a candidate. Normally parties try to agree [on] a common candidate to avoid complicating the issue.

The president is then elected by an electoral college (*bundesversammlung*) made up of 1,324 MPs and Federal state or *Land* deputies from Germany's lower house, the Bundestag and upper house, the Bundesrat.

There are three possible rounds of voting. However many candidates there are—and three would be a surprise—in the first two rounds a candidate must achieve an absolute majority to be elected. Candidates may drop out of the running after the first vote.

If voting continues for a third round, the president is elected by a simple majority.

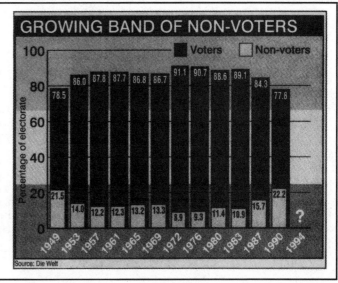

GROWING BAND OF NON-VOTERS

Source: Die Welt

As the opening shots in the election marathon were being fired, no one was prepared to admit this possibility. Instead jockeying for position and political profile has begun in the run-up to Germany's presidential elections due to be held at the end of May.

After bungling over Steffen Heitmann, Kohl's first choice of presidential candidate, the CDU has settled on Roman Herzog, president of the constitutional court, as the man they want to replace Richard von Weizsäcker.

Meanwhile, the FDP in an effort to raise its profile as a progressive party,

has announced that it intends to stick by its own candidate, liberal Hildegard Hamm-Brücher.

German presidents are selected by the votes of an electoral college comprising upper and lower houses of parliament. An absolute majority is preferred but a president can be elected on a simple majority in a third and final round of voting. On this basis Herzog seems virtually certain to be chosen.

But if polls are anything to go by, the presidential race has merely been added to the list of political choices that can be settled behind the scenes. The choice of

Herzog appears out of touch with the desires of most Germans. According to the *Stern* poll, 44 per cent want the SPD's candidate Johannes Rau to be president. Herzog polled 10 per cent, just ahead of the nine per cent of cartoonist and comedy actor Loriot. Other polls suggest that the president should be selected by popular vote.

Summing up Germany's prevailing political mood, *Die Zeit* chose to echo President Clinton's campaign call: "It's time for a change." The trouble is that nobody appears to have a clear idea of what that change should be.

A long year in German politics

BERLIN

This is a year of elections in Europe. General elections are due in Germany, Hungary, Italy and Sweden, and polls will be held throughout the European Union for the European Parliament. This week we look at the most election-studded calendar of all: Germany's. . . .

GERMAN governments, like German loaves, come in baffling variety: at the baker's, wheat, rye, oats, corn or barley, and any mixture thereof; in politics, Christian, Free or Social Democrats, as well as Greens and sundry smaller parties to right and left. The federal government is a coalition led by Helmut Kohl of the three centre-right parties (the Christian Democrats, the Christian Social Union and the Free Democrats, or liberals). Among the 16 *Länder* (state) governments, which often anticipate what is round the corner in Bonn, there are eight varieties of party combination, including just about every coupling save Christian Democratic-Green.

It sounds like a recipe for chaos. But Germany's mix-and-match coalitions, due in part to combining proportional and first-past-the-post elements in its electoral system, seem to work. Post-war German governments have tended, like German bread, to show the same dependable characteristics: a firm build, a resilient texture and tremendously long life.

Whether the same may be said in ten months' time, after a run of 19 elections culminating in the general one likely to be held on October 23rd, remains to be seen. On present showing, neither of the two biggest parties, the Christian Democrats and the Social Democrats, will alone win even close to the 50% of parliamentary seats needed to elect a new chancellor. Either will need partners, quite possibly each other—a "grand coalition", squeezing out smaller fry.

Such coalitions are commonly frowned on, though evidence about them is slim: the one federal grand coalition was back in 1966-69, a transitional affair bridging long periods of government led by conservatives (1949-66) and Social Democrats (1969-82). Neither Mr Kohl nor Rudolf Scharping, the leader of the Social Democrats, wants such a thing now, though they may not be able to avoid it. In any event, when, as now, one party controls the Bundestag and another the upper house, government often turns into a grand coalition in practice.

At the **Social Democrats'** headquarters in Bonn, talk of power-sharing with conservatives is treated as defeatist. Social Democrats are daring to think 1994 may be their year. And with some reason: Mr Kohl's exhausted government seems to lurch from one mishap to another. Unemployment is high and rising. Mr Scharping does not alarm middle-of-the-road voters (at the risk sometimes of putting them to sleep) and he has got his colleagues, at least on good days, to attack opponents rather than each other.

And who might Chancellor Scharping's partners be? The Greens, as in Hesse and Lower Saxony? Their pacifism is an obstacle. But Mr Scharping hints he could govern with individual Greens of *Realo* (realist) persuasion, such as Joschka Fischer, Hesse's environment minister. A "traffic-light" coalition, as in Brandenburg and Bremen?

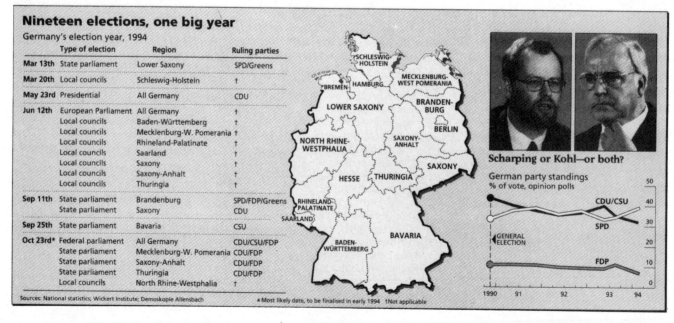

Nineteen elections, one big year

Germany's election year, 1994

	Type of election	Region	Ruling parties
Mar 13th	State parliament	Lower Saxony	SPD/Greens
Mar 20th	Local councils	Schleswig-Holstein	†
May 23rd	Presidential	All Germany	CDU
Jun 12th	European Parliament	All Germany	†
	Local councils	Baden-Württemberg	†
	Local councils	Mecklenburg-W. Pomerania	†
	Local councils	Rhineland-Palatinate	†
	Local councils	Saarland	†
	Local councils	Saxony	†
	Local councils	Saxony-Anhalt	†
	Local councils	Thuringia	†
Sep 11th	State parliament	Brandenburg	SPD/FDP/Greens
	State parliament	Saxony	CDU
Sep 25th	State parliament	Bavaria	CSU
Oct 23rd*	Federal parliament	All Germany	CDU/CSU/FDP
	State parliament	Mecklenburg-W. Pomerania	CDU/FDP
	State parliament	Saxony-Anhalt	CDU/FDP
	State parliament	Thuringia	CDU/FDP
	Local councils	North Rhine-Westphalia	†

Sources: National statistics; Wickert Institute; Demoskopie Allensbach   *Most likely date, to be finalised in early 1994   †Not applicable

Scharping or Kohl—or both?

German party standings
% of vote, opinion polls

CDU/CSU
SPD
GENERAL ELECTION
FDP

1990 91 92 93 94

That means Social Democrats (red), Free Democrats (yellow) and Greens. The risk with putting all lights on at a crossroads is of a Keystone-Kops pile-up.

A grand coalition with the Social Democrats as junior partner, as in Baden-Württemberg and Berlin? Mr Scharping would much prefer to be chancellor than number-two to Mr Kohl or his successor. Eager to typecast Mr Scharping as the ever-ready junior, Mr Kohl's men smother him with praise as "just the chancellor's sort".

Or a coalition with the liberals, as in Rhineland-Palatinate, where Mr Scharping is premier? Germany had a Social Democratic-Free Democratic coalition in 1969-82. It soured badly. Both sides swore "never again". But on the morning after October 23rd, who knows what wounds the lust for office may heal?

Until then, as most **Free Democrats** in Bonn agree, it would be suicide for their party even to hint at such a thing. Liberal voters on the whole prefer conservatives to Social Democrats as their second choice, though perhaps not so many of them as in the 1980s. Free Democratic ministers feel bruised by their senior partner. The new-year message from Count Lambsdorff, the party's veteran economics spokesman, agonised that Mr Kohl's party is not free-market enough—the latest of many similar heart-cries. The justice minister, Sabine Leutheusser-Schnarrenberger, complains of

the law-and-order policies of the Christian Democrats' tough interior minister, Manfred Kanther. But swing parties are born to suffer. When the liberals meet in September to announce their "coalition preference", nobody expects them to call for anything but more of the same.

And **Mr Kohl**? After 12 years as chancellor and 20 running his party, he has more arrows in his hide than St Sebastian (and Mr Kohl's pelt is not as thick as is commonly supposed). Yet those who recall the legend of that saint will know that the arrows, miraculously, did no harm: the martyr had to be finished off with an axe. Few Christian Democratic members of the Bundestag can be found with a kind word to say about Mr Kohl, who languishes frighteningly far behind Mr Scharping in opinion polls. Yet the sound of grinding axes is rare: election year is not the moment to kill the chief, and Mr Kohl has always been brutal with mutineers.

That the Kohl era is ending is plain to all. But eras end slowly in German politics and Mr Kohl means to be about a while yet. His election goals, as his advisers see it, are, in descending order: a conservative-liberal coalition, as now, where the chancellor is not numerically beholden to his junior partners; one where he is; or a grand coalition with Mr Scharping as vice-chancellor. When Social Democrats swear that Mr Scharping would never accept this, they should probably not be believed. When Mr

Kohl's people swear he would never agree to be number-two to Mr Scharping, they almost certainly should be. If Mr Kohl did go, one man widely mentioned as his successor is Wolfgang Schäuble, the Christian Democrats' parliamentary leader.

Mr Kohl hopes that by autumn Germany's economy will show growth, even if unemployment is not coming down. His party will play the card of experience in foreign affairs. It will stress "inner security". (Mr Schäuble has even suggested putting German soldiers on frontier duty against bands of refugees or gangsters from the east.) It will play on the theme that Germany, still struggling with the effects of unification in 1990, has had plenty of change for now.

There is a last, slim possibility: **a shattering of the old mould**, as in Italy in 1993. The two big parties' share of the vote has been falling for years. Small parties are everywhere in evidence (prompting some nervous souls in the big ones to call for pure first-past-the-post voting). These parties include the neo-fascist far right, ex-communists in eastern Germany and new independent centre-right parties, such as the Statt Party now governing with Social Democrats in Hamburg. Germany's version of the Italian Leagues? A few believe so. Most, however, think Germany's political bakery has not changed that much: protest-voting in state and local elections is one thing, picking governments in Bonn quite another.

The "Old" and the "New" Federalism in Germany[1]

Arthur B. Gunlicks
University of Richmond

I. INTRODUCTION

When the Wall came down on 9 November 1989, the two Germanies had dramatically different political systems. The most obvious of the differences could be found in the political party, administrative, and judicial systems and their ideological underpinnings as well as the contrasts these reflected in virtually all areas of public policy. Another major difference lay in the territorial-administrative organization of the two states, that is, in the federal organization of the West German Federal Republic and the unitary structures of the East German Democratic Republic (GDR). This difference was not in principle the direct result of the democratic-capitalist system in the West and the Communist-dominated party dictatorship in the East. Most democratic systems are also unitary states, and, at least in theory if not in practice, the Soviet Union and Yugoslavia were federal states under Communist party leadership.

With the fall of the Wall, the long-desired but unrealistic goal of German unification seemed within reach. At first, there was widespread agreement that unification would have to come slowly, not only because of anticipated objections by Germany's neighbors—and especially by the Soviet Union—but also because of the difficulty of uniting two states and societies that had gone off in very different directions after 1945. On 28 November 1989, Chancellor Helmut Kohl proposed a ten-point plan with unification as the final, long-range goal.

Soon after Kohl's statement, it became clear that unification would have to occur much sooner than almost anyone had thought. About 2000 people were leaving the GDR every day for West Germany, a situation which neither German state could tolerate for long. East German elections were moved up from May to March, and the prospect that unification might occur in early 1991 or even in 1990 began to sound less and less unrealistic.

What kind of state would a unified Germany be? It was clear, of course, that it would be a democratic capitalist welfare state, like the other states of Western Europe. But it was also clear that unlike France, Sweden or Great Britain, it would have to be a *federal* state, a requirement of the Basic Law (Article 79) not subject to amendment.

German Länder	Population* m	Seats in the Bundesrat after (before) unification	
North Rhine-Westphalia	16.7	6	(5)
Bavaria	10.9	6	(5)
Baden-Württemberg	9.3	6	(5)
Lower Saxony	7.2	6	(5)
Hesse	5.5	4	(4)
Saxony	5.0	4	(0)
Rhineland-Palatinate	3.6	4	(4)
Berlin	3.3	4	(4)
Saxony-Anhalt	3.0	4	(0)
Brandenburg	2.7	4	(0)
Schleswig-Holstein	2.6	4	(4)
Thuringia	2.5	4	(0)
Mecklenburg-West Pomerania	1.9	3	(0)
Hamburg	1.6	3	(3)
Saarland	1.1	3	(3)
Bremen	0.7	3	(3)
TOTAL	77.7*	68	(45)

*Population figures are for 1990

More important, perhaps, was the fact that there was a consensus in West and East Germany that a united Germany should be a federal state whatever the Basic Law said.

II. STATES AND *LÄNDER* IN GERMANY BEFORE UNIFICATION IN 1990

Why was there so much support for federalism? One answer would be that throughout their long history, with the exception of the twelve years of Hitler's Third Reich, Germans had only known some form of association of

 By Arthur B. Gunlicks. Written for *Annual Editions: Comparative Politics*, The Dushkin Publishing Group, Inc., 1993.

states. The Holy Roman Empire, which at least on paper lasted until 1806, was a semi-confederation of hundreds of mostly German states, including numerous city-states, and the German Confederation of 1815 was another loose collection of thirty-nine sovereign German states. The first real "German state" (if one ignores the federation of 1867) was a federation put together by Bismarck in 1871 by uniting twenty-five formerly sovereign states.

The collapse of Bismarck's Kaiserreich in 1918 led to the formation of the Weimar Republic, which was organized as a federation of first 18, then 17, states, now called *Länder*. When Hitler assumed power in January 1933, he not only established a one-party dictatorship but also eliminated the federal system.

At the conclusion of World War II in 1945, Pomerania, Silesia, and the southern half of East Prussia were given to Poland, while the northern half of East Prussia was annexed by the Soviet Union. What had been the middle quarter of Germany was placed under Soviet occupation, while the western half of the country was divided for occupation purposes among the United States, Great Britain and France. This western half became the Federal Republic of Germany in 1949, when the Basic Law, or constitution, was approved by the Western Allies and adopted by the parliaments of the previously created West German *Länder*. With the exceptions of Bavaria and the city-states of Bremen and Hamburg, these were not *Länder* with a long history of independence or autonomy but rather creations of the Allies. Lower Saxony, for example, was formed in 1946 by the British occupation authorities from the Prussian province of Hanover and the three small former *Länder* of Braunschweig (Brunswick), Oldenburg, and tiny Schaumburg-Lippe. North Rhine-Westphalia, Schleswig-Holstein, Hesse, the Rhineland-Palatinate, the Saarland, and Baden-Württemberg (formed in 1952) were also more or less artificial creations. West Berlin, of course, was a special case, and was legally though less in practice under Allied occupation until 1990.

Many people in the West were surprised to learn or had forgotten in 1989–1990 that the East Germans had also established five *Länder* between December 1946 and February 1947 and provided them with democratic constitutions. These went so far as to guarantee private property and free enterprise, but they also provided a number of social welfare rights.

The five *Länder* were (1) Mecklenburg, created from the old *Länder* of Mecklenburg-Schwerin, Mecklenburg-Strelitz, and Vorpommern (the western part of the Prussian province of Pomerania); (2) Brandenburg, formed from the Prussian province of Brandenburg that lay west of the Oder River; (3) Saxony-Anhalt, a combination of the former *Land* of Anhalt and the Prussian province of Saxony; (4) Thuringia, the pre-1933 *Land* that had been formed in 1920 from several old Thuringian principalities; and (5) Saxony, the old *Land* of Saxony with a long history as an independent kingdom.

In 1945 the Allies in Potsdam called for decentralized political structures and local self-government in post-war Germany. The creation of the five *Länder* in the Soviet Zone of occupation was a result of that agreement. The 1949 constitution of the newly established GDR also provided for a federal system with five *Länder*; however, by the early 1950s it was clear that the Socialist Unity Party (SED) and the Soviets preferred a highly centralized unitary state, and in July 1952 the five *Länder* were reconstituted in *Kreise* (counties) and fifteen *Bezirke* (districts), including East Berlin. In the process of drawing boundaries for these fifteen districts, the old *Land* boundaries were often ignored.

Soon after the Wall fell, people in the GDR began to agitate for the reestablishment of the East German *Länder* created after the War.[2] Even though three of five of these had had little or no tradition and the East German experience with them had been short-lived, there was evidence that most East Germans identified with them more than they did with the GDR (now—1993—there is talk of a certain GDR "nostalgia" which hardly existed in 1990).

The five *Länder* came into being on 3 October, the day on which German unification took place. East Berlin, however, was joined with West Berlin. In contrast to the five "territorial states" that held their first elections on 14 October 1990, elections in Berlin were not held until 2 December, when the new *Bundestag* (federal parliament) was elected. A new law contained provisions permitting additional boundary adjustments, and even before unification more than 140 cities and towns indicated they wished to change their territorial status. After 1990 other adjustments continued to be made by state treaties between the individual *Länder*. The fifteen *Bezirke* were abolished on 31 May 1990.

III. THE EXPERIENCE OF FEDERALISM IN THE WEST

A second important reason for the consensus concerning a united *federal* Germany lay in the generally positive experience with West German federalism. Of course, not all West Germans were entirely happy with federalism in a country about the size of the state of Oregon. They argued that federalism was too costly, inefficient, and unnecessary in a relatively small but densely populated country with little ethnic, cultural or religious conflict. Some complained that the federal system had been "imposed" on them by the Western Allies, ignoring the long tradition of federalism in Germany and the general agreement among the founding fathers of the West German state that some form of federalism was desirable. Some also complained that federalism was a "conservative" device to prevent uniform (and, of course, "progressive") standards in various policy areas, especially education. Finally, there were and are those who argue that as desirable as federalism might be in the abstract, modern technology, the welfare state, the demands for "uniform living conditions," and now increasingly the European Community, to name only some of the most obvious pressures, are requiring ever more centralization of policymaking.[3]

In spite of the doubters, evidence from opinion polls and other sources suggest that most Germans support strongly the federal system and, in contrast to federalism in the Kaiserreich and Weimar, identify it with a highly successful if imperfect postwar democratic Germany. With the weakening of the particularism that did exist before the War due to the millions of refugees who streamed into West Germany after being expelled from the Eastern territories or fleeing the GDR; the formation of new and artificially created *Länder*; the decline of religiosity; and the rise of a national welfare system, a national (and international) market, national television networks, and national standards for all kinds of activities, it might seem surprising that federalism would enjoy such support.

This support probably derives from a generally positive experience with federalism in practice rather than any kind of theoretical position. Thus a traditionally strong system of local government was preserved in the eight territorial *Länder* (i.e., excluding the city-states Bremen, Hamburg and West Berlin). Under federalism, German local governments and *Länder* were able to experiment with policies that were sometimes adopted elsewhere but other times were opposed in other regions. The traditional focus on administration even of most national laws by the *Länder* and local governments preserved important responsibilities for regional and local politicians and officials and probably reduced the bureaucratic "overload" alleged by many to exist in the highly developed—and mostly unitary—states of Western Europe.

The existence of *Land* parliaments in addition to local councils has provided voters with additional opportunities to influence policies and personalities through regional elections and multiplied many times the number of politicians who were successful in participating in politics above the local level but did not or could not serve in the *Bundestag*. *Land* cabinets as well as parliaments have provided politicians with practical political and administrative/managerial experience above the local level and with a base of operations not found in unitary states. The unique institution of the *Bundesrat* makes it possible for regional leaders to participate even in national affairs, since the *Bundesrat* considers all national legislation with the right of either a suspensive or an absolute veto. Indeed, today the *Bundesrat* has an absolute veto over more than 60 percent of all national legislation, i.e., those bills that affect the *Länder* in ways that permit the application of the absolute veto.

Regional leadership opportunities have contributed to the quantity and quality of political leaders available for national office. The existence of regional as well as local bases of political operations has also made it possible to create and maintain a noncentralized party system with regional leaders not infrequently willing to challenge the national leader or leaders. Federalism probably made it possible for some parties to come into existence (the Greens), for others to remain in existence (FDP), and for the major parties to lick their wounds and regenerate themselves (the CDU from 1969 to 1982 and the SPD since 1983). Thus federalism has served to promote and sustain party competition in ways that are not available to the British or French parties, for example.

IV. FEDERALISM IN THE UNITED GERMANY

As we have seen above, there seemed to be a popular consensus that federalism had been successful in the West German Federal Republic in spite of certain problems—not unlike developments and trends in the United States—that needed to be addressed if federalism were not to become a mere front for increasing central government control. It seems clear, however, that with unification and the addition of five new *Länder,* the challenges to German federalism will be even greater than before. Some of these challenges are discussed below.

More complex decisionmaking.—Federations are inherently complex systems. By definition they must resolve disagreements between central and regional authorities over the division of political and administrative powers. Disputes over taxes and revenues are endemic. High courts—in Germany the Federal Constitutional Court in Karlsruhe—are key institutions in conflict resolution in federal systems, but they have a limited role in making policy and accommodating interests on a routine basis. The institution designed to do this more than any other in Germany is the *Bundesrat*, an organ given the constitutional function of representing the interests of *Land* governments (and not the *Land* parliaments) in the policymaking process. According to the Federal Constitutional Court, it is not really a second house of parliament, even though it is often viewed as such. It is not a popularly elected body but rather one in which specially designated *Land* cabinet ministers cast from three to six block votes. The *Bundesrat* votes on all laws passed by the *Bundestag*, exercising an absolute veto over questions affecting the *Länder* (more than half of all bills) and a suspensive veto over other matters. In fact most disagreements between the *Bundestag* and *Bundesrat* are dealt with in mediating (conference) committee meetings called for the specific purpose of reaching a compromise between the two legislative bodies.

Before unification there were ten *Länder* with 41 votes in the *Bundesrat*, not counting West Berlin's 4 consultative votes. Each of the largest West German Länder—North-Rhine Westphalia, Bavaria, Baden-Württemberg, and Lower Saxony—received 5 votes; Hesse, Schleswig-Holstein, and the Rhineland-Palatinate received 4; and the Saarland, Hamburg, and Bremen received 3.

When the five East German *Länder* joined the Federal Republic, 3 votes were given to Mecklenburg-West

Pomerania and 4 each to the other 4 *Länder*. In order to reduce the disproportionate weight that the smaller West German *Länder* and the new *Länder* would have, and especially to prevent them from forming a two-thirds majority for the purpose of amending the Basic Law, the Unification Treaty of 31 August 1990 raised the number of votes for the largest *Länder* to 6 each. This has increased the total number of votes in the *Bundesrat* to 68. With about 21 percent of the total population of Germany, the five new *Länder* are still overrepresented with 28 percent of the votes. On the other hand, there is no East German *Land* that is large enough to receive 6 votes (which requires a population of 7 million) and serve as a partial counterweight to the large *Länder* in the West.

The expanded size of the *Bundesrat* will undoubtedly complicate the decisionmaking process and make the federal system even less transparent than it was with eleven *Länder*. The larger number of *Länder* will also make somewhat more unwieldy the various conferences of the *Land* prime ministers and functional ministers as well as the numerous bodies that meet within the framework of the joint tasks.

Länder consolidation.—The creation of five new *Länder* in the East has revived an old and divisive debate in Germany regarding a *Neugliederung* or re-ordering and re-organization of the *Länder*. In general the restructuring of *Land* boundaries in Germany has occurred only under severe pressure from the outside and/or as the result of war. Thus Napoleon was directly and indirectly responsible for reducing the number of German states from about 350 to 39 by 1815. Some states, e.g., Hanover, were annexed by Prussia in the 1860s as a result of the Austro-Prussian War. After World War II, the Allies created several new *Länder* by combining older, smaller *Länder* or turning parts of Prussia into new *Länder*.

In the late 1960s there was much discussion of territorial reform in Germany, including boundary reforms for the villages, towns, cities, counties, and, of course, the *Länder*. Major territorial reforms were enacted at the local level in the eight territorial *Länder*,[4] and a commission was formed to look at the *Land* boundaries. This commission, called the Ernst-Kommission, recommended major boundary changes. It proposed that the Federal Republic have either five or six *Länder*. Nothing ever came of these proposals, due in part to the Finance Reform of 1969 and the rise of "cooperative federalism."

Since early 1990 discussions concerning a re-ordering of boundaries and a reduction in the number of *Länder* have continued unabated. There is considerable support for the proposal to combine Berlin and Brandenburg into one *Land*, but proposals to incorporate the smaller and weaker *Länder* in the West, especially Bremen and the Saarland (Hamburg has indicated a willingness to consider consolidation with one or more of its neighbors), into larger neighboring *Länder* and to reduce the number of *Länder* in the East have led to heated debate. As an alternative there has also been some discussion of cooperative arrangements between *Länder* to promote common goals.

There are powerful arguments both for and against a redrawing of *Land* boundaries and a reduction in the number of *Länder* from 16 to 8 or 10.[5] It seems clear at the time of writing, however, that with the possible exception of Berlin and Brandenburg, there will be no consolidations or redrawing of boundaries. The *Länder* that are the most obvious targets in the West, namely Bremen and the Saarland, are the most vehemently opposed to consolidation; and it would not be easy to convince the *Länder* in the East that they should merge after having just been re-established.

Fiscal equalization.—One especially difficult problem is fiscal equalization, which exists in two forms: first, the transfer of funds from the federal government to the *Länder* and from them to the local governments; and, second, the transfer of funds from rich to poor *Länder* and from rich to poor local governments. This second kind of transfer does not exist in the United States. In Germany it serves to bring the poorer *Länder* up to a level of income that is close to the combined average of all the *Länder* and the local governments up to a level near the county average. There was much controversy in West Germany about the "fairness" of this complex system of fiscal equalization even before unification. Now it is clear that the much poorer new *Länder* in the East will need huge subsidies from the West for a decade or more, and this has made the West German *Länder* very nervous about their future revenues. As a result, there has been much discussion about a reform of the fiscal equalization system. This must take place before the beginning of 1995, or the older West German system will be put into place for all of Germany regardless of the negative effects on the old West German *Länder*.[6]

European Community.—Another major issue concerns the role of the *Länder* in the decisionmaking of the European Community.[7] As the only federal system in the EC, the German *Länder* have been caught in the dilemma of supporting European integration while at the same time finding it necessary to resist developments that threaten to or actually do undermine *Land* autonomy in certain functional areas. An important constitutional provision in this regard is Article 24 of the Basic Law, paragraph 1 of which states that "The Federation may by legislation transfer sovereign powers to inter-governmental institutions." This means that the federal government can transfer not only its own but also *Land* powers to the EC without the approval of the *Länder*, in spite of Article 79 which guarantees federalism in Germany. In addition, Article 235 of the EC Treaty grants "implied powers" to the EC, including education, broadcasting, and media, i.e., *Land* powers. Because of the growing influence of the EC in European policymaking in general, the *Länder* fear increasing marginalization.[8]

The fact is that the political situation for the *Länder* is not very good. The Federal Republic is a member of the

EC, not the *Länder,* and it is the member states that participate in the Council of Ministers and the EC Commission. The *Länder* execute European law, as they do federal law. But in the latter case they do so on their own responsibility and influence the legislative process in the *Bundesrat.* In contrast, the Council of Ministers can assign to the EC Commission the task of executing European law "even in those cases in which the German federal government would not be able to establish an executive agency due to the administrative powers of the *Länder.*"[9] There are also inherent limits on the degree of *Land* participation. The federal government cannot allow a *Land* prime minister to represent Germany in EC councils. Thus *Land* participation is limited in the final analysis to the national decisionmaking process.

Throughout 1992 and until the spring of 1993 a constitutional commission composed of representatives from the *Bundestag* and *Bundesrat* worked on a number of amendments to the Basic Law that will have the purpose of strengthening *Land* participation in the EC. These are discussed in greater detail below.

Constitutional reform at the national level.—A fourth major challenge facing the *Länder* is constitutional reform. Article 5 of the Treaty of Unification "recommends" that the *Bundestag* and *Bundesrat* take up the issue of constitutional revision, looking especially at provisions affecting the relationship between the *Länder* and the federal government and at the possibility of consolidating Berlin and Brandenburg under conditions that would be exceptions to the normal constitutional requirements. It also suggests that consideration be given to the issue of adding to the Basic Law certain state goals (*Staatszielbestimmungen*).

On 16 January 1992 the first meeting of a "joint constitutional commission" composed of 32 members of the *Bundestag* and 32 representatives from the *Bundesrat* met to begin their deliberations that are to be completed by the end of March 1993. The commission has had to deal with a large number of proposals for constitutional reform in addition to those suggested in the Treaty of Unification. Some changes have already occurred as a result of the provisions of Article 4 of the Treaty. Thus Article 23, under which the five new *Länder* joined the Federal Republic, has been repealed. The preamble of the Basic Law was changed to add the five new *Länder* to the list of *Länder* in Germany and to state that the Basic Law now applies to all Germans. The four largest *Länder,* all located in the West, were given 6 rather than 5 votes in the *Bundesrat.*

By the end of 1992 the constitutional commission had considered numerous proposals and agreed to recommend several important amendments. These were announced on October 16 and included provisions concerning both federal-state relations and EC-federal-*Land* relations. For the first time since 1949, amendments to the Basic Law have been proposed that would return powers from the federation to the *Länder.* Thus Article 72, which deals with

concurrent powers and has been used in fact to expand the federal role at the expense of the *Länder,* is to be changed so that in the future the federal government can claim a power only "if and when" it is necessary for the achievement of uniform living conditions or to maintain uniform legal standards. Agreement was also reached to recommend the amendment of Article 75, which deals with framework laws that in the past the federal government found possible to manipulate in such a way as to place considerable constraints on the *Länder.* A new provision would limit the right of the federal parliament to pass framework legislation that contains detailed regulations except under certain conditions. This change would affect in particular the federal regulations concerning higher education, which has been a traditional *Land* function. The commission recommended certain procedural amendments as well, namely that Article 76 be changed so that the *Bundesrat* may sometimes have nine, rather than six, weeks to consider cabinet bills before sending them on to the *Bundestag.* The time may be extended for "important reasons," such as the length of the bill, constitutional amendments, and measures that transfer sovereign powers to international organizations (namely the EC).

Of equal or even greater importance are commission recommendations concerning the EC, the federal government, and the *Länder.* For several years the *Länder* have been expressing growing fears that EC law and the EC bureaucracy are in the process of undermining the autonomy of the *Länder.* They have also expressed deep dissatisfaction over the right of the federal government under Article 24 to transfer sovereign powers, including *Land* powers, to international organizations.

To meet the concerns of the *Länder,* the commission has proposed a new Article 23 and a new Article 45 as well as amendments to Articles 24, 50 and 52. Article 23 deals explicitly with German encouragement of a united Europe. It authorizes the transfer of sovereign powers by the federal government to the European Union with the approval of the *Bundesrat.* Together with an amendment to Article 50, it calls for *Bundestag* as well as *Bundesrat* participation in decisionmaking concerning the European Union. The *Bundestag* would form a "European Committee" for these matters, according to the new Article 45, while the Article 52 would be amended to have the *Bundesrat* create a "European Chamber."

Constitutions in the Länder.[10]—Following their accession to the Federal Republic in October 1990, the five new *Länder* adopted temporary constitutions and established constitutional commissions for the purpose of drafting new permanent constitutions. By the middle of 1992, two *Länder*—Brandenburg and Saxony—had gone through the process of drafting, presenting to the public, and passing new constitutions, while a third *Land,* Saxony-Anhalt, had completed a "consolidated draft." Thuringia and Mecklenburg-West Pomerania did not introduce new constitutions until 1993.

In most respects the completed and draft constitutions of the new *Länder* are similar to those of the "old" ones. Thus, they all provide for democratic, parliamentary systems with a one-house legislature. But there are also numerous differences, e.g., in frequency of parliamentary elections, openness of committee meetings, provisions regarding the opposition, parliamentary majorities needed to elect judges, etc.

The new constitutions are similar in their focus on "progressive" basic rights (e.g., housing, employment, child care facilities) and certain "state goals" (e.g., clean environment). These new basic rights and state goals have become very controversial, with the proponents arguing they represent "modern" constitutional thinking and the opponents arguing that they are not enforceable law (courts cannot force the construction of housing or provide jobs) and therefore raise expectations that cannot be met.

The new constitutions also provide for popular initiatives and referenda, thus reflecting demands especially by the Left for more participatory democracy. These provisions have become controversial as well, in particular because of the relatively low signature requirements for petitions and lower thresholds for acceptance quotas for referenda. In contrast to the United States, a minimum percentage of the electorate, e.g., 25 percent, must favor a measure before it is considered to have passed. It should also be noted that no *Land* constitution permits referenda on public salary scales, budgets, or finances. While the focus of attention is now on constitution-making in the five new *Länder*, several "old" *Länder* are also engaged in amending or writing new constitutions. And, like the constitution-makers founders in the East, they are wrestling with controversial issues such as state goals, social and economic rights, and plebiscitary measures. Whether these issues are more symbolic and rhetorical than real, that is, whether they will really become subjects of future court challenges and parliamentary debates, remains to be seen.

V. CONCLUSION

When the two German states united on 3 October 1990, they faced the challenge of bringing together two societies that had lived under radically different political, social, and economic systems and political cultures for at least forty years. It was apparent from the beginning that the new Germany would look rather like the old West Germany, whereas very little of what had been the East German political and economic systems would survive. It was also taken for granted that, like the former West Germany, the new Germany would be a federal system. This was not only because of a long tradition in Germany of federal, confederal, or semi-confederal states or associations and Article 79 of the Basic Law which requires the federal organization of Germany, but also because of the generally positive experience and high regard for federalism that had developed in West Germany over the years.

With unification, German federalism faces a set of additional and in part new challenges. Among the most obvious of these are a more complicated decisionmaking process; demands for and opposition to a consolidation of the 16 *Länder* to 8 or 10; tax and fiscal equalization reform measures; the European Community; amendments to the Basic Law; and constitution-making in the new *Länder* and, to a lesser extent, in the old *Länder*.

To some extent "solutions" to some of the older problems and newer challenges of German federalism may be found in the proposals for constitutional revisions that were considered and recommended in 1992 and 1993 by the joint constitutional commission established in January 1992. These do seem to address seriously some of the problems of growing centralization in German federalism and threats to *Land* autonomy through the transfer of sovereign powers to the EC and through the actions of the EC bureaucracy. It is clear, however, that no constitutional amendments can answer all of the questions or deal with all of the issues affecting the health and future of German federalism. Federalism in Germany will remain an important subject for scholarly attention and dispute for a very long time to come.

NOTES

1. This is a shortened version of a chapter in a forthcoming book edited by Peter Merkl, *The Federal Republic of Germany at 45* (New York University Press, 1994).

2. For a more detailed discussion of plans and developments concerning the reestablishment of the Eastern *Länder*, see Arthur B. Gunlicks, "Federalism and German Unification," *Politics and Society in Germany, Austria and Switzerland* 4, No. 2 (Spring 1992), pp. 52–66.

3. See also Arthur B. Gunlicks, "Some Thoughts on Federalism and the Federal Republic," *German Politics and Society*, No. 15 (October 1988), pp. 1–7.

4. Arthur B. Gunlicks, *Local Government in the German Federal System* (Durham: Duke University Press, 1986), Ch. 4 and *Local Government Reform and Reorganization: An International Perspective* (Port Washington: Kennikat Press, 1981), Ch. 10.

5. For a discussion of pros and cons in English, see Arthur B. Gunlicks, "The Future of Federalism in a Unified Germany," in *The Domestic Politics of German Unification*, ed. by Christopher Anderson, Karl Kaltenthaler and Wolfgang Luthardt (Lynne Rienner Publishers, 1993), forthcoming. See also Uwe Leonardy, "Into the 1990s: Federalism and German unification" in *German Federalism Today*, ed. by Charlie Jeffery and Peter Savigear (New York: St. Martin's, 1991), pp. 143–147.

6. For a more detailed discussion, see my chapter in *The Domestic Politics of German Unification*.

7. Ibid.

8. Michael Burgess and Franz Gress, "German Unity and European Union: Federalism Repulsed or Revitalised?" in *Regional Politics and Policy*, forthcoming; for a list of policy areas in which the *Länder* see EC interference, see Rudolf Hrbek, "German federalism and the challenge of European integration," in *German Federalism Today*, pp. 86–87.

9. Klaus Otto Nass, "The Foreign and European Policy of the German *Länder*," *Publius: The Journal of Federalism* 19, No. 4 (Fall 1989), p. 181; for a somewhat contrasting view, see Hrbek, "German federalism," pp. 98–99.

10. For a more detailed discussion of old and new *Land* constitutions, see Arthur B. Gunlicks, "State Constitutions in Germany," in *State Constitutions around the World: a Comparative Study*, ed. James Thomson (Westport, CT: Greenwood Press, 1993), forthcoming.

THE FRENCH FUNK

Facing national elections, the country that put existentialism on the map is having a crisis that would make Sartre proud.

Alan Riding

Alan Riding is the Paris bureau chief of The New York Times.

It took long and agonizing debates, but the Chateliers finally decided to do the unthinkable on their farm deep inside the green heart of France. In an ancient stone barn that always held grain, they are now installing washing basins and toilets. And from their farmhouse, the view of sheep, gentle hills, woods and a medieval chateau will soon be filled by tents and mobile homes. The new campsite, though, is all that stands between them and bankruptcy.

"I live the land, the animals, the space," says Guy Chatelier, the farm's soft-spoken and bearded owner. "It's the end if we have to leave." But the day is getting closer. Two other sheep farms in this region of Vendée, in western France, south of Nantes, have already closed. And after the latest slump in mutton prices, the family of six is living largely off welfare payments and farm subsidies. "The campsite is our last hope," he says glumly.

Stories like this abound today. And although farmers represent only 6 percent of the work force, their cries for help are now spreading alarm throughout France. Almost every Frenchman believes his roots are buried in the provinces. And as *la france rurale* agonizes, a sense that the entire nation is losing another part of its identity feeds a deepening mood of pessimism.

Indeed, throughout French society unwanted change is sweeping away what was long taken for granted. Suddenly, it seems, the state is no longer the great protector, cities are being reshaped by third world immigration, the land's sacred *art de vivre* is under attack from hamburgers and the French language loses daily battles to English. Even France's self-proclaimed destiny as a great power no longer seems assured. "The French feel cut off from their past,"

explains Jean Raspail, a writer known for his monarchist views, "so their future makes no sense."

Today, if pre-election polling means anything, French voters will vent their frustrations by throwing the Socialist Party out of office. President François Mitterrand, the wily 76-year-old Socialist who was first elected in 1981, can stay in the Élysée Palace until his second seven-year term ends in 1995. But after today's first round and next Sunday's second round of voting, an overwhelming conservative majority seems certain to control the national Assembly. And Mitterrand will have to "cohabit" with a conservative Prime Minister.

Yet a new Government may not make the French feel much better about themselves. "It's not the opposition coming to power, it's the Socialists losing power," says Jean d'Ormesson, a writer and himself a strong critic of the Mitterrand years. "France does not have much hope in the upcoming change. You could say it's disappointed in advance. It's afraid that, in six to eight months, we will have a parliamentary majority that is almost as unpopular as the Socialists are today."

Outsiders are understandably puzzled. Britain's economic crisis, Italy's political crisis, Germany's identity crisis are all far worse than anything to be found in France. Yet, appropriately, France's *crise* seems to be almost existential, as if the French were mourning the loss of everything that made them proud to be French. "Sometimes when I hear my callers, I get the impression that all of France is paralyzed," Macha Béranger, who hosts a late-night radio call-in program, says. "Ten years ago, people were hesitant. Now they show real anguish."

Nostalgia for the past, so evident in the widespread public support for the farmers in their battle with the bureaucrats, is merely disguising fear of the future. The French feel let down by their legendary elites and lack confidence in themselves. They are abandoning the Socialists without embracing the conservatives. They were offered a future in Europe in a referendum last year, but their yes—51.4 percent to 48.6 percent—lacked conviction. "For 20 years, France has been pounded by change," Alain Duhamel, author of a new book called "The French Fears," notes. "I think it has simply destabilized many French."

Philippe Arnaud is a bookish-looking, 39-year-old farmer who grows grains and oilseeds on 75 acres of land in the Gers region of southwest France. He is better known, though, as a combative leader of Coordination Rurale, whose 10,000 followers routinely block railroad tracks and highways, dump produce in town squares and pelt Ministers with tomatoes. Last year, with more publicity than success, they even tried to besiege Paris with tractors to protest cutbacks in European Community farming subsidies. "We must always be ready to act," Arnaud says. "It's the only way we won't be forgotten."

Fear of a *jacquerie,* or peasants' revolt, of the kind that Arnaud might cheerfully organize, then, seems a plausible explanation for France's rejection of a farm trade agreement between the United States and the community last November. After all, the agreement is part of a global trade liberalization package that, if approved, would enormously benefit the rest of the French economy. What else, other than intimidation by the farmers, could explain why Paris would sink seven years of trade negotiations?

The reality is more complex. For years, rural France has been on the defensive. Its share of the population has fallen from 40 percent at the end of World War II to 6 percent today. Many villages have become ghost communities and few sons of farmers want to maintain centuries-old family vocations. When the French close ranks with the farmers, they are fighting to keep alive the identity of all true French.

Indeed, even in cities, the land never seems far away. Every student reads the stories of Marcel Pagnol's bucolic childhood in Provence. Two-thirds of the population has a parent or a grandparent who was brought up *en campagne.* In Parisian homes, the cheeses or pâtés or wines of some ancestral *pays* will always be preferred over others. The French Constitution even permits—and tradition requires—national politicians to serve also as mayor of a provincial town or village. The countryside still represents the best of France.

And so urban France is now proclaiming an attack on farmers as an attack on the very heart of France. "In the French imagination, the peasant farmer is a sort of nostalgic myth," d'Ormesson says. "He's like your cowboys, your American pioneers. He is part of the French subconscious that is still tied to the land." Pierre Nora, a noted historian, adds: "It's very curious, but France is a country for which *la terre* would mean something even if there were no more farmers left."

Yet for all this romanticism, defeat prowls la France rurale, as if time were finally catching up with a large farming sector that survived longer than in almost any other industrial nation. In Britain, the peasantry disappeared with the Industrial Revolution 150 years ago. In the United States, the rush to the cities began at the turn of the century. In France, though, the process has been slowed over the past 30 years by farming subsidies that first gave the country food self-sufficiency and then turned it into the world's second-largest food exporter after the United States.

Now the process is speeding up again. With 60 percent of the country's one million farmers over the age of 50, only 650,000 farmers will still be working in the year 2000. Those who keep going are under pressure to cut production. To receive Government aid, they must set aside 15 percent of their land. Even then, as a result of last year's reform of the European Community's common agricultural policy, over the next three years guaranteed prices for grains will fall by 29 percent and for beef by 15 percent. Large grain producers south of Paris will probably still flourish, but more than ever it is the small family farm that is struggling.

In the Vendée, a once-prosperous area of meadows and woods that spawned a royalist peasant counter-revolution in 1793, diversification rather than revolt is the chosen strategy for survival. And if the Chateliers are opening a campsite, Jean-Bernard Préault has begun baking brioches at this farm 30 miles away. "We make them with our own grain, butter and eggs," the stoutly build 35-year-old explains, offering a visitor a taste of the sweet loaf that is an essential part of local weddings, baptisms and first communions. Last year, his brioche Vendéenne à la ferme earned him an extra $15,000.

On their 350 acres near St. Denis la Chevasse, the four men of the Limousin family combine cattle, pigs and ducks fed on home-grown grain. But with a bank debt of $620,000 and a 25 percent drop in revenue since 1990, they too are worried. Yes, says Joel Limousin, the urban French do seem to care more these days. "But they have a romantic view," the 31-year-old farmer says. "They see agriculture as nature, full of little birds and trees. When they come here, they want to see farmers at work, they want to find a world that hasn't changed too much. For us, it's more a question of economics."

The drab suburbs, or *banlieues,* north of Paris were built to absorb the rapid urbanization that followed World War II. By now, though, many neighborhoods have been taken over by immigrants and, when possible, French families have chosen to move on. In Clichy-Sous-Bois, immigrant children fill local schools and families from some 30 third world nations crowd Government-owned apartment blocks.

"We can't take any more people," Christian Chapuis, a local official, says. "There's no more room, there's no more housing."

It wasn't meant to be like this. Back in the 1960's, the idea was that cheap immigrant labor from North Africa could help preserve the quality of French life. Instead, the immigrants changed France. They first brought different clothes, customs, food, language and religion. After immigration was halted in 1974, they could still bring wives and children. And even then, illegal immigration continued, with sub-Saharan Africans and Asians joining the large community from Algeria, Morocco and Tunisia.

Today, with an immigrant population of 4.2 million, plus 750,000 French-born children who have an automatic right to become French citizens, France has become a multi-ethnic and multi-cultural society. But many French have yet to accept this metamorphosis. They routinely blame immigration for high unemployment, rising crime and a housing shortage. Even more, they see it as a threat to their traditional way of life. They would like to turn back the clock. And since they cannot, they feel anger and resentment.

In the late 1970's, sensing the depth of discomfort with immigration, a burly former paratrooper, Jean-Marie Le Pen, founded the National Front around the slogan of "France for the French." And, by last year, he was drawing almost 14 percent voter support nationwide. Almost more important, though, other politicians began to echo him. Mitterrand said immigration had passed "the threshold of tolerance." Former President Valéry Giscard d'Estaing warned of an immigrant "invasion." Former Prime Minister Jacques Chirac commiserated with those living beside the "noise and smell" of immigrants.

While slowing the growth of the National Front, these mainstream politicians have made it respectable to be anti-immigrant. And France is still no closer to recognizing its new face. Instead, there are towns like Mantes-la-Jolie, 30 miles west of Paris, where 22,000 immigrants live in a crowded neighborhood called Val-Fourré surrounded by the homes of some 23,000 French. And they share only distrust of each other: one in three of the French here still vote National Front; one in three of the immigrant men are out of work.

As in many banlieues, though, Val-fourré's time bomb is ticking among its young. Most were born in France and know neither the language nor the land of their parents, yet they feel rejected by French society. With little hope of a job when they leave school, many slide into drug peddling and petty crime. "You should see how the police treat us if we go into town," Karim, a husky 22-year-old of Algerian parents, says with barely restrained fury. "They come up with their dogs and say, 'You know, they really like biting Arabs.' Then they'll ask us what we plan to steal. That's why there's so much hate here."

Yet the alternative of integration has little constituency among the French. A recent poll carried out by the National Consultative Commission on Human Rights said 21 percent of those questioned were "convinced racists" and another 34 percent were "tempted by racism." Even someone like Guy Bedos, a comedian who still considers himself a man of the left, is impatient. "We must stop allowing immigrants to pile up here," he says. He then adds softly: "I wouldn't have said that 10 years ago."

Executed with all the pomp and ceremony that this monarchical republic can muster, the bicentennial of the French Revolution on July 14, 1989, was a splendid affair, with world leaders virtually summoned to Paris to commemorate a turning point in European history and to pay homage to the France of today. Historians, though, may record it as France's last hurrah as Western Europe's leading political power. Four months later, the Berlin wall came down and Europe began to change beyond recognition.

Until then, France has had a "good" cold war. It emerged from German occupation to be treated as a victorious ally in 1945. It sold itself as a friend of poor nations and learned to display its independence—*marquer la différence*—by piquing Washington. More crucially, West Germany bowed to French leadership inside the European Community. And, with Britain ambivalent as ever about its place in Europe, France could believe it was, if not a superpower, at least a great power.

The crumbling of Communism, then, has badly shaken France's image of itself. The emergence of a single superpower has limited its room for maneuver in the third world. And in Europe, German unification has changed the balance of power to France's disadvantage. Paris has tried to compensate, participating in United Nations peace missions in Yugoslavia, Somalia and Cambodia as a way of demonstrating that it is still the only European nation with global reach. Yet it remains unsure of its status.

And it hasn't helped that its past is coming under critical scrutiny. The long-nurtured myths about French resistance to German occupation during World War II have been challenged by new information about the role played by the collaborationist Vichy Government in deporting Jews to Nazi death camps. France's defeat in Indochina in 1954 and its flight from Algeria in 1962 are being looked at afresh. Even France's success in controlling many of its former African colonies is now being viewed as a distasteful policy of supporting dictatorships.

In normal times, ordinary French might care little. Yet today, nervousness about a shrinking world role adds to deeper worries about France's very identity. "The French have always believed they should have a very important function in the world," says Daniel

Cohn-Bendit, a German intellectual who was a leader of the antigovernment student movement that rocked Paris in May 1968. "So it is difficult for them to accept anything less."

Indeed, if France could not match the nuclear might of Washington or Moscow, the French could at least claim cultural supremacy. Yet even its main cultural vehicle, its language, is retreating. French is no longer the language of diplomacy, nor even the lingua franca of European elites. In fact, such is the infiltration of English in France that a sentence was added to the French Constitution last year: "The language of the republic is French."

Silly? Perhaps. Yet whether in cuisine or movies or fashion or philosophy, *l'esprit français* has always prided itself on being the antithesis of everything Anglo-Saxon, the phrase for everything British or American. And while it is years since hamburger joints and American movies took over the Champs-Élysées, the advance of the English language is somehow more painful.

For France's leaders, the only place where the country can reassert its political and cultural identity is within the European Community. Strongly promoted by Mitterrand, then, the new push for regional unity that led to the Maastricht Treaty on European Union in December 1991 had the twin purposes of anchoring a united Germany in the West and of giving France a stronger forum in which to wield its influence.

After the treaty was rejected by Denmark in a referendum last June, Mitterrand saw his plan falling apart. Ever the gambler, he therefore decided to call his own referendum last September to demonstrate that France at least was committed to building a united Europe with a single currency and a common foreign policy. But he had another aim: to convince the French that France's destiny as *une grande puissance* was assured in a Europe that could stand up to the United States and Japan.

Instead, the referendum became a mirror of fears. Angered by cuts in community subsidies, farmers covered the countryside with signs saying "Non à Maastricht!" Many French voted against the treaty believing it would open the doors to greater immigration. Opponents of ratification warned that France would soon be governed by meddling, unelected "Eurocrats" in Brussels. And both sides tapped the ages-old specter of German domination.

For French leaders, it was a sobering experience. Although the treaty was narrowly ratified, almost half the voters—12.6 million people—signaled that they did not want change, that France's identity as a nation was in peril, that the country no longer set the agenda for Europe. Further, while modern France—Government and opposition leaders, business groups and newspapers—supported the treaty, old France—farmers, workers and senior citizens—voted no.

Today, things look little clearer. The Maastricht Treaty can only go into effect if ratified by Denmark, which is holding a new referendum on May 18, and by Britain, where a parliamentary majority is still not assured. If both approve it, France will at least have a blueprint to work from. But if either rejects it, France must look for a new place for itself in Europe. And French confidence in the future will be further bruised.

Brice Lalonde is probably one of the few happy politicians in France these days. Everyone seems sick of politics—the main parties are stuck with old leaders and several of the promising faces of yesterday have been muddied by corruption scandals. But with two decades in politics already under his belt, the balding 47-year-old environmentalist now looks set to become the principal beneficiary of the collapse of the Socialist Party.

His party, Génération Écologie, in alliance with the rival Greens—les Verts—could win more than 15 percent of the votes in today's election. And this would represent the largest pro-environment vote in any Western country so far. Yet, strangely, it will not mean France has gone "green." Rather, it will be another symptom of an ailing political system.

In the ´ecolos, as they are known in France, droves of disillusioned Socialists are finding a respectable place to seek refuge from a party that has let them down. And even Mitterrand, who in 1981 promised a new morality, concedes that financial scandals are the main reason for their desertion.

The scandals have been many. The outgoing Prime Minister, Pierre Bérégovoy, has admitted taking a $180,000 interest-free loan from a friend who was later indicted for insider trading. The Speaker of the National Assembly, Henri Emmanuelli, faces charges of illegal party financing. Bernard Tapie, an industrialist turned politician, resigned from the Cabinet after he was accused of embezzlement (he returned to his post after the case was settled out of court).

Laurent Fabius, the current First Secretary of the Socialist Party, was hurt by the still greater public outrage over the distribution to hemophiliacs of blood stocks known to be contaminated with the virus that causes AIDS—nearly 300 of the 1,230 infected in this way have died so far—when he was Prime Minister in 1985. Three health officials were convicted in the case last year, but the public demanded that senior politicians assume responsibility. So far, he has been unable to live down the scandal.

Many French, in fact, believe the country's entire political class is rotten. "Anyone who wants a public works contract from any regional council has to pay a kickback," the head of a construction company in Blois says. "It doesn't matter what party is in power. They're all the same." Conservative opposition leaders have been spared the embarrassment experienced by top

Socialists, but, according to Mitterrand at least, of 58 recent corruption scandals, 28 involved Socialists and 30 conservatives.

As they look for renewal of the political system, then, the French feel frustration. And on top of everything, the same old faces hang on. Mitterrand has been the main Socialist leader since the 1960's. Le Pen has been beating the same drum for 14 years. The leading conservatives are still the aristocratic Giscard d'Estaing—President between 1974 and 1981—and the ever-pragmatic Chirac—Prime Minister from 1974 to 1976 and 1986 to 1988.

The Socialists' front-runners for 1995 are no less familiar—Michel Rocard, Prime Minister between 1988 and 1991, and Jacques Delors, who heads the European Community's executive commission. Rocard, though, has understood that Socialists alone will not carry him into the Élysée. He has therefore promised "a political big bang" after the elections to form a movement of Socialists, reformed Communists, centrists and ecologists. And soon-to-be-jobless Socialists have promptly acclaimed him their new leader—although Rocard is himself in danger of losing his seat in the National Assembly.

It is from the ruins of the Socialist Party, however, that Brice Lalond also sees his chance to rise—if not to immediate power, at least to influence. A fluent English speaker whose mother is American, he feels inspired by the change of generation in Washington ("My friend, Al Gore," he name-drops). "We're jealous of the American system where anyone can rise to office," he says. "We have a new 1789 problem—we have a new *noblesse* that from Paris decides everything for everyone. But now the French are fed up."

After the elections, then, Lalond can expect to be wooed by Rocard, but he also plans to continue poaching among the Socialists as well as Giscard's Union for French Democracy with a view to expanding his own party. But if the French are to have hope again in their politicians, he says, they must be given something different. "I tell people here that to vote écolo is not just a vote for the environment," he insists, "but a vote for a new way of politics, for people who don't come from the elites."

Addressing the nation, traveling abroad, meeting friends in private, it is hard to tell that President Mitterrand's popularity has been hovering for 18 months around an all-time low. With some polls reporting that two out of three French would like him to retire, he remains his same aloof, acid and intelligent self.

With barely two years left in office, suffering—though not ailing—from prostate cancer, he clearly has some cards left up his sleeve. As President, he will remain in charge of foreign and defense policy, a point he has underlined by scheduling visits to both Washington and Moscow. At home, his principal job will be to name the head of the new Government. And, while the betting is that he will choose Edouard Balladur, an unexciting former Finance Minister backed by Chirac's Rally for the Republic party, he may be mischievous by offering it elsewhere.

More important to him, though, is to manage to leave office without looking like a defeated man. He may simply gamble that his own standing as an elder statesman will rise as the popularity of the new Government falls. But he may also want the ultimate vindication of being able to hand over power to a Socialist successor. Indeed, if Chirac and Giscard d'Estaing tear each other apart in their battle for the Élysée, someone else—perhaps Mitterrand's old rival Michel Rocard—might profit.

For the French, though, having emerged from a campaign almost bereft of ideas or debate, the prospect of two more years of campaigning is dismaying. While they worry about unemployment, immigration and the rural crisis, they see their politicians consumed by the scramble for office in 1995. "It's a long time since I believed in promises," Alfred Besseau, a dairy producer from the Vendée, says. "I don't see anything lifting the gloom of the farmers. I don't believe political parties can change much for the better."

Guy Bedos, the comedian, though, is encouraged. "We have always been treated like children by politicians," he says. "Now we're rebelling against our parents." Yet, as the old France disappears, what sort of new France will take its place? "We're going to have to become a less centralized, a more do-it-yourself society, perhaps more like the United States in some ways," Lalonde suggests. "But the real question is: How do we stay French into the next century? How do we maintain *la différence*?"

Notes of the month

France: the Right triumphs

At the end of March, France began its second experience of *cohabitation* – the co-existence of a President of the Left with a government drawn from the political Right – following the collapse of the Socialist Party in parliamentary elections. The election campaign was dull and without passion, not least because the outgoing Socialist government's defeat was widely predicted. Prominent Socialists had virtually conceded victory. Almost a month before the first round of voting on 21 March, the former Prime Minister, Michel Rocard, made a dramatic appeal for a renewal of the Left, a 'political "big bang"' that would sweep away old ideologies and labels appropriate to a different age, and erect in their place a new force, drawing on broader support, perhaps the progressive, pro-European social-democratic formation that Mr Rocard has long aspired to lead. The French daily, *Libération*, characterised his speech as a funeral oration for the Socialist Party. In the event, the predictions of its electoral collapse had not been exaggerated.

The alliance of the two formations of the mainstream Right, the neo-Gaullist *Rassemblement pour la République* (RPR) and the centre-Right *Union pour la Démocratie Française* (UDF), won more than three-quarters of the seats in the National Assembly.[1] It was the largest parliamentary majority since the establishment of the Fifth Republic in 1958; the most sweeping general election victory in France's democratic history. The Socialists and their immediate allies were the principal losers, collapsing from 282 seats in the outgoing Assembly to a mere 70. The Party's fist-and-rose symbol was removed from whole areas of the electoral map and many famous names, not least Michel Rocard himself, lost their parliamentary seats.

All things considered, the Communist Party fared rather better, losing several seats but gaining others, to arrive at a net loss of three seats. Their tally of 23 seats was quite enough to enable them to form their own official parliamentary group and the Party's veteran leader, Georges Marchais, held on to his own constituency that, at one stage, had looked to be under threat. Nonetheless, this election marked yet another step in the Party's historic decline. In percentage terms, it was well down on its score of 1988. The Communists' only solace was to have outdistanced the outgoing Socialist candidate in several constituencies, thus enabling them to minimise their overall losses.

Other forces on the Left were not so lucky. The poor showing of the ecologists was one of the great surprises of the first round of voting. This was to have been the year when the green wave broke through the doors of the National Assembly. Prior to the election, the Socialist Party had agonised about what sort of relationship to establish with the green alliance of *Les Verts* and *Génération Ecologie*. In January opinion polls were showing the Socialists and the ecologists as fighting neck and neck, both with around 19 per cent of the vote. Some figures in the mainstream Right seemed to be flirting with the ecologists, if only to compound the Socialists' problems. However, the green tide was already turning prior to the first round of voting. Only two candidates made it through to the second ballot and, despite respectable scores, neither was elected.

On the far right of the political spectrum, this election confirmed the persistence of the National Front as a player on the French political scene, but also its isolation. Although the Front's 12.4 per cent of the first ballot vote was a small improvement over the 9.65 per cent it won in 1988, the party of Jean-Marie Le Pen was unable to cash in on its solid first-round showing by actually winning seats at the second ballot. The Front's only outgoing Deputy, Marie-France Stirbois, was narrowly defeated at Dreux, and even in its southern bastions neither Mr Le Pen nor any of his lieutenants was able to secure victory. The National Front leader seized on the results as one more example of the iniquities of the electoral system in France, pointing to the fact that the Communists had won a significantly smaller percentage of the vote than the Front, but had over 20 seats in the National Assembly.

The vagaries of the two-ballot electoral system clearly amplified the success of the mainstream Right. Its overwhelming victory in terms of seats was not reflected in its overall share of the first-round ballot. The Right's score of just under 40 per cent of the votes cast was close to its showing at the first round of the 1981 legislative elections which saw the Left triumphant; and it was just behind the UDF and RPR's showing under a proportional voting system in 1986 – the election that ushered in the first period of *cohabitation*.

The sea-change in the Palais Bourbon does not correspond to a change of similar magnitude in the broader political landscape. The mainstream Right does not seem to have won over huge

From *The World Today,* Vol. 49, No. 5, May 1993, pp. 82-83. *The World Today,* published by The Royal Institute of International Affairs. Reprinted by permission.

numbers of the Left's traditional supporters. Many of them may have simply taken refuge in abstention, while others may have voted ecologist or even for the National Front. And indeed, the Front's performance at the first ballot hints at a potential problem for the mainstream Right at the presidential contest due in 1995. Jean-Marie Le Pen won over 14 per cent of the vote at the last presidential election in 1988, and he will be hoping to do at least as well next time around. If the battle were to be close and he advises his supporters to stay at home at the second ballot (thus depriving the mainstream Right of their support), he could do considerable damage to the chances of its candidate, Jacques Chirac.

Of course that presumes that the Left is able to run a credible candidate backed by an efficient political machine. The Socialists are clearly down, but are they also out for the immediate future? Can the Party rally its troops, broaden its appeal and help elect a successor to François Mitterrand in two years' time? The scale of their defeat was dramatic. The public rejected them for a variety of reasons, above all because of what was widely seen as their failure on the economic front. The widespread weariness with the political class as a whole was especially vented against the Socialists – a government that seemed to have run out of ideas and had become tainted by corruption and scandal.

The Socialists were unable to pass the psychological barrier of 20 per cent of the vote. It was a leap 20 years backwards, to the sort of score the party obtained in 1973, two years after its formation at the Congress of Epinay and one year after the signature of the Common Programme with the Communists. But its old ally has been terminally weakened and the ecologists remain too divided and too politically unstable to form the basis of an election-winning partnership. The immediate prospects are bleak. Their best presidential chance, Michel Rocard, could not even win his own parliamentary seat, and this could well weaken his voice in the struggle that lies ahead. There is a clear possibility that the Socialists may descend into an orgy of bitterness and recrimination – a battle between the various currents for the very soul of the Party.

However, the Right has its internal tensions too, where all eyes are similarly on 1995. The only real issue at the second ballot was the battle for dominance between the RPR and the UDF. Despite attempts by the supporters of the former President, Valéry Giscard d'Estaing, to keep more of their candidates in play than were really allowed under their electoral pact with the RPR, it was the neo-Gaullists who emerged triumphant. Their leader, Jacques Chirac, has virtually become the President-in-waiting. He immediately disagreed with his old rival, Giscard d'Estaing, as to how long that wait should be, urging President Mitterrand to take account of the voters' wishes and stand down immediately. Clearly an early presidential election would favour Mr Chirac. Giscard d'Estaing, on the other hand, needs time if he is to chip away at the Mayor of Paris's seemingly impenetrable position. The former President urged caution: if a constitutional crisis were to be precipitated, then the voters should have been told about it in advance. At the Elysée Palace Mr Mitterrand himself stressed that he would see out his mandate and expected to maintain his pre-eminence in defence and foreign affairs.

The battle for the succession has now begun and much depends on how far the new conservative government can impress the voters with its handling of the economy during the months ahead. The Right's two principal chiefs – Mr Chirac and Mr Giscard d'Estaing – have both remained outside the new Cabinet. Indeed, the second period of *cohabitation* may well be smoother than the first, not least because the two principal protagonists – the Prime Minister, Eduard Balladur, who is Mr Chirac's close associate, and President Mitterrand himself – are out of the running for 1995. Indeed, the very scale of the Right's success could give Mr Mitterrand some room for manoeuvre; a large majority giving ample scope for internal dissension within the right-wing camp.

With this very much in mind, Mr Balladur's Cabinet represents a careful attempt to achieve a balance between the main political forces. As well as the Prime Minister's post, the Gaullists hold the Foreign Affairs and Interior portfolios, while the UDF were given charge of the Ministries dealing with the Economy and Defence. This fair division of the spoils serves Mr Chirac's interests. Nobody can talk of an 'RPR-state', and by giving some of the younger centrist leaders government posts he has outmanoeuvred Mr Giscard d'Estaing. In overall terms, the government as a whole has a decidedly pro-European aspect despite the anti-Maastricht voice of the Interior Minister, Charles Pasqua. The other leading RPR critic of the treaty, Philippe Seguin, though not in the Cabinet, won a consolation prize, being elected President of the National Assembly.

This pro-European tone should ensure a large measure of continuity in policy. President Mitterrand has made it clear that this is his aim, and Mr Balladur is unlikely to have any problem with the President's desire to preserve the parity of the franc and the D-mark in the European currency system. Even in defence and foreign affairs, where some have predicted possible paralysis, there could be considerable room for agreement. The end of the Cold War has spelt a shift in the French security consensus, with politicians in many parties talking of closer links with NATO (while still falling short of full-scale reintegration into the Alliance's military command structure). Operations abroad, not least in the Gulf and in former Yugoslavia, have also demonstrated a pressing need for a greater number of professionals – as opposed to conscripts – in the armed forces.

The presidential election, however, is going to cast a long shadow in policy terms. One of the Balladur government's first measures is likely to be legislation to reform the Nationality Code to deal with the perceived problem of immigration. This is an overt attempt to deal with the concerns of a broad swathe of the right-wing electorate and, not least, the voters of the National Front, whose ballots may still play a crucial role in 1995.

JONATHAN MARCUS

NOTES

1. First-ballot percentage of vote: Communists 9.2%; Socialists 17.6%; Allies (MRG etc.) 2.44%; Ecologists 7.6%; RPR 20.4%; UDF 19.1%; Various Right 4.7%; National Front 12.4%. (Source: Interior Ministry). Final distribution of seats in the National Assembly: RPR 247; UDF 213; Assorted Right 24; Socialists 54; Allies in Presidential Majority 10; Left Radicals (MRG) 6; Communists 23.

The pedigree of Edouard Balladur.

Mr. French

Kenneth Weinstein

KENNETH R. WEINSTEIN is a research fellow at Hudson Institute in Indianapolis.

Edouard Balladur, the descendent of a long line of French merchants influential in the Ottoman Empire, is not especially bold. Friends who frequent his richly appointed Sixteenth Arrondisement townhouse, with its paintings by Braque, Kandinsky and Soulages, confess that Balladur's idea of cutting loose is to drink champagne on the rocks. But this level-headed man in his somber three-button suit has, in the middle of a deep recession, skyrocketed onto the political scene in France as the most popular prime minister of the last quarter-century. He's now the front-runner to succeed François Mitterrand as president of the Fifth Republic by perfecting a technique that may become emblematic of fin-de-siècle Western Europe: the politics of nostalgia.

In office since last April, Balladur, 63, has presided over an economy in collapse. Industrial output has shrunk; the franc has fallen; unemployment, at 12 percent, is still climbing. Yet, despite this and many policy reversals—including a retreat from a focus on budget austerity, backing off a plan to downsize Air France and dropping a bill to limit student housing subsidies—Balladur's popularity hovers in the mid-60 percent range. Part of this can be attributed to the welcome change he offers from the incompetence of the Socialists, who fell from office in last March's legislative elections. But it's also due to something else: in the face of easy, modern cynicism, Balladur has gained the trust of the French who see him as a throwback to the fondly remembered era of disinterested public service, strong families and iron-clad faith. He has assumed the Orleanist father-figure role unfilled since the death of his mentor, President Georges Pompidou. In 1987, while serving as

finance minister, Balladur had to be dissuaded from genuflecting upon the pope's arrival at Lyons Airport.

Balladur honed his political skills in the mid-1960s by handling industrial relations for then-Prime Minister Pompidou. During the May 1968 Paris unrest, Balladur kept his sangfroid while other officials flinched. He contributed to the Grenelle accords, which defused labor unrest by ensuring pay raises and reducing the work week. Bargaining in good faith with union leaders, he exhibited the trademarks of his current domestic success: a preference for "dialogue among social partners" over confrontation and a pathological willingness to compromise.

When Pompidou became president in 1969, Balladur became deputy secretary general of Elysée Palace, rising to secretary general in 1973. As Pompidou's health worsened, Balladur eventually came to run the Elysée in the dark days prior to and following Pompidou's death. In 1983 Balladur became the first to argue for "cohabitation," the power-sharing arrangement in which a prime minister of one party and a president of another hold office simultaneously. As ranking minister in Jacques Chirac's 1986-1988 government, he was to observe firsthand how that worked in practice. Mitterrand skillfully exploited economic stress, student riots and a transportation strike to undermine Chirac and defeat him in the 1988 presidential election.

As the 1993 legislative elections approached, Balladur was the only real person *"premier ministrable."* In addition to being a member of Chirac's inner circle, Balladur was acceptable to both Valéry Giscard d'Estaing's pro-European, center-right Union for the French Democracy (UDF) and the Euroskeptical elements of Chirac's Rally for the Republic (RPR). Balladur led RPR forces appealing for ratification of the Maastricht Treaty, but did so only while noting that a right-wing government would be responsible for enforcing the treaty. In office, he turned these skills to good effect. Even on the most divisive issue, the *franc fort* policy that tied France to high German interest rates, Balladur adroitly widened the European Rate Mechanism tunnel, effectively devaluing the franc while maintaining the ERM structure. This tactic kept further speculation at bay and reinforced the franc's market position. It also kept both conservative factions relatively happy.

Balladur, moreover, learned from Chirac's experience not to allow President Mitterrand and the left to capitalize on social discontent. He first attacked the $74 billion budget deficit, a result of high unemployment and rising social security costs. An austerity program, which pleased deficit-weary centrists, cut government spending and hiked taxes on tobacco, alcohol and the sources that finance social welfare benefits. He then announced the sale of twenty-one nationalized state industries, banks and insurance companies. Unlike Chirac's privatization, these sales were not inspired by ideology but by a need to bring money, approximately $95 billion, into government coffers. At the same time he deflated the economy, Balladur also bought off social unrest. In late May, as pressure grew to take concrete steps to improve soaring unemployment, Balladur launched sales of a bond to finance job creation and help out cash-strapped state industries. A compromise between further austerity and new expenses to stimulate economic growth and employment, the "Balladur bond" was a tremendous success, selling almost three times its original target of $7.3 billion.

He also gave in to organized labor in strategic fashion. Despite Air France losses totaling almost $1 billion a year, he scrapped a plan to phase out 4,000 positions at the airline when a two-week strike threatened to escalate. To appease farmers before heading into the final round of GATT talks, Balladur offered them an additional $275 million in subsidies.

While moving to the left on "social" issues, Balladur has moved to the right elsewhere. He has let Interior Minister Charles Pasqua run amok. Pasqua, the hardline interior minister in Chirac's 1986-1988 government and leader in the fight against Maastricht, appeals to voters of Jean-Marie Le Pen's National Front. On immigration, Balladur has largely let Pasqua have his way. Under Pasqua's guidance, the government has tight-

ened immigration and naturalization laws. The constitution has been amended so that asylum is now a prerogative of the state, not an individual right. This change enables France to deny entry to asylum-seekers refused entry elsewhere in the European Union. Moreover, while resident foreigners born in France used to automatically become citizens unless they expressed their desire not to do so, they must now declare allegiance to the republic to obtain citizenship. Even more significant have been Pasqua's measures to battle illegal immigration—including allowing mayors to nullify fraudulent marriages undertaken for immigration purposes—which have raised fears among France's half-million illegal immigrants.

Balladur also chose firmness in the GATT negotiations, while understanding and admitting that the agreement in many ways was a "trap": whereas opposing an agreement would have brought international isolation, giving in to international pressures for an unmodified GATT would have created a domestic crisis. Going into the GATT negotiations, Balladur needed to secure concessions while at the same time ensuring that an agreement was reached. He managed to get the United States to agree that the E.U. can reduce export subsidies more slowly, though still within the next six-year period. Moreover, Balladur has received assurances that the E.U. will indemnify farmers for land that will lay fallow as a result of GATT.

For the moment, Balladur has refused to talk presidential politics, saying he needs to stay focused on the economic crisis. And in fact, the recession remains his gravest threat. The government's own estimates show that unemployment will rise again next year, perhaps by as much as 240,000. And Balladur has not yet shown the courage to take all the difficult measures necessary to restore French competitiveness. But even if the slump intensifies, the polls suggest French voters are highly unlikely to return to Balladur's competitors on the discredited left: former Prime Minister Michel Rocard or Jacques Delors, president of the European Commission. In the last resort, the major reason many moderate French voters have placed their hopes on Balladur is because if his politics fails, there may be no alternative to a descent into something far worse. Pasqua—and what he stands for—is waiting in the wings. And nostalgia is for now a more palatable option than reaction.

Thoughts on the French Nation Today

Stanley Hoffmann

Stanley Hoffmann is Douglas Dillon Professor of the Civilization of France and Chairman of the Center for European Studies at Harvard University.

I

What is the present condition of the modern French nation which two centuries of conscious and conscientious efforts, from the Revolution to the present, have built around the *idea* of the nation? In the self-image of the French, as in the rhetoric of nationalism, there are two components: an internal one, which can be called national identity or specificity, and an external one, the nation-state.[1]

The revolutionaries and the Republicans of the nineteenth century tried to define France's national identity in political terms. What constitutes the nation is the social contract that set up a national, democratic polity; it was around those principles, transmitted by the school and the army, that foreigners were not merely "naturalized" but "nationalized," assimilated. But the initial voluntarism was enriched and modified by an increasing emphasis on historical continuity, on *l'h'eritage*. The weight of the past, a Burkean notion, was providing roots and substance to the abstract and somewhat formalistic notions derived from Rousseau. It is the combination of historical identity and political specificity which provided the formula of the French melting pot. In France, as in the United States, the absorption of immigrants has been a constant. Germany, however, remains reluctant to conceive of itself as a "country of immigration."[2] In both the United States and France—in the former because of the liberal tradition, in the latter because this is one point on which liberalism and Rousseauism converge, yet without merging—the distinction between the public and the private spheres means that the foreigner who becomes a national, and thereby a citizen, is supposed, in receiving all the rights of citizenship, also to accept the principles of legitimacy and government as well as the laws of his or her adopted country (explicitly in the United States, where these principles are not in dispute, implicitly in France), but can, in his or her private life, remain faithful to his or her customs and religion. The public person must speak English or French; the private one can keep speaking his or her language of origin. In both countries, the naturalization of foreigners was made easy: in France, this was accomplished through the use of jus soli as well as through voluntarism, i.e., requests for French nationality after a few years of residence.

But the French melting pot has never been quite like the American one. The United States *is* "a nation of immigrants"; France is a nation that attracts and incorporates immigrants. This is a major difference. It accounts for the waves of xenophobia which French historians are beginning to study[3]—against Italians and Belgians in the 1880s and 1890s, against Poles and refugees from Germany and Central Europe in the 1930s. After all, there were comparable waves in the United States. This accounts also for two distinctive features. First, because French nationality is not merely contractual—the signing on to the principles of the Constitution, as in the United States—but has a heavy historical component, the public dimension is *both* political and cultural: it entails the assimilation of French culture, which the school system was supposed to produce. Moreover, the political principles were more pointed or militant, as the result of long struggles; thus, the notion of citizenship entailed not only the separation of church and state, but also *la la'icit'e*, an aggressive *rejection* of the Catholic Church, precisely because of its old connections with and public role in prerevolutionary France, and its determination to have a say in public affairs. Second, although the French idea that the Republic integrates only individ-

From *Daedalus*, Summer 1993, pp. 63-79. Originally titled "The Nation, Nationalism, and After: The Case of France," from *The Tanner Lectures on Human Values,* edited by Grethe B. Peterson, pp. 215-282. Salt Lake City: The University of Utah Press, 1994. Reprinted by permission.

67

uals, not "communities," and does not "recognize" communities as public actors is one which many Americans would share, the private sphere is regarded, in France, with far greater suspicion than in America. It is the combination of these two differences which explains why the idea of "multiculturalism" remains repugnant to the French. There is only *one* French culture, and "separate" subcultures are not welcome insofar as they impede assimilation to the French culture.

To be sure, there are occasional similarities between American debates about, and resistance to, the demands of black militants who insist on group identity and groups rights and reject the model of individual integration, and French debates about the integration of Muslims. But America has a special and weighty problem with the blacks: they are Americans, and descendants of slaves forcibly brought to this country long ago. Claiming group rights is a way of obtaining at last the full range of individual civic and social rights that they were denied for so long. The Muslims are immigrants. And while the arguments about their "unassimilability," their ineradicable "difference," are no different from earlier anti-Italian or anti-Polish arguments, there is a novelty: Islam, as duly noted by Fernand Braudel, the eminent historian of the Annales School.[4] Islam is not only an "alien" religion (unlike Catholicism, Protestantism, and Judaism); it is a powerful culture (which, unlike Catholicism, has not been a major part of French culture), indeed "a way of life," and (like Catholicism in this respect) a code that includes the private *and* the public.

Hence the intensity of the debate about immigration. This time, French national identity is felt to be at stake by many more people than those who ranted about what the "invasion" from the East in the 1930s was doing to the French race (I am thinking of the French writer, Jean Giraudoux). There are two sources of worry. One is that many of the Muslims, particularly those who are deeply religious will be "unassimilable": either French identity will be deeply transformed if they become French, or they will be "a danger to the nation" if they are not assimilated.[5] The other worry is that the mechanisms which succeeded in assimilating men and women whose "cultural distance" from the French was often wide, are no longer as effective. The directives of the Ministry of Education about the civic and social values children must be taught may well be unchanged since Jules Ferry in the late nineteenth century.[6] It is the capacity of schools to transmit these directives which is questioned, partly because the content of French education has become less cultural and parochial, and more technical, that is to say mathematics and science count for more, history and the French classics for less, and partly because many primary schools are now predominantly frequented by the sons and daughters of immigrants in districts—urban and suburban—where they are most numerous, and from

whose schools the French have fled. There are other aspects of the "weakening of the French melting pot," as an important report has pointed out:[7] spatial segregation, the loss of influence of the Catholic Church on the Muslims, the flabbiness of French voluntary associations such as unions and parties (remarks which acknowledge the role the Church and the Communists, two organizations seen as "antinational" by many French, had played in the process of assimilation), and the decline of the army as an integrative body because of both shorter military service and the preponderance of technical expertise over civic training. All these factors make the Republican model of individual assimilation far more dubious. So, many foreigners want to become French but without assimilating, and the process that turned foreigners into Frenchmen is faltering. The nature of the "demand" has changed: it is tougher. The supply, too, i.e., the melting pot, has changed: it has softened.

The paradox is that the most common reaction, among intellectuals and politicians, from the conservative Catholic historian Pierre Chaunu, to the socialist leader Michel Rocard, via the Jewish sociologist Dominique Schnapper, is an act of faith in the very process which, all agree, no longer performs as it once had. "Integration will be easiest if the consciousness of French identity is strongest"[8] and such a reinforcement of national consciousness cannot be left to "the free play of the spontaneous forces of social life"[9]; the old distrust of private forces left to themselves is obvious here. A deliberate policy is needed, and it sounds most familiar. On the one hand, the goal of full integration is preserved—hence the rejection of the suggestion, made by Valéry Giscard d'Estaing among others, to make the jus sanguinis the exclusive mode of acquisition of French nationality—as well as the "voluntaristic" approach to the acquisition of French citizenship. When there is a contradiction between the two, the former prevailed until recently: hence the maintenance of the laws that granted French nationality automatically to certain categories of foreigners living in France. The new conservative majority has now sharply limited such cases and demanded formal and material evidence of will. On the other hand, a reinvigoration of the school and the army, as vehicles of civic training, is being demanded; little is said about how this is to be done. Around the need for full assimilation, France's two nationalist traditions, the Republican one and that of the far Right, curiously converge. It is true that the former wants to facilitate integration, the latter, which fears it, wants to make it more arduous; one stresses the political component of the melting pot, the other the cultural one. But there is a common enemy: the pluralism of multiculturalism. Jews who have become fully and proudly assimilated are, occasionally, the strange bedfellows of Catholic *int'egristes*.[10]

The episode of the *foulards islamiques* in 1988—the national debate about the insistence of three young Muslim girls on wearing a veil over their heads at school—showed both the French penchant for turning small incidents into grand symbolic issues, and the depth of the anxiety about Muslim distinctiveness. The defenders of the traditional mechanism of assimilation thought that such a demand was intolerable, because it challenged *la laïcité* in the very heart of the process of homogenization: the school system. American quarrels over multiculturalism, especially in schools and universities, have been followed with a certain amount of *Schadenfreude*.[11] What will happen to American national identity if the Hispanics, the blacks, and the Native Americans, among others, request a right to their separate cultures in the public realm (remember, it includes education for the French)? All these comments and warnings seem to suggest that whereas each wave of American immigrants contributes to and shapes American identity, French immigrants are asked to adopt a firmly preestablished French identity. Indeed, the social historian Gérard Noiriel boldly asserts that while the American melting pot began with the Revolution, the French one ended with it.[12]

And yet, there are genuine grounds for believing that France's capacity to assimilate immigrants has not been seriously impaired. Most of them speak French—part of the labor of integration is therefore unnecessary. Many of them, especially Algerians, appear to want integration, while preserving cultural and family links with their country of origin. This is neither an unreasonable demand nor an original one; it is not a fatal obstacle to assimilation. The power of the French culture, even in a "weaker" school system, remains enormous, and many elements of that culture are transmitted in the working place, and through the media and entertainment industries. Finally, for all the ideological resistance to the taboo of multiculturalism, all the Rousseauean suspicion of pluralism as a threat to *la volonté une,* a de facto pluralism has spread. It was always there in the private sphere, which is where people mostly live. But what is significant is the loosening of the Jacobin corset in the public sphere, and the lowering of the barrier between public and private. Regional government is gaining strength. The legislator's will can be declared unconstitutional by unelected judges. The French state encourages the building of mosques. The "private," i.e., Catholic, school system has, for many years now, been subsidized by the state and treated as part of the public service of education. When François Mitterrand tried to tighten state control over it, millions of Frenchmen marched, not in defense of the Church, but for the right of families to choose their children's schools. In the affair of the *foulards islamiques,* many Catholics and Jews—the former because the whole Republican model was built to *expel* the Church from the public domain, the

latter because of their own new restlessness about a model of *inclusion* that required assimilation but did not, in the horrible crunch of 1940–1944, protect them from discrimination and death—often supported the girls' request.

There is, thus, an increasing distance between the old Jacobin model, or straitjacket, and the modern French society and polity, but this distance does not doom the French melting pot. A certain amount of friendly tolerance for diversity might turn out to be as good a force for integration as the old Republican indoctrination. What is needed to keep the melting pot busy and effective is, in the first place, the prevalence of values of decency, sympathy, and universality in French society. This is why the refusal of right-wing parties to make deals with Jean-Marie Le Pen on the far Right, even though much of its electorate comes from theirs, is essential: the values common to liberalism and to the French (i.e., Jacobin) version of democracy are more important than the narrow model produced by the latter. In the second place, the success of the melting pot may be helped by the strength of French cultural identity, which remains as well established, and despite an apparent lack of public confidence, as solid as ever. It may be that the doubts about its strength are nothing other than pure and simple xenophobia, a rejection of the others not because they cannot or do not want to become "like us," but because we do not want them. In this respect, it cannot be said that the champions of the old model have always done their duty by combating repugnance for the "invaders."

II

Fears about not the substance but the potency of French national identity are also fed by questions about the European enterprise. European integration was initiated by the Fourth Republic, both as the best way to defend French interests now that France had slipped in rank and power, *and* as a bold endeavor in reconciliation (with Germany) and cooperation worthy of French ideals. The sacrifices of sovereignty entailed by supranationality had been, after the debacle of the European Defense Community, both reduced—insofar as the Common Market's Commission, unlike that of the Coal and Steel Community, was not a decision-making body—and delayed, because of the postponement of the introduction of majority rule in the Council. De Gaulle's *Blitzkrieg* against the European Economic Community's (EEC) Commission of 1965, when the latter tried to increase its powers, led to the Luxembourg compromise which eliminated the "threat" of majority rule in matters deemed of essential importance by a member. Under those conditions, the preservation of French independence seemed quite compatible with the construction of a West European entity in economic and monetary matters: the Community helped French modernization, French civil servants dominated its bureaucracy, and France was prima inter pares, the only nuclear Power of the entity, and a fully sovereign state next to a divided Germany with restrictions on its sovereignty. Moreover, in a world dominated by the Cold War, French military autonomy was widely seen as a great asset, offsetting whatever constraints the Community's rules might impose on French economic and financial freedom of maneuver. France was, in the eyes of many French leaders, still a Great Power: through Europe, by its presence outside Europe, especially in Africa, and by virtue of its nuclear nuisance power.[13]

A certain complacent pride began to evaporate in the 1980s. The socialist government's attempt to pursue a *dirigiste* policy of nationalizations and massive public spending disrupted France's balance of payments and trade and jeopardized France's ability to remain within the limits of the European Monetary System (EMS) established in 1978. The sudden awareness of the costs that would have been imposed by the pursuit of such a policy in the midst of a recession, when most of her European partners were tightening belts and fighting inflation, a huge loss of competitiveness and the need to insulate France from the EMS and the EEC's rules, revealed to the French both how much modernization and the abandonment of traditional industrial protectionism had made France dependent on the world market and especially the West European one, and the impossibility of pursuing an economic and financial policy that would be both independent and beneficial. Having finally chosen Europe and austerity—the latter because of the former—Mitterrand needed a new political initiative, and turned to a *relance* of Europe. It was, once more, presented as essential for French power and welfare. The switch to majority vote entailed by the Single Act of 1987 was accepted by Parliament with little turmoil: it was presented as a logical and necessary effect of the decision, unanimously made by the governments of the twelve members, to establish a single market by 1992. But clouds formed soon enough. The inevitable clash between sovereignty and integration, avoided since 1965, when the latter had been set back, could not be postponed any longer.

First, there was the problem of agriculture. The Common Agricultural Policy (CAP) imposed by de Gaulle had been a tremendous engine of modernization and expansion for French agriculture, just as the size of the rural population was falling to a new low. But the cost to consumers was high, and the accumulation of surpluses was exorbitant. When "Brussels," partly because of this, and partly under the General Agreement on Tariffs and Trade (GATT) pressure, began demanding a reform of the CAP, French farmers ceased seeing the Community as their savior and instrument,

and turned their anger against its new policies. The "transfer of competence" that had made Brussels, not Paris, the locus of France's agricultural policy was now seen as a fatal giveaway.

Second, it became gradually clear that the European Court of Justice was quietly but relentlessly giving a "Federalist" interpretation of Community competences, and establishing the superiority of Community over national legislation. The French Conseil d'Etat was the last to accept this, but it finally did. Effectiveness within the Community clearly required the enforceability of its norms, regulations, and directives in the Courts of the members. But French sovereignty, again, was being eroded.

Third, the reunification of Germany transformed the political context. The economic and monetary giant of the European Community (EC)—however hampered, temporarily, by a hasty policy of absorption of former East Germany that was supposed to be painless—was now a full "sovereign" state with enormous political weight. In the absence of the Soviet threat, France's exclusive card, the *force de frappe,* was devalued, and France's nuclear preference meant that Paris lacked the military freedom of action where it mattered: in the conventional domain. It was no consolation that Germany had voluntarily shackled its own freedom in this realm, since the addition of two *impuissances* left Western Europe still utterly dependent on the United States.

Fourth, the Maastricht treaty on European Union, despite its "essential conservatism," seemed to assault French sovereignty sufficiently, on three points, to oblige the government to ask the Constitutional Council for a judgment on its compatibility with the French Constitution. The Union was receiving the power to regulate the entry of non-EC nationals into the Community, possibly by majority rule in the future. The Monetary Union meant that France would have to give up both the franc and the theoretical autonomy of its financial policy, symbolized by the existence of the Bank of France, in exchange for a dubious share in the control of a European Central Bank which would be fully independent of governments, and a carbon copy of the Bundesbank. Indeed, in order to reach the nirvana of Monetary Union, France would have to meet the highly constraining "convergence criteria" Germany had demanded concerning inflation, interest rates, deficits, and public debts. The treaty also gave to EC nationals the right to vote in local elections and for the European Parliament in whatever country of the Community they were living in. This represented a breach in the historic French association of nationality and citizenship, on behalf of foreigners, whereas the only past dissociation—in colonies—had been at the expense of foreigners.

The Constitutional Council and the French Parliament, which had to revise the Constitution so as to make it compatible with the treaty, focused on these points (the new Title XVI reduces the right of non-French EC nationals to vote and to be elected to a possibility, and keeps them from becoming mayors or assistant mayors). The public debate, opened by Mitterrand's decision to submit the treaty itself to the public, and not merely to Parliament, went far beyond this. What emerged from the sound and fury were two central issues. The first was the need to choose between two radically different conceptions of sovereignty—the trickiest of all concepts. An "absolutist" one, which happened to be deeply engraved in French culture, from the days of the Old Regime *and* the proclamation of national sovereignty, logically led to a rejection of all the *abandons* and entrapments entailed by the infernal machine of the EC, with its treaties, its technocrats, and its judges. But the cost of keeping "free hands" risked being the lack of any hands at all: monetary sovereignty had already, de facto, been given up, and the champions of French independence were sufficiently lucid to realize that its recovery entailed jettisoning the EMS and weakening the single market altogether. However, the alternative economic policy they advocated, by imperiling French competitiveness and the franc through inflation and deficits, was no more attractive than in 1983, and no more likely to reduce unemployment than the official course.

A pragmatic and relative notion of sovereignty looked at it not as an indivisible substance but as a bundle of competences that could be gradually pooled or transferred to common bodies, so as to substitute the efficiency of the whole for the relative inefficiency of the members. But this raised as many questions as it answered. As Gaullist Senators put it in a request to the Constitutional Council,[14] which had adopted the pragmatic version in its ruling in April, "if sovereignty is no longer anything but an addition of competences, if one can successively remove them as one would the leaves of an artichoke, at what point, or at what degree, do we arrive at the heart?," a metaphor I had used many years ago![15] (The Council declined to answer.) Who was collecting these leaves? A classical "international organization . . . invested with powers of decision by virtue of transfers of competences consented to it by the member-states,"[16] as the Council put it, or, as many "European" jurists, contrary to the Council's opinion, see it, a supranational entity with a "distinct juridical order" of its own both superior to and part of the juridical order of the members? When the French Parliament, before the public debate on the treaty, amended the Constitution, it carefully avoided taking sides, and it just as carefully limited the "transfer of competences" to the establishment of economic and monetary union and to the setting of rules of entry into the Community.

The second issue which dominated the public debate was the famous democratic deficit. Here again, the Rousseauean, revolutionary, and Republican tradition weighed heavily. It attributes legitimacy only to decisions either taken by representatives of the nation, who have full legislative power, or controlled by these representatives. There is, so far, no European nation. The structure of the EC is such that decisions are taken either by "irresponsible" bureaucrats (the supranational Commission), or by ministers of the various member states who exert jointly the Community's legislative power. Even after Maastricht, which increases the European Parliament's powers, the Council will remain the main legislator, and the Parliament a body that can more easily plead and remonstrate than decide and control. Here, the defenders of the treaty were at a disadvantage. They could try to argue that a "transfer of competences" was a better choice for France than a jealous defense of sovereignty because a strong collective hand is better than a weak and empty national one. But there was no way they could argue that this transfer was to a fully democratic system. If the EC was just an international organization, the question of democracy was secondary, and the effectiveness of such an entity would continue to be impaired (the French government had to reassure Parliament that the Luxembourg compromise was still valid). If the new Union was going to become what its name implied, the absence of democratic institutions was a major handicap. The two countries most responsible for this were Britain and France—logically in the former case, since Britain is now the most ardent champion of national sovereignty, or rather, in Thatcherian words, the sovereignty of the British Parliament; but illogically in the French case, since it is the French government which wants the Union to have the broadest possible jurisdiction. The treaty's opponents were able to use the "democratic deficit" as a major part of their case. France, they said, was caught in an *engrenage* in which more and more decisions affecting her future were going to be taken by faceless figures operating on their own, and in which the representatives of the French people were being doubly dispossessed: by an Executive that defined the European policy of France all by itself (it is true that the French Parliament has debated European policy only rarely, but it is also true that these debates were remarkably ill-attended), and by European institutions that eat up, one by one, the leaves of the national artichoke.

III

The debate on Maastricht also raised two broader issues—one directly, the other indirectly. The first is the relation of the French nation-state to the European Community or Union. The Community, so far, is neither a classical Confederation, it goes way beyond, nor a Federal Union, it falls far short, nor an ordinary intergovernmental organization. The more it evolves, the more sui generis it becomes: its range expands, but its "supranationality" gets diluted (except insofar as the European Parliament's powers are grudgingly increased); its institutional structure becomes more Byzantine, its legal homogeneity more cracked. Pooled sovereignty means, in practice, that agents of the members behave both as guardians of national interests and as European trustees. To present the Community enterprise as a zero-sum game for the members is wrong. What the states "give up" is not necessarily lost, and much of what is "transferred" does not go to Brussels but to the private actors of the new European economy. Each of the members—by which I mean their governing elites—believes that, left to itself, the European small- or medium-size nation-state is doomed to being less prosperous at home and less effective abroad than if it pursues the complex course of European integration.

But this is not the whole answer. What is this course leading to? It has kept advancing, despite periods of stagnation and setbacks, partly for the reason just given, and partly because it has kept its ultimate configuration in the dark. Ambiguity, which preserves most alternatives, has been both the condition and the price of progress. But there is something about the French mind which resists ambiguity: the pragmatism and open-endedness of the "Monnet method" appeals more to businessmen, and often to bureaucrats, than to lawyers, political thinkers, and intellectual politicians. De Gaulle's insistence on setting goals, on eliminating alternatives, and on prescribing policies, while it always left room for pragmatic adaptation to "les circonstances," aimed at ruling out shackles on French hands. The formal anxiety about being governed from Brussels barely conceals a real anguish about being dictated by Bonn (or Berlin), entrapped in a Community that would be an extension of German might rather than, as was hoped originally, French power. Even though all the European nation-states are, in dozens of ways, dependent on each other, on the world economy, and on the country that still appears as having the greatest influence in shaping the world economy, namely the United States, some European states have greater means of affecting their milieu than others, and the new Germany is seen as potentially the most able to do so. There exists, at present, a gnawing fear of being caught in an enterprise that will either lead to a Federation in which the nation will lose its identity as a political unit, with its political powers going both upward, to the new central institutions of the Union, and downward, to the regions, or else result in a Baroque or Gaudiesque construction, multileveled and multispeed, manipulated above all by Germany. There is a fear that the Community begins to resemble much more the German model of Federalism and "so-cial market economy" than the French model of the unitary and regulatory state.

The second large issue is that of the relation of the French nation-state to the new global system that is now emerging. The French conception of political rule is heavily territorial: the soil, the hexagon, are inseparable from French conceptions of authority. But in the new system, as many observers have noted, "non-territorial functional space,"[17] as one of them inelegantly called it, is developing systems of regulation which are collective and apply to specific activities across geographical space. This "unbundling of territoriality" also takes the form of unregulated transnational economic and financial transactions. Both kinds affect all nations and states, but the hardest hit are, of course, those which participate the least or carry the least weight in the regulatory institutions or in the "transnationalized microeconomic links" and economic and financial flows, and those that find it hardest to conceptualize a system not based on sharp territorial demarcation. Nations such as the United States, Japan, potentially China, and perhaps Germany, although their capabilities are obviously uneven (among countries and among sectors), may be able to control the nonterritorial flows and institutions more than France. There is little solace to be found, for French men and women attached to the nation-state, in the emergence of so many new nation-states on the ruins of the former Soviet internal and external Empire, and of Yugoslavia. They are either eager to join the Community, or else are degenerating into an economic mess and violent conflict.

However, the French predicament is one that all nation-states will face (the worst is that of states that have not succeeded in becoming nations, either because, like Russia, they are still multinational, or because, like many African countries, they have failed to integrate their disparate and feuding elements). The nation-state has been a blend of cultural unity (often compatible, as in Britain, with the survival of regional cultures) and political unity; as Ernest Gellner has put it,[18] culture became the access card to citizenship and dignity. How far can these two elements be dissociated? What will happen to cultural identity if they are separated? And where should, or will, the political component of nationhood go in this divorce? To this last question, different countries may give different answers. Some, in Western Europe, for instance, may be quite ready for a leap into Federation; others (Switzerland, it appears) are not ready at all. If Auguste Comte's old principle still applies—that one can only destroy what one can replace—then the nation-state, including its political dimension, still has a bright future. There is, so far, no higher allegiance, nothing that replaces the nation as a legitimate source of social identity, even though, as the late Judith Shklar has pointed out,[19] the modern nation-state has so often been nothing but a war machine and a source of oppression for minorities and deviants. International institutions, although increasingly endowed with powers, remain utilitarian enterprises. They are not objects of loyalty. An entity such as the European Community is still, when it comes to allegiance, primarily a collection of cooperating national loyalties, with loyalty to "Europe" superposed on national loyalty (just as allegiance to Britain is over, say, loyalty to Scotland) only in the rare cases of devoted Eurocrats. It may well be that my judgment of 1965 still stands: the nation will survive, with diminished political powers, and those it will keep losing or has already lost will not go to a single, concentrated higher source. The model of modern state-building out of dispersed and overlapping earlier units may not tell us anything about the future. There may well be no European Federation, at least in the foreseeable future. Unless all the members of such a potential Federation are willing to begin by establishing both a genuine European electorate and an effective European Parliament, there will be no world state. But the surviving nation-state will bear little resemblance to the Rousseauean sovereign community, or even to the liberal Mazziniesque, Millian, or Wilsonian models of cooperating, homogeneous nation-states. It will no longer be possible to write a purely fierce and proud "hexagonal" history. A world of "pooled" and "unbundled" sovereignties, in which states collectively decide on the attribution and on the use of the powers which they put in common and which they are no longer strong enough to apply effectively all by themselves—even in the military realm—may well be the immediate future of the nation-state. It may be the natural result of an evolution marked both by increasing interpenetration and by the continuing elusiveness of that general society of humankind whose absence Rousseau had noted with, the cultural historian and theorist Tzvetan Todorov notwithstanding, more complacency than regret.[20]

As for French cultural identity, it has never been detachable from French political institutions and programs—it has always been tied to the state. The French state's abandonment of many of its powers over the French economy, the "Europeanization" or "globalization" of that economy, cannot therefore fail to affect French cultural identity. The French have in the past been proud of their unique economic "balance." This was a significant component of their sense of social distinctiveness, as well as a major component of Jules Michelet's nationalism, vis-à-vis England, and later of right-wing nationalism, especially in its anti-American incarnation. This singularity began to fade with post–World War II industrialization, urbanization, and the lowering of trade barriers. It is bound to vanish with the creation of a single European market open to the world. The very dispossession to which the state has thus consented will produce sharp reactions of

national sentiment and resistance, as in the case of French farmers, and renewed demands for greater state management and control of whatever can still be managed and controlled from Paris. But insofar as the strategic, high-tech sectors of the industry are concerned, regulation will make sense only at the European level. It may be true that the more European and global economic integration intensify, the greater will be the temptation to defend and to mythologize all the remaining social and political components of French national identity (just as global economic integration feeds the tendency of the "Eurocrats" to insist on Europe's distinctiveness—not always obvious—vis-à-vis the United States and Japan). However, the nationalist reactions are more likely to be similar to recurrent bouts of fever than returns to the dominant ideologies, policies, and practices of the self-contained past.

French national consciousness will therefore have to concentrate increasingly on such components of identity as, in the public sphere, the virtues of France's constitutional system—which, despite the consensus around it, are far from uncontroversial—as well as those of France's system of social protection, and the many elements of cultural distinctiveness still provided by French education, by the French intellectual tradition, by whatever persists in the French style of authority, by the sometimes frivolous, but permanent belief in the importance of high culture (which state policies have strengthened since André Malraux) as well as a certain art of life and leisure, a certain rapport with nature, a unique "agreement of earth and foot" (to quote from a character in Albert Camus' *Caligula*)—i.e., what the French have done and will continue to do with the imprint of their history and geography. What may, therefore, occur, is something that would be most welcome: the end of the need that Rousseau had posited—to choose between being a human being and being a citizen. The French revolutionary and Republican nationalism had tried, heroically but falteringly, to bridge the gap by making France the universal carrier of the citizen model. If the operational content of citizenship and sovereignty continues to shrink, then the emotional charge of a national feeling all too ready to veer into chauvinistic nationalism may shrink as well, despite occasional surges, and cosmopolitanism would no longer have to be either a chosen nation's "mission" or a term of insult.

ENDNOTES

1. This essay is an excerpt of the second of the Tanner lectures on "The Nation, Nationalism and After: The Case of France," delivered at Princeton University in March 1993, and to be published by the University of Utah Press.
2. See Gérard Noiriel, "Difficulties in French historical research on immigration," in Daniel L. Horowitz and Gérard Noiriel, eds., *Immigrants in Two Democracies* (New York: New York University Press, 1992), 66–79.

3. See especially Gérard Noiriel, *Le creuset fran͵cais* (Paris: Seuil, 1988), chap. 5, and Gérard Noiriel, *La tyrannie du national* (Paris: Calmann-Lévy, 1991). See also Rogers Brubaker, *Citizenship and Nationhood in France and Germany* (Cambridge, Mass.: Harvard University Press, 1992).

4. Fernand Braudel, *L'identit´e de la France,* vol. I (Paris: Arthaud-Flammarion, 1986), 195.

5. Noiriel, "Difficulties in French historical research on immigration," 74.

6. Quoted in Danielle Boyzon-Fradet, "The French education system: springboard or obstacle to integration," in Horowitz and Noiriel, eds., *Immigrants in Two Democracies,* 149.

7. "Rapport de la Commission de la nationalité," *Etre fran͵cais aujourd'hui et demain,* vol. II (Paris: Documentation française, 1988), 82ff. See also François Bourricaud, "1945–1992 La crise des référents," in J. F. Sirinelli, ed., *Histoire des droites en France,* vol. I (Paris: Gallimard, 1992), 567–99.

8. "Rapport de la Commission de la nationalité," 82.

9. Ibid., 86.

10. In a comparable vein, Paul Yonnet has written a book, *Voyage au Centre du malaise fran͵cais* (Paris: Gallimard, 1993), that requires particular attention. Rather than defending racism, he attacks antiracism. He charges foreign historians with having destroyed "le roman national français," along with French critics such as Bernard-Henri Levy, who has a "sick fear of French identity." He laments "the weakening of national sentiment," and the "decline of the representation of the nation's homogeneity." *Quotidien de Paris,* 2 February 1993.

11. See *Le D´ebat* 69 (March–April 1992).

12. In Horowitz and Noiriel, eds., *Immigrants in Two Democracies,* 73.

13. See my chapter on "French dilemmas and strategies in the new Europe," in Robert Keohane, Joseph Nye, and Stanley Hoffmann, eds., *After the Cold War* (Cambridge, Mass.: Harvard University Press, forthcoming, 1993).

14. Quoted in Alec Stone, "Ratifying Maastricht," *French Politics and Society* II (1) (Winter 1993): 83.

15. See "Obstinate or obsolete," in Stanley Hoffmann, *Decline or Renewal: France since the Thirties* (New York: Viking, 1974), 379.

16. Stone, "Ratifying Maastricht," 74.

17. John Gerard Ruggie, "Territoriality and beyond: problematizing modernity in international relations," *International Organization* 47 (1) (Winter 1993): 171.

18. In Ernest Gellner, *Culture, Identity and Politics* (Cambridge: Cambridge University Press, 1987), 6–28.

19. Unpublished remarks on nationalism.

20. Cf. Tzvetan Todorov, *Nous et les autres* (Paris: Seuil, 1989), 206 ff.

POLITICAL RENEWAL ITALIAN STYLE

Mark Gilbert

Mark Gilbert teaches in the Department of Political Science at Dickinson College in Carlisle, Pennsylvania, USA, and has written on Italian issues in Italian Politics and Society *and the* Political Quarterly. *He is currently writing a book, to be published in 1994 by Westview Press, on the collapse of the Italian party system 1987–93.*

The recent spate of bomb explosions in Florence, Rome and Milan has acted as a potent reminder that Italy is undergoing its most turbulent political crisis since the late 1970s. Whoever is responsible for planting the bombs, the purpose of the explosions is clear. The blasts are an attempt to intimidate the judges, politicians and thousands of ordinary people who are trying, with some success, to renew Italian democracy.

The underlying causes of the current upheaval are to be sought in the failure of post-war Italian governments to build a normal bond of mutual service and respect between the state and the citizen. The trains do not run on time, though this, in fact, is the least of the average citizen's problems. A more serious issue has been the ossification of the country's political class into a privileged *nomenklatura*. The complexities of the Italian political system, with its party lists, abundance of parties and permanent Communist opposition meant that Italian voters were either unwilling or unable throughout the Cold War to vote the country's governing parties out of power. This situation generated predictable results. By the mid-1980s, Italian politics was a by-word for corruption, jobbery, wasteful 'pork barrel' legislation and the pointless pursuit of personal power by the political elite.

Though this system had its defenders, it was inherently unstable. The first signs of public restlessness with the political system came in June 1991, through a referendum to simplify the electoral system and stamp out fraudulent voting procedures. One of the *nomenklatura*'s most glaring privileges was the possibility of using the immensely complicated party list system to manipulate election results. This made the huge victory won by the reformers, in the face of the open opposition of leading figures such as the former Socialist Prime Minister, Bettino Craxi, a symbolic affirmation of the public will for change. The long-serving government coalition, however, especially the christian Democrats (DC) and the Socialists (PSI), acted as if nothing had happened. Confident that their strangle-hold on the state television network and much of the press would enable them to mould public opinion during an election campaign, Italian leaders continued to play politics by the old rules. The then President, Francesco Cossiga, grasped that the parties were making a disastrous blunder, but his efforts to make them change their ways were undermined by his eccentric methods of presenting his views. As a result, the parties only discovered how far they had underestimated the strength of public opinion on the reform question in April 1992, when they were given an unprecedented drubbing in the national elections. The ruling coalition only obtained a majority in Parliament by the narrowest of margins, and the DC slid below 30 per cent for the first time since the war.

Yet, in retrospect, the parties must be glad that the election was held when it was. Since April 1992, the political fortunes of the old guard have gone from bad to worse as the judiciary, sniffing weakness, began rummaging through the dirtiest political laundry in the western world. The subsequent revelations of the *mani pulite* investigations in Milan, Rome, Venice and Naples have shocked even hardened cynics. It has become clear that since the early 1980s major public works contracts were awarded entirely on the basis of enormous under-the-counter 'contributions' to politicians from favoured businessmen; that most of these *tangenti* never reached the parties' coffers, and that many leading 'statesmen' were living far beyond their declared means. Worse still, a clear connexion between the political parties and organised crime seems to have been established. This is not a reference to the judicial woes of Giulio Andreotti, whose alleged friendship with the *capi* of the Sicilian mafia and reputed involvement in the murder, in 1979, of the journalist, Lino Pecorelli, has still to be fully investigated, let alone proved. Rather, it is a comment on the situation in Naples, where a flood of detailed confessions from repentant *camorristi* and disgraced politicians has shown beyond reasonable doubt that the political hierarchies of the city were working hand-in-glove with the principal crime families.

No democratic political system, however well-entrenched, could survive wrong-doing on this scale. Even the competence and personal honesty of Giuliano Amato, the Socialist academic who became Prime Minister after the April elections, could not prevent the Italians from switching their votes away from the traditional governing parties at every subsequent opportunity. The biggest beneficiary has been the *Lega Nord,* the populist movement often characterised, falsely, as neo-fascist. Despite (or perhaps because of) the occasional verbal intemperance of the party leader, Umberto Bossi, the *Lega*'s share of the national vote has mushroomed from about two per cent in 1990, to almost twenty per cent today. In December 1992, voters elected *Lega* pluralities in two important northern towns, Monza and Varese. In June 1993, the *Lega* took control of administration in Milan, recording the highest ever vote, thirty-nine per cent, for a single party, as well as of numerous other urban centres in the Po River Valley, Italy's industrial and commercial heartland. The coalition parties, meanwhile, suffered their *Caporetto.* The DC were the main victims of the *Lega*'s success in the north of the country, while their grip on the south was loosened by the left and by the neo-fascist *Movimento Sociale Italiano* (MSI). The party now stands at a post-war low of just eighteen per cent: a projected change of name to the *Partito Popolare* may not be enough to save it. The PSI is still worse off: bankrupt, divided and vilified by the press and by public opinion, it obtained less than five per cent of the votes in the June elections and is now facing a serious threat of extinction.

The *Lega,* however, has not been the only gainer from the collapse of the old regime. Public desire for change caused the electorate to vote by massive margins for a 'first past the post' electoral system in a national referendum held in April 1993; the leader of the referendum movement, Mario Segni, the son of a former President of the Republic and a long-time campaigner for a clean-up in Italian politics, now seems set to create a centrist force, the so-called *Alleanza Democratica.* This new party would attempt to act as a magnet for progressive Christians, members of the small but important Republican party, and disaffected socialists. More generally, it would establish a middle-class alternative to the *Lega,* whose supporters are predominantly lower-middle and working class. Segni seems also to be inching towards an accommodation with the only traditional political force which has survived the recent convulsions intact: the *partito Democratico della Sinistra,* the former communists.

The PDS has had a good 1993. Relatively few ex-communists have been arrested in the corruption scandals, giving the PDS a comparative reputation for honesty. Its election results, while not spectacular, have been encouraging: like the *Lega,* the PDS can count on a little under twenty per cent of the national vote. The party has also shown tremendous powers of endurance. The PDS was an infant exposed at birth to the bitter weather which followed the collapse of the former Soviet empire, but it has emerged hardier for the experience. The party leader, the much-maligned Achille Occhetto, deserves a great deal of the credit for this achievement. Showing great persistence, Occhetto has steered the PDS away from Marxism and towards a form of progressive social democracy which is attractive to many voters, but which may be impossible to realise in the context of Italy's devastated public finances.

This thumbnail sketch of recent political developments in Italy serves to underline a central point. For decades, Italians have said that they were governed by a *partitocrazia,* a government for and by the parties. Italy is now a fully-fledged *democrazia.* Sovereignty has quite genuinely been transferred to the people; the people have now got to decide what they will do with it. For the moment, power is in the hands of a caretaker government headed by Carlo Azeglio Ciampi, the former governor of the Central Bank, but it is generally conceded that this is a temporary solution. Italy will have to choose between the new centre—Segni and his allies; the revived left—the PDS; and the new right—the *Lega.* The most likely combination here is, as Segni has implied, a 'Stop the *Lega*' coalition between the new centre party and the PDS. Yet Segni, a lifelong anti-communist, is not an obvious ally of an ex-communist party, while the *Lega* is less explicitly right-wing than its colourful rhetoric and populist policies (reconstitution of Italy into three federal 'macroregions', privatisation and limits on immigration) sometimes make it appear.

To complicate matters further, other new parties can count on substantial followings in certain regions: the *Rete,* whose leading lights are the anti-mafia campaigners, Leoluca Orlando and Nando Dalla Chiesa, have strong support in Sicily, especially Palermo. Nor are the old parties wholly out of the reckoning. The DC, though wounded, remains the best-organised party in southern Italy and can count on a large client vote. *Rifondazione Comunista,* the group of hardline communists which split from the PDS after the dissolution of the old Italian communist party, enjoy substantial support in parts of the south and in big industrial cities like Turin. The MSI has done disturbingly well in recent elections, especially in Calabria, the 'toe' of the Italian boot. Even under Italy's new 'first past the post' electoral system, all these parties can be expected to have significant representation in the next Italian parliament. How such a parliament will be able to form a coherent government is a question to which there is no easy answer.

This climate of acute political uncertainty is compounded by the dire state of the national debt, which has reached 110 per cent of GNP, and the still un-won battle against the mafia (the arrest of Toto Riina earlier this year was, however, a body-blow from which the mafia will struggle to recover). Nevertheless, it would be a mistake to be too pessimistic about Italy's prospects. The political changes of the last eighteen months have been exhilarating, and are not merely a leap in the dark, as many Italian commentators profess to believe. The respected daily newspaper *La Repubblica* worried that Italy was being handed over to the 'new barbarians' in the wake of the *Lega*'s landslide victory in Milan, but it is hard to see this as other than upper middle-class *angst.* Whatever the *Lega*'s faults, it does possess a serious and thoughtful economic policy, is committed to European integration and has moderated its earlier, somewhat egoistic, demands for northern secession. The PDS and Segni show a similar willingness to think hard about the purpose of their political activity. After decades of government by men like Andreotti, whose most notorious remark is 'power wears out those who haven't got it', government by parties which want to treat politics as a means to an end can only make a refreshing change.

Italy's meltdown—and ours.

THE GODMOTHER

Martin Jacques

MARTIN JACQUES, formerly editor of *Marxism Today*, is a columnist for the *Sunday Times* of London.

Virtually every government in the democratic world is currently experiencing a crisis of credibility. Clinton, Kohl, Major, Yeltsin, Mitterrand: everywhere you turn the picture is the same. More disturbingly, opposition parties are faring no better. No one is yearning to vote for Labour in Britain or the Social Democrats in Germany. In the United States, Clinton's electoral victory was followed by a stunningly rapid implosion of political support; the Republican Party is in disarray; Congress is reviled; the most dynamic element of the American polity is the anti-party of Perot. In most of the former West, the ancien régime, with its anachronistic left-right split and party structures, has not given way to something new. It is creaking under the strain of its own inertia.

But there is one place that seems to have broken out of this pattern into something drastically new; one place where discontent has actually resulted in a complete political revolution, where perhaps the future of other Western countries can be seen in acute and extreme form. That country is Italy. Italy is the laboratory of post-1989 Western democracy. All the tendencies present elsewhere can be found there in exaggerated and dramatic form: the after-shocks of the end of the cold war, the delegitimation of traditional parties, the growth of money corruption, regional balkanization, cultural usurpation of political processes. Perhaps one way of understanding what is happening, or not happening, elsewhere is to look at the extreme case, the possible harbinger of what could happen everywhere.

Italy's position during the cold war was always an extreme case. After the war, the powerful Communist Party was a partner in the anti-fascist coalition, but in 1947, with the onset of the cold war, it was ejected from the government by the Christian Democrats and went into opposition. Thus was established the enduring pattern of post-

war Italian politics: the Christian Democrats always in power, the Communists always in opposition. It was, in effect, a de facto single-party system. Italy, in this sense, might be described as the only Eastern European state in Western Europe. In the Italian case, though, the Communists were in opposition, prevented for national and international reasons from participating in government. And unlike in the East, there were free elections, competing political parties and a vibrant civil society. Nevertheless, in a thousand and one different ways, Italy's democracy was shrunk and attenuated as a consequence.

The term single-party government, of course, is slightly misleading in the Italian case. The Christian Democrats always shared power with smaller parties such as the Liberals and the Republicans and, from the general election in 1963, most importantly of all, with the Socialists. But the Christian Democrats were always overwhelmingly the dominant partner: indeed, excepting the Socialists, the other outfits were rather like the satellite parties that cooperated with the Communists in Eastern European governments.

The constant succession of Italian governments in the postwar period became rather a joke in other Western countries, a by-word for instability. But this is utterly misleading. As in Japan, there may have been many governments and many prime ministers, but beneath this seemingly chaotic surface, exceptional stability prevailed. Governments came and went, fifty-two so far, but nothing much ever changed; the same party and the same people continued in power. Italy had the West's most stable political system. Italian politics may have given the impression of a melodrama, but in fact it was more like a stagnant pond, growing more putrid by the day.

Of course, as in the East, power in single-party government lies not with the government but with the party. The Soviet government counted for little compared with the Communist Party. Soon in Italy too, the real power lay not with the government but with the ruling parties, particularly the Christian Democrats, but also the Socialists. The parties became vast and bloated, with enormous resources, an extraordinary network of offices and great powers of patronage. They were like aristocratic fiefdoms. And, as a result, there grew up an extremely unhealthy relationship between government on the one hand and the state, business and civil society on the other.

Crucial to the power of the ruling parties was the state. The Italian state is no ordinary state. It accounts for around a quarter of GDP. It owns vast tracts of Italian industry; it was the key source of the patronage exercised by the ruling parties; all key state positions were party appointments, divided between the parties like the spoils of war. The vast majority of jobs, even secretaries, were the subject of patronage. Italy, like Eastern Europe, had its nomenklatura. And this nomenklatura, as in contemporary Russia, became inextricable from organized crime.

The relationship between the legal and the illegal state is crucial to an understanding of how the Christian Democratic regime worked. Only now is the story beginning to be told, and the details are still unclear. But it would appear that at the very heart of the regime was a secret, illicit relationship between the Christian Democrats and the Mafia. Giulio Andreotti, seven-time prime minister and the most powerful politician in postwar Italy, stands accused of being in effect the guardian and protector of the Mafia in Rome. The Christian Democrats' motivation requires little explanation: the Mafia helped deliver the Christian Democratic vote in the south, which became increasingly critical to its continued electoral dominance.

The picture I have presented, though, needs a little refinement. Italy, we must remember, is a recent creation, only finally being unified in 1870. Regional variations remain profound, with that between north and south the most acute. Italy to this day enjoys a weak sense of nation and a strong sense of region and city. The country's postwar political geography reflects these differences. The north and the south were the strongholds of the Christian Democrats, while central Italy—notably Emilia-Romagna and Tuscany—were the heartlands of the Communists. Bologna is the largest city in the West to have been governed uninterruptedly since the war by Communists.

During the '70s the Communists made steady advances; then in 1976 they made spectacular gains in the general election, winning almost a third of the vote. There was talk of a historic compromise between the Christian Democrats and the Communists. But it all came to naught, doused by the violence that was unleashed by the far right and the dark forces of the Italian state in the late '70s. Nevertheless, the steady Communist advance meant that the party slowly forced its way into the counsels of government at a regional and city level. As a result, it became part of the spoils system in some cities and even, in a very limited way, at a national level. It was still the outsider, but no longer the untouchable. The late '70s proved to be the Communist high-water mark. After

then, it very slowly began to decline. During the '80s the Christian Democrats maintained their dominance while the Socialists made steady advances, although their share of the vote never exceeded the mid-teens, compared with the Christian Democrats' low thirties and the Communists' high twenties.

1989 was the moment when the postwar system began to unravel. Until then, it had been frozen in the refrigerator of the cold war. But when the Berlin Wall was dismantled and communism collapsed, the entire political system lost its point. The Communist Party was thrown into crisis by events in the East. It began the search for a new identity, changed its name to the Democratic Party of the Left and was damaged by a split. But it was not to prove the main casualty of events in the East. With the Communist Party undermined and no longer the object of Western concern, the Christian Democrats' raison d'être suddenly evaporated. The entire political edifice, which had been constructed around the need to keep the Communists out of power, began to crumble. People slowly began to realize that the parties were no longer indispensable to work and life.

The first evidence of this process was the agony of the Communists. Then, in the north, the Lombardy League, anti-south, anti-Rome and separatist, began to gain ground in local elections. But the crucial moment came in early 1992 when the *tangenti* scandal broke in Milan. As in the case of Watergate, it had small and unlikely beginnings. Mario Chiesa, the head of Trivulzio, an old people's home in Milan, tried to get a small cleaning contractor, by the name of Luca Magni, to pay 10 percent of his contract as a kickback—to the Socialist Party. Rather than pay the kickback, which he could ill-afford, Magni went to the carabinieri, who set up a sting and caught Chiesa red-handed. It rapidly became clear that what had seemed like a freak occurrence was actually an insight into the way the whole system worked. As the old disciplines and accompanying loyalties broke down, so the guilty, like Chiesa, began to talk. The Trivulzio drop became a trickle and then turned into a torrent.

During the '80s Milan had been the powerhouse of Bettino Craxi's Socialist Party. It became clear that its enormous income was obtained overwhelmingly by illicit means, with the politicians helping themselves to a portion, often making themselves fabulously rich in the process. But what happened in Milan was true in many other places. At the center of tangentopoly, as it is known, were the huge state corporations such as Eni. In return for contracts, the managers, all political appointees, rewarded the parties and their politicians. In March of this year, the scandal spread south, to Naples and Palermo, and engulfed the Christian Democrats. But the charges here had a further dimension: leading Christian Democrat politicians were accused not only of receiving kickbacks, but also of complicity with organized crime, the Camorra in Naples and the Cosa Nostra in Sicily.

The magistrates are the heroes of the *tangenti* scandal, courageously taking on a system that previously had seemed beyond the law, the media and the people. It was they who began to lay bare the inner workings of the Italian state. The weakening of the old governing parties after 1989 together with the rise of the Northern League finally gave them the courage to act.

Italian politics is thus transformed. The old governing parties are thoroughly discredited; all but the Christian Democrats face extinction; even its future is in serious doubt. They now face the same kind of problems as those that confronted the ruling Communist Parties in Eastern Europe after 1989. The collapse of the old parties has led to the progressive dissolution of the old political identities that dominated the highly politicized Italian society. The sudden collapse of the old system has accelerated the decline of both the old bonds of class and religion and the left-right polarity. There is a search for new identities, of which, as in the Balkans, the most insistent have been regional. It is this that underpins the mushrooming support for the League.

Never before has a European democracy witnessed such a political upheaval. The governing class—politicians and businessmen alike—is being swept away. This is the first revolution in a mature European democracy. But this time the revolutionary heroes are not workers, peasants, students or even mullahs, but magistrates. Commentators are fond of comparing the present events in Italy to those of 1945 or 1968–69. But they are very different. The events of 1968–69, which were historically far less important than those of today, were marked by great demonstrations and strikes—the standard menu of Great Historical Events in the grand era of class politics. These are now almost completely absent. There are few outward signs that anything untoward is happening. The revolution is being played out in the courtrooms and on television. Talk shows have interacted with legal sanctions to create a political dynamic entirely outside the realm of traditional political structures. This is the first postmodern revolution.

Operation Clean Hands, as it is known in Italy, has made enemies of the powerful men who ran Italy in the postwar decades. During recent months car bombs have exploded in Florence, Rome and Milan. No one knows who perpetrated these outrages, but the conspirators are surely those who are most threatened by the reform movement. But it is difficult to believe they will succeed in derailing reform, as they did in the '70s. The scale of what is happening this time around is too sweeping, too deeply rooted, too popular. Again Eastern Europe provides a useful analogy. The velvet revolution in Czechoslovakia and the fall of the other regimes proved an unstoppable process even though it could hardly have been more profound and its enemies more powerful. And only in Romania was serious blood spilled.

If reform continues, what will be the likely result? Recently, we've begun to get a small glimpse of the future. An electoral law adopted at the beginning of August replaces the previous purist system of proportional representation with a combination of a first-past-the-post system for 75 percent of the seats and proportional representation for the other 25 percent. Its adoption clears the way for a general election to be held, probably early next year. With more than a fifth of

deputies under investigation in the kickback scandal, it is bound to result in a very different Senate and Chamber of Deputies.

The other key event was the mayoral elections in early June, which gave a clear hint as to the shape of the new political map. The Northern League emerged as the dominant force in the north—in Lombardy, Veneto, Piedmont and Liguria. The former Communists retained, even strengthened, their dominant position in the center—notably Emilia-Romagna, Tuscany, Umbria and the Marches. In the south the picture was more confused. The Christian Democrats were expected to emerge as dominant, but they suffered severe defeats—around Naples to the former Communists, and in Sicily to La Rete and the Democratic Alliance of Mario Segni (a former leading Christian Democratic who jumped ship in the spring). It looks as if Italy will be divided along regional lines to a far greater extent than in the past; the parallel again is the East and, most tragically of all, the neighboring Balkan peninsula.

These election results suggest that the new Italy will be divided into three regionally based antagonistic blocs—the League in the north, the former Communists in the center and the Christian Democrats in the south. The new electoral system is likely to encourage this process, because a first-past-the-post system rewards and accentuates regional strength. None of the three, however, is likely to emerge as strong enough to govern on its own. (The mayoral elections suggested national percentages of 17.8 percent for the Christian Democrats, 16.9 percent for the League and 12 percent for the reconstructed Communists.) A new government, therefore, is almost certain to require two of the three to cooperate in forming a new government. But which two? The Christian Democrats and the League, although both rightish, are bitter enemies. And the former Communists make unlikely allies for either of their rivals. The new Italy could be very unstable.

But there are other possible outcomes. If the mayoral elections are anything to go by, the new electoral system, together with the fragmented and fluid state of political alignments, could encourage new electoral alliances. These dominated the mayoral elections, with the former Communists being at the center of a kaleidoscope of alliances with a myriad of forces. The most likely possibility in this context is an arrangement between Segni's Democratic Alliance and the former Communists: what has been described as an "efficientist" alliance between progressive business and the liberal left. Such an alliance triumphed in the mayoral election in Turin and could conceivably form the basis of a new government. Neoliberalism has a distinct future in Italy, and maybe elsewhere.

Further down the road, there are other questions to be asked. Can the Christian Democrats survive? The party is trying to find a new role and identity and will rename itself the Popular Party before the election. But apart from the south, where patronage and clientelism live on, albeit in weakened form, its prospects look bleak. Then there is the Democratic Party of the Left, the former Communists. It did remarkably well in the mayoral elections, but as with the left everywhere, it no longer has a clear idea of what it stands for or where it is going. Finally, what will happen to the Northern League? This has been the Solidarity or Civic Forum of Italy, the outsider, the broad popular alliance that broke the old system. But unlike these, it is regionally based, hostile to the south, and therefore also regionally confined. Umberto Bossi, its leader, has been trying to play down its nationalistic and racist overtones in order to win broader support. Most populist alliances of this kind, however, tend to fracture when the time comes for them to assume office and responsibility. One thinks most especially of Perot.

Not so long ago, there was a naive belief that the problems stemming from the collapse of communism would be confined to the East. Italy, more than anywhere else, gives the lie to that belief. Indeed, Italy, with its de facto one-party system, the growth of regionalism, the trends toward fragmentation and the rise of the League, acts as some kind of bridge between Eastern and Western Europe in the transition to the post-cold war era.

It is now clear that the cold war had a restraining effect on the development of Western political systems. It didn't place them in the deep freeze, as in the East, but left them in the chill cabinet. During the cold war, society accepted disciplines and constraints that under normal circumstances it would have found unacceptable. Leaders enjoyed a prestige that only war can bestow. And the division between left and right remained the dominant polarity of Western politics, since it too reflected cold war reality. In Italy this arrestation of political development meant that while civil society was transformed, exploding in a plethora of media, style and culture, the political world was maintained in aspic. Indeed, because the political parties were so powerful, enjoying a stifling influence over civil society, this contradiction proved particularly acute; and its resolution particularly seismic. But Italy here only presents in extreme form what is a general Western problem that lies at the heart of our political crisis: politics is not as advanced as popular culture; it has not yet been fully transformed by the media revolution; it neither grasps the power of style nor harnesses the momentum of a dynamic and postideological civil society. It is ripe for meltdown. And Italy has led the way.

Political Revenge in Italy

Breakthrough elections anticipate lasting but daunting reform

Paul Cook

Paul Cook is a Ph.D. candidate in European studies as the Johns Hopkins School of Advanced International Studies. In 1993–1994 he was a Fulbright scholar living in Rome.

On Dec. 5, Italians voting in a second round of local elections advanced a revolution that is permanently changing the face of Italy's politics. In a cathartic process, a recession-plagued citizenry's resentment of the political class has turned into anger after revelations of shameless corruption on the part of the old political elite. Given a chance to throw the bums out, Italians are doing so with gusto.

For the first time, voters cast ballots directly for mayors in Naples, Palermo, Rome, Trieste, Genoa, and hundreds of smaller communities. Their votes have confirmed the imminent passing of the old political order. The national parliamentary elections to be held early next year are likely to end the dominance of the Christian Democratic Party and many of the centrist forces with which it shared the spoils of uninterrupted postwar rule. In its place, an unprecedented "bipartisan" system shaped in part by a new, two-ballot electoral process appears to be emerging in which voters can choose between clear alternatives.

New forces or parties long excluded from government dominated these elections. In only one, Palermo's, did a candidate win an outright majority and thus avert a runoff election. Leoluco Orlando, with his anti-Mafia La Rete party, capitalized on Sicilian fatigue with the old parties that had extended protection to the Cosa Nostra, pilfered public money, and neglected the city's social infrastructure.

Elsewhere, first-round elections held last month eliminated the once-dominant forces of government from contention. In the northern cities of Trieste, Venice, and Genoa, the second round elections pitted a coalition of leftist forces centered around the Democratic party of the Left (PDS), a social democratic party that has grown out of the old Italian Communist Party, against the neo-right wing Northern League. (The League advocates the division of Italy into separate nations. But its leader, Umberto Bossi, has recently called for the creation of three republics within a federated Italy, characterized by a reduced bureaucracy.) In all these cities, however, leftist coalitions won in the second round, electing mayors and city council majorities.

> *As much as the elections mark the passing of the old regime, they also suggest that the new political climate is polarized.*

Left-wing forces in Rome and Naples also were victorious. In these cities, their runoff opponent was the Italian Social Movement (MSI), an old nationalist-fascist party that has historically been strong in the south. The MSI benefited from many who were convinced that the PDS is a communist front; yet such logic failed to convince the majority. In Rome, Francesco Rutelli, an environmentalist with PDS backing, won 53.1 percent of the vote against MSI's party secretary Gianfranco Fini. In Naples, dyed-in-the-wool fascists had the opportunity to mark an "X" next to the name Mussolini (Alesandra); nonetheless, the left candidate, Antonio Bassolino, won with 55.8 percent of the vote.

As much as the elections mark the passing of the old regime, they also suggest that the new political climate is polarized. The fundamental political choice once lay between a bland center that offered an ever more corrupt stability and a Communist Party that only gradually retreated from its Stalinist past. Invariably that bland center prevailed. But its implosion, precipitated by mismanagement and corruption, as well as by the Soviet Union's collapse and the creation of a viable social-democratic alternative, has transformed the political map.

The great hope for the next system is that future governments will enjoy public mandates on clearly defined platforms. The great concern is that both the League and the MSI harbor revolutionary ambitions and are not viable options for most voters. Some analysts say that Italy now needs a modern, moderate conservative force, and many are looking to Mario Segni, a former Christian Democrat untainted by scandal, to build it.

The results of the Dec. 5 runoff elections are significant in other ways. That neither the regionalist League nor the hyper-nationalist MSI won in any large city in this latest round has forestalled a struggle pitting a wealthy separatist north against an impoverished nationalist south. The victorious left-wing forces are intent on ameliorating the conditions that have nurtured the separatist movements rather than cede to the facile temptation of national division. Yet even for the left, decentralization remains an important priority, although as a way to save, not break apart the country.

Economic revival and bureaucratic reform remain the greatest challenges for Italy's next government. Paring away the bureaucracy and privatizing state-owned firms calls for great sacrifice and contradicts the left's dogged defense of the powerful union movement. Acting quickly on this front might foment paralyzing strikes and civil disorder.

The public mandate on this central point is also ambiguous. Many voters are comforted by the notion of the state as an employer of last resort but dissatisfied with its inefficiency. If the left prevails in national elections early next year, its leaders are likely to argue that bureaucratic reform can proceed without layoffs; their first strategy will be to infuse the state with an ethic of public service. But this tactic is only a stopgap.

The bureaucracy is populated by clients of the old regime, and its structure is chaotic and antiquated; it will take more than prodding to infuse its ranks with an enlightened culture of public service. Yet the old patrons are rapidly vanishing, and the national fiscal crisis is narrowing the options for any government. Italy's partners in Europe are demanding that the government slash subsidies to publicly owned firms and reduce the debt, which now exceeds GNP. Bureaucratic practices and structures are thus bound to change, although not with the speed many optimists expect.

There is a final irony in these election results. For years American policymakers championed the Christian Democratic Party, which presidents from Truman to Bush viewed as an anticommunist bulwark. The Clinton administration may soon be dealing with the social-democratic PDS. That the two countries would maintain cordial relations in that event would provide further proof of the degree to which US perspectives on Europe have evolved in the post–cold war, and how far the former Communists have come in embracing both the form and substance of democracy.

Italy's 1994 Elections

Editor's Note: Toward the end of March 1994, Italy held its most important parliamentary elections in over four and a half decades. As a result, some observers spoke of the beginning of a Second Republic. The strategies and results of the pivotal contest were influenced by four major factors: (1) the manifest voter disgust with the corruption of the traditional governing parties; (2) the revamping of some of the old parties and the appearance of new populist protest movements; (3) the existence of gaps in the campaign broadcasting laws that gave special advantages to a media magnate turned politician; and (4) the use of new election rules that encouraged the formation of large electoral alliances. Three-quarters of the deputies were now elected by a plurality system of winner-takes-all, the rest by the old system of proportional representation.

The election served as an opportunity to get rid of participants in the national version of kleptocracy or *tangentopoli*. It resulted in a left-right polarization that crushed the old system of hegemony by the Christian Democrats and their smaller centrist allies. On the left, an alliance led by the increasingly social democratic PDS won 213 of the 630 seats in the lower house. This compared to 46 for the main centrist group, which included the Popular Party of former Christian Democrats. But the Freedom Alliance of the right triumphed by winning an absolute majority of 366 seats in the lower house as well as a near-majority in the less important upper house. It consisted of an incoherent and fractious combination of three main groups. The strongest was the three-month old populist *Forza Italia* (Go Italy) movement, created by media tycoon Silvio Berlusconi, who had been able to use a relentless television blitz to portray himself as Italy's savior from corruption, stagnation, and statism. The others were the neo-fascist and centralist National Alliance (formerly MSI), led by Gianfranco Fini, and the federalist or anti-centralist Northern League, led by Umberto Bossi. Berlusconi's expected coalition government of the right appeared headed for a rocky start.

Old sake in new bottles

Japan's election was only the first step in a process that will take years to change the nation

A welcome quiet descended on the streets of Japan last week as politicians abandoned the huge sound trucks that for 20 days had bombarded cities and villages with 90-decibel campaign messages. Instead, it was the politicians' turn to listen to the cryptic messages from their constituents, who on July 18 denied the conservative Liberal Democratic Party a parliamentary majority for the first time in 38 years.

"We have achieved our first goal," declared a triumphant Morihiro Hosokawa, an LDP rebel who heads the reformist Japan New Party, as the results came in. "We have put an end to the one-party rule of the LDP!"

But the election was not the rout many had predicted. While the LDP came away with only 223 seats in the House of Representatives, 33 short of a majority in the lower house of the Diet, Japan's parliament, it maintained its parliamentary strength at roughly preelection levels and won more than three times as many seats as its closest rival, the Socialist party. At LDP headquarters in Nagatacho in central Tokyo, party leaders spun the results beyond recognition. "Generally speaking, things are going well," said LDP Secretary General Seiroku Kajiyama, the man who had slammed the door on political reform and caused a split in the party a month earlier.

Beginning of the end? Yet as Japan's political turmoil moved off the streets and into the back rooms, where politicians began cutting deals to form a new government, it became clear that the election was merely the beginning of a process that will take years to reshape Japan's political landscape. The election broke the back of the party structure that had given Japan political stability since 1955, when the Liberal and Democratic parties were shoved into a merger under pressure from the influential and cash-rich Keidanren, the economic federation backed by big business. Japan's powerful House of Representatives now has nine minority parties jockeying for position, and only one thing is sure to emerge from the negotiations to form a new government: instability.

The results offer some superficial comfort to the LDP. Traditional voters did not abandon the party; it was the LDP's split that cut into its vote count. In fact, conservatives attracted more support than ever: Between them, the LDP and the splinter groups and parties led by LDP defectors won more than 60 percent of the popular vote and 64 percent of the seats in parliament.

Yet this is precisely why the election results are so dangerous for the LDP. For the first time, the party faces a credible conservative opposition led by skilled, experienced politicians. "I welcome the increase in strength of the conservative forces as a whole," said Keidanren Chairman Gaishi Hiraiwa, unconcerned by the prospect of an end to LDP rule.

Leading the reform charge is Ichiro Ozawa, chief strategist of the Japan Renewal Party (Shinseito). After losing an LDP factional struggle last December, Ozawa joined forces with former Finance Minister Tsutomu Hata to found the reform-minded Renewal party.

The patrician Morihiro Hosokawa is the head of the Japan New Party, another of the new reformist conservative groups. The 18th descendant of the feudal lord of Kumamoto, Hosokawa played one of his ancestors in a samurai movie. He is allied with Masayoshi Takemura, a kind, uncle-like figure with a distinctive common touch who for 11 years led a multiparty coalition as governor of Shiga prefecture.

While the LDP may be proud of mounting a well-fought campaign under difficult circumstances, the trends underlying the outcome—often obscured by Japan's convoluted multimember district system—portend deeper troubles ahead. To start with, reform-minded conservatives who split from the LDP were the overwhelming favorites with voters. Kazuo Aichi, a Japan Renewal Party candidate from Sendai city, received the largest number of votes ever given a single candidate in his district, even though voter turnout fell to a historic low. Of the 103 winning candidates from the three new reform parties, 48 took first place in their districts, nearly half the contests the three new parties entered.

The new parties did well even though the election was called on short notice, giving them little time to organize campaigns and leaving the LDP unchallenged in 31 of 129 electoral districts. The new conservative parties were aided by the self-destruction of the Socialist Party, which lost 64 Diet seats, but so was the LDP. Next time—perhaps later this year—the LDP will face a better-organized conservative opposition with more money and more candidates.

Loosening the old guard's grip

Support dropped for the Liberal Democratic Party in the July election, but overall backing increased for the conservative end of Japan's political spectrum

USN&WR—Basic data: Central Election Management Council (Japan)

Conservative parties

House membership	1990	1993
✓ Liberal Democratic Party	46.1%	36.6%
✓ Shinseito		10.1
✓ Japan New Party		8.0
✓ Sakigake (Harbinger)		2.6

Traditional opposition

House membership	1990	1993
✓ Socialist Party	24.4%	15.4%
✓ Komeito	8.0	8.1
✓ Communist	8.0	7.7
✓ Democratic Socialist Party	4.8	3.5
✓ United Social Democratic	0.9	0.7

Japan's two traditional parties are getting a smaller share of the vote

USN&WR—Basic data: Central Election Management Council (Japan)

Japan's House of Representatives 1993:
- Liberal Democratic Party 36.6%
- Other conservative parties 20.7%
- Other/independent 7.1%
- Other opposition parties 20.0%
- Socialist Party 15.4%

Japan's House of Representatives 1990:
- Liberal Democratic Party 46.1%
- Socialist Party 24.4%
- Other opposition parties 21.7%
- Other/independent 7.8%

DAVID S. MERRILL—USN&WR

More bad news. The LDP also failed to broaden its traditional base of support, mainly aging farmers whose votes are worth as much as three times more than urban votes in Japan's complex electoral system. Well-oiled LDP organizations in the countryside got out the vote as usual. In the nine mainly rural prefectures where voter turnout was highest, the LDP won 50 percent of the seats. But in the nine prefectures and cities where turnout was lowest, including Tokyo and Osaka, the LDP won only a third of the seats. In Osaka, Japan's second-largest city, the LDP won a pitiful five seats out of 28. With the agenda for political reform topped by a redistricting effort aimed at equalizing rural and urban votes, the LDP may find its foundation under assault.

The LDP also must fight to survive while some of its elders fight corruption charges. Last week, one of the party's most influential power brokers, 78-year-old Shin Kanemaru, pleaded innocent to charges that he failed to pay millions of dollars in taxes. Prosecutors said he took more than $9 million a year in secret contributions, mostly from construction companies.

The election also marked an important generational change in the parliament. The average age of Japan's representatives fell from 56.5 after the 1990 election to 53.9. But this understates the extent of the shift. The number of members born after World War II more than doubled, to 146. The average age of the parliamentarians in the three new conservative parties is 49, compared with 57 for the LDP. The JNP averages a politically adolescent 42, and Socialist and Communist legislators average nearly 60.

Compared with the LDP's party elders, the younger generation has been more outspoken, nationalistic and self-assertive, unencumbered by the humiliation of losing the war and the restrictions on Japan's sovereignty that followed. Younger politicians are likely to champion the interests of the urban consumers they represent against those of Tokyo's entrenched bureaucrats. And young LDP members are as impatient for change as the new opposition: Last week, in an angry public confrontation, the party's rank and file rejected a plan to let an ad hoc committee of party elders select a new leader to replace Prime Minister Kiichi Miyazawa.

The LDP party elders last week appeared to be caught in a time warp. First, Miyazawa, 73, made a desperate attempt to cling to power, even though his public-approval rating had fallen to nearly 5 percent, while the LDP split apart beneath him. Then, when Miyazawa finally resigned under pressure on July 22, the first person to throw his hat into the ring to replace him was Michio Watanabe, a 69-year-old factional leader who resigned as foreign minister earlier this year because of poor health. Next was Hiroshi Mitsuzuka, 66, who now heads the party's biggest faction.

By traditional calculation, both Watanabe and Mitsuzuka are due for the job, but both are deeply opposed to political reform and are apparently oblivious to the fact that the LDP has lost its majority. "There is a structure of power in the LDP that is out of sync with the public mood," says Prof. Gerald Curtis of Columbia University. "They just don't get it."

While LDP leaders embark on an unseemly factional squabble for control of a declining but still powerful party, seven opposition groups are edging toward a coalition with enough votes to force the LDP out of power. The final outcome is impossible to call. The best prediction: The sound trucks will be rolling again within a year, with voters casting ballots under reformed election rules.

STEVEN BUTLER IN TOKYO

A Prince of Politics Ascends

Japan's new prime minister was born an aristocrat but with a reformer's zealous heart. Some call him regal, others overbearing. Morihiro Hosokawa says he just wants to get things done.

Teresa Watanabe

Times Staff Writer

TOKYO—On the morning in 1945 that he was to face interrogation by the allies as a Class-A war criminal who failed to stop Japan from igniting a disastrous Pacific war, former Prime Minister Fumimaro Konoe put on a kimono and swallowed a dose of potassium cyanide to quietly kill himself.

Almost half a century later, in a strange quirk of history and fate, his grandson, Morihiro Hosokawa, stands at the very same helm to guide Japan through another turning point.

As he prepares to head the nation's first postwar government to break four decades of domination by the Liberal Democratic Party, it is the ghost of his grandfather's failure that drives the man who was elected Friday as prime minister of Japan.

Hosokawa—whose eclectic, almost eccentric aristocratic personality both charms and alienates those who know him—aims to be bold where his grandfather was weak, to shape history rather than be overwhelmed by it. Most of all, Hosokawa is determined to lead the march for reform in Japan, to stand up to established power cliques and appeal to the nation's conscience.

"The deepest thing I learned from my grandfather's tragic experience is that in times when you should speak out, you have to clearly speak out," he declared last year, shortly after establishing the reformist Japan New Party. "Now I am raising my voice. I can hear that voice of fate."

Fate has propelled him into one of the fastest rises in the history of Japanese politics: from a junior congressman to governor of a southern prefecture to the head of a fledgling minor party to prime minister in slightly more than two decades.

As Japan faces an uncharted future after the Cold War's collapse, Hosokawa is speaking out—against his country's political corruption, closed markets, powerful vested interests, high prices, shabby living standards and a tyrannical bureaucracy that has turned politicians into "sheep" and the populace into "cowards."

With his strong vision for reform, abundant confidence and proven ability to get things done, Hosokawa, 55, has the potential to become one of the most dynamic prime ministers Japan has ever known.

The question is whether he has the political skills to navigate the minefields awaiting him and the leadership to forge a workable coalition among eight parties rife with competing egos, ambitions and some sharp policy differences.

The parliamentary wrangling with the LDP, which delayed his election by one day, was just the first indication of what Hosokawa has acknowledged will be the "rough seas" he will encounter as he battles what is still Japan's largest single party.

Even within his own coalition, things won't be easy for him. Hosokawa must broker differences over issues ranging from rice imports to national security. He must take care not to appear to be the puppet of Ichiro Ozawa of the Japan Renewal Party, the politician whom many consider the real behind-the-scenes power.

His former ties to Kakuei Tanaka, the onetime LDP kingmaker who invented money politics, and to the scandal-tainted Sagawa Kyubin Co., have also raised questions about how clean this reformer really is. Sagawa rented one of Hosokawa's homes and gave him a loan and $238,000 in political contributions. (All was legally reported and Hosokawa says he has not taken money from them since 1991.)

If that weren't enough, his critics say Hosokawa is mealy-mouthed and constantly changes his mind. He also sometimes offends with a regal bearing befitting the eldest son born to the 18th generation of one of Japan's oldest and wealthiest lineages of feudal lords.

To this political prince, "everyone else has to be retainers," said Tetsuhisa Matsuzaki, a former Japan New Party official who was fired from his post in June. "People who stand for democracy, freedom of speech and fair competition are eliminated from his inner circle."

But Hosokawa's admirers see his changes of mind as open-mindedness and his reticence as political smarts. "He knows what's important, but until he is ready to say yes or no, he'll stay fuzzy. That is the way to survive in this country," said Yoshimi Ishikawa, a writer and adviser to the New Party Harbinger, which is closely allied with Hosokawa's Japan New Party.

Hosokawa is often compared to President Clinton by those who see a governor turned top national leader who listens well, has an enormous intellectual curiosity and soaks up everything from Chinese classical literature to robotics and biotechnology.

But like former President George Bush, Hosokawa also is a wizard with the telephone and boasts a far-flung network of powerful friends. And like Ross Perot,

From *Los Angeles Times*, August 9, 1993, pp. A1, A6, A8. © 1993 by The Los Angeles Times. Reprinted by permission.

his family's fabulous wealth gives him the independence to reject traditional machine politics and chart his own iconoclastic course.

Born in Tokyo to an aristocratic family that dates back to 1534, Hosokawa has a lineage that includes feudal lords, prime ministers and even one relative from the imperial family. His family's wealth was so substantial that his grandfather's private art collection could create a museum "similar to the Louvre," Hosokawa once said. He never carried money because everything he bought was paid for by the butler.

Growing up, he was surrounded by scholars, Buddhist masters, geisha, politicians, artists and other elites who came to visit his paternal grandfather, Moritatsu Hosokawa, a former politician with the upper house of Parliament. From him, Hosokawa learned to look for lessons in every encounter.

Lesson One: "The best way to study is to meet with top-class people in each field," Hosokawa wrote in a recent book. As a result, he surrounds himself with excellence, and his brain trust includes such corporate pioneers as Kyocera Corp.'s Kazuo Inamori, who single-handedly created the market for high-tech ceramics, and Daiei Corp.'s Isao Nakauchi, who shook up Japan's distribution system with discount retailing.

Lesson Two: "It's never too late to learn." Hosokawa was exposed early to a broad intellectual background and rigorous academic training. His father forced him to memorize the teachings of Confucius and the "Manyoshu," a collection of ancient Japanese poems. During the wartime electricity shortage, his father made him study by candlelight. Hosokawa hated the studies then, but they helped spark a lifelong thirst for knowledge.

He took up Chinese classical literature in his 30s; skiing and tennis in his 40s, and piano in his 50s. An intense student, he made a paper piano keyboard and practiced every morning in the car as he was driven to the governor's office.

That intellectual hunger helps him eagerly absorb new ideas.

When Mariko Mitsui, a feminist political activist, told him about Norway's system of affirmative action for women politicians, he immediately incorporated the idea into the Japan New Party's policies. He also sponsored a "politics school" to nurture women candidates and began aggressively recruiting women—

Profile: Morihiro Hosokawa

Background on the new prime minister of Japan:

■ **Age:** 55
■ **Birthplace:** Tokyo
■ **Education:** Rigorous at-home schooling in Japanese classics, culture; exposure to a range of intellectual, religious and artistic lights; Sophia University law school, 1963.
■ **Career:** Reporter of Asahi newspaper; began political career in 1971 with election to upper house of Parliament at age 33, becoming youngest member ever; elected governor of Kumamoto prefecture (state) in 1983; defected last year from ruling Liberal Democratic Party to form Japan New Party, a key player in toppling 38 years of LDP control; elected Friday as 79th prime minister.
■ **Personal:** Member of one of Japan's elite families, which traces its roots to feudal aristocracy; married in 1971 and has two daughters and a son; a quick learner with diverse interests, including music, classical literature, skiing, tennis and even a brief stint as a movie actor.

even calling his old newspaper, the Asahi, and asking editors to recommend bright women reporters who might be suitable candidates.

His eagerness for new experiences even led him to the big screen, where he appeared in two samurai movies.

Lesson Three: "To govern the country, you need a strong will not affected by emotion." One of Hosokawa's boyhood mentors was a Zen priest and college teacher who lived on one of the family estates in Kamakura, where the prime minister attended school. The master would fill the boy's head with vivid tales of Japanese history.

Hosokawa was particularly affected by the story of a famous warrior named Yorimoto Minamoto, who was said to have killed his brother, Yoshitsune, in a fit of jealousy and learned not to rule with passion.

The lessons show. Hosokawa is elegant, polite but eminently controlled.

When Kakuei Tanaka, his one-time political mentor, was arrested in the 1976 Lockheed bribery scandal, Hosokawa quickly cut ties with that faction, even though most other members remained loyal. To reformists, the action showed Hosokawa's sense of ethics and clearheaded judgment. But to others in Japan, where human relationships based on obligation and sympathy are key, Hosokawa can come across as a cold fish.

Lesson Four: "The only important thing in life is how you live." Hosokawa picked this up from another influential story learned from his Zen mentor about the final battle of Nobunaga Oda, a famous 16th-Century warlord. Before battle, he told his followers that life lasted only 50 years, a trifling moment in the course of the universe, so don't regret the past or worry about the future.

"He doesn't desire authority, money or fame," his wife, Kayoko, 50, has said. "He can throw out everything for whatever is necessary at the moment. For him, the here and now is very important."

Indeed, Hosokawa surprised the political world by giving up his parliamentary seat after two terms and his governorship after two terms, in stark contrast to typical politicians who hang on to power as long as they can. He has written that power corrupts after 10 years, and he discarded his jobs when he found new and better ways to achieve his goals of reform.

In 1963, Hosokawa was graduated in law from Sophia University. He set his sights on a political career from the start. To learn more about common people, however, he decided to work as a reporter for the Asahi newspaper despite his father's vehement objections.

He got a taste of low life when he was urinated on while covering a crime story. After his apartment was burglarized, he briefly moved into the Asahi newsroom, where he slept on a Ping-Pong table—in the nude—earning him the nickname "the Barbarian."

But he can't always escape his illustrious lineage. According to an account in the Shukan Asahi magazine, Hosokawa was once sent to cover an arson case while based in his newspaper's Kagoshima branch on Kyushu island. The police officer in charge happened to be a descendant of a family that had long served as the Hosokawa family's bird feeders. The officer, on seeing Hoso-kawa, blurted out: "I can't report a dirty story like crime to the young lord."

When Hosokawa persisted, the officer said: "Then it is my duty to give you a scoop."

In 1971, he married Kayoko Ueda, a fellow Sophia graduate who special-ized in surfing and English literature. She turned down his first proposal, in-stead moving to London to work for a trading company. But when they met by chance on a street in Rome, she felt the hand of fate and consented. They have two daughters and a son.

She is an activist in her own right, having served with the LDP's Kumamoto office and as vice chairwoman of the United Nations Children's Fund.

During the recent lower house elec-tion, her husband returned to Kumamoto only once so she recruited two relatives, signed up 500 volunteers and ran her husband's Japan New Party campaign herself. She says she supports the Japan New Party not because of her husband but because the party's policies agree with her own views.

Despite their mutual passion for poli-tics, there have been repeated rumors of marital strains over Hosokawa's alleged roving eye. The Shukan Shincho maga-zine recently reported that his wife be-came neurotic and returned to her parents' house because of Hosokawa's alleged affairs with party members, secre-taries, even his child's college-age tutor. He has denied all rumors, and she also denied leaving him over the rumored affairs.

In 1971, Hosokawa launched his politi-cal career as an upper house congress-man with the Liberal Democratic Party. From the start, he declared war on the bureaucracy, vowing to blast open the sys-tem with "dynamite." After 12 years, he quit and ran for governor of Kumamoto in 1983, where he won overwhelmingly.

As governor, Hosokawa distinguished himself as a relentless prefectural sales-man who helped bring several high-tech firms to what was a largely rural region. He also instituted some of the strictest water pollution standards in Japan and overturned the prefecture's longstanding opposition to lawsuits by Miyamata mer-cury poisoning victims, siding with them against the central government.

According to Japanese news accounts, Hosokawa attacked red tape, simplified documents and tried to drum efficiency into his bureaucrats by dispatching them to work stints at private companies. He got a group of executives to find ways to cut the budget 7% when his own bureau-crats said it could not be done.

Despite his energy, Hosokawa found many of his initiatives sty-mied by the oppressive central government.

As a result, Hosokawa decided the best way to fight the system was to return to the national political scene.

The Japanese public still seems to have plenty of questions about him. A local magazine gave him only a "C" grade for clean politics. And most people still don't seem clear on where he stands. A recent poll showed that 70% of those surveyed had qualms about him.

But Ishikawa, the writer, predicted that Hosokawa will make his mark on Japa-nese history—and remove the lingering legacy of his grandfather's ineffective-ness at a time of urgent national need. "He will speak up in a big way and try to make some drastic changes," Ishikawa said. "This is his fate from his family tree and blood history."

**Megumi Shimizu and Chiaki Kitada
of The Times' Tokyo bureau
contributed to this report.**

Editor's Note: On April 8, 1994, Morihiro Ho-sokawa resigned as Japan's prime minister. Mr. Hosokawa was elected with a voter man-date for change and a pent-up demand for new direction from the nearly four decades of political rule by the Liberal Democratic Party, which is considered protective of the bureau-cracy and big business in Japan. His resigna-tion came in response to the growing pressure over the scandal of his involvement in various previous financial dealings, which tainted his image of being an honest, reform-minded politician. What impact this will have on Japa-nese politics and Japan's role in the world is speculative. •

"[M]erely changing the rules of the game will not create a Japanese government capable of moving forward in domestic and foreign policy. The structural changes at home mean a leaner economy and government austerity. The changes in the world at large force Japanese leaders to embrace their proclaimed activism. . . . The problem for politics and diplomacy is that the end of one-party dominance in 1993 has yet to reveal a new political order that provides leadership, reform, and international impact."

Japan: The End of One-Party Dominance

STEPHEN J. ANDERSON

STEPHEN J. ANDERSON *has been a research fellow in Tokyo at the Asian Forum. He is teaching at the University of Virginia and is the author of* Welfare Policy and Politics in Japan: Beyond the Developmental State *(New York: Paragon House, 1993), as well as articles on the public policy, politics, and international relations of Japan.*

This summer the Liberal Democratic party lost control of Japan's government. Between a June 18 no-confidence vote and the August 9 inauguration of a coalition cabinet, the party and the Diet were in upheaval. Scandal, internal splits, electoral stalemate, and an opposition coalition were the immediate causes of the ruling party's fall after 38 years in power.

Observers had not predicted rapid change in the LDP or the individuals who had governed since 1955. Analysts had pointed to structural weaknesses in the Japanese party system, while the media focused on the personalities of the leaders. The outcome took everyone by surprise. As the old leaders lost control, a new coalition unexpectedly began to pursue reforms.

THE OLD GUARD

From October 1991 until summer 1993, Kiichi Miyazawa led the government as prime minister and head of the Liberal Democratic party. Elected party president as a compromise candidate by the LDP factions that together held a majority of the seats in the Diet, Miyazawa, like many other recent leaders of the party who had ascended to the prime ministership, owed his position to and relied on funds from party vice president Shin Kanemaru.

Until overwhelmed by scandals in 1992, Kanemaru managed the party's largest faction, which had previously been headed by Kakuei Tanaka and was until this year led by Noboru Takeshita, both former prime ministers. The faction especially depended on Kanemaru to raise money—including, among other methods, stock deals revealed during the infamous Recruit scandal of the late 1980s. Kanemaru met his downfall because of a second scandal that began with the discovery of payments by a Sagawa package express company to more than 60 politicians. Though scandals come and go in Japan, all the established political parties were caught in the web of the Recruit and the Sagawa scandals. In mid-1992 Kanemaru turned up at the center of the web, under suspicion of accepting 500 million yen ($4.2 million) in illegal campaign funds.

The LDP power broker was forced to resign from the Diet. He was joined in disgrace by former faction leader Takeshita, and both were asked to resign from the party because of scrutiny of past contacts with right-wing groups. With these resignations, it appeared that the scandal might be managed. This January Kanemaru admitted his guilt; he was fined less than $2,000 by the public prosecutor's office.

The settlement, however, created an uproar throughout Japan. It was condemned in the media and in 130 resolutions by local assemblies; a man outraged by it was arrested after throwing paint on the prosecutors' offices. In a reversal, Kanemaru's offices and residence were then raided by the prosecutors, who seized gold ingots, art works, and stock certificates. By March Kanemaru himself had been arrested, held in a small jail cell, and shown on television in a wheelchair after being hospitalized for diabetes. The ruling party had survived huge scandals in the past and the system had continued basically unaltered, but the negative publicity from this one, kept alive by new revelations throughout 1993, played a large part in the major political changes that were to follow.

REFORM AT LAST?

Political reform dominated public debate in the media and the Diet, but different groups gave different definitions of it. Japanese citizens wanted to end the back room deals of campaign financing and the "money politics" represented by Kanemaru and Tanaka and Takeshita before him, but extending to all the major political parties. Related reforms included changes in campaign laws, controls on individual candidate groups known as *koenkai*, and more complete disclosure of political contributions. Yet these objectives became secondary to revising the electoral rules for the House of Representatives, the Diet's powerful lower house. Reform, for the politicians, was limited to the rules of election, rather than involving anything that would disturb the delicate area of political contributions. Political reform thus came to focus on revising the electoral laws.

Under the 1947 constitution, the House of Representatives is invested with the ultimate powers of deciding on legislation, passing the budget, and electing the prime minister. Yet the body's election districts predate the constitution, relying on boundaries largely set in 1925. Districts have multiple members, meaning that between two and six Diet members are elected for each district. Imbalance between districts' population and number of Diet members gives greater weight to voters from nonsuburban districts—more than six to one in some cases. The imbalances have brought only piecemeal changes by court order, and the electoral system is now seen as unfair, irrational, and antiquated.

Doing away with the multimember districts is a key electoral reform problem. An alternative is medium or small districts with single members; this would strike at the way *koenkai* individual support groups have organized small segments of a district to ensure victory for their candidate. In addition, a separate system of proportional representation would imitate that used by the upper house, the House of Councillors, and provide for nationwide candidate lists set by each party. Under proportional representation, votes for a given party are counted, and candidates are awarded seats on the basis of a ranked party list. This system would yield the broad representation seen in the House of Councillors and would protect the smaller parties threatened by changes in House of Representatives districts. By late 1993, the favored proposal for reform was to elect 250 representatives by district and 250 by a nationwide vote using proportional representation.

ARCHITECTS OF A REVOLT

Among leading politicians, Ichiro Ozawa seized on the issue of reform. Ironically, Ozawa was the Liberal Democrats' heir apparent to the indicted Kanemaru; although he had formerly served as secretary general of the ruling party, he had distanced himself from the charges of corruption and the surrounding turmoil. As

Kanemaru's career fell victim to corruption charges, Ozawa's political fortunes rose when he broke with his faction, ostensibly over the issue of reform but partly for reasons of internal rivalry. Ozawa joined with former party finance minister Tsutomu Hata in forming a rebel group they called Reform Forum 21, which called on the prime minister to push for passage of immediate reforms. Yet Ozawa, the ultimate Liberal Democratic insider, was linked by opponents to the crimes of Kanemaru.

Prime Minister Miyazawa faced tremendous pressure to pursue reform. The internal pressure from the Hata-Ozawa group was matched by broad public disapproval. By June, Miyazawa's cabinet had less than 10 percent support in public opinion polls. Politicians were blamed for scandals and the lack of progress on reform, particularly during popular Sunday morning and late night news shows. As on "Meet the Press" or "Nightline" in America, Japanese politicians were called on to respond to criticism, face their opponents, and answer probing questions from journalists before the television cameras.

After a taped interview, Miyazawa was charged with being a "liar" when it came to his commitment to political reform. The prime minister had promised reform during the June Diet session in a television interview with journalist Soichiro Tahara. This pledge was to prove fatal. Clips from the interview were replayed repeatedly on television as evidence of Miyazawa's lying about reform and his inability to lead the government.

The defection of Ozawa and Hata at the end of the Diet session was a major blow to the prime minister. Miyazawa lost an unprecedented no-confidence motion when the rebels of the group paraded in front of the LDP leadership to cast their votes with the opposition and against their party; the final count was 255 to 220 against the Miyazawa government. No longer able to command a majority, the prime minister decided on immediate elections after the dissolution of the Diet.

On June 18 Miyazawa faced the cameras in a late night press conference to explain his call for elections. No compromise was possible, with most of the Liberal Democratic politicians unwilling to have their multimember districts altered by the electoral reform sought by forces behind the leadership of the Hata-Ozawa splinter group.

Two days later Hata and Ozawa defected to form a new party, Shinseito. LDP leaders decided to call snap elections for July 18 with the hope that their resources and organization would prevail; their opponents, on the other hand, planned a reshaping of the political world.[1] Among Japanese journalists, the idea of the "great man" driving political history pointed to Ichiro Ozawa as the person to bring an end to long-term rule by one party. At the same time, structural changes in

---

[1] See "Time for a Change," *Far Eastern Economic Review,* May 6, 1993, for an interview with the magazine's Tokyo bureau chief that charts Ozawa's later strategy.

electoral competition and international relations that had set new parameters for Japanese politics had to be acknowledged.

ELECTION STALEMATE?

The 1993 election ended the arrangement known as the 1955 system, a term used to commemorate the merger that year of socialist and nonsocialist parties that had allowed the Liberal Democrats to first prevail in national elections. By itself, the 1993 balloting was not an utter defeat of the longtime ruling party; instead, the pre-election defection and the rise of several new parties because of popular movements and LDP defections drained away sufficient votes so that a majority was beyond the reach of any single party. The election signaled a structural change in Japanese politics: the long-term decline of a two-party system was being succeeded by a period in which multiple parties must join in coalitions to form governments. The July 18 results were actually ambiguous, and potentially pointed toward a stalemate.

The key result from the election was the defeat of the largest socialist party. The Nihon Shakaito had recently announced a change in the official English translation of its name from the "Japan Socialist party" (a direct translation, by which it had long been known) to the "Social Democratic Party of Japan." But this did little to help it among voters. Though it formed the largest opposition bloc in the Diet, the party could no longer be counted on to win or to champion an opposition point of view in a two-party system. In 1989 the party enjoyed a brief surge of support at the polls as the result of a tax protest by small businessmen and the middle class. The party leader at the time, Takako Doi, the first woman to head a major party in Japan, led the 1989 victory in elections for the House of Councillors. Doi later won a nonbinding vote for prime minister in the Diet's upper chamber. But the July defeat was bitter for her party: from 141 seats in the 511-seat lower chamber, the party fell to only 77.

The results were mixed for the Liberal Democrats. The *koenkai* groups were seen as successful in their support of most LDP candidates, and the party remained the largest bloc in the House of Representatives, winning 223 seats outright. By August the LDP had gained the support of independents and controlled 228 seats, one more than the number it held in June after the defection. Nonetheless, 228 is short of the 256 that constitute a majority. The party lost its majority because of defection rather than the election, but the loss of the majority was a harsh reality for the leadership.

Several parties other than the LDP came off as winners in the election. The candidates from the new parties capitalized on the protests against scandal and calls for reform, and the alternative parties also challenged the traditional parties. The newcomers ben-

efited mostly from the decline of mainstream socialism, with the Democratic Socialist and Communist parties retaining 15 seats each. Among the established groups, the Buddhist-related Komeito used its neighborhood organization to gain a 7-seat increase, to 52 seats. But it was the new parties that had responded to and fueled the demand for political reform that won most of the redistributed Diet seats.

The media gave extensive coverage to the Japan New Party. In the July 1992 House of Councillors election, the party's first, it won 4 of the 126 upper chamber seats at stake. The party's leader, Morihiro Hosokawa, a former LDP governor of Kumamoto prefecture on the southern island of Kyushu, worked for the next year building a new party organization and recruiting candidates, including former television personalities, local leaders, and journalists to attract the support of younger and unaffiliated voters; the party won 36 seats in the House of Representatives in the July election. Hosokawa was joined by another former governor, Masayoshi Takemura, who had formed his own party in the Diet, the Sakigake party. With independents joining their bloc, the Japan New Party/Sakigake quickly reached the level of Komeito, controlling 52 seats.

Hata and Ozawa's Shinseito party was also successful. By August, Shinseito had gained a formidable 60 seats in the new Diet. Ozawa, hampered by people's association of him with scandal, decided not to attend the party's first press conference. Still, as secretary general he managed to raise funds, give candidates endorsements, and seek compromise on the creation of a non-LDP coalition. Shinseito benefits from having the most experience in national government among the new parties, as well as from its well-established candidates. In the new coalition, however, former ties by its members with the LDP meant trouble for the Shinseito candidate for prime minister, Tsutomu Hata.

None of the new parties had close to the LDP's plurality of seats in the House of Representatives. Commentators speculated that the Liberal Democrats might be able to form a new government, gathering some defectors back into the fold or even recruiting the Japan New Party to join a coalition. Such speculation died down only after internal debates revealed the depth of divisions within the LDP.

After the election results were in, the Liberal Democrats reorganized to prepare their response. In a vocal party meeting that was televised, subdued and shocked party elders listened to the loud and prolonged protests of younger members. In the race for party president, faction leader and Foreign Minister Michio Watanabe lost out to a reformed rebel, Yohei Kono. Kono had left the LDP in 1976 to act as a leader of the New Liberal Club, a splinter group, but had returned to serve as the chief cabinet secretary for the last Miyazawa cabinet. Now he was being elected party president so that he might become the reformer of the party that fell from power. In balloting that in previous years would have been to choose the new prime minister, Kono was selected as the party's first opposition leader.

The results of the national election showed a lack of confidence in the LDP government. All the other parties except the Communists took the opportunity to create a coalition. The shape of this coalition, with groups ranging from the left-wing socialists to right-wing conservative defectors, meant that political compromise was vital. But aside from the goal of ending LDP rule, observers saw little common ground among the coalition partners. Few prophesied success.

CREATING A COALITION THAT WORKS

The new parties avoided stalemate by agreeing about their cause: ending the long rule of the Liberal Democrats. Between July 18 and August 8 negotiators in intense sessions built a coalition without the Liberal Democrats, eventually backing a newcomer to the national scene. In Japan, explanations for the coalition's formation and choice of leaders range from the working-out of intensely personal politics to the changes facing the Japanese government and the issue of foreign relations after the cold war.

Speculation after the election was that compromise on the prime ministership and cabinet posts would give the jobs to experienced LDP rebels, at least. The rebels Hata and Ozawa were committed to forming a coalition government, with Hata emerging as a front-runner for prime minister. In the middle, between the LDP and the rebels, the newcomer, Morihiro Hosokawa of the Japan New Party—who had remained uncommitted throughout the campaign and after the election, fueling speculation he might join with the LDP—held the deciding vote.

The early negotiations were misleading to observers. At first the LDP defectors led by Tsutomu Hata remained the credible alternative for forming a coalition government headed by non-LDP politicians. But Hata, and Ozawa working on his behalf, proved unacceptable to the left-wing socialists of the coalition. Hata fell victim to longtime opponents, particularly the other established politicians who opposed these former LDP members because of their proximity to scandal. As negotiations continued only a newcomer such as Hosokawa remained an acceptable leader for the broad coalition.

Hosokawa agreed to join a coalition government only if he were named the new prime minister. He promised ministerial portfolios to Hata and his allies as well as to the socialists, including the post of speaker of the House for the Nihon Shakaito's former head, Takako Doi. Seven parties were awarded cabinet posts in the process of sealing the careful compromise. The broad coalition, including an additional party of 11 Diet members without portfolio in the upper house and two nonpoliticians in the cabinet, had created a government.

On August 8 new Prime Minister Hosokawa immediately staked his future on achieving electoral reform, implying, just as Miyazawa had before him, that he would resign if such reform did not pass. "I intend this cabinet not simply to lead the country for a brief interlude but rather to undertake the important mission of opening the way for a new era," Hosokawa proclaimed at his first news conference. In the first month of the new government, Hosokawa proved tremendously popular; public opinion polls showed him with a 70 percent approval rating. But by year's end the newcomer to national politics faced struggles over the electoral system and a budget bill that would test his political acumen.

The Japanese economy has been hurt by the worldwide recession. Analysts speak of a deflating "bubble economy" following from the high real estate and stock prices of the 1980s. Yet the finance ministry and cautious politicians have avoided further rapid expansion of the economy through public spending after three stimulus packages this year. But fiscal conservatism is not merely a matter of ideology, because Japan is also looking at rising entitlements. Japan has the most rapidly aging population of any advanced industrial society. While only 6 percent of the population was over the age of 65 in 1990, projections put the figure at 12 percent by the end of 1993 and show it doubling again in 30 years. By 2023, 24 percent of Japan's population will likely be over age 65, and of these, 15 percent will be over 75. The Hosokawa government pledged that it would stay the course for most LDP entitlements; it will probably not make major changes in other areas of public spending that might disturb the economy.

The problems of the new government were not wholly internal. Japan is sharing in the prolonged recession that in Europe and the United States has suppressed demand for Japanese exports. Japan faced adjustments for the appreciation of the yen, from 126 to the dollar in June 1992 to 105 or 106 to the dollar this October, that left businesses to cope with substantial instability for their international trade. Both these economic uncertainties and the political demands that Japan take on a larger international role meant that the coalition government had to move rapidly simply to keep up with world events.

THE QUEST FOR ACTIVIST DIPLOMACY

At the end of the cold war, Japan needs policies commensurate with its economic power and place in the world. Some of its leaders have called for an active foreign policy, yet Japanese diplomacy has remained cautious. In August the Foreign Ministry removed responsibility for security matters from the North American Affairs Bureau and placed it in a new general policy bureau designed to separate such matters from the American alliance.

Two years ago, Prime Minister Miyazawa was regarded as highly qualified to lead Japan in the international community. The senior statesman had served in a lengthy and broad-ranging list of leadership posts and spoke fluent English in which he would be able to articulate Japanese views. But anticipated successes were not achieved and his initiatives suffered a series of mishaps. In January 1992, Miyazawa was embarrassed when United States President George Bush became ill and fainted during a formal dinner in Tokyo. The pair had plans to announce a "global partnership," but instead the leaders of the world's two largest economies parted in confusion.

The muddle in relations with America did little to advance Japan's role in global politics. The Persian Gulf War early in 1991 had left Japan with lingering doubts about its position. UN allies had criticized Tokyo's contribution of money without personnel. By the time the 1992 elections for the Diet's upper house rolled around, debate focused on Japanese roles in peacekeeping efforts. The LDP eventually won a majority of 69 of the 126 contested seats, but the opposition ran strong and hard-hitting campaigns against the creation of a Japanese peacekeeping organization (PKO). (The 1947 constitution limits the Japanese Self-Defense Forces, which currently consist of 249,000 troops, to noncombat roles, and the opposition questioned the constitutionality of LDP-sponsored bills sending troops overseas.)

In the Diet the opposition protested the bill establishing the PKO through four all-night sessions, using a filibuster tactic known as the "cow-walk." Vocal opponents demonstrated and left-wing guerrilla groups set off explosions to protest the bill's passage in June 1992. Foreign critics, especially in China, South Korea, and Singapore, also cautioned against sending troops overseas.

Public opinion was divided on Japanese involvement in the UN peacekeeping effort in Cambodia. To deflect international criticism, the ruling party used the peacekeeping bill to create a new initiative under the UN umbrella and to encourage democratic elections in Cambodia. The peacekeeping troops of the newly constituted PKO force and civilian Japanese volunteers who went to Indochina did so at considerable risk. Japanese fears were to some extent realized with the deaths of several members of the national contingent: an election watcher was killed by a disgruntled worker, and then a policemen was killed and several were wounded by Khmer Rouge guerrillas. The dispatch overseas of members of the Japanese armed forces had raised fears of remilitarization both inside and outside

the country. Yet on balance, the effort has been rated a success because of the Cambodian election, the return of King Norodom Sihanouk, and the establishment of a new government.

In Cambodia, Japan showed leadership. In particular, Yasushi Akashi has served as the special representative leading the United Nations Transitional Authority in Cambodia. Akashi, a career diplomat who rose in the Japanese foreign ministry through his pursuit of challenging assignments, faced daunting tasks in the Cambodian peacekeeping effort, including the separation and disarming of warring groups including the Khmer Rouge.

PKO troops entered the limelight back home when sent to Cambodia. After Diet approval of the peacekeeping organization, troops had gone immediately to Sweden to train at UN facilities. Once in Cambodia, engineers built bridges, health care workers supported activities of the UN transitional authority in the country, and several thousand more PKO forces joined in policing and election monitoring. During New Year celebrations this year, Japan's national broadcasting company, reflecting popular interest, featured live, nonstop, dusk-to-dawn coverage from Angor Wat, Cambodia. In 1993 Japanese citizens became increasingly aware of and gave growing approval to the efforts to support stability in Southeast Asia.

THE US AND UN CONNNECTIONS

Relations between Japan and the United States are based on a mutual security treaty and economic ties that remain a pillar of world order. In July Miyazawa hosted a reassuring Group of Seven summit meeting attended by President Bill Clinton and leaders of the world's five other leading industrial nations. Miyazawa stressed the theme of global partnership in security, political cooperation, cultural ties, and scientific exchanges. Many Japanese preferred the Republican administrations of Reagan and Bush, yet they accepted the coming of a new Democratic government. The switch to the Democrats raised hopes among those Japanese who had long urged America to lower its budget deficit, improve infrastructure, and increase competitiveness. By the meeting's end, the Japanese and American chief executives had agreed on a bilateral trade framework that created some anticipation of improved economic ties.

During his visit to Tokyo, Clinton met with the future leadership. A United States embassy reception for political leaders overcame the ruling party's criticism and gave the president a chance to meet future deputy prime minister Hata Tsutomu and future prime minister Hosokawa. With their message of change for their countries, Clinton and Hosokawa had common ground on which to begin their relationship during a meeting at the UN in New York in September.

Since Miyazawa had weathered criticism of UN initiatives, Hosokawa committed himself to continue such policies. Officials hoped that foreign policy actions would allow for Japanese leadership based on economic competitiveness and overseas development assistance. Unofficial flows of capital and investment more than double the $10.95 billion in official aid from Japan in 1992 and the record-setting levels topping $11 billion for 1993. The September visit to the UN by Hosokawa and Foreign Minister Hata would affirm earlier Japanese commitments to that organization and the world.

Japan became more prominent in the UN. The UN High Commissioner for Refugees, Sadako Ogata, flew frequently to Cambodia, Iraq, and other crisis spots to survey international problems with the migration and mass movement of peoples. Indochina especially elicited support among the Japanese citizenry for moving toward more prominent UN roles. Japan gave $1.9 million in humanitarian aid to the former Yugoslavia and $15 million for famine relief to Somalia. Further, Japan considered future commitments to the Middle East, Bosnia, Africa, Latin America, and Russia, where Japanese interests are not directly at stake.

This past year Japanese diplomats remained firm about their territorial disputes with Russia. With the cold war over, Japanese and Russians sought to settle the question of the Soviet-occupied islands below the Kurile archipelago, which Japan argues had long been Japanese territories. After Soviet President Mikhail Gorbachev's 1991 visit to Tokyo, observers wondered about a direct swap of aid packages in return for two of the four disputed islands. In July 1992, Miyazawa secured the backing of the Group of Seven at a summit in Munich for his position demanding that Russia give back the islands, as Japan lawfully had sovereignty over them.

Russian President Boris Yeltsin, bowing to Sakhalin politicians and Russian parliamentarians who argued that further loss of territory would be a blow to national pride, abruptly canceled a long-planned visit to Japan in September 1992 but went to Tokyo later. Yeltsin was only grudgingly invited to the Group of Seven summit in Tokyo this July, and was coldly received in October after his violent crackdown on the renegade Russian parliament. Despite contributions pledged at the G7 meeting, Japanese aid to Russia will be limited by the territorial dispute, if not the doubts Japan's business community harbors about the long-term prospects for the Russian economy, considering the political situation. Russo-Japanese relations remain in stalemate.

Japan is poised to play a leading part in the Pacific Basin. Starting with careful diplomacy toward the Association of Southeast Asian Nations (ASEAN), Japan has supported the common positions of Asian countries. The movement toward regional organiza-

tions is a case in point. Since 1992 Japan has supported the government ministers meeting as the Asia-Pacific Economic Cooperation group, and the Pacific Economic Cooperation Conference, a forum for representatives from government, business, and academia; this year both groups established permanent secretariat offices in Singapore. Japanese backing for these seeks to increase economic cooperation in the region and initiate joint efforts to assure regional security; Japan is eager to move beyond bilateral relations with close neighbors and establish regional frameworks.

Japan supports the post-ministerial conferences of ASEAN to discuss security concerns. These talks after the meetings between ministers of the countries in the group are exploratory, and Japan remains committed to a security relationship with the United States. But the ASEAN meetings provide a new setting for regional actors to discuss differences over problems in Indochina and the Spratly Islands in the South China Sea, among other issues. In October Japan convened a meeting of ASEAN supported by the United States and Australia and attended by Hong Kong and South Korea on stopping the proliferation of weapons of mass destruction.

Toward China, Japan emphasizes favorable relations with its most populous neighbor. Japan was China's second-largest trading partner after Hong Kong, and China for the past several years has received more than $100 million annually in Japanese foreign aid. Japan also anticipates a generational shift in Chinese leadership. In October 1992 the Japanese emperor, Akihito, traveled to China in an effort to improve Sino-Japanese relations. Accompanied by officials working on long-standing disputes about wartime responsibility, the China visit was criticized by a vocal right wing in Japan after the emperor expressed regret for the "Pacific War."

This June, a wedding in the imperial family focused attention on its members' roles in Japan. The family heard quite a lot, mainly from right-wing groups, about the partner chosen by Crown Prince Naruhito, the future national symbol of state. For his bride, Masako Owada, a 29-year-old diplomat educated at Harvard and Oxford, the wedding celebration continued a bureaucratic struggle, as well as marking a great personal change; in a struggle over influence, Owada's father, the top bureaucrat in the Ministry of Foreign Affairs, where his daughter also worked, had clashed with the tradition-bound Imperial Household Agency, particularly over the funeral of Emperor Hirohito. The celebration also saw a career woman accept traditional roles in her commitment to the crown prince, and her generation saw it as an acceptance of traditional roles by a modern career woman. Owada, in an intensely personal and controversial article in the May 24 *Newsweek*,[2] was said to have overcome her reluctance to accept the prince's proposal after assurances from the Empress Michiko that a comfortable private life was possible for the imperial family.

FUTURE POLITICS

At year's end the Diet was poised to debate political reform and annual budget priorities. Japan remained in the most severe economic downturn it had experienced since the 1973 oil crisis. Hosokawa pressed forward with his goals for reform while holding together his broad coalition.

Under one possible scenario, the twin legislative battles over electoral reform and the annual budget bring on a crisis. If there is a deadlock and the schedule in December becomes tight, the coalition government may be forced to compromise on reform in order to pass the budget before the deadline. The result could be an early election and a new government for Japan.

A scenario in which electoral reform is deferred also holds the potential for conflict. If Hosokawa, along

---

[2]Bill Powell, "The Reluctant Princess," *Newsweek*, May 24, 1993, pp. 28–31. Conservatives in Japan criticized the article because it applied a probing and revealing style of journalism to the imperial family.

with the influential Ichiro Ozawa, who engineered the coalition and now helps manage it, decide to defer reform, the government might last well into 1994. But citizens and opposing politicians will quickly remind leaders of the pledge to pass reform and of decisions on other critical matters that cannot be deferred. Ozawa may provoke crisis himself in order to pursue a second election and his vision of a new two-party system led by Shinseito and the Liberal Democrats.

Structural change encourages electoral reform. In domestic politics, a reformed system that combines new, medium-sized districts and proportional representation might restore public confidence. Yet merely changing the rules of the game will not create a Japanese government capable of moving forward in domestic and foreign policy. The structural changes at home mean a leaner economy and government austerity. The changes in the world at large force Japanese leaders to embrace their proclaimed activism. Countries throughout Asia, if not in Latin America, Africa, and elsewhere, expect that Japan will fulfill pledges to overcome the past and fulfill the promises that its diplomats suggest. The problem for politics and diplomacy is that the end of one-party dominance in 1993 has yet to reveal a new political order that provides leadership, reform, and international impact.

Modern Pluralist Democracies: Factors in the Political Process

- Political Ideas, Movements, Parties (Articles 23 and 24)
- The Ethnic Factor in Western European Politics (Article 25)
- Women and Politics (Articles 26 and 27)
- The Institutional Framework of Representative Government (Articles 28–33)

Observers of Western industrial societies frequently refer to the emergence of a new politics in these countries. They are not always very clear or in agreement about what is supposedly novel within the political process or why it is significant. Although few would doubt that some major changes have taken place in these societies during the past couple of decades, affecting both political attitudes and behavior, it is very difficult to establish clear and comparable patterns of transformation or gauge their endurance and impact. Yet making sense of continuities and changes in political values and behavior must be one of the central tasks of a comparative study of government.

Since the early 1970s, political scientists have followed Ronald Inglehart and other careful observers who first noted a marked increase in what they called postmaterial values, especially among younger and more highly educated people outside the nonindustrial occupations in Western Europe. Such voters showed less concern for the traditional material values of economic well-being and security, and instead stressed participatory and environmental concerns in politics as a way of improving democracy and the general "quality of life." Studies of postmaterialism form a very important addition to our ongoing attempt to interpret and explain not only the so-called youth revolt but also some more lasting shifts in lifestyles and political priorities. It makes intuitive sense that such changes appear to be especially marked among those who grew up in the relative prosperity of Western Europe, after the austere period of reconstruction that followed World War II. In more recent years, however, there appears to have been a revival of material concerns among younger people. There are also some indications that political reform activities evoke less interest and commitment than earlier.

None of this should be mistaken for a return to the political patterns of the past. Instead, we may be witnessing the emergence of a still somewhat incongruent new mix of material and postmaterial orientations, along with old and new forms of political self-expression by the citizenry. Established political parties appear to be in somewhat of a quandary in redefining their positions, at a time when the traditional bonding of many voters to one or another party seems to have become weaker.

At this point, at least, it seems unlikely that Italy will set an example for many other democracies. Most established parties seem to have developed an ability to adjust to change, even as the balance of power within each party system shifts over time and occasional newcomers are admitted to the club. Each country's party system remains uniquely shaped by its political history, but there does seem to be some very general patterns of development. One frequently observed trend is toward a narrowing of the ideological distance between the moderate Left and Right in many European countries. It now often makes more sense to speak of the center-Left and center-Right respectively.

Despite such convergence, there are still some important ideological and practical differences between the two orientations. Thus the Right is usually far more ready to accept as inevitable the existence of social or economic inequalities. And it normally favors lower taxes and the promotion of market forces—with some very important exceptions, intended to protect certain favorite groups and values. The Left, by contrast, emphasizes that government has an important task in promoting opportunities, delivering services, and reducing social inequities. In some key domestic policy areas, such as that of higher and more progressive taxation or the relative concern for rates of unemployment and inflation, there will still be considerable differences between moderates of the Left and Right.

Even as the ideological distance between Left and Right narrows but remains important, there are also signs of some political differentiation within each camp. On the center-Right side of the party spectrum in European politics, economic neoliberals (who speak for business and industry) can be distinguished from the social conservatives (who advocate traditional values and authorities). European liberalism has its roots in a tradition that favors civil liberties and tolerance but that also values individual achievement and laissez-faire economics. For them, the state has an important but very limited role to play in providing an institutional framework within which individuals and social groups pursue their interests. Traditional conservatives, by contrast, emphasize the importance of social stability and continuity, and point to the social danger of disruptive change. They often value the strong state as an instrument of order, but many of them also show a paternalistic appreciation for welfare state programs that will keep the social net from tearing apart. In British politics, Margaret Thatcher promoted elements from each of these traditions in what could be called her own mix of business conservatism. The result is the peculiar tension between "drys" and "wets" within her own Conservative Party, even after she has ceased to be its leader. In France, on the other hand, the division between neoliberals and conservatives runs more clearly between the two major center-Right parties, the Giscardist UDF, and the neo-Gaullist RPR. In Germany, the Free Democrats would most clearly represent the traditional liberal position, while some conservative elements can be found among the Christian Democrats.

There is something of a split identity also among the Christian Democrats, who until recently were one of the most successful political movements in Europe after World War II. Here idealists, who subscribe to the socially compassionate teachings of the Church, have found themselves losing influence to more efficiency-oriented technocrats or success-oriented political managers. The latter seem to reflect little of the original ideals of personalism, solidarity, and subsidiarity that originally set the Christian Democrats off from both neoliberals and conservatives in postwar Europe.

On the Left, democratic socialists and ecologists stress that the sorry political, economic, and environmental record of communist-ruled states in no way diminishes the validity of their own commitment to social justice and environmental protection in modern industrial society. For them, capitalism will continue to produce its own social problems and dissatisfactions. No matter how efficient capitalism may be, they argue, it will continue to result in inequities that require politically directed reforms. Many on the Left, however, show a pragmatic acceptance of the modified market economy as an arena within which to promote their reformist goals. Social Democrats have long been known for taking such positions, but parties further to the left have also moved in that direction in recent years. Two striking examples of this shift can be found among the Greens in Germany and in what used to be the Communist Party of Italy.

Both center-Left and center-Right moderates face a dual challenge from populists on the right, who often seek lower taxes, drastic cuts in the social budget, and a curtailment of immigration, and neo-fascists on the ultra-right. The two orientations should be distinguished, as in Italy where the Northern League and the National Alliance represent positions that are polar opposites on such key issues as government decentralization (favored by the former, opposed by the latter). In part, the electoral revival of the right-wing parties can be linked to anxieties and tensions that affect some socially and economically insecure groups in the lower middle class and some sectors of the working class.

Women in politics is the concern of the third section in this unit. There continues to be a strong pattern of underrepresentation of women in positions of political and economic leadership practically everywhere. Yet there are some notable differences from country to country, as well as from party to party. Generally speaking, the parties of the Left have been more ready to place women in positions of authority, although there are some remarkable exceptions, as the center-Right cases of Margaret Thatcher in Britain and Simone Weil in France illustrate.

On the whole, the system of proportional representation gives parties both a tool and an added incentive to place female candidates in positions where they will be elected. But here too, there can be exceptions, as in the case of France in 1986 when women did not benefit from the one-time use of proportional representation in the parliamentary elections. Clearly it is not enough to have a relatively simple means, such as proportional representation, for promoting women in politics: There must also be a will among decision makers to use the available means for such a purpose.

This is where a policy of affirmative action may become chosen as a strategy. The Scandinavian countries illustrate better than any other example how the breakthrough may occur. There is a markedly higher representation of women in the parliaments of Denmark, Finland, Iceland, Norway, and Sweden, where the political center of gravity is somewhat to the Left and where proportional representation makes it possible to set up party lists that are more representative of the population as a whole.

In another widely reported sign of change, the relatively conservative Republic of Ireland has chosen Mary Robinson as its first female president. It is a largely ceremonial post, but it has a symbolic potential that Mary Robinson, an outspoken advocate of liberal reform in her country, is willing to use on behalf of social change. Perhaps most remarkable of all, the advancement of women into high political ranks has now touched Switzerland, where they did not get the right to vote until 1971.

Altogether, there is undoubtedly a growing awareness of the pattern of gender discrimination in most Western countries. It seems likely that there will be an improvement in this situation over the course of the next decade if the pressure for reform is maintained. Such changes have already occurred in other areas, where there used to be significant political differences between men and women. At one time, for example, there used to be a considerably lower voter turnout among women, but this gender gap has been practically eliminated in recent decades. Similarly the tendency for women to be somewhat more conservative in party and candidate preferences has given way to a more liberal disposition among younger women in foreign and social policy choices than among men.

In the fourth section of this unit, the authors compare a number of institutional arrangements: (1) essential characteristics and elements of a pluralist democracy, (2) some different forms of democratic constitutions, (3) two major systems of representative government, (4) different electoral systems, (5) the presidential and prime ministerial forms of executive, and (6) the recent revival of interest in a federal division of power.

The topic of pluralist democracy is a complex one, but Philipe C. Schmitter and Terry Lynn Karl manage to present a very comprehensive discussion of the subject in a short space. Robert Goldwin reminds us that most of the world's constitutions have been very short-lived. There has been a flurry of constitution-writing after the collapse of dictatorships in several parts of the world, and he suggests that the products may turn out to be more lasting if the drafters would consider carefully some basic questions. Above all, the constitution writers should remember to take into account the peculiarities of their own society. They can learn much that is useful from the experience of other countries, but they will find no valid universal formula for a good constitution. They would, in any case, court disaster if they ignored their own history by trying to begin with a completely clean slate.

Gregory Mahler focuses on the legislative-executive relationship of parliamentary and congressional systems, drawing mainly upon the British, Canadian, and American examples. He avoids the trap of idealizing one or the other way of organizing the functions of representative government. An article from *The Economist* examines the supposed advantages and disadvantages of different electoral systems, showing that proportional representation need not result in political instability or paralysis. Richard Rose compares the political executive in the United States, Britain, and France. He finds that each system has its own constraints upon arbitrary rule, which can easily become obstacles to prompt and decisive action.

A final article addresses the old problem of the optimal size and form of a governmental unit. Historical experience has not made it simpler to resolve this institutional conundrum. In modern times, the nation-state may well have become too small to deal effectively with the tasks of economic and monetary policy, let alone the provision of international security or the protection of the environment. At the same time, it often seems too large and centralized for dealing with matters better left to regional and local governmental units, as indicated by the electoral revolts in Italy and elsewhere. Britain is somewhat unusual among the larger European countries in not having developed a regional tier of government or anything resembling a regional policy. But Norman Orenstein and Kimberley Coursen go beyond this half-way house to consider full-blown examples of federalism. They underscore that the federal division of power has recently become very attractive for some countries that are on the brink of tearing themselves apart, because it combines the advantages of forming a union with the advantages of remaining in some ways separate. Here, also, James Madison might well have nodded in approval.

Looking Ahead: Challenge Questions

How do you explain the apparent centrist movement of parties of the moderate Left and moderate Right in recent years? How do Social Democrats present themselves as reformers of capitalism?

Why are women so poorly represented in Parliament and other positions of political leadership? How do institutional arrangements, such as election systems, sometimes help or hinder an improvement in this situation?

Would you agree with the inventory of democratic essentials as discussed by Philippe Schmitter and Terry Lynne Karl? What do you regard as most and least important in their inventory? What are some major traits of a good constitution?

What are some of the major arguments made in favor of the parliamentary system of government? What are the main arguments against and in favor of proportional representation?

A victim of outdated ideologies and lackluster leaders

The End of Politics

MARTIN JACQUES

THE SUNDAY TIMES

Britons all know that their government is extraordinarily weak. They know that John Major has been the most unpopular prime minister since records began. At any other time this century, the beneficiary would have been the opposition. Yet nobody believes that the Labor Party would make a better fist of things, either. The nation has lost confidence in politicians. We don't believe in them anymore. And the same applies elsewhere. It is difficult to think of a single political leader in the democratic world who is riding high. Governments everywhere are confronted with a crisis of credibility. The French elections saw the biggest defeat for the sitting government this century. German Chancellor Helmut Kohl is but a pale shadow of the figure that strutted the German scene in the heady days of reunification. In

Italy, the political class is discredited, the political system is disintegrating, and all the old governing parties are facing oblivion. Even in the United States, where, unlike in Europe, the people voted for a new kind of leader from a different generation, the president already finds himself an embattled figure.

What the hell is happening, you might ask. If this spectacle were confined to one country, it would be easier to explain, but that is not the case: It is almost a universal condition of the Western world. Two explanations are generally served up. First, recession makes governments unpopular, especially when they haven't got a clue what to do about it. We have had recessions before, though, and they have not led to this kind of political crisis. Second, the present generation of political leaders is, by historical standards, mediocre. But we have had mediocre leaders before, and it did not produce a universal collapse of confidence in the political class.

Shouldn't we be asking a rather more fundamental question altogether? Are we not witnessing a much more general crisis of politics as an activity, a clutter of institutions, and a body of people? There is plenty of circumstantial evidence.

Membership of political parties, not only in Britain but across the developed world, has long been in decline. The British Labor Party now has about 200,000 members, compared with 1 million in the early 1950s. The Conservative Party has more, but it, too, is shrinking. The days of the mass-membership party, with high levels of participation, are over. Fewer and fewer people believe in the party as a vehicle for change and as an object of their activities and affections. The vast and mushrooming range of alternatives—Greenpeace, the Royal Society for the Protection of Birds, the local health and fitness group, and Amnesty International—generally seem more attractive and a lot more useful.

Or consider this fact: The present generation of political leaders—Clinton, Major, Kohl, and Co.—may be the most unpopular bunch since the war. But political leaders have been suffering a steadily declining popularity rating ever since 1945, the most popular leaders being the immediate postwar generation—the Churchills, Attlees, Trumans, and Adenauers. Political leaders, in other words, command declining respect. When we watch the antics in the House of Commons, we are more likely to be appalled or alienated than impressed. Politics and politicians are now judged by more worldly standards. They stand before us like the em-

From the conservative "Sunday Times" of London.

peror with no clothes, stripped of the aura that once protected them.

Politics is like a declining sector of the economy: defensive, conservative, nostalgic, incapable of generating new ideas and practices, attracting fewer and fewer able people. Of all areas of society, the political world displays the least ability to learn. It remains male-dominated, resistant to new technology, and rooted in tradition. Society has changed, and politics has failed to keep pace. As a result, it is of declining importance in people's lives. People are less likely to take their identities from either parties or the state.

In the postwar decades, society was characterized by hierarchy and deference. People knew their place. Society consisted of large homogeneous blocs, with class as the foundation stone. Change was marked by certainty and predictability for individuals and institutions alike. But that world has slowly given way to something very different. Hierarchy and deference have been replaced by market-driven egalitarianism, where rank and title matter increasingly little. Certainty has been replaced by uncertainty. Previously, a company lived in the relative calm and safety of a national market; now there is no hiding place. Public-sector institutions such as hospitals and schools are similarly faced with growing uncertainty. And the same applies to people's lives: multiple careers, holidays in different places, and several partners are now *de rigueur*.

Homogeneity and class have been supplanted by diversity and multi-identity. We are confronted with a profusion of styles, ethnicities, identities. Society has become gloriously different. Order has given way to confusion. This is the pick-and-choose society. From food to holidays, from sport to fabrics, from sexual identity to clothes, we can choose as never before.

Society was once dominated by vertical structures that oozed hierarchy. Now society has gone lateral and horizontal. The old lines of connection and loyalty have been replaced. Crucial to this change has been the role of the media. Of course, television and the press are characterized by a certain hierarchy of their own, of editors and owners, controllers and producers. But that misses the point. The modern media have become the mirror, the interlocutor, the enabler of this new society. They are the source of information and opinion, symbol and humor. They have made people worldly rather than parochial. They have made society porous where once it was segmented. The media are now the template of society, defining success and failure in everything from sport to politics, from entertainment to ideas.

Politicians feel deeply uneasy about the change. The true object of their scorn is not this columnist or that program but what the media represent and symbolize in this new society. The media are the means by which political discussion and opinion, fact and revelation, are made universal. Governments and politicians can no longer control as they once did. As a result, they view the media with a mixture of fear and respect, resentment and anxiety. The politicians are fallen idols, and the media have played no small role in their downfall.

For politics, the most dramatic single aspect of the new culture is the decline of the state. In the postwar period, the state stood at the apogee of society, a source of respect and authority. The state was indubitably a commanding height,

and those who presided over it enjoyed commensurate prestige. Now the state has turned full circle and come to symbolize the past, inefficiency, and special interests. The implications for politicians have been profound. The state—national and local government—is where politicians do their business. It is their theater. Of course, as the left has always been rather more attached to the idea of the state as an instrument of change than has the right, so its decline has hurt the left more than the right. Taking the broad picture, though, this is nit-picking. The process has undermined the power and importance of all politicians.

But power has not only drained away from the state into, quite literally, thousands of groups within civil society. It has also seeped through the boundaries of the nation-state into the international ether. Things that the British government could do 30 years ago are no longer within its power. In some cases, no one or no body can exercise such control. In others, an institution such as the European Community has acquired some of the power. The decline of the nation-state and national sovereignty has eroded the importance of national politics.

There is another, rather different reason for the crisis of politics. European politics has been predominantly structured around the right-left polarity since the establishment of modern suffrage. There is ample evidence to suggest that the ability of this ideological system to explain the problems of society and offer solutions is in decline. Over the past 20 years or so, we have seen the rise of new issues such as gender, sexuality, and the environment, all of which transcend the traditional lines between left and right.

More recently, we have witnessed a growing crisis of the traditional bases of leftist politics. There are several ingredients: the demise of the Keynesian welfare model, the decline of the modern state and therefore the efficacy of state intervention, the rise of a more flexible and heterogeneous society, and the decline of the working class. Of these, the most important, arguably, is the latter. The industrial working class and its organizations furnished social-democratic parties, including Labor, with their culture, support, organizations, members, and voters. The decline of the working class has, unsurprisingly, thrown all socialist parties into crisis. But the consequences are far wider. If class was the central dynamic of the political system, then its decline disorganizes not only the left but also the right—and politics as a whole. When one pole is undermined, the other does not, by definition, remain unaffected.

The most obvious bipolar analogy is the cold war. The collapse of communism did not leave the West unscathed and unchallenged, as most expected in 1989. On the contrary, the demise of bipolarity has thrown the West into crisis. An overriding enemy provides a sense of purpose, helps to subordinate and discipline other potential conflicts, gives a clear moral framework, and furnishes a sense of identity. Without it, these questions rise to the surface in a new way, begging answers that are novel and profound.

The other dimension of the exhaustion of the left-right system is the decline of ideology. The 20th century has been dominated by grand ideologies: communism, socialism, fascism, neo-liberalism. In all cases, the hope kindled by them has been disappointed. As we approach the end of the millennium, there is, throughout the democratic world, a turn away from ideology toward pragmatism. Great transformative ideologies seem less and less appropriate in an environment of flux and uncertainty. The new era demands organizations able to engage in permanent innovation and experiment, whose natural habitat is a steep learning curve: exactly the opposite of the political party, which we once loved but now find increasingly uninteresting.

Historical crises are never the product of a single factor. They are a combination of long-term trends and short-term causes. The sheer tenaciousness of this recession, and the impotence of governments in the face of it, has created a general disillusionment in politicians and governments. More important, the end of the cold war has created a sense of malaise in the West, which has worsened as the Bosnia crisis has replaced the triumphalism of the Persian Gulf war.

So where is this crisis of politics leading? As always, it is easier to analyze a crisis than to predict its outcome. The added difficulty in this case is that this is a crisis of the old paradigm with no new paradigm yet in view. It would be wrong to assume that it will inevitably lead to some kind of apocalyptic change. That may happen; it is certainly what is occurring in Italy. More probable is a slow process of change and adjustment. This is likely to have two basic components. First, politics will come to occupy a less exalted position in society. This has already begun.

The second component is more intriguing. Politics must go through a process of reform that brings it more into line with how society has changed and is changing. That process, too, is already under way. A more open and pluralistic society suggests political parties that are more socially diverse in terms of membership, votes, and funding; that are not beholden in the same way to specific vested and material interests. Parties themselves are culturally anachronistic. Their decline is imposing powerful strains on the political system. The basis for the selection of candidates, policy, and, ultimately, governments is becoming increasingly narrow and unhealthy. Politics has effectively become the preserve of a small professional political class.

Yet it is difficult to imagine a political system without parties. Perhaps in time they will be looser and more porous, drawing people outside their ranks into decision-making, along the lines of the American model, and spawning leaders who have more diverse backgrounds, a wider range of cultural experience, and who, as a consequence, are able to speak to a broader constituency. But the decline of the political party and the shrinking importance of the formal political world suggest that there is a need for this to be complemented by forms of direct democracy as a means of enabling wider participation in the democratic process. The widespread use of referendums, for example, would allow more people to have a direct say in policy decisions while reducing the power of the parties. New television-based technology will soon revolutionize possibilities at local and national levels. Referendums would allow a little fresh air into a political system that now smells distinctly musty.

■ EUROPE'S SOCIAL DEMOCRATS

Identity Crisis
On the Left

NORMAN BIRNBAUM

Norman Birnbaum's most recent book is Searching for the Light: Essays in Thought and Culture *(Oxford).*

In June and July, I visited Germany, France and Spain in search of new ideas of socialism. I found, mostly, socialists. To be sure, many were trying to formulate new ideas—without much in the way of tangible results. Simply defending the view that property and the market ought to be subdued for the common good seemed difficult enough.

In Germany, the Social Democrats dream of a return to national office in 1994, the first time in twelve years. Their new chairman and candidate for chancellor, Rudolf Scharping, is persistent, sober and intelligent. To those who asked if he had a vision, he said that the party would do well if it could achieve its last, or even next to last, vision. He also insisted that the party move closer to the daily material concerns of ordinary Germans—away from the post-materialist values of the middle-class intellectuals who have come to replace trade unionists as the driving force in the party. He won his office in an unprecedented open election by the entire membership—which galvanized the party.

Still, the Social Democrats have not resolved the longstanding conflict between a membership interested in principles and a leadership obliged to compromise. By virtue of its control of the upper house of the legislature, the party has been in an unstable de facto partnership with Chancellor Helmut Kohl recently. Now Scharping is ready for agreement with Kohl on the use of the German armed forces for U.N. missions, which dismays plenty of Social Democrats, who fear a return to the militarization of foreign policy. Scharping clearly is ready for a governing coalition with either Kohl's Christian Democratic Union or the Free Democrats, often liberal on social questions but invariably devoted to the market. Many Social Democrats would prefer an alliance with the Greens, now merged with the old civil rights movement in what was East Germany. Scharping has won widespread assent in the party, however, for naming Oskar Lafontaine its chief economic spokesman. As candidate for chancellor in

1990, Lafontaine had warned that unification as conceived by Kohl would cause an economic crisis, and was washed away on a floodtide of national euphoria. He was right, of course, and now enjoys respect because he can count. He is also ready to count in new terms, and has proposed job sharing and reduced working hours. Lafontaine connects the party to new ideas of society. The issue of immigration influences German politics as race relations does in the United States, and many of the most racist are also the most threatened economically. Kohl knows this, and will fight the next election on the theme of Germany for the Germans—in hopes that it will make more palatable unemployment, cuts in social benefits and a higher tax burden on wage earners.

The Social Democrats, then, face a struggle on several fronts. They are slowly moving away from the assumption of continuous growth. After years of collaboration with German business, the party of Karl Marx actually has to confront issues of class. Descendants of the Enlightenment, they have to insist on republican ideas of citizenship when so many of their voters think of solidarity in ethnic terms. No immediate resolution of these tensions is in sight. Since a long period out of office has not accomplished renovation, perhaps a return to power would bring productive changes. It remains to be seen whether the party's tradition as a responsible custodian of order will dominate its self-image as a historical and moral vanguard.

Socialist parties are prisoners of their own past successes.

The Germans' French comrades will tell them that holding national office has ambiguous results at best. Self-criticism wasn't, however, the order of the day at the meeting of the party I went to in Lyons. It was intended to give ordinary members a chance to speak up. This meeting is a risky experiment, Michel Rocard told me; it could end in chaos. Instead, the participants obliged him, as new party leader, to distance himself from the argument that the party ought to be dissolved. Rocard had proposed that in a political equivalent of the cosmic "big bang" a new reformist alliance be formed. That was before he himself failed to win a parliamentary seat as the Socialists all but disappeared in the electoral black hole of March. In Lyons I spoke with municipal councilors and regional legislators, activists and teachers, unionists, even a locomotive engineer (most of whose workmates voted Communist). The party's leaders, they said, generally come from France's meritocratic elite; it is time to return to the party's original roots in society. Both in that sentiment and in the revivification of the party's base I sensed echoes of Germany. The first order of socialist business in Europe, then, is both familiar and simple: a return to democratic participation in the party.

My French interlocutors were insistent on the colossal failure of the Socialist governments of 1981-86 and 1988-93, with 12 percent of the labor force unemployed and no improvement in sight. The 1981 election was won on the theme *changer la vie*—alter the way we live—but the party's inability to guarantee the citizenry material security reduces its cultural and social ideas to ornamental status. Still, the delegates recognized that new economic strategies were necessary—that only a fundamental rethinking of industrial society could generate both new sensibilities and new policies. I was struck by their devotion to conceptions of enlarged citizenship, and by their persistence in adhering to a European future for France.

One large difficulty is that the European Community, once intent on bringing all of western and southern Europe up to the level of the most advanced societies, is now divided. European capitalists think the moment has come to push the level down. Meanwhile, immigration is as large a problem for France as for Germany. Despite the fact that one of every three French citizens has a grandparent born abroad, xenophobia is strong. The old French struggle between the universal ideals of the Revolution and a nation defined by blood and soil has resurfaced, and the right has made substantial inroads upon the left's traditional constituencies. Withal, the Socialists may win the presidency in 1995, the center-right proving to be divided and uncertain. Returning to office, however, will be decidedly easier than mastering the market.

At Lyons, the French cheered loudly when a message was read from Felipe Gonzalez, just re-elected to his fourth term as Spanish Premier—if as head of a minority government. In Madrid, I found the cheers rather muted. The new government is technocratic and will administer Gonzalez's continuing compromise with capital and the middle class. The Socialists campaigned by describing the major party of the right, the Popular Party, as "Franco's grandchildren." Memory won in the countryside and among the workers, but the urban middle class and the young responded to the 20 percent unemployment and economic stagnation and voted for the right. The Spanish situation is especially poignant because of the country's dependence upon the European Community. The countryside of Buñuel has disappeared, and in the villages, there are new houses, roads and schools (as well as ATM machines in four languages), with signs announcing that they come from the E.C.

Gonzalez has begun negotiations for a social pact with Spain's (weak) unions but has also initiated hostilities with the left wing of his party, led by Alfonso Guerra. The lines are confused. The group around Gonzalez has plenty of figures who agree on policy with Guerra, who considers that the modernization of socialism means its extension and not a belated adaptation to a destructive global economy. Guerra's program, however, is like Lafontaine's—still on paper. The Spanish Socialists, then, are in acute danger of self-destruction.

For the Spaniards, the wealthier French and the still wealthier Germans, it is clear that only European solutions will begin to solve their problems. That is why E.C. President Jacques Delors's proposal of $50 billion in social investment in the Community seems so compelling—and has attracted the bitter opposition of much of business. Still, all but the most stupid market ideologues know that it is only the disbursement of social benefits that keeps purchasing power at even its present diminished levels. The socialist parties are prisoners of their own past successes in modifying a capitalist model of consumption by adding social purposes. Having neglected both the pedagogic and social dimensions of solidarity, they face an onslaught on the welfare state from those who once joined them in a European consensus. The socialists' managerial habits of thought, in brief, are of little use to them. The European publics are angry and disoriented, unwilling to accept market models of society but unpersuaded that the socialists now have something productive to offer. The parties still command intellectual resources and residues of spiritual energy and moral tradition. It remains to be seen if they can activate them.

Western Europe Is Ending Its Welcome to Immigrants

John Darnton

Special to The New York Times

LONDON, Aug. 9—Fearfully, painfully, the nations of Western Europe are recognizing that immigration is probably the most explosive problem they face, and they are taking drastic steps to fend off unwanted foreigners.

France, Germany, Britain—all the Western European countries, from Sweden to Greece—feel that they are under siege as hundreds of thousands of poor people cross the newly opened borders of Eastern Europe or flee economically desperate countries in Africa and Southeast Asia.

Once grudgingly tolerated because they were willing to work in low-wage jobs like ditch digging or street cleaning, the newcomers are now seen as competitors, and many have become targets of wrath as the worst recession in decades tightens its grip. As a result, Western European governments are rushing to adopt new laws and strategies to shut out immigrants.

Tougher Tests for Asylum

To the distress of international organizations, the nations are also making it harder for refugees fleeing political persecution to find safe havens.

In a camp on the site of a former Belgian military barracks outside Cologne, 430 people from around the world await word on their fate, most

[This is the third in a 5-part series entitled *A Continent Adrift.* Ed.]

likely expulsion. After months of suspense, some have smashed the toilet plumbing and television sets in frustration.

"I don't know what to do," said Ali Ibrahim Jackson, a 19-year-old Liberian lounging against a wire fence in a bright blue track suit on a recent afternoon. Three months ago he stowed away on a freighter from Nigeria to Bremen with visions of becoming a soccer star.

"I can't go back," he said of Liberia, where a fragile cease-fire took hold last week after more than three years of civil war. "I walk the street and I'm a dead man."

Abandoning Postwar Ideal

There is no assurance that Western Europe will be able to close the door entirely, much less lock it. But in its efforts to do so, it is relinquishing a principle born from the ashes of World War II, that it should offer sanctuary to the world's persecuted and dispossessed.

"It's ironic: Europe was the inspiration for proper treatment of refugees the world over, and now they're trying to contain them," said Arthur Helton, who leads the refugee committee of the Lawyers Committee for Human Rights. "That raises a question—was asylum just a cold-war luxury all along? It seems so."

In their economic distress, Western Europeans are turning against the strangers in their midst, including the 2.8 million who are living

illegally in the 17 countries. In the European Community the unemployment rate is expected to pass 12 percent next year, meaning that 19 million people will be out of work.

Right-wing parties are trying to build constituencies by campaigning on a platform of expulsions of "foreigners." While there is little immediate danger that far-right parties will come to power on a national level, governments are shifting to the right on the immigration issue to blunt the threat.

Western European leaders are worried about rising xenophobia and racism and increasing attacks upon foreigners by neo-Nazis and skinheads. Nervously, they listen to the speeches of ideologues who hark back to a bygone era when their countries were supposedly homogeneous, comfortable, orderly and virtually all white.

But the changes in the ethnic makeup of Western Europe are already irrevocable. For generations Pakistanis have lived in Britain, Algerians in France and Turks in Germany, and even though they are regarded by some people as alien, they are there to stay.

'Fortress Europe'

The Open Doors Are Closing Hard

"Fortress Europe" is the name loosely given to the European Community's vision of a great domain of a dozen countries with no tariffs or borders to slow the internal flow of goods and people but big protective walls around the periphery.

A fortress mentality already exists.

In Europe's southern countries, where young people once went abroad to start new lives and wrote home about the prejudice they encountered, people are startled to find that they are now the hosts, and can themselves be bigoted toward newcomers.

In the Madrid suburb of Aravaca, thugs called "rapadas" break into an abandoned building where Dominican squatters are living, and one opens fire with a pistol. In Rome, "Nazi-skins" torch residences of foreigners and patrol the parks at night, beating up Africans who sleep there.

"I have no papers," said Joel Guehi, who came to Rome three months ago from the Ivory Coast. "I can get no work. I sleep in the park, and I'm scared every night."

Germany has revised its Constitution, eviscerating the well-known Article XVI. Symbolically a form of moral compensation for the Germans who found safe haven from the Nazis during World War II, the provision promised asylum to "people persecuted on political grounds." That clause was a loophole that brought in 438,000 immigrants last year. On July 1 the provision expired, and Germany's immigration policy became one of the most restrictive in Europe. The number of asylum applicants in July was about 10,000 lower than in June, and German officials expect the decline to continue.

France has given up on the almost mystical idea, traceable to the Revolution, that just being born on French soil was enough to qualify one as French. Now there is a more mundane requirement: To obtain citizenship, people born in France to non-French parents must formally apply between the ages of 16 and 21, a time when young men are called up for military service. And the rightist Interior Minister, Charles Pasqua, has proclaimed a goal of "zero immigration."

But no country has gone as far as Greece. Feeling overwhelmed by about 200,000 Albanians who slipped across the mountainous border over the last three years, the Athens Government recently seized upon the expulsion of a Greek Orthodox priest from southern Albania as a justification to round up and expel more than 25,000 Albanians. Some Greeks have taken to calling the police to provide addresses of illegal residents. Albanians say they have been beaten and robbed by police officers before being pushed across the border.

On Tuesdays and Fridays, busloads pass through the wire gate at the border checkpoint of Kakavia. An 18-year-old who was being escorted back by the border police on a recent Sunday was asked where he had been. He had spent four months in Crete, he said, clearing rocks from farmland and earning the equivalent of $17 a day in Greek drachmas. "Real money," he said.

Would he return? He smiled sheepishly, looked at his guards and said yes, he would.

The Numbers

Up to 2 Million Flow In Each Year

The numbers are inexorable.

A United Nations Population Fund report estimates that from 1980 to 1992 15 million people poured into Western Europe as migrants. Officials at the United Nations High Commissioner for Refugees roughly estimate that the number of newcomers is still running at between one and two million a year. For a region of some 300 million that exported its own people up until the 1970's, that seems to constitute an invasion.

Even the number of political refugees has mushroomed in Western Europe. Up until the mid-1970's there were about 30,000 a year, and most fit the definition of the 1951 Geneva Convention—that is, they had a "well-founded fear of persecution" in their home countries.

But as a side door for people fleeing economic deprivation, asylum requests rose dramatically, reaching 700,000 last year and costing governments an estimated $8.3 billion. In the decade through 1992, nearly three million applications for asylum. The vast majority were rejected, although the applicants almost always managed to stay on after appeals that lasted for years.

Unlike earlier postwar immigrants from southern Europe, many of the newcomers differ from longer-term inhabitants in skin color and religion. Millions of them did not assimilate, congregating instead in virtual ghettos on the outskirts of the cities.

The 2.6 million people in Britain considered members of ethnic minorities—5 percent of the nation's 56 million people—include West Indians, Bangladeshis, Indians, West Africans, Pakistanis and others. Almost half of them were born in Britain, and as British natives naturally identify themselves as British rather than, say, black African or black Caribbean. But they are not always viewed that way by whites.

The number of racially motivated incidents reported to the police in Britain has skyrocketed, from 4,383 in 1988 to 7,793 in 1992. In May Winston Churchill, the grandson of the wartime Prime Minister, called for a halt to the "relentless flow of immigrants," saying it was threatening to change Britain's way of life forever. Though his speech was condemned in editorials, he said that he had received 7,500 letters and that "they were 100 to 1 in support."

Even though many Britons seem to think immigrants are pouring in, that is no longer the case. "Primary immigration into this country ceased years ago—I mean, years ago," said Charles Wardle, the Home Office Minister responsible for immigration. Last year, 52,000 were admitted, because they were judged to have special skills, so they could be reunited with their families, or on other narrow grounds.

But globally, there is no prospect that pressure for migration will cease. A recent United Nations Population Fund report estimates that at least 100 million international migrants live outside the countries where they were born. The tide of people crossing borders to flee war, drought and economic misery "could become the human crisis of our age," it said.

Smuggling gangs fill boatloads of Chinese destined for California, Haitians take to the seas in rickety boats trying to reach Florida, and thousands of Africans step aboard planes destined for Europe. In one case, 156 Iraqis chartered an Egyptian airliner and flew to London to request asylum.

"There are no distances any longer in this world," said Dr. Manfred Matzka, Austria's Director of Immigration. "There are no islands."

Asylum

Tougher Path For Refugees

In Austria, the Traiskirchen camp, 20 miles outside Vienna, is known as the Ellis Island of the West. After the suppression of the 1956 uprising in Hungary, it took in 180,000 Hungarians; after the reform movement known as the Prague spring was crushed in 1968, 150,000 Czechs or Slovaks; after martial law was declared in Poland in 1981, 40,000 Poles. Passing through Traiskirchen was, former Chancellor Bruno Kreisky used to remark, the Austrian equivalent of the Nobel Prize.

But in June 1992, Austria adopted a new and complicated law that made political asylum very difficult to obtain. It deals quickly with "manifestly unfounded" cases—applicants with dubious claims—and sends them right back where they came from. It also asserts that anyone who comes through a "safe" country can be deemed to have found protection there.

The law was effective. In the first six months of 1992, there were 11,875 applications for asylum. In the first six months of 1993, there were only 2,490, a 75 percent decrease.

The same principles are now widely applied in Europe, where nine countries have grouped together in what is called the Schengen convention to "harmonize" restrictions. Western European countries have now declared surrounding countries "safe," so in effect no refugee can win asylum by coming overland through another country.

The chances of arriving through an airport are now minimal, too, because visa requirements have been imposed on some 110 countries. Many European countries insist that refugees passing through a transit lounge of another country are in effect "staying" there. Airlines that carry a passenger without a valid passport and visas face fines up to $3,000, a policy that Britain began in 1987.

"About the only way to get asylum these days is to land in a balloon in the center of the country with all your papers in order," quipped Hans Staudinger, a legal officer for the United Nations High Commissioner for Refugees in Vienna.

Countries are also demanding stringent proof that an asylum seeker is likely to be persecuted. This is not always easy to provide. "I was tried in absentia and condemned to death," said Thomas Kingston, a 26-year-old Liberian in a German camp. He added with a bitter smile, "they did not give me a copy of my sentence."

Given the new requirements, international organizations worry that governments will return bona fide political refugees to the countries that persecute them, often by bouncing them backward through the countries they passed through to get away.

Immigration officials reply that the goal is to weed out genuine political refugees from the economic migrants who have been abusing the asylum process and bring the system under control. "It's not a question of morals; it's wisdom," said Manfred Matzka, who put through the new Austrian laws. "In international migration there is a point at which it

becomes chaotic and there is no longer a means to control it."

One of the first cases decided under the tough new asylum policy that took effect in Germany on July 1 was that of a young Tamil from Sri Lanka, where young men of that mostly Hindu ethnic minority are often suspected of belonging to separatist guerrilla groups.

He arrived in Frankfurt and was able to show that he had been imprisoned in Colombo, the capital, five times. He was denied asylum on July 6 because, the decision papers say, "he was held only for short periods, and this does not constitute political persecution." The case is being appealed.

New Measures

Computer Checks And Troop Patrols

The Schengen agreement, under which all 12 community countries except for Britain, Ireland and Denmark are to dispense with internal borders and strengthen their parts of the community's external borders, is supposed to take effect in December.

But the accord is already causing anxiety, especially in France, which fears a flood of drugs from the Netherlands and a wave of illegal immigrants from Italy and Spain. To help allay such fears, the governments involved have agreed to give police officers extra powers to do things like check documents within 25 miles of the internal borders.

Like any fortress, "Fortress Europe" needs a moat, and the one that is being developed is a 20th-century version—a computer system called S.I.S. The system will maintain a data base so that the denial of asylum to an applicant in one country will be recorded everywhere. Another system, EURO DAC, which uses fingerprints for identification, will link police stations so "undesirables" can be quickly spotted.

But the countries are not waiting until Schengen goes into effect to take action against the flood of immigrants. Austria has sent 2,000 troops to try to seal the Hungarian border. Germany has bolstered its forces along the Polish border and installed infrared equipment to intercept the thousands from Lithuania, Belarus and other Eastern European countries who make it nightly across the Neisse, Europe's equivalent of the Rio Grande.

Germany sends planes full of deportees to Bucharest almost every day. In May it signed an agreement with Warsaw to send illegal immigrants back to Poland who are found to have passed through there—as many as 10,000 this year and an unlimited number in 1993.

Under Mr. Pasqua's direction, France is adopting the strictest measures of all—making it harder for foreigners to acquire French nationality through marriages of convenience, cutting back on work permits and refusing to allow additional wives from polygamous marriages into the country.

The debate over a bill to expand police powers to stop foreigners and check for documents almost completely sidestepped race, though it was on everyone's mind. How would French police officers be able to spot suspected foreigners? Perhaps, the bill's neo-Gaullist author, Alain Marsaud, disingenuously suggested, "If you are reading The New York Times on the street, you may be presumed to be a foreigner."

"The police already stop foreigners—they do it all the time now," said Zoubida Djelali, an Algerian doctor who works at a clinic run by the medical charity Doctors of the World. "They just go by the color of the face." Over the last two or three years, she said, she has witnessed a quiet crackdown on foreigners in areas like access to health care, the speed of rejection of asylum applications and interpretation of nationality requirements.

Of France's population of 57 million, about 4 million, or 7 percent, are foreigners, according to figures from the French Interior Ministry.

"They believe they'll be richer if

they toss us out," Dr. Djelali said. "They think there will be less unemployment. It's a fiction. Look at the work the foreigners do—maids, busboys, hauling wheelbarrows on construction sites. Underpaid or dangerous. The French won't take those kinds of jobs."

The Right

Trying to Preempt Demand for Curbs

The changes in France's immigration policy are not a response to a sudden surge in xenophobia. They represent campaign commitments by the two main conservative parties now in power to expropriate an issue that had long been exploited by Jean-Marie Le Pen's far-right National Front. Some 60 percent of France's foreigners are non-Europeans, mostly from Algeria, Tunisia and Morocco, and they are concentrated in the grimy industrial suburbs where the National Front pulls 30 to 40 percent of the vote in elections.

Almost every country has a burgeoning far-right party circulating anti-Semitic tracts and whipping up anti-foreign sentiment. There is the Freedom Party in Austria, the Republican Party in Germany, the Vlaams Blok in Belgium, the Falangists in Spain and the Northern League in Italy.

Germany's central intelligence office calculates that 41,900 of its citizens belong to far-right organizations, of which 6,400 are "militant and violence-prone." That figure does not include some 25,000 members of the Republican Party. In 1992, there were 2,584 proven acts of violence by the far right, a 74 percent increase over 1991. Of the rightist attacks, 88 percent were directed against foreigners, of whom seven died.

Whether the far-right parties are losing ground to the "responsible right," or actually gaining in stature as the establishment tries to accommodate the discontent stoked by the far right is debatable. But the tone of discourse points to other changes in

Western Europe, on a deeper, psychological level.

Western Europe is giving up its sense of itself as a civilizing corner of the world. After the horrors and guilt of the Holocaust and the Nazi occupation of much of Europe, the region has tried to compensate for the past by tending an image of itself as an assembly of decent societies. It may not have been the powerhouse on the world stage it once was, the argument ran, but at least it was a haven of toleration, democracy and respect for human rights.

Western Europe conceived of itself as a benign patron. It was inordinately proud of its medieval universities, of its cafes that nurtured conspiring Ethiopian Marxists, of its nightclubs that embraced expatriate black American jazz musicians.

Today that self-image seems increasingly untenable. There is still room for visitors and the occasional refugees, but the immigrants needed to keep the economies going are encountering more and more hostility. Western European countries are turning inward, some social critics worry, and becoming increasingly self-absorbed, intolerant and culturally hegemonistic.

A survey conducted by the European Commission and released on July 15 disclosed that for the first time, public opinion in the European Community had swung against immigrants from outside the 12 countries. Fifty-two percent of those polled said there were too many immigrants.

"There is a psychological backlash," said Ruprecht von Arnim of the United Nations High Commissioner for Refugees office in Brussels, "but the reason is not just racism, or economic difficulties. There was clearly the feeling that the countries had lost control over what was happening to them. The politicians picked up the anxieties of the people and carried them one step farther.

"I could see how looking in from the outside, a lot of people might think that these countries have lost their souls."

Frenchwomen Say It's Time to Be 'a Bit Utopian'

Alan Riding

Special to The New York Times

PARIS, Dec. 30—Women are no more fully represented in French politics today than they were after universal suffrage was finally introduced here 48 years ago, but a group of determined women—the French generally shy from the word "feminist"—is now intent on changing that.

Their goal is a law requiring that seats in the lower house of the French Parliament be shared equally by men and women. But on the way to achieving this, they must first win over the men who control the country's main political parties. And that will not be easy.

"It's illusory to think anything will come from the parties of their own accord," said Claude Servan-Schreiber, a journalist and one of the promoters of the initiative. "It would be entirely against their nature. Only public opinion can do this. Without public pressure, nothing will happen."

Debate in the Making

A debate, though, is in the making. Last month, 289 women and 288 men—a number chosen to symbolize the 577 members of the National Assembly—signed a petition published in Le Monde on Nov. 10 calling for "democratic parity" of the sexes. Michel Piccoli, an actor, and Sonia Rykiel, a designer, were among the signers.

A couple of weeks earlier, Michel Rocard, a former Prime Minister who now leads the Socialist opposition, said he would head his party's ticket in elections for the European Parliament in June only if it nominated an equal number of men and women as candidates for the 81 seats assigned to France.

But much ground must still be covered in the French Parliament. In March, 20 percent of candidates in the first round of parliamentary elections were women, but most came from tiny parties with no hope of victory. In the end, just 35 women won seats, representing 6 percent of the conservative-dominated National Assembly.

A new demand: parity in Parliament between women and men.

"We're at the same level as Greece and Turkey," said Françoise Giroud, a writer and former Government minister. "It's scandalous. That's why I think the campaign for parity is good. It's a bit utopian, but we're so far behind in France that everything should be tried."

Some other Western democracies do little better. Women now account for 8.1 percent of Italy's Chamber of Deputies, 9.1 percent of Britain's House of Commons, 11 percent of the House of Representatives (and 7 percent of the Senate) in the United

States and 15.7 percent of the lower house of the Spanish Parliament.

But women have a higher political profile in northern Europe. In their countries' main legislative assemblies, women hold 21.6 percent of the seats in Germany, 27.3 percent in the Netherlands, 32.6 percent in Sweden, 33.5 percent in Denmark and 38 percent in Norway.

As far back as 1979, a women's group within the French Socialist Party backed the idea of sexual parity in Parliament, though it was never adopted. In the 1980's the Green Party in both Germany and France also began picking equal

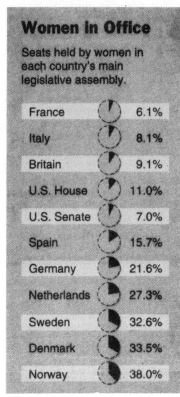

Women In Office

Seats held by women in each country's main legislative assembly.

Country	%
France	6.1%
Italy	8.1%
Britain	9.1%
U.S. House	11.0%
U.S. Senate	7.0%
Spain	15.7%
Germany	21.6%
Netherlands	27.3%
Sweden	32.6%
Denmark	33.5%
Norway	38.0%

The New York Times

numbers of men and women as candidates.

In the United States, a small group called "50/50 by 2000" has been active since 1988, promoting the idea of parity in Congress, the Cabinet and the Supreme Court by the end of the century. Its slogan has now been adopted by the National Association for Female Executives.

The new push in France dates back 18 months, to the publication of a book, "To Power, Women Citizens! Liberty, Equality, Parity," written by Mrs. Servan-Schreiber, Françoise Gaspard, a former Socialist legislator, and Anne Le Gall, a French lawyer.

"Exclusion of women has been part of France's political philosophy since the Revolution," said Mrs. Servan-Schreiber, who also publishes a newsletter called Parité-Infos. "Women of my generation—I am 55—didn't have to fight for the vote. But nothing has happened here since universal suffrage."

France was late in taking even this step. Women have voted in Russia since 1917, in Germany since 1919, in the United States since 1920, in Britain since 1928 and in Spain since 1931. But in France, they won this right only in 1944. Until then, it seemed, France's avowedly secular political system feared that the Roman Catholic Church could wield excessive influence through women who voted.

No Increase in Representation

What most startled Mrs. Servan-Schreiber, though, was the discovery that even though more women than men now vote, women hold the same proportion of parliamentary seats—6 percent—that they did in the assembly elected in 1945. And, in the interim, the share has never been higher and at times has fallen as low as 3 percent. After the elections in March, women of the parity movement demonstrated against the male stranglehold over Parliament.

A few women have gained prominence in French politics. In 1991, Edith Cresson, a Socialist, became the first woman to serve as Prime Minister, although she fared poorly in office. Simone Veil, former president of the European Parliament and the current Minister of Social Affairs, has long been a popular figure, but she is one of only three women in the current 30-member Cabinet.

Maurice Grimaud, a former Paris police chief, said he signed the petition calling for "democratic parity" because "we can't wait for it to happen naturally." He added, "Most politicians daren't say publicly that they're against the idea, but they're determined not to talk about it."

Olivier Duhamel, a well-known political scientist, nonetheless warned that sexual parity in representation introduced the notion of quotas, with the risk that the old and young or ethnic and religious groups might eventually also claim a right to be equally represented in Parliament.

But Mrs. Servan-Schreiber argues that men and women cannot be treated simply as categories. "They are the only two types of human beings that exist," she said, "so parity has nothing to do with this social class or if they are handicapped or if they belong to an ethnic group."

She said the plan is now for "committees for parity" to spawn a grass-roots movement, "which is rare here because everything always come from above." Eventually, she said, the committees, which already exist in Marseilles and Toulouse, should form a national collective.

But the real strategy is to persuade political bosses that women are a secret weapon as candidates. Mr. Rocard, at least, seems convinced; a recent poll said support for the Socialists would jump from 19 to 24 percent if they ran equal numbers of men and women.

"Sure, it's opportunism," Mrs. Servan-Schreiber said. "But it's his job to look for votes."

Women, Power and Politics: The Norwegian Experience

Irene Garland

Irene Garland, a Norwegian social scientist, lives in London.

Three Scandinavian countries all have more than one third of women representatives in their national assemblies. In Norway the Prime Minister is a woman as are 9 out of 19 cabinet ministers as well as the leaders of 2 of the other political parties.

Commentators trying to explain this phenomenon have looked back through history and pointed to the independence of Norwegian women as far back as the Viking era, when they kept the homefires burning while their menfolk were away plundering. Others have referred to more recent times. Outstanding women, however, are to be found in most countries at some time or another. The reason for Norwegian women being so successful in gaining political power must therefore be found somewhere else. My belief is that the explanation is of a practical nature and is to be found in the post-war era.

Common to the three Scandinavian countries is a structure of progressive social democracy and election systems based on proportional representation. If one compares the number of women in parliaments across the world, one finds that proportional representation is the single most important element for women to gain entry into politics. However, it was the ability to use this system to their advantage, and the fact that a group of women managed to agree on a common course across party lines, that made it possible to break the mold of the male dominated political scene in Norway.

A SPECTACULAR BEGINNING

The year was 1967 and Brigit Wiik—editor, author, mother and leader of the Oslo Feminist Movement—recalls in her book a chance meeting between herself and Einar Gerhardsen on the street in Oslo. Einar Gerhardsen was a leader of the Labor Party and had been Prime Minister almost continuously since the war. He was, at the time, in opposition, having lost the previous election. With the local elections coming up he agreed to a quota for women on the Labor party lists. In doing so he saw an opportunity to activate a new group of voters for his party, and when his agreement was presented to the party in power, they felt compelled to do the same. With the two largest parties both agreeing to give a quota to women, representatives from The National Advisory Council for Women, The Working Women's Association and the Oslo Feminist Movement, formed a group to lead the campaign to get women into politics by harnessing the female vote. They used a professional PR firm to lead the campaign—a first in Norway. The result surprised everyone; there was a national increase in women representatives of 50%, and whereas there had been 179 local communities without women's representation prior to the election, afterwards the number was reduced to 79. Subsequent campaigns further increased the number of women in local government by 50%—except for 1975.

From *Scandinavian Review,* Vol. 79, No. 3, Winter 1991, pp. 18-25. Reprinted courtesy of the American-Scandinavian Foundation.

2. FACTORS IN THE POLITICAL PROCESS: Women and Politics

WOMEN IN THE NATIONAL ASSEMBLY—THE STORTING

Though there was no campaign to elect women to the national assembly, there seems to have been a spill-over effect. Political parties were quick to recognize the advantage in gaining the female vote and soon extended the quota system to parliamentary elections.

Women's representation in parliament increased steadily from the 1969 election in parallel with what happened in the local elections.

WOMEN START WINNING THE ARGUMENTS

After the 1967 election the Central Bureau of Statistics started to separate voters by gender for the first time, and the 1970s saw an upsurge in research into the history of women's lives and living conditions. Young female researchers were for the first time given the opportunity and the funding to look into their own past, a hitherto ignored area of academic research, and much empirical data was collated during this decade. The history of women's lives ran to 18 volumes and a history of women writers to 3 volumes.

Once they gained entry into the corridors of power, women were increasingly taking up issues of importance to themselves and to the family. Such issues gained in importance by producing results at the ballot box. They could, therefore, not be ignored in party politics and as a result, became part of the overall political agenda.

Enabling policies such as the right to maternity leave and the ability to return to work after giving birth were important for women who wanted to have the choice between having a career and becoming a full-time housewife. With the increased number of women investing in higher education, going back to work was not only seen as a means of personal fulfillment, but became an economic necessity for those who needed to pay back their student loans. The availability of choice was also seen as central to the equality debate— why should men be able to have both a family and a career while women were forced to make a choice? The idea that there was such a thing as a "natural" place for a woman in the home despite qualifications or inclinations was rejected. If women were designed for domesticity by nature itself, then how could one explain the fact that women, given a chance, did very well in the outside world? The patriarchs were at a loss for an answer.

LAWS ARE CHANGED

The 1970s saw a number of typical feminist arguments being brought forward and legislation or common practices changed as a result. One such issue was the one over Miss and Mrs. Throughout the 1960s feminists had opposed the use of these titles and the alternative Ms. had not won approval. During the 1960s ardent feminists would reply to anyone asking if

THE INCREASE IN WOMEN'S REPRESENTATION

Local government elections	pre-1967	1967	1971	1975	1979
Women as a % of total	6.3	9.5	15	15	22.8
Parliamentary elections	1945–53	1969	1973	1977	1981
Women as a % of total	4.7	9.3	15	23.9	25.8

Maternity leave	2 weeks prior to confinement 30 weeks after confinement with full pay
Leave from work & the right to return	mothers have the right to a further year off work without pay
Paternity leave	fathers have the right to 2 weeks off work with pay, dependent on trade union agreement (applies to all civil servants)
Breast-feeding	mothers have their hours of work cut to accommodate breast-feeding
Children's illness	both parents have a right to 10 days off work with pay when a child under 12 is ill

	Born	Married	Children	Education
Gro H. Brundtland Prime Minister (Labor)	1939	1960	4	Degree in medicine; MA (Harvard)
Ase Kleveland Minister of Cultural Affairs (Labor)	1949	Cohabits	None	Part law degree; Studied music
Anne E. Lahnstein Leader, Centre Party	1949	1975	3	Social worker
Kaci K. Five Leader, Conservative Party	1951	1972	2	Political Science degree

they were Miss or Mrs. that it was none of their business whether they were married or not. These days no one would ask and such titles are not in general use.

Another issue was that of surnames upon marriage. Women regarded giving up their own names as losing their identities. The law on surnames has now changed so that couples can choose which name to use. Some prefer to keep their maiden name. Some couples take on her name after marriage instead of his, but many women prefer to attach their husbands' name to their own. The latter is the case with the three female party leaders. Children are no longer automatically given their fathers' surname—again it is subject to parental choice.

The debate on surnames formed part of a wider debate about the right to a separate identity for women after marriage. The argument was for women to be able to carry on with their own careers and not to take on the role of supporting player to that of their husbands. Marriage should not become synonymous with taking on the cooking, cleaning and entertaining in addition to their own jobs. Entertaining could equally well be done in a restaurant anyway. Men would have to grow up and stop relying on their wives taking over where their mothers had left off. Cooking and darning became part of every boy's curriculum at school—the emphasis was on enabling men to become self-sufficient.

This also extended to quotas being set for men in certain professions, such as nursing, which until then had been dominated by women.

WOMEN IN POWER TODAY

The quota system helped the Prime Minister, **Gro Harlem Brundtland**, on her way to power. When she became Prime Minister in 1981 for the first time, it was she who introduced the idea of 50/50 gender representation in the cabinet. Having formed her third government at the most recent election, she has taken with her a team of young and capable women. Mrs. Brundtland followed in her father's footsteps—he was a doctor and a cabinet minister—and has been involved in politics from an early age. She is known for her enormous capacity for work, and certainly her record of achievements bears witness to just this. In addition to working full time she has managed to raise a family of four children. Her first job was as a medical officer on the Oslo Board of Public Health. The first ministerial position came in 1974 when she was appointed Minister for the Environment. She was appointed leader of the Labor Party in 1981, the same year that she became Prime Minister at the age of 42, the youngest ever to hold this office.

Internationally she has served on The Palme Commission which published its report on "Common Security" in 1982. This was followed by her chairing the World Commission on Environment and Development whose report, "Our Common Future," was published in 1987. She has published many scientific papers and received numerous prizes in acknowledgement of her work in different fields.

The new leader of the Conservative Party, **Kaci Kullman Five,** also started in politics quite young. Her mother, an elegant looking lady in her 60s, is still active in the local conservative party in Baerum where Mrs. Five first started out. After serving as deputy leader locally, she joined the national party, and was elected to parliament in 1981. Her first major office was as Deputy Secretary of State for commercial affairs in the Foreign Office in 1989. Having a degree in political science, she has served on the standing committees for foreign policy and constitutional affairs and on the finance committee. She has also published a book.

The third female party leader is **Anne Enger Lahnstein** of the rural Centre Party, who comes from a farming background. She headed the national action against free abortion in 1978–79, and was a member of the Nordic Council from 1979 on, but she did not enter parliament until 1985. She was head of the Oslo Centre Party from 1980–83. From 1983 on, she served as the deputy leader of the national party until she took over as its leader this year.

Ase Kleveland, the new Minister of Culture, differs from the others in that she has not gone through the rank and file of a party. She studied classical guitar and music theory for a number of years and during the '60s and '70s was one of Norway's best known popular singers. Ms. Kleveland won the Norwegian finals of the Eurovision Song Contest and later hosted the TV program for this contest the year it was held in Norway. She headed the Norwegian Musician's Union for a period and her most recent job was as a manager of the first amusement park in Norway. She was due to take over as Cultural Director for the Olympics to be held in Lillehammer in 1994 on the very day she was offered her cabinet post.

COMBINING CAREER AND FAMILY

Combining career with family commitments is no easy task, though office hours in Norway are short—9 to 4—giving more time for both parents to spend with their children. The smaller towns and communities constitute less danger to children which also makes it easier on working parents. Often though, it would seem that having a husband with flexible working arrangements such as a researcher or a journalist helps, and there is no doubt that joint efforts are necessary when both parents work. Fathers do take a much greater part in the up-bringing of their children and in the running of homes, than previously. This "new" role for fathers has now become the norm.

The Prime Minister's children are all grown up now and she is in fact a grandmother, but her husband's job as a researcher and writer no doubt being able to work from home when the need arose, must have been a help. Anne Lahnstein's children are in their teens, only Kaci Five has a young child (8 years old), and she said in an interview that she had to work very hard in order to make time for the family—something she viewed as important. Her husband is an editor and doubtless has to take his turn in looking after the children.

SOUR GRAPES?

It is perhaps inevitable that dissenting voices be heard when so many women reach such high positions in society. Recently a study has been published suggesting that men are leaving politics in Norway because, since it has become dominated by women, it is also becoming a low-paid occupation. Men, it is claimed, are opting for the better paid, higher status jobs in the private sector.

With increased internationalization, they argue, there are many constraints on national assemblies, and important decisions are being made elsewhere; Parliament is no longer the power house it used to be.

Research by Ms. Hege Skjeie from the Institute for Social Studies, disagrees with these conclusions. It is quite true that politicians whose wages are part of the civil service wage scale are lower than those received for the top jobs in the private sector and also that many professions dominated by women are badly paid. However, wages in the state sector have always been considered low relative to private industry, and this was the case before women started to take an interest in a career in politics. Ms. Skjeie's studies found that the men leaving politics did so because of age—they had all served for quite some time. Others had in fact lost their seats or been ousted from positions of leadership within their parties—some by women. There was certainly no difficulty in recruiting young men into

politics, and as regards the power and status associated with politics one could point to Ase Kleveland, Minister of Culture, who had the choice between politics and the Olympic Committee, and chose politics in spite of its uncertainties.

"I'M ON QUOTA—AND I LOVE IT!"

There can be no doubt that it was the quota system that made it possible for Norwegian women to enter politics in such a big way. The power that comes from parliament cannot be underestimated—it has given weight to arguments that had been previously ignored and as such has changed social attitudes of both sexes to the roles and rights of men and women alike. This change could not have taken place without political backing and without such backing, it would not have received such broad social acceptance. However, it is clear that when women work together across party lines, as was the case in Norway during the early days, that is when they achieve the most. Campaigning is also necessary as the experience of 1975 showed—no campaign, no increase in women's representation. The clock cannot be turned back, but even in Norway many women feel that there is no ground for complacency.

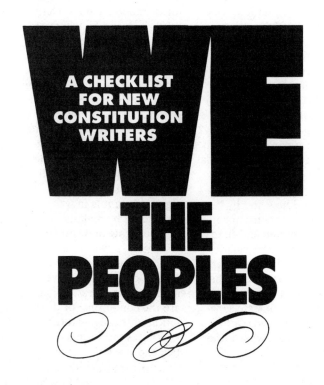

A CHECKLIST FOR NEW CONSTITUTION WRITERS

WE THE PEOPLES

ROBERT A. GOLDWIN

Robert A. Goldwin is a resident scholar at the American Enterprise Institute. He was director of AEI's Constitution Project. This article draws on the introductions of two of his books: Constitution Makers on Constitution Making *and* Forging Unity Out of Diversity.

AMERICANS ARE ACCUSTOMED to thinking of constitution writing as something done hundreds of years ago by bewigged gentlemen wearing frock coats, knee breeches, and white stockings, but for the rest of the world, constitution writing is very much an activity of the present day. The Constitution of the United States is now more than 200 years old, but a majority of the other constitutions in the world are less than 15 years old. That is, of the 160 or so written national constitutions, more than 80 have been adopted since 1975. This means that in the last few decades, on average, more than five new national constitutions have come into effect every year.

Some of these new constitutions are, of course, for new nations, but the surprising fact is that most were written for very old nations, such as Spain, Portugal, Turkey, and Greece. And now, in the old nations of Eastern Europe and possibly also in the Soviet Union or newly independent parts of it, new constitutions are about to be written to replace outdated, one-party constitutions.

Those who are responsible for writing these new constitutions know they need assistance. As Professor Albert Blaustein of Rutgers University Law School recently reported, many East European legal experts "haven't seen a constitutional law book for 45 years." They need not proceed without advice, though, because there are so many still-active, experienced constitution writers in scores of nations around the world that have recently adopted new constitutions. There are also experts in international constitutional law in the United States and in many other nations who would be only too glad to offer their services.

Nonetheless, except perhaps for narrow technical matters, outsiders, however expert, are limited in the help they can provide. A successful constitution must be deeply rooted in the history and traditions of the nation and its people, and its writers need a clear sense of what is central to the way the nation is constituted. For millennia, East European nations have been battlegrounds for innumerable invasions, conquests, and consequent migrations. As a result, there is a great mixing of peoples who cannot be sorted out even by computer-guided drawing of borders. These peoples, who

From *The American Enterprise,* May/June 1990, pp. 70-75. © 1990 by The American Enterprise Institute for Public Policy Research. Distributed by The New York Times Special Features. Reprinted by permission.

QUESTIONS FOR CONSTITUTION WRITERS

The Preliminaries

• How will delegates to the constitutional committee or constituent assembly be chosen? Will the new constitution be drafted by the legislative body or by a body chosen specifically for the purpose? If there is controversy about the method of selection, how and by whom will it be resolved?

• What will be the rules and procedures of the constitution-making body, once chosen, and how and by whom will controversies on this question be resolved?

Powers and Power Relationships

• What are the different branches of government, and what is their constitutional relationship? Are the executive and legislative branches separated or combined?

• Is there a single chief executive, or an executive cabinet, or some form of executive council? What are the executive powers, and how are they limited? Does the executive have some share in the legislative proc-

ess: for instance, do laws require his signature; does he have veto power, the right to propose legislation? Does the executive have treaty-making powers, the power to declare war, command of the armed forces, law-enforcement powers, some degree of responsibility to appoint judges, power of executive pardon or clemency? Are police powers national, or is there some form of local authority? How are the executive departments established, and how and by whom are the department heads appointed and fired? How are executive salaries determined? How is the chief executive chosen, and what is the term of office?

• Is the head of state separate from the head of government, and if so, what is the role of the head of state? How is the head of state chosen? What is the term of office? If a monarch, what is the role of the crown? Does the head of state act to dissolve the legislature, call for new elections, name a new prime minister?

• Is the legislature unicameral or bicameral? What is the principle of representation, or is there more than one principle (for example, some legislators chosen on

the basis of population, some by states or provinces)? What is the length of term for members? Under what conditions and by whom are new elections called? How are salaries of members determined and varied? Does the legislature have the power of the purse, taxing power, oversight powers, a role in executive and judicial appointments, budget-making powers, power over the monetary system, power to regulate domestic trade, foreign trade, a role in war making and treaty making, power to investigate and compel testimony, power to impeach executive and judicial officers? Do legislators have immunity from arrest? What are the conditions for dissolution of the legislature?

• What is the system of justice and law enforcement? What is the structure of the judicial system, and how and by whom is it established? In what ways, if any, are judges subject to legislative and executive controls? How independent are judges from executive and legislative control? How are judges appointed or elected and for what terms? Are judicial salaries protected? Do the courts of law have powers of judicial review of the consti-

tutionality of legislative and executive actions, or is there a separate constitutional court?

• To whom are the powers assigned for the conduct of foreign policy? To what extent are they shared, and on the basis of what principle? Where is the power assigned to declare war and to make and ratify treaties?

• Are there powers to suspend the constitution in emergencies? If so, by whom and under what conditions? Are there protections against abuse of emergency powers?

• Are all public officials required to take an oath of office to uphold this constitution?

• To what extent are the executive, legislative, and judicial powers separated, and by what provisions are the separations maintained?

• Is the national government unitary or federal, and if the latter, what form of federalism? Whether unitary or federal, is it centralized or decentralized, or some combination?

• What are the limits of the powers of the government and of the various branches and officers, and by what means are the limits sustained?

have no choice but to live side by side, are not necessarily able to love their neighbors. It seems as though everyone's grandfather was murdered by someone else's grandfather. As a result, most of these nations have diverse populations characterized by passionate hostilities. The constitutional task to make "one people"—to strengthen a sense of national unity by constitutional provisions—is a much greater concern for these nations.

Destructive Diversity

That all human beings are fundamentally equal is a central tenet of modern constitutionalism that is essential to all systems of political

liberty. To assert that we are all equal means, necessarily, that we are all equally human, sharing one and the same human nature. This view is widely held and advanced, sometimes as fact, sometimes as aspiration, and denied or disputed for the most part by those who are thought to be benighted, or bigoted, or both. The universality of human nature, the oneness of humankind, is a vital element of modern democratic thought.

And yet, wherever we look in the world, we see mankind divided into tightly bound groups, set apart by racial, religious, language, or national differences. The bonds of loyalty these differences engender often override all other considerations, including even the obli-

Elections and Political Parties

• By what methods are the various offices filled: direct popular election by universal suffrage or some indirect method; winner-take-all or some form of proportional representation? Which offices, if any, are not elective, and what is the method of appointment? Are there different methods of election or selection for different offices?

• What is the constitutional status of political parties, or is that left undetermined?

Nonpolitical Institutions

• What is the structure of the education system, and how is it supervised? Is the school system centralized, regional, local, or some combination? Are there provisions for ethnic, religious, or language schools? Are private schools allowed, and if so, what controls are imposed on them? Is the freedom of inquiry in university teaching and research protected?

• What are the provisions for the media? Are there government-owned, political party-owned, or privately owned newspapers, television channels, and radio stations? Are the media regulated or licensed? What protections are there for freedom of the press, and how are abuses prevented?

• What is the constitutional status of the military? Who is the commander in chief of the armed forces? How much and what form of civilian control is there?

• What is the role of religion? Is there an established church, and one or more official religions? Are there church subsidies from public funds, and if so, are they on a basis of equality or are they preferential? Is there separation of church and state? Is freedom of religion protected and by what means?

Rights

• Is there a bill of rights? What protections are there for the rights of individuals: speech, press, religion, peaceable assembly, habeas corpus, public trial, and so on? Is there equality of all persons, or are there constitutional preferences based on race, religion, sex, nationality, or different levels of citizenship? Are the rights primarily political and legal, or are social and economic rights included? Are the rights provisions stated negatively or affirmatively? Is there a list of duties of citizens listed, and if so, are the duties linked to rights? Are there protections of rights of aliens? What are the provisions for immigration and emigration? What is the status under the constitution of international declarations of rights? Are only the rights of individuals acknowledged, or are there also protections for the rights of religious, ethnic, racial, or regional groups?

• Are there different levels or kinds of citizenship; that is, are there qualifications or restrictions of voting rights, property rights, representation, access to education, or eligibility for public office based on race, sex, religion, language, or national origin? Do naturalized citizens have the same rights, privileges, and immunities as natural-born citizens? What are the naturalization provisions?

• Does the constitution specify any national or official languages? Are there provisions for schools, courts, government offices, churches, and other institutions to conduct their activities in languages other than the national or official ones?

The Economic System

• Does the constitution specify what kind of economic system shall prevail (for instance, that this nation is a socialist democracy or that the means of production shall be owned privately)? Are there provisions for managing the economy, or is a market economy of private enterprise assumed? What is the status of private property? What is the status of banks, corporations, farms, other enterprises? What are the regulatory and licensing powers? Are there government monopolies and, if so, what kind? What are the copyright and patent provisions? Is there protection against impairing the obligation of contracts?

• What is the status of international law and international organizations in relation to national laws and institutions? What is the legal status of treaties and other international obligations?

Final Questions

• What is the amendment process? Is it designed to make amending the constitution easy or difficult? Does the amending process include the people as a whole, or is it limited to the legislature and other officials?

• What is the process for ratifying the constitution?

---

gations of national citizenship. Whether or not we are "all brothers and sisters under the skin," two indisputable, and indisputably linked, facts are evident everywhere: first, there is a natural, powerful fraternal bond among persons who share the same religion, or race, or language, or nationality; second, the same inclusive bond commonly has the effect of excluding those who are different, engendering hostility toward "outsiders."

In almost all countries with diverse populations—and almost all countries around the world do have significant diversity—we see, not the "domestic tranquillity" spoken of in the preamble to the Constitution of the United States, but domestic hostility between fellow citizens of the same nation-states: Protestants and Catholics in Northern Ireland, Muslims and Christians in Lebanon, Jews and Muslims in Israel, blacks and whites in the United States, Flemish and French speakers in Belgium, Armenians and Azerbaijanis in the Soviet Union, Serbs and Albanians in Yugoslavia, Greeks and Turks in Cyprus, Hausas and Ibos in Nigeria—and this list does not come close to being exhaustive. Given historic animosities in many countries of Eastern Europe, diversity presents a problem for their constitution makers.

Citizens who are members of groups significantly different from others of the population can reasonably have grave concerns: fear for their safety, concern that they will not be allowed to participate in the political, social, and economic life of the nation, and fear that they will be restricted in the practices that are characteristic of their special way of life. To address these fears, many constitutions have special provisions, usually addressed directly to groups by name, assuring them of participation in the national life and guaranteeing freedom of religion or use of language, or promising preferences in education or employment on the basis of nationality or race. The dilemma such provisions pose, however, is that they raise the differences within the population to a constitutional status and tend thereby to identify, emphasize, and perpetuate the divisions within society. Our own constitution is silent in this regard, aiming for unity by assimilation.

No Universal Formula

Years of study of constitutions confirm what common sense would suggest: that there is no universal formula for a successful constitution. A sound constitution for any nation has to be something of a reflection, although more than that, of the essence of a particular nation, and this is inescapably influenced by the character of each nation's people, or peoples, and their history.

Constitution writers may wish to make a break with their past, to make a completely fresh start, but they never have the luxury of a clean slate. They start with a population having certain characteristics (for example, homogeneous or diverse), an economy tied to its geographic characteristics (a maritime nation or landlocked), neighboring nations (peaceful or warlike) that cannot be moved or ignored, and a history that has shaped their understanding of themselves and their national aspirations. The constitution must reflect all of these elements of the nation, and the more it is in accord with these national characteristics, the better the constitution will be.

One day in Athens some years ago, while talking to a Greek judge who is also a constitutional scholar, I referred to the newness of the Greek constitution. He asked me what date I put on it, and I, somewhat surprised, said, "1975, of course." "Yes, I understand," he said, "but you could also say 1863." "But," I replied, "Greece has had nearly a dozen constitutions since then." "Yes," he said, "that's right, but they are always the same." He was exaggerating, of course, but not much. When

Greece adopted its latest constitution, two issues were foremost, the roles of the armed forces and of the monarchy. However much Greek constitutions and regimes changed through the decades, these questions remained constant. There was not much leeway, not much discretion on many of the most important points. The same will be true for the nations of Eastern Europe.

Although there can be no universal formula for successful constitution writing—no canned answers that can be applied to any country in search of a new constitutional order—there are standard, universal questions that must be asked. A comprehensive list will include some questions that at first glance seem archaic or unnecessary to consider. Turkey or Portugal, for instance, did not have to dwell on the question of the role of the monarchy as Greece and Spain did, but considering how many modern nations are constitutional monarchies, it is not impossible that one or another East European nation might consider some form of constitutional monarchy before the turmoil is over.

Therefore, in the conviction that it is possible to develop a substantial, if not complete, list of the questions constitution writers must ask themselves in writing the constitution of any country, I offer this enumeration for guidance (see box).

A Rare Activity

The frequency of constitution writing tells us two things. First, constitutions are very important, and great investments of time and effort are needed to write them; and second, it is very difficult, and rare, to write a constitution that lasts—which is why there have been so many of them.

A complete list—and this one surely has omissions—gives no assurance of finding the right answers in writing a constitution. But an enumeration such as this provides reassurance that major issues will not be overlooked. It also reminds us what an extraordinary accomplishment our own 200-year-old Constitution is.

Making a constitution is a special political activity. It is possible only at certain extraordinary moments in a nation's history, and its success or failure can have profound and lasting consequences for a nation and its people. That is the challenge facing the constitution makers and the peoples of Eastern Europe.

WHAT DEMOCRACY IS . . . AND IS NOT

Philippe C. Schmitter & Terry Lynn Karl

Philippe C. Schmitter *is professor of political science and director of the Center for European Studies at Stanford University.* **Terry Lynn Karl** *is associate professor of political science and director of the Center for Latin American Studies at the same institution. The original, longer version of this essay was written at the request of the United States Agency for International Development, which is not responsible for its content.*

For some time, the word democracy has been circulating as a debased currency in the political marketplace. Politicians with a wide range of convictions and practices strove to appropriate the label and attach it to their actions. Scholars, conversely, hesitated to use it—without adding qualifying adjectives—because of the ambiguity that surrounds it. The distinguished American political theorist Robert Dahl even tried to introduce a new term, "polyarchy," in its stead in the (vain) hope of gaining a greater measure of conceptual precision. But for better or worse, we are "stuck" with democracy as the catchword of contemporary political discourse. It is the word that resonates in people's minds and springs from their lips as they struggle for freedom and a better way of life; it is the word whose meaning we must discern if it is to be of any use in guiding political analysis and practice.

The wave of transitions away from autocratic rule that began with Portugal's "Revolution of the Carnations" in 1974 and seems to have crested with the collapse of communist regimes across Eastern Europe in 1989 has produced a welcome convergence toward [a] common definition of democracy.[1] Everywhere there has been a silent abandonment of dubious adjectives like "popular," "guided," "bourgeois," and "formal" to modify "democracy." At the same time, a remarkable consensus has emerged concerning the minimal conditions that polities must meet in order to merit the prestigious appellation of "democratic." Moreover, a number of international organizations now monitor how well these standards are met; indeed, some countries even consider them when formulating foreign policy.[2]

WHAT DEMOCRACY IS

Let us begin by broadly defining democracy and the generic *concepts* that distinguish it as a unique system for organizing relations between rulers and the ruled. We will then briefly review *procedures*, the rules and arrangements that are needed if democracy is to endure. Finally, we will discuss two operative *principles* that make democracy work. They are not expressly included among the generic concepts or formal procedures, but the prospect for democracy is grim if their underlying conditioning effects are not present.

One of the major themes of this essay is that democracy does not consist of a single unique set of institutions. There are many types of democracy, and their diverse practices produce a similarly varied set of effects. The specific form democracy takes is contingent upon a country's socioeconomic conditions as well as its entrenched state structures and policy practices.

Modern political democracy is a system of governance in which rulers are held accountable for their actions in the public realm by citizens, acting indirectly through the competition and cooperation of their elected representatives.[3]

A *regime or system of governance* is an ensemble of patterns that determines the methods of access to the principal public offices; the characteristics of the actors admitted to or excluded from such access; the strategies that actors may use to gain access; and the rules that are followed in the making of publicly binding decisions. To work properly, the ensemble must be institutionalized—that is to say, the various patterns must be habitually known, practiced, and accepted by most, if not all, actors. Increasingly, the preferred mechanism of institutionalization is a written body of laws undergirded by a written constitution, though many enduring political norms can have an informal, prudential, or traditional basis.[4]

For the sake of economy and comparison, these forms, characteristics, and rules are usually bundled together and given a generic label. Democratic is one; others are autocratic, authoritarian, despotic, dictatorial, tyrannical, totalitarian, absolutist, traditional, monarchic, oligarchic, plutocratic, aristocratic, and sultanistic.[5] Each of these regime forms may in turn be broken down into subtypes.

Like all regimes, democracies depend upon the presence of *rulers,* persons who occupy specialized authority roles and can give legitimate commands to others. What distinguishes democratic rulers from nondemocratic ones are the norms that condition how the former come to power and the practices that hold them accountable for their actions.

The *public realm* encompasses the making of collective norms and choices that are binding on the society and backed by state coercion. Its content can vary a great deal across democracies, depending upon preexisting distinctions between the public and the private, state and society, legitimate coercion and voluntary exchange, and collective needs and individual preferences. The liberal conception of democracy advocates circumscribing the public realm as narrowly as possible, while the socialist or social-democratic approach would extend that realm through regulation, subsidization, and, in some cases, collective ownership of property. Neither is intrinsically more democratic than the other—just *differently* democratic. This implies that measures aimed at "developing the private sector" are no more democratic than those aimed at "developing the public sector." Both, if carried to extremes, could undermine the practice of democracy, the former by destroying the basis for satisfying collective needs and exercising legitimate authority; the latter by destroying the basis for satisfying individual preferences and controlling illegitimate government actions. Differences of opinion over the optimal mix of the two provide much of the substantive content of political conflict within established democracies.

"However central to democracy, elections occur intermittently and only allow citizens to choose between the highly aggregated alternatives offered by political parties . . ."

Citizens are the most distinctive element in democracies. All regimes have rulers and a public realm, but only to the extent that they are democratic do they have citizens. Historically, severe restrictions on citizenship were imposed in most emerging or partial democracies according to criteria of age, gender, class, race, literacy, property ownership, tax-paying status, and so on. Only a small part of the total population was eligible to vote or run for office. Only restricted social categories were allowed to form, join, or support political associations. After protracted struggle—in some cases involving violent domestic upheaval or international war—most of these restrictions were lifted. Today, the criteria for inclusion are fairly standard. All native-born adults are eligible, although somewhat higher age limits may still be imposed upon candidates for certain offices. Unlike the early American and European democracies of the nineteenth century, none of the recent democracies in south-

ern Europe, Latin America, Asia, or Eastern Europe has even attempted to impose formal restrictions on the franchise or eligibility to office. When it comes to informal restrictions on the effective exercise of citizenship rights, however, the story can be quite different. This explains the central importance (discussed below) of procedures.

Competition has not always been considered an essential defining condition of democracy. "Classic" democracies presumed decision making based on direct participation leading to consensus. The assembled citizenry was expected to agree on a common course of action after listening to the alternatives and weighing their respective merits and demerits. A tradition of hostility to "faction," and "particular interests" persists in democratic thought, but at least since *The Federalist Papers* it has become widely accepted that competition among factions is a necessary evil in democracies that operate on a more-than-local scale. Since, as James Madison argued, "the latent causes of faction are sown into the nature of man," and the possible remedies for "the mischief of faction" are worse than the disease, the best course is to recognize them and to attempt to control their effects.[6] Yet while democrats may agree on the inevitability of factions, they tend to disagree about the best forms and rules for governing factional competition. Indeed, differences over the preferred modes and boundaries of competition contribute most to distinguishing one subtype of democracy from another.

The most popular definition of democracy equates it with regular *elections,* fairly conducted and honestly counted. Some even consider the mere fact of elections—even ones from which specific parties or candidates are excluded, or in which substantial portions of the population cannot freely participate—as a sufficient condition for the existence of democracy. This fallacy has been called "electoralism" or "the faith that merely holding elections will channel political action into peaceful contests among elites and accord public legitimacy to the winners"—no matter how they are conducted or what else constrains those who win them.[7] However central to democracy, elections occur intermittently and only allow citizens to choose between the highly aggregated alternatives offered by political parties, which can, especially in the early stages of a democratic transition, proliferate in a bewildering variety. During the intervals between elections, citizens can seek to influence public policy through a wide variety of other intermediaries: interest associations, social movements, locality groupings, clientelistic arrangements, and so forth. *Modern democracy, in other words, offers a variety of competitive processes and channels for the expression of interests and values—associational as well as partisan, functional as well as territorial, collective as well as individual. All are integral to its practice.*

Another commonly accepted image of democracy identifies it with *majority rule.* Any governing body that makes decisions by combining the votes of more than half of those eligible and present is said to be democratic, whether that majority emerges within an electorate, a parliament, a committee, a city council, or a party caucus. For exceptional purposes (e.g., amending the constitution or expelling a member), "qualified majorities" of more than 50 percent may be required, but few would deny that democracy must involve some means of aggregating the equal preferences of individuals.

A problem arises, however, when *numbers* meet *intensities*. What happens when a properly assembled majority (especially a stable, self-perpetuating one) regularly makes decisions that harm some minority (especially a threatened cultural or ethnic group)? In these circumstances, successful democracies tend to qualify the central principle of majority rule in order to protect minority rights. Such qualifications can take the form of constitutional provisions that place certain matters beyond the reach of majorities (bills of rights); requirements for concurrent majorities in several different constituencies (confederalism); guarantees securing the autonomy of local or regional governments against the demands of the central authority (federalism); grand coalition governments that incorporate all parties (consociationalism); or the negotiation of social pacts between major social groups like business and labor (neocorporatism). The most common and effective way of protecting minorities, however, lies in the everyday operation of interest associations and social movements. These reflect (some would say, amplify) the different intensities of preference that exist in the population and bring them to bear on democratically elected decision makers. Another way of putting this intrinsic tension between numbers and intensities would be to say that "in modern democracies, votes may be counted, but influences alone are weighted."

Cooperation has always been a central feature of democracy. Actors must voluntarily make collective decisions binding on the polity as a whole. They must cooperate in order to compete. They must be capable of acting collectively through parties, associations, and movements in order to select candidates, articulate preferences, petition authorities, and influence policies.

But democracy's freedoms should also encourage citizens to deliberate among themselves, to discover their common needs, and to resolve their differences without relying on some supreme central authority. Classical democracy emphasized these qualities, and they are by no means extinct, despite repeated efforts by contemporary theorists to stress the analogy with behavior in the economic marketplace and to reduce all of democracy's operations to competitive interest maximization. Alexis de Tocqueville best described the importance of independent groups for democracy in his *Democracy in America*, a work which remains a major source of inspiration for all those who persist in viewing democracy as something more than a struggle for election and re-election among competing candidates.[8]

In contemporary political discourse, this phenomenon of cooperation and deliberation via autonomous group activity goes under the rubric of "civil society." The diverse units of social identity and interest, by remaining independent of the state (and perhaps even of parties), not only can restrain the arbitrary actions of rulers, but can also contribute to forming better citizens who are more aware of the preferences of others, more self-confident in their actions, and more civic-minded in their willingness to sacrifice for the common good. At its best, civil society provides an intermediate layer of governance between the individual and the state that is capable of resolving conflicts and controlling the behavior of members without public coercion. Rather than overloading decision makers with increased demands and making the system ungovernable,[9] a viable civil society can mitigate conflicts and improve the quality of citizenship—without relying exclusively on the privatism of the marketplace.

Representatives—whether directly or indirectly elected—do most of the real work in modern democracies. Most are professional politicians who orient their careers around the desire to fill key offices. It is doubtful that any democracy could survive without such people. The central question, therefore, is not whether or not there will be a political elite or even a professional political class, but how these representatives are chosen and then held accountable for their actions.

As noted above, there are many channels of representation in modern democracy. The electoral one, based on territorial constituencies, is the most visible and public. It culminates in a parliament or a presidency that is periodically accountable to the citizenry as a whole. Yet the sheer growth of government (in large part as a byproduct of popular demand) has increased the number, variety, and power of agencies charged with making public decisions and not subject to elections. Around these agencies there has developed a vast apparatus of specialized representation based largely on functional interests, not territorial constituencies. These interest associations, and not political parties, have become the primary expression of civil society in most stable democracies, supplemented by the more sporadic interventions of social movements.

The new and fragile democracies that have sprung up since 1974 must live in "compressed time." They will not resemble the European democracies of the nineteenth and early twentieth centuries, and they cannot expect to acquire the multiple channels of representation in gradual historical progression as did most of their predecessors. A bewildering array of parties, interests, and movements will all simultaneously seek political influence in them, creating challenges to the polity that did not exist in earlier processes of democratization.

PROCEDURES THAT MAKE DEMOCRACY POSSIBLE

The defining components of democracy are necessarily abstract, and may give rise to a considerable variety of institutions and subtypes of democracy. For democracy to thrive, however, specific procedural norms must be followed and civic rights must be respected. Any polity that fails to impose such restrictions upon itself, that fails to follow the "rule of law" with regard to its own procedures, should not be considered democratic. These procedures alone do not define democracy, but their presence is indispensable to its persistence. In essence, they are necessary but not sufficient conditions for its existence.

Robert Dahl has offered the most generally accepted listing of what he terms the "procedural minimal" conditions that must be present for modern political democracy (or as he puts it, "polyarchy") to exist:

1. Control over government decisions about policy is constitutionally vested in elected officials.
2. Elected officials are chosen in frequent and fairly conducted elections in which coercion is comparatively uncommon.
3. Practically all adults have the right to vote in the election of officials.
4. Practically all adults have the right to run for elective offices in the government. . . .
5. Citizens have a right to express themselves without the danger of severe punishment on political matters broadly defined. . . .
6. Citizens have a right to seek out alternative sources of information. Moreover, alternative sources of information exist and are protected by law.
7. . . . Citizens also have the right to form relatively independent associations or organizations, including independent political parties and interest groups.[10]

These seven conditions seem to capture the essence of procedural democracy for many theorists, but we propose to add two others. The first might be thought of as a further refinement of item (1), while the second might be called an implicit prior condition to all seven of the above.

8. Popularly elected officials must be able to exercise their constitutional powers without being subjected to overriding (albeit informal) opposition from unelected officials. Democracy is in jeopardy if military officers, entrenched civil servants, or state managers retain the capacity to act independently of elected civilians or even veto decisions made by the people's representatives. Without this additional caveat, the militarized polities of contemporary Central America, where civilian control over the military does not exist, might be classified by many scholars as democracies, just as they have been (with the exception of Sandinista Nicaragua) by U.S. policy makers. The caveat thus guards against what we earlier called "electoralism"—the tendency to focus on the holding of elections while ignoring other political realities.
9. The polity must be self-governing; it must be able to act independently of constraints imposed by some other overarching political system. Dahl and other contemporary democratic theorists probably took

this condition for granted since they referred to formally sovereign nation-states. However, with the development of blocs, alliances, spheres of influence, and a variety of "neocolonial" arrangements, the question of autonomy has been a salient one. Is a system really democratic if its elected officials are unable to make binding decisions without the approval of actors outside their territorial domain? This is significant even if the outsiders are relatively free to alter or even end the encompassing arrangement (as in Puerto Rico), but it becomes especially critical if neither condition obtains (as in the Baltic states).

PRINCIPLES THAT MAKE DEMOCRACY FEASIBLE

Lists of component processes and procedural norms help us to specify what democracy is, but they do not tell us much about how it actually functions. The simplest answer is "by the consent of the people"; the more complex one is "by the contingent consent of politicians acting under conditions of bounded uncertainty."

In a democracy, representatives must at least informally agree that those who win greater electoral support or influence over policy will not use their temporary superiority to bar the losers from taking office or exerting influence in the future, and that in exchange for this opportunity to keep competing for power and place, momentary losers will respect the winners' right to make binding decisions. Citizens are expected to obey the decisions ensuing from such a process of competition, provided its outcome remains contingent upon their collective preferences as expressed through fair and regular elections or open and repeated negotiations.

The challenge is not so much to find a set of goals that command widespread consensus as to find a set of rules that embody contingent consent. The precise shape of this "democratic bargain," to use Dahl's expression,[11] can vary a good deal from society to society. It depends on social cleavages and such subjective factors as mutual trust, the standard of fairness, and the willingness to compromise. It may even be compatible with a great deal of dissensus on substantive policy issues.

All democracies involve a degree of uncertainty about who will be elected and what policies they will pursue. Even in those polities where one party persists in winning elections or one policy is consistently implemented, the possibility of change through independent collective action still exists, as in Italy, Japan, and the Scandinavian social democracies. If it does not, the system is not democratic, as in Mexico, Senegal, or Indonesia.

But the uncertainty embedded in the core of all democracies is bounded. Not just any actor can get into the competition and raise any issue he or she pleases—there are previously established rules that must be respected. Not just any policy can be adopted—there are conditions that must be met. Democracy institutionalizes "normal," limited political uncertainty. These boundaries vary from country to country. Constitutional guarantees of property, privacy, expression, and other rights are a part of this, but the most effective boundaries are generated by competition among interest groups and cooperation within civil society. Whatever the rhetoric (and some polities appear to offer their citizens more dramatic alternatives than others), once the rules of contingent consent have been agreed upon, the actual variation is likely to stay within a predictable and generally accepted range.

This emphasis on operative guidelines contrasts with a highly persistent, but misleading theme in recent literature on democracy—namely, the emphasis upon "civic culture." The principles we have suggested here rest on rules of prudence, not on deeply ingrained habits of tolerance, moderation, mutual respect, fair play, readiness to compromise, or trust in public authorities. Waiting for such habits to sink deep and lasting roots implies a very slow process of regime consolidation—one that takes generations—and it would probably condemn most contemporary experiences *ex hypothesi* to failure. Our assertion is that contingent consent and bounded uncertainty can emerge from the interaction between antagonistic and mutually suspicious actors and that the far more benevolent and ingrained norms of a civic culture are better thought of as a *product* and not a producer of democracy.

HOW DEMOCRACIES DIFFER

Several concepts have been deliberately excluded from our generic definition of democracy, despite the fact that they have been frequently associated with it in both everyday practice and scholarly work. They are, nevertheless, especially important when it comes to distinguishing subtypes of democracy. Since no single set of actual institutions, practices, or values embodies democracy, polities moving away from authoritarian rule can mix different components to produce different democracies. It is important to recognize that these do not define points along a single continuum of improving performance, but a matrix of potential combinations that are *differently* democratic.

1. *Consensus:* All citizens may not agree on the substantive goals of political action or on the role of the state (although if they did, it would certainly make governing democracies much easier).
2. *Participation:* All citizens may not take an active and equal part in politics, although it must be legally possible for them to do so.
3. *Access:* Rulers may not weigh equally the preferences of all who come before them, although citizenship implies that individuals and groups should have an equal opportunity to express their preferences if they choose to do so.
4. *Responsiveness:* Rulers may not always follow the course of action preferred by the citizenry. But when

they deviate from such a policy, say on grounds of "reason of state" or "overriding national interest," they must ultimately be held accountable for their actions through regular and fair processes.
5. *Majority rule:* Positions may not be allocated or rules may not be decided solely on the basis of assembling the most votes, although deviations from this principle usually must be explicitly defended and previously approved.
6. *Parliamentary sovereignty:* The legislature may not be the only body that can make rules or even the one with final authority in deciding which laws are binding, although where executive, judicial, or other public bodies make that ultimate choice, they too must be accountable for their actions.
7. *Party government:* Rulers may not be nominated, promoted, and disciplined in their activities by well-organized and programmatically coherent political parties, although where they are not, it may prove more difficult to form an effective government.
8. *Pluralism:* The political process may not be based on a multiplicity of overlapping, voluntaristic, and autonomous private groups. However, where there are monopolies of representation, hierarchies of association, and obligatory memberships, it is likely that the interests involved will be more closely linked to the state and the separation between the public and private spheres of action will be much less distinct.
9. *Federalism:* The territorial division of authority may not involve multiple levels and local autonomies, least of all ones enshrined in a constitutional document, although some dispersal of power across territorial and/or functional units is characteristic of all democracies.
10. *Presidentialism:* The chief executive officer may not be a single person and he or she may not be directly elected by the citizenry as a whole, although some concentration of authority is present in all democracies, even if it is exercised collectively and only held indirectly accountable to the electorate.
11. *Checks and Balances:* It is not necessary that the different branches of government be systematically pitted against one another, although governments by assembly, by executive concentrations, by judicial command, or even by dictatorial fiat (as in time of war) must be ultimately accountable to the citizenry as a whole.

While each of the above has been named as an essential component of democracy, they should instead be seen either as indicators of this or that type of democracy, or else as useful standards for evaluating the performance of particular regimes. To include them as part of the generic definition of democracy itself would be to mistake the American polity for the universal model of democratic governance. Indeed, the parliamentary, consociational, unitary, corporatist, and concentrated arrangements of continental Europe may have some unique virtues for guiding polities through the uncertain transition from autocratic to democratic rule.[12]

WHAT DEMOCRACY IS NOT

We have attempted to convey the general meaning of modern democracy without identifying it with some particular set of rules and institutions or restricting it to some specific culture or level of development. We have also argued that it cannot be reduced to the regular holding of elections or equated with a particular notion of the role of the state, but we have not said much more about what democracy is not or about what democracy may not be capable of producing.

There is an understandable temptation to load too many expectations on this concept and to imagine that by attaining democracy, a society will have resolved all of its political, social, economic, administrative, and cultural problems. Unfortunately, "all good things do not necessarily go together."

First, democracies are not necessarily more efficient economically than other forms of government. Their rates of aggregate growth, savings, and investment may be no better than those of nondemocracies. This is especially likely during the transition, when propertied groups and administrative elites may respond to real or imagined threats to the "rights" they enjoyed under authoritarian rule by initiating capital flight, disinvestment, or sabotage. In time, depending upon the type of democracy, benevolent long-term effects upon income distribution, aggregate demand, education, productivity, and creativity may eventually combine to improve economic and social performance, but it is certainly too much to expect that these improvements will occur immediately—much less that they will be defining characteristics of democratization.

Second, democracies are not necessarily more efficient administratively. Their capacity to make decisions may even be slower than that of the regimes they replace, if only because more actors must be consulted. The costs of getting things done may be higher, if only because "payoffs" have to be made to a wider and more resourceful set of clients (although one should never underestimate the degree of corruption to be found within autocracies). Popular satisfaction with the new democratic government's performance may not even seem greater, if only because necessary compromises often please no one completely, and because the losers are free to complain.

Third, democracies are not likely to appear more orderly, consensual, stable, or governable than the autocracies they replace. This is partly a byproduct of democratic freedom of expression, but it is also a reflection of the likelihood of continuing disagreement over new rules and institutions. These products of imposition or compromise are often initially quite ambiguous in nature and uncertain in effect until actors have learned how to use them. What is more, they come in the aftermath of serious struggles motivated by high ideals. Groups and individuals with recently acquired autonomy will test certain rules, protest against the actions of certain institutions, and insist on renegotiating their part of the bargain. Thus the presence of antisystem parties should be neither surprising nor seen as a failure of democratic consolidation. What counts is whether such parties are willing, however reluctantly, to play by the general rules of bounded uncertainty and contingent consent.

Governability is a challenge for all regimes, not just democratic ones. Given the political exhaustion and loss of legitimacy that have befallen autocracies from sultanistic Paraguay to totalitarian Albania, it may seem that only democracies can now be expected to govern effectively and legitimately. Experience has shown, however, that democracies too can lose the ability to govern. Mass publics can become disenchanted with their performance. Even more threatening is the temptation for leaders to fiddle with procedures and ultimately undermine the principles of contingent consent and bounded uncertainty. Perhaps the most critical moment comes once the politicians begin to settle into the more predictable roles and relations of a consolidated democracy. Many will find their expectations frustrated; some will discover that the new rules of competition put them at a disadvantage; a few may even feel that their vital interests are threatened by popular majorities.

" . . . democracies will have more open societies and polities than the autocracies they replace, but not necessarily more open economies."

Finally, democracies will have more open societies and polities than the autocracies they replace, but not necessarily more open economies. Many of today's most successful and well-established democracies have historically resorted to protectionism and closed borders, and have relied extensively upon public institutions to promote economic development. While the long-term compatibility between democracy and capitalism does not seem to be in doubt, despite their continuous tension, it is not clear whether the promotion of such liberal economic goals as the right of individuals to own property and retain profits, the clearing function of markets, the private settlement of disputes, the freedom to produce without government regulation, or the privatization of state-owned enterprises necessarily furthers the consolidation of democracy. After all, democracies do need to levy taxes and regulate certain transactions, especially where private monopolies and oligopolies exist. Citizens or their representatives may decide that it is desirable to protect the rights of collectivities from encroachment by individuals, especially propertied ones, and they may choose to set aside certain forms of property for public or cooperative ownership. In short, notions of economic liberty that are currently put forward in neoliberal economic models are not synonymous with political freedom—and may even impede it.

Democratization will not necessarily bring in its wake economic growth, social peace, administrative efficiency, political harmony, free markets, or "the end of ideology." Least of all will it bring about "the end of history." No doubt some of these qualities could make the consolidation of democracy easier, but they are neither prerequisites for it nor immediate products of it. Instead, what we should be hoping for is the emergence of political institutions that can peacefully compete to form governments and influence public policy, that can channel social and economic conflicts through regular procedures, and that have sufficient linkages to civil society to represent their constituencies and commit them to collective courses of action. Some types of democracies, especially in developing countries, have been unable to fulfill this promise, perhaps due to the circumstances of their transition from authoritarian rule.[13] The democratic wager is that such a regime, once established, will not only persist by reproducing itself within its initial confining conditions, but will eventually expand beyond them.[14] Unlike authoritarian regimes, democracies have the capacity to modify their rules and institutions consensually in response to changing circumstances. They may not immediately produce all the goods mentioned above, but they stand a better chance of eventually doing so than do autocracies.

NOTES

1. For a comparative analysis of the recent regime changes in southern Europe and Latin America, see Guillermo O'Donnell, Philippe C. Schmitter, and Laurence Whitehead, eds., *Transitions from Authoritarian Rule*, 4 vols. (Baltimore: Johns Hopkins University Press, 1986). For another compilation that adopts a more structural approach see Larry Diamond, Juan Linz, and Seymour Martin Lipset, eds., *Democracy in Developing Countries*, vols. 2, 3, and 4 (Boulder, Colo.: Lynne Rienner, 1989).

2. Numerous attempts have been made to codify and quantify the existence of democracy across political systems. The best known is probably Freedom House's *Freedom in the World: Political Rights and Civil Liberties*, published since 1973 by Greenwood Press and since 1988 by University Press of America. Also see Charles Humana, *World Human Rights Guide* (New York: Facts on File, 1986).

3. The definition most commonly used by American social scientists is that of Joseph Schumpeter: "that institutional arrangement for arriving at political decisions in which individuals acquire the power to decide by means of a competitive struggle for the people's vote." *Capitalism, Socialism, and Democracy* (London: George Allen and Unwin, 1943), 269. We accept certain aspects of the classical procedural approach to modern democracy, but differ primarily in our emphasis on the accountability of rulers to citizens and the relevance of mechanisms of competition other than elections.

4. Not only do some countries practice a stable form of democracy without a formal constitution (e.g., Great Britain and Israel), but even more countries have constitutions and legal codes that offer no guarantee of reliable practice. On paper, Stalin's 1936 constitution for the USSR was a virtual model of democratic rights and entitlements.

5. For the most valiant attempt to make some sense out of this thicket of distinctions, see Juan Linz, "Totalitarian and Authoritarian Regimes" in *Handbook of Political Science*, eds. Fred I. Greenstein and Nelson W. Polsby (Reading Mass.: Addison Wesley, 1975), 175–411.

6. "Publius" (Alexander Hamilton, John Jay, and James Madison), *The Federalist Papers* (New York: Anchor Books, 1961). The quote is from Number 10.

7. See Terry Karl, "Imposing Consent? Electoralism versus Democratization in El Salvador," in *Elections and Democratization in Latin America, 1980–1985*, eds. Paul Drake and Eduardo Silva (San Diego: Center for Iberian and Latin American Studies, Center for US/Mexican Studies, University of California, San Diego, 1986), 9–36.

8. Alexis de Tocqueville, *Democracy in America*, 2 vols. (New York: Vintage Books, 1945).

9. This fear of overloaded government and the imminent collapse of democracy is well reflected in the work of Samuel P. Huntington during the 1970s. See especially Michel Crozier, Samuel P. Huntington, and Joji Watanuki, *The Crisis of Democracy* (New York: New York University Press, 1975). For Huntington's (revised) thoughts about the prospects for democracy, see his "Will More Countries Become Democratic?," *Political Science Quarterly* 99 (Summer 1984): 193–218.

10. Robert Dahl, *Dilemmas of Pluralist Democracy* (New Haven: Yale University Press, 1982), 11.

11. Robert Dahl, *After the Revolution: Authority in a Good Society* (New Haven: Yale University Press, 1970).

12. See Juan Linz, "The Perils of Presidentialism," *Journal of Democracy* 1 (Winter 1990): 51–69, and the ensuing discussion by Donald Horowitz, Seymour Martin Lipset, and Juan Linz in *Journal of Democracy* 1 (Fall 1990): 73–91.

13. Terry Lynn Karl, "Dilemmas of Democratization in Latin America," *Comparative Politics* 23 (October 1990): 1–23.

14. Otto Kirchheimer, "Confining Conditions and Revolutionary Breakthroughs," *American Political Science Review* 59 (1965): 964–974.

Parliament and Congress:

Is the Grass Greener on the other side?

Gregory S. Mahler

Gregory Mahler is chair of the Political Science Department at the University of Mississippi.

Aristotle long ago observed that man is a "political animal." He could have added that man, by his very nature, notes the political status of his neighbours and, very often, perceives their lot as being superior to his own. The old saying "the grass is greener on the other side of the fence" can be applied to politics and political structures as well as to other, more material, dimensions of the contemporary world.

Legislators are not immune from the very human tendency to see how others of their lot exist in their respective settings, and, sometimes, to look longingly at these other settings. When legislators do look around to see the conditions under which their peers operate in other countries, they occasionally decide they prefer the alternative legislative settings to their own.

Features which legislators admire or envy in the settings of their colleagues include such things as: the characteristics of political parties (their numbers, or degrees of party discipline), legislative committee systems, staff and services available to help legislators in their tasks, office facilities, libraries, and salaries. This essay will develop the "grass is greener" theme in relation to a dimension of the legislative world which is regularly a topic of conversation when legislators from a number of different jurisdictions meet: the ability or inability of legislatures to check and control the executive.

The Decline of Parliament

The theme of the "decline of parliament" has a long and well-studied history.[1] It generally refers to the gradual flow of true legislative power away from the legislative body in the direction of the executive. The executive does the real law-making — by actually drafting most legislation — and the legislature takes a more "passive" role by simply approving executive proposals.

Legislators are very concerned about their duties and powers and over the years have jealously guarded them when they have appeared to be threatened. In Canada (and indeed most parliamentary democracies in the world today), the majority of challenges to legislative power which develop no longer come from the ceremonial executive (the Crown), but from the political executive, the government of the day.

It can be argued that the ability to direct and influence public policy, is a "zero sum game" (i.e. there is only room for a

limited amount of power and influence to be exercised in the political world and a growth in the relative power of the political executive must be at the expense of the power of the legislature). It follows, then, that if the legislature is concerned about maintaining its powers, concerned about protecting its powers from being diminished, it must be concerned about every attempt by the political executive to expand its powers.

Others contend that real "legislative power" cannot, and probably never did reside in the legislature. There was no "Golden Age" of Parliament. The true legislative role of parliament today is not (and in the past was not) to create legislation, but to scrutinize and ratify legislation introduced by the Government of the day. Although an occasional exception to this pattern of behavior may exist (with private members' bills, for example), the general rule is clear: the legislature today does not actively initiate legislation as its primary *raison d'être*.

Although parliamentarians may not be major initiators of legislation, studies have indicated a wide range of other functions.[2] Certainly one major role of the legislature is the "oversight" role, criticizing and checking the powers of the executive. The ultimate extension of this power is the ability of the legislature to terminate the term of office of the executive through a "no confidence" vote. Another role of the legislature involves communication and representation of constituency concerns. Yet another function involves the debating function, articulating the concerns of the public of the day.

Professor James Mallory has indicated the need to "be realistic about the role of Parliament in the Westminster system."[3] He cites Bernard Crick's classic work, *The Reform of Parliament*: "...the phrase 'Parliamentary control, and talk about the 'decline of parliamentary control,' should not mislead anyone into asking for a situation in which governments can have their legislation changed or defeated, or their life terminated... Control means influence, not direct power; advice, not command; criticism, not obstruction; scrutiny, not initiation; and publicity, not secrecy."[4]

The fact that parliament may not be paramount in the creation and processing of legislation is no reason to condemn all aspects of parliamentary institutions. Nor should parliamentarians be convinced that legislative life is perfect in the presidential-congressional system. In fact, some American legislators look to their parliamentary brethren and sigh with envy at the attractiveness of certain aspects of parliamentary institutions.

Reprinted courtesy of *Canadian Parliamentary Review*, Winter 1985–86, pp. 19–21.

Desirability of a Congressional Model for Canada?

Many Canadian parliamentarians and students of parliament look upon presidential-congressional institutions of the United States as possessing the answers to most of their problems. The grass is sometimes seen as being greener on the other side of the border. The concepts of fixed legislative terms, less party discipline, and a greater general emphasis on the role and importance of individual legislators (which implies more office space and staff for individual legislators, among other things) are seen as standards to which Canadian legislators should aspire.

A perceived strength of the American congressional system is that legislators do not automatically "rubber stamp" approve executive proposals. They consider the president's suggestions, but feel free to make substitutions or modifications to the proposal, or even to reject it completely. Party discipline is relatively weak; there are regularly Republican legislators opposing a Republican president (and Democratic legislators supporting him), and vice versa. Against the need for discipline congressmen argue that their first duty is to either (a) their constituency, or (b) what is "right", rather than simply to party leaders telling them how to behave in the legislature. For example, in 1976 Jimmy Carter was elected President with large majorities of Democrats in both houses of Congress. One of Carter's major concerns was energy policy. He introduced legislative proposals (that is, he had congressional supporters introduce legislation, since the American president cannot introduce legislation on his own) dealing with energy policy, calling his proposals "the moral equivalent of war." In his speeches and public appearances he did everything he could to muster support for "his" legislation. Two years later when "his" legislation finally emerged from the legislative process, it could hardly be recognized as the proposals submitted in such emotional terms two years earlier.

The experience of President Carter was certainly not unique. Any number of examples of such incidents of legislative-executive non-cooperation can be cited in recent American political history, ranging from President Wilson's unsuccessful efforts to get the United States to join the League of Nations, through Ronald Reagan's contemporary battles with Congress over the size of the federal budget. The Carter experience was somewhat unusual by virtue of the fact that the same political party controlled both the executive and legislative branches of government, and cooperation still was not forthcoming. There have been many more examples of non-cooperation when one party has controlled the White House and another party has controlled one or both houses of Congress.

This lack of party discipline ostensibly enables the individual legislators to be concerned about the special concerns of their constituencies. This, they say, is more important than simply having to follow the orders of the party whip in the legislature. It is not any more unusual to find a Republican legislator from a farm state voting against a specific agricultural proposal of President Reagan on the grounds that the legislation in question is not good for his/her constituency, than to find Democratic legislators from the southwestern states who voted against President Carter's water policy proposals on the grounds that the proposals were not good for their constituencies.

Congressional legislators know that they have fixed terms in office — the President is simply not able to bring about early

elections — and they know that as long as they can keep their constituencies happy there is no need to be terribly concerned about opposing the President, even if he is the leader of their party. It may be nice to have the President on your side, but if you have a strong base of support "back home" you can survive without his help.

Are there any benefits to the public interest in the absence of party discipline? The major argument is that the legislature will independently consider the executive's proposals, rather than simply accepting the executive's ideas passively. This, it is claimed, allows for a multiplicity of interests, concerns, and perspectives to be represented in the legislature, and ostensibly results in "better" legislation.

In summary, American legislative institutions promote the role of the individual legislator. The fixed term gives legislators the security necessary for the performance of the functions they feel are important. The (relative) lack of party discipline enables legislators to act on the issues about which they are concerned. In terms of the various legislative functions mentioned above, congressmen appear to spend a great deal of their time in what has been termed the legislative aspect of the job: drafting legislation, debating, proposing amendments, and voting (on a more or less independent basis).

While many parliamentarians are impressed by the ability of individual American legislator to act on their own volition it is ironic that many congressional legislators look longingly at the legislative power relationships of their parliamentary brethren. The grass, apparently, is greener on the *other* side of the border, too.

Desirability of a Parliamentary Model

The "decline of congressional power" is as popular a topic of conversation in Washington as "the decline of parliamentary power" in Ottawa or London. Over the last several decades American legislators have sensed that a great deal of legislative power has slipped from their collective grasp.[5] Many have decried this tendency and tried to stop, or reverse this flow of power away from the legislative branch and toward the executive.

One of the major themes in the writings of these congressional activists is an admiration for the parliamentary model's (perceived) power over the executive. Many American legislators see the president's veto power, combined with his fixed term in office, as a real flaw in the "balance of powers" of the system, leading to an inexorable increase in executive power at the expense of the legislature. They look at a number of parliamentary structures which they see as promoting democratic political behavior and increased executive responsibility to the legislature, including the ability to force the resignation of the executive through a non-confidence vote. The regular "question period" format which insures some degree of public executive accountability is also perceived as being very attractive .

Critics of the congressional system do not confine their criticism only to the growth of executive power. There are many who feel there is too much freedom in the congressional arena. To paraphrase the words of Bernard Crick cited earlier, advising has sometimes turned into issuing commands; and criticism has sometimes turned into obstruction. This is not to suggest that congressional legislators would support giving up their ability to initiate legislation, to amend executive proposals, or to vote in a manner which they (individually) deem proper. This does suggest, however, that even congressional legislators see that independence is a two-sided coin: one side involves individual legislative autonomy and input into the legislative process; the other side involves the incompatibility of complete independence with a British style of "Responsible Government".

In 1948 Hubert Humphrey, then mayor of Minneapolis, delivered an address at the nomination convention of the Democratic Party. In his comments he appealed for a "more responsible" two party system in the United States, a system with sufficient party discipline to have *meaningful* party labels, and to allow party platforms to become public policy.[6] Little progress has been made over the last thirty-seven years in this regard. In the abstract the concept of a *meaningful* two party system may be attractive; American legislators have not been as attracted to the necessary corollary of the concept: decreased legislative independence and increased party discipline.

While American Senators and Representatives are very jealous of executive encroachments upon their powers, there is some recognition that on occasion — usually depending upon individual legislators' views about the desirability of specific pieces of legislation — executive leadership, and perhaps party discipline, can serve a valuable function. Congressional legislators are, at times which correspond to their policy preferences, envious of parliamentary governnments' abilities to carry their programs into law because MPs elected under their party labels will act consistent with party whips' directions. They would be loath to give up their perceived high degrees of legislative freedom but many of them realize the cost of this freedom in this era of pressing social problems and complex legislation. Parliamentary style government is simply not possible without party discipline.

A Democratic Congressman supporting President Carter's energy policy proposals might have longed for an effective three-line whip to help to pass the energy policies in question. An opponent of those policy proposals would have argued, to the contrary, that the frustration of the president's proposals was a good illustration of the wisdom of the legislature tempering the error-ridden policy proposals of the president. Similarly, many conservative Republican supporters of President Reagan have condemned the ability of the Democratic House of Representatives to frustrate his economic policies. Opponents of those policies have argued, again, that the House of Representatives is doing an important job of representing public opinion and is exercising a valuable and important check on the misguided policies of the executive.

Some Concluding Observations

The parliamentary model has its strengths as well as its weaknesses. The individual legislator in a parliamentary system does not have as active a role in the actual legislative process as does his American counterparts, but it is not at all hard to imagine instances in which the emphasis on individual autonomy in the congressional system can be counterproductive because it delays much-needed legislative programs.

The problem, ultimately, is one of balance. Is it possible to have a responsible party system in the context of parliamentary democracy which can deliver on its promises to the public, and also to have a high degree of individual legislative autonomy in the legislative arena?

It is hard to imagine how those two concepts could coexist. The congressional and parliamentary models of legislative behavior have placed their respective emphases on two different priorities. The parliamentary model, with its responsible party system and its corresponding party discipline in the legislature, emphasizes efficient policy delivery, and the ability of an elected government to deliver on its promises. The congressional model, with its lack of party discipline and its emphasis on individual legislative autonomy, placed more emphasis on what can be called "consensual politics": it may take much more time for executive proposals to find their way into law, but (the argument goes) there is greater likelihood that what does, ultimately, emerge as law will be acceptable to a greater number of people than if government proposals were "automatically" approved by a pre-existing majority in the legislature acting "under the whip".

We cannot say that one type of legislature is "more effective" than the other. Each maximizes effectiveness in different aspects of the legislative function. Legislators in the congressional system, because of their greater legislative autonomy and weaker party discipline, are more effective at actually legislating than they are at exercising ultimate control over the executive. Legislators in the parliamentary system, although they may play more of a "ratifying" role in regard to legislation, do get legislation passed promptly; they also have an ultimate power over the life of the government of the day.

The appropriateness of both models must also be evaluated in light of the different history, political culture and objectives of the societies in which they operate. Perhaps the grass is just as green on both sides of the fence.

Notes

[1] There is substantial literature devoted to the general topic of "the decline of legislatures." Among the many sources which could be referred to in this area would be included the work of Gerhard Loewenberg. *Modern Parliaments: Change or Decline?* Chicago: Atherton. 1971; Gerhard Loewenberg and Samuel Patterson, *Comparing Legislatures*, Boston: Little, Brown, 1979; or Samuel Patterson and John Wahlke, eds., *Comparative Legislative Behavior: Frontiers of Research*, New York: John Wiley, 1972.

[2] A very common topic in studies of legislative behavior has to do with the various functions legislatures may be said to perform for the societies of which they are a part. For a discussion of the many functions attributed to legislatures in political science literature, see Gregory Mahler, *Comparative Politics: An Institutional and Cross-National Approach* (Cambridge, Ma.: Schenkman, 1983, pp. 56-61.

[3] J. R. Mallory, "Can Parliament Control the Regulatory Process?" *Canadian Parliamentary Review* Vol. 6 (no. 3, 1983) p. 6.

[4] Bernard Crick, *The Reform of Parliament*, London, 1968, p. 80.

[5] One very well written discussion of the decline of American congressional power in relation to the power of the president can be found in Ronald Moe, ed., *Congress and the President*, Pacific Palisades, Calif.: Goodyear Publishing Co., 1971.

[6] Subsequently a special report was published by the Committee on Political Parties of the American Political Science Association dealing with this problem. See "Toward a More Responsible Two-Party System," *American Political Science Review* Vol. 44 (no. 3, 1950), special supplement.

ELECTORAL REFORM

Good government? Fairness?
Or vice versa. Or both

Italians want to junk proportional representation. Others could usefully adopt it. Which electoral system is best? The arguments are many. So are the answers

BRITAIN elects its House of Commons by the simplest possible system: single-member constituencies in which the front-runner wins, even if he has under 50% of the votes. In 1983, 7.8m votes, a quarter of the total, went to the "third party", the Alliance. It got 23 seats. The Labour Party got 8.5m votes—and 209 seats. No wonder half of all Britons say they would like a fairer system.

Italy uses systems of proportional representation (PR) that are elaborately fair. It has also had 52 governments, mostly coalitions, since 1945, all dominated by the Christian Democrats. Italian government is famously inept, its parties—not only the Christian Democrats—infamously corrupt. No wonder Italians have just voted massively to adopt the British system for three-quarters of their Senate seats; the Chamber of Deputies will probably go much the same way.

These two countries exemplify—in parody—the arguments about electoral reform. Britain's "first past the post" system (FPTP) nearly always produces a single-party government with an overall, and solid, Commons majority. Unless that party itself is split—as now, over the Maastricht treaty—the government can override all opposition. The result, given a decisive prime minister, should always be decisive government.

In contrast, look at Italy, Israel or Poland. Their PR is as fair as it comes. Umpteen parties, even tiny ones with 1-2% of the national vote, can win seats. With 3% or 4%,

they can make or break policies and governments, as Israel's religious parties notoriously have done. It sounds like a recipe for feeble government, with the tail—as the enemies of PR put it—wagging the dog.

The choice looks clear: good government or fair representation? In fact, not so. British governments have often been feeble; Israel's often decisive, even fierce. Italy's governments are unstable and inept; not so Germany's, although the Bundestag they rest on is shaped by PR. True, it keeps out small parties. Yet most post-1949 German governments have had a "tail", the Free Democrats (FDP).

As for the corruption now disgusting Italy's voters, its cause, arguably, is too long tenure of office, not the electoral system. Japan has no formal PR, but its ever-ruling Liberal Democrats are hardly clean. True, PR at times prevents complete clear-outs of government; but the parties that stay in office, despite swings among voters, are usually small, as in Germany (Italy is a special case; its large Communist party was not acceptable as an alternative in government to the Christian Democrats).

Corruption anyway springs more from the climate of society—and state control of the economy—than from any parliamentary arrangements. Most government in India (an FPTP country) is corrupt within weeks of taking office. The African minister

who is not, by British standards, corrupt, is acting very oddly indeed by African ones (or indeed by British ones of the 18th century: not to help one's friends—and oneself—is, like elective democracy, a recent, North European curiosity of human behaviour).

So FPTP offers no monopoly, or even guarantee, of good government. But neither does PR of fairness. Americans fret about many aspects of their political system, but not its fairness between parties; and—given that no third party exists—its results are decently proportional. Still not fair, maybe. All Americans have one vote, but of wildly different values: Alaska's 400,000 voters elect two senators, as do California's 23m. Yet why is that so? Because the founding fathers chose so. And few Americans are bothered by this either.

That is a reminder that fairness has many faces. As much as a party, the voter may want a given person to speak for him. FPTP allows for this. He may want one kind of person. Women hold few seats: in the late 1980s, about 30% in the Nordic PR countries, 5-20% in many others whose parties, in filling the party lists used in PR, take little, if any, note of this; and 5-15% in FPTP countries. Even fewer members come from poor, ethnic minorities. A few constitutions (India's, eg) reserve seats for them. Some American electoral boundaries are drawn to help them. Mostly, they must rely on accidents of geography, notably inner-city concentration.

Nor is the voter picking only his representative. He votes for certain policies, and—save in presidential systems—for a government; a serious one, not a bunch of clowns. A PR system could be as fair as Snow White in reflecting party support, and yet, at times, frustrate all these hopes. Would the result fairly represent the electorate?

It depends who, where and for what

America offers another reminder: that neither fairness nor effectiveness exists *in vacuo*. They depend on their context.

An elected body may spring from long democratic tradition or little, from a multi-cultural society or a homogeneous one. It may be national or local. It may be part of a two-house set-up (America gets territorial fairness in its Senate, demographic from the House). It may provide a government, as do European parliaments, or just legislate and oversee one, as in America. It may be mainly a sounding-board, like the 12-nation parliament of the European Community. And what is "right" here, or for one function, may be wrong there, or for another.

Britain offers an example. Its local government cries out for PR, since the national demography to which parties adapt is not reproduced locally. Voting in 1991 left 15 of 36 English "metropolitan" districts with councils that were 80%-plus Labour (nine of them 90%-plus). Of 296 "non-met"—less urban—councils, 31 had no Labour members, 35 no Liberal Democrats. Point made? Yet it proves nothing about the Commons.

With so many ifs and buts, it is easy to say if it ain't broke don't even think of fixing it. Who would today invent Britain's House of Lords, a jumble of hereditary peers, bishops and judges, plus assorted notables (or party hacks) picked by successive prime ministers? Yet, in its way, it works. If it can survive—and reforming it is a barely an issue in Britain—maybe anything can, even should.

Should? A wise country leaves well, or even only moderately well, alone. After Holland's PR elections, it can take months even to form a government. Yet few Dutchmen worry, any more than Americans do about Alaska. But when a majority (Italy) or a large minority (Britain) feels grossly ill-served or ill-treated, it is time to think again.

Beside Italy, Poland has recently opted for change. Its infant post-Communist democracy chose extreme PR, and in its late-1991 elections paid the price. In all, 67 "parties" fought; the best-placed won only 13% of the vote, and the legislature now includes 29—often shifting—groups. A new electoral law, though it too is PR-based, will limit such follies.

New Zealand, now using FPTP, may go the other way. A referendum last September backed a switch to PR (mainly, as in Italy, to punish politicians). Even Britain's Labour Party is looking at PR, if less because of Liberal complaints than of its own fears that FPTP—which in the past served it well—may leave its Tory rivals for ever running solid one-party governments on 40% of the vote.

Britain's love of FPTP is criticised beyond its borders, because, except in Northern Ireland, it elects members to the European Parliament by this system. So the Tory-Labour balance swings wildly, while large Euro-constituencies crush other national parties. In 1984, the Alliance won 18.5% of the Euro-vote, but no seats; ditto the Greens in 1989, with 14.5%. The result distorts not just British representation but the make-up of the whole parliament.

France's recent elections aroused worries about its two-round voting. This was de Gaulle's substitute for the instabilities of PR, only briefly replaced by PR again in the mid-1980s. Its results can be fair enough. Not this year. Right-wing parties, with 39% of the vote, took 80% of the seats. The National Front, with 12½%, got none. Nasty as the Front is, many Frenchmen doubt that democracy should leave so many voters voiceless.

Pros and cons

Italians' dislike of PR far outruns French or British anxieties the other way. That is natural: they identify it with lousy government. And bad government both hits the whole nation and impinges visibly and constantly on daily life; the disfranchisement felt by third-party voters does neither. Yet worries about FPTP and related systems go deeper. It is representative democracy, not good government, that is the essence of "western" politics. *The Economist*, discussing these issues two years ago, wrote flatly that

> And since the perception of fairness is the acid test for democracy—the very basis of its legitimacy—the unfairness argument overrules all others.

There is a more pragmatic reason. Politicians can, and in Europe mostly do, provide decent government with PR. Unless, as in America, history has dumped third parties, FPTP cannot, except by chance, and normally does not provide fair representation. Human wit can get round the faults of PR; it cannot—except in drawing electoral boundaries—act on the crude mechanics of FPTP.

Yet any shift toward PR must, if possible, avoid its faults in advance. Its critics list many, not all as solid as they sound:

• **Too complicated.** Nonsense. What some think the best system, the single transferable vote, is indeed complex. But the Irish can work it, so why not others?

• **Too many small parties.** That depends how far fairness is pushed. A threshold can hold numbers down: Germany's fierce 5% one has usually kept the Bundestag to just four parties, rarely five. Is it acceptable to exclude 4.9% of opinion—or, as recently in Eastern Europe, several times 4.9%? FPTP too can let in many small parties, if (but only if) each has a regional base.

• **Too many weak coalitions.** Coalitions, yes. Weak, maybe. PR produces both.

• **Too much power for small "pivotal" parties.** Germany's FDP is often cited. In 1982 it quit a coalition with the SDP and joined the CDU. Undemocratic? Six months later the policy shift that the FDP had sought was endorsed by the voters. The "tail-and-dog" case too is weak. On minor issues dear to them, small parties may get their way (as in Israel). On big issues, in politics as in physics, small bodies can only influence large ones, not rule them. West German unification-seeking softness toward Russia in 1989 is cited. That began with the FDP foreign minister; but it was backed by Chancellor Kohl.

• **Policy decided in inter-party haggling after an election, not by voters during it.** Often true, shamefully so in Italy, though its smoke-shrouded deals were more about posts than policy. But the idea that it is "unfair" for those who backed the biggest party in a coalition to see its policy then diluted is bogus: in politics as in marriage, if you cannot win outright, you must compromise.

• **Too much power for party bosses.** In party-list systems, that is nearly always true. But STV lets voters choose among a party's candidates; so does Japan's simple system. Any coalition adds to the power of party machines in government—and (notoriously in Italy, notedly in Germany) in patronage and appointment to public bodies, not least state television. One can argue whether or not one-party patronage, as in Britain, is even worse. A better answer is open under any system: less patronage.

• **Weak links between a member and his constituents.** This is true of PR using large electoral districts, not in the ones of 3-5 members used in Ireland (and Japan). Members of the Irish Dail feel pressure, they say, to look after constituents, because their support may slip away not only to rival parties but to other members of their own. British critics fear such a member may care only for a section of his constituents. That may happen; PR supporters, in reply, praise the voter's freedom to choose which member he turns to. Districts of 5-7 members, as in most of Belgium, Spain or France in its PR days, allow both PR and acceptable member/voter links.

Many answers

For countries seeking less PR, the considerations, curiously, are much the same, since not even the angry Italians want the pure milk of FPTP. For them too the trick is to find a balance between proportionality and the faults voters feel in their form of PR. They too must remember the many faces of fairness, and ask, in each case, what function the elected body serves, what they want to achieve (punishing politicians, however deservedly, is an inappropriate answer) and is it worth the upheaval? Only zealots think one solution fits every case.

Presidents and Prime Ministers

Richard Rose

Richard Rose is professor of public policy at the University of Strathclyde in Glasgow, Scotland. An American, he has lived in Great Britain for many years and has been studying problems of political leadership in America and Europe for three decades. His books include Presidents and Prime Ministers; Managing Presidential Objectives; Understanding Big Government; *and* The Post-Modern Presidency: The World Closes in on the White House.

The need to give direction to government is universal and persisting. Every country, from Egypt of the pharoahs to contemporary democracies, must maintain political institutions that enable a small group of politicians to make authoritative decisions that are binding on the whole of society. Within every system, one office is of first importance, whether it is called president, prime minister, führer, or dux.

There are diverse ways of organizing the direction of government, not only between democracies and authoritarian regimes, but also among democracies. Switzerland stands at one extreme, with collective direction provided by a federal council whose president rotates from year to year. At the other extreme are countries that claim to centralize authority, under a British-style parliamentary system or in an American or French presidential system, in which one person is directly elected to the supreme office of state.

To what extent are the differences in the formal attributes of office a reflection of substantive differences in how authority is exercised? To what extent do the imperatives of office—the need for electoral support, dependence upon civil servants for advice, and vulnerability to events—impose common responses in practice? Comparing the different methods of giving direction to government in the United States (presidential), Great Britain (prime ministerial and Cabinet), and France (presidential and prime ministerial) can help us understand whether other countries do it—that is, choose a national leader—in a way that is better.

To make comparisons requires concepts that can identify the common elements in different offices. Three concepts organize the comparisons I make: the career that leads to the top; the institutions and powers of government; and the scope for variation within a country, whether arising from events or personalities.

Career Leading to the Top

By definition, a president or prime minister is unrepre-

sentative by being the occupant of a unique office. The diversity of outlooks and skills that can be attributed to white, university-educated males is inadequate to predict how people with the same social characteristics—a Carter or an Eisenhower; a Wilson or a Heath—will perform in office. Nor is it helpful to consider the recruitment of national leaders deductively, as a management consultant or personnel officer would, first identifying the skills required for the job and then evaluating candidates on the basis of a priori requirements. National leaders are not recruited by examination; they are self-selected, individuals whose driving ambitions, personal attributes, and, not least, good fortune, combine to win the highest public office.

To understand what leaders can do in office we need to compare the skills acquired in getting to the top with the skills required once there. The tasks that a president or prime minister must undertake are few but central: sustaining popular support through responsiveness to the electorate, and being effective in government. Success in office encourages electoral popularity, and electoral popularity is an asset in wielding influence within government.

The previous careers of presidents and prime ministers are significant, insofar as experience affects what they do in office—and what they do well. A politician who had spent many years concentrating upon campaigning to win popularity may continue to cultivate popularity in office. By contrast, a politician experienced in dealing with the problems of government from within may be better at dealing effectively with international and domestic problems.

Two relevant criteria for comparing the careers of national leaders are: previous experience of government, and previous experience of party and mass electoral politics. American presidents are outstanding in their experience of campaigning for mass support, whereas French presidents are outstanding for their prior knowledge of government from the inside. British prime ministers usually combine experience in both fields.

Thirteen of the fourteen Americans who have been nominated for president of the United States by the Democratic or Republican parties since 1945 had prior experience in running for major office, whether at the congressional, gubernatorial or presidential level. Campaigning for office makes a politician conscious of his or her need for popular approval. It also cultivates skill in dealing with the mass media. No American will be elected president who has not learned how to campaign across the continent, effectively and incessantly. Since selection as a presidential candidate is dependent upon winning primaries, a president must run twice: first to win the party nomination and then to win the White House. The effort required is shown by the fact that in 1985, three years before the presidential election, one Republican hopeful campaigned in twenty-four states, and a Democratic hopeful in thirty. Immediately after the 1986 congressional elections ended, the media started featuring stories about the 1988 campaign.

Campaigning is different from governing. Forcing ambitious politicians to concentrate upon crossing and recrossing America reduces the time available for learning about problems in Washington and the rest of the world. The typical postwar president has had no experience working within the executive branch. The way in which the federal government deals with foreign policy, or with problems of the economy is known, if at all, from the vantage point of a spectator. A president is likely to have had relatively brief experience in Congress. As John F. Kennedy's career illustrates, Congress is not treated as a

Looking presidential is not the same as acting like a president.

means of preparing to govern; it is a launching pad for a presidential campaign. The last three presidential elections have been won by individuals who could boast of having no experience in Washington. Jimmy Carter and Ronald Reagan were state governors, experienced at a job that gives no experience in foreign affairs or economic management.

A president who is experienced in campaigning can be expected to continue cultivating the media and seeking a high standing in the opinion polls. Ronald Reagan illustrates this approach. A president may even use campaigning as a substitute for coming to grips with government; Jimmy Carter abandoned Washington for the campaign trail when confronted with mid-term difficulties in 1978. But public relations expertise is only half the job; looking presidential is not the same as acting like a president.

A British prime minister, by contrast, enters office after decades in the House of Commons and years as a Cabinet minister. The average postwar prime minister had spent thirty-two years in Parliament before entering 10 Downing Street. Of that period, thirteen years had been spent as a Cabinet minister. Moreover, the prime minister has normally held the important policy posts of foreign secretary, chancellor of the exchequer or both. The average prime

minister has spent eight years in ministerial office, learning to handle foreign and/or economic problems. By contrast with the United States, no prime minister has had postwar experience in state or local government, and by contrast with France, none has been a civil servant since World War II.

The campaign experience of a British prime minister is very much affected by the centrality that politicians give Parliament. A politician seeks to make a mark in debate there. Even in an era of mass media, the elitist doctrine holds that success in the House of Commons produces positive evaluation by journalists and invitations to appear on television, where a politician can establish an image with the national electorate. Whereas an American presidential hopeful has a bottom-up strategy, concentrating upon winning votes in early primaries in Iowa and New Hampshire as a means of securing media attention, a British politician has a top-down approach, starting to campaign in Parliament.

Party is the surrogate for public opinion among British politicians, and with good reason. Success in the Commons is evaluated by a politician's party colleagues. Election to the party leadership is also determined by party colleagues. To become prime minister a politician does not need to win an election; he or she only needs to be elected party leader when the party has a parliamentary majority. Jim Callaghan and Sir Alec Douglas-Home each entered Downing Street this way and lost office in the first general election fought as prime minister.

The lesser importance of the mass electorate to British party leaders is illustrated by the fact that the average popularity rating of a prime minister is usually less than that of an American president. The monthly Gallup poll rating often shows the prime minister approved by less than half the electorate and trailing behind one or more leaders of the opposition.

In the Fifth French Republic, presidents and prime ministers have differed from American presidents, being very experienced in government, and relatively inexperienced in campaigning with the mass electorate. Only one president, François Mitterrand, has followed the British practice of making a political career based on Parliament. Since he was on the opposition side for the first two decades of the Fifth Republic, his experience of the problems of office was like that of a British opposition member of Parliament, and different from that of a minister. Giscard d'Estaing began as a high-flying civil servant and Charles de Gaulle, like Dwight Eisenhower, was schooled in bureaucratic infighting as a career soldier.

When nine different French prime ministers are examined, the significance of a civil service background becomes clear. Every prime minister except for Pierre Mauroy has been a civil servant first. It has been exceptional for a French prime minister to spend decades in Parliament before attaining that office. An Englishman would be surprised that a Raymond Barre or a Couve de Murville had not sat there before becoming prime minister. An American would be even more surprised by the experience that French leaders have had in the ministries as high civil servants, and particularly in dealing with foreign and economic affairs.

The traditional style of French campaigning is plebiscitary. One feature of this is that campaigning need not be incessant. Louis Napoleon is said to have compared elections with baptism: something it is necessary to do—but to do only once. The seven-year fixed term of the French president, about double the statutory life of many national leaders, is in the tradition of infrequent consultation with the electorate.

The French tradition of leadership is also ambivalent; a plebiscite is, after all, a mass mobilization. The weakness of parties, most notably on the Right, which has provided three of the four presidents of the Fifth Republic, encourages a personalistic style of campaigning. The use of the two-ballot method for the popular election of a president further encourages candidates to compete against each other as individuals, just as candidates for the presidential nomination compete against fellow-partisans in a primary. The persistence of divisions between Left and Right ensures any candidate successful in entering the second ballot a substantial bloc of votes, with or without a party endorsement.

On the two central criteria of political leadership, the relationship with the mass electorate, and knowledge of government, there are cross-national contrasts in the typical career. A British or French leader is likely to know far more about government than an American president, but an American politician is likely to be far more experienced in campaigning to win popular approval and elections.

Less for the President to Govern

Journalistic and historical accounts of government often focus on the person and office of the national leader. The American president is deemed to be very powerful because of the immense military force that he can command by comparison to a national leader in Great Britain or France. The power to drop a hydrogen bomb is frequently cited as a measure of the awesome power of an American president; but it is misleading, for no president has ever dropped a hydrogen bomb, and no president has used atomic weapons in more than forty years. Therefore, we must ask: What does an American president (and his European counterparts) do when not dropping a hydrogen bomb?

In an era of big government, a national leader is more a chief than an executive, for no individual can superintend, let alone carry out, the manifold tasks of government. A national leader does not need to make major choices about what government ought to do; he inherits a set of institutions that are committed—by law, by organization, by the professionalism of public employees, and by the expectations of voters—to appropriate a large amount of the country's resources in order to produce the program outputs of big government.

Whereas political leadership is readily personalized,

government is intrinsically impersonal. It consists of collective actions by organizations that operate according to impersonal laws. Even when providing benefits to individuals, such as education, health care, or pensions, the scale of a ministry or a large regional or local government is such as to make the institution appear impersonal.

Contemporary Western political systems are first of all governed by the rule of law rather than personal will. When government did few things and actions could be derived from prerogative powers, such as a declaration of war, there was more scope for the initiative of leaders. Today, the characteristic activities of government, accounting for most public expenditure and personnel, are statutory entitlements to benefits of the welfare state. They cannot be overturned by wish or will, as their tacit acceptance by such "antigovernment" politicians as Margaret Thatcher and Ronald Reagan demonstrates. Instead of the leader dominating government, government determines much that is done in the leader's name.

In a very real sense, the co-called power of a national leader depends upon actions that his government takes, whether or not this is desired by the leader. Instead of comparing the constitutional powers of leaders, we should compare the resources that are mobilized by the government for which a national leader is nominally responsible. The conventional measure of the size of government is public expenditure as a proportion of the gross national product. By this criterion, French or British government is more powerful than American government. Organization for Economic Cooperation and Development (OECD) statistics show that in 1984 French public expenditure accounted for 49 percent of the national product, British for 45 percent, and American for 37 percent. When attention is directed at central government, as distinct from all levels of government, the contrast is further emphasized. British and French central government collect almost two-fifths of the national product in tax revenue, whereas the American federal government collects only one-fifth.

When a national leader leads, others are meant to follow. The legitimacy of authority means that public employees should do what elected officials direct. In an era of big government, there are far more public employees at hand than in an era when the glory of the state was symbolized by a small number of people clustering around a royal court. Statistics of public employment again show British and French government as much more powerful than American government. Public employment in France accounts for 33 percent of all persons who work, more than Britain, with 31 percent. In the United States, public employment is much less, 18 percent.

The capacity of a national leader to direct public employees is much affected by whether or not such officials are actually employed by central government. France is most centralized, having three times as many public employees working in ministries as in regional or local government. If public enterprises are also reckoned as part of central government, France is even more centralized. In the United States and Great Britain, by contrast, the actual delivery of public services such as education and health is usually shipped out to lower tiers of a federal government, or to a complex of local and functional authorities. Delivering the everyday services of government is deemed beneath the dignity of national leaders in Great Britain. In the United States, central government is deemed too remote to be trusted with such programs as education or police powers.

When size of government is the measure, an American president appears weaker than a French or British leader. By international standards, the United States has a not so big government, for its claim on the national product and the national labor force is below the OECD average. Ronald Reagan is an extreme example of a president who is "antigovernment," but he is not the only example. In the past two decades, the United States has not lagged behind Europe in developing and expanding welfare state institutions that make government big. It has chosen to follow a different route, diverging from the European model of a mixed economy welfare state. Today, the president has very few large-scale program responsibilities, albeit they remain significant: defense and diplomacy, social security, and funding the federal deficit.

By contrast, even an "antigovernment" prime minister such as Margaret Thatcher finds herself presiding over a government that claims more than two-fifths of the national product in public expenditure. Ministers must answer, collectively and individually in the House of Commons, for all that is done under the authority of an Act of Parliament. In France, the division between president and prime minister makes it easier for the president of the republic to avoid direct entanglement in low status issues of service delivery, but the centralization of government necessarily involves the prime minister and his colleagues.

When attention is turned to the politics of government as distinct from public policies, all leaders have one thing in common, they are engaged in political management, balancing the interplay of forces within government, major economic interests, and public opinion generally. It is no derogation of a national leader's position to say that it has an important symbolic dimension, imposing a unifying and persuasive theme upon what government does. The theme may be relatively clear-cut, as in much of Margaret Thatcher's rhetoric. Or it may be vague and symbolic, as in much of the rhetoric of Charles de Gaulle. The comparative success of Ronald Reagan, an expert in manipulating vague symbols, as against Jimmy Carter, whose technocratic biases were far stronger than his presentational skills, is a reminder of the importance of a national political leader being able to communicate successfully to the nation.

In the United States and France, the president is both head of government and head of state. The latter role makes him president of all the people, just as the former role limits his representative character to governing in the name of a majority (but normally, less than 60 percent) of the voters. A British prime minister does not have the symbolic obligation to represent the country as a whole; the queen does that.

The institutions of government affect how political management is undertaken. The separate election of the president and the legislature in the United States and France create a situation of nominal independence, and bargaining from separate electoral bases. By contrast, the British prime minister is chosen by virtue of being leader of the largest party in the House of Commons. Management of Parliament is thus made much easier by the fact that the British prime minister can normally be assured of a majority of votes there.

An American president has a far more difficult task in managing government than do British and French counterparts. Congress really does determine whether bills become laws, by contrast to the executive domination of law and decree-making in Europe. Congressional powers of appropriation provide a basis for a roving scrutiny of what the executive branch does. There is hardly any bureau that is free from congressional scrutiny, and in many congressional influence may be as strong as presidential influence. By contrast, a French president has significant decree powers and most of the budget can be promulgated. A British prime minister can also invoke the Official Secrets Act and the doctrine of collective responsibility to insulate the effective (that is, the executive) side of government from the representative (that is, Parliament).

Party politics and electoral outcomes, which cannot be prescribed in a democratic constitution, affect the extent to which political management must be invested in persuasion. If management is defined as making an organization serve one's purpose, then Harry Truman gave the classic definition of management as persuasion: "I sit here all day trying to persuade people to do the things they ought to have sense enough to do without my persuading them. That's all the powers of the President amount to." Because both Democratic and Republican parties are loose coalitions, any president will have to invest much effort in persuading fellow partisans, rather than whipping them into line. Given different electoral bases, congressmen may vote their district, rather than their party label. When president and Congress are of opposite parties, then strong party ties weaken the president.

In Great Britain, party competition and election outcomes are expected to produce an absolute majority in the House of Commons for a single party. Given that the prime minister, as party leader, stands and falls with members of Parliament in votes in Parliament and at a general election, a high degree of party discipline is attainable. Given that the Conservative and Labor parties are themselves coalitions of differing factions and tendencies, party management is no easy task. But it is far easier than interparty management, a necessary condition of coalition government, including Continental European governments.

The Fifth Republic demonstrates that important constitutional features are contingent upon election outcomes. Inherent in the constitution of the Fifth Republic is a certain ambiguity about the relationship between president and prime minister. Each president has desired to make his office preeminent. The first three presidents had no difficulty in doing that, for they could rely upon the support of a majority of members of the National Assembly. Cooperation could not be coerced, but it could be relied upon to keep the prime minister subordinate.

Since the election of François Mitterrand in 1981, party has become an independent variable. Because the president's election in 1981 was paralleled by the election of a Left majority in the assembly, Mitterrand could adopt what J.E.S. Hayward describes in *Governing France* as a "Gaulist conception of his office." But after the victory of the Right in the 1986 Assembly election resulted in a non-Socialist being imposed as premier, Jacques Chirac, the president has had to accept a change of position, symbolized by the ambivalent term *cohabitation.*

Whether the criterion is government's size or the authority of the national leader vis-à-vis other politicians, the conclusion is the same: the political leaders of Great Britain and France can exercise more power than the president of the United States. The American presidency is a relatively weak office. America's population, economy, and military are not good measures of the power of the White House. Imagine what one would say if American institutions were transplanted, more or less wholesale, to some small European democracy. We would not think that such a country had a strong leader.

While differing notably in the separate election of a French president as against a parliamentary election of a British prime minister, both offices centralize authority within a state that is itself a major institution of society. As long as a French president has a majority in the National Assembly, then this office can have most influence within government, for ministers are unambiguously subordinate to the president. The linkage of a British prime minister's position with a parliamentary majority means that as long as a single party has a majority, a British politician is protected against the risks of cohabitation à la française or à la americaine.

Variations within Nations

An office sets parameters within which politicians can act, but the more or less formal stipulation of the rules and resources of an office cannot determine exactly what is done. Within these limits, the individual performance of a president or prime minister can be important. Events too are significant; everyday crises tend to frustrate any attempt to plan ahead, and major crises—a war or domestic disaster—can shift the parameters, reducing a politician's scope for action (for example, Watergate) or expanding it (for example, the mass mobilization that Churchill could lead after Dunkirk).

In the abstract language of social science, we can say that the actions of a national leader reflect the interaction of the powers of office, of events, and of personality. But

in concrete situations, there is always an inclination to emphasize one or another of these terms. For purposes of exposition, I treat the significance of events and personality separately: each is but one variable in a multivariate outcome.

Social scientists and constitutional lawyers are inherently generalizers, whereas critical events are unique. For example, a study of the British prime ministership that ignored what could be done in wartime would omit an example of powers temporarily stretched to new limits. Similarly, a study of Winston Churchill's capacities must recognize that his personality prevented him from achieving the nation's highest office—until the debacle of 1940 thrust office upon him.

In the postwar era, the American presidency has been especially prone to shock events. Unpredictable and nonrecurring events of importance include the outbreak of the Korean War in 1950, the assassination of President Kennedy in 1963, American involvement in the Vietnam War in the late 1960s, and the Watergate scandal, which led to President Nixon's resignation in 1974. One of the reasons for the positive popularity of Ronald Reagan has been that no disastrous event occurred in his presidency—at least until Irangate broke in November 1986.

The creation of the Fifth French Republic followed after events in Vietnam and in Algeria that undermined the authority and legitimacy of the government of the Fourth Republic. The events of May 1968 had a far greater impact in Paris than in any other European country. Whereas in 1958 events helped to create a republic with a president given substantial powers, in 1968 events were intended to reduce the authority of the state.

Great Britain has had relatively uneventful postwar government. Many causes of momentary excitement, such as the 1963 Profumo scandal that embarrassed

---

The French tradition of leadership is ambivalent.

Harold Macmillan, were trivial. The 1956 Suez war, which forced the resignation of Anthony Eden, did not lead to subsequent changes in the practice of the prime ministership, even though it was arguably a gross abuse of power vis-à-vis Cabinet colleagues and Parliament. The 1982 Falklands war called forth a mood of self-congratulation rather than a cry for institutional reform. The electoral boost it gave the prime minister was significant, but not eventful for the office.

The miner's strike, leading to a national three-day working week in the last days of the administration of Edward Heath in 1974, was perceived as a challenge to the authority of government. The prime minister called a

general election seeking a popular mandate for his conduct of industrial relations. The mandate was withheld;
so too was an endorsement of strikers. Characteristically,
the events produced a reaction in favor of conciliation,
for which Harold Wilson was particularly well suited at
that stage of his career. Since 1979 the Thatcher administration has demonstrated that trade unions are not in-
vincible. Hence, the 1974 crisis now appears as an
aberration, rather than a critical conjuncture.

While personal factors are often extraneous to government, each individual incumbent has some scope for
choice. Within a set of constraints imposed by office and
events, a politician can choose what kind of a leader he or
she would like to be. Such choices have political consequences. "Do what you can" is a prudential rule that is
often overlooked in discussing what a president or prime
minister does. The winnowing process by which one indi-

Campaigning for office makes a politician conscious of a need for popular approval.

---

vidual reaches the highest political office not only allows
for variety, but sometimes invites it, for a challenger for
office may win votes by being different from an
incumbent.

A president has a multiplicity of roles and a multiplicity of obligations. Many—as commander in chief of
the armed forces, delivering a State of the Union message
to Congress, and presenting a budget—are requirements
of the office; but the capacity to do well in particular roles
varies with the individual. For example, Lyndon Johnson
was a superb manager of congressional relations, but had
little or no feel for foreign affairs. By contrast, John F.
Kennedy was interested in foreign affairs and defense and
initially had little interest in domestic problems. Ronald
Reagan is good at talking to people, whereas Jimmy Carter and Richard Nixon preferred to deal with problems on
paper. Dwight D. Eisenhower brought to the office a national reputation as a hero that he protected by making
unclear public statements. By contrast, Gerald Ford's
public relations skills, while acceptable in a congressman,
were inadequate to the demands of the contemporary
presidency.

In Great Britain, Margaret Thatcher is atypical in her
desire to govern, as well as preside over government. She
applies her energy and intelligence to problems of government—and to telling her colleagues what to do about
them. The fact that she wants to be *the* decision-maker for
British government excites resentment among civil servants and Cabinet colleagues. This is not only a reaction

to her forceful personality, but also an expression of surprise: other prime ministers did not want to be the chief
decision-maker in government. In the case of an aging
Winston Churchill from 1951-55, this could be explained
on grounds of ill health. In the case of Anthony Eden, it
could be explained by an ignorance of domestic politics.

The interesting prime ministers are those who chose
not to be interventionists across a range of government
activities. Both Harold Macmillan and Clement Attlee
brought to Downing Street great experience of British
government. But Attlee was ready to be simply a chairman of a Cabinet in which other ministers were capable
and decisive. Macmillan chose to intervene very selectively on issues that he thought important and to leave
others to get on with most matters. Labor leader Neil
Kinnock, if he became prime minister, would adopt a
noninterventionist role. This would be welcomed in reaction to Thatcher's dominating approach. It would be necessary because Kinnock knows very little about the
problems and practice of British government. Unique
among party leaders of the past half-century, he has never
held office in government.

In France, the role of a president varies with personality. De Gaulle approached the presidency with a distinctive concept of the state as well as of politics. By
contrast, Mitterrand draws upon his experience of many
decades of being a parliamentarian and a republican.
Pompidou was distinctive in playing two roles, first prime
minister under de Gaulle, and subsequently president.

Differences between French prime ministers may in
part reflect contrasting relationships with a president. As
a member of a party different from the president, Chirac
has partisan and personal incentives to be more assertive
than does a prime minister of the same party. Premiers
who enter office via the Assembly or local politics, like
Chaban-Delmas and Mauroy, are likely to have different
priorities than a premier who was first a technocrat, such
as Raymond Barre.

Fluctuations in Leaders

The fluctuating effect upon leaders of multiple influences is shown by the monthly ratings of the popularity of
presidents and prime ministers. If formal powers of office
were all, then the popularity rating of each incumbent
should be much the same. This is not the case. If the
personal characteristics of a politician were all-important,
then differences would occur between leaders, but each
leader would receive a consistent rating during his or her
term of office. In fact, the popularity of a national leader
tends to go up and down during a term of office. Since
personality is held constant, these fluctuations cannot be
explained as a function of personal qualities. Since there
is no consistent decline in popularity, the movement cannot be explained as a consequence of impossible expectations causing the public to turn against whoever initially
wins its votes.

The most reasonable explanation of these fluctuations
in popularity is that they are caused by events. They may

be shock events, such as the threat of military action, or scandal in the leader's office. Alternatively, changes may reflect the accumulation of seemingly small events, most notably those that are reflected in the state of the economy, such as growth, unemployment, and inflation rates. A politician may not be responsible for such trends, but he or she expects to lose popularity when things appear to be going badly and to regain popularity when things are going well.

Through the decades, cyclical fluctuations can reflect an underlying long-term secular trend. In Europe a major secular trend is the declining national importance of international affairs. In the United States events in Iran or Central America remain of as much (or more) significance than events within the United States. In a multipolar world a president is involved in and more vulnerable to events in many places. By contrast, leaders of France and Great Britain have an influence limited to a continental scale, in a world in which international relations has become intercontinental. This shift is not necessarily a loss for heads of government in the European Community. In a world summit meeting, only one nation, the United States, has been first. Japan may seek to exercise political influence matching its growing economic power. The smaller scale of the European Community nations with narrower economic interests create conditions for frequent contact and useful meetings in the European arena which may bring them marginal advantages in world summit meetings too.

If the power of a national leader is measured, as Robert A. Dahl suggests in *Who Governs?*, by the capacity that such an individual has to influence events in the desired direction, then all national leaders are subject to seeing their power eroded as each nation becomes more dependent upon the joint product of the open international economy. This is as true of debtor nations such as the United States has become, as of nations with a positive trade balance. It is true of economies with a record of persisting growth, such as Germany, and of slow growth economies such as Great Britain.

A powerful national leader is very desirable only if one believes that the *Führerprinzip* is the most important principle in politics. The constitutions and politics of Western industrial nations reject this assumption. Each political system is full of constraints upon arbitrary rule, and sometimes of checks and balances that are obstacles to prompt, clear-cut decisions.

The balance between effective leadership and responsiveness varies among the United States, Great Britain, and France. A portion of that variation is organic, being prescribed in a national constitution. This is most evident in a comparison of the United States and Great Britain, but constitutions are variables, as the history of postwar France demonstrates. Many of the most important determinants of what a national leader does are a reflection of changing political circumstances, of trends and shock events, and of the aspirations and shortcomings of the individual in office.

AS THE WORLD TURNS DEMOCRATIC, FEDERALISM FINDS FAVOR

*Norman Ornstein and
Kimberly Coursen*

*Norman Ornstein is a resident scholar in
social and political processes at the
American Enterprise Institute. Kimberly
Coursen is a research assistant at the
American Enterprise Institute.*

NO WORD IN POLITICAL THEORY more consistently causes eyes to glaze over than "federalism." Yet no concept is more critical to solving many major political crises in the world right now. The former Soviet Union, Yugoslavia, Eastern and Western Europe, South Africa, Turkey, the Middle East, and Canada are suffering from problems that could be solved, if solutions are possible, by instituting creative forms of federalism.

Federalism is not a sexy concept like "democracy" or "freedom"; it describes a more mundane mechanism that balances the need for a central and coordinating authority at the level of a nation-state with a degree of state and local autonomy, while also protecting minority interests, preserving ethnic and regional identification and sensibilities, and allowing as much self-government as possible. Federalism starts with governing structures put in place by formal, constitutional arrangements, but beyond that it is a partnership that requires trust. Trust can't be forged overnight by formal arrangements, but bad arrangements can exacerbate hostilities and tensions. Good ones can be the basis for building trust.

Why is federalism so important now? There are political reasons: the breakup of the old world order has released resentments and tensions that had been suppressed for decades or even centuries. Ethnic pride and self-identification are surging in many places around the globe. Add to this the easy availability of weapons, and you have a potent mixture for discontent, instability, and violence. There are also economic considerations: simply breaking up existing nation-states into separate entities cannot work when economies are interlinked in complex ways. And there are

> **Each country has unique problems that require different kinds of federal structures, which can range from a federation that is tightly controlled at the center to a confederation having autonomous units and a loose central authority.**

humane factors, too. No provinces or territories are ethnically pure. Creating an independent Quebec, Croatia, or Kazakhstan would be uplifting for French Quebecois, Croats, and Kazakhs but terrifying for the large numbers of minorities who reside in these same territories.

The only way to begin to craft solutions, then, is to create structures that preserve necessary economic links while providing economic independence, to create political autonomy while preserving freedom of movement and individual rights, and to respect ethnic identity while protecting minority rights. Each country has unique problems that require different kinds of federal structures, which can range from a federation that is tightly controlled at the center to a confederation having autonomous units and a loose central authority.

The United States pioneered federalism in its Union and its Constitution. Its invention of a federation that balanced power between a vigorous national government and its numerous states was every bit as significant an innovation as its instituting a separation of powers was in governance—and defining the federal-state relationship was far more difficult to work out at the Constitutional Convention in 1787.

The U.S. federalist structure was, obviously, not sufficient by itself to eliminate the economic and social disparities between the North and the South. Despite the federal guarantees built into the Constitution, the divisive questions of states' rights dominated political conflict from the beginning and resulted ultimately in the Civil War. But the federal system did keep conflict from boiling over into disaster for 75 years, and it has enabled the United States to keep its union together without constitutional crisis or major bloodshed for the 125 years

From *The American Enterprise*, January/February 1992, pp. 20-24. © 1992 by The American Enterprise Institute for Public
Policy Research. Distributed by The New York Times Special Features. Reprinted by permission.

since the conclusion of the War Between the States. It has also enabled us to meliorate problems of regional and ethnic discontent.

The American form of federalism fits the American culture and historical experience—it is not directly transferable to other societies. But if ever there was a time to apply the lessons that can be drawn from the U.S. experience or to create new federal approaches, this is it. What is striking is the present number of countries and regions where deep-seated problems could respond to a new focus on federalism.

A World in Ferment

• **The former Soviet Union.** Its crisis is particularly acute and salient now as Mikhail Gorbachev, Boris Yeltsin, and leaders of the other republics struggle to find a way to keep some remnants of a union together while allowing extensive political and cultural autonomy.

In the wake of the hard-line coup in August, Gorbachev proposed that the all-Soviet Congress of People's Deputies relinquish the bulk of its power to the 12 republics. The plan included the rough outlines of a central governmental system. The system was to consist of a State Council, responsible for foreign affairs, the military, defense, and law enforcement; a bicameral parliament, with voting members from each of the participating republics; and an Interrepublic Economic Committee, which would manage the economy and implement reform. Seven republics indicated that they would sign on.

Taken together, these changes represented a near-180-degree change from a strongly centralized government to one of the most decentralized confederations anywhere. Nevertheless, some of the largest republics persisted in the view that any degree of power held by the center was too much. Ukraine voted overwhelmingly for independence on December 1, and on December 8, Russia, Ukraine, and Byelorussia teamed up to create a "Commonwealth of Independent States." The trio of republics, which together comprise 73 percent of the population and produce 80 percent of the industrial output of what was the Soviet Union, declared that "the U.S.S.R. as a subject of international law and geopolitical reality is ceasing to exist."

Specifically, what the group has pro-posed is the establishment of "coordinating bodies" to control economic and foreign policy as well as the union's vast nuclear arsenal. In addition, the republics would share a common currency and common transportation and communications systems. The details are still sketchy, and they will undoubtedly meet with resistance, particularly from those who were not included in the negotiations leading up to this historic proposal.

The Gorbachev and the Commonwealth plans have some similarities: both are loose confederations of independent states that would join together for mutual advantage yet maintain a significant degree of autonomy over most issues. The difference between the two plans is one of degree. The greatest obstacle will be to define the precise relationship between the center and the republics.

Even when that is done, the new structure will have to deal with the simmering problem of ethnic distrust. A recent Times Mirror survey of three Soviet republics—Russia, Ukraine, and

> **In the former Soviet Union, the greatest obstacle will be to define the precise relationship between the center and the republics. Even when that is done, the new structure will have to deal with the simmering problem of ethnic distrust.**

Lithuania—showed strikingly high levels of animosity between ethnic groups. For example, four in ten Russians and Ukrainians said they had an unfavorable opinion of Azerbaijanis (by comparison, only 13 percent of white Americans hold unfavorable opinions of blacks).

In describing the Commonwealth proposal, Russian Foreign Minister Andrei Kozyrev raised the specter of ethnic fracturing when he said, "This is the only and possibly the last opportunity to avoid what has happened in Yugoslavia." Ethnic animosity creates difficulties between Soviet republics but also within them. The republics, after all, are not ethnically pure. Any federal approach, if there is to be one, will have to include some innova-tive forms of protection for minority populations.

• **Yugoslavia.** Here the problems start with ethnicity. The ethnic and political differences between Serbs and Croats have precipitated a bloody civil war, which is diverting attention from the deep divisions and suspicions between Bosnians, Macedonians, Slovenians, and Montenegrans.

The six republics that now make up Yugoslavia were created in the wake of World War I from the Ottoman and Austro-Hungarian Empires. After World War II, those six republics and two autonomous regions were forged into a federation under Marshall Josip Broz Tito. For nearly 50 years, his and his successors' harsh dictatorial control from Belgrade kept historic ethnic hatreds suppressed enough to keep the nation-state together.

In the late 1970s, in response to growing ethnic strife, the tightly controlled central government began to decentralize its activities. The individual republics and provinces were granted a great deal of autonomy, and representatives from the regions were given a say—through a de facto veto power—in economic and social policies decided at the federal level. But the new arrangements did not encourage any kind of cross-regional cooperation; ultimately, they resulted in a highly decentralized federation in which ethnic identities and inter-ethnic rivalries became increasingly institutionalized.

Tito's strong hand kept things together until his death in 1980, but his departure left a government unable to manage an integrated economy or to create any level of trust between republics or across ethnic lines. When the Communist Party, the only remaining entity sustaining the Yugoslav state, collapsed in 1990, the country fell apart. Had Tito created a loose confederation of states with economic incentives to cooperate and with legal and other guarantees built in for protection of ethnic minorities—and had he worked to infuse the central government with more of an ethnic mix—the country might have been able to cope with the revolutionary changes of the 1990s. Instead, there emerged a system of freely elected leaders in the various rival republics who are now pursuing their own agendas. Slovenia and Croatia have already declared their independence. While the situation in Slovenia stabilized after an initial period of violence, Croatia is a different story. The large number of ethnic Serbs living in Croatia, fearing to lose their own status, have resisted becoming a part of an independent state. They have been supported by Serbia, which controls the army, and the result has been a Serbo-Croatian civil war.

The situation is made even more complicated by the fact that the drive for a continuing central authority for a Yugoslav federation is coming mainly from Serbia, whose leader, Slobodan Milosevic, an unreconstructed communist and a Serbian nationalist, is not trusted by anybody except the ethnic Serbs.

It may not be possible to keep Yugoslavia from splintering into six or more separate fiefdoms, each eager to suppress the ethnic minorities that reside within its borders. If there is any chance to hold Yugoslavia together—as recent European action is designed to do—it will come through some innovative federal arrangement that guarantees ethnic safety and freedom, safeguards provincial autonomy, and yet retains some form of national economic coordination and sovereignty. Questions of minority rights are the first ones that have to be answered, but they will be followed by other knotty questions of economics, common foreign policy, and what kind of central authority can exist.

Ultimately, formulas for creative federalism may be needed in Czechoslovakia, Romania, Bulgaria, and other countries in Eastern and Central Europe that also have histories of ethnic dominance and conflict.

• **Canada.** The Quebec crisis demands a new balance of power between the central government in Ottawa and the provinces, something that was nearly achieved by the Meech Lake Accord in 1990 but is now in serious jeopardy. Prime Minister Brian Mulroney has created a new plan specifically aimed at preventing the secession of Quebec. It proposes the most comprehensive restructuring of Canada's federal system since the nation's founding in 1867. The plan would grant Quebec constitutional recognition as a "distinct" society, based on its unique language, culture, and civil law, but it also envisions sweeping changes in economic and political power between Ottawa and the provinces. Interprovincial trade barriers would be eliminated, and a new Council of the Federation would be installed to mediate

disputes that might arise between the provinces.

In exchange for this increase in central control, the provinces would be granted more influence over issues of national economic policy as well as greater authority over immigration and cultural matters. In addition, at the insistence of the western provinces, the current appointed Senate would be replaced by an elected, more representative, and more consequential upper house.

Meech Lake II, as Mulroney's new plan is called, has a better chance to succeed than the original accord. But it causes discontent in minority groups, such as Indians and Eskimos, and continues to be viewed with skepticism and even outright hostility by many of the western provinces. Several of these are now governed by the New Democrats, who are less wedded to the plan devised by the Progressive-Conservative prime minister.

Meech Lake II would grant Quebec constitutional recognition as a "distinct" society, but it also envisions sweeping changes in economic and political power between Ottawa and the provinces.

• **South Africa.** The issue here is not only minority rights but also political balance. Any long-term solution to the political crisis in South Africa has to provide some sense of assurance and some real and meaningful political role for the white minority, at the same time providing full political rights and a full political role for the black majority. Both the African National Congress (ANC) and President de Klerk have offered their own plans. There are similarities: both institute universal suffrage; both propose a bicameral parliament, with one house elected by population and the other organized on regional lines; both establish an independent judiciary and a bill of rights.

But there are major differences between the plans. De Klerk's plan calls for a decentralized system for nine regions rather than the four provinces that now exist, with a central government headed by an executive council rather than by a powerful single president. The ANC plan

envisions a much more centralized system than de Klerk's, with a strong executive able to appoint his own prime minister. Negotiations between de Klerk and the ANC will include discussions not only about federal political arrangements and guarantees for blacks and whites but also about the degree of central control over the economy.

• **Hong Kong.** As the result of a 1984 treaty, Britain will turn control of Hong Kong over to the People's Republic of China in 1997. The treaty guarantees that the Chinese government will not interfere in Hong Kong's economic system, that it will be "one country, two systems"; however, the language of the treaty is vague and open to a variety of interpretations. Because of Tiananmen Square, there is widespread fear in Hong Kong and doubt that China will honor the letter or the spirit of the treaty. Thus, there has been increased emigration and substantial capital flight from Hong Kong, and some are predicting political and economic chaos before the turn of the century.

To keep Hong Kong a free-market democracy while bringing it into the orbit of the People's Republic may require more innovative forms of federalism. There are many incentives for China to explore such options—more than just the economic one of keeping alive the goose that lays the golden egg of hard foreign currency. There is also the desire to find a form of governance for Hong Kong that might be a model attractive enough to make a political, federal alliance possible between the People's Republic and the Republic of China on Taiwan.

• **The Middle East.** The peace conference in Madrid in October and the talks in Washington in December were times for posturing, deciding who is represented, who is representing the represented, and how to proceed from there. The underlying issue—resolving the Arab/Israeli conflict—has yet to be addressed. When it is, the resolution of the Palestinian/Israeli component will inevitably turn to how to govern the West Bank and Gaza—how Jews and Arabs can co-exist politically, economically, and socially.

Some form of co-federation, with shared governance, will have to be on the table. The issue would be much easier to resolve if Jordan east of the Jordan River were considered the base of a

Palestinian state, making the West Bank an ancillary, not a central, territory. But Jordan's role aside, creative federalist solutions for these disputed territories is a must. They might include some form of co-citizenship with Israel, Jordan, and the West Bank itself; they might include some innovative economic arrangements. Federalism may also be invoked to resolve the Golan Heights dispute with Syria.

• **Western Europe.** The Soviets and others are carefully watching Europe's attempt at economic and political union known as Europe '92. Their interest is more than geopolitical. In a way, the European Community faces a situation similar to that faced by struggling nations around the world. The EC consists of a group of ethnically and culturally diverse nation-states attempting to establish an integrated and coordinated economic and political system. The compromise reached at the historic meeting in December 1991 may serve as a model of sorts for other countries experimenting with both democracy and new forms of federalism.

The European Community has been predicated primarily on common economic interests. The 12 member-states have already agreed that by January 1, 1993, the EC will be a single economic market, with free movement of capital, goods, and services among its members, making it the most powerful trading bloc in the world. Members have also agreed, more problematically, to establish a common currency and a regional central bank.

Real political union is a less certain proposition. There is a consensus that economic union has to be complemented by some common political structure. But the Europeans divide sharply over whether the community should become a tightly knit federation with central political control over foreign and defense policy and legal matters as well as economic ones, or whether it should be a loose confederation of independent states linked primarily for economic reasons. Germany and France prefer the former, Britain the latter. Eventually, the inherent French suspicion of the Germans may move them into a closer alliance with the British.

> **There is also the desire to find a form of governance for Hong Kong that might be a model attractive enough to make a political, federal alliance possible between the People's Republic and the Republic of China on Taiwan.**

Even after the departure of Margaret Thatcher and her tough anti-Community rhetoric, the British have continued to make clear their deep reluctance to embrace the centralized system of majority rule that the French have proposed. Currently, the European Commission, the executive arm of the EC, operates under a system of unanimous rule in which each member-state retains a veto power. The British are adamant about keeping this system intact. The bigger issues of political power aside, arguments going on now over standards and regulations for transcontinental construction, disputes over how to handle defense and regional security, and questions of whether and when Eastern European nations should be invited to join the Community suggest that it will be a long time before a true European federation takes shape.

Summary

In the final analysis, nations and regions will hold together or come together in the modern world if their economic interests demand it. Even then, the potential for self-destruction, atomization, substantial bloodshed, even all-out war, is very great. A common interest in economic advancement provides the incentive to try to find structural solutions to political and social problems. But it is a delicate matter to find structures that can allay primal fears of genocide, legitimize emerging national identities, and divide up economic and political powers and goodies in a fashion that will be seen as fair to everybody. It is here that creative federalism can play its role.

The United States may be able to at least point the way. Our innovations in decentralized federal arrangements as well as our experience in sorting out powers and rights between Washington and the states could well be adapted to many troubled situations elsewhere today. One especially significant American example may well turn out to be the U.S. Senate. Creating a second legislative chamber with real authority, prestige, and legitimacy, that is divided along state (or regional, or ethnic, or racial) lines, may be an initial way for shaky unions to balance their centrifugal forces and centripetal needs.

Creative structures alone will not solve the problems of a prostrate Soviet central economy, keep Serbs and Croats from murdering one another, or bring blacks and whites together in South Africa, much less Palestinians and Israelis in the Middle East. While creative federalism may not be enough, it is surely essential for peaceful transition and successful governance.

Europe—West, Center, and East: The Politics of Integration, Transformation, and Disintegration

- **The European Union: From EC to EU (Articles 34–37)**
- **Revamping the Welfare State (Articles 38 and 39)**
- **Post-Communist Central and Eastern Europe (Articles 40 and 41)**
- **Russia and the Other Post-Soviet Republics (Articles 42–45)**

Most of the articles in this unit are in some way linked to one or the other of two major developments that have fundamentally altered the political map of Europe in recent years. The first of these major changes is the long-term movement toward supranational integration of many western European states within the institutional framework of the European Community, or EC, which officially became the European Union, or EU on November 1, 1993. Here the development has primarily been one by which sovereign states piecemeal give up some of their traditional independence, especially in matters dealing with economic and monetary policy.

The second major challenge to the established European state system is far more abrupt and goes in another, far more disruptive, direction. It consists of the more recent and rapid disintegration brought about by the sudden collapse of Communist rule in Central and Eastern Europe. Here states, nations, and nationalities have broken away from an imposed system of central control, and now assert their political and societal independence from the previous ruling group and its communist ideology.

A closer look at the countries of Western Europe reveals that they have their own internal problems, even if in a far less acute form than their counterparts to the East. Their relative prosperity rests on a base built up during the prolonged postwar economic boom of the 1950s and 1960s. By political choice, a considerable portion of their affluence was channeled toward the public sector and used to develop generous systems of social services and social insurance. Between the early 1970s and the mid-1980s, however, Western industrial societies were beset by economic disruptions that brought an end to the long period of rapidly growing prosperity. The last half of the 1980s marked some improvement in the economic situation throughout most of Western Europe, partly as a result of some favorably timed positive trade balances with the United States.

The earlier economic shock that first interrupted the prolonged postwar boom had come in the wake of sharp rises in the cost of energy, linked to successive hikes in the price of oil imposed by the Organization of Petroleum Exporting Countries (OPEC) after 1973. In the 1980s, OPEC lost its organizational bite, as its members began to compete against each other by raising production and lowering prices rather than abiding by the opposite practices in the manner of a well-functioning cartel agreement. The resulting improvement for the consumers of oil helped the West European economies recover, but as a whole they did not rebound to their earlier high growth rates. The short Gulf War did not seriously hamper the flow of Middle East oil in 1991, but it once again underscored the vulnerability of Europe to external interruptions in its energy supply.

Because of their heavy dependence on international trade, West European economies are especially vulnerable to the kind of global recessionary tendencies we have encountered during the past few years. Another important challenge to these affluent countries is found in the stiff competition they face from the new industrial countries (NICs) of East and South Asia, where productivity is higher and labor costs remain much lower.

A related issue is how the increase in international trade within and outside the European Community will affect the established social market economies of continental Europe. The economic gains derived from international competition could have a positive consequence, by providing a better base for consolidating and invigorating the social welfare systems, as described by Joel Havemann. However, a different scenario seems to be starting in which there will be a drastic pruning and reduction in social services, carried out in the name of efficiency and international competitiveness. As the article by Roger Cohen pointed out, there are other demographic and economic challenges to the corporatist and welfare state arrangements that appear to have served these countries so well for so long.

Prudent observers had long warned about a premature celebration of "Europe 1992," which really refers to the abolition on restrictions in the flow of goods, capital, services, and labor by January 1, 1993. They suggested that the slogan served to cover up some remaining problems and some newly emerging obstacles to the full integration of the Community. The skeptics seemed at least partly vindicated by the setbacks that have followed the EC's supposedly decisive "leap" forward during its Maastricht meeting in December of 1991. The Maastricht Treaty foresaw the further supranational integration of the member nations during the 1990s, providing for a common monetary system and a federal European Reserve Bank as well as common policies on immigration, environmental protection, external security, and foreign affairs. In three of the twelve member countries—Denmark, Ireland, and France—ratification of the treaty was tied to the outcome of national referendums. In the first of these expressions of the popular will, Danish voters in June 1992 decided by a very slim majority of less than two percent to reject the treaty. A huge Irish majority in favor of the treaty was followed by a very slim French approval as well. The negative Danish vote seemed to have the effect of legitimating and releasing many reservations in other member countries. But in May 1993, Danish voters approved a modified version of the agreement, and some weeks later British Prime Minister John Major was able to hammer together a fragile parliamentary majority in the House of Commons. The last formal hurdle to the Maastricht Treaty was passed in Germany, where the Constitutional Court turned down a legal challenge. But the difficult ratification process had revealed widespread political resistance that will continue to hamper the course toward a federal union.

As several of the articles in this section point out, European Union has effectively reached a crossroads. The European nation-state has turned out to have more holding power than some European federalists had expected, especially in a time of economic setbacks and perceived threats to the social order. The absence of a coherent West European response to the violent ethnic conflict in former Yugoslavia has added a further reason for doubt concerning the EC's imminent progression toward an elementary form of political federation. For these and other reasons, the present seems to be a time for new thought and debate about the European Union's further goals and its route for reaching them, as Stanley Hoffmann and Roger Kaplan both suggest.

While much academic and political ink has been spilled on the problems of a transition from a market economy to state socialism, we have little theory or practice to guide East Europeans who are moving in the opposite direction. A new and major theoretical issue, which has important policy consequences, thus concerns the best strategy for restructuring the economies of the former communist countries.

A debate has been carried out in the former Soviet Union during the past few years. In some ways, it could be argued that Mikhail Gorbachev failed to opt clearly for an economic reform. He seemed not only to have been ambivalent about the means but also about the ends of his *perestroika* or restructuring of the centrally planned economy. He remained far too socialist for some born-again marketers in his own country, while communist hard-liners never forgave him for dismantling a system in which they had enjoyed at least a modicum of security and privilege.

Gorbachev appears to have regarded his own policies of *glasnost* or openness and democratization as essential accompaniments of perestroika in his modernization program. He seems to have understood (or become convinced) that a highly developed industrial economy needs a freer flow of information along with a more decentralized system of decision making, if its component parts are to be efficient, flexible, and capable of self-correction. In that sense, a market economy has some integral feedback traits that make it incompatible with the traditional Soviet model of a centrally directed, authoritarian command economy.

Most importantly, glasnost and democratization gave ethnic minorities in the Soviet Union, who had a territorial identity, an opportunity to demand autonomy or independence. The death knell for the Soviet Union sounded in 1991, when the Ukrainians, who constituted the second largest national group in the Soviet Union after the Russians, demanded independence.

In a very real sense, then, Gorbachev's political reforms ended up as a threat not only to the continued leadership role by the Communist Party but also to the continued existence of the Soviet Union itself. Gorbachev seems to have understood neither of these ultimately fatal consequences of his reform attempts until quite late. This explains why he could set in motion forces that would ultimately destroy what he had hoped to make more attractive and productive. The attempted coup against the reformer and his reforms, in August 1991, came far too late and was too poorly organized to have succeeded. In fact, the would-be coup d'état became instead a coup de grace for the Soviet Communists and, in the end, the Soviet Union as well. Somewhat reluctantly, Gorbachev declared the party illegal soon after he had been returned to office by the resistance, led by Russian President Boris Yeltsin, who had broken with communism earlier and far more decisively.

After his formal restoration to power, Gorbachev became politically dependent on someone who had once been his protégé and then became his bitter critic before turning out to be his rescuer. It was a remarkable development, which is explained by Adam Ulam in his review of the unraveling of the Soviet Union. But Gorbachev had by then become a transitional figure, as some observers concluded right after the abortive coup. His own days as Soviet president were numbered, when the Soviet Union ceased to exist at Christmas 1991. It was replaced by the Commonwealth of Independent States, a very loose union without any important institutional framework to hold it together. Almost from the outset, the CIS seemed destined to be a transitional device. At best, it could serve as a useful link between the former Soviet republics, as they negotiate what to do with the economic, military, and other institutional leftovers of the old system and try to shape new and useful links to each other for the future.

Specialists on the former Soviet Union disagree considerably in their assessments of the current situation or what brought it about. One of the hotly debated issues concerns President Yeltsin's decision in September 1993 to use a preemptive strike to break a deadlock between his government and a majority in the Russian Parliament. When a majority of the legislators, who had been elected over two years earlier, persisted in blocking some of his major economic reforms, Yeltsin dissolved Parliament and called new elections to be held in December 1993.

The electoral result was a political boomerang for Yeltsin, in the form of a major setback for the forces backing rapid and thoroughgoing market reforms. The new Parliament, based on a two-ballot system of elections, is highly fragmented, but nationalists and former communists occupy pivotal positions in the Duma. By the beginning of 1994, it appeared likely that President Yeltsin would play a more subdued role than previously and that a new government would pursue more cautious reform policies. It is unclear whether the nationalist surge in strength, which seems based on a demand for cracking down on crime and social disorder, would have serious foreign policy implications. But neither the ultra-right nor the former communists, who rejected drastic market reforms, seemed unwilling to return to a centrally planned economy. In that limited sense, at least, the long Soviet chapter of Russian history appeared to have been closed, even though the experience would continue to disturb the pattern of the country's future development,

Looking Ahead: Challenge Questions

What are the major obstacles to the emergence of a more unified Europe?

What is the evidence that the economic problems of Western Europe are not just cyclical but also structural in origin?

What are the main problems facing the newly elected governments in Eastern and Central Europe?

Was Gorbachev mistaken in believing that the Soviet Union could be reformed without being dissolved? How did he and Yeltsin differ in their views about reform before the abortive coup in August 1991?

Why did Boris Yeltsin call an early parliamentary election in December 1993, and how did its outcome represent a setback for the market reformers?

The maths of post-Maastricht Europe

FROM OUR BRUSSELS CORRESPONDENT

With the Maastricht treaty ratified all round, we look ahead to the problems the European Community will face as it takes on new members.

WILL Europe now leave its "period of waiting and gloom"—the apt phrase of the European Commission's president, Jacques Delors—and fulfil the promises of the Maastricht treaty? After the judgment on October 12th of Germany's Constitutional Court, no legal impediment remains to the Treaty on European Union agreed on almost two wearying years ago. There will, the treaty says, be co-operation on policing, a common foreign and security policy and, by 1999 at the latest, an economic and monetary union (EMU).

Promises, promises. The practical impediments are clear to all. Just as the horrors of former Yugoslavia mock the dream of a common foreign policy, so Europe's economic malaise imperils the ambitions of EMU. The criteria for EMU are low inflation, low budget deficits, a stable exchange rate and a public debt limited to 60% of a country's gross domestic product. No country at present meets all those criteria and precious few seem likely to within the Maastricht timetable—not even Germany, once it has taken full account of the costs of unification in its public debt (as it is due to in 1995). Without Germany, no one thinks there can be EMU. So the period of waiting may be over, but gloom will still envelop Europe's leaders when they meet at a special "celebratory" summit on October 29th.

The question is whether the gloom will distract them from an issue that in practice looms more important than the improbable targets of the Maastricht treaty: how to accommodate a growing list of applicants for membership that ranges from Austria, Norway, Finland and Sweden, potential entrants in 1995, to Turkey, Poland, Malta

EC arithmetic

	Population (m)	Votes in council
Germany	80.6	10
Britain	57.9	10
France	57.5	10
Italy	56.9	10
Spain	39.1	8
Holland	15.2	5
Greece	10.3	5
Belgium	10.0	5
Portugal	9.8	5
Sweden*	8.6	4 or 5
Austria*	7.9	4 or 5
Denmark	5.2	3
Finland*	5.0	3
Norway*	4.3	3
Ireland	3.5	3
Luxembourg	0.4	2

Source: European Commission   *Applicants

and others later. Should the club change its rules as it grows bigger?

The answer depends on who is being questioned. The EC has never been a Community of equals. Of the six founders, France, West Germany and Italy had large populations, Holland, Belgium and Luxembourg small ones. The trick of the founding fathers was to introduce a system of checks and balances that has survived to this day. Big countries have more votes in the decision-making Council of Ministers so they cannot be out-voted by a gaggle of small ones. But small countries are protected from big-country bullying by a system of weighted voting. It takes 54 of the council's 76 votes to get a "qualified", or decisive, majority—so small countries need to amass only 23 votes to form a "blocking minority".

So far this has worked well. The arithmetic means that the big five, even though they represent two-thirds of the Community's population, cannot out-vote the small seven. To reach a qualified majority the big five need the support of at least two small states. Similarly, minnows in search of a qualified majority need to get three big states on their side. The basic principle is that a qualified majority represents 70% of the Community's population.

But expand the Community (or "Union", as Maastricht would have it) and the arithmetic will work differently. Of the score of new applicatants, only Turkey and Poland have populations large enough to join the present big five. So the balance of power will start shifting to small countries. The inclusion of Austria, Sweden, Finland and (assuming its voters agree) Norway will enable eight countries representing only 12% of the Community's population to block the wishes of eight countries representing 88%.

Hence the desire of Britain and, less publicly, Germany (which, after unification, ought to have more than ten votes) to start an early debate on the balance of power. Hence, too, the desire of small states to postpone the debate until their ranks are increased by the new entrants.

The number of votes in the Council of Ministers is not the only issue dividing big and small. At the moment, the presidency of the council—which carries the responsibility for organising the EC's affairs—goes from

From *The Economist*, October 16, 1993, pp. 51-52. © 1993 by The Economist, Ltd. Distributed by The New York Times Special Features. Reprinted by permission.

Last harrumph for Maastricht

FROM OUR SPECIAL CORRESPONDENT IN KARLSRUHE

"EXCELLENT, excellent," chortled one of Chancellor Helmut Kohl's officials after the public reading on October 12th of the unanimous 85-page verdict by which Germany's Constitutional Court said Yes to the Maastricht treaty. The court's expected ifs and buts were less restrictive than Mr Kohl's government had once feared. The decision would allow (markets permitting) monetary union without strings.

By rejecting the three main complaints against the treaty as inadmissible or unfounded, the eight judges of the court's second bench removed the last legal obstacle to German ratification. This enabled the president to sign the treaty and Germany to join its 11 European partners in full ratification.

The Karlsruhe court first dismissed the complaint that the European Union created by Maastricht involved a dissolution of German national sovereignty. The treaty, it said, establishes not a "European state" but a *Staatenverbund*—a league of states, each of which preserves its national identity while sharing many once-sovereign powers.

Second, turning to the so-called "democratic deficit" (ie, the idea that the European Community's elected institutions are too weak compared with its executive ones), the court rejected the Greens' call for a referendum on Maastricht but insisted that "democratic control" should grow in step with European integration. The European parliament must play its part in this, said the court, especially if members come to be elected throughout Europe under the same voting rules (which they are not now). But the court made clear that the more important institution, as far as the German constitution was concerned, was the German parliament.

Third, the court was not impressed by fears that Maastricht might abolish the D-mark and push Germany into monetary union at the end of the decade against its will. There is, the court said, nothing automatic about the final step to monetary union. Strict economic convergence criteria have to be met first.

And those, the judges said, cannot legally be weakened without a decision by the German government with the advice of the Bundestag.

Germany's loudest Euro-enthusiast, Helmut Kohl, can be pleased with all this. The court's view of Maastricht is close to the government's own, though whether it is as close to what Mr Kohl once wished for is another matter. Mr Kohl remains as Europhile as ever. It seems an exaggeration to claim, as did Manfred Brunner, one of the losing plaintiffs who had hauled the treaty before the Constitutional Court, that "Kohl's Europe with this ruling is dead." But the chancellor has become more circumspect about what is achievable in the short term.

As for the future shape of the Community, the court gave scant comfort to federalists. It took a restrictive view of the "implied powers" clause of the treaty, which gives the EC the powers it needs to carry out its tasks. And it said that the future EC cannot create revenues on its own for new tasks that it sets itself.

---

one country to another for a term of six months. Add too many new members and the big countries will have to wait for years before their turn comes again. Unless the procedure is changed, there will be a period from mid-1996 until the end of 1999 during which a sequence of seven small countries (and three in a row will be new members) will hold the presidency.

Nor are the big countries amused by the prospect of a larger commission. At the moment each big country provides two commissioners, each small country one. The result is a commission of 17. Give each new entrant a commissioner, and the body will become ever more unwieldly.

What is to be done? In August Karl Lamers, parliamentary spokesman on foreign affairs for Germany's Christian Democrats, suggested a "double majority" for the Council of Ministers: a majority of member states representing a majority of the EC's population. For matters that now require unanimity, he suggested a "super-qualified" majority: four-fifths or three-quarters of the member states representing four-fifths or three-quarters of the Community's population. Other proposals are to cut the number of commissioners from the current 17 to ten, which would mean the big countries having one each and the small countries having to rotate commissioners be-

tween them; and to rotate the presidency of the council between big and small members (a British idea that is also favoured by Germany).

Doubtless there will be more ideas yet—and doubtless the wrangling will dismay the Euro-enthusiasts, especially those who hanker for a future beyond the Maastricht treaty, a federal Europe with the sort of powerful parliament that few EC governments, big or small, are yet keen on seeing. But the enthusiasts should not be too disheartened. For all its faults, and for all the gloom, the European Union is still a club that others want to join.

European Union: Now What?

Roger Kaplan

Roger Kaplan is editor of Freedom Review.

On New Year's Day 1993 the European Single Market went into effect, achieving the promise of economic union among the twelve-nation Economic Community. Thus ended a chapter in European history, one that began in 1950 when Frenchmen Robert Schuman and Jean Monnet declared that cooperation must exist on the ground before it could be achieved politically.

And on 1 November, All Saints' Day, the European Community, still referred to by many as the "European Economic Community" or the "Common Market," officially became the European Union. Thus began, on a Christian holiday founded in sorrow but touched by hope, a new chapter in European history.

Many were too hardup to notice. The looming failure of EuroDisney, a two-year old theme and amusement park that had been launched on a wave of optimism about the internationalization of business and culture, the collapse of the Renault-Volvo merger, and the continuing layoffs in such basic industries as steel and textiles, seemed an apt symbol of the times, and if the point needed stressing, it was done by German Chancellor Helmut Kohl, who rebuked his countrymen for abandoning their characteristic work ethic: "Germany is not an amusement park," he said. But attempts at forging new deals among the "social partners," usually stressing more work and fewer benefits, were angrily rejected by workers in Belgium, Spain and France, and had mixed success in Italy and Germany. The Swiss, Norwegians, Swedes, Finns, and even the Austrians (striving for respectability) doubted whether their governments, all of which had applications pending or under review to join the EU, had the right idea. In the southern countries, Italy and Spain in particular but France as well and Greece more ambiguously, voters disgusted with the corruption rotting away their democratic polities threw the rascals out. Looming over this odd mix of unity and rancor was the biggest issue of all: the Yugoslav war—and the failure of Europe, of the European Union, to do anything about it.

To be sure, the new Union, as a political concept, was not under strain, partly because the British and the Danes—along with currency speculators—convinced the Europeanists that Europe, institutionally, politically and economically is not an all-or-nothing proposition: it can advance at different speeds, with individual states deciding when to participate fully in joint economic or security institutions. The EU's difficulties were inherent in the member states themselves, problems stemming from the exhaustion of the welfare state in recessionary times, the weakening of civic and family values, and the frustrations of being, to simplify only slightly, the world's most prosperous region and politically weakest entity. Throughout the fall European governments dealt with strikes that were motivated more by insecurity about existing employment and benefits than by demands for better deals. These, as well as the continuing political violence in Northern Ireland, Spain and Italy, horrifying but limited, reminded Europeans that the good society was still in the making. The wars in the Balkans and the Caucassus, and massacres, mayhem and armed subversion in former African possessions were like a bitter reproach to the European wish, expressed in everything from protectionist stances in successfully completed GATT negotiations (a victory for EU cohesiveness) to recurrences of anti-Americanism and Japophobia, to be left alone in the little corner from which they once ruled the world.

Thus, even as the Single Market gave Europeans the unified economic space promised since the 1957 Treaty of Rome, they

---

On New Year's Day 1993 the European Single Market went into effect. Thus began a new chapter in European history. Many were too hardup to notice.

From *Freedom Review*, Vol. 25, No. 1, January/February 1994, pp. 53-57. © 1994 by Freedom House, New York, NY 10005. Reprinted by permission.

sought protection from Japanese cars, American movies, and Polish produce, not to mention foreign bodies in general. Interestingly enough, they were unable, or unwilling, to protect their currencies from market fluctuations, which battered the French, Swedish, Spanish, Italian, Portuguese and British currencies to the point where the SME (or ERM, the mechanism for keeping currencies, inflation rates, and interest rates closely in line) was several times pronounced dead (it lives, just). They revised their constitutions to restrict asylum seekers and ordinary migrants from points east and south, in keeping with the EU Treaty's single border.

Tough times in the amusement park

The sense that the new Union has a brittle foundation was underscored by labor unrest. Trade union members have been waiting, and waiting some more, for tangible benefits of the "social chapter" which the moderate Left, notably French President Francois Mitterrand and European Commission President Jacques Delors, have been describing, since they proposed it ten years ago, as the indispensable counterweight to the liberalized market which they, men of the Left, put in place in the late 80s.

It is worth noting that criticism of neo-laissez-fairism, which European leaders felt they had no choice but to embrace in order to keep up with the U.S. and Japan, is by no means confined to the labor movement and its allies on the social democratic and socialist Left. There is a deep conservative tradition in Europe which, also, denounces the individualistic ethic, which they delight in referring to by such epithets as "casino" or "savage" capitalism or (still) "Reagano-Thatcherite ultraliberalism," or more simply, the "jungle." Without the Soviet threat, this conservative tradition is more readily able to break with its erstwhile classical liberal allies. This explains (in part) the strains in the conservative-liberal coalition (CDU-FDP) in Germany, or the angry call by the conservative president of the French National Assembly, Philippe Seguin, to resist the "social Munich" caused by liberal monetary policies (meaning tight money and a strong currency) designed to keep European currencies on track toward convergence.

Ironically indeed, "ultraliberalism" did not make good politics in the year of the Single Market. France's new conservative prime minister, Edouard Balladur, extolled the role of the (albeit leaner) state. John Major's difficulties stem in part from his need to balance the claims of the Thatcherite legacy and those of the Tory state-interventionists like Michael Heseltine (who led the revolt against Thatcher in 1992).

The Europeans' sense of their countries and their new Union as morally vacant places stems in part from being out of sorts, out of purpose, and out of cash. But no one doubted, either, that in the

---

German Chancellor Helmut Kohl rebuked his countrymen for abandoning their characteristic work-ethic: "Germany is not an amusement park."

---

one large moral enterprise that was available for the immediate taking, namely to intervene in the Yugoslav wars, Europe failed: not for lack of knowledge, and probably not for lack of public indignation and will, but for lack of political will.

Toward Union

There had been some close calls on the way to Union, with the French approving the Maastricht Treaty in a September 1992 referendum by the narrowest of margins, and the Danes approving it, in a May referendum, only after rejecting it in 1992. In Great Britain's House of Commons the Treaty was approved 292-112 in May, but only after the "Eurosceptics" nearly undercut John Major's government. And it was not until October that the German constitutional court decided the Treaty did not contradict that country's Basic Law.

Winning is what counts, but most Europeanists, not to mention their more enlightened detractors, knew that in many ways Maastricht was already behind the curve. The unreadable Treaty of Union is not a document to which anyone would spontaneously swear allegiance. "It is a bad treaty," said former German Chancellor—and unimpeachable Europeanist—Helmut Schmidt, "in which the fundamental issues are mixed up with less important ones." For Europeanism to remain credible, its champions know they need to look good, and fast. But the mud of political and economic stagnation was thick in Europe in 1993, and despite acts of heroism—notably in Italy, where a brave band led a popular revolt against political-gangster corruption—it was not the most inspiring year on record.

The Maastricht Treaty confers "European citizenship" on citizens of member states, which should, by and by, allow Italian residents of London, for example, to stand in local, and eventually national, elections. This pleased the Left but displeased the Right. Actually, in many countries the cleavage was less between Left and Right than between "nationals" and "Europeanists." But both of these schools included unnatural allies united only in their dislike of liberal centrists like German Chancellor Helmut Kohl and Spanish Prime Minister Felipe Gonzalez, who best represent the European project in its Maastricht Treaty phase. Both on the extreme-liberal Right (what American calls libertarianism) and on the radical Left (which today has little foothold in the mainstream socialist parties, including Italy's ex-Communist Democratic Party of the Left, PDS), the new EU is viewed as a system to favor big business and labor. Yet this is in line with the social democratic civilization, based on private enterprise and statist redistribution, which produced nearly fifty years of peace and prosperity. The question is whether the model is spent and the union without a fresh purpose.

To be sure, there is the matter of personalities, too. Men like Kohl, *a fortiori* François Mitterrand and Jacques Delors, are haunted by memories of Europe's wars. A younger leadership was emerging in 1993, represented by many members of British Labour Party leader John Smith's shadow cabinet, or by the young (born 1947) leader of the German SPD, Rudolph Scharping (following the resignation for truth-fudging several years ago of the minister-president of Schleswig-Hollstein Bjorn Engholm). A former leader of the Jusos (young Socialists) and the minister-president of Rhine-Palatinate (Kohl's job in the 70s), Scharping takes Europe for granted, but by the same token cannot be expected to expend great enthusiasms on it. On the other hand, Gro Harlem Brundtland, whose Labor party won (again) in Norway, wants her country to join, as does her liberal-conservative neighbor in Sweden, Carl Bildt. The Danish referendum, in which all the parties, trade unions, media, and business associations urged a "yes," reflected the difference between elites and public opinion in Scandanavia. The Swiss are generally pro-Europe at this point in opinion surveys, but they rejected membership in the EEE[1] in a referendum. Some of this lessening of the Eurosteam is doubtless sensible, reflecting a pragmatic approach to a still uncertain future. Thus even as German Chancellor Helmut Kohl used "new chapter" rhetoric to greet the day, British Prime Minister John Major—who belongs to Scharping's generation—warned against the "politics of illusion" that the Euro-enthusiasts fostered.

Power to whom?

The Treaty of Union goes beyond free trade zonism to prepare the way for full monetary union and a single defense and foreign policy. Countries, notably Great Britain and Denmark, that do not like this do not have to participate. The principle of a Europe moving at several gears is accepted, though it remains to be seen how this will work out in the growing body of European law, which takes precedence over national law, so long as it does not contradict national constitutions: an ambiguity that will take years to work out, and much lawyering. Josef Joffe of the Süddeutsche Zeitung says the Court maintained the primacy of national parliaments over Europe's parliament.

This institution, located at Strasbourg and directly elected since 1979, saw its powers enhanced under the Treaty, notably in that it can veto decisions of the Council of Ministers (the Union's executive, of which the Commission is the arm). But, absent some precedents, it is unclear how this is going to work out, or whether this will result in more democratic governance, as its partisans claim. There is a left-wing current of anti-Maastrichism which says the Treaty is technocratic and anti-democratic and favors reinforcing the Parliament even more. But there is also a current which dislikes the idea of one more level of government, and a remote one at that.

Although Europe, the project, and the much-maligned Eurocrats in Brussels, got a good pounding between the signing of the Treaty in February 1992 and its final ratification in the fall of 1993, politicians in power took most of the heat for the unemployment crisis. Liberal economists blame the high costs of labor, including the high costs of laying off workers. Voters blame it on incumbents. Strasbourg property values may be rising, but politics are still local.

Shock at the polls

The first shock at the polls came in France in March. The governing Socialists knew they were in trouble. They had called for a yes on the Maastricht Treaty, which President Mitterrand had submitted to referendum, the previous September, and they very nearly lost it. The party split on the issue, with the "republicans" breaking ranks. Though of course all socialists consider themselves to be in the republican tradition, the term increasingly is appropriated by the heirs of the Jacobin line, centralizing and statist, who oppose the more liberal approach of party-leader Michel Rocard.

The Left's ostensible constituency, salaried workers, voted against Maastricht. But the Socialists were unprepared for the tidal wave that hit them in March. The new Assembly contained 57 Socialists, 12 independent Lefts, 24 Communists, and 460 liberal-conservatives. Apart from the rout, the campaign's significance for the Left was that the Greens were bleached out, even as they, along with the Socialists, introduced the share-the-work theme that has become popular throughout the EU as a putative

way to create jobs. Also, the rout allowed Rocard (who lost his seat) to wrest the party from the last Mitterrandist faithful.

Neither British Prime Minister John Major nor German Chancellor Helmut Kohl had to face the voters, and each was doubtless grateful for that. Major, despite a surge in the British economy after a prolonged recession, had more than enough trouble with the "Thatcherites" in his Tory party, and had to keep an eye on the rising stars of the new Labour party leadership, such as John Smith, John Prescott and Gordon Brown.

Helmut Kohl often appeared to be in trouble, with the CDU losing local elections steadily to the SPD and facing the very real, if still improbable, possibility of national defeat in 1994. Kohl, who had made himself the champion of rapid reunification after the fall of the Berlin Wall, was rebuffed in the eastern Land of Brandenburg, which was carried by the ex-Communist candidate in December. Kohl also had to contend with a right-wing, led by the Bavarian CSU leader Edward Steubel, who called for less Europe and more Germany. The chancellor supported the Saxon Steffen Heitmann for the presidency, a post that in Germany is important for the moral authority that it represents. Outgoing president Richard von Weizsaecker is one of the most respected men in Germany and has spoken out forcefully against the neo-Nazi violence that has been directed at foreigners in the past two to three years.

But Heitmann, chosen by Kohl as a symbol of reconciliation between eastern and western Lander, gave the impression that he believes Germans should stop apologizing for their past. This may or may not have a basis in common sense, but Germans do not expect it of the president of the Bundesrepublik. Heitmann's supporters said it was a typical case of national hypocrisy, but the Saxon leader withdrew. Kohl is likely to nominate another easterner, Richard Schroder, but he will have to contend with the Social Democrat candidate, Johannes Rau (minister-president of North Rhine-Westphalia), as well as the Free Democrat spoiler, Hildegard Hamm-Bruchher.

In Spain, Prime Minister Felipe Gonzalez had a close call in June elections, and his PSOE found itself without an absolute majority in the Cortes for the first time since 1982. The Socialists have been hurt by kick-back scandals, and Gonzalez played his personal popularity to the hilt to carry the elections. He also placed the top anti-corruption prosecutor, Jose Garzon, high on his party list, to show that bad apples did not reflect institutional rot. His new government, formed with Catalan and Basque votes but not ministerial participation, was dominated by Socialist "renovators" (liberals).

Europe, however, was not an issue, since there is a broad pro-European consensus in Spain. This is partly because Europe represents the opening to the world—and to freedom—that was not possible during the Francoist decades, but it is also because Spain, like Portugal (and Ireland, southern Italy, and Greece), benefits handsomely from the EU's development programs, known as the

---

The unreadable Treaty of Union is not a document to which anyone would spontaneously swear allegiance.

---

structural funds and the new (since Maastricht) cohesion funds. Whether these work better than the schemes to "develop" Third World countries on which they are modeled has not yet been proven, but they are appreciated in the places for which they are designed, such as Andalusia, Greece, Ireland, and the eastern German Lander.[2]

European welfare and subsidies are easily criticized. As much as 15 percent of the EC budget may be embezzled. No one is sure. Over half of the EC budget goes to agriculture (5 percent of west Europe's population), and it is simply impossible to get at the bottom of agricultural fraud, let alone do anything about it.

To these criticisms the Europeanists reply that what is needed is more Europe, not less. A bureaucracy responsible to a strengthened executive and a stronger Parliament, with help from an effective Europolice organization, can attack fraud (and drug trafficking, which did not wait for 1993 to take advantage of more permeable borders). Raymond Barre, the former French prime minister, believes that Poland and other central European countries should be brought in without delay, and the countries of the EFTA (Norway, Sweden, Finland, Austria, Switzerland) as soon as they want to. Barre argues that even the countries of eastern Europe should be brought in as soon as possible, that is to say as soon as they demonstrate their active (not rhetorical) commitment to democracy, human rights, free circulation of people, money and goods.

Europe, superficially, does not look depressed. Cities are clean, high-speed trains run on time, crime is low by American standards, free health care is available. But when you get beyond the spic-and-span downtowns you find enough misery to understand that comparisons with the 30s are not out of line. The crucial difference is the social safety net. But this is straining under the impact of prolonged unemployment combined with tears in the social fabric due to weaker family structures, less disciplined educational system, drugs and, according to some, diminished church attendance.

There are about 18 million unemployed in the EU and there may be 20 million by the end of 1994.[3] Carlos Ferrer Salat, chairman of UNICE (the European employers' federation), says: "Europe has the most costly and rigid labour market in the world and Spain"—he is from Barcelona—"has the most costly and rigid market in Europe."

Some of this, no doubt, is disguised. Spain, for example, officially has an unemployment level of 20 percent (triple the official U.S. rate and ten times the official Pacific rim rate) but more people seem to be working there than in France, which has about 12 percent. It seems that in less mature welfare states, people learn to make do with mixes of official benefits and unofficial jobs. At any rate, the debate on "managing work" spread across Europe in 1993, and its outcome may influence European competitiveness (and thereby its ability to sustain acceptable levels of prosperity) in the years ahead.

The work debate, though it focuses for rhetorical convenience on working time is, more deeply, a debate about the relationship between productivity and society. In France, Michel Rocard says you must work less to produce more jobs, but with less income, at

---

There are about 18 million unemployed in the EU and there may be 20 million by the end of 1994.

---

least until productivity increases. The liberals say there is no need to have national, let alone European, working-time regulations;

what is needed is more flexibility. The Germans are beginning large-scale experiments in working-time modifications, notably at Volkswagen, where a four-day week was instituted in October, with 10 percent pay-cuts (management had asked for 20 percent) and a day for job retraining.

VW represented the strength of the German social pact, but Kohl warned that the country is living beyond its means. Construction workers demonstrated against reductions in their "bad weather" benefits. They are compensated when the weather keeps them off the job and under new proposed rules, this benefit would only apply to the winter months.

Concerned about the viability of their social democracies, the Europeans knew they had to maintain some sort of global credibility. The EU calls for a single foreign and security policy (Pesc), and one of the first things it did was to offer Serbia a relaxation of the U.N.-imposed sanctions if it eased up (or persuaded the Bosnian Serbs to ease up) on territorial claims in Bosnia. Many observers felt this was a fitting way to end a year in which the putative new superpower had let a slaughter take place under its figurative nose, but here again, the Europeanists could plead that something could have been done had there been "more" Europe. Until the EU came into being, they say, Europe, as a political entity, had no competence in the matter. And did the "unilateralists" offer anything better? The champions of "NATO's new missions?" The globalists of the U.N.? The EU, in inviting the U.S. and the Russian governments to join them for an ultimate (one more time) effort at getting the parties to make a deal was, it can be said, at least, picking up reality where it came in.

Keeping it safe for natives

The EU is also supposed to organize a common internal security policy. In practice this means, in the short term, getting control of Europe's borders. As in other matters, this produced a cleavage between the "little Europe" protectionists and the "new superpower" visionaries. The best way to keep out waves of huddled masses, the latter say, is to help them help themselves. But the needs are great and the demands never-ending. In North Africa, half the population is under thirty and unemployed, and fanatics are bidding for power. Across much of eastern Europe, misery and war stalk the lands.

However, the debates over immigration also touch upon the issue of what it means to be a Frenchman, or a German, or a Dane—or a European. To many little-Europe men, particularly on the Left and among the Green parties, nationalism is old hat when not mischievous. Multicultural, multiethnic societies are better. In the middle, the mainstreams of the CDU and the SPD put together legislation to simultaneously restrict immigration and facilitate the acquisition of citizenship. Until recently it was almost impossible to acquire German citizenship, but the idea now is to make it possible for those who do get in to become integrated, rather than create non-German communities living apart from the rest of society.

Indeed, integration is very much on the agenda in France as well, after several years during which multiculturalism ("the right to be different") was fashionable. The French also have tightened immigration rules and have made the acquisition of citizenship more difficult, in order to distinguish between applicants who want to be Frenchmen and those who need a place to stay.

On the surface, this stiffening of the national idea, and of notions of civic responsibility that accompany it, runs counter to the pan-Europeanism of the pro-Maastricht Euroenthusiasts. In the past several years, and particularly this past year as European nations had to get their laws in harmony with the European directives that render the Single Act operational, there was a great deal of "We are Europeans" rhetoric, complete with the Ode to Joy (the EC, and now EU, anthem) as background music. A reaction was inevitable.

One positive aspect of the inward turn has been to take a fresh look at the corrupt practices that to some degree could be tolerated in expansive years but that became intolerable in lean ones. Particularly in the Latin countries, judges (state prosecutors) went after politicians, businessmen and gangsters engaged in countless variations of the basic kickback. In Italy the process has been close to revolutionary. The Christian Democratic and Socialist Parties have been all but wiped out, as leaders up to and including seven-time Christian Democrat Prime Minister Giulio Andreotti (DC), under investigation for links with the mafia, and the country's longest-serving prime minister, socialist Bettino Craxi (PSI), investigated for municipal corruption in Milan, lost their credibility. President Oscar Luigi Scalfaro attacked politicians' attempts to vote themselves an amnesty, and Pope John Paul II went to Sicily to attack the mafia. At least 3,000 people were in jail or under arrest by mid-1993, with even great names of Italian business like Carlo de Benedetti and Raul Gardini—who committed suicide—implicated in the *mani puli* (clean hands) investigations.

Italy's citizen revolt

The citizens' revolt in Italy, with the prosecutors in the vanguard, demonstrated that "republican virtue" and "responsibilities of citizenship" at some point have to go from talk to action. *Arrestateli tutti* (arrest them all) was the slogan, showing the citizens getting in step behind the marshals in a country supposedly too blase for virtue. But it was not just a matter of confounding the cliches. Getting behind the marshals could mean getting killed, and the marshals themselves, notably the courageous anti-mafia judges, including Giovanni Falcone and Paolo Borsalino (both murdered in 1992), often paid with their lives. Leoluca Orlando, the successful anti-mafia, anti corruption mayoral candidate in Palermo, Sicily, was frequently in hiding.

Thoughtful observers, native and foreign, doubt the war against the mafia can be won in a decisive sense. But "the octopus" can be weakened by repeated blows at its leadership, its markets, and at the political-business elites with which it does business. In this regard the capture of Salvatore "Toto" Riina, the boss of all bosses, in Palermo, in January, was of great symbolic, as well as substantial, importance. Riina is suspected of having ordered the Falcone assassination as well as the murder, ten years ago, of the *carabinierri* general Carlo Alberto Dalla Chiesa (who had dismantled the terrorist Red Brigades.) Both men's wives were murdered at their sides, lending some bitter piquancy to Riina's family-values poses in the courtroom.

Already in 1992, the state had sent 7,000 soldiers to Sicily, passed tough anti-Mafia laws and intensified the *pentiti* (informer-protection) program, often in cooperation with U.S. law-enforcement. The most famous informer, Tommaso Buscetta, claims Craxi took $29 million in bribes in Milan and says Andreotti himself was the mafia's top inside fixer in Rome. It is difficult to over-emphasize the heroism of Italian law-enforcement in this deadly game because, as terrorist bombings showed, there is absolutely no safety from the mafia, no matter how high you are. When Andreotti

said he feared for his life (implicitly suggesting that he did indeed know certain things about the mafia-state links), no one laughed.

Italian voters, in a stunning April referendum, signaled they had enough of a system in which the spoils and patronage had come to eclipse governance almost entirely. The vote, with a 77 percent turnout, represented "a shocking indictment of the political class and the political system that have controlled Italy for almost half a century," observed the *Economist's* John Andrews. The typical trade-off was the exchange between the DC and the mafia in the south, and particularly in Sicily: votes in exchange for public money, parceled out by local bosses. Thanks to men like Leoluca Orlando and Nando Dalla Chiesa (the general's son), this arrangement may be over.

In the November municipal elections, one of the biggest landslides in western Europe in living memory, the traditional parties were beaten, with the important exception of the ex-Communists, now called the Democratic Party of the Left, which openly proclaimed its allegiance to the north-European social-democratic values (at Strasbourg they sit on the democratic left benches, unlike the French comrades). The ex-PCI had not been implicated in municipal corruption as much as the other parties (though they ran many cities and some observors claim they played the system just like the others), and of course they had never belonged to the ruling coalitions at the national level, the *partitocracia*. Moreover, the DC could no longer wave the anti-Communist, anti-Soviet flag, as they had done for fifty years. Indeed, evidence that the Cold War was no longer a factor in Italian politics was shown by the strong showing of the MSI (neo-fascists) in Naples and their photogenic standard bearer, Alessandra Mussolini. (She lost the runoff to the PDS candidate.) With the fascists on one side and the ex-Communists on the other, the Cold War center had not held.

The *partitocracia* remains in power at the national level, but with the government of Carlo Azeglio Ciampi (who left the Bank of Italy in May) essentially in a caretaker role. The old-order parties, overwhelmed by revelations about past abuses both venal and political, are doing their best to limit the scope of political and financial reform. However, Ciampi has exploited Italy's precarious position, and the repeated attacks on the lira, to rally a consensus for a tough budget package based on a tax hike and spending cuts that would keep the public sector deficit below 9 percent of gross domestic product. The bets were that he would get the budget passed by the end of the year (as required by law) and keep to the political calendar which calls for a new parliament to be elected, with new rules and new constituency boundaries, next March.

Whether this means Italy will become politically polarized remains to be seen; but neither the MSI, which has never disowned its Mussolinian heritage, nor the PDS, which has broken with the Stalinist past, appears to be be tempted by anti-democratic solu-

---

Many doubt the war against the mafia can be won in a decisive sense. But "the octopus" can be weakened by repeated blows at its leadership and its markets.

---

tions. Arguably more troublesome for the country's political future is the fact that Italy remains two distinct countries, economically and otherwise. This may not be enough reason to break up this newcomer among European nation-states, as the Northern League's Umberto Bossi would like, but it underscores the political challenge faced by Italy's reforming patriots. In Lombardia, Veneto or Piedmont, you are for most practical purposes in Bade-Wurtenberg or Sussex or Geneva; in Calabria and Campania and Sicilia you almost could be in North Africa. Of course, this statement is grossly proximate: in Veneto or in Tuscany you are, in fact, in Veneto or Tuscany, and in Sardinia and Basilicata you are in Sardinia and Basilicata. Nonetheless, these socio-economic gaps underscore the limits of integration-via-economics. There seems to come a point where a rising tide does not carry all boats, it leaves some boats stranded. At this point, politics must take over.

Jean Monnet knew this, and he expected the political leaders to take over from the economic building-block men. Well, the Single Market is in place and the Treaty of Union ratified. If there are Europeans with vision, let them stand up and be counted.

Notes

1 - The EEE, or EEA, for European Economic Area, is the coordinating body of the EC and the EFTA.

2 - The cohesion funds are supposed to go to regions where income is less than 75 percent of the EU average, but no government can resist this sort of pork so they make deals whereby "poor" areas that are in fact very close to average get pieces of the action as well.

3 - Eurostat, the EC's (now EU's) raw research arm, said the unemployment level in June was 11.5 percent, about 17 million, and rising, compared to "only" 8.4 percent in 1990.

Goodbye to a United Europe?

Stanley Hoffmann

Stanley Hoffmann is Douglas Dillon Professor of the Civilization of France and Chairman of the Center for European Studies. He is at work on a book about French nationalism and, with Michael J. Smith, on a book about ethics and international relations.

1.

When the leaders of the twelve members of the European Community signed the Treaty on Monetary and Political Union in Maastricht in December 1991, the project of a United Europe, which began in 1950 under the inspiration of Jean Monnet, seemed to be making spectacular progress. A single currency, a common monetary policy, and an independent central bank were to be established in stages before the end of the century, thus bringing to its logical conclusion the design for a single European market that had been proposed in the mid-1980s.[1] The powers of the Community were also to be extended to deal with a broad range of policies concerning health, consumer protection, the environment, crime, immigration, labor relations, diplomacy, and defense. Even though Britain had refused both to accept the new social provisions of the treaty and to join the full monetary union, agreement on so vast an expansion of community activities was hailed as a great success.

Yet the signing of the Maastricht treaty marked the beginning of a serious crisis, which has led to a new wave of pessimism about Europe's future, both on the Continent and in the US.

The pessimism comes from a variety of different troubles. Every Western European economy is stagnant, the result both of the worldwide recession and the huge costs of German unification. Partly as a result, the main European governments are concentrating on their domestic difficulties and programs. Two other sources of the European malaise may be more difficult to deal with in the long run. One is often referred to as the Community's "democratic deficit," the much-resented distance between the bureaucracies that administer the EC and the European voters who are affected by it. Perhaps the deepest problem of all concerns the relation of the traditional nation-state to a new United Europe.

The ambitious plans that are now falling apart were the product of another recession—the one that hit Western Europe after the oil crisis of 1973 and resulted in years of "Europessimism," fluctuations in exchange rates, and stagnation in the development of the Community. Even Britain's entry into the EC didn't help, since the British spent, in effect, ten years—between 1974 and 1984—renegotiating the terms on which they had been admitted. In 1978, the French President Valéry Giscard d'Estaing and the West German Chancellor Helmut Schmidt took the initiative to set up a European Monetary System (EMS) that would create monetary stability by narrowing the range of exchange rate fluctuations among the members' currencies. This seemed one of the more striking European successes of the postwar period. Devaluations and reevaluations of currency were not ruled out, but they became increasingly rare. Britain, which had at first stayed out, finally joined the EMS in 1990. The EMS was to be the basis on which a full monetary union, ultimately with a common European currency—an objective toward which Jaques Delors, the president of the EC's Commission, had been working for years—was going to be built.

Progress toward monetary union, as defined at Maastricht, required that the members' economic and fiscal policies would converge with regard to inflation, interest rates, deficits, debts, and currency stability. The treaty set up guidelines that participants in the enterprise were to meet, and, as has been the case during the 1980s, these corresponded to the preferences and policies of the German Bundesbank. Maastricht was supposed to continue the process by which both Britain and (after the grand reversal of the Socialists' economic policy in 1983) France pursued economic strategies, including high interest rates, that aimed at monetary stability and at reducing inflation. Even when the American recession began to reach Europe, these policies continued.

But German reunification, beginning in 1989, destabilized the EMS. Chancellor Kohl's decision to establish a one-to-one exchange rate between the Deutsche mark and the Ostmark and to accept wage parity between the workers of the Federal Republic and the far less productive workers of the former Democratic Republic led to enormous reductions in income, employment, and production in the East, and obliged the German government to transfer huge amounts of public funds there. Kohl's reluctance to raise taxes resulted in large borrowing and a big deficit; the rise in Germany's inflation (which had preceded unification) worsened. The independent Bundesbank reacted by raising its interest rates by six percentage points in five years in order to combat inflation. But this obliged Germany's partners in the EMS to raise their own interest rates in order to prevent an outflow of funds from their countries to Germany and to preserve the stability of their own currencies, the result being lower economic growth and higher unemployment.

In Britain and France, politicians, economists, and businessmen (such as Jacques Charvet, the head of Peugeot, in France) began to question the wisdom both of sacrificing growth to sustain artificial exchange rates and of following the dictates of the Bundesbank, which had become the de facto European Central Bank, yet acted only according to its view of the German national interest. Also the international money markets, computerized and deregulated, began to sell gigantic amounts of currencies that appeared overvalued, such as the peseta, the lira, and the pound. The central banks that tried to defend their currencies by purchasing large amounts of them on the market simply did not have the reserves to succeed in doing so. The daily turnover in currency markets reached $900 billion, while the reserves of the G7 nations amounted to less than a third of this sum.

In early September 1992, the European governments failed to agree on an official currency realignment that would have slightly adjusted the value of currencies in relation to the market. The French objected because of possible negative effects on the difficult campaign to get the French public to vote for the Maastricht treaty, the British because they insisted, in vain, that the Germans reduce interest rates. This led to the uncontrolled devaluation of the pound, the lira, and the peseta, and to Britain and Italy's withdrawal from the EMS after the Bank of England's failure to support

the pound even after spending half of its reserves.[2]

The EMS is not dead. With much help from the Bundesbank, the French were able to resist the markets' onslaught on the franc, and thus to keep their currency within the margins of fluctuation required by EMS. As long as EMS is alive, there is a chance for monetary union, but it is clear that Britain, now embarked on a policy of reduced interest rates and monetary autonomy, will not rejoin it in the near future. Nor will Italy, Greece, and Spain, among others, meet the "convergence criteria" set up by EMU. There will be increasing pressure on the Bundesbank, particularly from the French, to lower German interest rates so that these rates can be lowered in France and elsewhere, and the way opened to more growth and reemployment.

If the Bundesbank resists French pressures, the French politicians who argue against any further sacrifice of the French economy on the altar of monetary stability will gain influence. Moreover, the entire experience has strengthened the position of those in Germany who oppose the Maastricht treaty, believing that the dilution of the power of the Bundesbank in a European Central Bank, accompanied by a disappearance of the German national currency, would be a mistake. Thus, even a European Monetary Union limited to the stronger currencies among the twelve EEC nations remains at the mercy of the recession. If the recession prolongs the agony of East Germany's merger with West Germany, which is the cause of the Bundesbank's reluctance to lower interest rates, and one of the causes of the unemployment crisis in France,[3] the chances of organizing a European Monetary Union will be slim. But should the Bundesbank become more lax, Germany's own ability to meet the criteria for economic convergence would be even more compromised. The great step toward a monetary union planned at Maastricht now appears to have been premature.

What the financial crisis has shown is the impossibility of bringing about monetary union without a close coordination of national economic policies—and the fact that, at present, there is a huge discrepancy between a single, deregulated market set up and

monitored by the Community and the tax, labor, monetary, and other economic policies that are still in the hands of the national governments. When these governments are determined to pursue the same type of economic policy—as was the case of France and Germany in the 1980s—the EC can make progress; but when the governments are incapable of pursuing the kind of policy preferred by the Bundesbank (as with Italy) or rebel against it (as with Britain), such progress stops.

Resuming the quest for monetary union will require that the governments of Western Europe put their respective economic houses in order. But if they concentrate on politically difficult domestic issues, such as lowering unemployment, they are likely to give less attention to all the other aspects of European unification, and indeed to become all the more impatient with them.

The governments of the EC's "big four" have all turned inward. Of these countries, Italy has always been the most strongly and sentimentally enthusiastic about European unification—but also the least capable of enforcing the rules and directives of the EC because its government has been so disorganized and inefficient. Its regional institutions are sometimes more competent, but Italy is the one country whose regions have no representation in Brussels.[4] Moreover, the current apocalyptic crisis in Italian politics, which has undermined the entire postwar political leadership and the constitutional system, will only reinforce the need to concentrate on domestic matters. To shift from an increasingly corrupt system of unaccountable public enterprises and patronage to a new, reformed Italian administration will be painful and tricky. Under prodding from a public that has long been complicit and cynical but finally has become fed up, such a shift will have to be carried out by the very people who have become targets of popular wrath, the beneficiaries of the old order. A successful economic reform might allow Italy to rejoin the European Monetary System and to put itself in shape for the European Monetary Union—but this would be an immense task, in view of Italy's debts and deficit.

The British concentration on domestic affairs and hostility to Europe extends beyond John Major's government, which decided that British growth must prevail over European monetary cooperation. Along with most conservatives, Major believes that the Thatcherite victory over trade unions has to be protected from the proposed EC labor charter with its liberal provisions on such matters as union rights and powers and factory conditions, which are abhorrent to British employers.

The genteel resentment of Britain's postwar decline—relative not only to France but even to Italy—which was so evident in the 1960s and 1970s, and which had been among the sources of Mrs. Thatcher's appeal, has not disappeared. It has only been supplemented by an awareness of the dark sides of Thatcherism (the gap between the richer and poorer parts of England) and of its failures (in industry or education), and by the discrediting of once sacred institutions, including the monarchy. None of this has made the British keener to participate in the EC. Nostalgia for Britain's "finest hour," in 1940, and for the days of empire, is still there. The special concessions Major had obtained at Maastricht, as well as the monetary crisis of last September, seem only to have strengthened the British tendency to want to have the advantages of being in the European "club" and the single market, but only as long as they do not clash with American policies and the British sense of distinctiveness. Britain's enthusiasm for extending the EC to the newly liberated countries of Eastern Europe derives largely from the old and constant British desire to turn the Community into little more than a free trade area with as few common rules and policies as possible.

The new French government has, by contrast, renewed France's strong commitment to the EC, to the European Monetary Union, and to a common European security system. The prime minister, Edouard Balladur, by his statements and appointments has subtly constrained his "boss" Jacques Chirac, who is expected to run for president in 1995, and has been known to veer opportunistically from statements of shrill nationalism to proclamations of good Europeanism. Balladur's mission is to manage the economy, with its three million unemployed, in such a way as not to undermine Chirac's chances in 1995, and this concern will determine his attitude toward the EC. If the EC can be used to provide tangible benefits for France (a reduction of interest rates by the Bundesbank, for instance), it will be applauded. If it tries to impose sacrifices on French farmers, because of the preference that most EC members (including Germany, if not German farmers) have for a GATT agreement on freer agricultural trade, even at the expense of a very small part of the French peasantry, the EC will be resisted. It is most unlikely that the government will accept a compromise that would cost Chirac, a former minister of agriculture, the votes of France's farmers, most of whom vote for the right but were against Maastricht.

As for Germany, it will hold many elections next year—local, state, and federal—and its government will have to deal above all with an electorate whose mood has been soured by the most serious recession in the postwar era, by the flood of refugees who have sought asylum (and against whom the growing far-right movements have turned their violence), and by the nasty revelations of the Stasi files in the East, which have worsened the climate of suspicion and resentment. The psychological gap between the West Germans, proud of their economic performance and of their ability to confront and repudiate the Nazi past, and the East Germans, accused of having bad working habits and a bad conscience as well, has not been closed. The many insecurities that afflict the public of a country whose internal tensions have, in the past, spelled trouble for much of Europe, are now central concerns of Germany's tired and divided government, which has only one year and a half to go. The government's main party, the Christian Democrats, has been slipping badly in the polls and in votes in state elections.

The overriding need felt by leaders throughout Western Europe to concentrate on domestic difficulties and to try, during a time of economic troubles, to cope with widespread public impatience with politicians, their stilted language, unfulfilled promises, and scandalous behavior, helps to explain why the Maastricht treaty may become a dead letter. So do the decline, except in England, of "established" parties (in France last month, the Socialists and the moderate right got only 57 percent of the vote) and the rise of extremism in Italy, France, and Germany. Instead of the common European policy on asylum called for by the end of 1993, new German legislation unilaterally declares that refugees who come to Germany from its eastern and southern neighbors do not deserve asylum.

As for a common European foreign policy and defense, nothing has done more to tarnish the prestige of the EC than the disastrous tragedy in Yugoslavia. The most "activist" of the EC members, Germany, prematurely pushed for recognition of Slovenia and Croatia. Germany has been the most indignant about Serbian crimes in Croatia and Bosnia, while remaining the one state that is constitutionally unable to fight outside its borders. (Hence the limited significance of the Franco-German Army Corps.) Those countries that can fight, such as Britain and France, have had no desire to go beyond humanitarian involvement. The EC's impotence and its eagerness to dump Yugoslavia on the UN reflect, once again, its members' overriding domestic political preoccupations.

2.

Such a conclusion may seem unfair, since diplomacy and defense, unlike agriculture or the single market, are still matters in which the EC members can act only when they are unanimous. But here we come to the third kind of crisis. The machinery of the EC has become increasingly complex and opaque. One of the reasons why the majority of the Danes and almost half of the French said no to the Maastricht treaty in 1992 was that the text was nearly incomprehensible. Drafted after the heads of state and government had left Maastricht, it was written by and for lawyers and bureaucrats and required legal experts to explain it.

The more clarification was provided, the more it became apparent that with the extension of the Community's competence came a vast tangle of procedures—cases in which decisions can be taken by a two-thirds majority, cases requiring unanimity, cases in which a two-thirds majority can decide because of a unanimous decision to allow it to do so—creating an almost impenetrable maze. Few Europeans really understand how the EC works. It has a dense network of committees on which bureaucrats serve both as national agents and European civil servants, and an extremely cumbersome machinery. The Commission, charged with taking initiatives and applying decisions, is made up of supposedly independent leaders appointed by the members. The Council, composed of government representatives, is a legislative body, quite distinct from the Parliament in Strasbourg, whose discussions, budgetary deliberations, and "co-decisions" on some matters with the Council are barely comprehensible to the public.

Hence the widespread lament about a "democratic deficit." The Council is the chief legislator, while the popularly elected Parliament has only very limited powers. The Commission, set up by the governments but basically not accountable to them or to the Parliament, is the main organ for taking initiatives and drafting regulations. The almost three hundred measures that were needed to create by 1993 a single market for goods, services, capital, and people were drafted by the Commission, submitted by it to the Council, which turned them into three hundred directives and regulations; these were then discussed by the Parliament, and referred to the member countries for enforcement by the national bureaucracies.

Such a setup is obviously very different from that of a federal democracy. During the negotiations over political union, not only the UK and France but the EC Commission opposed any dramatic increase in the Strasbourg Parliament's powers. The UK and France wanted, of course, to preserve the Council's preeminence because they can use it to assert national interests. But why was the Commission hostile to giving more power to the Strasbourg Parliament as well? The parliamentarians were said to be given to ceaseless, irresponsible talk. But how can they be expected to be anything else if they have no real powers?

Even more serious is the problem of the relations between the EC's institutions and national institutions. National parliaments in the EC countries, where parliamentary government is the norm, feel doubly dispossessed. Everywhere in Western Europe, it is the executive—i.e., the cabinet—that initiates the main legislative acts and sets the course for the nation. Quite unlike the system in the US, parliaments have only the choice between overthrowing the cabinet (and thus often risking their own dissolution) and accepting the cabinet's proposals. The transfer of an increasing number of state functions to Brussels has already reduced the sphere in which national parliaments can act and under the Maastricht treaty they would be reduced even further. These functions, moreover, are to be carried out not by a supranational parliament, but by the representatives of the national executives.

Quite understandably, a backlash has occurred. In amending the French constitution so as to make it compatible with Maastricht, the French Senate insisted that EC legislation be submitted to the French Parliament. But it also said that the French Parliament could do no more than pass "resolutions" approving or disapproving the EC's decisions, which often take the form of complex package deals, negotiated in Brussels, that cannot usefully be dealt with by a simple parliamentary resolution. If similar resolutions are passed by parliaments in other countries this would lead to paralysis rather than to a closing of the democratic gap.

An attempt was made at Maastricht to appease such fears of dispossession by invoking the principle that the Community should deal only with what cannot be handled "effectively" at the national level. But of course much of politics is itself a struggle among people with conflicting views precisely about the level on which decisions should be taken. This "principle of subsidiary," borrowed from Catholic thought, is of no help: it does nothing to make the EC more democratic, and could do much to provoke a constant tug of war between the national states and the EC.

The Byzantine complexity of the whole structure will be aggravated by the increasing heterogeneity of the EC, which will grow even further if new members join. One now hears talk of a "flexible Europe" in which all members will have to sign the same charter, but exceptions, transitory periods, and special provisions will be granted to those who otherwise wouldn't or couldn't join. Denmark, for instance, has obtained a special deal aimed at making a "yes" vote in the forthcoming referendum more likely. Under it, Denmark accedes to the Maastricht treaty but not to most of its provisions. The more Byzantine the structure, the less democratic it will be.

Two proposals are being made to deal with the democratic deficit. There could be a second house of the Parliament, composed of delegations from the national parliaments. This would associate these delegates more closely with what goes on in the EC. However, this arrangement would only intensify and duplicate a flaw of the present system: the Parliament is elected not so much as a truly *European* assembly, but as a collection of *national* deputies, who run, in their respective countries, on purely national slates, and campaign not on European but on national issues. A truly European assembly would presuppose not nationwide slates of candidates but slates elected by smaller constituencies, and composed not only of natives, but of people of different nationalities.[5] This would be a second way of dealing with the democratic deficit—if, and only if, the election of such an assembly was accompanied by a major expansion of its powers. Indeed, without such an increase, neither method would resolve the issue.

Most of the European governments have been reluctant to increase the Strasbourg Parliament's powers and to change its makeup not only because they are the major beneficiaries of the "democratic deficit" but because both reforms would clearly turn the EC in a federal direction. The reforms would thus dissipate the deliberate ambiguity that has characterized the Community since the beginning and has allowed it to proceed despite the different conceptions that exist among and within its members about its goals. Is the EC destined to become a federal state, more or less on the American model, or is it to be a particularly active regional organization, governed by its members? In other words, is the purpose of the enterprise a transfer of sovereignty from the nations to the new entity, or is it to pool the sovereignties of the members, in a way that acknowledges their growing inability to reach national goals by purely national means, yet does not oblige them to transfer sovereignty to a superior power?

The reality is somewhere in between. The two "federal" bodies that are supposed to represent the common interest—the Commission and the Parliament—are weaker than the Council dominated directly by governments. On the other hand, especially with the increasing practice of making decisions in the Council by two thirds majorities (as opposed to unanimity), the transfer of final authority in some important matters (agriculture, external trade, competition policy) to the Community, and the largely completed establishment of a single market, the EC has more of a federal character than any other regional organization that has ever been organized. It is a unique experiment, but its very uniqueness has provoked a profound doubt and distrust about the relation of the Community to the national states and public. The debates on Maastricht in Denmark, France, and now Britain have brought such feelings to light. Their sources are not difficult to understand.

First, in recent years, the activities of the Brussels bureaucrats have expanded, often in somewhat absurd ways, literally regulating ways of making cheese. As a result, Europeans tend to believe that Brussels already dictates, as Jacques Delors imprudently predicted, 80 percent of what affects their daily lives. But in fact Brussels firmly controls little more than agriculture, the elimination of regulations that hamper competition and trade among Community members, and trade with countries outside the Community. The EC does not try to establish uniform standards and rules. As long as certain minimum standards set by the Community are observed (for instance for health and safety or environmental protection) each state is simply obliged to recognize as valid the standards and regulations set up by each of its partners. The public, suffering from unemployment and connecting it to high interest rates, tends to blame the EC for what are, basically, still national policies.

The Maastricht treaty, for all its verbiage, was a modest treaty (even insofar as EMU is concerned, in view of the conditions and stages specified in the treaty), but it was overpromoted as a major advance.

This made the discontented members of the public—who blamed layoffs and cuts in subsidies on the single market and on reforms in the EC's bloated agricultural policy—even more suspicious of the next stages. Even if the EC's procedures were more democratic, it would be a target of expressions of social and economic unhappiness: in every democracy, it is the government and the bureaucracy that are held responsible for events or trends they often can't control. In fact, the powers given up by European states have not all been transferred to the EC's institutions; many have gone to the private investors and speculators who are central to the European economy and to world finance. Indeed, the single market is a boon to industry and especially to multinational enterprises. They have exerted far greater influence on the recent development of the Community than the labor unions, which have been weakened by the recession. This in turn strengthens the objections of those who believe that the duly elected representatives of the various member countries are no match for the combined power of unelected European bureaucrats and businessmen.[6]

Secondly, the relation of the nation-state to the Community is not everywhere the same. For many years, the French, who dominate the Brussels bureaucracy, saw in the EC a vehicle for French influence and for imposing restraints on the power of West Germany. Today, and for good reasons, the fear of Germany dominating the Community has replaced (as also in Denmark) the old fear of an unshackled Germany outside the Community. Especially after unification increased the relative weight of Germany among the Twelve, the Federal Republic's economic and financial might has made the EC an instrument of German influence. It has done so both through Bonn's willingness to dispense funds to (and thus obtain business from) the poorer members of the Community, and by using its influence to maintain a decentralized EC whose institutions resemble those of the Federal Republic far more than they resemble those of France.

It may seem excessive to say that, in the EC, what Germany wants, it gets, especially since the German government remains determined not to want anything that would cost it the external support it deems indispensable. Basically, however, Germany does get much of what it wants, and what it doesn't want doesn't get done. The European Community has been central to the rise of Germany. It has lifted Bonn step by step from its constricted and shriveled sovereignty of 1949, to its full legal sovereignty in 1990.

For Britain, which never even began to win its bet on finding new channels of influence through the Community (largely because of its own ambivalence), and for France, which has found the post–cold war world far less hospitable than the "order of Yalta" it once so vigorously denounced,[7] the Community is beginning to look much less desirable. For Britain it seems more like a cage from which the country is trying to liberate itself. For France it is worth staying in the EC as long as Germany is in it, but the French have increasing doubts about who is the guard and who is the captive. Hence the appeal, during the French referendum campaign over Maastricht, of those who said they were not "against Europe," but only against "Maastricht's Europe." They argued for a different kind of Europe that would extend farther East *and* allow for greater French independence at the same time.

This nostalgia for independence results not only from a geopolitical fear of being diminished. It springs from a third and more ideological or mythical consideration, powerful both in France and in the UK. Both are countries in which the nation has been created by, and remains inseparable from, the state—in contrast to the national history of Germany and Italy. The British ideological tradition, revived by Mrs. Thatcher, associates the notion of parliamentary sovereignty within the United Kingdom (however empty of substance it is in reality) with that of Britain's external sovereignty, i.e., its power to act without constraint in Europe.

France's Rousseauistic, Jacobin, and Republican tradition, evoked by

De Gaulle and, in 1992, by the Gaullist Philippe Séguin, the new speaker of the National Assembly, combines France's claim to external sovereignty with its insistence on the domestic sovereignty of the people (another potent myth). Most of the governments of the Twelve have, pragmatically, treated external sovereignty quite differently—as a bundle of powers that could be traded off and pooled. In most EC nations the institutional setup of the Community has diluted the strength of parliamentary or popular sovereignty at home. But in France and in the UK, much of the public remain attached, in a Danish commentator's phrase, to a view of sovereignty as "something like virginity": it is not divisible.[8]

Nations like France and the UK, where the state is seen as the source of rights and duties, and as the source of the nation itself, can only interpret the distinction which the EC encourages between the nation and the state (whose powers are now shared with the EC) as a dangerous and disturbing trend. The distinction points, indeed, to a European state, but one without a European nation, since there are still no European mass media, parties, interest groups (except in business), or public. The establishment at Maastricht of a common European citizenship is only a formal first step. Without such a European nation, many feel, so to speak, denuded, for the national state is losing power, but the European would-be state, uncomfortably straddling nations with diverse traditions and interests, seems incapable of defining a common policy in matters as vital as defense and diplomacy, as the failure in Yugoslavia shows.

In France and the UK, by contrast with Germany, the state was seen and embraced as the founder and guardian of the nation. Its weakening and replacement by a weak multinational pseudo-superstate only increase fears about national identity. The same fears are already inflamed by the influx of "others," such as immigrant workers and refugees, or by the "Americanization" of popular culture,

or by the decline of traditional ways of life, whether of British miners, French peasants, or small shopkeepers throughout the continent. The Community had been celebrated as a way, the only one perhaps, to preserve "European distinctiveness," particularly from American pressures and cultural influences, but of course the bureaucrats in Brussels could never do this. It is not surprising that in the 1992 debates on Maastricht, the treaty's opponents blamed the EC for every threat to national identity, for yielding to American policy over GATT or to American television imports, as well as for opening borders to more immigrants (a charge that had little basis in the treaty).

Countries like France and the UK, whose identity was shaped early and whose people see the nation as a long-defined and completed entity, have far greater difficulty accepting the implications of an ever-expanding Community than, say, Germany, which like the US, although in a very different way, tends to see itself as unfinished and continuously developing. The Germans' almost permanent uncertainties about German identity somehow make it easier for them to endorse a European identity which is equally uncertain and unfinished. French and British certainties about their national past and character are being shaken, and the EC is seen as one of the culprits.

This does not mean, in either case, that the policy of European integration will be abandoned: there is no turning back. But resistance to integration, fed by the EC's institutional flaws, is likely to increase as the EC's powers expand. So will the gap between the European governments, for whom joint action (or inaction) has become second nature (especially since it is often unchecked), and their citizens, who wonder where their governments are taking them and who benefits and who loses, from the march to an unknown destination. Western Europe today is a collection of bruised nations, whose states have traded visible and distinctive power for diffuse col-

lective influence.[9] It is not surprising that so many Europeans find it difficult to identify with a "Europe" that remains a purely economic and bureaucratic construction and shows few signs of becoming a nation.

---

[1] See Robert O. Keohane and Stanley Hoffmann, editors, *The New European Community* (Westview Press, 1991).

[2] I have relied on the account in David Cameron's still unpublished paper "British exit, German voice, French loyalty: defection, domination, and co-operation in the 1992-93 ERM crisis," March 1993.

[3] There are other causes: the world recession, of course, the unstoppable decline of traditional industries in the mid-1980s, the need to be competitive abroad (a need made more acute by deregulation and the policy of tying the franc to the mark), which led to large-scale layoffs in a country where labor costs are high.

[4] See Paul Ginsborg, "Lo stato italiano: transformazione o transformismo," *La Rivista dei Libri*, March 1993.

[5] Only the Italian Communists have put distinguished foreigners on their list in elections to the European Parliament.

[6] See Nicholas Hildyard, "Maastricht: the Protectionism of Free Trade," *The Ecologist*, Vol. 23, No. 2 (March–April 1993).

[7] See S. Hoffmann, "French Dilemmas, and Strategies in the New Europe," in Joseph Nye, Robert Keohane, and Stanley Hoffmann, editors, *Europe After the Cold War* (Harvard University Press, forthcoming next month).

[8] Ulf Hedetoft, *Sovereignty, Identity and War in 90s Europe*, Department of Languages and Intercultural Studies (Aalborg: Aalborg University, 1993), especially pp. 14–38.

[9] See Wolfgang Merkel, *Integration and Democracy in the European Community: The Contours of a Dilemma*, Working Paper 42 (Madrid: Instituto Juan March de Estudios e Investigaciones, 1993).

Reinventing the politics of Europe

Anthony Hartley

Anthony Hartley, former Editor of *Encounter* and now Contributing Editor (Europe) for the *National Interest* in Washington, is a close student of European Community affairs and a former EC official. His previous contribution to *The World Today*, on the Clinton presidency, appeared in the February 1993 issue.

Once again the European Community has been ploughing through rough seas. No sooner had the Maastricht Treaty been ratified in Britain, by a process akin to Chinese water-torture, than a wave of speculation forced the devaluation of the French franc in circumstances that were as humiliating and politically uncomfortable as they were for John Major, Britain's Prime Minister, when the pound suffered a similar fate in October 1992. This time the European Monetary System (EMS) was altered to allow a fluctuation around the central rate of 15 per cent (instead of 2.5 per cent). Effectively the system itself was abolished, and the European currencies were left to float, apart from the continued link between the D-Mark and the Dutch florin. As the economic correspondent of *Le Monde* put it: 'The speculators have won. The EMS is badly damaged, Europe deeply weakened.'[1]

Since the crisis voices have not been lacking to proclaim that all may yet be well. For France's Prime Minister, Edouard Balladur, the Brussels agreement of 2 August has preserved the EMS and maintained the value of the franc through the mutual efforts of France and Germany. More recently Sir Leon Brittan, EC Commissioner for External Trade, has expressed his belief that the Maastricht timetable can still be kept. Yet these attempts to 'save the phenomena', a phrase used by the defenders of the Ptolemaic system of astronomy, are hardly convincing. The Editor of the *Rheinischer Merkur*, Thomas Kielinger, found a simpler and more artistic explanation: 'What we saw this week, however, was the triumph of Lancelot "Capability" Brown over Le Nôtre, the triumph of English landscape gardening over French geometrical rigidity.'[2]

The fact is that, at a time of falling European gnp, of heavy unemployment and of divergence between the principal European economies (most notably between Germany and the rest), any effort to set EC states on a forced march towards monetary union was bound to end in a debilitating failure. The monetary programme agreed at Maastricht was designed for another and more familiar world – a world of prosperity and full employment. At Maastricht neither the depth of the depression nor the results of German reunification were perceived. The link with the dominant and virtuous D-Mark, which had been intended to be the foundation-stone of the new system, turned out to be a link with pain – the measures adopted by the Bundesbank to counter post-reunification inflation. On 'Black Wednesday' this proved too much for Britain and Italy; on 30 July it proved too much for France.

But present European difficulties are wider spread than the obscuring of the monetary panel of the Maastricht diptych. The signing of that treaty almost coincided with the recognition by Germany of Croatia and Slovenia (23 December 1991). The announcement of future common foreign and security policies for a putative European Union saw the Yugoslav crisis well under way – a crisis which seemed to offer an opportunity for Europeans to show their mettle as peacekeepers and arbitrators. Indeed, some Community spokesmen seemed positively to welcome the occasion. Mr Jacques Poos, the Luxembourg Foreign Minister, led the euphoria with the rallying cry: 'This is the hour of Europe. Not the hour of the Americans.'[3]

What happened in Bosnia and elsewhere was rather different. World opinion and the United Nations have been seen to be powerless to prevent massacre and counter-massacre or to punish those who have used 'ethnic cleansing' as the instrument of a policy of expansion. By late 1993, much of Bosnia had been 'cleansed' of Moslems, despite the involvement of UN forces; a peace agreement still eludes Lord Owen; and UN sanctions do not seem to have discouraged President Slobodan Milosevic from pursuing a 'Greater Serbia'. The European Community, meanwhile, has distinguished itself neither by its unity nor by its efficiency. An original split between Britain and France, who wished to preserve a Yugoslav state, and Germany, which did not, was followed by the dispatch of small numbers of British, French and Spanish troops to Bosnia and Croatia on humanitarian missions. Britain and France have been united in resisting further military involvement in a civil war, while the German press has urged military intervention – though acknowledging that it would be constitutionally impossible and politically inappropriate for Germany to join any such operation.

Far from demonstrating the ability of a European Union to extinguish bush-fires kindled on its frontiers, the Yugoslav crisis has shown (1) that member states of the European Community are likely to have different interest and objectives when faced with trouble in Eastern Europe and elsewhere; and (2) that the laborious diplomatic negotiations, necessary to produce a carefully crafted formula to obscure such disagreements, delay the instant action required to seize even a fleeting opportunity of deterring aggression to a point where decisions always come too late. The stern test of Yugoslavia has undermined the European Community's claim to act effectively in a crisis involving European security and eroded the credibility of the new common foreign and security policies. The United States, on the other hand, remains the only credible intervener, an essential ingredient for effective resistance to aggression.[4]

Thus the two main provisions of the Maastricht Treaty have had discredit cast upon them, even before final ratification of the

From *The World Today*, Vol. 49, No. 11, November 1993, pp. 202-205. *The World Today*, published by The Royal Institute of International Affairs. Reprinted by permission.

agreement was permitted by Germany's Constitutional Court. Now the European Community has entered upon yet another internal conflict over the world trade negotiations in the framework of the so-called Uruguay Round of the General Agreement on Tariffs and Trade (GATT). France's refusal to accept the 1992 Blair House agreement between the United States and the EC on the agricultural sector of the GATT negotiation risks provoking a serious split in the Community and the failure of the negotiation, with the evil consequences that this would bring for world trade and the already depressed economies of Western Europe. At the time of writing it is impossible to tell how things will go and whether the Uruguay Round will be completed by mid-December 1993. The United States, in the person of its trade negotiator, Mr Mickey Kantor, has said that 'interpretation or clarification of Blair House cannot be a guise for modifying the terms of the agreement'.[5] Sir Leon Brittan's flying visit to Washington, to see whether some minor concessions on the American side were not possible, does not seem to have produced anything on the agricultural issue.

A concession, if it comes, will be left until the last moment. But France's Prime Minister, Edouard Balladur, is no De Gaulle. A small bone to fling to the farming lobby is certainly what he wants. For he must know that a French veto on a GATT agreement would not receive German support. On important issues Bonn has always supported the United States.

Can some of the devices that have been suggested – exemption of present EC agricultural stocks from the cuts in subsidised exports, 'back-loading' of such cuts – be used to reach a solution? The American negotiators also have their farmers to consider and, moreover, have been irritated by France's questioning of what, for the American side, is an agreed compromise. Mr Kantor's view is that French objections are not a matter for him but an internal EC dispute.

Mr Balladur is, therefore, faced by a choice between what will be, in effect, a retreat or causing a rupture that will damage France's industry and strain the working of the European Community. His difficulties illuminate the present confused state of European politics, where the twin pressures of unemployment and immigration have produced a disagreeably xenophobic brand of populism. The fall of the franc and the disappearance of the EMS were a humiliating setback for French policy, which had inflicted hardship on French citizens in order to sustain the parity with the D-Mark. French politicians and officials were disagreeably surprised by what happened. They had never believed that the Bundesbank would refuse to support the franc, and commentators found it hard to decide whom to blame most: 'Anglo-Saxon speculators' or 'egotistical German bankers'.[6]

The GATT issue provides another scenario where France can be seen as assailed by the United States and its European sympathisers. In addition, the presidential election is only 18 months off, new laws on immigration may require a referendum, unemployment stands at 3,215,800 (11.7 per cent) and seems likely to reach 12 per cent by the end of the year.[7] No wonder that the 'new policy' recommended by Philippe Séguin, Speaker of the National Assembly and an effective campaigner against the Maastricht Treaty, should find support, particularly with Mr Séguin's own Gaullist party, the *Rassemblement pour la République* (RPR), or that over 50 per cent of French citizens

should now say that they would vote against the treaty in any new referendum.[8]

A nationalist and protectionist reaction to events since German reunification makes life more difficult for Mr Balladur, but also for the European Community. For, all over Europe, the apparent inability of governments to master unemployment and their own financial affairs is producing a confused populism that increasingly ignores established political parties and is sceptical of the remedies presented by politicians, bankers, trade union leaders and European officials. In Italy this cynicism takes the form of advocacy of a breakup of the present Italian state. In Britain, Mr Major's government has plunged in the polls, while the Labour opposition is felt to be boring. In France and Germany there have been outbreaks of xenophobia, attacks on Turkish or Arab immigrants or the burning of foreign produce in transit.

The tensions shared by European societies are producing a destabilisation of political institutions, not excluding those of the European Community. Blame for economic difficulties rubs off on to Community policies. High interest rates accompanying membership of the EMS can be held responsible for unemployment, as can Community social policies that increase labour costs and discourage employers from taking on new employees. The existence of the Community and its Brussels institutions has come to appear irrelevant to the problems created by economic depression, if not responsible for them, in that the drive to European Monetary Union (EMU) implied an attempt to impose deflationary policies on countries whose real economic situation required the opposite.

What should the European Community do to restore its credibility in the eyes of its citizens? Despite protestations to the contrary, it is clear that the Maastricht Treaty will require modification, to say the least, and that its timetable for monetary union is unlikely to be kept – if, indeed, its objectives can be realised at all in a time-span of under 20 years. After the recent experience of Britain, France and Italy, it is improbable that European political leaders will be willing once again to take the risk of trying to achieve 'convergence' by going against the grain of the world economic conjuncture. As for the common foreign and security policies, meetings of ministers will continue, and so will attempts to harmonise purely diplomatic activity or to pursue joint staff talks in the Western European Union (WEU). But the limits to this process are soon reached. Once it is a matter of intervention or 'peacekeeping', no government is going to allow the extent of its participation to be determined by anyone other that itself or its own parliament. It is impossible to imagine that, within any European organisation – never mind the name – Britain or France would allow the use of their armed forces to be decided by even qualified-majority voting on the part of countries, many of whom hardly possess any effective military capacity at all.

In the face of such considerations, should the European statesmen continue the struggle to 'help' history? Maastricht was an attempt to consummate in a few years processes which were bound to take far longer to achieve – if, indeed, success were possible in present-day Europe. If European leaders now decide to have another shot at EMU, will not the same fate await it? Can they accelerate common foreign and security policies which, if they are to be effective, must be the result of habit and use? Above all, should the Community constantly be setting itself deadlines which it then fails to keep, with the inevitable consequences for its credibility in the eyes of Europe's citizens?

'Time,' wrote Hugo von Hofmannsthal, 'is a strange thing.' It is also an essential ingredient in the preparation of lasting political change. Instead of the constant hurry and bustle of summits, ministers' meetings and complex timetables, accompanied by seemingly endless legislation coming off the production line, might it not be better to allow Europe to evolve at a pace and in a direction more adapted to the comprehension of its citizens? In retrospect it seems extraordinary that the Maastricht plan for Europe's future should have ignored the two principal matters of present concern to citizens of the European Community: unemployment and instability in Eastern Europe, to which recent events in Moscow have given an added urgency. It is strange that so strenuous a discussion on Europe in the year 2000 should have neglected the main features of its present political and economic conjuncture. The answer is, of course, that the ideas of Maastricht were gestated a decade or more back and were intended for a different world from the one that now exists after the collapse of Soviet power.

Meanwhile, as statesmen ponder the ruins of the EMS, political events are moving on. The future shape of the Community will depend on whether it is capable of catching up with these or whether it will lag behind change, offering the remedies of the 1970s and 1980s for the problems of the 1990s. A number of trends in European and international politics, while not bearing directly on the shape of European institutions, are nevertheless likely to influence the characteristics of the Community over the next decade:

● Increasing instability in Eastern Europe, particularly in Russia and Ukraine, will alarm other European states which, however, will be unequally affected and will, in any case, be unable to 'intervene', except by diplomatic means.

● Germany is likely, therefore, to become more and more preoccupied by such events as the West European country most exposed to their consequences in the shape of economic chaos and, possibly, a flow of refugees. This will not necessarily imply less support in Bonn or Berlin for the European Community, but it will mean more distraction from it and more urgency in its extension to the East. The German government's move to Berlin will play its part here.

● Over the next two years those European leaders most attached to the original 'Carolingian' Europe – Delors, Kohl, Mitterrand – seem likely to disappear. Their successors will probably see Europe's future in rather a different light from that of the immediate successors of the 'founding fathers'.

● There are already divergences in the way member states view foreign policy. Britain has a relationship with the United States which can be called 'special', provided that this is not taken to mean the possibility of invariably exercising influence in Washington. Germany is developing its own 'special relationship' with Russia and other East European countries. France and Italy are rivals for influence around the Mediterranean basin. The end of the Cold War has liberated such aspirations to more characteristically national policies on the part of Community member states.

● The logical conclusion of recurring GATT rounds will be a symbiosis between free-trade areas such as the EC and the North American Free Trade Area (NAFTA) – if it survives its passage through Congress. This will be good for the world's economy but will lessen Europe's sense of specificity.

Other trends could be added to these factors, which are helping to reinvent the politics of Europe. But even without taking into consideration, for instance, the evident weakening that is taking place in the Franco-German relationship, or the increasing impossibility of considering economic developments in any other than a global framework, those mentioned above are enough to encourage expectation of a Europe evolving on rather different lines from hitherto, casting aside some old orthodoxies to gestate a system that is less rigid and less ponderous.

In a recent *Economist* article, Mr Major correctly identified the real tasks facing Europe today.[9] If the European Community is to prosper, it must deal with unemployment and use its best endeavours to help the new democracies of Eastern Europe. To this Mr Delors has replied by an appeal to the European Community's 'founding fathers' who, he believes, aimed at the construction of a federal state.[10] This conception sees Europe as becoming a 'power' in the traditional sense of the word, an enlarged nation-state with a central bureaucracy, a single government and Parliament and single policies. It is a view that inclines easily to protectionism in that a Europe, with a trade policy sharply defined against competitors, would, it is thought, become more acutely conscious of its own identity. Moreover, European federalists usually present their model, not in terms of American federalism, about which they know little, but simply as a wider European state whose tendency is to draw power to the centre and impose a *Gleichschaltung* on laws and institutions.[11] Mr Major perceives a Community wider in its extent, less centralised in its machinery, and where there would be variations in what is required of each member state; a Community whose economic area would gradually blend into others to the East and West. It would be a Community which would pay more attention to the immediate problems of Europe and spend less time on constitutional changes which can prove divisive and destabilising in individual countries.

Which of these views of Europe's future is more likely to be realised? They both have their contradictions. Mr Major favours enlargement and less constitution-building. But enlargement, leading to a Community of some 20 states, will destroy the present system of decision-making, and something will have to be put in its place. Mr Delors looks to an eventual federation, but wishes to maintain the technocratic power of the European Commission. France and Germany advocate pushing ahead with integration, but wish to decrease the influence of the smaller countries. The argument on the future of the European Community is liable to become hopelessly embroiled, with little in the way of clear political principle about it.

The difficulty for the federalists is that theirs is an 'all-or-nothing' argument. But, since neither governments nor peoples seem prepared to move towards the 'all' of a European government, they are condemned to a series of fiercely contested compromises ending, all too often, in small symbolic gestures – a European passport or changes in nomenclature. The risk they run—and what now appears to have happened—is the neglect of real politics and an undue reliance on legal formulae. Political leaders, on the other hand, have their being in real politics. When their interests and their electorate require it, they will flout traditional European orthodoxy. They are happier with the European Council than with the European Parliament or the Commission, except when a small country believes that supranational bodies give it more of a hearing than it would otherwise receive. Maastricht, in any case, will probably be the last hurrah of federalism, a treaty pushed ahead by France's desire to restrain a newly unified Germany, and Germany's wish to start on its new course of untrammelled independence with European credentials to its credit.

It looks, therefore, as though the pragmatic, illogical view of a Community muddling through to some form of confederation for which there is no model – certainly not that of the nation-state – would correspond most nearly to events. There is, fortunately, much about Europe's future that we cannot foresee. For instance, will the peoples of the new candidate states – the Scandinavian countries and Austria – vote in favour of entry at their respective referendums? Not if the Community shows no signs of being able to cope with economic depression. Will the European Community emerge as something more like the Holy Roman Empire than the Roman Empire? Pragmatists are often accused of lacking idealism. But the Geneva of GATT has as much going for it in terms of human welfare as the Strasbourg of the European Parliament. The dimly perceived vision of a free-trade area extending halfway round the world does not lack ambition or daring. After Maastricht the European Community finds itself at the beginning of a long historical process whose final result remains uncertain. It is important not to confine it to the mould of theoretical assertions.

NOTES

1. *Le Monde*. 3 August 1993.
2. *The Times*, 7 August 1993.
3. *International Herald Tribune*, 30 June 1991.
4. On the limitations and dangers of peacekeeping, see Laurence Martin, 'Peacekeeping as a Growth Industry', *The National Interest*, No 32, Summer 1993.
5. *Financial Times*, 22 September 1993.
6. In the issue of *Le Monde* of 30 July 1993, that paper's Brussels Correspondent writes of the 'attacks of Anglo-Saxon speculation' which he sees as being encouraged by the *Financial Times*. On 3 August 1993, two days after the Brussels agreement, *Le Monde* speaks of the '*diktat* of Bonn and Frankfurt'.
7. See the *Wall Street Journal*, 30 September 1993. It should be remembered that, since France has conscription, some hundreds of thousands of young men are taken out of the labour market each year. France has never known unemployment at this level. Between the wars the highest figure was 374,000. See André de Lattre, *Politique économique de la France depuis 1945* (Paris: 1966), p. 437.
8. M. Séguin's views were presented in a speech on 16 June 1993 (*Le Monde*, 18 June 1993) and include attacks on free trade, high interest rates and the *franc fort*, the diminution of social benefits and the run-down of the public sector.
9. John Major, 'Raise your eyes, there is a land beyond', in *The Economist*, 25 September 1993.
10. This was hardly true of Konrad Adenauer. He was critical of supranational bureaucracy and commented that he was becoming somewhat tired of European Union, adding: 'If the birth pangs are already so difficult, one can hardly reckon on living children.' See Hans-Peter Schwarz, *Adenauer: Der Staatsmann 1953-1967* (Stuttgart: 1991), p. 737.
11. For instance, Brussels favours harmonised company law as essential to a Common Market. In the United States, this is left to the individual states, but these variations do not seem to affect adversely the operation of the internal market.

DIAGNOSIS: HEALTHIER IN EUROPE

By most standards, Western Europeans are in better medical shape than Americans. And costs are sharply lower. But bureaucracies and under-the-table payments mar the system.

Joel Havemann

Times Staff Writer

BRUSSELS—For someone with a potentially fatal disease, Regine Delvaux is exceptionally healthy. A diabetic for 26 of her 37 years, Delvaux holds down a part-time office job in Brussels and, in the past four years, has been able to adopt two young children.

She owes her active life to the Belgian national health system, which, like those of other Western European governments, guarantees that virtually all Belgians are insured and pays the lion's share of the costs. That means Delvaux receives virtually free care, including the regular insulin she needs to fend off kidney failure, blindness and the other scourges that diabetes can bring.

The contrast with the United States is striking. Europeans have better access to health care than Americans, an estimated 35 million of whom are uninsured. By most objective measures, they are healthier.

And what is most extraordinary, Europe actually spends less for health care—about one-third to one-half less in most countries—than the United States. The U.S. health bill, growing far faster than overall inflation, will reach something like $800 billion this year, or about 13.5% of the nation's entire economic output.

No wonder President-elect Bill Clinton is looking at Europe as he seeks to redeem his campaign promise to overhaul the U.S. health care system. Clinton has promised to require employers to provide insurance to all workers, to guar-

antee public insurance for those who do not work and to set a national limit on overall health-care spending.

Most Western European countries already do all this.

Clinton and his health-care planners will not want to copy everything they find across the Atlantic. European-style health care is hardly trouble-free.

Inflexible bureaucracies sometimes interfere with the delivery of care. Some doctors, unwilling to settle for government-prescribed fee schedules, take part of their payments under the table. For a minor operation to correct nearsighted-

ness, a Brussels clinic charges not only the official rate of about $300 but also another $900 in unreported cash.

Medical services are rationed, especially in countries that spend relatively little on health care. In Britain, which spends less than all but the poorest Western European nations, the elderly frequently wait two years for hip replacements and cataract operations.

Even in the Netherlands, which spends 30% more per person than Britain for health care, a recent survey found that one-third of all hospital admissions came only after excessive waits. At the same

---

Who Pays the Freight?

Here is the share of health care spending paid by governments and by private individuals and insurers, 1989:

	Governments	Private
France	75%	25%
Germany	72	28
Britain	87	13
Italy	79	21
Netherlands	73	27
Sweden	90	10
United States	**42**	**58**

HOW DOCTORS ARE DOING

The average after-tax income of general practitioners in 1985, the latest year with available data:

France	$24,700
Germany	48,200
Britain	27,900
Netherlands	32,400
Sweden	22,200
United States	**77,900**

Reliable figures for salaries of Italian doctors were not available.
Sources: American Medical Assn., Organization for Economic Cooperation and Development

---

time, under pressure from health care providers and patients, the Dutch government pays for such dubious treatments as herbal medicine and psychic healing.

In a range of European countries, rising costs have triggered reform movements that have a distinctly American flavor. The Netherlands, for example, is edging toward competition between insurance companies in an effort to introduce incentives to control costs.

Yet for all the flaws, analysts on both sides of the Atlantic rank European health care miles ahead of America's. "What can Europeans learn from Americans about the financing and organization of medical care?" asked Alain C. Enthoven, a health-care financing specialist at Stanford University. "The obvious answer is, 'Not much.' "

The reasons that America spends more and gets less are legion: uncontrolled use of sophisticated medical technology, massive administrative costs, expensive malpractice insurance and higher-paid doctors, to name a few.

All this is rooted in the uniquely American pioneer experience and distrust of big government. The legacy is an every-man-for-himself approach to health care. Except for the elderly and the very poor who are enrolled in Medicare and Medicaid, those on the receiving end of the health care system get what they—or their employers—can pay for.

"In America, part of your population is accustomed to getting every available medical technology," said Henk ten Have, a professor of medical ethics at Catholic University in Nijmegen, the Netherlands. "But another large part gets no care at all."

COLLECTIVE CARE

Health care in Europe, by contrast, is grounded in collective responsibility. European governments either directly provide most health care, as in Britain, or require that everyone be insured, while paying for most of their citizens' insurance, as in Germany.

Either way, European countries operate on the same principle that governs public education in the United States: All of society benefits from a healthy citizenry, and all of society should shoulder the costs.

It is an attitude that Abram de Swaan, a University of Amsterdam sociologist,

Health Care: America vs. Europe

For all the flaws, analysts on both sides of the Atlantic rank European health care far ahead of what the U.S. offers.

Americans Spend More . . .

(health expenditures per capita, 1990)

United States	$2,566
France	1,543
Germany	1,487
Sweden	1,479
Netherlands	1,266
Italy	1,234
Britain	974

. . . but Are Less Satisfied . . .

(share of persons who believe the health care system works pretty well and only minor changes are needed)

United States	10%
Netherlands	47
France	41
Germany	41
Sweden	32
Britain	27
Italy	12

. . . and Achieve Poorer Results

(infant mortality rates per 1,000 births, 1990)

United States	9.2%
Italy	8.5
Britain	7.9
Germany	7.5
France	7.2
Netherlands	6.9
Sweden	5.9

Sources: Organization for Economic Cooperation and Development; Robert J. Blendon, Harvard School of Public Health

traces back 150 years to cholera epidemics that broke out in urban slums throughout Europe and claimed the lives of the rich as well as the poor. Out of self-protection more than charity, Europe developed modern sewage systems. Now cholera is largely under control, but the principle of collective responsibility remains intact.

"The social welfare systems in West European countries promote the dignity and well-being of all persons and the welfare of society as a whole," said

Reinhard Priester of the Center for Biomedical Ethics at the University of Minnesota. "In contrast, the United States embraces individualism, sees provider autonomy as the preeminent value and neglects community-oriented values."

In only two of the 24 industrial nations that make up the Organization for Economic Cooperation and Development does the government pay for less than half of the health care. Those two are the United States and Turkey.

In Western Europe, by contrast, all governments pick up at least two-thirds of health care costs. Each country has its own approach.

In Britain and Sweden, the government owns and operates most of the health care system, with the money coming largely from income tax revenue. Most other countries offer a mix of public insurance and compulsory, government-subsidized private insurance, with the government's contribution coming from a Social Security-like tax on employers and workers.

The Netherlands relies relatively heavily on private insurance. But even there, the 70% of the population at the bottom of the income scale is covered mostly by public insurance; for the rest, a combination of public and private insurers pays most of the bills.

No matter what the system, patients may generally choose their doctors, and they can buy supplementary insurance to cover what their government-financed insurance does not. Most governments dictate what doctors may charge, and some play a role in determining what procedures are appropriate to diagnose and treat particular conditions.

PATIENT SATISFACTION

To Americans, the European approach might seem heavily centralized, bureaucratic and rigid. But Europeans are happier with their approach than Americans are with theirs.

A 1990 study by the Harvard School of Public Health found that only 10% of Americans said their "health care system works pretty well." That put the U.S. system squarely at the bottom of the 10 nations included in the survey.

Of the six European countries surveyed, satisfaction levels ranged from 47% in the Netherlands to 12% in Italy. Canadians, whose national health insurance system is much more European than

American, were the most satisfied of all, with a 56% rating.

These ratings square with the few objective ways of measuring national health. Although America's diverse population, with its many minority groups, makes comparisons with more homogeneous Europe somewhat uncertain, it is nevertheless true that the United States falls consistently below Western European nations in infant mortality rates and life expectancy.

Europe achieves these results even though it spends substantially less for health care than the United States—typically 7% to 9% of national economic output, compared with America's 13.5%. Central to Europe's approach is a technique that seems unthinkable in the United States: Governments set strict health-care budgets, and local health authorities must live within their allowances.

"The strict planning systems for hospital care in Switzerland and the Netherlands, the two European systems most similar to those of the United States, are the major reason why expenditures are constrained in these countries," said Bengt Jonsson, a health specialist at the Stockholm School of Economics.

With strict health-care budgets, Europe has escaped America's uncontrolled growth in the purchase of medical technology. Two nearby European hospitals may not both buy the same piece of sophisticated machinery unless they can show a clear need; instead, one gets the equipment, and the patients at both hospitals use it.

Dr. Niek Klazinga, an official with the Dutch National Organization for Quality Assurance in Hospitals, said a single hospital in Houston three years ago had 13 sophisticated and expensive magnetic resonance imaging machines, more than all of the Netherlands.

American hospitals, armed with the latest medical gadgetry, are compelled to use it to recoup the cost. "When a patient with a headache is told that he needs a brain scan to make sure he doesn't have a tumor, his natural reaction is, 'Where do I lie down?'" said Arthur L. Caplan, director of biomedical ethics at the University of Minnesota.

In most of Europe, by contrast, the expensive brain scan may be used as a last resort—or not at all. In the Netherlands, every neighborhood has a general practitioner who serves as the gatekeeper to medical technology.

"General practitioners know that 70% of all headaches are emotional," Klazinga said. Before they permit brain scans to check for tumors, he said, they test all other possible causes.

Joseph Newhouse, a professor of health policy at Harvard, estimates that "technological change, or what might loosely be called the march of science and the increased capabilities of medicine," accounts for at least half the explosive growth of U.S. medical costs in the last half-century.

Robert Brook, senior health services researcher at the RAND Corp. in Santa Monica, said the use of costly technology often does not help and sometimes is downright dangerous to patients' health.

"Perhaps one-third of the financial resources devoted to health care today are being spent on ineffective or unproductive care," Brook and Kathleen Lohr of RAND's Washington office wrote recently.

FOOTING THE BILL

Technology aside, Europe is more willing to pay for preventive care than is the United States, where the uninsured generally benefit from no such care at all and even those with insurance sometimes find reimbursement unavailable.

Americans, and especially the poor, must typically get sicker than Europeans before they can get the care they need, said Jean-Pierre Poullier, a health policy analyst with the Paris-based Organization for Economic Cooperation and Development. That has the perverse effect, he said, of jacking up the cost of their treatment when they finally get it.

Diabetes provides a stark example. Dr. Ann Owen, an American who was born and trained as a physician in the United States but has specialized in treating diabetics in Belgium since 1983, said uninsured or underinsured diabetics in the United States often have no access to the insulin they need to control their blood sugar. Nor can they afford to care for the non-life-threatening complications of their disease.

"That means many people have to go into a coma before they can get treatment," Owen said. "By then, they need intensive care at a hospital, and in a few days you're up to $50,000."

"In Belgium," she added, "insulin is considered so essential to life that it's available for free."

Delvaux, the long-term diabetic, is glad it is. Since 1989, when the Belgian government set up a special program for diabetics, Delvaux has also been reimbursed for most of the costs of her regular doctor visits and blood sugar tests. "I have hardly had to pay more than a couple of hundred francs [about $7] a month," she said.

Thanks to her regular treatment, which includes a steady supply of insulin that is administered by a pump permanently implanted in an underarm, she has not been hospitalized for about 20 years.

In Los Angeles, Felipe Perez shows what might have happened to Delvaux. Perez, 39, has a less serious form of diabetes. Although he does not require regular insulin, he would benefit from other forms of routine treatment.

But as one of America's 35 million uninsured persons, he does not receive it. Two years ago, Perez lost his paid health insurance when he was laid off from his city job. Once last year he went to a community health clinic in Lincoln Heights and was prescribed medication for his diabetes. But he couldn't afford to buy it.

Earlier this year, he landed a part-time job with Los Angeles County as a home health-care worker for the elderly, but he gets no health benefits himself.

As a consequence, he found himself at L.A. County-USC Medical Center for the better part of a week recently so that doctors could treat an infection in his underarm that, because of his diabetes, had grown to the size of a walnut. The cost, most of which will be absorbed by the hospital: about $5,500.

DOCTORS' PAY

Medical salaries are another part of the cost-quality equation. General practitioners in the United States earned an average income of $77,900 in 1985 after covering their expenses but before paying taxes, according to the American Medical Assn.'s most recent data. That compares with $48,200 in Germany, $32,400 in the Netherlands, $24,700 in France and $19,700 in Belgium.

The United States has fewer doctors for its population than most European countries, with the notable exception of

Britain, and its supply of registered nurses falls at about the European average.

Yet its health care system employs more people than Europe's—especially those who sell health insurance and administer claims. "Behind every hospital bed in the United States is a clerk filling out forms," said Poullier of the OECD.

Jack A. Meyer, an analyst with New Directions for Policy, a Washington research group, said administrative costs soak up 22% of U.S. health-care spending. The American urban landscape, said Caplan of the University of Minnesota, is dotted with insurance company towers (Prudential, John Hancock) and even an entire city (Hartford, Conn.).

"We have a huge administrative bureaucracy to keep the rich from having to share costs with the poor, the healthy from having to share costs with the sick and the able-bodied from having to share costs with the disabled," Caplan said.

European nations avoid a substantial share of these administrative costs because they do not make such distinctions. At least in this respect, their decision to make health a collective rather than an individual responsibility actually saves money. **Times staff writer Somini Sengupta in Los Angeles contributed to this story.**

Europe's Recession Prompts New Look at Welfare Costs

Roger Cohen

Special to The New York Times

THE HAGUE—Hans vander Valk, a former assistant professor at Delft University, is suffering from an ailment that has attained epidemic proportions in the Netherlands: stress. So he has stopped working and for the last three years has been collecting $1,630 a month in disability benefits.

"The doctor said I was suffering from stress because I was so worried about obtaining research money and so obsessed with colleagues' talking behind my back, I was finding it very hard to relax," Mr. vander Valk, a 48-year-old physicist, said. He is vaguely contemplating some other line of work, but meanwhile is assured of his disability pay until the age of 65.

STRESS TERMED SUBJECTIVE

Rene Jansen, an official at the Ministry for Social Affairs, said 912,000 people, or about 18 percent of the work force of the Netherlands, receive disability pay. Confounding the stereotype of a nation of placid burghers, nearly a third of those recipients suffer from "stress."

"The thing about stress," Mr. Jansen said, "is that it is extremely subjective."

What is starkly clear is that the ballooning costs of social welfare programs for the disabled, the infirm, the elderly and the unemployed in Europe are threatening the Continent's economic future. In Spain, there is now one person receiving a social security benefit for every one working.

SYSTEM UNDER STRAIN

As a result the welfare state, the crowning achievement of Social Democratic and Christian Democratic governments in postwar Europe and a model from which the Clinton Administration wants to borrow, is under unprecedented strain.

While it has safeguarded Western Europe from the extremes of poverty and alienation that haunt many American cities, the system has become so costly—often adding as much as 50 percent to labor costs through payroll taxes—that it may be shutting Europe out of business in an increasingly competitive global economy.

"Every time we're asked to give up a benefit, we're told we're now in direct competition with Taiwan," said Bill Tynan, an official of Britain's Amalgamated Engineering and Electrical Union. "The message from executives to workers is, if you don't cede on labor costs, we're going elsewhere."

Swissair has done just that with one of its business units. As of July 1, the company moved part of its accounting department to Bombay from Zurich. About 50 jobs were lost in Switzerland; the same number were created in India.

"There are highly trained people in Bombay, we're connected directly to them through our data network, and they work for a fraction of the cost of the Swiss," said Herbert Schmell, a Swissair spokesman. "We expect a saving of about $5 million."

Such business decisions underscore a fundamental question facing the European welfare state: Have the rapid changes in the world economy rendered Europe's system, with its high wage costs and comprehensive social security

benefits, unsustainable? Or is a European recession simply causing serious financial problems that will pass when recovery comes?

"Either, as I believe, Europe's comprehensive social security coverage will emerge intact from Europe's recession, or we are at the beginning of an economic and cultural revolution that will throw the whole system into doubt," said Frédéric Oudea, an official who oversees Government benefits at France's Budget Ministry. "If it is the latter, if Swissair is pointing the way, then the social consequences will be dire."

CUTBACKS: FALLING RESOURCES TURN THE TIDE

Europe's recession and soaring unemployment have certainly placed new strains on benefits. Most European social insurance programs are financed through payroll taxes on workers and employers, so the fewer salaried workers there are, the less money flows into social security budgets. But the more people out of a job, the more unemployment benefits there are to pay, so resources are dwindling as demand soars.

The number of unemployed in the European Community, whose economies as a whole are expected to shrink five-tenths of 1 percent this year, has already risen to 18.1 million from 14.3 million in 1991 and is expected to reach at least 19 million next year. The financial impact on welfare programs in the 12 member nations has been severe.

But other forces are also prompting questioning of the structure of Europe's welfare states, even as President Clinton considers measures that would bring the United States closer to the European model, like a payroll tax to extend medical care to all American citizens, an increase in unemployment benefits and a higher minimum wage.

The rapid aging of the population—Western Europeans, like Americans, are living longer—is squeezing pension plans. Because older people spend more on health, the aging is also contributing to sharply rising medical costs in many European countries.

In France, a recent study projected that the deficit in the Government pension budget would soar from about $3.5 billion today to about $35 billion by 2010 if radical reforms are not enacted, because the ratio of active to retired people is shrinking fast. Overall, France's deficit on its annual $280 billion comprehensive social security budget is likely to grow from $7 billion today to $17.5 billion by the end of next year unless new revenue is found.

"The tendencies are catastrophic," Mr. Oudea said.

Similar shortfalls are reported throughout Western Europe.

From Sweden, until recently the paradigm of the welfare state, to Italy, with its swelling budget deficit, laws are being passed to cut the range and cost of welfare programs. Sweden has already adopted a measure raising the age for pension eligibility from 65 to 66 and eliminating sick pay for the first day of work missed. In Italy, the pensionable age has also been raised, and some limits have been imposed on free medical care for people with higher incomes.

The German Government, which has had to cope with the exceptional costs of unifying east and west, recently proposed cutting benefits for the unemployed. While people of the former East Germany have had to forsake the guaranteed employment and the cast-iron, cradle-to-grave social safety net provided by the Communist system, they have been largely integrated into the social security systems of the west, at great cost to the Bonn Government. Eastern Germans have lost their free day care and free homes for the aged, but they still have substantial protection.

In France, the conservative Government that took over in March has pushed through a range of measures to control costs, like lowering retirement payments, reducing reimbursement for medical expenses and shortening the period during which the unemployed can receive jobless benefits.

"We can't have people working for 8 months and then receiving 15 months' of unemployment benefits, as they do today," a French official said.

In the Netherlands, the rules governing disability benefits have been tightened as of Aug. 1, with the aim of cutting more than $2 billion from the disability budget. Definitions of incapacity to work will be stricter, medical examinations will be more rigorous, and in some cases, payments will be lowered from 70 percent of the last wage earned to 70 percent of the minimum wage.

"Before, the top priority was protection for people," said Mr. Jansen, the Social Affairs Ministry official in the Netherlands. "Now the priority is avoiding fraud, getting people back to work as fast as possible, and encouraging citizens to supplement national insurance with private insurance policies."

Of course, such measures set off fierce opposition. Mr. Jansen was speaking in a fifth-floor office that could be reached only by a stairway because a bomb planted by a Dutch terrorist group had recently blown up the ministry's elevator shaft. The group has been protesting changes in social benefits and in labor laws as well as an effort by the Government to crack down on the hiring of illegal immigrants.

But even when the public approves of cuts in benefit programs, experts are questioning whether the basic concept of comprehensive, or at least far-reaching, social protection is still tenable.

JOB MARKET: BENEFITS REDUCE NEW HIRING

Benefits programs add enormously to wage costs and tend to make industries less competitive in an economy that technology and high-speed communications have made genuinely global. There is also growing evidence that the cost of benefits makes employers extremely hesitant to hire new people. In France, for instance, an employer paying the current monthly minimum wage of 4,830 francs—about $810 at current exchange rates—will incur total wage costs of about 8,500 francs, or about $1,420, once payroll taxes for social security programs have been included.

A German manufacturing worker costs employers about $26.89 an hour, of which benefits account for 46 percent. In contrast, the average hourly pay of an American worker, $15.89, and benefits, about 28 percent of the wage, are much lower.

In 1992 alone, unit labor costs in the European Community grew 4.1 percent, compared with 2.4 percent in Japan and 1.4 percent in the United States, according to figures supplied by the Organization for Economic Cooperation and Development.

"With the social charges so high for an employee, I just can't afford to take on new people," said Gerard Dumontant, the owner of the Hôtel de Longchamp in Paris, who has cut his staff to 35 people from 45 over the last three years. "People are far too protected by society, and they have lost their sense of personal responsibility."

In Madrid, another small businessman, José Paniagua, the owner of an auto repair shop, explained with similar exasperation that it had become too costly and risky for him to hire more workers. He would like to increase his work force from four to five, but his tax bill would rise by about 25 percent. Spanish law also makes it very difficult, and expensive, to fire anyone.

"So if I need an extra worker, I'm forced to do it illegally," he said. "I bring him in on a Saturday morning, lock the door, and pay him in cash under the table."

Mr. Paniagua said the scope of social security programs made illegal practices inevitable. As an example he cited his brother-in-law, who has a profitable 300-acre farm in Andalusia but is able to collect unemployment benefits of about $900 a month each for his wife and two children.

Such is the extent of welfare fraud in Spain, where unemployment officially runs at over 20 percent, that a joke was widely heard in the countryside during the recent election campaign: "We have to beware of these politicians. They are threatening to reduce unemployment!"

Underlining such distortions, the Organization for Economic Cooperation and Development warned bluntly in a report published this month that generous unemployment benefits could be adding to long-term joblessness in Europe. "In many countries, the unemployment benefits system, rather than providing temporary support to job-seekers while they re-establish themselves in the labor market, has also become a means for long-term income support," the report said.

COMPETITION: FLIGHT OF JOBS RAISES WARNINGS

In some cases, benefits designed to cushion society from social problems seem to be worsening those ills. In effect, social security systems are deterring corporations from offering what many people view as the greatest single greatest source of security to an individual—a full-time job.

Indeed, in Spain, new full-time jobs have become a rarity because of the protection guaranteed workers. Dismissing anyone is so costly and so complex—usually involving lengthy mediation by the Labor Ministry and payment of at least 45 days' wages for each year worked—that corporations have resorted to hiring temporarily. More than 35 percent of the Spanish labor force is working on temporary contracts of a maximum of three years.

"It is very hard, in a modern economy of rapid change, to manage a company that you cannot adjust," said Gonzalo Hinojoso, the chief executive of a big Madrid clothing and retail company called Cortefiel. "That is why we have to use a lot of temporary labor, even though it is far from ideal."

In 1986, Cortefiel shifted some production of apparel from Spain to Morocco, where labor costs are about 25 percent of Spanish levels, social security taxes are minimal, and hiring and firing is far more flexible. "In this way, we can compete against textile manufacturers in the Far East," Mr. Hinojoso said.

European labor leaders fear that this trend is permanent. "Industry now just consists of financiers taking a look at the world and seeing where they can make the most profit," said Christian Muller, a labor official at the Hoover vacuum cleaner factory near Dijon, France. "Well, it costs 55 francs an hour for a specialized worker in France, compared with about 5 francs in Poland and one franc in Russia. The calculation doesn't take long."

Mr. Muller predicted "civil war" should the movement of jobs out of Europe and reductions in benefits continue. "We're going toward an American system," he said, "and it just won't work here."

He has reason to be bitter. His job and 617 others at the Hoover plant were eliminated earlier this year when the Maytag Corporation, which owns Hoover, decided to transfer production to Scotland, where labor and social security costs are about 37 percent lower than they are in France. The factory in Dijon is to close early next year.

But at the same time, Maytag secured concessions from its Scottish plant, at Cambuslang, by threatening to move production to France. Labor unions agreed to slash the bonus for working a night shift, eliminate some overtime payments, and increase the work week by 50 minutes. They also agreed that newly hired employees should have a two-year probationary period with no sick pay or pension contributions paid by the employer.

Such strong-arm tactics seem likely to spread. Faced by growing competition, corporations in Europe are desperate to cut costs.

Such companies have some backing from Britain's Conservative Government, which wants to encourage the move to roll back the welfare state. "Labor markets are the crux of Europe's economic woes—over-rigid, overregulated and over-priced," Kenneth Clarke, the Chancellor of the Exchequer, declared in July. "The first step must be for European Community governments to look at the whole range of extra costs we force on business by excessive regulation."

RESISTANCE: ANY CHANGES WILL COME SLOWLY

Other governments are taking a different tack. France, for instance, wants to force developing countries to improve their social security programs and thereby raise their labor costs. The alternative, President François Mitterrand argues, should be trade sanctions against those nations.

Though Western Europe's current model, for many reasons, no longer seems to be working, change appears certain to be slow. Europeans are deeply attached to their social protection: they like their free ambulance rides, their nine free ultrasound examinations per pregnancy, their five weeks of paid vacation and their generous pension plans. Even as unemployment rises and jobs migrate to other countries, Europeans will fight to keep these benefits, and politicians will hesitate to propose any change that looks like a dismantling of the welfare system.

A deep-seated conviction still exists among many people that Europe has got some things right that the United States has wrong. This sentiment was summed up last year by Mr. Mitterrand when he commented that the Los Angeles riots illustrated "that the social needs of any country must not be neglected."

Even as the Clinton Administration considers a wider social safety net and the Europeans a more stringent system, profound differences seem likely to persist.

"In the United States, work is regarded as a path to fulfillment," said Emilio Ontiveros, a Spanish economist. "Here, it is regarded more as a divine malediction, and social security is what makes it bearable."

And Now the Hard Part

George Zarycky

George Zarycky is Central European specialist for Freedom House.

During Poland's 1989 round-table negotiations between Solidarity and the ideologically bankrupt Jaruzelski junta, a farmer atop his wagon was asked by a Western news crew what should be done with the Communists. Without hesitating, he silently pointed to a line of trees along the road and made a gesture suggesting a noose. Just four years later, the Communists had staged a dramatic comeback. In September's national elections, the "post-Communist" Democratic Left Alliance (SLD) swept 171 of 460 seats in the Sejm. At its nucleus are the Social Democracy of the Republic (SdRP), the direct successor of the Communist-era Polish United Workers Party (PUWP), and the former official OPZZ trade union federation. Its coalition partner, the Polish Peasant Party (PSL)—a descendent of the PUWP's long-time satellite, the United Peasant Party—gained 132 seats. The new government of Prime Minister Waldemar Pawlak, the thirty-four-year-old PSL leader who served briefly as prime minister from June-July 1992, included 16 of 21 cabinet ministers who are former members of the PUWP or the old Peasant Party. The SDL-PSL coalition enjoys a comfortable 66 percent majority, almost enough to pass a constitution and overrule a presidential veto.

How did the Communists go from the gallows to governing in a country whose post-war history was so thoroughly anti-Communist and anti-Russian? Though widely anticipated, Poland's turn to the Left at a time when so-called "shock therapy" reforms gave it the fastest growing economy in Europe has raised serious questions. Would the new government roll back key market programs? What of ambitious plans to privatize or close money-losing state enterprises? Did the election signal a popular nostalgia for paternalistic centralism that eliminated class and income disparities through a bogus egalitarianism based on shared hardships? After five prime ministers, four governments, three national elections and two parliaments did Poland's election results presage a tropistic regional trend toward a more familiar authoritarianism and order?

Politics: the Polish paradox and beyond

Poland's nod to self-styled "post-Communist" Communists was part of a marked regional resurgence or continued popularity of left-socialist, "reform- neo- ex-Communist" national hybrids. A recent poll showed that over 70 percent of the population in East-Central Europe believed the state should provide a place to work, as well as a national health service, housing, education, and other services. But in the four years since the collapse of the East bloc, the countries of East-Central Europe—while facing the same broad challenges of dismantling a forty-year-old, Soviet-imposed totalitarian and centralized system—have diverged along indigenous historical, cultural and geographic factors into states where democracy is relatively strong and those where democracy has yet to take firm root.

In Poland, Hungary, Slovenia, the Czech Republic, and to some extent Slovakia, post-Communist Communists have emerged as pro-market, pro-competition and pro-reform socialists, not unlike left-wing parties in Western Europe. Poland's SDL seems part of a long socialist tradition and, unlike the rural-based PSL, appears committed to privatization and market reforms, albeit at a slower pace. In Hungary, where the centrist ruling Hungarian Democratic Forum (MDF) has purged its ultra-nationalist component but continues to slip in the polls, the death of Prime Minister Jozef Antall can only boost the prospects of the reform-Communists who oversaw the 1988 palace coup that ousted the hard-line Kadar regime and are viewed by many as capable, pro-market technocrats. Czech Communists, badly splintered between ultra-hardliners and moderates, still make up the second-largest parliamentary block.

In much of East-Central Europe, the forty-plus year interregnum of Soviet rule could not completely destroy pre-Communist infrastructures as well as literal and psychological avenues to the West.

What most of these countries have in common—and what attenuates but does not completely eliminate an authoritarian backlash—is a vibrant and entrenched civil society, functioning (though often chaotic) multi-party parliaments and other democratic institutions, several free-and-fair elections under their belts, and other indices of genuine pluralism. So while the Czechs, for example, still grapple with the composition of a constitutionally mandated upper house, laws get passed and signed. (With the exception of impoverished Albania's Democratic Party, nowhere does one-party have over half the seats and can rule alone). What's more, these countries, despite weak party structures, often obstructionist political-social elements, and constitutional gray areas have thus far steadfastly and rather successfully stuck to an incremental path of democratic change and market transition, much of it on the fly. This in itself is rather remarkable just four years after the disintegration of orthodox regimes, the collapse of the Warsaw Pact military alliance and the Council for Mutual Economic Assistance (CMEA) trading bloc, and with war raging in the Balkans. In much of East-Central Europe, the forty-plus year interregnum of Soviet rule could not completely destroy pre-Communist infrastructures as well as literal and psychological avenues to the West.

On the other side of the Communist constellation are states where members of the *ancien regime* and *nomenklatura* have retained prominent positions in government and where important democratic political institutions, for various historic-social-cultural reasons are stunted or non-existent. In Romania, the ruling Party of Social Democracy of Romania (PSDR), led by President and former Ceausescu ideologue Ion Iliescu, is essentially opposed to loosening the government's grip on the economy and is tethered to its ultranationalist and leftist coalition allies. Opposition movements and parties are fragmented into scores of organizations. The Bulgarian Socialist Party (BSP) has, with 106 seats, only 11 less than the badly fractious Union of Democratic Forces (UDF) which was ousted from power after losing a non-confidence motion in 1992. Like Romania, Bulgaria has been sluggish in implementing market reforms, and this year's draft budget was criticized by reformers for offering too much aid to a wide range of inefficient state enterprises and for giving continued control of the economic sector to the former nomenklatura, including members and former members of the BSP.

The ongoing conflagration in the Balkans continues to define politics in Croatia, Macedonia, Bosnia-Herzegovina and the rump-Yugoslavia (Serbia and Montenegro). The regime of former Communist Gen. Franjo Tudjman in Croatia has used the war as a pretext to purge moderate elements from the ruling Croatian Democratic Union (HDZ), tighten its grip on the media, and arrest political opponents. Major economic reforms are on virtual hold. Serbia's strongman Slobodan Milosevic has used television and truncheons to cow democratic opponents and his erstwhile allies of the fascist-nationalist Serbian Radical Party led by Seselj. Rump-Yugoslavia's economy is a basket case, the banking system has all but collapsed, inflation hovers at triple digits, and reform in any sense of the word is nowhere on the horizon. Bosnia lies plundered and helpless, victimized by Serbian and more recently Croatian aggression. Macedonia, with its substantial Albanian minority and a troubled history of Bulgarian, Greek and Serbian machinations, remains a tinderbox, though the presence of some 300 U.S. troops along its border with Serbia has helped keep things calm for now.

Is communism back?

Is communism back to stay in East-Central Europe and what are the regional ramifications? Poland's political crisis grew out of

parliamentary gridlock exacerbated by the fact that 29 parties were represented under a 1991 electoral system that wasn't modified until 1993. As a result, the moderate government of Prime Minister Hanna Suchocka never enjoyed the support of a stable majority. Paradoxically, President Lech Walesa's decision to dissolve parliament and call for new elections came amid sustained economic progress. GDP rose by over 4 percent in 1993. Industrial production was 7.6 percent higher in the first six months of 1993 than in the comparable period the year before. While unemployment was about 15 percent and climbing by mid-year, private sector employment accounted for 60 percent of the workforce. There were 1.7 million private firms and figures showed that in 1992 private sector jobs compensated for the 500,000 that vanished in the state sector.

While privatization of giant state enterprises had yet to be implemented, the economy was definitely on the upswing. Yet 56 percent of citizens polled felt the country was moving in the wrong direction. How come?

For one thing, while nearly half of Poles are employed in the private sector, there is a persistent perception—a legacy of communism—that new wealth and rich businesses are inherently corrupt or in the hands of the old *nomenklatura*. Moreover, as RFE/RL's Louisa Vinton has pointed out, another holdover of the Communist's gigantism mindset is that wealth and value are determined by the size of an enterprise and the number of employees, and that the huge though inefficient state firms are a cornerstone of Poland's national economy, long providing job security and other benefits regardless of the output of work. Throw in an innate fear of domination by foreign interests, and privatization looks less attractive to many. These debilitating factors are also present in varying degrees in Hungary, the Czech Republic, Slovakia, Slovenia, indeed everywhere in the region where governments have had trouble with or been reluctant to dismantle giant, money-losing enterprises.

The Communist political and industrial order—once derided as ossified and out-of-touch—has proven much more resilient and adaptable than predicted.

The continued appeal of socialist-left solutions have marginalized not only the center, but right-wing nationalists as well. In Poland, the big losers were parties closely linked to the conservative, socially intrusive policies of the Catholic Church on abortion and other issues. In Hungary, the MDF purged the right-wing, anti-Semitic clique led by Istvan Csurka, whose 1992 essay blamed the country's ills on Jews, international bankers and liberals and suggested a resurgence of a Greater Hungary. However, similar rantings continue to have appeal in Romania, where ex-Communists fine tuned their message with populist-nationalist demagogy, appealing to anti-Hungarian and anti-Semitic passions and xenophobia.

The post-Communist trend has been accompanied over the last few years by the concomitant weakening of the broad-based coalitions that toppled Communist regimes and launched market reforms. Bulgaria's UDF is badly factionalized and Romania's Civic Alliance has splintered. In the Czech Republic, voters abandoned the Civic Forum. In Slovakia, the Public Against Violence commands no support. In Poland, Solidarity—which initiated the no-confidence vote—was shut out of the Sejm, capturing seven seats in the 100-member Senate. President Walesa's moderate Non-Party Block to Support reform barely cleared the 5 percent hurdle, capturing just 20 seats.

These movements, which opened their societies to the prospects of democracy, now find themselves far from power. The diminished popularity of many liberal-intellectual groups, while unfortunate, is understandable and may actually signal maturation rather than regression. The dissidents symbolize an older era that many people would rather forget. They reminded non-dissidents of their own quiescence during the Communist era. For others, they represent warriors from a struggle already won. Some of the internecine conflicts within the democratic movement were part of an evolutionary process of political differentiation. Nevertheless they did dissipate the strength of post-Cold War political groupings. Coincidentally, Communists regrouped, utilizing existing structures and networks, discipline and shared ideology. The Communist political and industrial order—once derided as ossified and out-of-touch—has proven much more resilient and adaptable than predicted.

Lustration loses its luster

A controversial factor in the political resiliency of former Communists has been the reluctance of governments to pursue aggressive de-Communization. The Czech Republic's much-debated "lustration laws," aimed at excluding senior Communists officials from holding certain political or public offices, were vehemently attacked in the press and by international human rights groups on civil liberties and constitutional grounds. Over the last two years, Bulgaria has proposed several measures to exclude ex-Communist leaders from political, security, business and educational institutions, but the drafts met stiff resistance from Socialists and democrats alike. This February, the Constitutional Court did uphold the so-called Panev Act that bars persons connected with "the supreme structures of the former Bulgarian Communist Party and security services" from holding "managerial offices at scientific establishments, such as chiefs of departments, deans, rectors, and chief editors of serials." The law, which caused an outcry among some human rights groups in the West, did lead to the removal of several thousand formerly communist-affiliated academic staff from managerial positions. Meanwhile, several prominent Bulgarian Communists were prosecuted and convicted for criminal offenses, including former Communist leader Teodor Zhivkov, and former prime ministers Andrei Lukanov and Georgi Atanasov.

Poland resisted an across-the-board housecleaning, with some democrats even acknowledging the Party's role in keeping Soviet tanks at bay. Many Hungarians still appear to view the ex-Communists as early advocates of economic and political reform. In Romania, the government and other institutions continue to be permeated by ex-Communists, partly because few capable figures in the country are entirely untainted by the Ceausescu years.

The issue of de-communization and the rule of law remains nettlesome throughout the region, creating legal and moral contretempts. While witch-hunts and revenge-motivated purges would ultimately exacerbate social tensions and undermine democracy, it is clear that civic education, a greater sensitivity to the social repercussions of rapid economic transformation, and re-

striction on high-level former Communists who engaged in clearly illegal activities be integral to any meaningful transition.

Bumps on freedom's road

The possible ascent of the Left and its effect on the consolidation of democratic gains in much of East-Central Europe is an open question. While Poland's SDL has assured that their aim is not retrenchment but reform with a "more social face," and that they are committed to foreign investment, the conclusion by some Western analysts that they represent "social democracy" may be overly sanguine. Future economic progress—in Poland and elsewhere—is contingent upon privatizing the state sector, the pace and scope of which now seem less certain. And while there are definite independent institutional constraints that can prevent Poland's new government from too radically altering the country's economic course, the pervasive differentiation between rich and poor and growing social discontent could lead to conflicts over the rate of reform that whet the authoritarian appetite.

More immediate threats to further democratization stability and security were such issues as failure to draft and adopt post-1989 constitutions, deteriorating economic conditions, corruption, ethnic tensions—both domestic and regional—and control and character of the broadcast media. Future political developments in Russia were a critical factor in efforts by most East-Central European countries to formulate military policy, seek greater regional security cooperation and/or strive for full integration in the North Atlantic Treaty Alliance (NATO), the European Community (EC) and other European institutions.

The symbiosis between democratization and market reforms remained a key dynamic in charting the area's present and future course.

A less tangible challenge facing the region's governments was overcoming growing cynicism, voter apathy and gloom among citizens who appear to have lost faith in the political process, probably because they expected democracy and freedom to translate into instant economic improvement. A disturbing trend throughout much of the region was the percentage of unrepresented voters in national parliaments. In Hungary, Poland, the Czech Republic and Slovakia, relatively unfragmented parliaments were achieved by inadvertently disenfranchising large numbers of voters. In Bulgaria, the Czech Republic and Slovakia, a quarter of the voters chose parties which failed to clear electoral thresholds. While these figures would not be overly alarming in established democracies, the inherent potential for parliamentary instability and voter alienation is worrisome where democracy is so new. An eventual shake-out of marginal, "paper" parties and unwieldy coalitions should improve stability, particularly when and if voters and leaders realize how many parties essentially share the same basic beliefs.

Another destabilizing factor was ongoing corruption in government, particularly relationships between the *nomenklatura* and private business interests. In Romania, the infamous Caritas pyramid scheme was launched in collusion with right-wing politicians from ethnically tense Transylvania, including rabid nationalist Gheorghe Funar of the Party of Romanian National Unity (PRNU).

Much of what's left of rump-Yugoslavia's economy is in the hands of the government-criminal mafia. So-called *nomenklatura* privatization has also caused popular resentment at the exploitation of power and privilege by the new elite in Poland, Hungary, the Czech Republic, Slovenia and elsewhere. As mentioned, some of this frustration has awakened nostalgia for more authoritarian methods to restore order and stamp out graft.

This year also saw the intensification of the struggle for media reform. From Hungary and the Czech Republic to Croatia and Romania opposition groups claimed government control of television and radio denied them equal access. In Hungary, a year-long "media war" over control of radio and television resulted in several dismissals, including the suspension by state television of a liberal editor of a late-nights news program and his replacement by a pro-government journalist. In Slovakia and Romania, the broadcast media, while nominally independent, are in effect controlled by people loyal to the government and the ruling party. In October, MPs of the ruling Movement for a Democratic Slovakia moved to dismiss the head of Slovak Television, complaining that it was too critical of the government. In March, the director of Czech Radio resigned, citing as a reason interference by the Board of Radio Broadcasting. In Serbia and Croatia, television is used by the government as an instrument of propaganda and misinformation, with air time virtually denied anti-government voices.

Finally, democracy and human rights were undermined by escalating reports of discrimination and ethnic violence around the region. Gypsies were favorite targets of attack and bias in housing, employment and education from Hungary to Romania to the Czech Republic. Serbia continued its repression of 2 million ethnic Albanians in Kosovo. Romanian-Hungarian relations remained tense over the substantial Hungarian minority in Transylvania, which has pressed for greater autonomy and self-administration. For its part, Hungary has expressed concern about the 600,000-strong Hungarian minority after the Czechoslovak breakup. While full-blown ethnic violence was limited to the former Yugoslavia, ethnic and minority issues were a potential flashpoint throughout the region.

Economies: engines of democracy?

An important signpost of future social and democratic development was the state of national economies. Throughout East-Central Europe, the symbiosis between democratization and market reforms remained a key dynamic in charting the area's present and future course. And the overall picture offered a mixed bag.

In the three years following the overthrow of old-line Communist regimes, the countries of the region experienced a prolonged and precipitous fall in output. With the collapse of COMECON, most export markets disappeared virtually overnight. Living standards dropped dramatically, though not as sharply as is usually assumed. Inflation and unemployment sailed up as price liberalizations and dislocations took hold. Public resentment toward "shock therapy" reforms or market mechanisms lead to political squeamishness or indecision, as did the persistence of the old-guard *nomenklatura* protecting its turf.

By year's end, Poland, Hungary, the Czech Republic, Slovakia, and Slovenia had the largest private sectors and the most readily convertible currencies in the region and relatively low rates of inflation. Between them, they attracted some $13 billion in foreign investment 1992-93. Throughout the region, governments, through voucher schemes and other plans, managed to oversee

the privatization of mostly small businesses and enterprises. In Poland, the private sector's share of GDP in 1992 was 45 percent and 60 percent of total employment; in the Czech Republic, it was 20 and 23 percent; in Hungary, 40 and 16.7 percent. In Romania, it was 25 percent of GDP, and 20 percent in Bulgaria.

And while all East-Central states generally had problems with macroeconomic stabilization, budgetary issues, the slow pace of privatization of state property and enterprises, dysfunctional post-Communist banking and financial systems, as well as unresolved issues dealing with regional economic integration and trade, progress was recorded to varying degrees. Poland, Hungary, the Czech Republic, Slovenia, and, to some extent, Slovakia, have come closest to institutionalizing a viable market system. Bulgaria and Romania continue to be plagued by political gridlock, hyperinflation, plummeting output, and continued dominance of state ownership. Political elites in Serbia, Croatia and the other Yugoslav successor states have placed national security and nation-building above economic transition. Some economists predict that the worst of the economic transition has yet to come. The European Bank for Reconstruction and Development reported that it might take East-Central Europe thirty-five-years to catch up with per capital levels in the OECD.

Important questions remain: will citizens of East-Central Europe accept the fact that there are no overnight economic miracles, that the road to capitalism will be long and painful, and that austerity and social dislocation will continue in the foreseeable future? If the economic engines sputter and die, can democracy survive? Yes and probably not. A determining factor in the economic outcome is the role of the West. Thus far, the West's role has been muddled. Hundreds of millions of assistance dollars have been wasted on high-paid western consultants and trainers, instead of empowering local groups. The economic recession in Europe and Germany's costly absorption of East Germany have stymied substantial investment and closed EC markets to goods and products from the former East Bloc. As Josef Olesky of Poland's victorious SLD told the Western press: "Poland's economy depends on fast export growth. How can the West expect us to grow and not buy our goods? This situation naturally contributed to estrangement of the workers and more votes for us."

All this and NATO too?

Looming over these crucial processes is the shadow of a dangerous nemesis. Toward the end of the year, there were diplomatic flurries throughout the region as leaders and foreign ministers petitioned Euro-statesmen and U.S. secretaries of state and defense, Warren Christopher and Les Aspin, to quit talking about new partnerships for peace and enlargement doctrines and admit Europe's former Warsaw Pact nations as full members into NATO. In making the Czech Republic's case, President Vaclav Havel in October spoke of the country's precarious security situation due, not to the ongoing war in the Balkans, but to the unstable situation in Russia. Throughout much of East-Central Europe, there was a wary focus on Russia, with officials expressing real fear of a resurgence in Moscow of empire-restoring, Communists-nationalists. Ironically, one sure way lingering nostalgia for a Communist past would vanish overnight is if hardline Communist-nationalists oust Boris Yeltsin.

By year's end, prospects for expanding NATO to include any former East Bloc countries, including the oft-vaunted Visegrad Four (Poland, Hungary, the Czech Republic and Slovakia) had receded.

Yet, in barring membership, the U.S. and its allies continued to resist East-Central Europeans forging their own collective security alliances to fill the vacuum. Any possible threat from Russia aside, Romania, Bulgaria, Hungary, among others, continued to express deep concerns about the threat of an expanded Balkan War.

And then there's Bosnia

As the year ended, so too did any real hope for resolute action by Europe or the U.S. to end Bosnia's agony. The bankruptcy of ideas and groveling before Serbia reached unexplored lows when European negotiators suggested that they would lift the sanctions against Serbia—which had driven the Serbian economy to its knees and were the only punitive steps against Belgrade's aggression—if Milosevic could use his good offices to bring Bosnia's murderous Serbs into line and get them to agree to give up a little more of the land taken by force and genocide. The new administration in Washington seemed all too willing to wash its hands of the whole affair, blaming the Europeans, recalcitrant Bosnian Muslims, and lack of consensus for its own lack of leadership.

On the ground, the Bosnian position grew more untenable, as the Muslim's erstwhile Croatian allies turned their guns around and made their own rapacious land grab. Diplomatically, Muslims were being painted as the heavies, obstructionist and difficult when they refused to give away sovereignty rights that no one but themselves had the courage and moral fortitude to defend. They were being chastened for not buying into Lord Owen's vision of what was fair and proper.

As for the East-Central Europeans, virtually shut out of the peace-process, the peril of civil and territorial strife related to Bosnia was real enough. War spreading to Macedonia could ultimately involve Bulgaria, Greece, and Serbia. Bulgaria has its own tensions with the large Turkish minority. An explosion in Kosovo would draw in Albania and possibly Turkey. A new Croatian-Serbian conflict is by no means far-fetched. Meanwhile, millions of civilian refugees from Hungary to Croatia are taxing humanitarian and relief systems as yet another winter settles in.

Equally as menacing, the Bosnia conflict has, to many, legitimized the use of force without fear of international reprisal to settle ancient ethnic and territorial scores. Hungarians are concerned about their minorities in Slovakia and Romania. Romanian pretensions to Moldova could lead to conflict with Russia and Ukraine. The fate of Polish minorities in western Ukraine, Lithuania and Russia could further complicate relations with these states. And then, of course, there are the simmering conflicts in the former Soviet Union.

For all of its many problems, there is reason for guarded optimism about the ability of this region to overcome the formidable obstacles to democratization and market reforms left over after the collapse of four decades of Communist rule. What seems clear is that forces of regression and reaction, though weakened, should not be counted out just yet. Poland's post-Communist Communists may yet prove to be benign caretakers of a smooth transition. Citizens from Budapest to Bucharest may be sagacious enough to understand that what seems like anarchy or chaos is part of a prolonged process to fine-tuning democracy, that gangsterism and corruption are as much by-products of the old system as the new, and that whatever illusions they may have had about living almost as well as the West under communism were just that—chimerical—and that in many ways they are closer to the developing world than to Europe.

But there must be sagacity and commitment from the West as well. The nations of East-Central Europe need meaningful assistance. They need markets for their goods. They need help with infrastructure. They need to be encouraged and fully integrated in Europe's economic and security structures, regardless of the concerns of Russia or others. The West has failed them in Bosnia, failed miserably. We must do better as this turbulent, eventful century draws to a close.

The murderous intensity of newly fanned ethnic hatreds in the post-Soviet sphere surprised most, who considered such antagonisms confined to history textbooks. As Steven Burg points out, however, nationalism in all its forms is very much alive and, ironically, in some instances catalyzed by elements of the democratic forces that have swept the region.

Nationalism Redux: Through the Glass of the Post-Communist States Darkly

STEVEN L. BURG

STEVEN L. BURG *is an associate professor of politics at Brandeis University. This article is based on the forthcoming* Nationalism and Democracy in Post-Communist Europe: Challenges to American Foreign Policy, *which was supported by the Twentieth Century Fund.*

The wanton violence of the fighting taking place in the Balkans and the Caucasus (Armenia, Azerbaijan, and Georgia) has brought death and destruction to Europe on a scale not seen since the end of World War II; it threatens to destabilize not only the continent but other international communities. Because political boundaries rarely match ethnic boundaries, conflicts based on calls for ethnic self-determination inevitably threaten to involve neighboring states. And, as has been seen in the Balkans and Caucasus, once initiated, the violence of ethnic-based conflicts is easily escalated by individual acts of brutality into widespread death and destruction.

Failure to contain the conflicts that have already broken out, forestall future ones, and secure the democratization of the successor states of the former Soviet bloc would have a negative effect on the direct economic, political, and security interests of the West. Left unattended, the rise of nationalist regimes in eastern Europe, and the consequently increasing political appeal of nationalism in western Europe, may stimulate further violence by neo-Nazi and other ethnocentric groups in the West. The strong reactions such developments would bring from responsible governments, if sustained for long periods, might themselves become real threats to the foundations of liberal democracy. The military issues raised by continuing conflicts in the East, and intra-alliance differences over them, may stall the deeper development of the European Community and perhaps even erode the basic cohesiveness of NATO. It would almost certainly deal a powerful setback to the process of establishing a security framework among the North American, west-

ern European, and post-Communist states to replace the obsolete security architecture of the cold war.

The appeals of nationalist-separatist groups to the principle of national self-determination challenge the principles of state sovereignty, territorial integrity, inviolability of borders, and noninterference that have been central to the post–World War II international system. This challenge must be addressed if peaceful mechanisms for the resolution of ethnic conflicts are to be established, and the stability of the international system is to be preserved. This will inevitably require the careful redefinition of these postwar principles and the obligations arising out of them. The conflict between nationalism and democracy in the post-Communist states also presents a direct challenge to the ability of the United States to make human rights principles central to the international system.

FROM CONTAINMENT TO INVOLVEMENT

As long as the Communist leadership in Moscow exercised hegemony over the states of eastern Europe, the United States and its allies had only limited involvement in the region. The artificial stability the Soviet Union imposed on the domestic and international relations of eastern Europe was also found in states outside direct Soviet control, where independent Communist regimes created domestic stability by force and refrained from upsetting the political balance between East and West. Although ideologically opposed to communism, the West accepted the apparent certainties of Soviet domination of the region and refrained from direct attempts to undermine it.

Although the United States adopted a strategy of "containment," it consistently refrained from becoming directly involved in the internal affairs of the Soviet bloc countries. Even when faced with outbreaks of popular unrest or mass opposition to Communist rule (as was the case in Hungary in 1956, in Czechoslovakia in 1968, and in Poland in 1979 and 1980), the West refrained from intervening directly. Paradoxically, it was the onset of détente and the collaborative Soviet-American effort to ratify the status quo that created new opportunities for change in eastern Europe.

In 1975, 35 countries—including those from the Soviet bloc, western Europe, and the United States—concluded the Helsinki Final Act. Although the Helsinki agreement ratified the international status quo, it also provided the basis on which the West and, more important, domestic groups in the Communist states, could pursue political changes in eastern Europe. The Helsinki Final Act included 10 basic principles that were to be used to evaluate the actions of the signatory countries. These included some that ratified the postwar configuration of states in Europe by establishing their sovereignty and territorial integrity, affirming the inviolability of their borders, and mandating nonintervention in their internal affairs. Other principles committed the signatories to peaceful relations by disavowing the threat or use of force and calling for the peaceful settlement of disputes; the principles also committed them to respect "human rights and fundamental freedoms" and "the equal rights of peoples and their right to self-determination." The act further established the right of peoples to determine their political status. In effect, the Helsinki principles made Western concepts of individual liberty and collective democracy the political standard, and applied that standard to all the signatory states, from the countries of North America to the Soviet Union.

One consequence of the Helsinki agreement, certainly unanticipated in the East and perhaps in the West as well, was the formation in the Communist countries of small but active dissident grass-roots political organizations to uphold these political standards. The increase in cultural contacts between East and West that followed the act also reinforced a process already under way among the broader, nondissident social elites in the East: the development of increasingly liberal political values and growing national consciousness. This liberalization of values and new emphasis on national identity contributed—once Soviet President Mikhail Gorbachev's attempt to reform the Soviet system had introduced new opportunities for grass-roots political activity—to the re-emergence of national movements aimed at the establishment of independent states; in the end it also contributed to the collapse of communism.

The apparent marriage of liberalism and nationalism in the Communist states in the 1970s and 1980s echoed a similar marriage between these forces in Central Europe in the mid-nineteenth century. That alliance led to the devolution of power to nationalist leaderships, but failed to produce democracy. The implosion of the Soviet domestic political order, the emergence of independent states in the former territory of the Soviet Union, and the emergence of new regimes in eastern Europe has produced an analogous devolution of power to the state. As a result, nationalism has again become a powerful legitimating force for new governments with uncertain bases of popular support. It remains to be seen whether these post-Communist regimes will be able to transform the bases of their legitimacy from nationalist to democratic principles. The increased salience of nationality has rekindled many of the ethnic issues of the late nineteenth and early twentieth centuries. And these, as they have in the past, may yet lead some of these states to more authoritarian arrangements.

A BAD FIT: NATIONALISM AND DEMOCRACY

The commitment and ability of a government to guarantee individual rights is a necessary element in solving any ethnic conflict. As the scholars Larry Diamond and Juan Linz have pointed out, "for all their procedural messiness and sluggishness, [democracies] nevertheless protect the integrity of the person and the freedoms of conscience and expression."[1] Such protection is essential to ending the threat felt by individuals in situations of intergroup conflict and establishing interethnic peace. But the establishment of stable democratic regimes in the post-Communist states is also strategically important to Western security; democratic regimes are the strongest social foundations on which to build an international security framework.

The development of democratic regimes in eastern Europe and the former Soviet Union, and the construction of a new framework for Euro-Atlantic security, are best served by linking Western aid to local efforts to establish democracy. It cannot be taken for granted that, because Communist authoritarianism has given way to more open electoral processes and governments, the new regimes are "democratic." The loosening and even abandonment of state censorship and state-imposed limits on individual expression have indeed permitted the emergence of a multitude of citizens organizations of varying size and interests. And the introduction of competitive electoral politics has stimulated the formation of independent political parties. These expanded freedoms of expression, participation, and organization are essential to the democratization process. But the degree to which government institutions are becoming instruments for the representation of social interests and can impose accountability on the national leadership, not to mention the extent to which individual rights are protected, varies greatly from state to state.

---

[1]Larry Diamond, Juan Linz, and Seymour Martin Lipset, "Preface," in Diamond et al., eds., *Democracy in Developing Countries, Vol. 4: Latin America* (Boulder, Colo.: Lynne Rienner, 1989).

It is not clear that democratic regimes will be consolidated even where elements of democracy have already been established. In some cases greater openness has accelerated political and cultural polarization: witness the open expression of extreme nationalist, ethnocentric, and anti-Semitic sentiments, the organization of political movements based on these sentiments, and the eruption of violent ethnic conflict across the region. Local political leaders need to address this explosion of ethnic tensions, and Western assistance must support their efforts to do so in ways that help moderate conflict and ensure the effectiveness of democratic institutions.

Nationalism is distinguished from social movements that arise among other aggrieved groups by the powerful emotions associated with it. In extreme cases, nationalist movements evoke a willingness to fight and die on behalf of the cause. This derives from the notion that what is at issue is group "survival." Nationalist movements, however, cannot be understood as solely "primordial" in nature. They are most often also organizational vehicles for the articulation of arguments over rights, goods, status, power, and other material and political issues. Hence, the conflicts between Serbs and other groups in the former Yugoslavia, and between Armenians and Azerbaijanis in Nagorno-Karabakh may be exceptional cases by virtue of the disproportionately powerful role primordial hatred has played and the extreme violence that has taken place. Their ultimate solution, however, must involve the redress of grievances over rights, status, and power that also motivate and mobilize the populations—and especially their leaders—in these conflicts.

The strength of nationalist political movements, the popular appeal of avenging long-held ethnic grievances, and the resultant escalation of ethnic conflict impede the transition from authoritarianism to democracy. Democratization involves the creation of stable political institutions and processes "that make conflict, change, and conciliation possible without institutional collapse."[2] Nationalist conflict suppresses the importance and, in some cases, even the emergence of multiple issues, demands, and interests as nationalist leaders try to subordinate all other issues. Nationalist movements usually demand autonomy and seek a separate existence, denying the reality of commonalities, shared interests, or even mutual dependence. Ethnically based claims to autonomy thus strike at the heart of the process of democratization, since they compete with individual rights-based legitimation of a liberal democratic order.

The political organizations characteristic of nationalist movements, and the state institutions and processes they spawn are therefore ill-suited to the conciliation of competing demands. They tend to adopt exclusivist rather than inclusivist policies, and tend to extremism rather than moderation. In this way the politics of nationalism are contrary to the essence of the liberal democratic process.

The enormous hardships that have been imposed on the people of eastern Europe and the former Soviet Union by the transition from central planning and state ownership to market-based economies make it difficult, if not impossible, for governments to win popular support on the basis of the material benefits they can deliver. This heightens the effectiveness of a government's appeals to national sentiments. The declaration of "sovereignty," the establishment of cultural supremacy, or even the threat of military action are promises more easily delivered than an improvement in the standard of living. Moreover, such acts strengthen the state's power and secure the positions of political incumbents far more effectively than efforts to institutionalize civil liberties, which would facilitate criticism of the government and the activities of an opposition.

Attempts to legitimate even democratically elected governments through appeals to nationalism may unsettle relations between neighboring states. Expressions of concern for minority communities of ethnic brethren in neighboring countries, no matter how carefully constructed, may raise the specter of irredentist claims and stimulate nationalist responses among the neighboring ethnic majority. Given the changing historical/political status of territories throughout eastern Europe and the former Soviet Union, real and imagined irredentist issues claims represent sources of potentially serious interstate conflict.

Nationalist legitimation of new states may also lead to actions that impede the development of internal democracy. Several post-Communist governments have attempted to redress the ethnic grievances of the majority or eponymous population through legislation that effectively discriminates against minorities. Already, new citizenship laws, laws on language rights, voting rights laws, and other legislation have heightened tensions between dominant and minority groups. The popular support these measures evoke suggests how difficult it is to establish a broad social and political commitment to the pluralistic concept of civil society that underlies Western liberal democracy. The prospect of successfully establishing the political culture of tolerance for differences that underlies American democracy, for example, appears to be especially limited.

The post-Communist regimes are experiencing a broad, multidimensional transition from the enforced integration, artificial homogeneity, and stability of communism to the more open and pluralistic patterns of public discourse and behavior associated with incipient democracy. The rapid multiplication of political groups and organizations, the narrowness of

[2]Ibid., pp. 385–386.

support for most of them, and in some cases the obviously satirical if not cynical intention behind their formation suggest that the eastern European and post-Soviet states are undergoing processes of social and political fragmentation. With only a few notable exceptions, political organizations and institutions in these states have yet to bring together diverse groups and reconcile their conflicting interests. Their inability to do so may reflect the absence of interests that bind their populations together. At the very least it suggests that such interests are now far less important to the population than those that divide them.

Even where common economic interests, for example, might provide a pragmatic basis for linking constituencies to a common administrative and political center, the power of nationalist-separatist sentiments among the populace makes it difficult for local leaders to act on them. Indeed, even the distribution of economic interests and resources themselves may be in dispute, held to be illegitimate legacies of the old regime for which contemporary compensation is due. In competitive elections, greater support—and therefore greater political power—may be gathered by exploiting the coincidence of regional economic differences and inclinations toward ethnic self-assertion than by advocating economic compromise and political unity. The perception of material conflicts in ethnic terms by the mass populace, the acceptance or exploitation of such ethnic definitions by elites, and the frequency with which conflicts defined this way produce violence, make the resolution of differences over the distribution of government functions and over economic and other issues much more difficult to achieve. If liberal democracy depends on the mastery by political leaders of the art of compromise, then a successful transition to democracy is made more difficult in eastern Europe because the new countries' leaders, facing populations whose nationalist aspirations are unconstrained by other competing interests and aspirations, enjoy little leeway in which to develop this art.

THE TIES THAT DIDN'T BIND

In the post-Soviet states, the former Yugoslav states, and in Czechoslovakia, the transition from authoritarianism was turned into a simultaneous "end of empire" process. Once seen this way, intellectual, economic, and other groups who might otherwise have been inclined to support a transition to democracy were drawn toward more nationally determined positions. The Slovenian and Croatian challenges to rule from Belgrade, for example, stimulated a conservative and even reactionary response among some Serbs, whose earlier support for democratization proved less powerful than the appeal of Serbian nationalism. Similarly, the opportunity to establish an independent state proved more appealing to democratic activists in

Slovenia than the task of democratizing a common Yugoslav state. In Czechoslovakia, the alliance of Czechs and Slovaks opposed to communism soon disintegrated and electoral support in both Slovakia and the Czech Republic shifted to leaders and parties intent on pursuing regional interests at the expense of continued federation.

The rush to redress long-suppressed national grievances has also led in some cases to the partial legitimation, or re-legitimation of the antidemocratic aspects of national political history. The Fascist and Nazi collaborationist regimes established in Hungary, Slovakia, and Croatia during World War II have been the object of public, and in some instances de facto official re-valuation by nationalist leaders. New governments in Lithuania and Slovenia have pardoned Nazi collaborators. These actions are one dimension of the reaffirmation of collective identities, and a reflection of the powerful urge to reject any negative judgments of them. They also reflect, however, how weak concerns are for individual and human rights in the contemporary politics of the region. The still overwhelming strength of collective identities makes efforts to distinguish between national-cultural communities and the actions of individuals, especially when they are government officials, very difficult. And such distinctions are essential to the success of a transition from nationalist to democratic bases of legitimation.

The supporters of democratization in the region thus confront a vexing dilemma: the collapse of authoritarianism has unleashed forces that make the establishment of liberal democracy difficult. Yet to suppress these forces would require actions that might make democracy impossible. Some accommodation of the national aspirations of local populations is essential in order to avoid violence, to strengthen the legitimacy of new democratic institutions, to motivate these populations to endure the sacrifices associated with transition and, not least of all, because of the moral virtue of doing so.

Democratically inclined leaderships in the region are, therefore, confronted with the task of establishing an enforceable boundary between democratically acceptable and unacceptable political behavior. This is an immensely difficult political challenge. Debate over this issue continues in the United States even after 200 years of institutionalized democratic experience. It should not be surprising, therefore, that this is so difficult to achieve in the post-Communist states. It is clear that these states cannot depend on either a mass civic culture or on their own accumulated legitimacy to insulate them from popular discontent; moreover, they do not have the resources to deliver sufficient benefits to their people to counterbalance the social, economic, and political hardships that confront them.

THE NEED FOR INTERNATIONAL ATTENTION

The fate of democracy in the successor states of eastern Europe and the former Soviet Union depends on both internal conditions and the international environment. On the international level, the wars in the former Yugoslavia and rising ethnic tensions elsewhere have stimulated efforts to find a new framework for international peace and security and the collective mechanisms to enforce it. The conflict in Yugoslavia has revealed the weaknesses of the Conference on Security and Cooperation in Europe (CSCE), or the "Helsinki process." They have contributed to concerns about the need to strengthen the peacemaking and peacekeeping capabilities of the UN. And they have underscored the importance of direct bilateral and multilateral negotiations among the post-Communist successor states to address and eliminate potential sources of conflict between them.

Despite the differences that have arisen, negotiations among the democratically elected governments of eastern Europe and their active engagement in the CSCE and other international organizations have contributed to peaceful relations among them. Their behavior reflects, in part, the powerful norms of negotiation, compromise, and peaceful behavior that prevail among democratic governments. Their behavior also stands in sharp contrast to that of authoritarian states, governments, and organizations in the region, which have resorted to force to achieve their goals. Events in the former Yugoslav states, in the Caucasus, and in Moldova make it clear that the use of force in pursuit of nationalistic goals threatens the stability of neighboring states and raises the prospect of direct military involvement by outside actors, including the West. The costs and controversy such involvement would create place a premium on preventing and resolving these conflicts before they turn violent. The peaceful character of dispute resolution between democratically elected governments, therefore, gives the United States and its allies a strategic interest in the consolidation of democracy in the post-Communist states that parallels their interest in establishing an international security framework.

Post-Communist Europe thus presents the United States and its European allies with important and difficult foreign policy challenges. More direct involvement in the region seems essential. This requires coordination with European allies, whose own interests in the region may, in some cases, differ from or even conflict with those of the United States. The task of meeting these challenges must be met in ways that contribute to the further integration of the Euro-Atlantic community, and especially to the institutionalization of mechanisms for the prevention and peaceful resolution of conflict.

American policy must support the development of democratic governments in the region. It can do so directly and through multilateral arrangements. American efforts must be multidimensional, addressing the social and political dimensions of democratic development, as well as providing direct economic assistance. Policies toward individual states must reflect the nature of the threat to democracy in that state. And where democracy is threatened by interethnic conflict, special efforts must be devoted to building counterweights to the appeals of nationalism.

Clearly, any external power—European or American—that attempts to impose solutions in these conflicts will find it difficult to achieve success. The challenge to the United States and its allies, therefore, is to find ways to structure conditions in such a way that the conflicting parties themselves recognize incentives to resolve their disputes and become willing to initiate and sustain efforts to defuse ethnic tensions. The Yugoslav crisis demonstrates the importance of concerted international action to prevent and resolve conflicts before they turn violent.

American policy must support the development of an international framework for the prevention and peaceful settlement of conflict in the Euro-Atlantic community. This will require a multilateral effort to reconcile the conflicting principles of sovereignty, territorial integrity, noninterference, human rights, and self-determination on which conflicting claims in specific cases are based. This effort, while difficult, can be coordinated with and reinforce efforts to promote the democratic development of new governments. Because no framework for peace can prevent all conflicts, the United States must also consider ways to strengthen, through the UN and regional organizations, the peacekeeping and peacemaking resources of the international community, both as a means of encouraging parties to accept negotiated solutions and in case enforcement action becomes necessary.

Although the dramatic events of recent years heighten the temptation to resort to political hyperbole, the West *does* confront a historic opportunity to encourage the democratic development of the formerly Communist regimes and aid in the emergence of a new framework for maintaining peace in the expanded Euro-Atlantic community. The collapse of communism by itself does not guarantee this will happen. The strength of nationalisms throughout the region provides a powerful instrument for the construction of new authoritarian regimes. The prospect of a nationalist authoritarian government in Russia, for example, offers dangers many orders of magnitude greater than those already created by such a government in Serbia. Ameliorating the nationalist threat to democracy in the post-Communist states, therefore, must be seen as a strategic goal of American foreign policy, one to which an appropriate level of American attention and resources need to be devoted.

> "It would be naive to think that even the wisest and most far-sighted [reform] policy. . .could have avoided trouble [in the Soviet Union]. Still, when the trouble came, it would not have had to be as far-reaching and seemingly intractable had Gorbachev [been] more sensitive to the problems of the multinational state emerging from autocracy and repression." In the end, "he [found] himself in the position of the sorcerer's apprentice: unable to stop the very forces he had evoked."

Looking at the Past:
The Unraveling of the Soviet Union

ADAM B. ULAM

ADAM B. ULAM *is director of the Russian Research Center and Gurney Professor of History and Political Science at Harvard University. This article is adapted from* The Communists *by arrangement with Charles Scribner's Sons, an imprint of Macmillan Publishing Company.*

Were glasnost and perestroika merely the means through which Mikhail Gorbachev sought and hoped eventually to achieve personal dictatorship? Or, on the contrary, was he from the beginning a thoroughgoing liberal, intent on replacing Communist party rule with democracy, one whose earlier cautions and reservations were designed to reassure the more conservative of his followers? Or did he try to change his course only when he realized that the price of democracy might be the dissolution of the Soviet state?

The most reasonable hypothesis is that his original intentions were somewhere between those two extremes. Glasnost was not to be an end in itself but the means to clear the path to thorough reform of the state and society. Socialism would remain the foundation of the system. In politics the Communist party would remain supreme, but it would be internally democratized and would rule through persuasion rather than coercion. In the economy, overcentralization and the "command administrative" system would give way to "market socialism," the exact meaning of which was probably not clear to Gorbachev himself but stood for something that would allow for private initiative and foreign investments.

In the spring of 1988, Gorbachev, who was three years into his tenure as party general secretary, may well have felt that the debate about the party's sinful past had gone too far. But at the same time he undoubtedly must have expected that society's attention would now be turned to the ambitious plan of constitutional and political reconstruction that he was about to propose. Glasnost had enabled him to discredit or immobilize the opponents of perestroika within the party councils. Now it was time to turn to the tasks at hand. It was only later, after the elections of 1989, that the proponents of reform realized how much damage historical debate had done to the spell—if that is the word—that the party had exercised over society. And after another year, and with the territorial integrity of the Soviet Union threatened, the general secretary would have appreciated what a famous American baseball player once said: "Don't look back. Something may be gaining on you."

But by mid-1988 Gorbachev stood at the height of his popularity at home and abroad. To the world he was the man who by creating an entirely new atmosphere in East-West relations had exorcised the specter of nuclear war. No one but the extreme doctrinaires begrudged him as yet the promise of perestroika and the new spirit of openness that pervaded the Soviet Union. The general secretary's assimilation of certain traits of Western political style, such as taking his wife along on his state visits abroad, must have created some head shaking among the party stalwarts, but by the same token it enhanced his popularity among the progressive elements of society. The same was true about his gradual dismantling of the apparatus and phraseology of proletarian internationalism. The people at large, if not the remaining ideologues and some generals, welcomed the government's pledge to withdraw Soviet troops from Afghanistan by February 1989 and thus conclude what had been an endless and unpopular war.

THE UNRAVELING BEGINS

Against this generally pleasing picture were portents of trouble. One touched on the possibility of remaking

From *Current History* magazine, October 1992, pp. 339-346. Adapted from *The Communists* by Adam B. Ulam. © 1992 by Adam B. Ulam. Reprinted with the permission of Charles Scribner's Sons, an imprint of Macmillan Publishing Company.

the party so that it would fit into the scheme of things to come. The other was a preview of what would be the Achilles' heel of perestroika in the Soviet Union: the nationalities question. What happened in the Caucasus in February 1988 foreshadowed the unraveling of the pattern of authority that for seven decades had held the multinational state together.

The ethnic mosaic that is the Caucasus had been the scene of national and religious hostilities since time immemorial. That "prison house of nationalities," as Lenin called czarist Russia, could not for all of its authoritarian character eradicate the most recurrent of these conflicts between the Muslim Tatars, or as they would be classified in Soviet times, Azerbaijanis, and the Christian Armenians. Racial, religious, and socio-economic factors had all fueled the tension between the nationalities, which periodically would erupt into bloody clashes. The coming of Soviet power brought with it the eventual creation in the Caucasus of three union republics—Georgia, Armenia, and Azerbaijan—but the old ethnic mix and the resultant tension persisted.

According to the canon of Marxism-Leninism, with these major nationalities being given their own states, national animosities should have subsided, since the real cause for all the ostensible manifestations lay in the economic and political enslavement of all the nationalities under the czars' reign. Against such prognoses ethnic troubles continued, even though Communist rule proved much more effective in preserving its own version of law and order than the czar did. Still, if ethnic enmities were an unwitting reaction to the frustrations of life under a despotic rule, that was truer of much of the Soviet period than before the Revolution. And with Stalin's death, the repressed national aspirations of the peoples of the Caucasus (as elsewhere) began to be aired in public, at first timidly, but with the onset of perestroika, quite boldly.

Officially, Nagorno-Karabakh had the status of an autonomous region within the Azerbaijan republic. Ethnically, it was a predominantly Armenian enclave (some 80 percent of the population of 180,000), separated from Armenia by territory inhabited by the Azerbaijanis. For years, representatives of the district's majority, as well as those of Armenia itself, had been petitioning Moscow for the transfer of the district to the latter. All such pleas were met with bureaucratic indifference. As the Armenian party head was to complain at the nineteenth party conference in June 1988: "The sources of the existing situation are found in the complex. . .problems arising from the distortion of the nationality policy during the periods of the cult of personality, and of stagnation." In other words, under Stalin nobody would have dared to complain; under Brezhnev nobody would listen.

The "existing situation" to which the Armenian chief referred was that of virtual warfare between the two "fraternal" republics of the Soviet Union over possession of the tiny enclave. As perestroika proceeded, so did the Armenians' insistence that the district be joined to their republic, a demand that ran into obdurate resistance by Azerbaijan officials. Riots erupted in the area in February. That in turn led to huge demonstrations in Yerevan, the capital of Armenia, in which crowds estimated at nearly a million participated (the total population of the republic being around 3 million). Quite apart from the disputed district, there were a lot of Armenians living in Azerbaijan towns. And on February 27, in one of them, a clash between the two nationalities left at least 32 dead, the great majority of them Armenians. Their fellow nationals now began to flee Azerbaijan, while in Armenia mass protests escalated. Confronted by the crisis, Gorbachev appealed to both nations for calm, but privately complained that the Armenians "were stabbing perestroika in the back." Troops were sent to Armenia to enforce order. To its people this signified that Moscow, as before, favored the cause of their hereditary antagonists.

The subsequent course of the Azerbaijan-Armenian conflict lies outside this study. Suffice it to say that all the Kremlin's efforts to resolve it—use of force, persuasion, the temporary imposition of direct rule from Moscow—proved unavailing. It has festered to this day. What is pertinent to our theme is that the initial phase of the crisis illuminated the vulnerability of the Communist system, especially during the attempts to liberalize it, to the enmities of the ethnic groups within the Soviet state.

This is not to argue that democratization ought not to have been tried, or that the old ways could have been continued for long without bringing an even more violent explosion of national enmities and secessionist demands than that which would rack the Soviet Union from 1989 on. But Gorbachev and his aides underestimated the gravity and urgency of the nationalities problem.

In itself, at least to an outsider, the issue in contention in the Caucasian dispute could appear preposterously small to have triggered such serious and mournful consequences. In the past a peremptory order from Moscow had led on occasion to the resettlement of a population several times the size of that of the unfortunate district. But in this situation, as on other issues, the post-1953 Soviet regime was not able to sustain such a level of repression. By 1988 the celebrated paradox from *Through the Looking-Glass* was applicable to the situation in the Soviet Union: the regime would have to run very fast to keep in the same place. Freely translated, it carried a lesson that Gorbachev should avoid half-measures. Perestroika could not be accomplished through democratization. It could either set a course toward real democracy or it would run into trouble. The nationalities issue is a good case in point. If in 1987 and 1988 the Kremlin had offered an imaginative plan to restructure the Soviet Union by granting real and substantial autonomy to the 15 republics, it would have, in all likelihood, been spared the subsequent demands for full independence. Events and the people's reaction to them showed that the Balts, the Georgians, and others who would have been content in 1988 if the Soviet Union had become a real rather than a fictitious federal commonwealth, would two years later be satisfied with nothing short of independence.

RESTRUCTURING THE PARTY-STATE

But the crucial consideration on this issue, just as on practically every other in Soviet life, was to be the role of the party. *Legally,* the republics and hence the major nationalities, did not need any new powers. Under the existing constitution (proclaimed by Stalin in 1936, amended slightly under Brezhnev in 1977) they enjoyed powers far surpassing those of the American states, including the right to secede from the union. But up until now the constitution was a part of the mythology of Soviet life, rather than anything having really to do with the rights of the union republics, or for that matter, with those of the individual citizens. The country was ruled by the party, and that again did not mean rule by its 19 million members, for the party statute was also a part of the mythology. Real power resided with the 20 to 25 men at the top of the party hierarchy, and as of 1988 they were chosen, just as under Brezhnev in the era of stagnation, by co-optation.

If perestroika was not to turn out to be just a show, all this had to be changed. Hence Gorbachev's first words to the 5,000 delegates to the nineteenth party conference that opened June 28, 1988: "The basic task [that faces us] is how to deepen and make irreversible the revolutionary perestroika that has been initiated and has been developing under the leadership of the party."

At the conference, the general secretary proposed and the conference agreed to establish a new political system in the Soviet Union, one that would combine democracy *and* one-party rule. How could a seasoned politician and a man endowed with his intelligence entertain such a fantastic notion? Some speakers at the conference tried to tell him, delicately and indirectly, that the idea was as hard to realize as squaring the circle. But Mikhail Sergeievich was a party man not only by profession but also emotionally.

Those seemingly incongruous bedfellows, democracy and one-party rule, were to be united under the auspices of the new Soviet constitution, whose general outline was presented at the conference. It was too much to expect that any constitution, no matter how finely crafted, could by itself smooth the path of perestroika. But quite apart from the glaring incongru-

ity of its two main motifs, the new constitution would turn out to be a most unwieldy political instrument, with several of its provisions impractical or obsolete already by the time it came into force.

The central and most awkward feature of this Rube Goldberg-like contraption was to be the Congress of People's Deputies. Two-thirds of this assembly of 2,250 representatives was to be elected by popular suffrage and one-third by "social organizations," a description encompassing such diverse organizations as the Communist party (100 delegates), the Academy of Sciences (20), and the Society of Philatelists (1). The Congress would meet annually and select one-fifth of its membership to constitute the Supreme Soviet; the two-tiered standing legislature would be expected to function like a Western-style parliament.

What was behind the cumbersome scheme was obvious. The Soviet state was to have real elections for the first time since 1918. Those 1,500 popular seats could—most of them would—be contested, rather than, as before, having just one candidate sponsored by the party. Thus quite a few, perhaps a sizable number, of the people elected by universal suffrage might turn out to be independents, critical of this or that aspect of the regime. But a great majority of those 750 deputies sent to the Congress by "social organizations" were bound to be individuals toeing the party line, and hence Gorbachev loyalists. There was to be the best of all possible worlds: democracy secured, one-party rule safeguarded, and an (almost) freely elected legislature with a firm proregime majority. In any event, it did not turn out that way. Even on the procedural side there would be great confusion as to the powers of the Congress concerning the Supreme Soviet. The story of prerevolutionary Russia's brief experience with parliamentarism (1906–1917) should have taught Gorbachev that you really cannot combine genuine parliamentarism with what might be called semiautocracy.

In general, however, the nineteenth party congress resulted in considerable success for Gorbachev. The party conference followed the counsel of neither the right nor the left. It voted for the middle course, which was, for all Gorbachev's language about its revolutionary character, exactly what the general secretary expected from perestroika.

Mikhail Sergeievich stood at the apogee of his career by the end of 1988. For all the ominous portents we have listed, it still would have required special prophetic powers to predict that within one year his leadership would be challenged, that party authority would have suffered a catastrophic blow, and that the Soviet Union would be in the process of losing its Eastern European empire, with its own unity endangered by separatist and nationalist forces.

One event accelerated all those developments and made them erupt simultaneously on the Soviet scene:

3. EUROPE—WEST, CENTER, AND EAST: Russia and Post-Soviet Republics

the elections for the Congress of People's Deputies, which took place in March 1989 and which marked a watershed in Soviet history, perhaps even more significant than the events of March 1985, when Gorbachev came to power.

We spoke before about the damage done to the reputation of the Communist party because of what glasnost has revealed about its past and also because of the loss of a sense of mission. What happened as the result of the elections went, however, much further. It was a veritable body blow to the role of the party, one from which it would not recover.

If one pay attention merely to numbers, the election may well have appeared as justifying Gorbachev's expectations. The great majority of the successful candidates were in principle supporters of perestroika. The diehard party conservatives were for the most part defeated. Superficially, the results justified the prediction Gorbachev made while casting his own ballot on March 26—"Elections will carry us and perestroika far forward"—and *Pravda*'s headline the morning after: "Millions Vote for Perestroika—A Vote of Confidence for the Policy of Regenerating Soviet Society." But the numbers do not begin to tell the whole story.

Properly understood, the vote was one of nonconfidence in the Communist establishment. That the party was able to secure a majority of sorts was due first of all to the complex electoral procedure, to the undoubted tampering with the ballots in several places in the provinces, and of course to those seats reserved to the "social organizations" where the nomenklatura could be expected to score heavily—and by and large it did, though there were also some surprises for the regime. (Thus, despite considerable pressure on the Academy of Sciences *not* to elect Andrei Sakharov, he was eventually voted in.) But the overall impression had to be one of spectacular setbacks dealt to the party, with humiliating defeats of several of its notables. This was most obvious in the big cities, where it would have been difficult to tamper with the ballots or indulge in other chicaneries. The unofficial (there was no longer an official) party slate in Moscow and Leningrad was trounced. Many party bosses were repudiated by the voters in what had been their little kingdoms.

But even the spectacular defeats of the Communist establishment figures were overshadowed by the victories of those who were identified with the antiestablishment. Outstanding among them was Boris Yeltsin, who in a district coterminous with Moscow received 6 million votes, crushing the party hack put up against him. In the Baltic republics, reformers grouped in "popular fronts"—regional organizations based (though not explicitly) on the ethnic principle—secured the majority of the seats, the Lithuania one, Sajudis, winning in 31 out of 39 districts. Communist leaders in those areas had to go along with the local nationalist aspirations in order to be elected. Those aspirations,

demands for much wider autonomy or full independence, surfaced in other areas of the vast land.

The sum total of the developments centered around the elections to the Congress of People's Deputies spelled the end of the Communist party's domination of Soviet politics and of the entire one-party political culture. The party would remain an important element in Soviet politics, but it definitely ceased to be the decisive one.

The results of the elections had thus to be a blow to Gorbachev. He had hoped to nurse Soviet democracy through its infancy. He was suddenly confronted by an unruly adolescent. How much the results of the elections unnerved the leadership was demonstrated before the Congress of People's Deputies assembled. A peaceful demonstration in Tbilisi, Georgia, with the marchers carrying banners with nationalist slogans, was brutally dispersed by the troops of the local military districts. For reasons still not fully explained, soldiers resorted to the use of toxic gas and physically assailed the demonstrators. At least 20 demonstrators were killed, with many more injured. Orders for repression on that scale had to come from the center, and it is still not clear who issued the order to send in troops, and why, and whether Gorbachev himself was involved. The Georgian tragedy was only the most publicized of the many incidents of violence caused by ethnic tensions that were becoming endemic over large areas of the Soviet Union. As it was, the Tbilisi affair gave a powerful stimulus to the independence movement in Georgia.

AND PERESTROIKA?

Where, in what was becoming an increasingly chaotic situation, was perestroika? By the end of 1989 it had definitely ceased to be, if it ever was, a systematic program of reforms and had become a synonym for changes, some of them intended by the government, others to which it had been pushed by extraneous factors. What was also occurring was what might be called rebellion perestroika, such as was inherent in the various units of the federal system adopting reforms on their own and pressing for independence.

Gorbachev's position had undergone a considerable alteration. He was still enormously popular in the West, where he was credited, and on good grounds, with bringing an end to the cold war and, somewhat less justifiably, with consciously helping Eastern European countries get rid of their Communist regimes. But at home his popularity began to decline. This was largely, though not completely, because of the worsening economic situation.

The task of bringing the Soviet economy out of the doldrums and setting it on a steady course that would lead to immediately recognizable benefits in raising the standard of living and the amelioration of the environment would have overtaxed the resources of the most resolute leader, even one with absolute power. Gorbachev's position from 1989 on fitted neither of these criteria. He had reluctantly accepted that the old dogmas of Marxism-Leninism had to be jettisoned. Soviet economists now virtually unanimously proclaimed that ideological superstitions were doing immeasurable harm to the well-being of the Soviet people and the vitality of the economy. The remedies were to be found in the free market, the open path to private initiative, and the dismantling of the entire collective-state farm system that had been the curse of Soviet agriculture for more than five decades. Most of the measures to implement those goals, while salutary in the end, were bound in the "short run" (conceivably taking years) to cause considerable hardships and unrest among the people. All of them involved tremendous administrative problems, as well as the overcoming of long-standing practices and prejudices.

Many of the difficulties could have been avoided if Gorbachev, like Stalin or even Brezhnev, could just crack the whip and be obeyed—if for example, prices on the necessities of life could be doubled overnight, and the people could be expected to suffer in silence rather than strike and riot. Now, with political power diffused and the regime no longer awesome, the Soviet consumer was unlikely to acquiesce in having his already unsatisfactory standard of living lowered still further and to suffer it in silence. Even without the government's resorting to measures of the kind described above, the worsening economic situation brought strikes, such as that by miners in the summer of 1990, on a scale unimaginable only a few years before.

With the fervor of neophytes, growing numbers of Soviet economists began to embrace the gospel of free enterprise. For them all the dangers and difficulties of the transition to the free market paled against the urgency of changing the old economic ways that had brought the country to the brink of disaster. The people, went their argument, would put up with an interlude of hardships if at the end of the road there was a clearly discernible goal of a free and dynamic economy, no more shortages of basic commodities, no more shoddy goods, and the overall appearance of a Soviet society no longer reminiscent of that of a third world country.

Mikhail Sergeievich's attitude toward a free-market economy remained similar to his view about the possibility of introducing democracy in the Soviet Union: yes, up to a point, but certainly not right away. And so progress toward economic perestroika was episodic and inconsistent. Joint ventures with foreign entrepreneurs were authorized but were intermittently overregulated. The same went for cooperative enterprises. Privatization of Soviet industry was proclaimed to be a legitimate goal, but again bureaucratic hurdles were erected in the path of its realization.

Mid-1989 concluded the first, and in retrospect, hopeful, phase of perestroika. With the meeting of the Congress of People's Deputies in May, the focus of political activity shifted not necessarily to the legislative bodies but certainly away from the Communist party. What had been the struggle to remake the state and society would soon be preempted by another and desperate effort by Gorbachev to preserve as much as possible the existing structure of Soviet power and to cling to the vestiges of the Communist creed. The great reformer became simultaneously and incongruously a defender of the status quo on issues such as the rights of the republics versus those of the center.

With the decline of the Communist party one would have expected the rise of another movement that would aspire to guide Soviet society. Once Gorbachev's popularity began to wane, there should have been some rivals aspiring to the top post. Yet it was a peculiarity of Soviet politics under perestroika that it produced no party seeking power at the all-union level. There was a profusion of fronts, blocs, and even parties, but practically all of them had regional constituencies and goals. It was characteristic that even democratically inclined members of the first Congress of People's Deputies who banded together called their association the interregional *group*. Somehow the term "party" had taken on a pejorative meaning. In June 1917 at the All-Russian Congress of the Soviets, one speaker declared that there was no single party ready to assume the staggering burden of governing what had been the Russian Empire. Lenin aroused universal merriment and disbelief when he shouted from the benches that yes! there was such a party—his own. What was said in 1917 was true also of the perestroika period.

NATIONALISM RAMPANT

We must return to the Achilles' heel of the Soviet system: the nationalities question. The travails of the Soviet Union and communism were reminiscent of those Russian dolls in which, after detaching the top segment of the figurine, one finds successively smaller and smaller dolls. The breakdown of the unity and ideological mission of the movement revealed and accentuated the tensions within the smaller entity—the socialist bloc. And with that bloc disintegrating and then reduced to the Soviet Union itself, its own unity and survival became subject to increasing pressures.

Gorbachev had had his hands full fighting the battle of perestroika on several fronts. Still, one must note his lack of foresight when it came to the issue of nationalities and preserving the unity of the country. As a statesman setting out to remake his society, he should have remembered how in prerevolutionary Russia every attempt to liberalize the autocratic system and any advance toward glasnost, no matter how modest, would bring the nationalities problem to the surface and pose a quandary for the central government. Any relaxation of the regime would prompt the inmates to try to break out of their "prison house of nationalities." The Soviet period brought the nationalities formal equality and the fiction of a federal state. The primary and avowed purpose of perestroika had been to make those rights—so impressive on paper, so irrelevant to the actual process of Soviet politics—real.

It would be naive to think that even the wisest and most far-sighted policy on that count could have avoided trouble. Still, when the trouble came, it would not have had to be as far-reaching and seemingly intractable had Gorbachev and his associates shown themselves more sensitive to the problems of the multinational state emerging from autocracy and repression. He had tried to democratize the Soviet political scene while retaining the dominant role of the Communist party; he now proposed to reform the economy and yet somehow preserve its socialist character. Likewise, Gorbachev planned to turn the Soviet Union into a real federation while preserving undiminished the powers of the union. He would find himself in the position of the sorcerer's apprentice: unable to stop the very forces he had evoked. And while in regard to political and economic reforms the architect of perestroika would let himself be pushed far beyond where he originally proposed to stop, he would prove much more recalcitrant when it came to preserving undiminished the Union of Soviet Socialist Republics.

That the virus of independence should manifest itself first and most violently among the population of Lithuania was both unexpected and logical. Unexpected because of the relatively tiny size of the Lithuanian nation, and because the economic and geographic situation of the republic would make its complete separation from the Soviet Union fraught with great hardships for its inhabitants. One would have expected nationalist aspirations to explode more readily among the Ukrainians, the second-largest ethnic group in the Soviet Union, their republic having ample resources and meeting other conditions for a separate state existence. Stronger secessionist ambitions might have been expected also in Georgia, with its long history of independent statehood, or in Moldavia, where after its annexation in 1940 the Kremlin had renamed the Romanian-speaking majority of the population Moldavians.

At the same time, once the atmosphere of fear that had pervaded preperestroika Soviet politics abated, it was quite natural for Lithuania to surge to the forefront of those Soviet political entities seeking sovereignty and for the spokesmen of its people to define this term as implying secession from the Soviet state. Despite their previous inclusion in the Russian Empire and their forcible annexation in 1940, the three Baltic countries had remained the least politically assimilated parts of the Soviet Union. Of the three, Lithuania has

the highest percentage of native inhabitants among the population, and its people have shown themselves remarkably resistant to foreign domination, be it cultural or political. Even so, Latvia and Estonia were not far behind their fellow Baltic land in asserting, though more cautiously, their right to seek independence. In May 1990 all three adopted legislation proclaiming their sovereignty.

In the Soviet Union, 1990 thus might be called the year of sovereignty and, by the same token, the testing time for the survival of the union itself. This is not the place to give a detailed account of the effort to preserve some form of the union, a struggle that ended with its disintegration. What is pertinent for us is the connection between that process and the decline of communism as a world movement, the abdication by its Soviet branch of its universal mission. Here the causal relation is unmistakable. No sooner did the rulers of the Soviet Union explicitly abandon the mission to remake the world in a Marxist-Leninist image than power began to slip out of their hands. With communism no longer able to sustain the fiction that it was the wave of the future, the Communist party could no longer act as the glue which held the multinational state together.

THE MOMENT OF TRUTH

The Communist era in the country first known as Russia and later on as the Soviet Union began with the successful putsch of November 7, 1917, and concluded with the abjectly unsuccessful one of August 19, 1991. The first was a daring move by a handful of zealots leading a motley crowd of soldiers, workers, and sailors, not only to seize power but to ignite the fires of world revolution; the latter, a clumsy attempt by a junta of aging oligarchs to reimpose the Communist version of law and order, not in the name of any revolutionary ideas, but to preserve the power and privileges of a decrepit bureaucracy. The failure of the putsch reaffirmed what had been said earlier: an attempt to reinstall dictatorship in the Soviet Union of 1991 would prove even more difficult than steering the state toward effective democracy and an orderly economy.

"A wretched country; they don't even know how to hang properly," a nineteenth-century Russian revolutionary was reputed to have exclaimed when the hangman's rope broke under his weight. And now conspiratorial skill appeared to have been completely missing in such alleged experts of the craft as Vladimir Kryuchkov, head of the KGB, and Minister of the Interior Boris Pugo (himself with a long KGB background). They failed to move with dispatch, to secure such people bound to oppose the coup as Russian President Boris Yeltsin and former Foreign Minister Eduard Shevardnadze; within hours Yeltsin was on the Moscow streets calling on the citizens to rise against the junta and for a general strike. In Leningrad another dauntless reformer, its mayor, Anatoli Sobchak, galvanized even larger crowds to stand up for democracy. In 70 hours the foolish enterprise was over; seven of the junta arrested, one a suicide, and a shaken Gorbachev being flown back to Moscow after being detained in the Crimea.

Could a more professionally staged coup have succeeded? Those who would lean to that conclusion could point to the fact that most of the civilian government personnel (including virtually the entire council of ministers) and the higher military ranks initially supported the putsch. Most of the local party bosses did likewise, some of them being among the active plotters. And among the leaders of the non-Russian republics there were quite a few who for the first few hours adopted a wait-and-see attitude. But the essential condition for the success of such a venture—firm support by the officer corps, the KGB, and the party state machinery—was lacking. Ever since 1989, power in the Soviet Union had become too diffused to be scooped up by one sudden blow, and then through the years of glasnost Soviet society had become, if not exactly democratic, too agitated to remain passive in the face of this blatant attempt to turn the clock back.

On October 13, 1964, Nikita Khrushchev had been the generally venerated leader of the Soviet state and people; on October 14 it was announced that through a secretly arrived decision by some 12 to 15 people (in the Politburo) he had become an emeritus, and the attitude of the mass of the people remained one of complete indifference. Now it was different. Soviet men and women, including those in uniform, felt themselves to be citizens, and though most of them may have had scant sympathy for Gorbachev or concern for constitutional proprieties, they would not passively accept such presumption by a bunch of faceless bureaucrats. "We older folk used to express what we really thought by whispering in the kitchen. Now our children spoke out loudly in the city's streets and avenues," a Soviet journalist exultantly wrote.

One should not overromanticize what happened between August 19 and 22. Had the coup been carried out more efficiently, had not some army units taken Yeltsin's side, the plotters might have succeeded in seizing Moscow and Leningrad. But that would have meant bloodshed and a civil war, which the Kryuchkov clique could not have won.

"Gorbachev Returns to Power," proclaimed Western press headlines on August 23. He did return, but the president's power, already severely constricted before the coup, was now at its nadir. Yeltsin, the hero of the hour, vetoed Gorbachev's appointments of new ministers and forced him to accept those he himself nominated. The triumphant president of the Russian republic could not resist the temptation of publicly humiliating the president of the Soviet Union. At a session of the Russian parliament he kept interrupting Gorbachev's speech and bossing him around. Gorbachev's first utterances on his return showed his unawareness that the political situation and the public mood were now greatly different than they had been on August 18. He still expressed his belief that the Communist party should not only continue to exist but also act as a leading force in Soviet society, still thought that the outdated Treaty of the Union should provide the basis for the future Soviet Union; yet at the very same time Yeltsin was decreeing the suspension of all party activities on the territory of the Russian republic and shutting down its press organs. Heads of the other republics, anxious to compensate for their ambivalent reaction to the putsch, hastened to follow in Yeltsin's footsteps. "Does Gorbachev understand that he has returned to what is now a different country?" a newspaper perspicaciously asked.

Rather belatedly, Mikhail Sergeievich did understand. Within a week of his rescue he laid down the office of the general secretary and called upon the Central Committee of the Communist party of the Soviet Union to dissolve itself. By this time the appeal appeared superfluous: all over the Soviet Union the party's offices were being raided and shut down, its archives and files, as well as those of the KGB, seized by the local authorities. What for 70 years had been hailed as "the pride and conscience of the nation," "the vanguard of the world proletariat"—the celebrated and mighty Communist party of the Soviet Union—for all practical purposes ceased to exist; its formal dissolution would come merely as a death certificate. All over the vast land crowds were dismantling statues of Lenin and other Communist notables. Along with those momentous developments there arose a very practical question: Who would inherit the enormous wealth of the party, estimated at upward of five billion rubles?

But that question seemed trivial when compared with another problem of inheritance. It was the Communist party that had, though in the last three years increasingly shakily, held the Soviet Union together. Who or what could inherit that function? The trauma of August 19–21 made explicit what had been implicit ever since March 26, 1989: the Soviet Union was falling apart and it would take a quite unexpected turn of events to arrest the trend. As it was, during those post-August 21 days all the non-Russian republics, led by the largest of them, the Ukraine, hurriedly proclaimed their independence. Again that term, like "sovereignty," could as yet be interpreted in various ways, expressing the desire of at least some of them not necessarily to break off all the ties with Moscow but, rather, to have the Soviet Union transformed into a loose form of confederation. But there could be no mistaking the resolve of the three Baltic republics to acquire the full paraphernalia of independent statehood. And even before Gorbachev and the Congress of the People's Deputies grudgingly acquiesced in their secession, foreign countries began to recognize formally the independence of Lithuania, Latvia, and Estonia.

The impetus to full independence among the non-Russians was undoubtedly strengthened not only by the putsch, but also by Yeltsin's incautious behavior following its failure. By bossing Gorbachev around, by giving a strong impression at least initially that Russia was intent on dominating what remained of the Soviet Union, the president of the Russian republic could not but intensify the long-standing fears and resentments among other nations of the Soviet Union. Especially injudicious was Yeltsin's threat—to be sure, almost immediately withdrawn—that were some other republics to opt entirely out of the union, Russia might demand border rectification, that is, to claim those areas of sister republics where ethnic Russians constitute a high proportion of the populations. Said the head of Kazakhstan, Nursultan Nazarbayev, "Kazakhstan will never acquiesce in becoming an 'appendix' of another region, will never accept the role of being a 'younger brother' of another nation."

As August gave way to the following months, the tumult and confusion receded and Yeltsin and Gorbachev joined in an attempt to find what was still salvageable from the Soviet Union. Among the people the elation of the post-putsch days began to give way to a sober realization of the trials and dangers ahead. There could be no doubt now that perestroika had failed, that what had been conceived as restructuring had the effect of a demolition. As Anatoli Sobchak phrased it: "Our great mistake during those six years had been to try to reform what was unreformable." There was a hurried effort, through yet another constitutional improvisation, to patch up the foundering Soviet ship of state, but this failed and by December the union had totally dissolved, with 11 of the 15 former republics forming a loose association in what was called the Commonwealth of Independent States (Georgia and the Baltics declining to join).

A LOOK AHEAD

The lesson of the year of revolutions, 1917, teaches that the overthrow of an autocracy does not by itself clear the path to democracy. The crowds that demonstrated their jubilation over the overthrow of czarism were no less inspired by the passion for freedom than those that during the August days, answering the appeal of Yeltsin and Sobchak, poured onto the streets of Moscow and Leningrad (restored to its old name, St. Petersburg, in one of the last acts of the Congress of People's Deputies). Enthusiasm alone, however, is not a sufficient foundation for a stable democratic society. The budding democracy of the 1917 Russia, which Lenin himself called the freest state in the world, failed to develop a network of institutional defenses, and hence succumbed rather easily to the Bolshevik coup in November.

To show reservation about the changes in the Soviet Union is to realize the horrendous harm that communism has done to societies over which it had ruled, and especially to the Soviet Union. If with Stalin dead and buried, Stalinism still had clung to Soviet policies, then with the Communist party of the Soviet Union in shambles its legacy—the disastrous condition to which it had brought society—still stands in the way of the former Soviet republics' quest for democracy. And by the same token this legacy poses a threat to the world order: a fragmented Soviet Union, its parts now independent states, some of them not inconceivably under a dictatorship, that might prove a no lesser danger to international stability than that which had been posed by the Soviet Union at the height of its power. For almost 50 years we had worried about what the "Communists" might do to us. Now the West is concerned, and justifiably so, about the consequences of what the Soviets had been doing to themselves.

Communism drew its strengths and appeal from the claim that it was the only ideology and movement that could rise above nationalism and establish a peaceful and stable state. Ever since 1948 that boast, as we have seen, was repeatedly refuted by events. And it is an irony of history that the claim of communism being a force for peace among nations should finally be laid to rest in its birthplace.

THE HANGOVER

Boris Yeltsin prevailed in October, but his chances of building a democracy are increasingly threatened by a rising tide of corruption and anarchy.

David Remnick

RUSSIANS have been building Potemkin villages since the time of Catherine the Great. Now, as they slop paint over the charred parliament building known as the White House and fix its windows, they have nearly finished one on the banks of the Moscow River. Two years ago, the building, in all its sprawling vulgarity, was the scene of the greatest historical triumph since the end of the Second World War—the defeat of a Bolshevik coup and the fall of the old regime. Overnight, the Russian White House became a symbol of liberty more vivid than the Bastille: the storming of the Bastille had not been on CNN; Boris Yeltsin standing on a tank was. Last month, Yeltsin won another victory at the White House, not by defending it but by bombarding it. After an armed mob led by Albert Makashov, a rebel military commander and an avowed Stalinist, attacked the Russian television center and nearly took it, Yeltsin swayed the reluctant Army to side with him. It was not until after Yeltsin made a secret, late-night trip to the Defense Ministry that the military decided to put its full force behind the President. Because Yeltsin came so close to losing power to a leadership that would have been infinitely worse than his, nearly all of Russia has expressed relief. But there is no sense of celebration. There were funerals this time, not fireworks.

The hangover in Moscow is deadening. Everywhere I go—from the Central Market to the villages outside town, from newspaper offices to Kremlin anterooms, where aides sit around dully watching music videos—there is a sense of hope-lessness about political life. There are no heroes, no great expectations. "The October events," as they are called here, obliterated any shred of triumphalism left from the defeat of the August coup of 1991. The relatively easy verities of the old political struggle—good versus bad, reformers versus reactionaries, democrats versus Communists—have dissolved into a bitter soup of uncertainty. The charred parliament building is by no means the only deflating symbol of the recent events. State television reported sobering news about the Madonna of Vladimir, one of the most cherished works of art in Russian history. When Alexey II, the Patriarch of Moscow and All Russia, became involved in the futile negotiations between Yeltsin and the parliament he had disbanded, the Church ordered the delicate twelfth-century icon brought by minibus from the Tretyakov Gallery to the Cathedral of the Epiphany to "bless" the talks. The exposure to the weather left the priceless icon badly damaged.

Even as the papers are filled with news of Yeltsin's plans for a new, two-chambered parliament, or Duma, and elections on December 12th to fill it, Russia is under no delusion about being a democratic country. Intellectuals and government officials who were once prepared to enjoy the moral clarity of First Amendment absolutists now claim that a country as unstable as Russia cannot afford the luxury of having newspapers that support armed insurrection. Yeltsin's government ordered the closing of fifteen far-right newspapers for their support of the rebellion, and allowed *Pravda* to resume publication only after it agreed to replace its editor-in-chief. Aleksandr Yakovlev, who was the leading advocate for a free press within the Gorbachev inner circle, told me, "You just cannot compare our situation with that in America, where there is stability. *Pravda* cannot be considered merely an opposition paper when it calls for workers' detachments to come to the White House—that is an open call to arms. There is as much blood on the hands of the editor of *Pravda* as there is on General Makashov's."

Nor at the Kremlin is there any sense of pure victory. Narrow escape is more like it. "We were on the verge," Andrei Makarov, a Presidential adviser, told me. "We won by accident." In conversations I had with four of Yeltsin's aides, all of them admitted that their hopes for a smooth, swift transfer from a Communist dictatorship to a free-market democracy had been shattered. The fall of the old regime, which was so morally satisfying, turns out to have left the new regime in an impossible moral position. The choice is stark: behave with the manners of a Western democrat and risk allowing the current anarchy to overwhelm Russia or else take "decisive measures" and risk smothering Russia's newborn civil society in the cradle. Now the talk is of a transitional regime of "enlightened authoritarianism" or "administrative democracy" or some such hybrid that makes no secret of the need for a prolonged concentration of power in the Presidency.

The Kremlin's political sales force is working furiously to emphasize the need for order. "The hand of power cannot be totally weak," Yeltsin's legal adviser Yuri

From *The New Yorker*, November 22, 1993, pp. 51-52, 54-55, 57-58, 60, 62-65. © 1993 by David Remnick. Reprinted by permission.

Baturin told me one afternoon. "When the use of power was necessary during the October events, it was impossible to use it right away, because the so-called power ministries—defense, security, police—were hesitating. If they had used their force more quickly, the victory would have been accomplished sooner, with less blood."

But Yeltsin's advisers also admit that in trying to restore some degree of order in Russia there is always a danger of drifting into iron rule. "Like Gorbachev's perestroika, everything now, in the development of democracy, is being guided only from above," said Georgi Satarov, a member of the Presidential Council, which is a body of experts that meets whenever Yeltsin wishes. "It is very easy to slip into dictatorship. There are no checks. Monopolistic rule is responsible for checking itself, and this self-restriction has to hold somehow before there can be real checks and balances. There can be little steps toward dictatorship, each one seeming small in itself, but the trend can drag us into dictatorship. This can happen. But, insofar as I know the President and his motives, I do not think he has any intention of becoming a dictator."

There are more than enough people who have called on Yeltsin to become an unabashed autocrat. A poll published recently in *Izvestiya* showed that three-quarters of all Muscovites welcomed the brief state of emergency that followed the October events, and wanted to see it prolonged indefinitely. Yeltsin's new press minister stunned Moscow's media corps with an announcement that the government's job was to define "state ideology" and the reporters' job was to spread it. A popular satirist named Aleksandr Ivanov, a favorite of Yeltsin's, told the President, seriously, at a meeting of writers that he really ought to become a strongman, a Russian version of Chile's Augusto Pinochet. Fortunately, Yeltsin has not extended his admiration of Ivanov to the point of taking his advice. "Many people in Russia think they admire Pinochet, but they have no idea why," Leonid Radzikhovsky, a political writer for the weekly magazine *Stolitsa*, told me. "All they know is that Pinochet shot a lot of Communists, and they would like to shoot Communists. But that's all they know."

EVEN if Yeltsin were inclined to become the leader of a full-scale authoritarian regime—and he is not—he wouldn't be able to manage it. Although some of his advisers point to South Korea and parts of Latin America as places that built potential democracies under authoritarian rule, the analogy falls flat before Russian realities. Despite the military's decisive role in October, the Army has no Latin-American-style ambitions for juntadom; the generals would much rather win higher wages and other social guarantees than take the upper hand in politics. Nor can Russia rely on an Asian work ethic or on Asian efficiency, to say nothing of a tradition of democratic political culture—a feature of life in Chile before Pinochet. Russia has to make democracy with Russians.

The truth is that Yeltsin, or any leader who emerges as his potential successor, has the nearly impossible task of trying to build a democracy in conditions of almost complete social and economic anarchy. Aleksandr Rutskoi and Ruslan Khasbulatov, the leaders of the anti-Yeltsin uprising in October, may be in jail, but theirs is not likely to be the last episode of rebellion or violence. Even those who accept—or, at least, are resigned to—Yeltsin's notion of transition understand that the anger and disillusion throughout Russian society are growing ever worse. The dulling realities of Soviet society—equality in poverty, stability of repression—have come unwound, and now Russia is a scene of radical polarization. The fondest wish of the Russian reformers in 1991 was that out of economic change would emerge a large middle class and a business élite, which would become the main constituencies for further change. There are no signs of this happening. Instead, Russians have watched with fury and envy as a small percentage of people have grown rich—gaudily rich—in an environment of almost general chaos and criminality. Capitalism in Russia has produced far more Al Capones than Henry Fords, more Luca Brasis than Ward Cleavers. In fact, the economy hardly merits the name of capitalism at all, since it operates largely outside the framework of law.

There is not a single field of activity, not a single institution, free of the most brutal sort of corruption. Russia has bred a world-class Mafia. According to

Luciano Violante, the chairman of Italy's parliamentary committee of inquiry into the Mafia, Russia is now "a kind of strategic capital of organized crime from where all the major operations are launched." He said that Russian mob leaders had held summit meetings with the three main Italian crime organizations, from Sicily, Calabria, and Naples, to discuss drug-money laundering, the narcotics trade, and even the sale of nuclear material. Russia, he added, "has become a warehouse and clearing house for the drug market."

The new Russian mobsters, who are involved in everything from arms sales to banking, have learned to work with former officials in the highest ranks of the Communist Party and the K.G.B. as well as with mob bosses abroad. There is little doubt that the ministries of Yeltsin's government—especially in areas like foreign trade, customs, tax collection, and law enforcement—are also thoroughly corrupt. According to Yuri Boldyrev, who was until recently the government's chief investigator into corruption, the decay in state and public institutions now "goes beyond the limits of the imagination."

A ten-page report drafted by police and security ministries and submitted to Yeltsin early this year described how senior military officers who were based for years in the former East Germany have been involved in huge embezzlement schemes. The officers set up their own companies to buy food and liquor, transported as military supplies, and then sold them on the free market in Poland and Russia. Sales were estimated at a hundred million Deutsche marks—fifty-eight million dollars. In another case, Air Force Major General Vladimir Rodionov and his deputy, Colonel Georgi Iskrov, were charged with using military aircraft for commercial flights and keeping the proceeds.

Yeltsin has not been averse to admitting what is before the eyes of everyone. Last February, according to a report by Victor Yasmann, of Radio Liberty, he said in a speech to the heads of the central and regional law-enforcement agencies that two-thirds of all commercial and financial enterprises in Russia—and forty per cent of the individual businessmen—were engaged in some form of corruption. He added that in 1992 two billion dollars had simply "disappeared" from the budget of the Ministry of Foreign Economic Relations. Even the anti-Mafia investigators are suspect. In October of 1992, an Interior Ministry chief was arrested for taking a million-ruble bribe. A subsequent search of his home found eight hundred and five thousand rubles more in cash.

Foreigners trying to do business in Russia have become easy targets. A friend told me about a Westerner who was caught in traffic in Moscow and, as he inched along, lightly touched the bumper of the car ahead of him. A man dressed mainly in jewelry and leather leaped from the car, ran up to the foreigner's window, stuck a revolver in, and said, "Buy my car now or I will kill you!" The foreigner, an experienced resident of Moscow, knew well that this mafioso was not joking. He went home, gathered up all the cash he could find, and bought the car. The following week, the same unfortunate man was travelling to St. Petersburg on the midnight train. Someone drugged him, and when he woke up in the morning all his valuables were gone.

Law enforcement, too, is a bitter joke. Mobsters often have more troops and more powerful weapons than the police. Army officers and recruits, desperate for cash, are only too glad to sell guns, rocket launchers, and grenades to the highest bidder. It is not unknown for members of Mafia gangs in southern Russia to use a tank to settle an especially stubborn account. And at a time when nearly everyone is impoverished—including police, jailers, and judges—the likelihood of successful prosecution is minuscule. Vladimir Rushailo, the chief of the Moscow Police Department, said, "Even if we manage to jail an influential member of the Mafia, his fellow-bandits immediately unleash a campaign pressuring victims, witnesses, judges, public assessors. And they do this quite freely. Clearly, the criminals are much more inventive than the lawmakers."

No matter which parties dominate the new parliament—and the blocs range from free-marketeers to unapologetic Communists—none are going to be able to provide Russia with a magic formula to clear away the rubble of the old system, cope with the anarchy of the present, and bring on a new prosperity. For example, no one has come up with a satisfactory answer to the question of what to do with gigantic factory cities like Magnitogorsk, in the Urals, whose entire economy is built around a product—in this case, steel—that no one wants or can use. The choices are harsh. A purely economic answer would be to shut down the plant and let tens of thousands of people find work in the new economy—which hardly exists. The moderates would phase in new technology to modernize the plant—with funds that do not exist. The Communists, presumably, would keep things chugging along toward the abyss. In the meantime, the workers of Magnitogorsk and their children visit clinics and drink "oxygen cocktails"—concoctions of fruit juice and sugar infused with oxygen—to soothe their poisoned lungs. There are hundreds of such cities, places built around factories or mines or collective farms, which are the economic equivalent of the living dead. Eventually, Russia will have to recognize the hard fact that much of its overmilitarized, largely obsolete economy will go bankrupt—quickly or slowly. The unemployment to follow will be immense. Political unrest may not be far behind.

Perhaps the constituency that has been most stunned by the course of Russia in the two years since the collapse of the old regime is the liberal intelligentsia—the array of writers, artists, academics, and journalists who were at the forefront of the perestroika era. For centuries, Russian intellectuals had been a kind of shadow government, a moral prod to the czars and, later, the Communist Party. When Pushkin stood up to Alexander I, or Sakharov to the General Secretary, they were asserting a belief in the power of truth and the individual against a brutal system. Perhaps the apotheosis for the liberal intelligentsia came in 1989, when one intellectual after another was elected to the Soviet legislature: at its first gathering, a Dostoyevski scholar called for Lenin to be removed from his tomb and buried in the ground; a short-story writer outlined the rot of the Soviet economy; a novelist described the horrors of Chernobyl. For years, American writers like Philip Roth would return from the Soviet Union and Eastern Europe marvelling at the importance of literature there. Roth once remarked that in the West everything is permitted and nothing matters, and in the East nothing is permitted and everything matters. Now in the East everything goes—and the intelligentsia matters less than it ever has.

One afternoon, I went to the ramshackle offices of Znamya (Banner), which was one of the leading literary and political monthlies in the Gorbachev years, to see the deputy editor, Natalya Ivanova. I had been visiting Ivanova as a reporter on and off for six years, and had never known her to be so pessimistic. At first, I thought the reason for her pessimism might be the fate of Znamya and the other literary monthlies. Where once they sold a million or more copies, in the late nineteen-eighties, none now sell more than eighty thousand or so. Where once the best-seller lists were filled with titles from Solzhenitsyn, Orwell, and Brodsky, they are now litanies of mass-lit. Larisa Vasilieva, a Russian pop-historian, has made a fortune with "Kremlin Wives," a look at the seamy world of political boudoirs in the Communist era. Rex Stout may now be the most popular foreign novelist in the country. "People want a little pleasure," one writer told me. "If they have to read about one more concentration camp, they'll die."

But Ivanova was worried about more than the statistics of culture. It was inevitable, she realized, that once the regime fell the abnormal importance (and outsized popularity) of serious literature would fade. "We can all accept the idea that the only people reading now are the ones who read for nonpolitical reasons," Ivanova said. "Now you see the rise of advice columns, personal ads, Harlequin romances. Well, that's O.K. What is unexpected is the general degradation of culture and of the intelligentsia itself. Its dominant position is now held by this new class of so-called businessmen, and they have no class at all. This new bourgeoisie is made up mostly of speculators stealing from the country."

Ivanova showed me the galley proofs of an article of hers called "Double Suicide," which she was getting ready for publication in Znamya. It is an angry piece, in which she accuses her fellow-artists and fellow-thinkers of being more interested in "the course of the dollar" than in "moral problems," of bowing humbly before a new and vulgar image of what the Bolsheviks used to call "the shining future." Where once the Russian landscape was littered with one kind of propaganda—"We Are Marching Toward Leninism," etc.—television, radio, and the newspapers are now filled with propaganda of a different kind: advertisements for unaffordable luxuries, fantastic commercials geared toward lives that hardly exist. One minute, you are *Homo sovieticus*, surrounded by the aggressive blandness of Communism; the next minute, you are watching a Slavic Russ Meyer vixen sucking on a Maraschino cherry and telling you which casino to visit. There is something profoundly irritating about ads for investment funds or American cat food in a country where the vast majority of the citizens are living in poverty. A year or two of exposure to American-style commercials has produced what decades of Communist propaganda could not: genuine indignation on the part of honest people against the excesses of capitalism. But the intelligentsia is bewildered by it all and incapable of providing moral guidance. "People struggled for a new life, and it turned out that this life deceived them," Ivanova said sadly.

For the young, there is just no sense, no prestige, in pursuing intellectual careers. At Moscow State University, it is suddenly a cinch to gain admission to the humanities departments; everyone wants to learn finance. The endless ethereal conversations around the kitchen table, the wonderful no-show jobs at academic institutes, the big audiences for poetry readings—that world is dwindling. Another friend, the political scientist Andrei Kortunov, remarked to me, "What we had under Gorbachev and for the years before was like the ecological system in Australia before the English brought their dogs and rabbits. We had this weird, authentic, original kind of culture. The intellectuals were even a privileged class. But when the English came, with their dogs and rabbits, the ecological system decayed. I suppose we need to go through this period of consumerism and pop culture, just as they are doing in Poland and Czechoslovakia. The question is whether Russia will ever be able to preserve even part of the old ecology—its distinctive intellectual character."

One night, I took the journalist Leonid Radzikhovsky to dinner at the plush Italian restaurant in the Kempinski, a new, German-owned hotel across from the Kremlin. Hotel restaurants used to be a unique variety of torture for the foreign visitor—places where you might be told that every dish but one, on a ten-page menu, was unavailable. The new hotels are islands of foreign luxury. Radzikhovsky, for his part, looked around suspiciously, as if waiting to be thrown out. When I asked him about the lost world of the Russian intelligentsia, he betrayed no wistfulness. "I am a cynic maybe, a realist," he said, "but there is no more moral authority in Russia. Russia is a country in the stage of primitive accumulation of capital. Look around you, at this restaurant. What will dinner cost? At least a hundred dollars, right? An average Moscow salary for at least a month. In the nineteenth century, there were landlords and peasants and no thought of mixing them. But now everyone thinks he has a right to have dinner at the Kempinski. And everyone wants it. This is *all* anyone thinks about. People don't think about novels or plays or poetry. If it is true that everything in America is about dollars, it is even truer now in Russia. This is a hungry country, and it wants to be fed."

Radzikhovsky used the phrase "primitive accumulation of capital" not out of any desire to lionize Karl Marx, though he was quoting him, but, rather, to make the point that Russia would have to go through many stages of development, generations, before it ever became, as Russians say, "a normal country." As he forked his way through a plate piled high with tiramisu ("What sort of cake is this?"), he mentioned he was thinking about running for the new parliament.

"I was at one of the congresses for a new bloc, Russia's Choice, and I was one of those writing the platform," he said. "It was all about order and combatting crime. Two years ago, we would have been writing only about the necessity of freedom and democracy. But who is a democrat and who is not is unclear. It was the rebels inside the White House last month who were describing themselves as 'defenders of the constitution' and 'defenders of democracy.' Yeltsin is no democrat, but he's not going to establish authoritarian rule, either. And I'm not a democrat, because I have no clear idea of what it means. I don't like Fascism, that's true, but how would I, a Russian, have a clear idea of what democracy means?"

Before paying the check, I asked Radzikhovsky if his circle of political friends had given themselves a name. Yes, he said. Loosely translated, the circle was called Demskitz—Democratic Schizophrenics.

THE other day, I went to visit Leonid Batkin, a historian, whose involvement in the movement toward democracy in Russia was evidently so compelling to the authorities that, beginning in the mid-eighties, the K.G.B. had assembled a five-volume collection of his phone conversations. Batkin had won this peculiar honor for being one of those political-academic heroes of the Gorbachev era, but now, he said, all that was in the past. "That wasn't politics," he said. "That was history."

Like most of the other democracy activists I talked to in Moscow, Batkin was relieved that Yeltsin had prevailed in the October events, but he was convinced that Yeltsin in 1993 was beginning to look like Gorbachev in 1990—erratic, confused, reaching the end of the line as an effective leader. "As with Othello, it is time for Yeltsin to leave the stage, and that will come," Batkin said. "For the problems we face, we need a politician with the range of someone like Franklin Roosevelt. We need someone shrewd, intelligent, imaginative, someone who can change direction. We have no such figure ready on the horizon, because until very recently serious people in this country just did not do politics." Now, Batkin said, it was finally time for Russia to develop a professional class of politicians: the era of revolutionary giants and moral saints was over. "If Andrei Sakharov had lived to the present day, he would not have the same effect he did when he was able to impress the whole country with a speech. The time has come for institutions—real politicians and parties. Politics now is not a matter of saying the unsayable. It is a professional activity, and so far most of the professionals are still from the old regime."

The runner-up to Yeltsin in the polls these days is the young economist Grigori Yavlinsky, who is gaining popularity but is still not well known in the provinces. Sergei Shakhrai, a Kremlin legal adviser at odds with Yeltsin over a number of issues, is also too young to be taken seriously as a national figure. The Prime Minister, Viktor Chernomyrdin, projects a kind of bland bureaucratic competence, but it is hard to imagine the public rallying around his listless banner and dubious commitment to reform.

The politics of Russia is now so deeply depressed that the only person I could find who expressed delight in it was Aleksandr Prokhanov, who is the erstwhile editor of *Dyen* (*Day*), a far-right paper that had called for armed uprisings against Yeltsin and has now been ordered closed. Because Prokhanov has ties to the most nationalist elements in the military, he is often called "the nightingale of the General Staff." For as long as I have known him, he has been titillating his visitors with outrageous threats of coups d'état. His predictions have been on the mark. In October, Prokhanov stayed with Rutskoi in the White House until the last day, then left for the offices of *Dyen* to try to put out a final issue.

At his apartment one morning, Prokhanov told me that Russia's interference in the civil war in Georgia, its recent moves to control the press, its general drift toward a harder line showed that Yeltsin was adopting the right-wing agenda. "I am gloating," he said. "In an authoritarian regime, sentimental liberals will not survive." Prokhanov vowed that the "patriotic forces" would eventually bring down Yeltsin and prevail. "Hitler in 1933 also dissolved the Reichstag, but he didn't have to pay for it until 1945," he said.

I said that many people in Moscow were worried that the forces that had surrendered at the White House would now go underground and carry out terrorist attacks. Would that happen?

"I'd be crazy to talk with you about terrorism," Prokhanov answered, but he added that he could not rule it out, any more than he could "rule out the explosion of nuclear power stations." In the land of Chernobyl, those were not comforting words.

So this is how Russia lives now—under threat, veering uncertainly between authoritarian impulses and democratic ambitions. When the people go to the polls on December 12th, they will vote "yes" or "no" on a new constitution now being drafted by a commission whose coördinator is Boris Zolotukhin, a lawyer who defended political prisoners under Soviet rule. The President, for his part, is making sure that Presidential powers are clear and immense. After promising to face the voters in June, Yeltsin has, with little explanation, declared his intention to finish his current term, which runs to 1996. Politics, to say nothing of his health, are not on the side of his endurance. Meanwhile, the government has yet to decide where the new parliament will sit. At the White House, only the façade has been repaired.

The Russian Elections

Weimar on the Volga

FROM OUR MOSCOW CORRESPONDENT

After the success of Vladimir Zhirinovsky's neo-fascist party in Russia's general election, we look at how this will affect Russian politics.

THE day before Russia went to the polls, Yegor Gaidar described the decision facing voters thus: "The choice for Russia is the evolution of Germany after the first world war, or after the second world war." The next day, Russia's dispossessed vented their anger at the reforms that he had introduced by choosing to go back to the first war.

The similarities between this election and that held to the Reichstag in September 1930 are alarming. Heinrich Brüning, then German chancellor, was awkward before large audiences and spoke uninspiringly of sacrifices to be endured. Mr Gaidar led a bloodless campaign for Russia's Choice, the largest pro-reform party, refusing to make populist promises. Paul Hindenburg, the German president, decreed that, "As a matter of principle, the Reich president does not intervene in the election campaign." Boris Yeltsin refused to support any party, preferring to stay above the fray.

So the outcomes proved similar. The Nazis, which had won 809,000 votes in 1928, grabbed 6.4m (18% of votes cast) in 1930. Polls commissioned at the beginning of Russia's election campaign said that Vladimir Zhirinovsky, the leader of the absurdly misnamed Liberal Democratic Party, would win 2% of the vote. Instead he won one-fifth of votes cast for the 225 seats in the State Duma (the lower house of the new Russian parliament) to be filled by proportional representation.

Mr Zhirinovsky denies that he is a fascist. But his party espouses policies of xenophobia,

anti-Semitism, militarism and corporatism that seem strikingly fascist. That, though, was not his attraction to most voters. Rather, it was his campaigning style. Whereas his rivals wasted free television time on boring monologues, Mr Zhirinovsky proved a mas-

ter of the medium. He spent over 300m roubles ($250,000) to ensure that he was on television more than any rival, appearing one night with a bottle of vodka and a condom—"All that Gorbachev left us"—another with flowers and a box of chocolates to "prove" his feminist credentials.

Though his opponents dismissed him as a clown, his message sank in:

> The Russian people have three choices. We can either chose what we have now by voting for Gaidar and Yavlinsky [the leader of the other main pro-reform party]; or we can chose to go backwards by voting for the Communists. My party represents the third choice.

This appealed most to those who have lost from the reduction of state subsidies and gained nothing from the introduction of market forces. They are the armed forces; people living in far-flung parts of the country (coal miners in the Arctic circle) where economic activity is carried on only because of subsidies; and people who live in the rustbowls of Russia. Mr Zhirinovsky told them that "the dark times are over." They wanted to believe him.

Prince of darkness

His prescriptions for ending the darkness are not reassuring. He set out his economic plan in his party's newspaper shortly before the election. The Liberal Democrats' economic priorities will be to stop all aid to the former republics of the Soviet Union; to stop the conversion of arms factories and to export weapons to anyone who can afford them; and to "liquidate the 5,000 organised gangs" that allegedly control the economy. These three measures ought to double Russia's living standards in three to four months, wrote Mr Zhirinovsky.

The election does not put Mr Zhirinovsky in command of the levers of power: the new constitution which was adopted by referendum on December 12th prevents that (see box on page 191). Actually, it is far from clear that Mr Zhirinovsky wants to be running policy for the time being. His goal is to wield the extended powers of the president under the

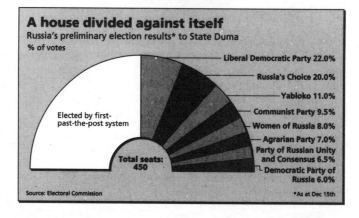

A house divided against itself
Russia's preliminary election results* to State Duma
% of votes

Elected by first-past-the-post system

Total seats: 450

Liberal Democratic Party 22.0%
Russia's Choice 20.0%
Yabloko 11.0%
Communist Party 9.5%
Women of Russia 8.0%
Agrarian Party 7.0%
Party of Russian Unity and Consensus 6.5%
Democratic Party of Russia 6.0%

Source: Electoral Commission

*As at Dec 15th

From *The Economist*, December 18, 1993, pp. 45-47. © 1993 by The Economist, Ltd. Distributed by The New York Times Special Features. Reprinted by permission.

Framework or frame-up?

Russia's new constitution, approved by just 52% of votes cast (28% of eligible voters), is often said to create a dictatorial presidency. Does it?

RUSSIANS have voted for a strong presidential regime, giving the president the whip hand in government appointments and policy-making, subject to confirmation by parliament. In case of disagreement, the president has the greater power, because he may issue decrees and directives, as well as call referendums, without legislative checks.

Elected for a maximum of two four-year terms, the president is head of state, commander-in-chief and head of the security council. Thus, rather like the French and American presidents, he has the upper hand in making foreign and defence policies. He may also declare war on foreign countries, provided only that he "informs" parliament, which cannot rescind his decisions. (In America, by contrast, Congress declares war.) He may also declare states of emergency or martial law inside Russia, subject to confirmation by parliament's upper house. It is unclear what happens if parliament refuses consent. This ambiguity may prove a strong temptation to authoritarianism.

The president nominates his prime minister and deputy prime minister. His candidates must then be approved by the lower house of parliament. If parliament rejects a candidate, the president may ignore it twice; after a third rejection, the president may dissolve the lower house and call a new election. The idea is to stop parliament undermining government policies by dictating ministerial appointments, as it did in 1992-93.

The president may sack his government without asking parliament. He nominates the head of the central bank, the prosecutor-general and high-court judges, all subject to parliamentary confirmation. He is also the main authority in mediating disputes between central and local government, and between the various branches of government.

Impeaching a president is difficult, even if he apparently seeks to subvert the constitution. This seems intended to stop a replay of 1992-93, when parliament stood ready at the drop of a hat to impeach the president for infringing the old constitution. Under the new one, the only ground for impeachment is treason or serious crime. To start a case, the president must stand accused by one-third of the lower house of parliament; a two-thirds majority in both houses is needed to make the accusation stick. It will be hard to impeach the president (as it is in America). But not impossible.

So too with constitutional change. In 1992-93, parliament fought the president by constantly amending the constitution. So this has been made hard. The main clauses may be altered only by agreement between the president, two-thirds of the lower house of parliament, three-quarters of the upper house, and two-thirds of the 89 regions and republics of Russia. This is meant to be a step towards stability. Ending chaos by such a strong tilt in favour of the president gives him immense power.

Yet parliament has ways to offset presidential authority. The upper house, the Council of the Federation, has 178 members, two from each region and republic in Russia. It has jurisdiction over relations between the centre and regions, including border changes and the use of the army (all important in Russian politics). The upper house may also examine legislation passed by the lower house; any law involving economic or defence policies needs its approval. This is a constraint upon the lower house, where Vladimir Zhirinovsky's power lies. In the upper house, Mr Yeltsin's supporters are more influential.

The lower depths

The lower house, called the State Duma, has 225 members elected by proportional representation, and 225 by first-past-the-post voting. It has to approve the government's fiscal and monetary policies, and oversee government appointments. It can draft budgetary laws, but not independently, only with the government's consent.

If there is to be a vote of no confidence in the government, the Duma holds it. The first time round, the president may simply reject the vote. If within three months the Duma passes another no-confidence motion, the president must either dismiss the government, or dissolve parliament and call a new election.

Two clauses give the Duma some protection against arbitrary dissolution. First, the president may not dissolve it after a no-confidence vote during its first year (the idea being to prevent the president holding repeated elections until he gets a parliament he likes). Second, the Duma cannot be dissolved if it is considering impeachment charges, or during a nationwide state of emergency.

Protection and interpretation of the constitution are entrusted to a Constitutional Court. Courts are to be independent, judges appointed for life. But the fact remains that all political arrangements must be tested by use. The rather similar constitutions of the United States and France work as well as they do, not just because of their drafting, but because they rest upon democratic traditions, a judiciary whose independence is taken for granted, and functioning multi-party systems. It will be some time before Russians have those assets.

new constitution. Rather than be tarred with responsibility for hard times ahead, Mr Zhirinovsky will use his power base in the new Duma to launch a bid for the presidential election, which must be held by June 1996.

The reformers are split on how to deal with his challenge. The leaders of Russia's Choice take the moral high ground. They refuse to countenance negotiations with fascists. They argue that as soon as Brüning began negotiating with Hitler in 1932, Weimar was lost. Mr Zhirinovsky returns the sentiment and has demanded that Mr Gaidar, Andrei Kozyrev (the foreign minister) and Anatoly Chubais (the privatisation minister) be sacked. Machiavellian reformers argue that the best way to neutralise Mr Zhirinovsky would be to co-opt him into government, giving him an impossible job—such as fighting crime—and thus exposing him as a windbag. Mr Yeltsin will have to decide.

As more results from the election are confirmed, they reinforce the arguments of the anti-negotiators. Results from far-off places, where extremists did well, were announced soon after the polls closed. They

Zhirinovsky's A-Z

FROM OUR MOSCOW CORRESPONDENT

HERE are the thoughts of Vladimir Wolfovich Zhirinovsky, in his own words*, on:

The army. What an army needs are armed conflicts, both inside and outside the country. Only wars will revive the Russian army.

Russia's neighbours. We should only threaten regions from where Russians are being expelled with the possibility of doing the same to their people living in Russia. Take Azerbaijan. Five hundred thousand Russians used to live there. Now only 100,000 remain, but a million Azeris wander around Russia. So, to begin with, we should expel 400,000 Azeris and deport them to Baku. If they harm the Russians there, we would expel the whole million of them. One must not forget that democracy also implies violence.

The West. We say to Bill Clinton, stop while there is still time and do not repeat the mistakes of Hitler and Napoleon. You Americans must leave the Balkans and Middle East. The world will thank you. If you do not, one fine day you will find yourself on a court bench facing another Nuremberg. The Germans are interfering in Russia now, but if a German looks at Russia the wrong way when I'm in the Kremlin, you Germans will pay for all that we Russians built up in Germany.

The East. I would bomb the Japanese. I would sail our large navy around their small island and if they so much as cheeped, I would nuke them.

Jews. Our voters are tired of so many non-Russian faces on television. They want some Slav faces with Russian accents ... Sometimes Russia has been overwhelmed by anti-Semitism. This phenomenon was provoked only by the Jews themselves. Russia is a kind nation.

Childhood and youth. I grew up in a world where there was no warmth—not from my parents, not from friends or teachers. I felt somehow superfluous, forever in the way, an object of criticism.

Marriage. If I had found a loving woman, perhaps I would have expended half of my energy, or most of it, on her. [Mr Zhirinovsky is married, with one son.]

Feminism. Our party will find husbands for all unmarried women.

Astrology. I was born in 1946, the year of the dog. Dogs are faithful, sincere and always at your service. My party will never betray our voters.

Presidential elections (due to be held in 1996). I will be 50 in 1996. Being elected president will be a nice birthday present.

---

* From Mr Zhirinovsky's autobiography, speeches and interviews given during and after the election campaign.

The final tally

Russian State Duma (lower house of parliament)

	PR lists			
	% votes cast	Seats	Constit-uencies	Total*
Russia's Choice	15.38	40	30	70
Liberal Democrats	22.79	59	5	64
Communists	12.35	32	16	48
Agrarian	7.90	21	12	33
Yabloko	7.83	20	3	23
Civic Union	1.92	-0	1	1
Democrats	5.50	14	-	14
Dignity and Charity	0.70	0	2	2
Russian Unity and Accord	6.76	18	1	19
Women of Russia	8.10	21	2	23
Russian Movement for Democratic Reforms	4.06	0	4	4
Parties not listed above	-	-	14	14
Independents	-	-	129	129

*Does not add up to 450 because in six constituencies election declared illegal

From *The Economist*, January 8, 1994, p. 55.

Weeks late, final figures for Russia's general election have been published. As forecast, Vladimir Zhirinovsky's Liberal Democratic Party won the largest share of the vote. Yet Russia's Choice won more seats. This happened because Russians had two votes: one for a list of candidates for seats to be filled on proportional-representation rules (Mr Zhirinovsky did well here); another for single-member constituencies (Russia's Choice did well here). But no coalition is likely to be able to form a stable majority.

gave the impression that Mr Zhirinovsky's party had won twice as many votes as Mr Gaidar's. Results from the main population centres, where the reformers did well, were much slower to come in. They changed the picture.

In Moscow, Russia's Choice won an estimated 37% of votes cast, as well as a majority on the city's 35-man council. (Control of the capital is a big advantage in Russian politics.) Russia's Choice has also been the most successful at getting its men into the 225 seats in the Duma elected according to first-post-the-post rules. Of 193 results known by December 16th, 27 seats had been won by Russia's Choice, only five by Mr Zhirinovsky's men. (More than 100 were won by independents, whose presence will make the new parliament unpredictable.) When the final results are released, Russia's Choice will emerge as the largest single party in the new parliament, followed by the Liberal Democrats. Between them, the pro-reform parties will be able to muster the one-third of votes needed to block any attempt by parliament to override presidential decisions.

The Yeltsin era begins to end

Though the results may not be as bad as they seemed at first, Mr Zhirinovsky will still have one of the loudest voices in the new parliament. Mr Yeltsin's current dilemma is that the only sure way to neutralise Mr Zhirinovsky is to get the economy growing. That will mean taking tough decisions which, in the short term, may increase the number of his new rival's sympathisers.

Although the constitution gives Mr Yeltsin the power to push on with reform, this course could end in another confrontation with parliament unless Mr Yeltsin is careful to build up coalitions to support his policies. If he were to fail and the confrontation turned nasty, as the last one did, Mr Yeltsin could not rely on the support of the army, which voted heavily for Mr Zhirinovsky.

Nor can Mr Yeltsin any longer be confident of beating opponents in a presidential election. One exit poll carried out on December 12th found that 39% would vote for Mr Yeltsin as president, but 52% would vote for "someone else".

This election may therefore mark the beginning of the end of the Yeltsin era. Those who want to reform Russia now have two and a half years to show to a majority of Russians that they will benefit from reform—and to find a leader who can out-campaign Mr Zhirinovsky. . . .

The road to ruin

Whether Russia or the West is mainly to blame, the brave attempts at reform under Boris Yeltsin have come to a halt. The worst may be yet to come

MOSCOW

AS RUSSIA turns its back on reform, the recriminations begin about who is to blame. Jeffrey Sachs, who resigned on January 21st as an adviser to the Russian government, condemns the West and particularly the International Monetary Fund (IMF). The purpose of aid to Russia, insists Mr Sachs, should be political: to keep reformers in power. The West failed to support the reformers, and lost them. The IMF, which prefers economic criteria, argues that the Russian government made promises that it failed to keep.

However the West may have failed Russia and itself, Mr Sachs's version of events, and the IMF's, both rely on views of the Russians' own behaviour. Mr Sachs believes that the reformers did what could reasonably have been expected of them. The IMF believes that more could have been done, but was not. To decide who is right, consider the achievements and missed opportunities of six distinct phases.

• **Before August 1991. Was the inheritance too crushing?** Even by post-communist standards, Russia came with an unusually difficult economic legacy. The reformers inherited a budget deficit running at 31% of GDP, foreign-exchange reserves down to three hours-worth of import cover, and a collapse of trade with Soviet republics. The industrial base was huge and loss-making. Monopolies choked the economy. Nothing had been done to reform agriculture, a central failure of Mikhail Gorbachev's.

Largely because Mr Gorbachev had not believed in the market economy, his own attempts at reform were counterproductive. By August 1991, he had reviewed and rejected 13 reform programmes, including the radical "500-day" plan of September 1990. Mr Gorbachev's record was one reason why

western analysts were not more readily enthusiastic about Boris Yeltsin: they had already seen too many Russian reform plans come and go.

Even then, the economy was by no means the worst of Russia's problems. The country faced a humiliating retreat from empire both in Eastern Europe and in the former Soviet states; and it needed to build a democracy from scratch without any of the tradition on which, say, the Czech Republic could draw. It also had to do all this without a functioning government, because, more so than other Soviet republics or the East European satellite states, Russia had little in the way of government machinery separate from that of the Soviet Union. When Soviet power collapsed, Russia had nothing.

For all these reasons, reform in Russia was always going to be harder than anywhere else. But that did not mean it was doomed from the start. Reform can thrive on crisis, when crisis provides opportunities for decisive action by small, determined groups. At the start, Russia did have a small group of people with a clear idea of what to do (though divisions quickly emerged among them). They retained popular support for a surprisingly long time. As late as September 1992, half the population wanted reforms to be speeded up.

• **August 1991-January 1992. Did the reformers waste their first opportunity?** In principle, all reformers' freedom of action is greatest at their moment of taking office, because harsh decisions can then be blamed on their predecessors. But Russia's dire inheritance limited opportunities from the outset. Ideally, in the view of Grigory Yavlinsky, who had helped write the 500-day programme for Mr Gorbachev, the dismantling of monopolies should have come

before the liberalising of prices. But with the central-planning system in collapse, price liberalisation could not be delayed.

Partly because of this, and partly because some of the reformers were less keen than others, the first Yeltsin team failed to make the most of its early opportunities. It refused to free energy prices, ensuring both that oil output would continue to fall and that the decision to raise prices later would be politically more difficult. It allowed local authorities to maintain some price controls, limited mark-ups in state shops, and resisted full opening to foreign trade.

But in the circumstances, it is surprising just how much the early government did achieve. It freed most prices without riots, sharply reduced shortages and, by cutting the budget deficit, hauled the country back from the edge of hyperinflation.

There is a strong case, in fact, for saying that the reformers' crucial early error was a political one: they would have been far cleverer to have secured new parliamentary elections at once, not two years later amid falling living standards and intense political wrangling. But in August 1991 Alexander Rutskoi and Ruslan Khasbulatov, who were to lead parliament's insurrection two years later, were standing shoulder to shoulder with Boris Yeltsin on the balcony of the White House celebrating Russia's victory over Soviet communism. In early November parliament granted Mr Yeltsin emergency powers to introduce reform by decree. At that point the government seemed to have all the means it needed.

Nor would an early election alone have resolved what became Russia's biggest political problem of 1992-93: the constitutional chaos created by an uncertain division of powers between parliament and president, which set both camps fighting for control over monetary, fiscal and industrial policy. To have pre-empted that development would have required a new constitution as well as a new parliament—a tall order in Russia's first few months as an independent state.

It can be argued, therefore (as Mr Sachs makes a good job of doing), that the Russian reformers did as much in the early months as could reasonably have been expected of them. They might have done much better still with western aid—but they did not get it. Teams of bureaucrats descended on Moscow in the winter of 1991. Their decisions were dreadful.

The IMF wrongly advised the Russians not to set up a separate currency, advice that later cost Russia 10% of its GDP as other republics issued rouble credits that Russia felt obliged to cover. It also insisted, wrongly, that Russia did not need balance-of-payments support, though imports had dropped by 45% in 1991. Advisers from the G7 group of leading economies meanwhile seemed simply to ignore the astonishing shift in Russian economic policy, and focused instead on Soviet foreign debt, insisting that the new government should hand over its last kopek's-worth of foreign exchange in debt service. No one seriously discussed economic stabilisation. "Aid" in those days meant food parcels.

In April 1992, as the danger of missed opportunity became palpable, George Bush announced $24 billion in aid. Even this failed to arrive. Of its central element, $4.5 billion due to come from the World Bank and IMF, the bank lent $670m but did not disburse it until 1993. The IMF's standby arrangement was not approved until August, when the fund lent $1 billion on condition that the money be held in reserves, not spent. For the rest, the Bush package consisted of short-term loans at market interest rates which helped exporters to Russia at a high cost to the Russian budget.

• **June 1992-March 1993. Did Boris Yeltsin fail the reformers?** This western niggardliness took its toll in the summer of 1992. By July, Yegor Gaidar, arch-reformist and acting prime minister, had cut monthly inflation to 9%. Russia was within striking distance of stability. But the austerity policies which made that possible had also met fierce opposition from industrial bosses, who launched their own political party.

Western aid could have helped Mr Gaidar soften the impact of his policies; but the IMF loan was not then signed. Without it, he faced a dangerous confrontation with the industrialists' lobby in parliament.

Mr Gaidar decided to retreat, hoping to stay in office and so protect the fledgling privatisation programme. He bought himself a few vital months, but only at the cost of acquiescing in a soaring inflation rate. By December, he was out. Worse, he left behind him a new and profligate central-bank

chairman, Viktor Gerashchenko, who was to play a leading role in undermining reform over the next 18 months. Recommending Mr Gerashchenko was Mr Gaidar's biggest mistake; his motive remains a mystery.

This first departure of Mr Gaidar raised a more fundamental question: could things have been different had Boris Yeltsin supported the reforms more forthrightly? To answer that question, take a step back.

One of the few features common to successfully reforming countries has been a leader with a clear sense of where he wants his country to go and a willingness to stick by his purpose when the going gets rough—Vaclav Klaus, or Lech Walesa, for example. In defence of Boris Yeltsin, it might be said that he was resolute in the 1991 coup; he was bold enough to promote Mr Gaidar when most of his other advisers were urging caution; and he was willing to fight for Boris Fedorov as central-bank governor rather than Mr Gerashchenko. But on balance periodic acts of strength have not outweighed Mr Yeltsin's systematic weakness.

First, Mr Yeltsin lacks a consistent view of where he wants Russia to go. In 1990-91 he was willing to settle for a Russia within the Soviet Union, albeit with increased powers. In 1991, he talked of westernising Russia, turning it into a liberal democratic state. Now, he is talking about reviving a strong Russian state. While Mr Klaus relentlessly pursues membership of the European Union for the Czech Republic, Mr Yeltsin's trimming reflects something of Russia's Eurasian ambivalence.

Second, though willing to show courage in a crisis, Mr Yeltsin has failed to provide the steadier and more sustained leadership that would have enabled reformers to survive at other times. To do this, short of imposing authoritarian rule, Mr Yeltsin should have organised a presidential party of reform. Here, Mr Klaus has argued, lies the new Russia's greatest political failure.

By the hot summer of 1992, Mr Yeltsin had abandoned his initial "policy of breakthrough", which had meant acting as his own prime minister and putting himself in the front line of reform. Instead, he reacted to parliament's attacks on his policies by trying to stay above the fray, bringing an industrialist into government here, slipping a reformer back there, more like a feudal monarch than a modern head of state.

Worse, he attempted to bypass parliament by setting up rival centres of power, giving increased authority to his own entourage and to a body called the security council which had ill-defined but wide-ranging powers. He did this for fear that he himself might be brought down by attacks on his reforms. But he succeeded only in worsening the constitutional muddle inherited from the Soviet system, producing by the winter of 1992-93 a deadlock between president, government, parliament and central bank.

• **March-September 1993. Why wasn't the**

deadlock resolved? Even some of Mr Yeltsin's closest advisers were not sure what he was going to say when he went on television on the evening of March 20th 1993. The parliamentary session, just ended, had severely trimmed his powers. Nothing had been done to give any fresh impetus to reform, and some past gains were eroding. By the beginning of 1993, monthly inflation, at 27%, was soaring again.

Against this grim background, Mr Yeltsin's resolution reasserted itself. He declared that on April 25th there would be a vote of confidence in his performance.

Pessimists argued that regional opposition would block the referendum, or that no one would bother to vote. Even Mr Yeltsin's new prime minister, Viktor Chernomyrdin, thought a majority would vote against the president's economic policies. They were wrong. Nearly 60% of voters backed Mr Yeltsin, and 53% backed his economic policies. Yes votes carried 66 of Russia's 88 provinces and republics, destroying the claim that swathes of Russia were anti-Yeltsin.

The referendum gave Mr Yeltsin the freedom to tilt the balance of power in government against the conservatives brought in by Mr Chernomyrdin; and in favour of Mr Fedorov, by then the finance minister, and of Anatoly Chubais, in charge of privatisation. Here was a second opportunity for breakthrough.

At first the signs looked good. The G7 promised Russia a second aid package, this time of $28 billion. Anders Aslund, a Swedish economist who served as an adviser to Mr Fedorov in 1993, says America's policies towards Russia, steered by Lloyd Bentsen and Larry Summers at the Treasury, were now "first rate". Mr Aslund also gives the IMF, criticised by his colleague, Mr Sachs, the benefit of the doubt: "The IMF did more to support reform than most agencies—it actually lent Russia some money."

But the IMF could only be expected to support economic policies that were likely to work—which excluded Mr Gerashchenko's central bank. In July 1993, when Mr Yeltsin was on holiday and Mr Fedorov was in America, Mr Gerashchenko announced a confiscatory monetary reform. The operation was (characteristically) bungled; inflation increased.

By fighting the central bank at every step, Mr Fedorov managed to reduce the credits it handed out from 42% of GDP in the fourth quarter of 1992 to 25% in the third quarter of 1993. He abolished import subsidies, which had gobbled up 13% of GDP in 1992, and cut subsidies to other former Soviet states to under 4% by late 1993. But Russia was still missing its IMF targets.

At this point, if the purpose of aid to Russia should have been—as Mr Sachs argues—fundamentally political, then more should have come from the G7. For various reasons, it did not. Some of the G7 countries were in recession. Germany had provided half of all aid to Russia since 1991 and was unwilling to give more. Japan was locked in a dispute over the Kurile islands. So the G7 hid behind the IMF; and the Russian government added to its own problems by blocking (out of indecision) World Bank loans intended to finance social spending.

Above all, it was clear by the autumn of 1993 that fundamental reform would be impossible so long as parliament continued to vote for open-ended spending. It was parliament that forced the crisis. It tabled motions for a budget which, if adopted, would have brought hyperinflation. Then, it began to debate stripping Mr Yeltsin of his remaining powers.

• **September-December 1993. Why did the election go wrong?** Mr Yeltsin launched a pre-emptive strike. On September 21st he dissolved parliament, announcing that an election for a new one, and a referendum on a new constitution, would be held on December 12th. This gave the reformers two months to rally public support.

They did too little, partly because the April referendum had lulled some into thinking that people would support them come what may. Others gaily assumed that the self-interest of an emerging class of property-owners would ensure that liberal democracy followed automatically. Whatever the reason, most of the reformers campaigned miserably.

They split into four groups, with the three smaller ones treating the largest, Russia's Choice, as their main enemy. "No democratic party identified the people as its target group," says Mr Aslund. "They lectured people like old-style communists."

The one man who can claim to have campaigned as a true democrat—in the sense that he raised questions which troubled ordinary voters and supplied attractive, if insane, answers—was an extreme nationalist, Vladimir Zhirinovsky. He picked up 15m protest votes from people frustrated by all established politicians, old-guard communists and thrusting democrats alike.

This may not have been a vote against economic reform itself. Yuri Levada, who runs a polling firm, believes that the most consistent support for Mr Zhirinovsky came from men aged 25-40, most of whom earned above-average wages. Their main concern, says Mr Levada, was law and order. Mr Zhirinovsky's core support relied much less on the unskilled, elderly and unemployed—the losers from economic reform.

If so, then the best way to counter Mr Zhirinovsky would be to continue with economic reform while cracking down on crime. The worst way would be for the Russian government and its western supporters to lose their nerve about reform and so make social disorder worse. Yet that second course is the one the government seems to have chosen, in part because of another ill-timed intervention from the West.

• **January 1994. Is reform dead?** During a visit to Moscow shortly after the election, Vice-President Al Gore said the IMF was being too tough in its policy advice to Russia. Strobe Talbott, Bill Clinton's main adviser on Russia, then went so far as to coin an anti-reform slogan, claiming that Russia needed "less shock, more therapy". These remarks, which came as Mr Yeltsin was pondering a new government, were a "stab in the back" for reform, says Mr Fedorov. With even America seeming to soften on reform, Mr Chernomyrdin pounced—forcing out of government all the top reformers except Mr Chubais; Mr Fedorov's departure on January 26th completed that process.

The result, for the time being at least, is that after a series of short-lived and fractious coalitions, Russia now has a united government dominated by industrial lobbies. There remains no obvious figure with the power to block their special pleading to slow reform.

This does not necessarily imply an absolute reversal of all that reform has achieved. Central planning is dead, and the private sector that has sprung up over the past two years will not be snuffed out easily. But the post-election shift does mean the end of sensible macroeconomic policies and the demise of those in government who wanted genuinely free markets. Worse, it gives power to those who believe Russia has nothing to learn from other countries. This could indeed make Russia unique if it leads to the triumph of a political madman, Mr Zhirinovsky, in the 1996 presidential election.

The Third World: Diversity in Development

- **Politics of Development (Article 46)**
- **Latin America: Mexico (Articles 47 and 48)**
- **Africa (Articles 49 and 50)**
- **China (Articles 51 and 52)**
- **India (Article 53)**
- **Newly Industrialized Countries (Articles 54 and 55)**

The Third World is an umbrella term for a disparate group of states, often called developing or less developed countries (LCDs). Their most important shared characteristic may well be what these countries have *not* become—namely, relatively modern industrial societies. Otherwise they differ considerably from each other, in terms of both history and politics as well as present socioeconomic conditions and prospects.

Originally the term Third World referred to countries—many of them recently freed former colonies—that chose to remain nonaligned in the cold war confrontation between the First World (or Western bloc) and the Second World (or communist bloc). It was common to speak of "three worlds," but the categories of first world and second world themselves never gained wide usage. They make very little sense today in view of the collapse of communist rule in Central and Eastern Europe, including Russia and the other former Soviet republics.

Most of the Third World nations also share the problems of poverty and, though now less frequently, rapid population growth. However, their present economic situation and potential for development vary considerably, as a simple alphabetical juxtaposition of countries such as Angola and the Argentines, Bangladesh and Brazil, or Chad and China illustrates. An additional term, Fourth World, has therefore been proposed to designate countries that are so desperately short of resources that they appear to have little or no prospect for self-sustained economic improvement. Adding to the terminological inflation and confusion, the Third World countries are now often referred to collectively as the "South" and contrasted with the largely industrialized "North." Most of them in fact are located in the southern latitudes of the planet—in Latin America, Africa, Asia, and the Middle East. But Greenland would also qualify for Third World status along with much of Russia and Siberia, while Australia or New Zealand clearly would not. South Africa would be a case of "uneven" or "combined" development, as would some Latin American countries where significant enclaves of advanced modernity are located within a larger context of premodern social and economic conditions.

Sometimes called the Group of 77, but eventually consisting of some 120 countries, the Third World states once linked themselves together in the United Nations to promote whatever interests they may have had in common. In their demand for a New International Economic Order, they focused on promoting changes designed to improve their relative commercial position vis-à-vis the affluent industrialized nations of the North. This common front, however, has turned out to be more rhetorical than real. It would be a mistake to assume that there is a necessary identity of national interest among these countries or that they pursue complementary foreign policies.

The collapse of communist rule in Europe has had a profound impact on the ideological explanation of Third World poverty and on the resulting strategies to overcome it. The Soviet model of modernization, which until recently fascinated many Third World leaders, now appears to have very little of practical value to offer these countries. The fact that even the Communists who remain in power in China have been willing to experiment with market reforms, including the private profit motive, has added to the general discredit of the centrally planned economy. Perhaps

even more important is the positive demonstration effect of some countries in Africa and Latin America that have pursued more market-oriented strategies of development. On the whole, they appear to have performed better than some of their more statist neighbors. That may help explain the intellectual journey of someone like Michael Manley, the former prime minister of Jamaica, who broke away from the combination of dependency theory and socialist strategies that he had once defended vigorously. During the 1980s, Manley made an intellectual U-turn as he gained a new respect for market economics, without abandoning his interest in using reform politics to promote the interests of the poor. More recently, Jorge G. Castañeda has called upon the Left in Latin America to abandon utopian goals and seek social reforms within "mixed" market economies.

Latin America illustrates the difficulty of establishing stable pluralist democracies in many parts of the Third World. Some authors have argued that its dominant political tradition is basically authoritarian corporatist rather than competitively pluralist. They see the region's long tradition of centralized authoritarian governments, whether of the Left or Right, as the result of a unitary bias in the political culture. From this perspective, there is little hope for a lasting pluralist development, and the current trend toward democratization in much of Latin America is unlikely to last. Today, however, the cultural explanation for the prevalence of authoritarian governments in Latin America appears to meet with more skepticism than it did a few years ago.

In much of Latin America there has been a turn toward a greater emphasis on market economics, replacing the traditional commitment to strategies that favored statist interventions. Of particular interest to Americans is the attempt by President Carlos Salinas of Mexico to move his country toward a more competitive form of market enterprise. At the same time, he has been hesitant to move from economic to political reform. His reluctance is understandable, since such a shift could erode the hegemony of his own long-ruling party, the PRI, and give new outlets for protest in a time of enormous socioeconomic dislocations. But critics of Salinas argue that his approach is too technocratic in its assumption that economic modernization can be accomplished without a basic change of the political system.

The successor to Salinas will be chosen in what promises to be a hard-fought presidential election in August 1994. The PRI's first candidate, Luis Donaldo Colosio, was assassinated in March 1994. His place was taken by Ernesto Zedffio, an economist who fits the technocratic mold of recent Mexican leaders. He will presumably continue the basic economic policies of Salinas, but it could prove difficult to continue ignoring the demands for more meaningful political reform. His chief rivals for the presidency will be the candidates of the left Democratic Revolutionary Party (PRD) and the conservative National Action Party (PAN). For all the parties, the peasant uprising in southern Mexico at the beginning of 1994 will serve as a point of reference, although they are likely to draw different policy conclusions about land reform and economic redistribution.

South Africa faces the monumental task of introducing democracy in a multiracial society where the ruling white minority has never shared political or economic power with black Africans or Asian Immigrants. A new transitional constitution was adopted in late 1993, followed by the first multiracial national elections in April 1994. Outgoing President Frederik de Klerk will go into history as an important reformer, but his political work cannot possibly please a broad cross section of South African society. His reforms have simply gone much too far and too fast for a privileged white minority, and they have not gone nearly far nor quickly enough for many more who demand policies that would promote much more than formal racial equality. His successor is expected to be Nelson Mandela, whose historical task may turn out to be even more difficult. In addition to his undisputed leadership qualities, two of Mandela's best political cards would appear to be the fact that while he clearly represents the aspirations of a long-repressed majority, he has also managed to retain the respect of a sizable number of the white minority. It will be important that he continue to bridge the racial cleavages that otherwise threaten to ravage South African society.

After the parliamentary elections, it will be necessary to seek accommodation through some institutional form of power-sharing. Keeping such a coalition government together will be only one of many problems. In order for the changes to have much meaning for the long-suppressed majority, it will be necessary to find policies that reduce the social and economic chasm separating the races. The politics of redistribution will be no simple or short-term task, and one may expect many conflicts in the future. Nevertheless, for the first time since the beginning of colonization, South Africa now offers some hope for a major improvement in interracial relations.

China is the homeland of over a billion people, or more than one-fifth of the world's population. Here the reform Communists, who took power after Mao Zedong's death in 1976, began much earlier than their Soviet counterparts to steer the country toward a relatively decontrolled market economy. They also introduced some political relaxation, by putting an end to the recurrent ideological campaigns to mobilize the masses. In their place came a domestic tranquillity such as China had not known for over half a century. But the regime encountered a basic dilemma: it wished to maintain tight controls over politics and society while reforming the economy. When a new openness developed in Chinese society, comparable in some ways to the pluralism encouraged more actively by Gorbachev's glasnost policy, it ran into determined opposition among hard-line Communist leaders. The aging reform leader Deng Xiaoping presided over a bloody crackdown on student demonstrations in Beijing's Tiananmen Square in May 1989. The regime refuses to let up on its tight political controls of society, but it has continued to loosen the economic controls. In recent years, China has experienced a remarkable economic surge with growth rates that appear unmatched elsewhere in the world.

India is often referred to as a subcontinent. With its almost 800 million people, this country ranks second only to China in population and ahead of the continents of Latin America and Africa combined. India is deeply divided by ethnic, religious and regional differences. In recent years, Hindu extremists have become politicized and now constitute a threat to the Muslim minority as well as the secular foundation of the state. For the vast majority of the huge population, a life of material deprivation seems inescapable. However, some policy critics point to the possibility of relief if the country's struggling economy were freed from a long tradition of heavy-handed state interference. The potential for political crisis looms over the country. In 1992

the national elections were marred by the assassination of Rajiv Gandhi, the former prime minister and leader of the Congress party. Prime Minister P. V. Narasimha Rao, the political veteran who took charge of a tenuous minority government after the election, has followed in the steps of other reform governments in the Third World by adopting more market-oriented policies. This attempt to bring India, with its long tradition of heavy state regulation and protectionism, into the world economy bears careful watching.

The Newly Industrialized Countries (NICs) are the subject of the two final articles in this unit. They have received much attention as former Third World nations that have succeeded in breaking out of the cycle of chronic poverty and low productivity. It is not fully clear what lessons we can draw from the impressive records of the four or five "tigers" or "dragons"—Singapore, Hong Kong, South Korea, Taiwan, and possibly Thailand or Malaysia. Some observers have suggested that their combination of authoritarian politics and market economics have provided a successful mix of discipline and incentives that have made the economic takeoff possible. Others point to the presence of special cultural factors in these countries (such as strong family units and values that emphasize hard work, postponement of gratification, and respect for education), which supposedly encourage rational forms of economic behavior. It would also be possible to cite some geopolitical and historical advantages that helped the NICs accumulate investment capital at a critical phase. The subject is of great importance and it seems bound to become one of the main topics in the field of study that we call the politics of development. These countries are clearly of interest as possible role models for economic development. They can also serve as examples of how authoritarian, political, and social traditions can be reformed in tandem with the development of a more affluent consumer society. The authors give a perspective on the new industrial countries by carefully reviewing the debate concerning the relative contributions made to their remarkable economic development by market forces, state intervention, and cultural and social factors.

Looking Ahead: Challenge Questions

Why is the term Third World of little analytical value? What have these countries in common, and how are they diverse?

How do explanations of Third World poverty and slow development differ in assigning responsibility for these conditions to external (foreign) and internal (domestic) factors?

What is dependency theory, and why has it had so much appeal, especially in Latin America?

Why do economic development and representative government run into such difficulties in most of Latin America and much of Africa?

What are some of the major political, economic, and social problems that South Africa still has to face in overcoming the legacy of apartheid?

How do you explain China's relative success in turning toward market reforms for their economy, as compared to the Soviet Union?

How has India managed to maintain itself as a parliamentary democracy, given the many cleavages that divide this multi-ethnic society?

What can the new industrial countries of Asia teach us about the possibility of economic modernization and democratic reform?

LET'S ABOLISH THE THIRD WORLD

It never made much sense, and it doesn't exist in practice.
So why not get rid of it in theory?

Sometimes language lags history. Take the Third World. Did we ever have another name for the poor, unstable nations of the south? In fact, the Third World is a 1950s coinage, invented in Paris by French intellectuals looking for a way to lump together the newly independent former European colonies in Asia and Africa. They defined *le tiers monde* by what it wasn't: neither the First World (the West) nor the Second (the Soviet bloc). But now the cold war is over, and we are learning a new political lexicon, free of old standbys like "Soviet Union" that no longer refer to anything. It's a good time to get rid of the Third World, too.

The Third World should have been abolished long ago. From the very beginning, the concept swept vast differences of culture, religion and ethnicity under the rug. How much did El Salvador and Senegal really have in common? And what did either share with Bangladesh? One of the bloodiest wars since Vietnam took place between two Third World brothers, Iran and Iraq. Many former colonies remained closer to erstwhile European metropoles than to their fellow "new nations."

Nevertheless, the Third World grew. Intellectuals and politicians added a socioeconomic connotation to its original geopolitical meaning. It came to include all those exploited countries that could meet the unhappy standard set by Prime Minister Lee Kuan Yew of Singapore in 1969: "poor, strife-ridden, chaotic." (That was how Latin America got into the club.) There's a tendency now to repackage the Third World as the "South" in a global North-South, rich-poor division. To be

sure, in this sense the Third World does refer to something real: vast social problems—disease, hunger, bad housing—matched by a chronic inability to solve them. And relative deprivation does give poor nations some common interests: freer access to Western markets, for example.

But there are moral hazards in defining people by what they cannot do or what they do not have. If being Third World meant being poor, and if being poor meant being a perennial victim of the First and Second Worlds, why take responsibility for your own fate? From Cuba to Burma, Third Worldism became the refuge of scoundrels, the "progressive" finery in which despots draped their repression and economic mismanagement. Remember "African socialism" in Julius Nyerere's Tanzania? It left the country's economy a shambles. A good many Western intellectuals hailed it as a "homegrown" Third World ideology.

Paternalism is one characteristic Western response to a "victimized" Third World. Racism is another. To nativists such as France's Jean-Marie Le Pen or Patrick Buchanan, "Third World" is a code phrase for what they see as the inherent inferiority of tropical societies made up of dark-skinned people. Either way, the phrase Third World, so suggestive of some alien plant, abets stereotyping. "The Third World is a form of bloodless universality that robs individuals and societies of their particularity," wrote the late Trinidad-born novelist Shiva Naipaul. "To blandly subsume, say, Ethiopia, India, and Brazil under the one banner of Third Worldhood is as

absurd and as denigrating as the old assertion that all Chinese look alike."

Today, two new forces are finishing off the tattered Third World idea. The first is the West's victory in the cold war. There are no longer two competing "worlds" with which to contrast a "third." Leaders can't play one superpower off the other, or advertise their misguided policies as alternative to "equally inappropriate" communism and capitalism. The second is rapid growth in many once poor countries. The World Bank says developing countries will grow twice as fast in the '90s as the industrialized G-7. So much for the alleged immutability of "Third World" poverty—and for the notion that development must await a massive transfer of resources from north to south. No one would call the Singapore of Lee Kuan Yew poor, strife-ridden or chaotic: per capita GNP is more than $10,000, and its 1990 growth rate was 8 percent. South Korea, Taiwan and Hong Kong also have robust economies, and Thailand and Malaysia are moving up fast.

American steelmakers have recently lodged "dumping" complaints against half a dozen Asian and Latin American countries. Cheap wages explains much of these foreign steelmakers' success, but the U.S. industry's cry is still a backhanded compliment. "A nation without a manufacturing base is a nation heading toward Third World status," wrote presidential candidate Paul Tsongas. But Tsongas was using obsolete imagery to make his point: soon, bustling basic industries may be the *hallmark* of a "Third World" nation.

Patina of modernity: Nor can the Third World idea withstand revelations about what life was really like in the former "Second World." It was assumed that, whatever the U.S.S.R.'s political deformities, that country was at least modern enough to give the West a run for its money in science and technology. In fact, below a patina of modernity lay gross industrial inefficiency, environmental decay and ethnic strife. Nowadays, it's more common to hear conditions in the former Soviet Union itself described as "Third World," and Russia seeks aid from South Korea. Elsewhere in Europe, Yugoslavia's inter-ethnic war is as bad as anything in Asia or Africa. The United States itself is pocked with "Third World" enclaves: groups with Bangladeshi life expectancies and Latin American infant-mortality rates.

A concept invoked to explain so many things probably can't explain very much at all. The ills that have come to be associated with the Third World are not confined to the southern half of this planet. Nor are democracy and prosperity the exclusive prerogatives of the North. Unfair as international relations may be, over time, economic development and political stability come to countries that work, save and organize to achieve them. Decline and political disorder come to those who neglect education, public health—and freedom. The rules apply regardless of race, ethnicity, religion or climate. There's only one world.　　　　　CHARLES LANE

Mexico's Efforts at 'Salinastroika' Omit Needed Political Reforms

The myth of a 'Mexican miracle' fades in wake of Chiapas revolt

David Clark Scott

Staff writer of The Christian Science Monitor

MEXICO CITY

The New Year's Day Indian rebellion in Mexico is sparking a debate here over a basic tenet of President Carlos Salinas de Gortari's administration: economic reform before political reform.

"Salinastroika" is the term used by critics. It's the Mexican version of *perestroika* (restructuring) but without *glasnost* (political opening). Comparatively minimal political reforms have been accompanied by five years of economic growth, falling inflation, reduced debt, the privatization of inefficient state enterprises, record foreign investment, sweeping agricultural reform, and the crowning achievement: the North American Free Trade Agreement (NAFTA).

The free-market reforms embodied in the so-called "Mexican miracle" have been touted by the United States as the model for Latin America. While some Salinas critics see the Chiapas revolt as a failure of the economic reforms to benefit one of Mexico's poorest states, many blame a lack of democracy.

"Salinas was seen as the little Superman south of the border, able to change 'everything' without having to resort to populism," says historian Lorenzo Meyer, a Salinas critic at the Colegio de Mexico. "Meanwhile, the authoritarianism, corruption, repression, and electoral fraud were kept in the background. Now everyone is aware inside and outside Mexico that Salinas is not a little Superman."

It is argued that extreme poverty is not confined to the 1 million Indian farmers in Chiapas. Government figures show 17 million Mexicans live below the poverty line and have complaints similar to those of the rebels. And even though the Salinas administration has pumped more money into Chiapas via antipoverty programs in the last two years than almost any other state, it is there that the peasants took up arms rather than seeking redress through the political system. But why?

One answer comes from rebel "Major Mario" interviewed Jan. 15 by several Mexican newspapers. "We won't be voting

MEXICAN POVERTY: *A boy in Matamoros scavenges a garbage dump. Government figures show that 17 million Mexicans live below the poverty line and have complaints similar to those of the Chiapas rebels.*

MELANIE STETSON FREEMAN – STAFF

[in the August presidential elections] because they're fixed. Our brothers have voted for the PRI and got nothing. They've voted for the PAN [National Action Party] and nothing. They've voted for the PRD [Democratic Revolutionary Party] and got nothing."

Economist Roberto Salinas León, a proponent of Salinas economic policies, blames the frustration on the "feudal and highly corrupt structures of the Institutional Revolutionary Party [PRI] machinery." He notes that NAFTA "is supposed to reflect Mexico's status as a booming first-world country. The Chiapas revolt is a violent, but unquestionable, indication that much third-world political backwardness remains to be addressed."

Officially, the PRI won 98 percent of the Chiapas ballots in 1976. In 1982 and 1988, 90 percent of the vote went to the PRI. But the uprising begs the question: How real is PRI support?

When approached by journalists after an aerial bombardment near San Cristóbal de las Casas, a frightened woman and her daughter emerged from a thatched hut waving their voter registration cards (which have no information about party affiliation) as if they were tickets to safety: "We're PRI, we're PRI."

"As long as the local *caciques* [political bosses] delivered Chiapas to the PRI, no one at the national level questioned how they got the vote. Now, you're seeing the fruits of frustration sown by past policies. How else can you explain a revolt in the most PRI of states?" Mr. Meyer says. "The unavoidable conclusion is that an overwhelming part of the vote is fiction or fraud." PRI officials say that an armed uprising by 1,500 to 2,000 Chiapas Indians is not representative of views of the remaining 3.2 million state residents.

Alfonso Flores Zarate, director of the Interdisciplinary Consulting Group, a Mexico City political research firm, says rebel demands for land redistribution, better health care, improved education, and more jobs have received the most attention. But Mr. Zarate considers the political demands "very important."

In their "Declaration of War," the Zapatista National Liberation Army (EZLN) communiqué says that the Indians have been denied the "right to freely and democratically elect our officials." A Jan. 6 Zapatista communiqué states: "The serious state of poverty shared by our compatriots has a common cause: lack of liberty and democracy. We consider genuine respect for liberty and the democratic will of the people are indispensable requisites for the improvement of economic and social conditions." It also calls for "a guarantee of clean elections."

Zarate notes that the rebel demands for clean elections are likely to figure prominently in the major presidential candidates' campaigns. The specifics of those demands—not yet fully outlined in the indirect negotiations begun this week—may favor the opposition parties who now smell a chance to end the six-decade reign of the PRI.

The Jan. 11 official campaign launch of PRI presidential candidate Luis Donaldo Colosio—normally a publicity bonanza for the ruling party—has been overshadowed by the Chiapas crisis. There is speculation that peace negotiator Manuel Camacho Solís—passed over by Salinas for the PRI candidacy—may be substituted for Mr. Colosio if he can reach a peaceful solution quickly. But most political pundits discount the rumor.

Still, the political repercussions of the Chiapas crisis are likely to continue to be felt here and abroad. On Jan. 18, the governor of Chiapas, Elmar Setzer Marseille resigned.

Last week, the Secretary of the Interior Ministry (another ex-Chiapas governor) was fired and replaced by former human rights ombudsman Jorge Carpizo McGregor. Mr. Carpizo's appointment is likely to bolster the credibility of the Mexican elections, Zarate says.

"I'm sure it's scary for the pot-bellied old guard of the PRI to have an honest guy like Carpizo in charge of the elections," says John Bailey, a Georgetown University political scientist.

In Argentina, another free-market reformer, President Carlos Saúl Menem, put his military and police forces on alert Jan. 13 as a precaution against a similar rebellion occurring there.

The revolution continues

MEXICO CITY

President Salinas's economic reforms and free-trade policies are fundamentally sound. But his successor, to be elected in August, should read the bloody Chiapas rebellion as a warning that political reforms are also needed urgently

AS CARLOS FUENTES, a novelist, has noted, just when Mexico was moving closer to North America, its rulers were forcibly reminded that parts of their country still belonged to Central America. On January 1st, the day the North American Free-Trade Agreement (NAFTA) sent trade barriers tumbling between Mexico, the United States and Canada, a previously unknown guerrilla group was seizing half a dozen towns in the southern state of Chiapas and bloodily rewriting the political agenda.

President Carlos Salinas and his team of free-market reformers have been nastily shaken. Basking in international applause for his liberal economic policies, Mr Salinas had been looking forward to ending his six-year term on a high note and handing over smoothly to his heir-apparent, Luis Donaldo Colosio,* candidate of the ruling Institutional Revolutionary Party (PRI) in August's presidential election. Instead, thanks to the intervention of the Zapatist National Liberation Army, as the guerrillas call themselves, Mexico faces a turbulent year in which the social costs of economic reform, and of the lack of a properly functioning democracy, have suddenly acquired new prominence.

The Zapatists take their name from Emiliano Zapata, a peasant leader who fought to defend village lands during Mexico's 1910-20 revolution; they claim to have been preparing their present campaign for years, drawing on social injustices which are particularly acute in Chiapas where a third of the population is Indian and many of the rural poor have lost their land to cattle barons with political clout. When the Zapatists launched their attack, officials tried at first to dismiss them as a small bunch of agitators. But it took the army four days to drive them back into the mountains; and even then, with more than a hundred dead, there was no sign that the rebels suffered a decisive defeat. In fact, they may have two thousand or more well-drilled fighters, their nucleus drawn from Mexicans who fought as volunteers with Nicaragua's Sandinists and El Salvador's left-wing guerrillas in the Central American wars of the 1980s.

Nobody expects the rest of Mexico to rise in armed rebellion. But already the Zapatists have taken some of the gloss off Mexico's economic transformation by exposing the flawed political base on which it rests and by denouncing the unequal distribution of its rewards. They have also humbled a government accustomed to ignoring opposition. Mr Salinas himself began by calling for their surrender, then quickly changed tack. He sacked his hard-line interior minister, Patrocinio Gonzalez, a former governor of Chiapas; declared a unilateral ceasefire; and sent Manuel Camacho, his foreign minister and most experienced negotiator, to open talks.

The Salinas solution

Even before Chiapas, sceptics feared that Mexico was condemning itself to having to sprint in a competitive world when much of its economy was still learning to walk unaided. NAFTA, momentous as it is for Mexico, is merely a trade agreement which in itself can guarantee neither growth nor prosperity and which involves none of the social and regional funds that the European Union offers its poorer members. The pressures and strains of forced economic adjustment must be borne by Mexico alone: and, with the Zapatists' leader, Comandante Marcos, denouncing NAFTA from a seized hotel balcony as a "death sentence" for Mexico's Indians, small wonder if some foreign investors, still counting their profits from the recently soaring stockmarket, began to have second thoughts about just how great those pressures and strains might be.

Mr Salinas's economic policies have widened already-huge disparities of wealth. Mexico now has seven dollar-billionaires, according to *Forbes* magazine—as many as Britain. Some have grown rich from a privatisation programme which brought large capital sums to the state but which also converted public monopolies into private ones. At the other extreme, despite sharply increased social spending by the government, 16% of Mexico's population—13.5m people—is officially classified as living in "ex-

[*Luis Donaldo Colosio was assassinated on March 23, 1994. President Carlos Salinas selected Ernesto Zedillo Ponce de León, an American-trained economist, as new presidential candidate of Mexico's governing party. Ed.]

treme poverty" and another 23.6m as "poor". The government claims, improbably, that unemployment is only 3.7%; private-sector economists say that 25-30% of the labour force is out of work or scraping a living in the informal economy.

In the countryside, where most of the poor live, reform has so far done little to end chronic stagnation. Almost a quarter of the population works in agriculture, but it receives only 8% of national income. The government has begun to phase out its last significant crop subsidy, on maize. Instead, it will make cash payments to farmers, encouraging them to switch to more profitable crops. Though sensible in economic terms, this policy will pose political challenges by speeding the drift from the land—and provide more fuel for the Zapatists or their like.

Importantly, the Zapatists claim to be fighting not only for their land and culture, but also for free elections—a rare departure for Latin American guerrillas. If they fail, they should at least ensure an unusually complicated year for the PRI, which has ruled Mexico since the 1920s under various names and never lost a national election.

The PRI's designated candidate for the August presidential election, Mr Colosio, who used to be Mr Salinas's social development minister, has been pushed into the background by the Chiapas revolt. Some even suggest that if Mr Camacho, who was Mr Colosio's closest rival for the nomination, succeeds in pacifying Chiapas, he could make his own bid for the presidency, perhaps as an independent. Mr Colosio has his work cut out to show that he can win the election convincingly (as Mr Salinas did not in 1988) and without recourse to his party's long tradition of ballot-box fraud.

Mr Colosio may be helped by a divided opposition. Mr Camacho aside, his main challenger is likely to be Cuauhtemoc Cardenas, a left-of-centre former PRI leader who some believe won more votes than Mr Salinas in 1988. The conservative National Action Party (PAN) is fielding a skilled parliamentarian, Diego Fernandez de Ceval-

los, as its candidate, and has strong pockets of regional support. Also working in Mr Colosio's favour will be the fact that, despite two electoral reforms under Mr Salinas, the system still favours the PRI. The government controls the electoral authority; the party enjoys privileged television coverage and—opponents claim—access to state resources.

Mr Colosio, or whoever else wins the August election, will find himself running an economy changed in some areas beyond recognition under Mr Salinas. The budget has been in surplus; foreign debts have been renegotiated; private investment has become the driving force of what was previously a state-led economy; import tariffs have been cut—the highest is now 20%, compared with more than 100% ten years ago; inflation, running at 159% annually in 1987, fell to 8% in 1993; more than 390 state-owned companies have been privatised, raising $23 billion; the constitution has been amended to allow communal farmers to own their land and do deals with private investors; regulations hindering private business have been systematically scrapped.

Mr Salinas's crowning achievement, Mexico's accession to NAFTA, surmounted a history of prickly nationalism and set his country on a course of economic integration with the United States which will be difficult and expensive for any future Mexican government to change. Now, 11 years after Mexico's moratorium triggered the Latin American debt crisis, the process of structural adjustment is almost complete. With NAFTA in place, optimists are hoping for economic growth strong enough to bring Mexico into the developed world some time early in the next century.

NAFTA and after

But for these high hopes to be realised, Mexico's businesses will first have to compete with America's, and survive. For the moment, that prospect appears at least as daunting as it does inspiring. Despite Mr Salinas's reforms and an inflow of about $25 billion in foreign capital, Mexico's GDP

probably grew by only about 0.5% in 1993, down from 2.6% in 1992. In the third quarter of 1993, output shrank by 1.2%, the first drop since 1986. While bigger companies raise cheap funds on international capital markets and prepare to take on the world, smaller ones are struggling to cope with real interest rates of up to 15% and thousands have gone bust.

Officials attribute the present slowdown mainly to a sluggish world economy and to the prolonged uncertainty over NAFTA's fate in Congress which held up investment decisions: after growing by 20.4% in 1992, private investment rose by only 2.8% in the first three quarters of 1993. The government expects a rebound to 6.4% in 1994: so long as political violence does not spread, this may prove an underestimate. NAFTA should improve Mexico's credit rating (and so make its borrowing cheaper), though Chiapas has probably caused American rating agencies to hold off upgrading Mexican debt from speculative to investment quality.

Recovery will also get a boost from the government's decision, with one eye on the presidential election, to spend its budget surplus. Some of the extra money will go to the poor. Fulfilling a promise made to Bill Clinton to help smooth NAFTA's passage, workers on the minimum wage will receive an extra 14-17% this year, partly through a new negative income tax for low earners.

The challenge facing Mr Salinas's successor will be to sustain growth without yielding to inflationary pressures. Failure will be painful: Mexico's economy needs to grow by 5-6% in real terms each year merely to provide jobs for the 1m new workers entering the labour market. Growth provides the best hope of reducing income inequalities and increasing domestic savings, thus lessening Mexico's dependence on foreign capital. But the next government will also have to resist pressures to deal with social problems simply by opening its chequebook—a self-discipline which should be helped by a new law giving the central bank greater autonomy in credit policy.

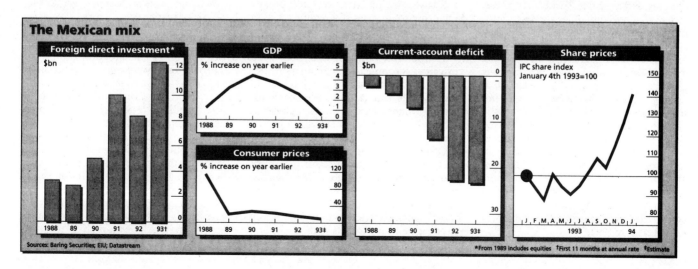

The Mexican mix

Foreign direct investment* — $bn — 1988, 89, 90, 91, 92, 93†

GDP — % increase on year earlier — 1988, 89, 90, 91, 92, 93‡

Consumer prices — % increase on year earlier — 1988, 89, 90, 91, 92, 93‡

Current-account deficit — $bn — 1988, 89, 90, 91, 92, 93‡

Share prices — IPC share index January 4th 1993=100 — J F M A M J J A S O N D J / 1993 94

Sources: Baring Securities; EIU; Datastream   *From 1989 includes equities †First 11 months at annual rate ‡Estimate

In practice, Mexico's capacity to achieve sustainable growth will depend on three related variables: microeconomic reforms to raise productivity; the current account deficit; and post-NAFTA capital inflows.

First, productivity. Big companies have worked hard in the past three or four years to become more competitive. They have shed peripheral businesses, cut workers and found foreign partners with new technologies and markets. Some have expanded into the United States or elsewhere through acquisition. Many are now highly efficient. Their efforts have contributed to a steady productivity rise in manufacturing industry, up 19% between 1990 and 1992. But many smaller companies have barely begun to work out what they need to do to compete, and are holding the economy back. Guillermo Ortiz, deputy finance minister, admits that the process has taken "longer than we thought it would—the inefficiencies and distortions in the productive apparatus were much greater than we realised."

Growth has also been slowed because Mexico's more open and competitive environment has obliged many firms to scrap plant and machinery installed in the protectionist era sooner than would normally have been the case; and to adjust to sharp changes in the relative prices of capital, labour, energy and imported goods. Energy prices, for example, are now 50% higher in real terms than they were in 1982. Capital was also cheaper then, and many imported goods were inaccessible. According to Jesus Reyes Heroles of GEA, an economic consultancy, companies in industries such as textiles, leather goods and petrochemicals were stuck with the wrong technology when relative prices changed. Despite a growth in investment from 17% of GNP in 1988 to 22% in 1992, the economy's capital stock is barely bigger than it was a decade ago.

Restructuring has been made harder during the past year by the tough combination of a faster-than-expected fall in inflation, high real interest rates and an appreciating real exchange rate. To the first of those, lower inflation, companies are now adjusting. Interest rates are set to fall: Baring Securities, a stockbroker, forecasts the peso interbank lending rate falling from 19% to 11% during 1994. That leaves the exchange rate. The peso was undervalued in the late 1980s when trade liberalisation began, so the initial impact on competitiveness was slight. Since then, the government has emphasised productivity as a means to raise competitiveness, while profiting from a firm currency to cut inflation and to break inflationary expectations. That policy is more controversial now that the biggest cloud over Mexico's growth prospects is a current-account deficit that reached $22.8 billion, or 6.8% of GDP, in 1992.

Miguel Mancera, president of the central bank, argues that the deficit is not inherently dangerous, because it is associated with the inflow of foreign funds, swelling the capital account, rather than expansionary fiscal or monetary policy. "It only becomes a problem because people think it's a problem," Mr Mancera says. Perhaps; but market perceptions do matter, and inflows could cease or reverse, making the deficit harder to finance. And, though import growth has slowed along with the economy, Mexican companies have shifted, probably permanently, to a greater dependence on imports. Officials point out that Mexico's non-oil exports have been growing faster than those of South Korea and Singapore since 1985, but there are also fears that the export-growth rate of 15% recorded in the first eight months of 1993 will fall sharply once the domestic market revives.

Rogelio Ramirez de la O, an economic consultant, says that each unit of investment in Mexico since 1988 has pulled in 1.8 units of imports, while the equivalent figure for Chile has been only 1.1. He argues that with NAFTA in place and the budget balanced, Mexico can afford to tackle the current-account deficit by letting the peso slide further against the dollar, without reviving inflation; a fall to the bottom of the band fixed by the central bank would mean a devaluation against the dollar of about 13% over the next 18 months. Without that, says Mr Ramirez, concern about the current account will dog growth again in 1995.

Finishing the job

Even if foreign investors do stay enthusiastic about Mexico, and growth is sustained without too much strain on the balance of payments, there are still many areas the next government needs to address to help Mexican companies compete. They include:

• **Deregulation.** Although the federal government has cut through swathes of red tape, state and municipal governments have been more grudging. A typical example: road haulage is now deregulated in federal law, allowing lorries to travel on any route, but some states still require goods to be re-loaded on to local transport for the final leg of their journey.

• **Monopolies.** Many still exist, public and private. A "competition commission", set up by the government last year, has been all but invisible—not least in December when the government decided to award 62 vacant television frequencies to Televisa, a private near-monopoly, without public tender.

• **Infrastructure.** Although labour costs in Mexico are low, poor infrastructure keeps transport and energy costs high. Private investors financed 4,000 kilometres of new motorway, but found that the high tolls deterred traffic. Ports, airports and railways all need big new investments.

• **Industrial policy.** The Salinas government dislikes it in principle, but officials have not always resisted it in practice. Mr Reyes Heroles argues for a disciplined blend of credits and information-sharing rather than crude subsidy.

But most of this relatively fine tuning will be academic if the government fails to maintain civil peace. The message of Chiapas is that bolder social and political reforms are needed. Mr Salinas's administration made a start on the former, but barely touched the latter. It increased social spending by almost 85% in real terms, much of that new money going via Solidarity, a high-profile anti-poverty agency. But to make any significant impact on poverty, Mr Salinas's successor will have to ensure that money is spent more wisely and impartially. Solidarity has too often allowed political criteria to dictate the direction of its disbursements.

Education is just as vital. Mr Salinas put more money into it, but quality and content still have a long way to go. Good universal education will be the precondition for a more productive workforce and for the redressing of what will otherwise be entrenched and perhaps worsening inequalities. Despite all its recent changes, much of Mexico remains locked in a feudal culture, accustomed to being told what to do—whether by an Aztec king, a Spanish viceroy or a PRI bureaucrat.

Feudal attitudes are at their most entrenched in far-flung places like Chiapas. Though more Solidarity money has gone there than anywhere else, its impact has often been neutered by the iron control of local PRI bosses whose main concern is with keeping the vote-machine well oiled: improbably, Mr Salinas was declared to have won 89.9% of the Chiapas vote in 1988.

By treating too much of Mexico too often as still its fief, the PRI may be storing up trouble. At the most recent municipal elections in Chiapas in 1991, for example, Mr Cardenas's opposition party believed it had won in the towns of Ocosingo and Las Margaritas. Mr Gonzalez, then the state governor, had other ideas. He jailed 153 Cardenas supporters in the two towns and awarded victory to the PRI. It may not be coincidence that both towns were among those occupied earlier this month by the Zapatists.

NAFTA and Chiapas should probably now be pulling Mexico in the same direction: towards a more responsive and efficient—and therefore open—political system which would place Mexico on a more equal footing with its other North American partners. A more inclusive political system might also be the best way for Mexico to lock in its gains from economic reform, by dissuading the poor and angry from venting their frustration by extra-political means.

"As a result of its economic marginalization and relatively feeble attempted [economic] reform, Africa is in many respects lost between state and market. It wanders between ineffective states and weak markets, both domestic and international, and the latter are increasingly indifferent."

Africa: Falling Off the Map?

Thomas M. Callaghy

Thomas M. Callaghy *is an associate professor of political science at the University of Pennsylvania; he is coeditor, with John Ravenhill, of* Hemmed In: Responses to Africa's Economic Decline *(New York: Columbia University Press, 1993). This article is a revised and updated version of a chapter in* Africa in World Politics, *2d edition, edited by John Harbeson and Donald Rothchild (Boulder, Colo.: Westview Press, paperback, 1994; cloth, 1995), and appears by permission.*

In the mid-nineteenth century, after the end of the slave trade and before the imposition of direct colonial domination, Africa found itself both marginalized from the world economy and highly dependent on it. A leading historian of Africa has pointed out this paradox, and noted that it operated in the opposite direction as well: the world's "increasing involvement in the African economy. . .[was] at odds with the decreasing economic importance of Africa" for the world economy.[1] At the end of the twentieth century, this paradox still holds; in fact, it is truer now than it was in the pre-colonial period.

Africa's increased marginalization has been both economic and political-strategic, but the former is most significant. Africa is no longer very important to the international division of labor or to the major actors in the world economy—multinational corporations, international banks, the economies of the major Western countries or those of the newly industrializing countries such as South Korea, Taiwan, Brazil, and Mexico. Africa generates a declining share of world output. The main commodities it produces are becoming less sought after or are more effectively produced by other third world countries. Trade is declining, nobody

[1]Ralph Austen, *African Economic History* (London: James Currey, 1987), pp. 102, 109. In this article, Africa means sub-Saharan Africa minus South Africa.

wants to lend, and few want to invest except in selected parts of the mineral sector.

Africa's per capita income levels and growth rates have declined since the first oil crisis in 1973, while its percentage of worldwide official development assistance rose from 17 percent in 1970 to about 38 percent in 1991. Since 1970, nominal gross domestic product has risen more slowly than in other developing countries, while real GDP growth rates have dropped dramatically since 1965.

Other developing countries performed better in spite of the poor world economic climate, especially in the 1980s. For the period 1982–1992, average annual GDP growth for Africa was 2 percent; for South Asia, the most comparable region, it was a little over 5 percent, while the East Asian rate was 8 percent. The rate for all developing countries was 2.7 percent. The per capita GDP rates are even more revealing: Africa, 1 percent; South Asia, 3 percent; and East Asia, 6.4 percent. The World Bank's baseline projections for the decade beginning in 1992 are more optimistic, projecting annual GDP growth of 3.7 percent for Africa, but the bank's estimates for Africa have often proved overly hopeful, and the assumptions of the current forecast are startling. They assume less unfavorable external conditions, including a break in falling commodity prices; more liberalized world trade regimes; and no real decline in the growth of industrial countries; less civil strife; improvement in economic policies and implementation; a higher percentage of foreign investment; the continuation of current foreign aid; and no major adverse weather! The forecast does, however, anticipate a 50 percent rise in the number of poor people, from 200 million to 300 million, making Africa the only region in the world with an overall increase in poverty.

In addition, African export levels have stayed relatively flat or have actually declined since 1970, while those of other developing countries have risen significantly. For example, the continent's share of developing-country agricultural exports slumped from 17 percent to 8 percent between 1970 and 1990, with South and East Asian exports expanding rapidly. Africa's marginalization becomes more startling when its performance is compared with that of other low income regions, particularly South Asia. The difference between the two is striking for per capita GDP growth; Africa's has slipped markedly while that of South Asia has climbed slowly but steadily as the African population growth rate continues to rise while that of South Asia has begun to decline.

The most important differences, however, relate to the level and quality of investment. Africa's investment as a percentage of GDP declined in the 1980s, while that of South Asia continued to increase despite the difficult economic conditions of the decade. South Asia followed better economic policies, and above all provided a much more propitious socioeconomic and political environment for investment. This is most vividly manifested in the rate of return on investment: in Africa, the rate fell from almost 31 percent in the 1960s to just 2.5 percent in the 1980s, while in South Asia it inched steadily upward, from 21.3 percent to 22.4 percent.

Given this dismal economic performance, both substantively and comparatively, it is not surprising that world business leaders take an increasingly jaundiced view of Africa. As one business executive said to this author, "Who cares about Africa; it is not important to us; leave it to the IMF [International Monetary Fund] and the World Bank." Some observers have referred to this phenomenon as "postneocolonialism." For the most dynamic actors in a rapidly changing world economy, even a neocolonial Africa is not of much interest anymore, especially after the amazing changes wrought in Eastern Europe and elsewhere beginning in 1989. According to this viewpoint, the African crisis really should be left to the international financial institutions, and if their salvage effort works, fine; if not, so be it, the world economy will hardly notice.

Thus, whatever one thinks about the role of foreign business and capital, it is important to remember that Africa increasingly imposes enormous difficulties for them, such as political arbitrariness and administrative, infrastructural, and economic inefficiency. Because foreign capital has the considerable ability to select the type of state with which it cooperates, it is very doubtful that Africa will play any significant role in current shifts in the patterns of production in the international division of labor. For most businesspeople from abroad Africa has become a sinkhole that swallows their money with little or no return. Two arresting facts further underscore Africa's marginalization: the amount of external financing through bonds for East

Asia in 1991 was $2.4 billion, and for South Asia $1.9 billion, while it was zero for Africa; and flight capital as a percentage of GDP at the end of 1990 was 15 for South Asia, 19 for East Asia, and 28 for developing Europe and for Central Asia, while it was 80 for Africa.

Disinvestment, in fact, has emerged as a trend. During the 1980s, for example, 43 of 139 British firms with industrial investments in Africa withdrew. Ironically, the retrenchment has in part been due to economic reforms that have done away with overvalued exchange rates and import tariff protection. The British firms were unwilling to inject new capital to make their investments efficient by world standards of competitiveness. While Japan is now the major donor, it is not likely to be a major investor in Africa; in the 1980s, for example, the number of Japanese commercial companies operating in Kenya dwindled from 15 to 2.

The second aspect of Africa's marginalization is at the strategic level, which has also had negative economic consequences. Africa has become of much less interest to the major world powers with the dramatic changes in the international arena, especially the end of the cold war. As one senior African diplomat put it, "Eastern Europe is the most sexy beautiful girl, and we are an old tattered lady. People are tired of Africa. So many countries, so many wars." The rise of warlords in regional and civil wars similar to those in nineteenth-century Africa has challenged the very notion of the nation-state borrowed at independence in the 1960s. Eritrea's independence from Ethiopia, made official last year, and the potential breakup of countries such as Zaire, raise the potentially inflammatory issue of redrawing old colonial boundaries sacrosanct for 30 years. External intervention on the scale seen in Somalia recently is not likely to be repeated; the malign neglect applied to the greater Liberian, Angolan, and Sudanese civil wars is likely to be the more common reaction to such conflicts.

THE NEW NEOCOLONIALISM

Yet in other ways Africa has become more tightly linked to the world economy. This increased involvement has two aspects: an extreme dependence on public actors from outside Africa, particularly the IMF and the World Bank, in the determination of African economic policy; and the liberal or neoclassical thrust of the policy so developed, which pushes the continent toward more intense reliance on and integration with the world economy. Both these aspects are directly linked to Africa's debt crisis.

In 1974 total African debt was about $14.8 billion; by 1992 it had reached an estimated $183.4 billion, or about 109 percent of Africa's total GNP. (In comparison, in South Asia it was 36 percent, and in East Asia 28 percent.) Much of the recent rise has come through borrowing from international financial institutions, especially the IMF and the World Bank, that has been associated with economic reform programs sponsored from outside, usually referred to as structural adjustment. In 1980 debt through international financial institutions constituted 19 percent of the total, whereas by 1992 it accounted for 28 percent. This cannot be rescheduled and significant arrears are accumulating, with the result that IMF and World Bank assistance to some countries has been cut off. Much of the rest of Africa's debt is bilateral or government-guaranteed private medium- and long-term debt and thus is rescheduled by leading Western governments through the Paris Club, and not by the private banks as in Latin America. Countries cannot obtain Paris Club rescheduling relief without being in the good graces of the IMF and the World Bank.

Despite its relative smallness by world standards, the enormous buildup of African debt puts terrible strains on fragile economies. By the end of the 1980s the debt was the equivalent of 350 percent of exports. Africa's debt service ratio (debt service owed as a percentage of export earnings) averaged a little less than 30 percent by the mid-1980s. By 1992 it still averaged more than 25 percent, with some African countries showing much higher rates; Uganda's, for example, was 80 percent. The debt service ratios would be significantly lower, however, if African export growth had kept pace with the performance of other less developed countries. Only about half of debt service owed is paid in any given year, which tends to dampen foreign direct investment.

Given such debt, African countries have benefited from rescheduling concessions such as longer terms and grace periods, lower interest rates, and the rescheduling of previously rescheduled debt. Between 1989 and 1991, about $10 billion in concessional debt, especially that incurred by the continent's low-income nations, was written off by Western countries, including the initially unwilling United States. Despite strong pressure from the IMF, the World Bank, various UN agencies, and private organizations such as Oxfam, most of the major donor countries are still resisting significant debt cancellation.

As in other areas of the third world, this external debt burden and the consequent desperate need for foreign exchange have left African countries highly dependent on a variety of actors from outside the continent, all of which have used their leverage to "encourage" economic liberalization. This process, which some have referred to as "the new neocolonialism," means intense dependence on international financial institutions and major Western countries for the design of economic reform packages and for the resources needed to implement them. Specific economic policy changes are requested in return for the lending of resources. The primary intent of these economic reform efforts is to more fully integrate African economies into the world economy by resurrecting the primary-product export economies that existed at independence and making them work better this time by creating a more "liberal" political economy.

The track record of IMF and World Bank economic reform in Africa since the early 1980s has been quite modest. Ghana under the authoritarian military government of Jerry Rawlings has been about the only case of sustained economic transformation, and it is still fragile. Even African countries that traditionally did relatively well economically in the postcolonial period are now in considerable trouble—Nigeria, Kenya, Ivory Coast, Cameroon, and Senegal have grave economic problems and weak or failed economic reform efforts.

As a result of its economic marginalization and relatively feeble reform efforts, Africa is in many respects lost between state and market. It wanders between ineffective states and weak markets, both domestic and international, and the latter are increasingly indifferent. Many African officials fail to realize just how unimportant Africa is becoming to the world economy. Many are still looking for a quick fix, while the last decade of world history shows that one does not exist. If African countries are to survive, changes must be made. If not, changes in the world political economy will continue to pass Africa by, with very serious long-term consequences for the people of the continent.

DEBATING WHAT TO DO

By the end of the 1980s, with obstacles to reform on all sides, the key question remained: what should Africa do to cope with its devastating economic crisis? The answer from outside, led by the World Bank, was to persevere with the thrust of reforms while making modifications to make them work more effectively. Many Africans remained unconvinced. This fundamental disagreement had simmered quietly throughout the decade behind what appeared to many as a growing consensus around a modified neo-orthodox position.

This disagreement erupted with surprising vigor in what could be called "the bloody spring of 1989." A major battle ensued between the World Bank and the UN's Economic Commission for Africa (ECA) as the former tried to defend structural adjustment and the latter attack it and present its own alternative strategy. Both sides made inappropriate claims. The record of structural adjustment was not nearly as strong as the World Bank tried to make it appear. On the African side, the ECA's "alternative framework" was a warmed-over version of earlier statist and "self-reliant" policies that were vague, often contradictory, and could not be implemented under the best of conditions—all linked to staggering demands for money and other resources. Many Africans were still running from the world economy while looking for a shortcut to development.

By late 1989 the visceral emotions of the bloody spring had been substantially tamed, though without resolution of many of the underlying disagreements. One of the main pacifying factors was the World Bank's release of its long-awaited "long-term perspective study," *Sub-Saharan Africa: From Crisis to Sustainable Growth*, which had been drafted following extensive consultation with Africans—from government officials and entrepreneurs in both the formal and informal economies to the heads of African private volunteer organizations. The report demonstrated that the World Bank had learned many lessons from the attempts at structural adjustment in the 1980s, especially the desperate need for institutional change and for a slower, more sequenced transition that recognized the sociopolitical obstacles to change. Its major themes were that Africa requires an enabling environment— above all, technical and administrative capacity (both state and private) and better political governance.

The report sought a second-generation development strategy in which the state listens carefully to the market even if it does not precisely follow it. Although not put in these terms, this strategy would attempt a move away from the predatory and inefficient mercantilism of the first 30 years of independence and back toward a more productive and efficient, though limited, version of what some have called "benign mercantilism"—that is, toward a more productive tension between state and market.

From the African point of view, this second-generation strategy is clearly a second-best one. But critics of structural adjustment, both inside and outside Africa, do not have a viable alternative to this modified version of neo-orthodoxy. The current African state does not have the capabilities for the more interventionist versions of benign mercantilism represented by South Korea and Taiwan. Governments can, and should, work in that direction, but the transition will be slow and uneven.

Creative tinkering with the neo-orthodox strategy by both African governments and the IMF and World Bank could begin to move the continent in useful directions. The long-term perspective study seemed to represent a step down that road. Ultimately it is not just a question of finding the "precarious balance" between state and market or state and society, but rather of searching for the balance between state, market, and the international arena.

This author would argue that the debate was reignited because many of the nice-sounding "lessons" of *From Crisis to Sustainable Growth*, which were meant to placate a variety of critics, have either been very difficult to implement or the IMF and the World Bank have simply not tried to do so seriously. Largely this is

because structural adjustment requires difficult tradeoffs that most opponents refuse to face squarely. Structural adjustment cannot be all things to all people; if it could, there would be no crisis.

DEMOCRACY AND ECONOMY

The three-way balance between state, market, and the international arena has proved hard to achieve. In part this is because the international arena has a habit of presenting new and unexpected challenges for African rulers. While *From Crisis to Sustainable Growth* was initially well received by many Africans, it contained a time bomb called governance—the issue of how African states are ruled—which has brought considerable new tension and uncertainty to relations between Africans and influential groups from outside, and to economic policy.

With the shifts in the world since 1989, especially in Eastern Europe but also in Central America and South Africa, and the search for a new direction in foreign policy to replace containment—what the Clinton administration has recently called "enlargement" of the world's free community of market democracies— governance has been transformed by the major Western industrial democracies into a strategy for the promotion of democracy. The convergence of these two policy thrusts—one largely technocratic from the World Bank, the other distinctly political from the major powers—has posed a real dilemma for Africa.

Political conditionality, or making bilateral assistance and loans from international financial institutions conditional on domestic political changes, greatly increases African dependence on outside actors. Many African leaders fear this, including a few who are committed to economic reform. Guinea's finance minister, Soriba Kaba, for example, recently complained about the proliferation of conditions that African regimes have to face, "especially relating to governance and performance," saying that "application of these criteria, without agreed parameters and precise definitions, may be used as a pretext to reduce the volume of resource flows to our continent."[2] Some leaders resist energetically, such as Zaire's Mobutu Sese Seko; others, such as Kenya's Daniel arap Moi and Cameroon's Paul Biya, stall while playing charades with critics both inside and outside their countries.

However, a major contradiction may indeed exist between economic and political conditionality, one that Western governments either do not see or ignore. The primary assumptions appear to be that economic structural adjustment and political liberalization are mutually reinforcing processes, and that since authoritarian politics in large part caused the economic malaise, democratic politics can help lift it. Yet evidence from the second and third worlds over the last decade does not support such optimism. This is not to

---

[2]Cited in "The IMF and the World Bank: Arguing about Africa," *Africa Confidential*, vol. 34, no. 20 (October 8, 1993), p. 3.

say that authoritarian regimes can guarantee economic reform or even produce it very often. Nor is it to say that economic reform under democratic conditions is impossible; it is just very difficult.

Presumptions about the mutually reinforcing nature of political and economic reform in Africa rely on an extension of neoclassical economic logic: economic liberalization creates sustained growth, growth produces winners as well as losers, winners will organize to defend their newfound welfare and create sociopolitical coalitions to support continued economic reform. This logic, however, does not appear to hold for Africa, even under authoritarian conditions, much less under democratic ones.

The winners of economic reform in Africa are few, appear only slowly over time, and are hard to organize politically. The neoclassical political logic of reform is too mechanistic for Africa; there are real "transaction costs" to organizing winners, and not just infrastructural ones. Other organizational bases of political solidarity exist—ethnic, regional, religious, linguistic, and patron-client—that make mobilization around policy-specific economic interests difficult in much of Africa.

Some have argued that Africa does not have a democratic tradition, but in fact it has a vivid one, although its day was brief and ended in failure, and the reasons for its demise have not disappeared. The periodic reemergence of democratic regimes in Ghana and Nigeria over the last two decades indicates that old patterns of politics reappear with amazing vigor; political liberalization is not likely to guarantee the appearance of new political alignments that favor sustained economic reform.

The progress of democratization in Africa has been very uneven. Outside actors tried political conditionality in Kenya only to have it undermined by the maneuvering of the Moi government and the inability of the opposition to come up with a single presidential candidate and slate of legislators. In Zambia, where a full transition did take place in late 1992, the new government of Frederick Chiluba has been confronted with political factionalism, renewed corruption, ethnic and regional tension, and uneven economic performance, despite good intentions and help from abroad.

Is this version of the "thesis of the perverse effect"—that political liberalization might have a negative impact on the chances for sustained economic reform—likely to hold across the board for Africa? No, it is not. It is important to assess particular countries. But if not handled properly, political conditionality might well impede rather than facilitate Africa's relinking to the world economy in more productive ways. The widespread emergence of what UCLA professor Richard Sklar has called "developmental democracies" is not likely in Africa any time soon.

Finally, the actions of Western governments in other areas of the world will be important. Many Africans, for example, are likely to see recent support for Russian President Boris Yeltsin's accumulation of executive power and manipulation of constitutional and electoral practices, largely in the hope of getting more coherent economic reform, as highly hypocritical: one standard for strategically important Russia and another for marginal and dependent Africa.

ENDING AS THEY BEGAN

With or without political conditionality, what are the prospects that African countries will engage successfully in economic reform and establish more a productive relationship with the world economy? The answer appears to be that simultaneous marginalization and dependence are likely to continue, and probably increase, for most countries. A few, with hard work, propitious circumstances, and luck, may begin to improve their situation. Differentiation among African states, long evident, may well increase; a few countries will stay in the third world and do relatively better economically, while most will continue to descend. The countries likely to do better are those that are already more advantaged, partly because of better performance over the last 30 years: Kenya, Ivory Coast, Cameroon, Nigeria, Zimbabwe, and possibly Senegal. As noted above, however, even these cases are now fragile, largely for political reasons. A handful of countries in serious decline, such as Ghana, may be able to reverse course, but chances for this are even more tenuous.

A quiet debate is under way among Western officials and business executives about what to do with Africa. Should they provide some resources to all countries to create a sort of international social safety net for declining countries, which then become de facto wards of the world community, or should they "pick a few and work with them," as one Western official has put it? With the first option, it is not at all clear how effective such an international safety net would be, as the recent intervention in Somalia has shown. With the second option, resources would be concentrated in countries that have some good prospects for sustained economic performance, and possibly some strategic importance—Nigeria and Zimbabwe, for example. This is a delicate political task, however, and the recent performance of both of these countries might give one considerable pause.

The trajectory of individual countries will be affected by both internal and external factors. On the internal side, the degree of effective "stateness"—the technical and administrative capabilities to formulate and implement rational economic policies—will be crucial. On average, Africa has the lowest level of state capabilities of any region in the world. As the IMF and the World Bank have begun to realize, it takes a relatively capable state to implement their neo-orthodox economic reform consistently over time. To sustain a solid base in the international political economy, a country needs a high degree of "stateness," including the crucial ability to bargain with all types—private business groups, states, and the international financial institutions. Whether "stateness" will emerge or increase in many places, however, is questionable; certainly political dynamics will play a vital role in arriving at a productive balanced tension between state and market and between state and society. Some African leaders, such as Jerry Rawlings in Ghana, have begun to understand this.

Although it is largely a self-help world, external factors are also very important. They revolve around two central issues. First is the degree of openness of the world political economy. Second is the degree to which both sides fulfill their part of the "implicit bargain" between international financial institutions and the major Western countries and Africans: if African countries successfully reform their economies with the help and direction of the IMF and the World Bank, then new international private bank lending and direct foreign investment will be made available.

John Ruggie has characterized the current international political economy as one of "embedded liberalism," in which the major Western countries intervene in their domestic economies to buffer the costs of adjusting to shifts in the world economy. A precarious openness, based on liberal economic norms, is maintained, despite increasing tensions. Others, such as Robert Gilpin, see the world moving toward an increasingly conflictual and closed international political economy, which might be characterized as "malign mercantilism." Africa's prospects would not be very bright under a shift from embedded liberalism to malign mercantilism by the major Western powers. Despite its marginalization and dependence, Africa desperately needs openness in the world economy; in fact, the neo-orthodox adjustment strategy is predicated on it. Whether some form of benign mercantilism would benefit Africa is also open to question.

Chances for fulfillment of the "implicit bargain" may not be much better, however. Because private actors in the world economy increasingly pass Africa by, Western countries and the international financial institutions will continue to play central roles. If African countries are to have any hope of making economic progress, these actors must help to fulfill this bargain, primarily through increased aid levels and substantial debt relief. Given the domestic politics of Western industrial democracies, debt relief might be the easier route to take, since it is more politically malleable. But major debt relief has not occurred, and there are signs that aid levels may decline as these Western countries become increasingly preoccupied with domestic problems and those of more important regions.

Because resources are scarce, aid and debt relief should be given only to those actually undertaking difficult economic reforms and without being tied automatically to political change. The Jerry Rawlingses of Africa should be supported; nonreforming leaders should not. It is not clear, however, how many leaders like Rawlings actors outside Africa can actually support at the level required for sustained economic change. Since such reform is difficult, stop-and-go cycles are a fact of life, and external actors need to learn to adjust to them more effectively. The primary obstacle is how to cope with a huge debt and substantial arrears to the IMF and the World Bank without setting precedents with worldwide implications.

Finally, given the enormous obstacles confronting African countries, undue optimism and inflated expectations about what is possible in Africa can be dangerous. Slow, steady, consistent progress is preferable. Neither international nor African policymakers can unduly hasten, control, or speed up social processes such as institution and capacity building. Change is incremental, uneven, often contradictory, and dependent on the outcome of unpredictable socioeconomic and political struggles. Policymakers must try to bring about important changes, but they need to retain a sense of the historical complexity involved. Today's policy fads can easily become tomorrow's failed initiatives.

Africa really is caught between a rock and a hard place when it comes to the world economy and the international state system, and all will have to work extremely hard to alter this fact. Although pessimism about Africa is appropriate analytically, try they must, for not trying to keep Africa from falling off the map could have even worse consequences for its long-suffering peoples.

562

South African Parliament Adopts New Constitution

Kenneth B. Noble

Special to The New York Times

CAPE TOWN, Dec. 22—South Africa's Parliament finally approved a new interim constitution, officially ending centuries of white domination, but the proceeding ended on a sour note today as pro-apartheid whites and conservative blacks threatened to boycott the country's first multiracial elections in April.

The legislature's strong endorsement of the constitution—237 votes to 45—was a boon to the spirits of Government negotiators and leaders of the main opposition group, the African National Congress, who had been badly shaken in recent days by mounting opposition to the pact.

But as of tonight, it was uncertain whether a formidable coalition that includes Afrikaner separatists, white supremacists, fervent anti-Communists and Chief Mangosuthu Gatsha Buthelezi, leader of the Zulu-based Inkatha Freedom Party, would take part in the balloting.

As delegates debated the new constitution, a group of pro-apartheid whites stood up and sang the country's soon-to-be-replaced national anthem. But the atmosphere inside the chamber was generally restrained as the members effectively voted the white-dominated parliament out of existence.

Many Conservatives Bitter

But this troubled land is still riven by fierce racial, ethnic and regional divisions, and the enactment of the constitution stirred feelings of bitterness among many conservative South Africans.

Two days of talks here between the Government and the African National Congress on one side, and the Freedom Alliance on the other, failed to resolve their differences, most of which hinge on questions of self-determination and regional autonomy.

At a news conference this morning, Ferdi Hartzenberg of the pro-apartheid Conservative Party vowed to wage a "liberation struggle" if demands for an autonomous white homeland were not met. He told journalists that he was convinced such a struggle would succeed.

"The fact that the Afrikaner nation, the Zulu nation and the Tswana nation are not accommodated means there is not a solution at this stage," he said. Afrikaners are descendants of the early Dutch settlers, while Zulus and Tswanas are two of the country's major black groups.

'A Political Grave'

But Cyril Ramaphosa, the secretary general of the African National Congress, said any leader who failed to participate in the electoral process would be "digging a political grave for himself."

Moreover, President F. W. de Klerk has said he is willing to use force if necessary to prevent the holdouts from disrupting elections.

Proponents of the constitution tried to put the best face on the vote today. "Now, for the first time, the future holds the promise of a better tomorrow," said Nelson Mandela, the congress leader, who also noted that this would be the last Christmas under white rule in South Africa.

Next year, he added, must "be the year in which all South Africans, regardless of race, creed or gender, must take hands and work together to bring an end to the terrible violence that is tearing our country apart," he said in a statement. Mr. Mandela was en route to a Christmas vacation in the Bahamas.

Mr. de Klerk said today's parliamentary session, which may be the last under white rule, should not be grieved over.

No 'Legitimacy Problem'

"It is not the end, but a new beginning," he said. There would be another Parliament, "but this time a Parliament without a legitimacy problem."

The vote today effectively ended years of negotiations that began in Mr. Mandela's jail cell during his three decades of imprisonment for attempting to overthrow apartheid. Over the last two years the negotiating process has become a grueling political struggle involving up to 26 political parties and Government bodies.

Much of that effort was directed at creating a formula that would calm whites who fear for their safety and property under a black government without giving minorities the power to paralyze democracy.

The result was a nearly 200-page constitution that will serve as South Africa's supreme law until an elected assembly can write a permanent version. It promises minority parties seats in a 27-member Cabinet for the first five years, and accepts the notion of protecting the jobs and pensions of white soldiers and civil servants. It is backed up by a long list of "fundamental rights" with a powerful constitutional court.

The architects of apartheid created 10 tribal homelands, which are almost wholly dependent on handouts from South Africa. Four of the homelands were persuaded to accept independence, a status unrecognized by an country except South Africa, while the remainder are described as self-governing.

Threats from the right cast a shadow of uncertainty.

Some of the homeland leaders now insist that South Africa has no authority to take back the independence it gave them. And they have been joined in their opposition to the new constitution by pro-apartheid whites who are fiercely opposed to majority rule.

Whites in the Freedom Alliance insist they will only feel secure if they attain an autonomous homeland, while blacks like Chief Buthelezi want to preserve an array of powers given them under the apartheid system. Chief Buthelezi, chief minister of the KwaZulu homeland, is also its Minister of Police, a role that gives him command of a force that critics call a private army. He also acts as Minister of Finance, which allows him to dispense patronage among a wide network of influential chiefs.

A United South Africa

But the architects of the new constitution firmly rejected the idea of splitting the country into sovereign, ethnically based homelands, saying that would amount to another version of apartheid. Thus, the homelands are to disappear when the new constitution takes effect, immediately after elections in April.

The next opportunity to resolve these differences will come early next year. The Government and the African National Congress have held out the possibility that the constitution could be amended if their foes agree to recognize its legitimacy and participate in the nonracial elections, which are set for April 27. If they agree to take part, another parliamentary session could be called.

Rowan Cronje, the chairman of the Freedom Alliance, voiced disappointment that agreement could not be reached before parliament voted on the constitution, but he said an "open door had been made possible" that could allow the alliance to achieve its demands.

But although Government and African National Congress negotiators expressed satisfaction that the process had not broken down completely, they privately hold out little hope that the conservative groups will be persuaded to participate in the elections.

Fierce Factional Battles

That prospect worries South Africans who have already endured a reign of terror during the last decade. More than 13,000 people have died in political violence, much of it linked to rivalries between supporters of the African National Congress and Inkatha or vigilantes operating outside the direct control of the political organizations. Some evidence has also indicated that the security forces have aided pro-Inkatha militants in clashes with congress supporters.

Much of the country is awash in weapons. Many of the guns were supplied years ago by South Africa to anti-Communist rebels in Mozambique and are now flowing back across the border. Others are said to spill from the caches stowed by the African National Congress when it suspended its guerrilla war against apartheid.

If the dissidents boycott the elections, the potential for continuing violent disruption is enormous. Some political experts here fear that such violence could give South Africa's powerful military and security forces a ready pretext for a takeover.

In China, Communist Ideology Is Dead, but Party Shell Lives On

Chinese see party as only assurance of public order and rising prosperity

Sheila Tefft

Staff writer of The Christian Science Monitor

BEIJING

Ideologically, the former newspaper editor admits, communism in China is dead. But the party lives on, he says, not because Chinese like the aging Communist leadership, but because there is no substitute.

"China is culturally different from the Soviet Union and Eastern Europe. Even though the beliefs are gone, the shell is still there, because no one is willing to take the lead in damaging the shell," says the editor, who lost his job for supporting political protests in 1989. "No one will touch the shell because it is already empty. It will collapse by itself."

In today's China, Marxism-Leninism may be passé. But no one is betting on an imminent demise of the ideologically bankrupt Communist Party.

Despite economic liberalization, which has opened China to foreign investment and trade and undermined the command economy, the party continues to attract membership among young and old, according to official reports.

In 1992, membership rose almost 5 percent to 52 million members as applications, largely from the rural peasantry rather than urbanites, have jumped sharply in the past two years. Despite years of political oppression under the Communists, Chinese still regard the party as the only source of public order and, in recent years, of prosperity, international stature, and peace.

Chinese analysts say that many people worry about a possible cutoff of economic reforms, which have dramatically raised living standards, and are uneasy about the imminent leadership transition that will follow the death of ailing supreme leader Deng Xiaoping.

Although many Chinese resent Mr. Deng and the ruling Communists for the brutal suppression of pro-democracy protests four years ago, they view the party as the only force able to shepherd the country in its transition to capitalism.

For the time being, the party also remains in control of patronage and advancement in China's vast welfare state, which many Chinese workers are afraid to jettison for the uncertainties of the marketplace.

"Despite all the propaganda about the market economy, the government still retains a lot of control over people's lives. And, conditioned all these years in the ways of the command economy, many people don't

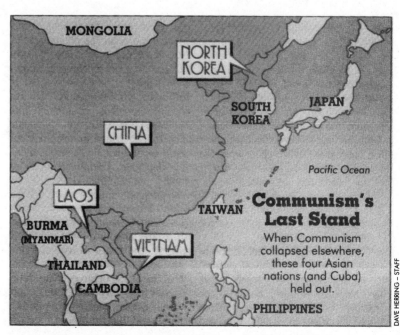

Communism's Last Stand

When Communism collapsed elsewhere, these four Asian nations (and Cuba) held out.

DAVE HERRING – STAFF

want to give it up," says a Western diplomat in Beijing.

"I don't like Deng, but I hope he lives as long as possible to give the reform and opening to the outside world more time to take root," says a university business professor in Beijing.

Although authoritarianism seems entrenched for now, Chinese analysts say, that hardly means that all is well for China's leaders. Pushing the limits of their autonomy, regional leaders have balked at central government efforts to rein in speculative loans and real estate developments and central attempts to collect more tax revenues from provinces and localities.

The party also grapples with a wave of corruption that is unprecedented in more than four decades of rule and erodes its once widespread grass-roots support.

In August, President and Party General Secretary Jiang Zemin declared war on corruption, setting off a national investigation and crackdown on corrupt local leaders and a series of executions. Of late, though, under pressure from influential provincial leaders whose support is crucial to the center, Beijing has backed off in its crusade, Western diplomats say.

Ultimately, party leaders will have to face the potentially explosive issue of how to handle the legacy of the Tiananmen Square crackdown on June 4, 1989, when hundreds of Chinese were massacred on the streets of Beijing.

One signal of a party shift over Tiananmen could come with a decision on the future of Prime Minister Li Peng, who was sidelined with a heart attack this year.

"The only reason Li Peng stays is because he is regarded as a symbol and had a direct hand in June 4. If he is removed, people will know that the party is addressing the issue of June 4. And that will set off a chain reaction," a Chinese political observer says.

"Though nobody will openly acknowledge it, what is practiced in China today is not socialism but capitalism. Regardless of whether it is Deng himself, his enemies, people who
benefit from the reforms, or those who are hurt by them, everyone knows this. Deng's
opponents may raise the 'anti-capitalist' banner after he dies, but it is already too late."

The Long March from Mao: China's De-Communization

LIU BINYAN

LIU BINYAN *served as a special correspondent for the Chinese
Communist party newspaper* Renmin ribao *from 1979 to 1987.
While at the paper Liu became well known for his investigative
reporting on corruption in the party. He was expelled from the
party in 1987. He is presently serving as chairman of the executive committee of the Princeton China Initiative. A collection of
his essays has been published as* China's Crisis, China's Hope
*(Cambridge: Harvard University Press, 1990). This article was
translated from the Chinese by David M. Kamen.*

Since 1989, Communist regimes in Eastern Europe
and the Soviet Union have collapsed one by one,
leaving only China with an apparently flourishing
Communist government. China's Communists have not
only managed to remain in power, but have even induced rapid economic growth while maintaining relative social stability during the last few years. How has
this been possible? And what is the future of the party,
and the China that it rules?

THE ROOTS OF AMBIVALENCE

The Chinese Communists (and their Vietnamese
counterparts as well) are unique among the world's governing Communist parties in that they came to power
only after more than 20 years of bitter fighting. The honesty and high moral standards displayed by the Chinese
Communists for their first few years in power starkly
contrasted with the darkness and corruption of pre-1949
Kuomintang rule—so much so that all the nearly un-
bearable problems that had plagued China for so long
seemed obliterated overnight. For the Chinese people,
the Communists and Mao Zedong became not only
great liberators, but the very embodiments of truth, justice, and morality.

The absolute authority and public trust the Communist party enjoyed during the 1950s and 1960s made almost all Chinese eager to join. The best people from

every level of society, from the intelligentsia to the workers, became party members and cadres. Even though in
following Mao they may have made numerous mistakes
(which they have come to regret), many of them had the
people's welfare at heart as they waged successive ideological struggles against "erroneous" political lines; large
numbers even suffered Mao's ruthless persecution.
When Deng Xiaoping rehabilitated the victims of previous upheavals in 1979, the former party members who
regained their political rights numbered in the hundreds
of thousands; quite a few resumed leadership duties.

Many middle-aged and older Chinese still remember
the Communists' outstanding record of political accomplishments between 1949 and 1956. This is largely due
to the fact that even after Mao had led the Chinese people into disasters, many party members and cadres
stayed true to their ideals and stood with the people in
an attempt to mitigate these disasters, or worked to oppose the bad cadres in the party.

This explains why the Chinese frequently view the
party with a split perspective. People will occasionally
complain, for example, that local magistrate so-and-so
(usually a party member) is "very bad and ought to be
shot, but the local party secretary is a good person; we
like him." Even during the upheavals of 1988 and 1989,
when people reviled the party from all sides, they would
never have condoned a slogan such as "Down with the
Communist party!"

Much about the Chinese Communists would be
unimaginable in other countries. In its first three
decades of rule, the party had no need for a state-secu-
rity organization like the KGB. During the famine of
1959–1961, which Mao engineered, at least 40 million
people died, but there was no rebellion. Far from abandoning the party after it launched the decade-long disaster known as the "Great Proletarian Cultural
Revolution," the people actually pinned their hopes on
Deng Xiaoping and his clique. Even after Deng decided
to unleash an unprecedented massacre in the capital in

1989, the people continued to tolerate the Communist regime.

Compared to their former Soviet counterparts, Chinese Communists are less rigid and dogmatic, and are more interested in obtaining practical results. In pursuing a major goal, they are likely to be more flexible on side issues, and at times even willing to make major concessions or accept faits accomplis that they dislike. People at all levels of the party hierarchy thus often get away with merely feigning obedience to their superiors.

This flexibility extends to China's political mechanisms, which are also slightly more pliant than were those of the Soviet Union. As a result, Deng's policy of "holding fast to the Four Basic Principles" (which are hardly distinguishable from Maoism) can co-exist with his policy of economic liberalization.* This is the basis for the way Deng Xiaoping and the Chinese people in general behave in society: there are things one can do but not talk about, others one merely talks about but does not actually do. Deng has launched campaigns against "bourgeois liberalization" on four separate occasions, yet the freedom enjoyed by the Chinese people continues to grow.

Depending on their temperament and attitudes, the actions Chinese leaders take in the regions or departments they are in charge of may depart from the limitations imposed by the system. For example, a few months after Mao launched an intensive nationwide campaign of agricultural collectivization in 1956, the secretary of a county party committee in Zhejiang province dared to propose a plan for setting farm-output quotas on the basis, not of cooperatives, but individual households (*baochan dao hu*); his superior, the secretary of the provincial party committee, actually implemented it temporarily on a trial basis. (Deng himself dared not fully authorize this system until 1979.)

Similar situations became even more common after the Cultural Revolution. The chaos of that period had brought party activities to a halt for as long as five years; almost all party cadres were stripped of their positions, deprived of their rights, and subjected to ruthless ideological denunciations (which often included physical humiliation and torture). As a result, the will and morale of the Chinese Communist party, previously known for its "iron discipline," were enormously damaged. Different political factions arose within the party, and corruption among party cadres grew significantly, all of which had a devastating impact on the political and economic system in the aftermath of the Cultural Revolution. Considerable liberalization had taken place within the party even before Deng launched his reforms in 1979, which is why there was less resistance within the party to reforms than there was from within the Soviet Communist party to reforms in the Soviet system.

These distinctive aspects of Chinese political practice are among the reasons why China's Communists have found their way out of their crises and avoided a total collapse of the system. Since the introduction of economic reforms, the trend toward the localization of political authority has greatly intensified; local leading cadres can respond to a political crisis by making more independent decisions (which include some concessions to popular demands), thus enhancing local stability and lessening the impact of the crisis. While the overall system remains unchanged, each province and district will gradually become more politically, economically, and culturally diversified.

All this is evidence of a unique and fascinating phenomenon now taking place in China. Though nobody will openly acknowledge it, what is practiced in China today is not socialism but capitalism. Regardless of whether it is Deng himself, his enemies, people who benefit from the reforms, or those who are hurt by them, everyone knows this. Deng's opponents may raise the "anti-capitalist" banner after he dies, but it is already too late.

A CYCLE OF CORRUPTION

From the very beginning of his economic reform effort, Deng faced a host of problems. The reforms did raise the people's standard of living; 800 million peasants were released from semi-serf status as the era of "People's Communes" ended, greatly alleviating popular dissatisfaction with the Communists. But economic liberalization brought with it demands for ideological and political liberalization; Deng's repeated campaigns against "bourgeois liberalization" and his refusal to let the people promote social reform stirred popular discontent and resistance.

The economic reforms and China's opening to the outside during the 1980s gave party officials greater opportunity to abuse their power; resistance to reforms from within the party decreased as a result. But party corruption also gave rise to popular demands for political reform and the introduction of the rule of law, which Deng and his clique had no intention of carrying out.

As the economic reforms progressed, they revealed abuses in the political system ever more clearly. Political reform would necessarily present a threat to the vested interests of the bureaucracy. As the representative of that group, Deng had already shown by the mid-1980s that he had no interest in pursuing even the most elementary political reforms; without political reforms to improve government efficiency and credibility (and stem official corruption), his economic reforms were inevitably weakened and compromised.

All this culminated in the Tiananmen movement of 1989.

Deng resorted to military force to suppress the pro-

*Editor's note: The "Four Basic Principles" to be upheld are: the socialist road; the dictatorship of the proletariat; Communist party leadership; and the leading role of "Marxism-Leninism-Mao Zedong thought."

democracy movement in Tiananmen Square in order to preserve the Chinese Communist regime. The June 4 massacre and the massive purge that followed badly hurt the forces of democracy, but Deng's own power and prestige, the reforms he had promoted, and the regime itself were also grievously wounded.

In the four years since 1989, the reform process of the previous decade has been almost completely repeated, only faster and more intensely. In many ways China has come full circle, and has returned to the conditions prevailing on the eve of the 1989 pro-democracy movement.

Corruption among party officials is now much more serious. In 1990, cases of bribery and graft were double what they were in 1989, and these abuses of power have become open and systematic (in the routine operations of party and government organs, fixed prices have been set for various categories of bribes). Cadres at various levels, their children, and people with powerful connections are recklessly plundering the nation's wealth and resources, becoming millionaires or billionaires through trading in stocks or real estate.

China's economy has certainly undergone rapid growth, mainly in the coastal regions, but at a heavy cost. Income gaps have widened alarmingly between the urban rich and poor, between the cities and the countryside, and between coastal and inland regions. In particular, the declining incomes and increasing burdens (including exorbitant taxes, forced contributions, and fines or other forms of punishment) afflicting several hundred million peasants are causing a growing number to resort to violence, which frightens the party Central Committee out of its wits. At the same time, tens of millions of workers at state-run enterprises are facing the threat of unemployment as state-owned enterprises become increasingly uncompetitive and economically irrelevant.

In order to pander to Deng's decrees and in the desire for private gain, bureaucrats throughout China have blindly increased investments without considering the economic impact; at the same time, most state-run enterprises continue to operate at a loss. The result has been a skyrocketing fiscal deficit and the printing of far more money in far greater quantities than planned. Inflation has reached a new peak; many urban residents are panic-buying goods and materials, and a large number of local banks have been forced to suspend operations because of runs on their deposits. These conditions are almost identical to those in 1988—especially the high inflation, which was a direct cause of the 1989 Tiananmen movement.

China has once again reached a crossroads.

A FIFTH ASIAN TIGER?

A peaceful and gradual transition to democracy is still possible in China, and this is what the majority of Chinese hope for. But the death of Deng Xiaoping (generally expected in the next year or two) may remove a major source of China's stability while simultaneously stirring up other forces of destabilization. In 1992, Deng stripped General Yang Shangkun and his half brother Yang Baibing of their influential positions on the party's Central Military Commission, and carried out the most extensive purge of the armed forces since 1949; the resultant dissatisfaction in the military could lead to real problems after Deng's death.

A full-scale civil war does not appear likely. Regional differences in development and local conditions mean that change in China will take place differently in each province and region. Prospects for peaceful change are better in the coastal areas, while varying degrees of disorder appear inevitable in inland areas. In fact, two rebellious outbreaks at the county-seat level have already occurred this year; one, in Sichuan province, involved an estimated 10,000 disgruntled farmers, who stoned members of the People's Armed Police.

It is an illusion to think that China can become another Singapore or Taiwan by relying solely on economic growth without political reform and democratization. Those who cling to this illusion ignore two important facts about China:

First, mainland Chinese are different from Chinese living outside the country; more than 40 years of Communist rule have cut them off from Chinese cultural traditions. Mao successfully wiped out the sources of authority that traditionally maintained stability in China and replaced them with the party as the sole authority; that sole authority has now vanished as well. Today the only sources of authority in the minds of the mainland Chinese are their own personal instincts and desires.

At the same time, the Chinese Communists also wiped out social morality and religion, destroyed education, and left the law so compromised that it no longer commands respect. Thus there are neither internal nor external restrictions on the people's behavior. The corruption of party and government officials is driving the corruption of the entire society.

For more than 40 years, Mao pushed the Chinese people toward awakening through actions aimed at creating the opposite effect. Twice he pushed them into hopeless impasses (the 1959–1961 famine and the Cultural Revolution). He stripped them of their freedoms, stifled their hopes, and gave them no choice but to become the party's "docile tools." But precisely because he did his job only too well, the Chinese people have finally awakened from their sleep of several thousand years and realize that they are human beings with a right to defend their individual freedoms and interests and to strive for their individual development. Deng's reforms have further loosened the bonds imposed on the individual.

This is why Chinese society now has such abundant energy, though this energy can be a constructive force or a frighteningly destructive one. The people no longer abjectly obey anyone who tramples on them, which is an enormous and historic step forward. Some Chinese officials complain that the Chinese have become "people of cunning and violence"; this makes a certain amount of sense, in that the people are much smarter now, and much braver. Such Chinese would never accept the kind of autocratic leadership practiced by Singapore's Prime Minister Lee Kuan Yew, nor would they submit to Singapore's coercive social system.

The second major factor that must be kept in mind about China is that Taiwan, Singapore, and Hong Kong do not have anything remotely comparable to mainland China's enormous Communist bureaucracy and its total monopoly on the nation's economy and resources. The Communists' rapaciousness and unrestricted political power, combined with the mutual protection provided by networks of personal connections throughout this bureaucracy, result in criminal behavior that generally goes unpunished.

WHAT CHINA NEEDS

That the Chinese people have tolerated the rule of a bureaucratic clique since 1989 is partly due to the enormous political pressure it exerts, and partly to the improvements in the people's material well-being during this period. In addition, despite the lack of political freedom, the regime does not generally interfere in people's private lives; in the economic and cultural spheres at least, the scope of individual "liberty" has expanded. In contrast to Mao, Deng has allowed people's lives to become a bit richer, and has also permitted them to be a little happier. A capable person in China now has a much broader range of choices in terms of lifestyles and future prospects. Finally, the social and economic chaos that have followed the Soviet Union's and Eastern Europe's revolutions have led the Chinese to cherish their current stability. Indeed, stability has become Deng's trump card, a card that he uses to intimidate the Chinese people: "If my regime ever falls, China will inevitably fall into chaos and civil war!"

But this impasse is of the Communists' own making. They do not permit an alternative political force to exist legally, or even let people organize themselves for nonpolitical goals; yet their own regime has become so corrupt and incompetent that it cannot even perform the most basic administrative functions.

It will not be long before the people of China see the awful crisis this sort of "stability" is creating for their future. Since 1989 the regime's social control has gradually slackened, which could allow more room for civil society to function for the people's benefit. For the moment, the regime's information blockade prevents people from learning about the struggles carried on elsewhere in China, or gaining an adequate understanding of the regime's current difficulties; they thus have insufficient confidence in their own power to effect change.

But the inevitable power struggles at the top after Deng dies, combined with social disruption brought on by economic crises, will soon force China's intellectuals and the talented people scattered throughout society to realize that they must mobilize themselves, throw off the restrictions imposed by the regime, and organize the people by legal means (based on the civil rights granted to them in China's constitution). This will be necessary in order to defend the rights and interests of the people, satisfy their needs, and protect their personal security and property. The people will have to take over many of the functions that the regime is presently incapable of handling.

This will be a movement by the Chinese people to govern, protect, and save themselves. It is also the only way to re-kindle the people's love for their nation and native land, and change the antisocial psychology and behavior that now results in people venting their hatred of the regime on society at large. (One of the most disastrous consequences of the Communists' total control of China's society and people has been that many Chinese now think of their own country as something belonging to the Communists, and that they themselves have no connection to it.) Moreover, a mass self-salvation movement of this kind would gradually teach the Chinese how to live democratically.

A desirable path such as this would allow China to avoid chaos and would transform the Chinese, not into a "cunning and violent" people, but into a constructive force made up of responsible citizens.

"[India's] most significant achievement since independence has been to demonstrate that democracy can survive in a poverty-stricken nation," says Sumit Ganguly. But "[n]ot since the sanguinary days of independence and the 1947 partition that created Pakistan has Indian society been so polarized."

India: Charting a New Course?

SUMIT GANGULY

SUMIT GANGULY, *a professor of political science at Hunter College and the Graduate Center of the City University of New York, is a fellow at the Woodrow Wilson International Center for Scholars in Washington during 1993–1994. A grant from the United States Institute of Peace provided research support for this article. The author is grateful to Rajan Menon and Andrew Polsky for their comments on an earlier draft.*

The specter of irrelevance in the emerging world order haunts the Indian state. Mainly because of flawed and short-sighted policies, the country is besieged by a legion of problems, none of them easily solved. With the end of the cold war, many of the familiar moorings of India's foreign policy have been sundered. The nation finds itself adrift. If India is to play a role commensurate with its size and economic potential, its leaders will have to demonstrate considerable dexterity in tackling the new challenges on the domestic front and abroad. Failure to do so may well result in India's permanent relegation to the status of a crippled giant.

SECULARISM AND ITS DISCONTENTS

Not since the sanguinary days of independence and the 1947 partition that created Pakistan has Indian society been so polarized. The emergent division along religious lines poses an extremely significant challenge to the secularism on which the modern Indian state was founded.

Relations between the dominant Hindu community, which makes up nearly 80 percent of the population, and the largest minority group, the Muslims, who make up more than 11 percent, are arguably at their lowest ebb in the post-independence era. Hindu-Muslim animosity is not simply a function of "ancient hatreds" with deep atavistic roots, nor is it a purely

"modern hate."[1] Relations between the two communities have oscillated over the centuries between harmony and unremitting conflict. Harmonious periods have given rise to syncretistic movements such as Sufism. Religious fanaticism—as during the rule of the Muslim Mughal Emperor Aurangzeb, for example— has bred outright oppression and violent iconoclasm. The recent recrudescence of Hindu-Muslim violence stems from the attempts of various political parties, the right-wing Hindu revivalist Bharatiya Janata party (BJP) in particular, to exploit the historical record for short-term political ends.

Why is religious affiliation, a specific facet of ethnic identity, suddenly coming to the fore in India? Oddly enough, it can be argued that the spate of violence is an indicator of the success of Indian democracy. Because of the continued if fitful extension of the franchise, long-quiescent minorities are beginning to demand and claim their rightful privileges in society. The expansion of educational and employment opportunities through "positive discrimination" (affirmative action) programs has significantly improved the lot of segments of minority communities. The increased assertiveness and the slowly improving socioeconomic status of minorities have sown misgivings among many in India's dominant group. More than any other party, the BJP has sought to play on the fears and anxieties these developments have aroused among the Hindu majority, whipping up communal hatred and fomenting bloody conflict.

Party ideologues have deftly directed their ire against some of the real and perceived shortcomings of Indian

---

[1] The term comes from Suzanne Hoeber Rudolph and Lloyd Rudolph, "Modern Hate," *The New Republic*, March 22, 1993, pp. 24–29.

secularism—which the BJP calls pseudosecularism. It points to the example of the government's handling of the Shah Bano case. In 1986 the Indian Supreme Court upheld a lower court that had directed that alimony be paid to a divorced, indigent Muslim woman, Shah Bano. The ruling contravened Muslim personal law (Shariah), which does not require the payment of alimony. Faced with an outcry from the more conservative Muslim clergy and some Muslim politicians, the governing Congress party of Prime Minister Rajiv Gandhi overturned the Supreme Court decision through an act of parliament. Gandhi's energy minister, Arif Mohammed Khan, a Muslim, resigned in protest, charging the party with focusing on the political arithmetic of the conservative Muslim vote.

More recently, the abject failure of the government under Prime Minister P. V. Narasimha Rao to prevent the destruction of the Babri Masjid, a fourteenth-century mosque in the town of Ayodhya in the northern state of Uttar Pradesh, demonstrated the erosion of the state's commitment to the secular ideal. On December 6, 1992, members of two of the BJP's more militant associates, the grass-roots groups Vishwa Hindu Parishad and Rashtriya Swayam Sevaks, attacked and destroyed the mosque (which had long been in a state of desuetude). The ostensible reason for the attack was that the mosque had been built on the ruins of an ancient temple that consecrated the putative birthplace of Lord Rama, one of the principal gods of the Hindu pantheon; according to BJP ideologues, the mosque had been constructed after the wanton destruction of the temple during Muslim rule.

Nothing can exculpate the BJP for allowing its associates to call for the mosque's demolition, which inspired militant Hindus to destroy it, but the political background of the conflict must be understood. The site has been a source of contention throughout the twentieth century. In December 1949, Hindu activists broke into the mosque and placed two icons of Lord Rama inside. Excited by the notion that Lord Rama had returned to his birthplace, crowds began flocking to the area. The local authorities, whose sympathies lay with the activists, refused to remove the icons, despite explicit instructions from Uttar Pradesh government officials. Both Hindu and Muslim groups then filed suit to obtain rights of worship at the shrine.

The inordinately slow pace of the Indian judicial system, coupled with the intractable character of the dispute, bottled up the problem for well over 30 years. In 1984, however, the Vishwa Hindu Parishad revived the issue when it organized a procession to Ayodhya. It is widely held that Congress party stalwart Arun Nehru, in an attempt to undercut the BJP, put pressure on a local judge to open the site to public worship. When this was done in February 1986, sectarian rioting ensued. At this point the Vishwa Hindu Parishad openly called for the destruction of the mosque.

The Babri Masjid Action Committee, an organization of Muslim politicians and activists, responded by demanding the removal of the icons and the opening of the mosque for prayers. Blatantly courting the Hindu vote, Gandhi hinted during the 1989 election campaign that he was sympathetic to the militant Hindus' case. The stage was set for a confrontation that culminated in the events in Ayodhya and subsequent Hindu-Muslim violence in other Indian cities early last December. At least 1,200 people were killed and 4,000 wounded—most of them Muslims.

What Myron Weiner in his 1962 book on India called "the politics of scarcity" has also enabled Bharatiya Janata to broaden its political base. Economic modernization in the country has created more opportunities and resulted in increased social mobility. But this expansion has not been commensurate with growing demands for political participation and economic advancement; indeed, India's institutional capacity for dealing with these demands has been stretched to the breaking point. Consequently the BJP once again has been able to channel the frustrations of the Hindu population, now highly politically mobilized, against the "pampering" of minorities who allegedly have benefited disproportionately from the government's largess.

The rise of a group like Bharatiya Janata that proclaims an antisecularist manifesto is not a uniquely Indian phenomenon. In recent years what appears to be a global challenge to the secular state has emerged. The resurgence of ethnoreligious sentiment has gone against the expectations of both Marxian and Weberian social science, which had contended that the forces of modernization would efface ethnic identities. If anything, the reverse now appears to be the case—far from erasing ethnic differences, the dislocating effects of modernization seem to reinforce them. Anxious lest they lose their identity and become subsumed in the homogenized masses, members of ethnic groups often come together and seek to establish ethnic solidarity as a source of solace and belonging.

THE KASHMIR CONUNDRUM

The Bharatiya Janata party's antisecularist ideology has made it even more difficult for Prime Minister Rao's weak and ineffectual government to come to grips with a number of compelling problems facing the Indian state. One of the most intractable of these is the ethnically based insurgency in the Muslim-dominated Kashmir Valley in the northwestern state of Jammu and Kashmir. Despite applying considerable force over the past four years, the Indian government has not been able to quell the rebellion.

A range of insurgent groups currently operate in the province, covering an ideological spectrum from the fundamentalist Hizb-ul-Mujahideen, which wants union with Pakistan, to the notionally secular Jammu and

Kashmir Liberation Front, which favors independence, to militants who would be happy with a modicum of autonomy for the province. The insurgency has no central command, and the various militant groups are sometimes at cross purposes. It is widely believed that the Hizb-ul-Mujahideen has received substantial material support from both official and private sources in Pakistan. Recent press reports in India suggest that a sizable number of Afghan mujahideen have also joined the insurgents. All the militant groups are well armed and enjoy varying degrees of support from the local population.

The government estimates the total number of deaths in Kashmir since the beginning of the insurgency at around 6,000; private sources put the figure at somewhere between 7,500 and 10,000 dead. The harsh counterinsurgency tactics employed until recently by paramilitary forces operating under the Home Ministry—including wanton killings, deaths of detainees in custody, and the occasional use of torture—have further alienated ordinary Kashmiris (although the government has now replaced paramilitary units with two regular army battalions and has taken steps to punish those engaged in rampant violations of human rights in Kashmir).

An examination of the origins and evolution of the insurgency provides considerable insight into the decline of political institutions in India in the face of widespread political mobilization. Kashmir's special status is enshrined in Article 370 of the Indian constitution. Among its many provisions, the article prohibits non-Kashmiris from purchasing immovable property in the state—with the obvious purpose of preventing non-Muslims from migrating to and permanently settling in Kashmir, thereby altering its demographic composition (Muslims form the majority population). Throughout a succession of governments in New Delhi, this central provision of Article 370 has been kept intact. However, unlike the rest of India, where most elections, whether state or national, have been largely free and fair, a number of national governments have engaged in electoral fraud and abuse in Kashmir. Political skulduggery has marked virtually every election in the state, made possible by the political quiescence of several generations of Kashmiris. But by the late 1980s a new generation had emerged in Kashmir—one that had benefited from increased education and greater exposure to the media and thus was far more politically aware.[2] Specific circumstances dovetailed with this general background to give rise to the insurgency.

[2]For an extended discussion of Kashmir's special status and its integration into the Indian Union, see Sumit Ganguly, *The Origins of War in South Asia: The Indo-Pakistani Conflicts since 1947* (Boulder, Colo.: Westview, 1993). On electoral irregularities, see Ganguly, "Avoiding War in Kashmir," *Foreign Affairs,* vol. 89 no. 5 (Winter 1990–1991).

The politics of Kashmir gave rise to the forces that finally opened the swelling reservoir of discontent. The Kashmir National Conference has dominated the political scene since 1947. Sheik Mohammed Abdullah, the party's founder, was incarcerated several times after exciting the wrath of the central government. In 1975 Prime Minister Indira Gandhi reinstated him as chief minister of the state in return for a series of political compromises. In 1982 Abdullah passed on his mantle to his son, Faroukh Abdullah, a political neophyte who had been a practicing physician in Britain. The son not only lacked his father's stature and political instincts but was also perceived as venal and incompetent. In 1984 Rajiv Gandhi's government dismissed Faroukh Abdullah's government on grounds of mismanagement and corruption. There may well have been ample evidence of both, but given the low standard of probity the central government had long tolerated in Kashmir, such failings could hardly be deemed exceptional. Two years later the same national government decided to forge an alliance of convenience with the deposed leader and recall him to office. This had the effect of reducing Faroukh Abdullah to a mere stalking-horse for the Congress party in Kashmir.

Both the dismissal and the reinstatement had an alienating effect on the new generation of Kashmiris. They correctly deduced that the Congress party government in New Delhi had little or no regard for democratic procedures and niceties when it came to its attempt to obtain a toehold in the state's politics. But despite the Indian government's rank opportunism, the mounting sense of injustice in Kashmir might never have taken a violent turn had it not been for the 1987 elections. During this state-level contest, the Congress party, in concert with the Kashmir National Conference, systematically engaged in widespread electoral abuses, mainly to keep the opposition Muslim United Front from obtaining a substantial share of the vote. With the last avenue for the expression of political discontent effectively blocked, significant numbers of young Kashmiris turned to violence.

Apologists for the Indian government are at pains to point out that the insurgency would not have started up without Pakistani interference. Pakistan's role in aiding and abetting the insurgency is undeniable, but the Congress party government's actions encouraged external involvement. After all, between 1972 and 1989 separatist sentiment in Kashmir lay completely dormant, and no amount of Pakistani instigation shook Kashmiri loyalty to the Indian state.

The situation in Kashmir continues to simmer. For much of 1993 internal government squabbling has limited the ability of national policymakers to formulate a coherent strategy to deal with the conflict. Union Home Minister S. B. Chavan (who is in charge of maintaining domestic order and overseeing police, paramilitary forces, and prisons, among other things), has been at odds with the minister for internal security, Rajesh Pilot; though unable to conceive of any alternative course, Chavan has resented the junior minister's attempts to start a political dialogue with some of the militant groups. In September an Indian government initiative to rekindle the political process in Kashmir sent a group of prominent journalists, senior retired army officers, and administrators to the state to assess the people's grievances and discuss the possibility of a political dialogue with the insurgents, but the outcome is still extremely problematic. With divided counsel at the highest quarters, bureaucrats in the Home Ministry in New Delhi and in Srinagar, the capital of Kashmir, have been given little useful guidance. The status quo prevails, with its heavy reliance on various paramilitary forces and the Indian army to maintain a semblance of civil order.

Bharatiya Janata's intransigence has also made the government less willing to take bold steps—such as declaring an amnesty for the insurgents in preparation for meaningful negotiations on Kashmir. It is to the government's credit that it has steadfastly refused to acquiesce to the BJP's repeated demand that it revoke Article 370.

Finally, the present minority government desperately wants to ensure its own survival, and a great deal of political capital and energy are being consumed to that end. In late July the government narrowly survived a no-confidence vote in parliament. The Communist Party of India gave three main reasons for introducing the motion: the government's willingness to accede to the demands of the World Bank and the International Monetary Fund on economic restructuring, its propensity to consort with sectarian forces, and the "all pervading corruption" in its ranks. The final charge stems largely from the accusations of Harshad Mehta, a Bombay stockbroker who has been indicted in the largest stock market scandal in India's history. Mehta has contended that in 1991 he gave the equivalent of $371,000 to Prime Minister Rao as a form of "political insurance." The government, as might be expected, has denied the allegation and sought to refute it; whether or not the incident actually took place, dealing with the political fallout has proved to be a major distraction.

A COLD WAR WORLD DESTROYED

The Indian government's troubles are not confined to the domestic front. The end of the cold war has left India in a singularly unenviable position. Its long-standing quasi alliance with the Soviet Union has abruptly come to a close; clearly Russia is not impelled by the strategic imperatives that cemented the Indo-Soviet relationship. An array of benefits has been canceled. India can no longer rely on the support of a veto-wielding superpower in the United Nations Security Council on the crucial Kashmir question, and it has

also lost its principal supplier of a panoply of advanced weaponry, and at highly concessionary rates. This has been a blow to the Indian armed forces, since much of their equipment is of Soviet origin. The paucity of spare parts and supplies, coupled with Russian insistence on payment in hard currency and India's tightened budget, has affected battle-readiness as well.

The changed situation has forced India to try to improve relations with China. This project, first undertaken during Rajiv Gandhi's tenure in office, has now taken on new urgency. India's desire for good relations with the People's Republic extends beyond the loss of Soviet protection. The 1962 war with China over the northern Himalayan border was a rout for the Indian military. Today the Indian forces along the Sino-Indian border are better prepared and better equipped than ever before. But India has had to reduce deployments in the Himalayas and assign the troops to various internal security duties, and these commitments are unlikely to diminish markedly in the foreseeable future. Thus maintenance of good relations with China—and the avoidance of border clashes especially—has taken on particular importance. In addition, India has sought to improve relations with the United States and the western European nations, albeit in a fitful and grudging fashion.

A second broad foreign policy consequence of the cold war's end involves the Nonaligned Movement, which India, under the leadership of Prime Minister Jawaharlal Nehru, helped found. With the cold war's demise the movement has lost all meaning. Old habits, however, do tend to die hard. Some Indian proponents of nonalignment are desperately attempting to breathe new life into this now moribund concept. One of their arguments holds that nonalignment ensures a state's ability to maintain an independent stance in the conduct of its foreign policy. This contention is entirely unexceptional, but it can hardly serve as the basis for a multilateral movement. The second position—a more coherent argument—holds that the Nonaligned Movement can become a platform for airing North-South issues, and that India should take a leading role in this enterprise.

Adopting this confrontational role could have disastrous consequences for India. In fact, rarely has there been a more inopportune time for pursuing such a strategy. After years of isolation from the international economic system while in pursuit of an import-substitution strategy for industrialization, India has finally embarked on an attempt to open its economy to foreign investment. To that end it has also sought to dismantle the labyrinthine regulations that have governed labor practices, investment priorities, and the expansion of industrial capacity. Championing North-South causes at a global level would inevitably conflict with India's attempts at economic liberalization internally and externally. India would become identified with rigid positions on such questions as intellectual property rights at the General Agreement on Tariffs and Trade negotiations, which could well have a detrimental effect on foreign investment in India.

TWO GIANTS REGARD EACH OTHER

A hospitable foreign investment climate would enable India to attract significant investment from the United States, India's largest trading partner. A substantial American stake in the Indian market could provide the basis for an expanded relationship between the two countries. The task of forging new ties will not be easy. If deftly managed and freed from the rhetorical excesses of the past, it could yield important benefits to both sides. Failure to do so could lead to yet another round of shattered hopes and bitter recriminations.

As India continues with its colossal economic liberalization program it will need multilateral assistance; American support for "soft financing" from the World Bank and the IMF will remain crucial. The United States also remains India's best possible source for advanced technology in areas such as electronics, genetic engineering, and space research. This argument holds despite the American intervention in July that prevented the Russian space agency Glavcosmos from selling cryogenic engines to the Indian Space Research Organization, a deal that violated the United States–sponsored Missile Control Technology Regime. Further, the United States is the only outside power of any consequence that can play a useful role in resolving the Kashmir dispute.

Currently, there appears to be gradual recognition in New Delhi of the importance of the United States in Indian foreign policy calculations. Several small indicators suggest a willingness to maintain a positive tenor to the relationship despite occasional discordant notes. For example, when the cryogenic rocket engine deal collapsed, New Delhi protested in the mildest possible terms. Also, the United States attack on Iraqi intelligence facilities in July not only elicited no protest from New Delhi but even received a sympathetic response; in the past, India's decisionmakers would have roundly condemned the attack in an expression of third world solidarity.

This is not to suggest that the Indo-American relationship does not have its pitfalls, or that it is currently robust. Differences exist, and the present areas of cooperation are limited. The principal divergence of views centers on the question of nuclear proliferation in South Asia. Despite pressure from the United States, India continues to insist it will not sign the nuclear Non-Proliferation Treaty, which it sees as discriminatory. India's argument is simple. The treaty prohibits countries that do not yet have nuclear weapons from acquiring them, but it places no restric-

tions on the nuclear states. Furthermore, Indian decisionmakers argue that India faces a threat from a nuclear-armed China.

United States nonproliferation policy, which had been fitfully pursued during the 1980s, has acquired renewed vigor at the end of the cold war. American concern about nonproliferation in South Asia stems from the incipient nuclear arms race between India and Pakistan. The United States is sensitive to India's concern about a possible Chinese threat, but concerns about an unrestrained arms race in South Asia continue to animate American policy.

The stated positions of the two sides appear intractable. New Delhi's protestations about the Chinese threat notwithstanding, a quest for great power status is the underlying reason for India's desire for nuclear weapon capability. To pursue the larger goal of nonproliferation, the United States will need to address this; failure to do so will only lead to deadlock on this critical issue. As Stephen Cohen, a specialist on South Asian security, has suggested, one possible option may be to offer India a permanent seat on the UN Security Council. Senior Indian diplomats suggested to this writer last October that such an arrangement might be acceptable.

A second irritant in the relationship proceeds from the human rights situation in India. Faced with increasing pressures from their constituencies, various members of Congress are urging the Clinton administration to take a tougher stand on violations of human rights in India. These pressures are not likely to abate, but unlike with the nonproliferation issue, the Indian government can move with considerable dispatch in addressing this problem. The vast majority of the human rights violations for which India has been criticized constitute blatant infringements of provisions in its own constitution; addressing these lapses calls only for rigorous enforcement of the country's existing laws. Consequently the government can, if it so desires, easily deal with jingoistic sentiment that holds India is bowing to American pressure on the human rights issue.

As the end of the century approaches India stands at a crossroads. Its most significant achievement since independence has been to demonstrate that democracy can survive in a poverty-stricken nation. Three central questions for the future now confront the Indian state. Can it tackle the seemingly endemic problem of poverty through its new strategy of economic liberalization? Is it resilient enough to cope with the recent wave of ethnoreligious assertion and still maintain its secular credentials? And finally, can its institutions for making foreign policy as well as its leadership summon up sufficient skill, imagination, and courage to discard long-held shibboleths and effectively deal with a markedly altered world order?

Miracles beyond the free market

Michael Prowse

The biggest challenge for economists today is understanding the extraordinary success of east Asia. The region has nearly quadrupled per capita incomes in the past quarter of a century—a record unparalleled in economic history. On present trends it may begin to overtake much of the industrialised west early in the 21st century.

If its startling success could be replicated elsewhere, billions of people in developing and formerly communist countries could look forward to improved living standards. And the hope, eventually, of eliminating the scourge of grinding poverty would seem less quixotic.

Yet the region is as puzzling as three-dimensional chess. It has done far better than conventional theories predict, even allowing for such quantifiable pluses as macroeconomic stability, high rates of investment and a focus on exports. There is just no generally accepted explanation for its main distinguishing feature—supercharged rates of productivity growth.

The puzzle is deepened by the region's lack of homogeneity. The high-fliers are far from being carbon copies. At one extreme, Hong Kong has pursued a broadly free market approach; at the other, South Korea has intervened in just about every way conceivable. And the magic formula for growth has entirely eluded some countries in the region, such as the Philippines.

At the World Bank in Washington, an exhaustive analysis of the "Asia miracle" is nearing completion. Bank staff are distilling lessons from Japan, the four "tigers"—South Korea, Taiwan, Hong Kong and Singapore—and the so-called "cubs"— Malaysia, Thailand and Indonesia. They have also taken a look at the recent explosive growth in parts of southern China.

The study was undertaken partly at the instigation of Japan, the bank's second-largest shareholder, which has long wanted to play a bigger role in policy design. Japan has been critical of aspects of conventional World Bank/International Monetary Fund prescriptions and, justifiably, believes more attention should be paid to its own outstandingly successful development strategies—which formed a model for much of east Asia.

In 1991, Japan's Overseas Economic Co-operation Fund told the bank it was putting too much emphasis on deregulation and privatisation and made a case for selective import protection in developing countries and for the use of subsidised credits as a tool in industrial policy.

Mr John Page, a senior member of the bank's Asia miracle team, says the Japanese criticism struck a chord because the results of market-oriented reforms had often proved disappointing in developing economies. By cutting budget deficits, eliminating market distortions and shrinking government, client countries had stabilised their economies. But too often they had not achieved a virtuous cycle of rapid growth; they still lay "at the bottom of the league table relative to east Asia". The question became: "What now?"

The bank's benchmark for judging Asian policies is not an extreme free market philosophy, which would have the public sector shun responsibility for just about everything bar national defence. It is rather the less controversial "market friendly" strategy set out at length in the bank's 1991 World Development Report.

This clearly delineates the role of markets and the state. Development would be fastest, it claimed, when government concentrated on two jobs: maintaining macroeconomic stability through conservative fiscal and monetary policies; and investing in people through public education, training and healthcare programmes.

Beyond this, developing countries should rely on market forces. They should create as competitive as possible a regime in industry, commerce and the financial sector. And they should eliminate all barriers to trade and foreign investment. The core idea is that governments should focus on the things only they can do and leave everything else to markets.

It turns out that most of the Asian high-fliers have adopted a more permissive attitude to the role of government. Indeed, Mr Page argues that the success of the region can best be understood in terms of a "strategic growth" model that focuses more on what has to be done to achieve rapid growth than on who should do what.

On the strategic theory, development will be rapid provided countries find a way of: accumulating capital rapidly; allocating resources efficiently; and catching up technologically.

But there is no presumption that any of these functions should be reserved exclusively for the private sector. The miracle economies appear to have used a mixture of market incentives and state intervention in each of these areas:

• Accumulation. Gross domestic investment averages a startling 37 per cent of GDP in east Asia against an average of 26 per cent in developing countries as a whole. Yet this advantage was not won purely by adhering to the market-friendly approach.

The region has admittedly created a positive climate for business investment by pursuing conservative fiscal and monetary policies—inflation has averaged 9 per cent over the past 30 years, less than half the rate in other developing countries. The public sector has also invested effectively in people (enrollment in primary education far exceeds levels elsewhere, as does attention to vocational education), although it has not spent an atypical proportion of national income on social services.

But most of the Asian high-fliers have also interfered with market mechanisms.

They have limited the personal sector's ability to consume and heavily regulated the financial sector so as to ensure a predictable supply of low-cost capital for industry. Mechanisms for forcibly shifting resources from consumption to investment vary—Japan, South Korea and Taiwan, for example have maintained stringent controls on consumption and housing. The net effect, however, is the same everywhere: an abnormally high rate of savings.

• Efficient allocation of resources. Governments have striven to ensure that the most important market of all—that for labour—is flexible, if not fully competitive. Wages have largely reflected market supply and demand, partly because trade unions have been suppressed. Focusing hard on success in export markets has also imposed crucial competitive discipline and prevented domestic prices for industrial inputs moving far out of line with world markets.

Yet bank research indicates governments have also intervened vigorously. While less protectionist than the third world as a whole, few accepted western free-trade principles. Many have used import controls to protect strategic sectors (for example, quotas in South Korea, high tariffs in Thailand) and showered offsetting subsidies on export industries. At one time or another state-owned industries have played an important role in many of the economies, including South Korea, Taiwan, Indonesia, Singapore and Thailand. Many have not hesitated to direct the supply of credit to particular sectors. Both South Korea and Taiwan provided automatic credit for exporters in the early stages of development.

• Technological catch-up. The lesson again is that remarkable productivity growth only partly reflects market-oriented policies. Singapore, Malaysia, Thailand and, to some degree, Taiwan, have welcomed foreign investment. Early developers such as Japan and South Korea used other devices, such as licences letting them copy foreign technology. But unlike many other developing countries none tried to rely on home-grown technology.

However, all high-fliers intervened selectively to promote particular industries, with varying intensity and success. The process of trying to shift industrial output towards high-valued-added sectors is described by enthusiasts as "getting prices wrong in order to create dynamic comparative advantage".

South Korea provides a wealth of examples of aggressive and successful intervention. The government's most audacious move was perhaps to create from scratch a domestic steel industry despite foreign donor opposition and lack of private-sector enthusiasm. The state-run business went on to become the world's most efficient steel producer.

An internal bank memo sums up South Korea's record: "From the early 1960s, the government carefully planned and orchestrated the country's development. . . . [It] used the financial sector to steer credits to preferred sectors and promoted individual firms to achieve national objectives. . . . [It] socialised risk, created large conglomerates (chaebols), created state enterprises when necessary, and moulded a public-private partnership that rivalled Japan's."

Singapore provides another classic example of directed growth. When private sector companies failed to respond to opportunities identified by bureaucrats, state-owned or controlled groups were often pushed to the fore, the memo says. The bank has documented selective interventions throughout the region, even in supposedly free market Hong Kong.

The Asian example poses a dilemma for bodies such as the IMF and the World Bank, especially in former communist countries. Does it still make sense to advocate a form of "shock therapy"—the doctrine that deregulating and privatising everything as fast as possible is the optimum policy? Or should they recommend east Asia's slower, more interventionist path to economic maturity? It all depends on whether east Asia's deviations from orthodoxy can be replicated.

There are some grounds for caution. Mr Vinod Thomas, the bank's chief economist for east Asia and an architect of the market-friendly strategy, points out that government activism outside east Asia has produced dismal results. A distinction should also be drawn between the earlier "northern tier" of Asian high-fliers—Japan, South Korea and Taiwan—and the later "southern tier" of Malaysia, Thailand and Indonesia.

Until the 1980s, countries such as South Korea were able to promote exports and protect imports without provoking much criticism. But pressure for a more level playing field has since grown intense. Broadly speaking, the southern tier of later developers has pursued more market-oriented policies than the first wave of Asian stars. Industrial interventions have also tended to be less successful. A bank memo describes Malaysia's efforts as "by and large a costly failure" and Thailand's as "largely ineffective".

Less tangible political and cultural factors may also be crucial. Most Asian high-fliers benefited from long periods of stable (if authoritarian) political rule. This encouraged long-term horizons. Public-sector bureaucracies have also tended to be more able and less corrupt than in most other third world countries. Governments were thus unusually well placed to implement development strategies.

Policymakers were also remarkably pragmatic; if a policy did not work it was rapidly dropped. South Korea, for example, went through several phases. It was relatively market-oriented in the early 1960s, became highly interventionist during the "heavy and chemical industries" drive of the 1970s, and then reverted to greater reliance on market forces in the mid-1980s. No region, it seems, has been less weighed down by ideology or more willing to seek advice from abroad.

The bank has only just begun the politically charged process of drawing conclusions from mountains of research papers. But senior officials believe the study may lead to a new paradigm for development in the 1990s. The evidence confirms that the miracle economies did indeed "do things differently". In many instances, "government played a big role, trade was not open and financial markets were repressed", concedes Mr Thomas.

"If we're right," says Mr Page, "the economic policy arsenal has many more weapons than we suspected." Mr Thomas agrees: the lesson from east Asia is that "you need a government guiding hand; you cannot just abdicate development to the private sector". He predicts that the bank will pay more attention to the role of institutions and to the potential for partnerships between the public and private sectors.

The most encouraging aspect of the Asian story, officials say, is that habits and institutions crucial for economic success were created rather than inherited. To raise the social standing of entrepreneurs, for example, South Korea had to overcome its Confucian traditions, which had glorified the scholar-bureaucrat. Singapore raised its savings rate from 1 per cent in 1965 to more than 40 per cent today. The implication is that sufficiently determined governments can work similar miracles in other places.

The causes of the East Asian economic miracle have been the subject of intense debate. Is it the invisible hand of the free market left to itself? Or is it partly because government "technocrats ... did a lot of what neoclassical economists say bureaucrats cannot do well: they picked industries for special promotion, [treating] particular industries at any one time (information, electronics, and biotechnology today, for example) as the natural successors to the bridges and lighthouses of Adam Smith's day—which Smith thought too critical for the general welfare to be left to market forces."

The Visible Hand:
The State and East Asia's Economic Growth

ROBERT WADE

ROBERT WADE is *a fellow of the Institute of Development Studies at the University of Sussex and was recently a visiting professor of politics at MIT. He is the author of* Governing the Market: Economic Theory and the Role of Government in East Asian Industrialization *(Princeton: Princeton University Press, 1990).*

What accounts for East Asia's outstanding economic success?[1] Professional economists and international financial institutions hold that the East Asian economies have succeeded mainly because their governments followed economic policies that did not obstruct the natural growth-inducing processes of capitalist market economies. Governments elsewhere in the developing world have failed to exercise such restraint, and their citizens have paid dearly for it.

This "neoliberal" view emphasizes the importance of East Asia's near free trade regime, undistorted exchange rate, conservative government budgeting, high real interest rates, and free labor market. Hong Kong is the paradigm.

But over the past decade considerable evidence has come in that questions this view. This evidence suggests that Taiwan and South Korea did not have unusually liberal trade regimes; that in some respects their public sectors were unusually large; that South Korea's high real interest rates prevailed for only a few years (1967–1971), after which they were very low or negative; that both states tightly controlled the financial system (South Korean banks were owned by the state until the early 1980s, Taiwan's are only now in the process of nominal privatization); and that both governments carried out policies to promote specific industries using subsidized and targeted credit, fiscal concessions, and protection to alter profit functions

(along with quite a lot of arm-twisting) in order to induce or cajole more resources into targeted sectors than would have otherwise flowed in the absence of such "distortions."

Faced with this evidence, neoliberal economists have revised the core interpretation in one of three ways. Some simply acknowledge that South Korea, for example, had relatively high protection from, say, 1960 to 1985, but then pass on without stating what implications this has for the neoliberal prescription for nearly free trade. This is the simplest response.

Other neoliberals have come to agree that South Korea and Taiwan were not cases of laissez-faire—that the state did take an "active role" in the economy. But in specifying the content of that active role, they emphasize only the provision of public goods, such as education, and say little about state policies that distorted prices or blocked market exchanges. This keeps the explanation consistent with the neoliberal prescription of what governments should and should not do while making a rhetorical concession to the new sympathy for intervention.

A third group acknowledges these various interventions and price distortions, but then says that the distortions were sufficiently balanced to cancel each other out; the distortions in effect "simulated" a free market. This group further implies that if the whole array of distortionary policies were withdrawn at a stroke there would be no more than short-term effects on resource allocation. In World Bank economist Frederick Berger's words, "I believe that the crux of the [South] Korean example is that the active interventionist attitude of the state has been aimed at applying moderate incentives which are very close to the relative prices of products and factors that would prevail in a situation of free trade."

The trade theorist Jagdish Bhagwati combines the second and third responses. "The Far Eastern economies (with the exception of Hong Kong) and others that have come close to the EP strategy [EP means export promotion, the strategy consisting of getting the average effective exchange rate for imports approximately equal to that for exports] have been characterized by *considerable government activity* in the economic system. In my judgement, such intervention can be of *great value,* and almost certainly has been so, in making the EP strategy work successfully."

What are the components of this "considerable government activity" that has been "of great value"? The interventions of great value are those that establish the necessary confidence in the minds of producers that the government's commitment to an export promotion strategy is serious (but Bhagwati gives no indication of what precisely these interventions are). He mentions in passing that the export promotion strategy does not preclude import substitution in selected sectors, but gives no attention to this combination. In this fashion Bhagwati recognizes the fact of considerable government "intervention" in the East Asian cases, but then implies that insofar as those interventions helped more than they hindered, they did so by creating and reinforcing some of the neoclassical growth conditions. Interventions that do not meet this criterion are treated as by the first group: acknowledged but ignored as being of no consequence for the theorems or the recipe.

Neoliberal economists are thus able to say that they know that South Korea, Taiwan, and Japan have not been paragons of laissez-faire; state intervention was, however, mostly consistent with neoliberal principles (it simulated a free market); and any interventions that are inconsistent with those principles were unimportant enough to ignore—no more than "window dressing." But there is no evidence for this last proposition; it follows from an assumption that the theorems must be right, so that anything inconsistent with the theorems can (in the context of a successful case) be ignored.

Two Kinds of State-Market Interactions

Behind this neoliberal interpretation—both the simple and the revised versions—lies a theory that views most of the interactions between states and markets as a vicious circle:

- More and stronger state action subverts or distorts markets (other than the provision of public goods and, in Bhagwati's formulation, policies that enhance producers' confidence that the government will stick to an EP strategy).

- The gainers in such subverted markets use their gains to subvert the state.

The solution is a compressed state, with smaller shares of GNP flowing through state channels of allocation, allowing healthier markets. The East Asian and Latin American countercases are taken to show the truth of both sides of the argument.

Outside the mainstream is a more miscellaneous body of analysts, many of whom emphasize the role of the state. These "statists" see state-market interactions as a virtuous circle:

- More and stronger state action aids more efficient and sustainable markets by providing infrastructure, education, enforcement of property rights, commodities subject to both large economies of scale and diseconomies of private monopoly regulation, and early investments in high-entry-barrier industries important to the economy's future growth.

- The incentives, rivalry, and feedback of these markets in turn help keep state actors effective and efficient.

The difference between East Asia and Latin America lies not in the size of the state, but in East Asia's more disciplined use of state power to foster the national economic interest.

In the general case, there is clearly truth in both arguments: bigger and better markets do often need bigger and better states, while bigger states do often seek to control or eliminate markets.

The state-market dilemma directs our attention to two large questions about East Asia that may help us supersede the stale old "states or markets" debate. From the first horn of the dilemma, what have East Asian states done to widen and improve the workings of markets, especially the ability of markets to generate growth or new resources—as distinct from their ability to generate efficiency in the use of existing resources? (And as a subquestion, how much of this is consistent with neoliberal prescriptions as to what governments should and should not do?) From the second horn of the dilemma, what has disciplined the state in East Asia not to subvert or remove markets, at least not to the extent of impeding growth? Why has there not been massive "government failure"?

The State and Growth

A "governed market" was the key feature of industrial policy in South Korea and Taiwan. This is a system of mostly private enterprises competing and sometimes cooperating under state supervision in the context of heavy investment in education.

In this system there were both large amounts of direct state intervention and large amounts of competition. The competition came mainly in export markets, the domestic market being (as we shall see) somewhat buffered by protection. State intervention was guided neither by the half-light of economic theory nor by the preferences of vote-seeking politicians. Rather, technocrats paid close attention to the industries needed to boost military self-sufficiency; to the Japanese model, including specific organizational arrangements; to results in export markets; and to private demand for imports of capital and intermediate goods. With criteria derived from these sources, they did a lot of what neoclassical economists say bureaucrats cannot do well: they picked industries for special promotion, encouraging resources into them beyond what individual companies were prepared to risk. They treated particular industries at any one time (information, electronics, and biotechnology today for example), as the natural successors to the bridges and lighthouses of Adam Smith's day—which Smith thought too critical for the general welfare to be left to market forces.

With governed markets, South Korea and Taiwan managed to obtain the economies of scale that come from acting in a wide economic space (the international market), plus the innovations induced by competititon, plus some buffering of the domestic market from international competition, and some reduction of risks or increases in profits in industries that the government deemed important for the economy's future growth. Both countries were able to ride the wave of internationalization while at the same time imposing a politically determined directional thrust on domestic resource allocation, integrating and transforming the production structure faster than would have occurred had the controllers of capital been allowed to operate in an unconstrained logic of global profit maximization.

No other developing countries achieved this combination. China, India, and the countries of eastern Europe, for example, had plenty of direct state intervention (of a less strategically focused kind), but little competition; and minus eastern Europe they had a much less sustained commitment to raising skill levels.

Let us consider two domains of state action in East Asia: education and protection. Education provided and regulated by the state is generally considered to be consistent with the neoliberal recipe because of its public good characteristics; protection is generally considered to be quite inconsistent.

GUIDED KNOWLEDGE

One of the most striking things about South Korea, Taiwan, and even more so Japan is the increase in the ratios of skilled to basically skilled to unskilled people in the labor force over the past 40 years. This is measured not just in terms of level of education attained, but in terms of the content of the education, with a high proportion of the total in engineering or science. In a population of 20 million, Taiwan's junior colleges produced over 20,000 graduates with engineer-

ing diplomas annually during the 1980s, the universities another 10,000 bachelor-level engineers a year (nearly twice as many as the United States in relation to population). About 25 percent of all university graduates since 1960 have been engineers (law graduates, 1.2 percent). Science and engineering students together accounted for more than one-third of post–high school graduates during the 1960s, and over half by the 1980s.

Rapidly rising skill levels are fundamentally important in the East Asia story. Their particular importance derives from some recent research on North-South trade in manufactures, which concludes that this trade "is based almost entirely on differences in the availability of human skills. . .[and] not on differences in the availability of capital."[2] That is to say, comparative advantage, in the context of North-South trade in manufactures, rests largely on the skill composition of the labor force, and shifts in a country's comparative advantage in the direction of higher wages are dependent on increases in the ratio of skilled to basically skilled to unskilled labor.

Behind this view is the argument that product categories can be ranked in terms of the skill mix needed for their production, and the categories that are "appropriate" to a country at any one time (in the sense of being in line with comparative advantage) can be determined by comparing the product's skill requirements with the skill composition of the labor force. This is because the ratio of skilled to basically skilled to unskilled people determine the scarcity and relative cost of different levels of skill, and therefore the viability of investments that require different combinations of these skill levels. It was the onrush of technically educated people into the labor force of South Korea, Taiwan, and Japan that lowered the relative cost of skilled labor, allowing investments in progressively more skill-intensive, higher wage activities to be viable.

What about government education policy? The influx of skilled people was not simply the result of citizen preferences. The government steered the demand for education through a series of manpower plans. In Taiwan the actual results—in terms of expansion of enrollments in different subjects, the balance between private and public schooling, the overall rate of expansion, the proportion of GNP allocated for education—have corresponded fairly closely to the targets of these plans. Moreover, many of the targets have run counter to citizen demand. For example, post–junior high school enrollments in vocational institutions expanded much faster than enrollments in academic institutions, raising the ratio of vocational to academic places from 40:60 in 1963 to 69:31 in 1986. The growth of academic institutions has been deliberately restrained. But the rate of private return on education in the academic institutions has

East Asia Profiles

	Population 1990 (in millions)	Population growth rate, 1980–1990 (in percent)	GNP per capita, 1990 (in US dollars)	GDP growth rate, 1980–1990 (in percent)
Japan	124	0.6	25,400	4.1
South Korea	43	1.1	5,400	9.7
Taiwan	20	1.3	8,000	7.7
Hong Kong	6	1.4	11,500	7.1
Singapore	3	2.2	11,500	6.4
China	1,134	1.4	370	9.5
US	250	0.9	21,800	3.4

Source: World Bank, *World Development Report 1992* (New York: Oxford University Press, 1992). Taiwan data are from *Taiwan Statistical Databook* (Taipei: Council for Economic Planning and Development, 1992).

been calculated to be higher than that on education in the vocational institutions, suggesting that the restriction on expansion of the academic institutions runs counter to private demand. In sum, maximizing individual preference was not the goal of the Taiwanese government's education policy.

PROTECTING THE MARKET: THE TAIWANESE EXAMPLE

Nor did East Asian governments allow consumer preferences to prevail in international trade. All three East Asian countries have had closely managed trade regimes (although Japan removed most state-sponsored protection between 1970 and 1980). East Asia's trade regimes are inconsistent in major ways with even a modified neoclassical account of what constitutes a good trade regime.

Taiwan is often presented as an exemplar of a liberal trade regime. The main evidence for this view is the study by Lee and Liang using data from as long ago as 1969.[3] This study does indeed show Taiwan as having at that time a relatively low average level of protection, especially for manufacturing. But there are two basic problems. If we disaggregate even a little, we find that Lee and Liang's results show significant differences in the extent to which various industries are spurred on by policy-based incentives, and significant differences between industries in the incentives to export or sell domestically.

Second, methodological problems mean that we have to be cautious about accepting the study's results at face value. In particular, certain assumptions and omissions have the effect of either making the amount

of inter-industry incentive bias seem lower than it really is (that is, of concealing the true degree of incentive nonuniformity), or of making the average level of protection seem lower than it actually is.

Some other evidence for later periods suggests substantial protection. In 1984, after waves of much vaunted "liberalization," 54 percent of Taiwan's imports by value were still covered by various nontariff barriers. The most comprehensive barriers required prior approval of an import by the domestic producer of substitutes or a government department. All steel imports, for example, had to be approved by the large public enterprise steel-making company, China Steel, until 1987. Moreover, the average legal tariff in 1984 was 31 percent, about the same as the developing country average of 34 percent for tariffs and other trade charges. Yet because Taiwan's tariffs had come down before 1984 much faster than the developing country average, we can infer that Taiwan's average legal tariff before then had been higher than the developing country average.

In the neoclassical argument, protection has four main harmful effects:

• High protection eases or removes pressure on domestic producers to lower their costs to international levels.

• High protection makes for high dispersion in protection levels between industries, resulting in unplanned and undesirable differential incentives.

• High protection harms exports and domestic agriculture.

• High protection induces rent-seeking, which causes social losses.

We consider just two of these effects here. How was protection arranged so that it did not eliminate international competitive pressure on domestic producers, and so that it did not harm exports? The key point is that protection policies operated in the context of strong government emphasis on exports. The government (here I refer to both South Korea and Taiwan) created a special regime for exporters that enabled them to obtain imported inputs quickly and at near-world prices. This was supplemented by a facility that covered much or all of their working capital requirements at lower than normal bank loan rates. Both these facilities operated according to well-established rules, and were automatically available to exporters.

More broadly, the government took export performance as a factor in providing resources. If a firm wanted help for one reason or another (perhaps to avoid penalties for building a factory outside a land zoning plan), its request would be more favorably viewed if it could point to good export performance. Exporting became a "focal point" of government-business relations. Firms therefore sought to export not just to get the various export incentives, but also to build up "credit" in their future dealings with government. In this sense there was a government-created export "culture."

Even firms enjoying protected domestic sales were under pressure to export. Indeed, the sheltering of their domestic sales allowed them to practice discriminatory pricing, charging higher prices on domestic sales and using the higher profits to subsidize exports. In 1979 the average total cost of the Pony, a Hyundai car, was $3,700; the domestic price was $5,000; the price abroad was $2,200. Similar dual pricing continued at least to the late 1980s.

Even some heavy upstream industries (where firms directly exported little and where they have enjoyed substantial protection) have been under competitive pressure to lower costs to international levels. If their prices rise above the cost of import substitutes, exporters can petition the government to allow more imports, and they will probably have some success. (The allowable proportion of imports in the total use of a chemical, for example, may be raised from 40 percent to 60 percent for a limited period.) In other words, the protection given through nontariff barriers is not unconditional. The government often sponsors negotiations between upstream firms and downstream user firms (in petrochemicals, for example). These are aimed at balancing the interest of upstream firms in having a reliable base of domestic demand against that of downstream firms in getting inputs at world market prices.

This balance expresses the compromises between the competitiveness of present-day exports and the government's conviction that the industrial structure should shift toward higher value-added activities faster than unguided market forces alone would produce. To soften the trade-off between present and future, the government devotes considerable resources to assessing the long-run prospects of various technologies, goods, and foreign markets, as well as providing plenty of current market information to domestic producers and foreign buyers.

Still another use of this strategy of quantitative trade management to aid industrial transformation can be seen in the following case. A large multinational was producing in Taiwan a product that required a chemical with unusually high purity. Domestic makers could not supply the chemical with the purity required, and the company was allowed to import what it needed. At a certain point, the Industrial Development Bureau official who supervised that part of the chemical chain thought that production at the higher level of purity was within the technological capability of Taiwan-

based makers. He discussed the possibilities with the Taiwanese makers and also with the multinational. He encouraged the latter to complete a purchasing agreement with the domestic makers to guarantee them sales if they made the requisite investment in plant and skills. The multinational was doubtful. But after awhile, it found that its applications to import the chemical, previously approved automatically, began to be delayed—and the delays began to lengthen. It got the message; it entered into a purchasing agreement with the domestic suppliers, and they upgraded their capacity.

This strategy—which has been used across the industrial spectrum in Taiwan— shows how Taiwanese industrial policy officials can nudge the production structure into more sophisticated activities. But note that the necessary condition for this strategy to work was that the domestic maker had to be able—within not too long a time—to produce to the required standard of purity and at not much above the world market price.

In short, the means by which protection is administered suggest how the shape of Taiwan's protection regime and its integration into a wider export and industrial transformation strategy may have offset the predicted neoclassical costs of protection on domestic costs and exports. Protection administered in this fashion may even have helped to accelerate the shift of comparative advantage into higher value-added activities, by means of a "learning-by-doing" effect on skills.

East Asian trade regimes, and their industrial policies more generally, gave government officials, often men and women in their thirties, much discretion. From the neoliberal treatment of government-in-general, we would expect that this discretion would have been systematically misused. Yet it would be hard to argue that it has happened on a scale that significantly retarded growth in South Korea and Taiwan. This brings us to the second horn of the state-market dilemma.

WHAT HAS DISCIPLINED THE STATE?

Bigger states are often capable of and interested in removing, controlling, or intervening in markets in ways that obstruct economic growth. In neoclassical economics there are three broad arguments that explain such a tendency.

- The information available to public officials is inherently more limited or inaccurate than that available to decentralized private agents. This questions the ability of government to carry out its intentions, whatever they might be.

- Government intervention creates super-normal

profits (rents) for whose capture private agents use resources "wastefully" or "unproductively" in growth-inhibiting ways. This likewise questions the ability of government to implement policies with the intended net effects since the costs, once broadened to include the unproductive use of resources to capture government-created rents, are likely to exceed the benefits.

- Government officials tend to seek objectives only distantly related to the ostensible public purposes of their agencies, especially since their behavior is less constrained by anything analogous to the profit imperative that motivates businesspeople. This argument questions the extent to which the real interventions of government are in line with the publicly stated ones.

According to the neoclassical view, as government becomes larger and more active, the net impact of its growing attempts to change the economy's composition is likely to harm growth for reasons that relate to information, rents, and the discrepancy between ostensible and real bureaucratic objectives. What has checked these tendencies in East Asia? This is the jackpot question.

There is no simple answer. We can make some headway and avoid a completely ad hoc, regionally specific, and historically unique kind of explanation (for example, "Confucian values") by looking at the East Asian facts through the lens of the three neoclassical arguments about "government failure."

THE INFORMATION GAP THAT ISN'T

The information problem has been eased in several ways. First, the civil service is still an elite career; this helps overcome compliance and asymmetric information problems in bureaucratic agencies. (English-speakers take note: it is in the English-language countries—the United Kingdom, the United States, Canada, Australia, and New Zealand—where vigorous efforts were made during the 1980s to move away from the concept of an elite civil service with lifetime employment.)

Second, central officials draw on expertise and information located in the forest of state enterprise "research and service" organizations surrounding the core economic bureaucracy. For example, when Taiwanese officials need to make decisions about protection in the electronics field, they get advice from the Electronics Research and Service Organization (ERSO), which had a staff of 1,700 in 1987. Research and service organizations like ERSO employ specialists more flexibly than the central government service can.

Third, the government makes substantial investments in acquiring information and making it available. Officials can know within 48 hours what has been imported and exported from the country, for example. In Taiwan, the Industrial Development Bureau officials responsible for monitoring various economic sectors spend several days a month making factory visits up and down the country. An export quality control scheme requires the inspection of each exporting factory at least once a year by a team of experts in quality control, who grade the factory's quality control system (the higher the grade the lower the inspection fee). Through both channels (factory visits by Industrial Development Bureau officials and export quality control officials), the government can make decisions based on detailed knowledge of production conditions and capabilities—though not about finances, which firms are much more secretive about. These devices are a kind of substitute for the government-industry "deliberative councils" that have been more common in Japan and South Korea.

Finally, there is the architecture of the industrial policies themselves. Several forms of public help are made conditional on performance, which is tracked with relatively easy-to-monitor indicators, such as exports, or the gap between domestic and international prices. This also eases the information problem.

In short, information is abundantly available to central economic bureaucrats. And information asymmetries between top decisionmakers and lower level officials, and between the state and target groups, are checked by the civil service's eliteness (which aids compliance within it), by performance indicators, and by the sheer variety of information sources.

THE ECONOMICS OF CORRUPTION AND STATE MYOPIA

What about the other neoclassical preoccupations that government officials will use their discretion over budgets and permissions to pursue goals only distantly related to the publicly stated ones, and that even if well intentioned, their interventions will generate rents to whose capture private agents will divert resources "unproductively"?

Again, we can find several factors at work in Taiwan that inhibit these effects. The high level of talent attracted into government service, specifically those with technical training, has already been mentioned. This means, among other things, that government officials steer their conduct by norms of intellectual and professional integrity. At the same time, they are not caught between rival interest groups lobbying for favors. Economic interest groups have little autonomy, while the civil service has a lot from the legislature. (Officials are, however, subject to monitoring from centers outside the core bureaucracies, namely, the research and service agencies.) And the press is fairly free to make economic—but not political—criticisms of the government. Industrial officials study the business press with care.

Moreover, the performance conditions attached to government assistance discipline not only the recipients but also the givers. Government officials know that their own behavior can be assessed in relation to the same performance indicators. If a firm can show that its ability to meet performance conditions on exports, for example, is being impaired by incompetent or bribe-seeking officials, it has another channel of recourse. Indeed, performance conditions give officials clearer indicators of what they are meant to be doing and give them an incentive to help "their" firms meet those conditions. Performance conditions thus not only help the information problem; they also help the "bureaucratic self-seeking" and "private agent rent-seeking" problems.

So while officials have certainly conferred rents (by giving more help to some firms or industries than others), the resources devoted to rent-seeking have been limited because the chances of modifying government allocations through kickbacks are not high. Moreover, the industrial rents conferred by government have often facilitated higher productivity growth because of the wider competitive-cooperative incentive structure facing rent-capturing firms, and because the government has often (but not always) been able to withdraw the rent-creating interventions when necessary.

This then helps us to understand why "government failure" in the market might be less in Taiwan and South Korea than neoclassical theory would predict. But neoclassical theory is rooted in the institutional structure of the West, and takes for granted certain features that should not be taken so in a broader comparative context. For example, we need to be explicit that for centuries, Taiwan and South Korea have had economies based on markets and (mostly) private-property. Unlike Russia, China, Vietnam, and others, South Korea and Taiwan never took their undoubted admiration for the state to the point of having it make shoes and provide haircuts. The control of most of the economy's productive assets by private capitalists meant that government officials had to pay close attention to how their decisions affected profits if the government's military and developmental objectives were to be achieved.

In another way, however, Taiwan and South Korea are closer to the "socialist" cases than to the West. Until very recently their government structure had not met even the minimal condition of democracy: that the ruling party can, potentially, lose power through elections. Civil society has also been kept deliberately weak. In terms of civil and political rights, Taiwan and South Korea came no higher than halfway down a ranking of middle-income countries by civil and political rights during the 1970s and early 1980s. The absence of democracy and civil society has made it easier for government officials to carry out their intentions. But what has kept those intentions consistent with national economic growth objectives (in contrast to the case of Myanmar, for example)?

THE HISTORICAL CONTEXT

At this point in the argument we need to step up the causal chain from the "proximate" causes and back into the domain of those historically more specific and contingent. Taiwan and South Korean officials operate with cultural models of power and authority that have been generated by centuries of experience in the centralized polity and economy of the Chinese empire and the Korean kingdom.[4] The cultural models have been reinforced by Japanese colonialism, by the organizational exigencies of fighting wars, resisting siege, and (in the case of Taiwan but not South Korea) being perceived as alien by the native population.

Taiwan and South Korea are "part countries"—both face a credible threat to their continued existence from the part torn off. The sense of an external threat and the urge to do better than the other side may have compensated for the lack of internal competition between a domestic opposition party and the state. After all, the governments of most developing countries knew that they could fail economically and not risk the survival of the government *and* the state and nation itself. In contrast, South Korea and Taiwan knew that without quick economic growth and social stability, the ultimate horror of economic and political collapse was a possibility. This led them to devise an unusually close coupling between national security and economic strength. As in Japan, the economic bureaucracies were initially given responsibility for directing resources that enhanced manufacturing's ability to shift to military production, an objective subsequently extended, with the same "must do" mentality, to joining the club of advanced Western nations as fast as possible.

Here the "neighborhood" effect of being near Japan has been important. Japan provided a textbook on how to catch up—a textbook with which the Taiwan and South Korean rulers have become well acquainted. It provided a tangible model of what a disciplined state could achieve both militarily and economically, and that model contributed to the development of a mission-oriented organizational culture in key government agencies. And independent of government policies, the Taiwanese and South Korean economies benefited from spillovers from Japan's high-speed growth, spillovers that, inkblot-like, were spatially concentrated. (How important this "inkblot" or neighborhood effect was I do not know.)

These historical and cultural conditions generated the pressure for a coherent national economic strategy and the ability to implement the strategy. Above all, they help to explain why Taiwan and South Korea have met the central proximate condition of government "success": that those intervening in the market on behalf of the national interest had the national interest at heart; were talented enough to translate between broad goals and policy specifics; had accurate information about the capacities and behaviors of private agents and their own subordinates; and took the goals and authority of the organizations they worked for as the bases for their own actions.[5]

AN EAST ASIAN MODEL
FOR THE DEVELOPING WORLD?

What does the foregoing suggest about the chances that other developing countries can transform their economies and raise incomes fast enough to shoot up the global economic hierarchy at something approaching the rates of South Korea and Taiwan? It suggests that the chances are a good deal slimmer than the neoliberal account would have us believe. For one thing, the world economy today is less expansive than when, in the 1960s and 1970s, South Korea and Taiwan gained momentum. For another, the political conditions for establishing and sustaining the key policy combination of competition, direct state intervention, and education are too stringent to be met by many other states. The stringency of this combination is consistent with evidence on the rarity of a country moving from periphery to semiperiphery, or from semiperiphery to core over the past five decades.

However, we have to take note of some pointers that lead to a more optimistic conclusion. Several of the key institutional arrangements in East Asia are the result not of deep historical trends or "culture," but deliberate and fairly recent design. One thinks of Japan's industrial relations system, some parts of which were put in place in the 1920s and 1930s (plant unions and gradual extension of white-collar privileges—security of employment and incremental salary scales—to blue-collar workers), but institutionalized as a national system only as recently as the early 1950s in response to intense labor-management conflict. Japan's economic bureaucracy and other public sector organizations (such as the police, post office, and navy) were designed after close study of Western models in the late nineteenth century. South Korea and Taiwan based many of the organizational arrangements for their industrial policy on modified Japanese models from the 1950s and 1960s.

These arrangements are now "available" for other catch-up countries to copy. Of course, major organizational change is rarely voluntary in the sense of policymakers thinking such change would be to their country's advantage. It generally comes at a time of economic distress and social conflict. But when people try to resolve conflicts they tend to choose from among alternatives already familiar to them on the basis,

partly, of their knowledge of how alternatives work elsewhere. The superior economic performance of East Asia gives legitimacy to efforts in other parts of the world to adopt some elements of that region's organizational arrangements.

Malaysia, Thailand, Indonesia (population nearly 260 million), and the southern coastal provinces of China (Guandong and Fujian, population 100 million) have been growing quickly since the 1980s. Their growth is partly "at the invitation" of the East Asians, who are investing heavily. Can it be sustained? Perhaps some Latin American countries, squeezed by foreign debt and Asian competition in potential export markets, are descending from the semiperiphery to the periphery, leaving space in the semiperiphery for a few of the Asian newcomers to move into. Perhaps Britain, with the most ill-educated labor force of all the core countries and a long-standing commitment to an overvalued exchange rate, is steadily dropping out of the core toward the semiperiphery, leaving space for others, such as Taiwan, South Korea, Singapore, Spain, and perhaps parts of eastern Europe.

Perhaps. But on the minus side, note two facts. One is the global recession, seen in the decline in annual rates of world GDP growth from 4.9 percent in 1960–1970, 3.5 percent in 1970–1980, to 2.9 percent in 1980–1989. This makes it more likely that growing trade from countries newly integrating into the world economy will constitute trade diversion rather than trade augmentation, which is presumably more difficult to do. Growing protection in the West, induced by the global recession, reinforces this tendency.

The second fact is that Southeast Asia's industrialization is dominated by foreign investors, who have so far developed ties with domestically based suppliers and users to a remarkably small degree. For example, Thailand's "investment rush" of the late 1980s was driven largely by foreign investment; 75 percent of the investment projects by value approved by the Thai Board of Investments were from foreign firms, half of which were Japanese. The local content of consumer electronics goods produced by Japanese firms directly investing in Thailand and Malaysia in 1988 was only about 30 percent, and locally procured parts came mainly from transplanted Japanese parts markers. Taiwan and South Korea at an equivalent time in their industrialization were much less dominated by foreign firms, and those foreign firms that were there were more closely anchored in the domestic economy, thanks partly to government actions to make it happen (recall the case of the high purity chemical in Taiwan).

If the prospects for large-scale replication are small, this does not mean that newly industrializing countries cannot learn a great deal from the successful East Asian cases. The most transferable knowledge is at the level of specific institutional design. For example, if some protection for domestic industries is to be maintained, it is essential to exempt imports of inputs for exports from tariffs, allowing exporters to receive inputs at world market prices. Taiwan and South Korea have a great deal of experience on how to organize such a tariff-rebate scheme, which newcomers would be crazy to ignore.

WHAT THE ANSWERS ARE

The Role of Industrial Policies

South Korea, Taiwan, and Japan show that selective industrial promotion need not be inimical to rapid industrialization. Whether they show that selective industrial promotion can itself accelerate industrialization in such a way as to bring net social benefits is still an open question. There is no conclusive evidence either way. My own judgment is that the balance of evidence is in favor of the argument that selective industrial policies as practiced by these three countries did assist their internationally competitive industrialization.

To make the point more precise, we need to distinguish between two types of government "intervention": leading the market and following the market. Following the market means government assists some of the projects that private businesspeople want to undertake at current prices. Leading the market means that the government initiates projects that private businesspeople would not undertake at current prices. Leading in turn comes in two degrees: initiating projects that are unviable at current prices but viable at proper shadow prices (L1), and initiating projects that are unviable even at "proper" shadow prices (L2).[6] Looking at the role of government in East Asian industrialization, we see a pattern of government intervention shifting between these roles in some industries over time, while in other industries we find little if any intervention—not even regulatory. It seems likely that most of the government's leadership of the market was of the L1 type. But there are some cases of L2 that turned out to be successful, the Korean steel industry being the most celebrated example. In any case, whether doing L1 or L2, the government's role in industrial promotion went far beyond the neoliberal recipe.

Where the central proximate condition for industrial policy success, given above, cannot be even minimally met, it would be foolish for a government to try L2; and even L1 has to be done very selectively. Most industrial promotion should be the case where the government follows the market, with export performance or the gap between domestic and international prices the dominant criterion for continued assistance.

Education

Raising a country's ratios of skilled to basically skilled to unskilled people is the most effective way to shift comparative advantage in the direction of activities that support higher incomes.

Trade Policy

Trade policy ("outward orientation," "inward orientation") is of secondary importance in explaining trade patterns relative to skill mix and natural resource endowment. A trade regime that is, overall, "trade neutral" (that is, which meets Bhagwati's EP condition) is consistent with substantial differences between industries in the extent to which they are spurred on by industrial policy incentives, and in the extent to which they have incentives to sell abroad or in the domestic market. One of the most important topics for research is how, practically and theoretically, this combination can be achieved—and how reconciled with rules of a global trading regime. The vast neoclassical literature on trade policy is wrong to treat protection as a unitary phenomenon. The costs of protection depend heavily on organizational mechanisms and the conditions with which it is granted. The incentive effects of different protection "contracts" require more study, especially identifying the conditions in which protection can be expected to stimulate investment and learning-by-doing.

Trade Protection and Social Protection

Protection in East Asia was used not only as an instrument of industrial promotion, but also as a means of buffering the population from the risks stemming from entering the international market (as well as to raise revenue). As governments in the region have reduced protection, they have also bolstered expenditure on domestic insurance in the form of welfare and transfer payments. In an article in a 1991 volume of *International Organization*, Robert Bates et al. found evidence in a sample of 32 low- and middle-income countries that "the higher the level of terms-of-trade risk that a nation faces in international markets, the more likely it is to increase trade barriers," and that "the greater the social insurance programs mounted by a nation's government, the less likely that government is to block free trade." The force of this point is reinforced by the new international competition that has made it possible for a set of industries located in one country to wipe out competitors in another country in half a decade, posing enormous adjustment problems, a phenomenon of which Adam Smith and David Ricardo were entirely innocent.

The Organization of Direct State Intervention

South Korea, Taiwan, and Japan used "pilot agencies" to exercise foresight and strategic planning in a way that private businesspeople could not afford to cultivate. These pilot agencies (MITI in Japan, the Industrial Development Bureau in Taiwan, and the

Economic Planning Board in South Korea) were located in the heartland of government, where they acted as a lobbyist for a long-term perspective on national issues. They were staffed by some of the best talent available (and most of their officials were not economists). They had control over only a small amount of resources, much of their influence coming from their ability to persuade the resource controllers to support projects, for which their position in the heartland of government was crucial. However, our knowledge of the organization and operation of the economic bureaucracies of East Asia is remarkably thin.[7]

State-Society Relations

The pilot agency, in turn, formed part of a state apparatus that had a high measure of autonomy from the rest of the society (before the 1970s in the case of Japan). This is of course a stringent political condition. A more corporatist organization may be a feasible and attractive substitute for state autonomy, and is still likely to be more effective than the "free trade" of United States–style political pluralism, which tends to produce the damaging immobilism seen in United States domestic policy.

Democracy and Human Rights

The East Asian states did not allow resource allocation to be determined only by decentralized businesspeople operating in the logic of global profit seeking. Above all they mediated the external transactions of the owners and managers of capital in such a way as to generate an intense cycle of investment and re-investment within the national borders; and they further subjected this investment to priorities determined through a political process (a nondemocratic one in the case of South Korea and Taiwan, an anomalously democratic one in the case of Japan).

Against this experience, we should be concerned at the current uncritical embrace of "democracy" and "human rights" as the political correlate of the economic doctrine of "free markets." Not only the new European Bank for Reconstruction and Development but also the old and ostensibly "nonpolitical" multilateral financial institutions such as the World Bank and IMF are now beginning to make "democracy" and "human rights" a condition for their loans, implicitly modifying their own previous notion of sovereignty.

Yet political changes promoted under the banner of democracy and human rights open the way for the controllers of transnational capital to exercise still greater influence over a country's political development. Human rights are being defined to include the right to use one's economic assets almost however one wishes, so that restrictions on asset use of the kind East Asian states routinely impose come to be seen as violations of basic human rights. "Democratic rules" readily allow outside groups to pour money into national electoral competition in an effort to determine the result (as was the case recently in Nicaragua).

These principles together can justify arrangements that, ironically, undercut the nation-state as a political center where compromises are hammered out between the groups of people who live there. In particular, they can make it difficult to reach and enforce compromises that entail restrictions on the use of capital, especially transnationally mobile capital. Yet without some such restrictions, and without an effective political center, it is unlikely that, in late twentieth-century conditions, a country can quickly stride up the world economic hierarchy. That, at least, is what the East Asian experience suggests.

---

[1]Much of the data and the arguments in this article come from Robert Wade, *Governing the Market: Economic Theory and the Role of Government in East Asian Industrialization* (Princeton: Princeton University Press, 1990). See also the author's "East Asia's Economic Success: Conflicting Paradigms, Partial Insights, Shaky Evidence," *World Politics*, January 1992.

[2]Adrian Wood, "A New-Old Theoretical View of North-South Trade, Employment and Wages" (Discussion Paper 292, Institute of Development Studies, Sussex University), p. ii.

[3]T. H. Lee and K. S. Liang, "Taiwan," in Bela Balassa, et al., *Development Strategies in Semi-industrial Economies* (Baltimore: Johns Hopkins University Press, 1982), ch. 10.

[4]See, for example, Lucian and Mary Pye, *Asian Power and Politics: The Cultural Dimensions of Authority* (Cambridge: Belknap Press, 1985).

[5]My account is obviously highly stylized. For further discussion, see Wade, op. cit., chapters 7 to 10, especially pp. 333–342.

[6]Shadow prices are market prices adjusted for market imperfections so as to more accurately reflect real scarcities.

[7]But see Chalmers Johnson's classic, *MITI and the Japanese Miracle: The Growth of Industrial Policy, 1925–1975* (Stanford, Calif.: Stanford University Press, 1982).

Comparative Politics:
Some Major Trends, Issues, and Prospects

- **The Democratic Trend: How Strong, Thorough, and Lasting? (Articles 56 and 57)**
- **The Turn Toward the Market: What Role for the State? (Article 58)**
- **Ethnic and Cultural Conflicts: The Political Assertion of Group Identity (Articles 59–61)**

The articles in this unit deal with three major political trends or patterns of development that can be observed in much of the contemporary world. It is important at the outset to stress that, with the possible exception of Benjamin Barber, none of the authors predict some form of global convergence in which all political systems would become alike in major respects. On closer examination, even Barber turns out to argue that a strong tendency toward global homogenization is offset by a concurrent tendency toward intensified group differentiation and fragmentation.

Thus the trends or patterns discussed here are neither unidirectional nor universal. They are situationally defined and therefore come in a great variety of forms and "mixes." They may well turn out to be temporary and at least partly reversible. Moreover, they do not always reinforce one another, but show considerable mutual tension. Indeed, their different forms of development are "the very stuff' of comparative politics, which seeks an informed understanding of the political dimension of social life by making careful comparisons across time and space.

After such cautionary preliminaries, we can proceed to identify three recent developments that singly and together have had a very important role in changing the political world in which we live. One is *the democratic revolution,* which is sweeping much of the world. This refers to a widespread trend toward some form of popular government which often, but not always, takes the form of a search for representative, pluralist democracy in countries that were previously ruled by some form of authoritarian oligarchy or dictatorship.

Another trend, sometimes labeled *the capitalist revolution,* is the even more widespread shift toward some form of market economy. It includes a greater reliance on private enterprise and the profit motive, and involves a concurrent move away from heavy regulation, central planning, and state ownership. But this need not mean laissez-faire capitalism. The social market economy, found in much of Western Europe, allows a considerable role for the state in providing services, redistributing income, and setting overall societal goals. In some of the Asian communist-ruled countries, above all China, we have become used to seeing self-proclaimed revolutionary socialists introduce a considerable degree of capitalist practices into their formerly planned economies. Some wits have suggested that it is time to speak of "Market-Leninists."

The third major trend could be called *the revival of ethnic or cultural politics.* This refers to a growing emphasis on some form of an exclusive group identity as the primary basis for political expression. In modern times, it has been common for a group to identify itself by its special ethnic, religious, linguistic, or other cultural traits and to make this identity the basis for a claim to rule by and for itself. The principle of national self-determination received the blessing of Woodrow Wilson, and it continues to have a democratic appeal, even though some critics warn against the potential dangers that may stem from a fractious politics of ethnocracy. They detect a collectivist or antipluralist

potential in this form of political expression, and point out that it can contribute to intolerance and conflicts among groups as well as between the group and the individual.

The articles in the first section cover democratization as the first of these trends, that is, the startling growth in the number of representative governments in recent years. Even if this development is likely to be reversed in some countries, we need to remember how remarkable it has been in the first place. Using very different criteria and data, skeptics on both right and left for a long time doubted whether representative government was sufficiently stable, efficient, accountable, attractive, or, ultimately, legitimate to survive or spread in the modern world. It would be instructive to review their more recent discussion of the 1970s and early 1980s, not in order to refute the pessimists but to learn from their insights as well as their oversights.

Samuel Huntington is one of the best known observers of democratization, who in the past emphasized the cultural, social, economic, and political obstacles to representative government in most of the world. In the aftermath of the collapse of communist regimes in eastern and central Europe, he has identified a broad pattern of democratization that began in the mid-1970s, when three dictatorships in southern Europe came to an end (Greece, Portugal, and Spain). In the following decade, democratization spread to most of Latin America. Central and Eastern Europe followed, and the trend has also reached some states in East and South Asia as well as Africa.

In a widely adopted phrase, Huntington identifies this trend as the "third wave" of democratization in modern history. The first "long" wave began in the 1820s and lasted about one century, until 1926, a period during which the United States and 28 other countries established governments based on a wide and eventually universal suffrage. In 1922, however, Mussolini's capture of power in Italy began a period of reversal, which lasted until the early 1940s. During these two decades, the number of democracies fell from 29 to 12, as many became victims of dictatorial takeovers or military conquests.

A "second wave" of democratization started with the Allied victory in World War II and continued during the early postwar years of decolonization. This wave lasted until about 1962 and resulted in the conversion of about two dozen previous authoritarian systems into democracies or quasi-democracies, sometimes of very short duration. There followed a second reverse wave, lasting from 1962 to 1973. During this period, the number of democracies fell from 36 to 30 and the number of non-democracies increased from 75 to 95 as various former colonies or fresh democracies fell under authoritarian or dictatorial rule. In the mid-1970s the "third wave" of democratization got its start.

At the beginning of the 1990s, Huntington counted about 60 democracies in the world, which amounts to a doubling of their number in less than two decades. It is an impressive change, but he points out that the process is likely to be reversed once again in a number of the new democracies. His discussion supports the conclusion that democracy's advance has always been a "two steps forward, one step back" kind of process. The expectations associated with the coming of democracy are in some countries so high that disappointments are bound to follow. Already, the "third wave" democratic advances in countries like the Sudan, Nigeria, Algeria, Haiti, and Peru have been followed by authoritarian reversals. There are ominous signs of an authoritarian revival in some parts of the former Soviet Union.

Huntington's rule of thumb is that a democratic form of government can be considered to have become stable when a country has had at least two successive peaceful turnovers of power. Such a development may take a generation or longer to complete, even under fortunate circumstances. Many of the new democracies have little historical experience with a democratic way of life. Where there has been such an experience, it may have been spotty and not very positive. There may be important cultural or socioeconomic obstacles to democratization, according to Huntington. Like most other observers, he sees extreme poverty as a principal obstacle to successful democratization.

Robin Wright points to another precondition for a viable pluralist democracy. Wright examines the importance of civil society—a rich associational network of intermediary groups between the individual and the state. Like many other observers, Wright finds that such a "middle" is often missing in the new democracies that have emerged on the ruins of repressive authoritarian or totalitarian systems.

The second section covers the trend toward capitalism or, better, market economics. Here Gabriel Almond explores the connections between capitalism and democracy in an article that draws upon both theory and empirical studies.

Almond's discussion can be linked to a theme emphasized by some contemporary political economists. They point out that the economic competition between capitalism and socialism, in its communist form of state ownership and centralized planning, has become a largely closed chapter in history. The central question now is which form of capitalism or market economy will be more successful. A similar argument is made by the French theorist Michel Albert, who also distinguishes between the British-American and the continental "Rhineland" models of capitalism. The former is more individualistic, antigovernmental, and characterized by such traits as high employee turnovers and short-term profit-maximizing. It differs considerably from what the Germans themselves like to call their "social market economy." The latter is more team-oriented, emphasizes cooperation between management and organized labor, and leaves a considerable role for government in the setting of general economic strategy, the training of an educated labor force, and the provision of social welfare services.

The third section deals with the revival of the ethnic and cultural dimension in politics. Until recently, relatively few observers foresaw that this element would play such a fractious role in the contemporary world. There were forewarnings, such as the ethnonationalist stirrings in the late 1960s and early 1970s in peripheral areas of such countries as Britain or Spain. It also lay behind many of the conflicts in the newly independent countries of the Third World. But most Western observers seem to have been poorly prepared for the task of anticipating or understanding the resurgence of politicized religious, ethnic, or other cultural forces. Many non-Westerners were taken by surprise as well. Mikhail Gorbachev, for example, grossly underestimated the centrifugal force of the nationality question in his own country.

The politicization of religion in many parts of the world falls into this development of a politics of identity. In recent years, religious groups in parts of Latin America, Asia, sub-Saharan Africa, Asia, and Europe have variously set out on the political road in the name of their faith. As Max Weber warned in a classic lecture shortly before his death, it can be dangerous to seek "the salvation of souls" along the path of politics. The coexistence of people of divergent faiths is possible only because religious conviction need not fully determine or direct a person's or group's politics. When it does, it can add an element of fervor and an unwillingness to compromise that makes it difficult to live harmoniously with people who believe differently.

There is an important debate among political scientists concerning the sources and scope of politics based on ethnic, religious, and cultural differences. Samuel Huntington argues forcefully that our most important and dangerous future conflicts will be based on clashes of civilizations. In his view, they will be far more difficult to resolve than those rooted in socioeconomic or even ideological differences. His critics, including the German Josef Joffe, argue that Huntington distorts the differences among civilizations and trivializes the differences within civilizations as sources of political conflict. Chandra Muzaffar, a Malaysian commentator, goes much further by contending that Huntington's thesis provides a rationalization for a Western policy goal of dominating the Third World.

In the final article, Benjamin Barber brings a broad perspective to the discussion of identity politics in the contemporary world. He sees two major tendencies that threaten democracy. One is the force of globalism, brought about by modern technology, communications, and commerce. Its logical end station is what he calls a "McWorld," in which human diversity, individuality, and meaningful identity are erased. The second tendency works in the opposite direction. It is the force of tribalism, which drives human beings to exacerbate their group differences, become intolerant, and engage in holy wars or "jihads" against each other. Barber argues that globalism is at best indifferent to democracy, while militant tribalism is deeply antithetical. He argues in favor of seeking a confederal solution, based on democratic civil societies, which could provide human beings with a nonmilitant, parochial communitarianism as well as a framework that suits the global market economy fairly well.

Looking Ahead: Challenge Questions

What is meant by the first, second, and third waves of democratization? Describe the reversals that followed the first two.

Where are most of the countries affected by the third wave located? What factors appear to have contributed to their democratization?

Is there a possible tension between the values of liberal democracy and those of majoritarian or community democracy?

In what ways can market capitalism and liberal democracy be said to be mutually supportive?

Why is it so difficult to resolve political conflicts that arise from the political assertion of an exclusive religious or ethnic identity?

What does Benjamin Barber mean when he warns that democracy is threatened by globalism and tribalism?

A NEW ERA IN DEMOCRACY
DEMOCRACY'S THIRD WAVE

SAMUEL P. HUNTINGTON

Mr. Huntington is professor of government at Harvard University.

Between 1974 and 1990, at least 30 countries made transitions to democracy, just about doubling the number of democratic governments in the world. Were these democratizations part of a continuing and ever-expanding "global democratic revolution" that will reach virtually every country in the world? Or did they represent a limited expansion of democracy, involving for the most part its reintroduction into countries that had experienced it in the past?

The current era of democratic transitions constitutes the third wave of democratization in the history of the modern world. The first "long" wave of democratization began in the 1820s, with the widening of the suffrage to a large proportion of the male population in the United States, and continued for almost a century until 1926, bringing into being some 29 democracies. In 1922, however, the coming to power of Mussolini in Italy marked the beginning of a first "reverse wave" that by 1942 had reduced the number of democratic states in the world to 12. The triumph of the Allies in World War II initiated a second wave of democratization that reached its zenith in 1962 with 36 countries governed democratically, only to be followed by a second reverse wave (1960-1975) that brought the number of democracies back down to 30.

At what stage are we within the third wave? Early in a long wave, or at or near the end of a short one? And if the third wave comes to a halt, will it be followed by a significant third reverse wave eliminating many of democracy's gains in the 1970s and 1980s? Social science cannot provide reliable answers to these questions, nor can any social scientist. It may be possible, however, to identify some of the factors that will affect the future expansion or contraction of democracy in the world and to pose the questions that seem most relevant for the future of democratization.

One way to begin is to inquire whether the causes that gave rise to the third wave are likely to continue operating, to gain in strength, to weaken, or to be supplemented or replaced by new forces promoting democratization. Five major factors have contributed significantly to the occurrence and the timing of the third-wave transitions to democracy:

1. The deepening legitimacy problems of authoritarian regimes in a world where democratic values were widely accepted, the consequent dependence of these regimes on successful performance, and their inability to maintain "performance legitimacy" due to economic (and sometimes military) failure.

2. The unprecedented global economic growth of the 1960s, which raised living standards, increased education, and greatly expanded the urban middle class in many countries.

3. A striking shift in the doctrine and activities of the Catholic Church, manifested in the Second Vatican Council of 1963-65 and the transformation of national Catholic churches from defenders of the status quo to opponents of authoritarianism.

4. Changes in the policies of external actors, most notably the European Community, the United States, and the Soviet Union.

5. "Snowballing," or the demonstration effect of transitions earlier in the third wave in stimulating and providing models for subsequent efforts at democratization.

I will begin by addressing the latter three factors, returning to the first two later in this article.

Historically, there has been a strong correlation between Western Christianity and democracy. By the early 1970s, most of the Protestant countries in the world had already become democratic. The third wave of the 1970s and 1980s was overwhelmingly a Catholic wave. Beginning in Portugal and Spain, it swept through six South American and three

From *Current*, September 1991, pp. 27-39. From "Democracy's Third Wave," as it appeared in *Journal of Democracy*, Spring 1991, pp. 12-34.

Central American countries, moved on to the Philippines, doubled back to Mexico and Chile, and then burst through in the two Catholic countries of Eastern Europe, Poland and Hungary. Roughly three-quarters of the countries that transited to democracy between 1974 and 1989 were predominantly Catholic.

By 1990, however, the Catholic impetus to democratization had largely exhausted itself. Most Catholic countries had already democratized or, as in the case of Mexico, liberalized. The ability of Catholicism to promote further expansion of democracy (without expanding its own ranks) is limited to Paraguay, Cuba, and a few Francophone African countries. By 1990, sub-Saharan Africa was the only region of the world where substantial numbers of Catholics and Protestants lived under authoritarian regimes in a large number of countries.

THE ROLE OF EXTERNAL FORCES

During the third wave, the European Community (EC) played a key role in consolidating democracy in southern Europe. In Greece, Spain, and Portugal, the establishment of democracy was seen as necessary to secure the economic benefits of EC membership, while Community membership was in turn seen as a guarantee of the stability of democracy. In 1981, Greece became a full member of the Community, and five years later Spain and Portugal did as well.

In April 1987, Turkey applied for full EC membership. One incentive was the desire of Turkish leaders to reinforce modernizing and democratic tendencies in Turkey and to contain and isolate the forces in Turkey supporting Islamic fundamentalism. Within the Community, however, the prospect of Turkish membership met with little enthusiasm and even some hostility (mostly from Greece). In 1990, the liberation of Eastern Europe also raised the possibility of membership for Hungary, Czechoslovakia, and Poland. The Community thus faced two issues. First, should it give priority to broadening its membership or to "deepening" the existing Community by moving toward further economic and political union? Second, if it did decide to expand its membership, should priority go to European Free Trade Association members like Austria, Norway, and Sweden, to the East Europeans, or to Turkey? Presumably the Community can only absorb a limited number of countries in a given period of time. The answers to these questions will have significant implications for the stability of democracy in Turkey and in the East European countries.

The withdrawal of Soviet power made possible democratization in Eastern Europe. If the Soviet Union were to end or drastically curtail its support for Castro's regime, movement toward democracy might occur in Cuba. Apart from that, there seems little more the Soviet Union can do or is likely to do to promote democracy outside its borders. The key issue is what will happen within the Soviet Union itself. If Soviet control loosens, it seems likely that democracy could be reestablished in the Baltic states. Movements toward democracy also exist in other republics. Most important, of course, is Russia itself. The inauguration and consolidation of democracy in the Russian republic, if it occurs, would be the single most dramatic gain for democracy since the immediate post-World War II years. Democratic development in most of the Soviet republics, however, is greatly complicated by their ethnic heterogeneity and the unwillingness of the dominant nationality to allow equal rights to ethnic minorities. As Sir Ivor Jennings remarked years ago, "the people cannot decide until somebody decides who are the people." It may take years if not decades to resolve the latter issue in much of the Soviet Union.

During the 1970s and 1980s the United States was a major promoter of democratization. Whether the United States continues to play this role depends on its will, its capability, and its attractiveness as a model to other countries. Before the mid-1970s the promotion of democracy had not always been a high priority of American foreign policy. It could again subside in importance. The end of the Cold War and of the ideological competition with the Soviet Union could remove one rationale for propping up anti-communist dictators, but it could also reduce the incentives for any substantial American involvement in the Third World.

American will to promote democracy may or may not be sustained. American ability to do so, on the other hand, is limited. The trade and budget deficits impose new limits on the resources that the United States can use to influence events in foreign countries. More important, the ability of the United States to promote democracy has in some measure run its course. The countries in Latin America, the Caribbean, Europe, and East Asia that were most susceptible to American influence have, with a few exceptions, already become democratic. The one major country where the United States can still exercise significant influence on behalf of democratization is Mexico. The undemocratic countries in Africa, the Middle East, and mainland Asia are less susceptible to American influence.

Apart from Central America and the Caribbean, the major area of the Third World where the United States has continued to have vitally important interests is the Persian Gulf. The Gulf War and the dispatch of 500,000 American troops to the region have stimulated demands for movement toward democracy in

PROMOTION OF DEMOCRACY

Kuwait and Saudi Arabia and delegitimized Saddam Hussein's regime in Iraq. A large American military deployment in the Gulf, if sustained over time, would provide an external impetus toward liberalization if not democratization, and a large American military deployment probably could not be sustained over time unless some movement toward democracy occurred.

The U.S. contribution to democratization in the 1980s involved more than the conscious and direct exercise of American power and influence. Democratic movements around the world have been inspired by and have borrowed from the American example. What might happen, however, if the American model ceases to embody strength and success, no longer seems to be the winning model? At the end of the 1980s, many were arguing that "American decline" was the true reality. If people around the world come to see the United States as a fading power beset by political stagnation, economic inefficiency, and social chaos, its perceived failures will inevitably be seen as the failures of democracy, and the worldwide appeal of democracy will diminish.

SNOWBALLING

The impact of snowballing on democratization was clearly evident in 1990 in Bulgaria, Romania, Yugoslavia, Mongolia, Nepal, and Albania. It also affected movements toward liberalization in some Arab and African countries. In 1990, for instance, it was reported that the "upheaval in Eastern Europe" had "fueled demands for change in the Arab world" and prompted leaders in Egypt, Jordan, Tunisia, and Algeria to open up more political space for the expression of discontent.

The East European example had its principal effect on the leaders of authoritarian regimes, not on the people they ruled. President Mobutu Sese Seko of Zaire, for instance reacted with shocked horror to televised pictures of the execution by firing squad of his friend Romanian dictator Nicolae Ceauşescu. A few months later, commenting that "You know what's happening across the world," he announced that he would allow two parties besides his own to compete in elections in 1993. In Tanzania, Julius Nyerere observed that "If changes take place in Eastern Europe then other countries with one-party systems and which profess socialism will also be affected." His country, he added, could learn a "lesson or two" from Eastern Europe. In Nepal in April 1990, the government announced that King Birendra was lifting the ban on political parties as a result of "the international situation" and "the rising expectations of the people."

If a country lacks favorable internal conditions, however, snowballing alone is unlikely to bring about democratization. The democratization of countries A and B is not a reason for democratization in country C, unless the conditions that favored it in the former also exist in the latter. Although the legitimacy of democratic government came to be accepted throughout the world in the 1980s, economic and social conditions favorable to democracy were not everywhere present. The "worldwide democratic revolution" may create an external environment conducive to democratization, but it cannot produce the conditions necessary for democratization within a particular country. *WORLDWIDE DEMOCRATIC REVOLUTION*

In Eastern Europe the major obstacle to democratization was Soviet control; once it was removed, the movement to democracy spread rapidly. There is no comparable external obstacle to democratization in the Middle East, Africa, and Asia. If rulers in these areas chose authoritarianism before December 1989, why can they not continue to choose it thereafter? The snowballing effect would be real only to the extent that it led them to believe in the desirability or necessity of democratization. The events of 1989 in Eastern Europe undoubtedly encouraged democratic opposition groups and frightened authoritarian leaders elsewhere. Yet given the previous weakness of the former and the long-term repression imposed by the latter, it seems doubtful that the East European example will actually produce significant progress toward democracy in most other authoritarian countries.

By 1990, many of the original causes of the third wave had become significantly weaker, even exhausted. Neither the White House, the Kremlin, the European Community, nor the Vatican was in a strong position to promote democracy in places where it did not already exist (primarily in Asia, Africa, and the Middle East). It remains possible, however, for new forces favoring democratization to emerge. After all, who in 1985 could have foreseen that Mikhail Gorbachev would facilitate democratization in Eastern Europe?

In the 1990s the International Monetary Fund (IMF) and the World Bank could conceivably become much more forceful than they have heretofore been in making political democratization as well as economic liberalization a precondition for economic assistance. France might become more active in promoting democracy among its former African colonies, where its influence remains substantial. The Orthodox churches could emerge as a powerful influence for democracy in southeastern Europe and the Soviet Union. A Chinese proponent of *glasnost* could come to power in Beijing, or a new Jeffersonian-style Nasser could spread a democratic version of Pan-Arabism in the Middle East. Japan could use its growing economic clout to encourage human rights and democracy in the poor countries to which it makes loans and grants. In 1990, none of these possibilities seemed very likely, but after the surprises of 1989 it would be rash to rule anything out.

A THIRD REVERSE WAVE?

By 1990 at least two third-wave democracies, Sudan and Nigeria, had reverted to authoritarian rule; the difficulties of consolidation could lead to further reversions in countries with unfavorable conditions for sustaining democracy. The first and second democratic waves, however, were followed not merely by some backsliding but by major reverse waves during which most regime changes throughout the world were from democracy to authoritarianism. If the third wave of democratization slows down or comes to a halt, what factors might produce a third reverse wave?

Among the factors contributing to transitions away from democracy during the first and second reverse waves were:

1. the weakness of democratic values among key elite groups and the general public;

2. severe economic setbacks, which intensified social conflict and enhanced the popularity of remedies that could be imposed only by authoritarian governments;

3. social and political polarization, often produced by leftist governments seeking the rapid introduction of major social and economic reforms;

4. the determination of conservative middle-class and upper-class groups to exclude populist and leftist movements and lower-class groups from political power;

5. the breakdown of law and order resulting from terrorism or insurgency;

6. intervention or conquest by a nondemocratic foreign power;

7. "reverse snowballing" triggered by the collapse or overthrow of democratic systems in other countries.

Transitions from democracy to authoritarianism, apart from those produced by foreign actors, have almost always been produced by those in power or close to power in the democratic system. With only one or two possible exceptions, democratic systems have not been ended by popular vote or popular revolt. In Germany and Italy in the first reverse wave, antidemocratic movements with considerable popular backing came to power and established fascist dictatorships. In Spain in the first reverse wave and in Lebanon in the second, democracy ended in civil war.

The overwhelming majority of transitions from democracy, however, took the form either of military coups that ousted democratically elected leaders, or executive coups in which democratically chosen chief executives effectively ended democracy by concentrating power

in their own hands, usually by declaring a state of emergency or martial law. In the first reverse wave, military coups ended democratic systems in the new countries of Eastern Europe and in Greece, Portugal, Argentina, and Japan. In the second reverse wave, military coups occurred in Indonesia, Pakistan, Greece, Nigeria, Turkey, and many Latin American countries. Executive coups occurred in the second reverse wave in Korea, India, and the Philippines. In Uruguay, the civilian and military leadership cooperated to end democracy through a mixed executive-military coup.

In both the first and second reverse waves, democratic systems were replaced in many cases by historically new forms of authoritarian rule. Fascism was distinguished from earlier forms of authoritarianism by its mass base, ideology, party organization, and efforts to penetrate and control most of society. Bureaucratic authoritarianism differed from earlier forms of military rule in Latin America with respect to its institutional character, its presumption of indefinite duration, and its economic policies. Italy and Germany in the 1920s and 1930s and Brazil and Argentina in the 1960s and 1970s were the lead countries in introducing these new forms of nondemocratic rule and furnished the examples that antidemocratic groups in other countries sought to emulate. Both these new forms of authoritarianism were, in effect, responses to social and economic development: the expansion of social mobilization and political participation in Europe, and the exhaustion of the import-substitution phase of economic development in Latin America.

Although the causes and forms of the first two reverse waves cannot generate reliable predictions concerning the causes and forms of a possible third reverse wave, prior experiences do suggest some potential causes of a new reverse wave.

First, systemic failures of democratic regimes to operate effectively could undermine their legitimacy. In the late twentieth century, the major nondemocratic ideological sources of legitimacy, most notably Marxism-Leninism, were discredited. The general acceptance of democratic norms meant that democratic governments were even less dependent on performance legitimacy than they had been in the past. Yet sustained inability to provide welfare, prosperity, equity, justice, domestic order, or external security could over time undermine the legitimacy even of democratic governments. As the memories of authoritarian failures fade, irritation with democratic failures is likely to increase. More specifically, a general international economic collapse on the 1929–30 model could undermine the legitimacy of democracy in many countries. Most democracies did survive the Great Depression

POTENTIAL CAUSES

of the 1930s; yet some succumbed, and presumably some would be likely to succumb in response to a comparable economic disaster in the future.

SHIFT TO AUTHORITAR-IANISM
Second, a shift to authoritarianism by any democratic or democratizing great power could trigger reverse snowballing. The reinvigoration of authoritarianism in Russia or the Soviet Union would have unsettling effects on democratization in other Soviet republics, Bulgaria, Romania, Yugoslavia, and Mongolia and possibly in Poland, Hungary, and Czechoslovakia as well. It could send the message to would-be despots elsewhere: "You too can go back into business." Similarly, the establishment of an authoritarian regime in India could have a significant demonstration effect on other Third World countries. Moreover, even if a major country does not revert to authoritarianism, a shift to dictatorship by several smaller newly democratic countries that lack many of the usual preconditions for democracy could have ramifying effects even on other countries where those preconditions are strong.

If a nondemocratic state greatly increased its power and began to expand beyond its borders, this too could stimulate authoritarian movements in other countries. This stimulus would be particularly strong if the expanding authoritarian state militarily defeated one or more democratic countries. In the past, all major powers that have developed economically have also tended to expand territorially. If China develops economically under authoritarian rule in the coming decades and expands its influence and control in East Asia, democratic regimes in the region will be significantly weakened.

Finally, as in the 1920s and the 1960s, various old and new forms of authoritarianism that seem appropriate to the needs of the times could emerge. Authoritarian nationalism could take hold in some Third World countries and also in Eastern Europe. Religious fundamentalism, which has been most dramatically prevalent in Iran, could come to power in other countries, especially in the Islamic world. Oligarchic authoritarianism could develop in both wealthy and poorer countries as a reaction to the leveling tendencies of democracy. Populist dictatorships could emerge in the future, as they have in the past, in response to democracy's protection of various forms of economic privilege, particularly in those countries where land tenancy is still an issue. Finally, communal dictatorships could be imposed in democracies with two or more distinct ethnic, racial, or religious groups, with one group trying to establish control over the entire society.

All of these forms of authoritarianism have existed in the past. It is not beyond the wit of humans to devise new ones in the future. One possibility might be a technocratic "electronic dictatorship," in which authoritarian rule is made possible and legitimated by the regime's ability to manipulate information, the media, and sophisticated means of communication. None of these old or new forms of authoritarianism is highly probable, but it is also hard to say that any one of them is totally impossible.

OBSTACLES TO DEMOCRATIZATION

Another approach to assessing democracy's prospects is to examine the obstacles to and opportunities for democratization where it has not yet taken hold. As of 1990, more than one hundred countries lacked democratic regimes. Most of these countries fell into four sometimes overlapping geocultural categories:

1. Home-grown Marxist-Leninist regimes, including the Soviet Union, where major liberalization occurred in the 1980s and democratic movements existed in many republics;

2. Sub-Saharan African countries, which, with a few exceptions, remained personal dictatorships, military regimes, one-party systems, or some combination of these three;

3. Islamic countries stretching from Morocco to Indonesia, which except for Turkey and perhaps Pakistan had nondemocratic regimes;

4. East Asian countries, from Burma through Southeast Asia to China and North Korea, which included communist systems, military regimes, personal dictatorships, and two semi-democracies (Thailand and Malaysia).

The obstacles to democratization in these groups of countries are political, cultural, and economic. One potentially significant political obstacle to future democratization is the virtual absence of experience with democracy in most countries that remained authoritarian in 1990. Twenty-three of 30 countries that democratized between 1974 and 1990 had had some history of democracy, while only a few countries that were nondemocratic in 1990 could claim such experience. These included a few third-wave backsliders (Sudan, Nigeria, Suriname, and possibly Pakistan), four second-wave backsliders that had not redemocratized in the third wave (Lebanon, Sri Lanka, Burma, Fiji), and three first-wave democratizers that had been prevented by Soviet occupation from redemocratizing at the end of World War II (Estonia, Latvia, and Lithuania). Virtually all the 90 or more other nondemocratic countries in 1990 lacked significant past experience with democratic rule. This obviously is not a decisive impediment to democratization—if it were, no countries would now be democratic—but it does make it more difficult.

Another obstacle to democratization is likely to disappear in a number of countries in the 1990s. Leaders who found authoritarian regimes or rule them for a long period tend to be-

LEADERSHIP CHANGE

come particularly staunch opponents of democratization. Hence some form of leadership change within the authoritarian system usually precedes movement toward democracy. Human mortality is likely to ensure such changes in the 1990s in some authoritarian regimes. In 1990, the long-term rulers in China, Côte d'Ivoire, and Malawi were in their eighties; those in Burma, Indonesia, North Korea, Lesotho, and Vietnam were in their seventies; and the leaders of Cuba, Morocco, Singapore, Somalia, Syria, Tanzania, Zaire, and Zambia were sixty or older. The death or departure from office of these leaders would remove one obstacle to democratization in their countries, but would not make it inevitable.

Between 1974 and 1990, democratization occurred in personal dictatorships, military regimes, and one-party systems. Full-scale democratization has not yet occurred, however, in communist one-party states that were the products of domestic revolution. Liberalization has taken place in the Soviet Union, which may or may not lead to full-scale democratization in Russia. In Yugoslavia, movements toward democracy are underway in Slovenia and Croatia. The Yugoslav communist revolution, however, was largely a Serbian revolution, and the prospects for democracy in Serbia appear dubious. In Cambodia, an extraordinarily brutal revolutionary communist regime was replaced by a less brutal communist regime imposed by outside force. In 1990, Albania appeared to be opening up, but in China, Vietnam, Laos, Cuba and Ethiopia, Marxist-Leninist regimes produced by home-grown revolutions seemed determined to remain in power. The revolutions in these countries had been nationalist as well as communist, and hence nationalism reinforced communism in a way that obviously was not true of Soviet-occupied Eastern Europe.

One serious impediment of democratization is the absence or weakness of real commitment to democratic values among political leaders in Asia, Africa, and the Middle East. When they are out of power, political leaders have good reason to advocate democracy. The test of their democratic commitment comes once they are in office. In Latin America, democratic regimes have generally been overthrown by military coups d'état. This has happened in Asia and the Middle East as well, but in these regions elected leaders themselves have also been responsible for ending democracy: Syngman Rhee and Park Chung Hee in Korea, Adnan Menderes in Turkey, Ferdinand Marcos in the Philippines, Lee Kwan Yew in Singapore, Indira Gandhi in India, and Sukarno in Indonesia. Having won power through the electoral system, these leaders then proceeded to undermine that system. They had little commitment to democratic values and practices.

Even when Asian, African, and Middle Eastern leaders have more or less abided by the rules of democracy, they often seemed to do so grudgingly. Many European, North American, and Latin American political leaders in the last half of the twentieth century were ardent and articulate advocates of democracy. Asian and African countries, in contrast, did not produce many heads of government who were also apostles of democracy. Who were the Asian, Arab, or African equivalents of Rómulo Betancourt, Alberto Llera Camargo, José Figueres, Eduardo Frei, Fernando Belaúnde Terry, Juan Bosch, José Napoleón Duarte, and Raúl Alfonsin? Jawaharlal Nehru and Corazon Aquino were, and there may have been others, but they were few in number. No Arab leader comes to mind, and it is hard to identify any Islamic leader who made a reputation as an advocate and supporter of democracy while in office. Why is this? This question inevitably leads to the issue of culture.

CULTURE

It has been argued that the world's great historic cultural traditions vary significantly in the extent to which their attitudes, values, beliefs, and related behavior patterns are conducive to the development of democracy. A profoundly antidemocratic culture would impede the spread of democratic norms in the society, deny legitimacy to democratic institutions, and thus greatly complicate if not prevent the emergence and effective functioning of those institutions. The cultural thesis comes in two forms. The more restrictive version states that only Western culture provides a suitable base for the development of democratic institutions and, consequently, that democracy is largely inappropriate for non-Western societies. In the early years of the third wave, this argument was explicitly set forth by George Kennan. Democracy, he said, was a form of government "which evolved in the eighteenth and nineteenth centuries in northwestern Europe, primarily among those countries that border on the English Channel and the North Sea (but with a certain extension into Central Europe), and which was then carried into other parts of the world, including North America, where peoples from that northwestern European area appeared as original settlers, or as colonialists, and laid down the prevailing patterns of civil government." Hence democracy has "a relatively narrow base both in time and in space; and the evidence has yet to be produced that it is the natural form of rule for peoples outside those narrow perimeters." The achievements of Mao, Salazar, and Castro demonstrated, according to Kennan, that authoritarian regimes "have been able to introduce reforms and to improve the lot of masses of people, where more diffuse forms of political authority had failed."

Democracy, in short, is appropriate only for northwestern and perhaps central European countries and their settler-colony offshoots.

The Western-culture thesis has immediate implications for democratization in the Balkans and the Soviet Union. Historically these areas were part of the Czarist and Ottoman empires; their prevailing religions were Orthodoxy and Islam, not Western Christianity. These areas did not have the same experiences as Western Europe with feudalism, the Renaissance, the Reformation, the Enlightenment, the French Revolution, and liberalism. As William Wallace has suggested, the end of the Cold War and the disappearance of the Iron Curtain may have shifted the critical political dividing line eastward to the centuries-old boundary between Eastern and Western Christendom. Beginning in the north, this line runs south roughly along the borders dividing Finland and the Baltic republics from Russia; through Byelorussia and the Ukraine, separating western Catholic Ukraine from eastern Orthodox Ukraine; south and then west in Romania, cutting off Transylvania from the rest of the country; and then through Yugoslavia roughly along the line separating Slovenia and Croatia from the other republics. This line may now separate those areas where democracy will take root from those where it will not.

WESTERN CULTURE THESIS

A less restrictive version of the cultural obstacle argument holds that certain non-Western cultures are peculiarly hostile to democracy. The two cultures most often cited in this regard are Confucianism and Islam. Three questions are relevant to determining whether these cultures now pose serious obstacles to democratization. First, to what extent are traditional Confucian and Islamic values and beliefs hostile to democracy? Second, if they are, to what extent have these cultures in fact hampered progress toward democracy? Third, if they have significantly retarded democratic progress in the past, to what extent are they likely to continue to do so in the future?

CONFUCIANISM

Almost no scholarly disagreement exists regarding the proposition that traditional Confucianism was either undemocratic or antidemocratic. The only mitigating factor was the extent to which the examination system in the classic Chinese polity opened careers to the talented without regard to social background. Even if this were the case, however, a merit system of promotion does not make a democracy. No one would describe a modern army as democratic because officers are promoted on the basis of their abilities. Classic Chinese Confucianism and its derivatives in Korea, Vietnam, Singapore, Taiwan, and (in diluted fashion) Japan emphasized the group over the individual, authority over liberty, and responsibilities over rights. Confucian societies lacked a tradition of rights against the state; to the extent that individual rights did exist, they were created by the state. Harmony and cooperation were preferred over disagreement and competition. The maintenance of order and respect for hierarchy were central values. The conflict of ideas, groups, and parties was viewed as dangerous and illegitimate. Most important, Confucianism merged society and the state and provided no legitimacy for autonomous social institutions at the national level.

In practice Confucian or Confucian-influenced societies have been inhospitable to democracy. In East Asia only two countries, Japan and the Philippines, had sustained experience with democratic government prior to 1990. In both cases, democracy was the product of an American presence. The Philippines, moreover, is overwhelmingly a Catholic country. In Japan, Confucian values were reinterpreted and merged with autochthonous cultural traditions.

Mainland China has had no experience with democratic government, and democracy of the Western variety has been supported over the years only by relatively small groups of radical dissidents. "Mainstream" democratic critics have not broken with the key elements of the Confucian tradition. The modernizers of China have been (in Lucian Pye's phrase) the "Confucian Leninists" of the Nationalist and Communist parties. In the late 1980s, when rapid economic growth in China produced a new series of demands for political reform and democracy on the part of students, intellectuals, and urban middle-class groups, the Communist leadership responded in two ways. First, it articulated a theory of "new authoritarianism," based on the experience of Taiwan, Singapore, and Korea, which claimed that a country at China's stage of economic development needed authoritarian rule to achieve balanced economic growth and contain the unsettling consequences of development. Second, the leadership violently suppressed the democratic movement in Beijing and elsewhere in June of 1989.

In China, economics reinforced culture in holding back democracy. In Singapore, Taiwan, and Korea, on the other hand, spectacular growth created the economic basis for democracy by the late 1980s. In these countries, economics clashed with culture in shaping political development. In 1990, Singapore was the only non-oil-exporting "high-income" country (as defined by the World Bank) that did not have a democratic political system, and Singapore's leader was an articulate exponent of Confucian values as opposed to those of Western democracy. In the 1980s, Premier Lee Kwan Yew made the teaching and promulgation of Confucian values a high priority for his city-state and took vigorous measures to limit and suppress dissent and to prevent media criticism of the government and its policies. Singapore was thus an authoritarian Confucian anomaly among the wealthy countries of the world. The interesting question is whether it will remain so now that Lee, who created the state, appears to be partially withdrawing from the political scene.

TAIWAN AND KOREA

In the late 1980s, both Taiwan and Korea moved in a democratic direction. Historically, Taiwan had always been a peripheral part of China. It was occupied by the Japanese for 50 years, and its inhabitants rebelled in 1947 against the imposition of Chinese control. The Nationalist government arrived in 1949 humiliated by its defeat by the Communists, a defeat that made it impossible "for most Nationalist leaders to uphold the posture of arrogance associated with traditional Confucian notions of authority." Rapid economic and social development further weakened the influence of traditional Confucianism. The emergence of a substantial entrepreneurial class, composed largely of native Taiwanese, created (in very un-Confucian fashion) a source of power and wealth independent of the mainlander-dominated state. This produced in Taiwan a "fundamental change in Chinese political culture, which has not occurred in China itself or in Korea or Vietnam—and never really existed in Japan." Taiwan's spectacular economic development thus overwhelmed a relatively weak Confucian legacy, and in the late 1980s Chiang Ching-kuo and Lee Teng-hui responded to the pressures produced by economic and social change and gradually moved to open up politics in their society.

In Korea, the classical culture included elements of mobility and egalitarianism along with Confucian components uncongenial to democracy, including a tradition of authoritarianism and strongman rule. As one Korean scholar put it, "people did not think of themselves as citizens with rights to exercise and responsibilities to perform, but they tended to look up to the top for direction and for favors in order to survive." In the late 1980s, urbanization, education, the development of a substantial middle class, and the impressive spread of Christianity all weakened Confucianism as an obstacle to democracy in Korea. Yet it remained unclear whether the struggle between the old culture and the new prosperity had been definitively resolved in favor of the latter.

THE EAST ASIAN MODEL

The interaction of economic progress and Asian culture appears to have generated a distinctly East Asian variety of democratic institutions. As of 1990, no East Asian country except the Philippines (which is, in many respects, more Latin American than East Asian in culture) had experienced a turnover from a popularly elected government of one party to a popularly elected government of a different party. The prototype was Japan, unquestionably a democracy, but one in which the ruling party has never been voted out of power. The Japanese model of dominant-party democracy, as Pye has pointed out, has spread elsewhere in East Asia. In 1990, two of the three opposition parties in Korea merged with the government party to form a political bloc that would effectively exclude the remaining opposition party, led by Kim Dae Jung and based on the Cholla region, from ever gaining power. In the late 1980s, democratic development in Taiwan seemed to be moving toward an electoral system in which the Kuomintang (KMT) was likely to remain the dominant party, with the Democratic Progressive Party confined to a permanent opposition role. In Malaysia, the coalition of the three leading parties from the Malay, Chinese, and Indian communities (first in the Alliance Party and then in the National Front) has controlled power in unbroken fashion against all competitors from the 1950s through the 1980s. In the mid-1980s, Lee Kwan Yew's deputy and successor Goh Chok Tong endorsed a similar type of party system for Singapore:

> I think a stable system is one where there is a mainstream political party representing a broad range of the population. Then you can have a few other parties on the periphery, very serious-minded parties. They are unable to have wider views but they nevertheless represent sectional interests. And the mainstream is returned all the time. I think that's good. And I would not apologize if we ended up in that situation in Singapore.

A primary criterion for democracy is equitable and open competition for votes between political parties without government harassment or restriction of opposition groups. Japan has clearly met this test for decades with its freedoms of speech, press, and assembly, and reasonably equitable conditions of electoral competition. In the other Asian dominant-party systems, the playing field has been tilted in favor of the government for many years. By the late 1980s, however, conditions were becoming more equal in some countries. In Korea, the government party was unable to win control of the legislature in 1989, and this failure presumably was a major factor in its subsequent merger with two of its opponents. In Taiwan, restrictions on the opposition were gradually lifted. It is thus conceivable that other East Asian countries could join Japan in providing a level playing field for a game that the government party always wins. In 1990 the East Asian dominant-party systems thus spanned a continuum between democracy and authoritarianism, with Japan at one extreme, Indonesia at the other, and Korea, Taiwan, Malay-

DOMINANT-
PARTY SYSTEM

sia, and Singapore (more or less in that order) in between.

Such a system may meet the formal requisites of democracy, but it differs significantly from the democratic systems prevalent in the West, where it is assumed not only that political parties and coalitions will freely and equally compete for power but also that they are likely to *alternate* in power. By contrast, the East Asian dominant-party systems seem to involve competition for power but not alternation in power, and participation in elections for all, but participation in office only for those in the "mainstream" party. This type of political system offers democracy without turnover. It represents an adaptation of Western democratic practices to serve not Western values of competition and change, but Asian values of consensus and stability.

Western democratic systems are less dependent on performance legitimacy than authoritarian systems because failure is blamed on the incumbents instead of the system, and the ouster and replacement of the incumbents help to renew the system. The East Asian societies that have adopted or appear to be adopting the dominant-party model had unequalled records of economic success from the 1960s to the 1980s. What happens, however, if and when their 8-percent growth rates plummet; unemployment, inflation, and other forms of economic distress escalate; or social and economic conflicts intensify? In a Western democracy the response would be to turn the incumbents out. In a dominant-party democracy, however, that would represent a revolutionary change. If the structure of political competition does not allow that to happen, unhappiness with the government could well lead to demonstrations, protests, riots, and efforts to mobilize popular support to overthrow the government. The government then would be tempted to respond by suppressing dissent and imposing authoritarian controls. The key question, then, is to what extent the East Asian dominant-party system presupposes uninterrupted and substantial economic growth. Can this system survive prolonged economic downturn or stagnation?

ISLAM

"Confucian democracy" is clearly a contradiction in terms. It is unclear whether "Islamic democracy" also is. Egalitarianism and voluntarism are central themes in Islam. The "high culture form of Islam," Ernest Gellner has argued, is "endowed with a number of features—unitarianism, a rule-ethic, individualism, scripturalism, puritanism, an egalitarian aversion to mediation and hierarchy, a fairly small load of magic—that are congruent, presumably, with requirements of modernity or modernization." They are also

generally congruent with the requirements of democracy. Islam, however, also rejects any distinction between the religious community and the political community. Hence there is no equipoise between Caesar and God, and political participation is linked to religious affiliation. Fundamentalist Islam demands that in a Muslim country the political rulers should be practicing Muslims, *shari'a* should be the basic law, and *ulema* should have a "decisive vote in articulating, or at least reviewing and ratifying, all governmental policy." To the extent that governmental legitimacy and policy flow from religious doctrine and religious expertise, Islamic concepts of politics differ from and contradict the premises of democratic politics.

Islamic doctrine thus contains elements that may be both congenial and uncongenial to democracy. In practice, however, the only Islamic country that has sustained a fully democratic political system for any length of time is Turkey, where Mustafa Kemal Ataturk explicitly rejected Islamic concepts of society and politics and vigorously attempted to create a secular, modern, Western nation-state. And Turkey's experience with democracy has not been an unmitigated success. Elsewhere in the Islamic world, Pakistan has made three attempts at democracy, none of which lasted long. While Turkey has had democracy interrupted by occasional military interventions, Pakistan has had bureaucratic and military rule interrupted by occasional elections.

The only Arab country to sustain a form of democracy (albeit of the consociational variety) for a significant period of time was Lebanon. Its democracy, however, really amounted to consociational oligarchy, and 40 to 50 percent of its population was Christian. Once Muslims became a majority in Lebanon and began to assert themselves, Lebanese democracy collapsed. Between 1981 and 1990, only two of 37 countries in the world with Muslim majorities were ever rated "Free" by Freedom House in its annual surveys: the Gambia for two years and the Turkish Republic of Northern Cyprus for four. Whatever the compatibility of Islam and democracy in theory, in practice they have rarely gone together.

Opposition movements to authoritarian regimes in southern and eastern Europe, in Latin America, and in East Asia almost universally have espoused Western democratic values and proclaimed their desire to establish democracy. This does not mean that they invariably would introduce democratic institutions if they had the opportunity to do so, but at least they articulated the rhetoric of democracy. In authoritarian Islamic societies, by contrast, movements explicitly campaigning for democratic politics have been relatively weak, and the most powerful opposition has come from Islamic fundamentalists.

ECONOMIC
PROBLEMS
　　In the late 1980s, domestic economic problems combined with the snowballing effects of democratization elsewhere led the governments of several Islamic countries to relax their controls on the opposition and to attempt to renew their legitimacy through elections. The principal initial beneficiaries of these openings were Islamic fundamentalist groups. In Algeria, the Islamic Salvation Front swept the June 1990 local elections, the first free elections since the country became independent in 1962. In the 1989 Jordanian elections, Islamic fundamentalists won 36 of 80 seats in parliament. In Egypt, many candidates associated with the Muslim Brotherhood were elected to parliament in 1987. In several countries, Islamic fundamentalist groups were reportedly plotting insurrections. The strong electoral showings of the Islamic groups partly reflected the absence of other opposition parties, some because they were under government proscription, others because they were boycotting the elections. Nonetheless, fundamentalism seemed to be gaining strength in Middle Eastern countries, particularly among younger people. The strength of this tendency induced secular heads of government in Tunisia, Turkey, and elsewhere to adopt policies advocated by the fundamentalists and to make political gestures demonstrating their own commitment to Islam.

Liberalization in Islamic countries thus enhanced the power of important social and political movements whose commitment to democracy was uncertain. In some respects, the position of fundamentalist parties in Islamic societies in the early 1990s raised questions analogous to those posed by communist parties in Western Europe in the 1940s and again in the 1970s. Would the existing governments continue to open up their politics and hold elections in which Islamic groups could compete freely and equally? Would the Islamic groups gain majority support in those elections? If they did win the elections, would the military, which in many Islamic societies (e.g., Algeria, Turkey, Pakistan, and Indonesia) is strongly secular, allow them to form a government? If they did form a government, would it pursue radical Islamic policies that would undermine democracy and alienate the modern and Western-oriented elements in society?

THE LIMITS OF CULTURAL OBSTACLES

Strong cultural obstacles to democratization thus appear to exist in Confucian and Islamic societies. There are, nonetheless, reasons to doubt whether these must necessarily prevent democratic development. First, similar cultural arguments have not held up in the past. At one point many scholars argued that Catholicism was an obstacle to democracy. Others, in the Weberian tradition, contended that Catholic countries were unlikely to develop economically in the same manner as Protestant countries. Yet in the 1960s, 1970s, and 1980s Catholic countries became democratic and, on average, had higher rates of economic growth than Protestant countries. Similarly, at one point Weber and others argued that countries with Confucian cultures would not achieve successful capitalist development. By the 1980s, however, a new generation of scholars saw Confucianism as a major cause of the spectacular economic growth of East Asian societies. In the longer run, will the thesis that Confucianism prevents democratic development be any more viable than the thesis that Confucianism prevents economic development? Arguments that particular cultures are permanent obstacles to change should be viewed with a certain skepticism.

Second, great cultural traditions like Islam and Confucianism are highly complex bodies of ideas, beliefs, doctrines, assumptions, and behavior patterns. Any major culture, including Confucianism, has some elements that are compatible with democracy, just as both Protestantism and Catholicism have elements that are clearly undemocratic. Confucian democracy may be a contradiction in terms, but democracy in a Confucian society need not be. The real question is which elements in Islam and Confucianism are favorable to democracy, and how and under what circumstances these can supersede the undemocratic aspects of those cultural traditions.

Third, cultures historically are dynamic, not stagnant. The dominant beliefs and attitudes in a society change. While maintaining elements of continuity, the prevailing culture of a society in one generation may differ significantly from what it was one or two generations earlier. In the 1950s, Spanish culture was typically described as traditional, authoritarian, hierarchical, deeply religious, and honor-and-status oriented. By the 1970s and 1980s, these words had little place in a description of Spanish attitudes and values. Cultures evolve and, as in Spain, the most important force bringing about cultural changes is often economic development itself.

ECONOMICS

Few relationships between social, economic, and political phenomena are stronger than that between the level of economic development and the existence of democratic politics. Most wealthy countries are democratic, and most democratic countries—India is the most dramatic exception—are wealthy. The correlation between wealth and democracy implies that transitions to democracy should occur primarily in countries at the mid-level of economic development. In poor countries democratization is unlikely; in rich countries it usually has already occurred. In between there is a "political transition zone": countries in this middle economic stratum are those most likely to transit to democracy, and most countries that transit to democracy will be in this stratum. As countries develop economically and move into the transition zone, they become good prospects for democratization.

In fact, shifts from authoritarianism to democracy during the third wave were heavily concentrated in this transition zone, especially at its upper reaches. The conclusion seems clear. Poverty is a principal—probably *the* principal—obstacle to democratic development. The future of democracy depends on the future of economic development. Obstacles to economic development are obstacles to the expansion of democracy.

The third wave of democratization was propelled forward by the extraordinary global economic growth of the 1950s and 1960s. That era of growth came to an end with the oil price increases of 1973-74. Between 1974 and 1990, democratization accelerated around the world, but global economic growth slowed down. There were, however, substantial differences in growth rates among regions. East Asian rates remained high throughout the 1970s and 1980s, and overall rates of growth in South Asia increased. On the other hand, growth rates in the Middle East, North Africa, Latin America, and the Caribbean declined sharply from the 1970s to the 1980s. Those in sub-Saharan Africa plummeted. Per capita GNP in Africa was stagnant during the late 1970s and declined at an annual rate of 2.2 percent during the 1980s. The economic obstacles to democratization in Africa thus clearly grew during the 1980s. The prospects for the 1990s are not encouraging. Even if economic reforms, debt relief, and economic assistance materialize, the World Bank has predicted an average annual rate of growth in per capita GDP for Africa of only 0.5 percent for the remainder of the century. If this prediction is accurate, the economic obstacles to democratization in sub-Saharan Africa will remain overwhelming well into the twenty-first century.

The World Bank was more optimistic in its predictions of economic growth for China and the nondemocratic countries of South Asia. The current low levels of wealth in those countries, however, generally mean that even with annual per capita growth rates of 3 to 5 percent, the economic conditions favorable to democratization would still be long in coming.

In the 1990s, the majority of countries where the economic conditions for democratization are already present or rapidly emerging are in the Middle East and North Africa (see Table 1). The economies of many of these countries (United Arab Emirates, Kuwait, Saudi Arabia, Iraq, Iran, Libya, Oman) depend heavily on oil exports, which enhances the control of the state bureaucracy. This does not, however, make democratization impossible. The state bureaucracies of Eastern Europe had far more power than do those of the oil exporters. Thus at some point that power could collapse among the latter as dramatically as it did among the former.

In 1988 among the other states of the Middle East and North Africa, Algeria had already reached a level conducive to democratization; Syria was approaching it; and Jordan, Tunisia, Morocco, Egypt, and North Yemen were well below the transition zone, but had grown rapidly during the 1980s. Middle Eastern economies and societies are approaching the point where they will become too wealthy and too complex for their various traditional, military, and one-party systems of authoritarian rule to sustain themselves. The wave of democratization that swept the world in the 1970s and 1980s could become a dominant feature of Middle Eastern and North African politics in the 1990s. The issue of economics versus culture would then be joined: What forms of politics might emerge in these countries when economic prosperity begins to interact with Islamic values and traditions?

In China, the obstacles to democratization are political, economic, and cultural; in Africa they are overwhelmingly economic; and in the rapidly developing countries of East Asia and in many Islamic countries, they are primarily cultural.

ECONOMICS VERSUS CULTURE

ECONOMIC DEVELOPMENT AND POLITICAL LEADERSHIP

History has proved both optimists and pessimists wrong about democracy. Future events will probably do the same. Formidable obstacles to the expansion of democracy exist in many societies. The third wave, the "global democratic revolution" of the late twentieth century, will not last forever. It may be followed by a new surge of authoritarianism sustained enough to constitute a third reverse wave. That, however, would not preclude a fourth wave of democratization developing some time in the twenty-first century. Judging by the record of the past, the two most decisive factors affecting the future consolidation and expansion of democracy will be economic development and political leadership.

Most poor societies will remain undemocratic so long as they remain poor. Poverty, however, is not inevitable. In the past, nations such as South Korea, which were assumed to be mired in economic backwardness, have as-

TABLE 1. *Upper and Middle Income Nondemocratic Countries—GNP Per Capita (1988)*

Income level	Arab-Middle East	Southeast Asia	Africa	Other
Upper income (>$6,000)	UAE[a] Kuwait[a] Saudi Arabia[a]	Singapore		
Upper middle income ($2,000–5,500)	Iraq[a] Iran[a] Libya[a] Oman[a,b] Algeria[b]		(Gabon)	Yugoslavia
Lower middle income ($500–2,200)	Syria Jordan[b] Tunisia[b]	Malaysia[b] Thailand[b]	Cameroon[b]	Paraguay
$1,000 --				
	Morocco[b] Egypt[b] Yemen[b] Lebanon[b]		Congo[b] Côte d'Ivoire Zimbabwe Senegal[b] Angola	

Source: World Bank, *World Bank Development Report 1990* (New York: Oxford University Press, 1990), 178–181.
[a]Major oil exporter.
[b]Average annual GDP growth rate 1980–1988 > 3.0%.

tonished the world by rapidly attaining prosperity. In the 1980s, a new consensus emerged among developmental economists on the ways to promote economic growth. The consensus of the 1980s may or may not prove more lasting and productive than the very different consensus among economists that prevailed in the 1950s and 1960s. The new orthodoxy of neo-orthodoxy, however, already seems to have produced significant results in many countries.

Yet there are two reasons to temper our hopes with caution. First, economic development for the late, late, late developing countries—meaning largely Africa—may well be more difficult than it was for earlier developers because the advantages of backwardness come to be outweighed by the widening and historically unprecedented gap between rich and poor countries. Second, new forms of authoritarianism could emerge in wealthy, information-dominated, technology-based societies. If unhappy possibilities such as these do not materialize, economic development should create the conditions for the progressive replacement of authoritarian political systems by democratic ones. Time is on the side of democracy.

Economic development makes democracy possible; political leadership makes it real. For democracies to come into being, future political elites will have to believe, at a minimum, that democracy is the least bad form of government for their societies and for themselves. They will also need the skills to bring about the transition to democracy while facing both radical oppositionists and authoritarian hard-liners who inevitably will attempt to undermine their efforts. Democracy will spread to the extent that those who exercise power in the world and in individual countries want it to spread. For a century and a half after Tocqueville observed the emergence of modern democracy in America, successive waves of democratization have washed over the shore of dictatorship. Buoyed by a rising tide of economic progress, each wave advanced further—and receded less—than its predecessor. History, to shift the metaphor, does not sail ahead in a straight line, but when skilled and determined leaders are at the helm, it does move forward.

The 'Missing Middle' of Democracy

People, not ideologies, are the building blocks of the new politics, say visionary experts on 'civil society.'

Robin Wright

Times Staff Writer

WASHINGTON—On the West Bank, Palestinian teachers, students and parents quietly run underground schools and college courses to replace those closed by military authorities.

In the overcrowded refugee camps of the Gaza Strip, young women operate nonprofit child-care facilities, while Islamist groups offer welfare and social services. In East Jerusalem, the al-Hakawati speakers group holds regular debates on legal, human rights and other topical issues.

Throughout the occupied territories, volunteers have created scores of local "health committees" that provide rudimentary care for those who can't get to or afford conventional treatment. And professional unions offer a mechanism for everything from pooling resources to regulating services, while writers' and scientists' syndicates provide forums for exchanging ideas and innovations.

As Palestinians prepare for the long road to self-rule, this mosaic of grassroots organizations may be even more important than Yasser Arafat in determining whether a stable, pluralist society is eventually created in the West Bank and Gaza.

But groups like these may also provide a key to broader stability in the post–Cold War world. For they are at the core of what political strategists call "civil society"—a term increasingly used worldwide to describe a new vision of social and political organization built around people rather than ideologies.

Civil society is the product of groups both formal and informal, ranging from local sports associations to international human rights organizations, from trade unions to women's bridge clubs and from chambers of commerce to wildlife protection movements.

Together, they form the "missing middle" that can fill the vacuum between the state and its people, according to Naomi Chazan, a political scientist at Hebrew University in Jerusalem.

As in the Palestinian case, civil society offers a means of participating before the ballot. In struggling democracies from Poland to Peru, it offers a means of having impact beyond the ballot.

And in places as different as Brazil's tropical Amazon and Siberia's arctic hinterlands, the diverse and disparate groups provide various means to draw people into a system, give them a stake, protect their rights and project their demands—thus stabilizing societies, peacefully.

The fabric woven by civil society could eventually replace the majority in "majority rules." In places where there is no longer a classic, single-minded majority, interactive groups may provide a stronger glue to hold fragmenting societies together, social scientists predict.

The growth of civil society reflects one of the most fundamental shifts in power since the onset of global change in 1989, according to Augustus Richard Norton, a Boston University political scientist and director of the Civil Society in the Middle East project.

"The state system—with its armies and diplomatic privileges and sovereignty—survives. But parallel to the state system now is a system of non-sovereign or non-state actors, sometimes local but sometimes crossing boundaries, because the communications revolution has enabled them to maneuver around state restrictions and laws and surveillance," he said.

In the decades ahead, civil society is likely to be the strongest barometer of democratic change. As a rule, the more numerous, engaged and diverse a community's civil organizations, the more likely pluralism will take root and survive. And the more civil groups people belong to, the greater a society's stability.

"Sustaining democracy requires more than just reforming laws to open up the political system or creating a large middle class," Norton added.

"It also requires opening up political space where contending opinions are given a voice. The real home of democracy is civil society, because without a vibrant and autonomous civil society, elections no matter how pristine, no matter how mechanically perfect, are unlikely to produce durable results."

Group life is nothing new nor, really, is civil society. The concept is as old as the ancients who coined the term. And for centuries the world's great thinkers, from Montesquieu and Marx to Adam Smith and Hegel, have debated the role of grass-roots and other non-governmental organizations in lofty treatises.

What distinguishes the situation today are the dimensions and diversity of new groups that are emerging. The 1993 U.N. Human Development Report describes "an explosion of participatory movements or non-governmental organizations. . . . People's participation is becoming the central issue of our time."

Trade unions have provided much of the impetus for the wave of democratization of the 1980s, particularly in Poland,

Bulgaria, South Korea and several Latin American countries.

The citizens groups Civic Forum and Public Against Violence were critical to the success of Czechoslovakia's 1989 "Velvet Revolution," providing a means of empowering people and challenging the state. And the 1989 pro-democracy uprising at Beijing's Tian An Men Square was the product of a civil society struggling to emerge in China.

In the United States, which probably has the world's richest civil society, the right of free association in groups beyond government control may be taken for granted. But it is new in most parts of the world. And it is growing.

Kenya now has 23,000 women's groups alone. India's Tamil Nadu state has 25,000 registered grass-roots organizations. And the Philippines has at least 12,000 community associations or cooperatives, according to the U.N. report.

Internationally, groups not tied to states are becoming global players in the 1990s. The London-based human rights group Amnesty International is now "more powerful than 90% of the world's states," Norton contends. International Physicians for the Prevention of Nuclear War won the Nobel Peace Prize in 1985, while Doctors Without Borders, Save the Children and a host of other international organizations are more involved in global crises than most Western nations. They're also often a jump ahead of the United Nations.

In a break with the past, most of these groups are not controlled, manipulated or financed by nations. And in varying degrees, they are changing global political life on at least three levels.

A STAKE IN THE SYSTEM

First, they are bringing people from the bottom of society into the system—and in turn changing the middle and top.

Egypt offers an extreme example. About 750,000 people live in mausoleums of Cairo's largest cemetery, known as the City of the Dead, due to a chronic housing shortage. The only people lower on the social ladder are poor migrants from Egypt's desert oases who squat on the cemetery's fringe. They're called *Zabbaleen,* or garbage people.

For years, the *Zabbaleen* lived nocturnally, picking up refuse as an illegal livelihood. By dawn, they'd disappeared into their squalid and also illegal shanties.

Even City of the Dead residents looked down on them.

But in the late 1980s, the *Zabbaleen* began organizing. They've since obtained a license to operate legally—and during daylight. The government agreed to provide water and electricity to their area. And as a recognized group, they've changed their image: Rather than being an embarrassment, they're now seen as people contributing to the city's life and cleanliness.

"Associational life in the past—unions and professional groups—was always dominated by the middle class. The new development is that the lower classes are now mobilizing in their own interests too," explained Saad Eddin Ibrahim, an Egyptian sociologist and publisher of the monthly Civil Society newsletter, which circulates around the world.

"And they are slowly changing the way of life and the balance of power in Egypt."

At the time of President Gamal Abdel Nasser's death a generation ago, Egypt was home to about 7,000 groups, many of them under heavy state control or influence. Today, Egypt boasts 21,000 diverse organizations, the majority free, Ibrahim said.

Emerging civil societies are also empowering minorities—and allowing them to integrate without forcing a surrender of their separate identity.

Over the last three years, the Amazonia Working Group has pulled together more than 140 of Brazil's small and isolated communities, from Indian tribes to rubber tappers, in an umbrella advocacy movement. It now has eight regional offices, according to Marcel Viergever, a U.N. development specialist. Once powerless, the minorities are together gaining clout on political and environmental issues.

On the other side of the Equator, the 15,000 indigenous Chukchi of Siberia's Arctic Chukotka Peninsula—powerless for centuries against Russian imperial and Soviet Communist rule—have started to take on both the state and the Russians, who now outnumber the Chukchi 8 to 1 in their ancient tribal area. They're campaigning to restrict wildlife hunting and eliminate a local nuclear power station, urging that funds instead be used to research energy alternatives.

"We're trying to make non-indigenous people understand that in coalition we can create a better environment for all, not just the Chukchi," said Oleg Egorov, the Chukchi's new lobbyist.

A plethora of groups has also been crucial to female empowerment in the 1990s.

In Yemen, for example, the formation of several new women's organizations resulted in 50 female candidates in parliamentary elections last April. Against all odds—since they were either independents or small-party candidates in a male-dominated, staunchly Muslim country—two won, crossing a threshold.

"Through civil organization people are able to express at the grass-roots level their preferences and their aspirations. Once they have a stake, then they're hooked. So civil society influences the pattern of political development and ensures its survival," said Saraswathi Menon, an Indian sociologist in the U.N. Human Development Program.

GADFLY TO THE NATION

Second, people's organizations are increasingly vehicles for changing the functioning of nations. In addition to holding governments accountable, they, rather than the nation, often take the lead in solving problems.

Among the most dynamic Palestinian groups in the occupied territories is Law in the Service of Man or Al-Haqq, a human rights group formed in the 1980s and widely praised by Amnesty International and others.

Al-Haqq, which uses Palestinian lawyers, business people and academics on a voluntary basis, documents and goes to court over abuses. Even before a Palestinian authority is elected, a group is already in place to monitor its practices—although staunchly Palestinian, Al-Haqq has kept sufficient political distance from all parties to be a fair arbiter of democratic and human rights standards, both Palestinian and American experts claim.

"Civil society is simultaneously arrayed against the state and engaged with the state in setting the boundaries of public power," explained Peter Lewis, author of "Political Transition and the Dilemma of Civil Society in Africa."

"Throughout the continent, independent political and social forces have emerged to challenge moribund authoritarian-patrimonial regimes of many varieties," Lewis added. "Churches and organized labor, lawyers and students, market women, academics, physicians, journalists, business elites and a host of other interests may be identified among the growing realm of associational participation."

Zambia's young trade union movement was critical in ending almost three decades of one-party rule. Its role was acknowledged in 1991 presidential elections, won by trade union leader Frederick Chiluba.

In the Middle East, the rise of political Islam is also based on its ability to provide a range of associations and social services, particularly in countries unable to meet citizens' needs yet unwilling to allow change.

Since 1970, the number of groups in the 21-nation Arab world has soared from some 20,000 to 70,000, according to Ibrahim, the Egyptian sociologist. Vast numbers are Islamist.

In Jordan, Egypt and other Arab states, Islamists have organized schools and clinics, assembled networks for youth and women, offered training and jobs, generally fostering an atmosphere of participation through Islamist groups.

"As the state retreats from providing services and housing and so on, people are recognizing that they must organize to provide alternatives. In the process, they demand a share in decision-making at the community level," Ibrahim said. "That's the wave of the present and the future."

According to the U.N. report, free participation in civil society and the economy is not a luxury but an imperative for the survival of nations. "If states are to survive, they will have to establish new relations with their people," it warned.

RESOLVING CONFLICTS

Perhaps the biggest test of many emerging civil societies is their ability to deal with conflicts, combat crime, and counter ethnic and nationalist passions, particularly in the Third World and former Communist states.

On the one hand, the proliferation of civil organizations offers new means to cope with those nagging problems.

Although efforts to disarm Somalia's warlords dominate the headlines, for example, U.S. and U.N. diplomats have also been working quietly to pull together people with common interests—merchants, intellectuals, women and others—to form a series of associations that go beyond clan divisions.

"Building civil society provides leaders who have their own constituencies with common interests," explained former U.N. envoy Mohammed Sahnoun. "People begin to listen to them rather than the warlords as they see an alternative leadership which is long-term and rational and in which they have a stake."

Among Palestinians, ideological differences run deep among diverse political groups—from Marxist to Islamist and from moderate pro-peace to radical rejectionist. But because virtually every party supports or is linked to aspects of civil society—ranging from Islamist health care groups to leftist women's self-help groups—the long-term prospects for stability triumphing over violence are considered by many to be high.

"People at all levels already have a practical stake in a system," said Mohammed Hallaj, head of the Palestinian Research and Education Center in Washington.

Accordingly, for places such as the former Yugoslav republics, Afghanistan and the embattled Nagorno-Karabakh region of Azerbaijan, experts advocate encouragement of broad-based associations that reach beyond the primordial bonds fueling strife.

"The goal is to have people associate in several groups so no singular source of identity will lead to conflict with a rival. Multiple associations provide different channels for expression, action and support and move people away from parochial or tribal perceptions," said sociologist Menon.

On the other hand, the U.N. report conceded that civil society has limitations. "Building these institutions takes time—and constant renewal if they are not to become instruments for a small elite to manipulate the levers of power," it said.

For instance, religious groups may provide social services and mobilize adherents to participate in politics. Yet the result in some cases—either directly or indirectly—can be to exclude people of other religions.

"Self-interest, prejudice and hatred cohabit with altruism, fairness and compassion," Norton said, "sometimes making unrestrained free play of civil society a chilling thought."

Capitalism
and
Democracy*

Gabriel A. Almond

Gabriel A. Almond, professor of political science emeritus at Stanford University, is a former president of the American Political Science Association.

Joseph Schumpeter, a great economist and social scientist of the last generation, whose career was almost equally divided between Central European and American universities, and who lived close to the crises of the 1930s and '40s, published a book in 1942 under the title, *Capitalism, Socialism, and Democracy*. The book has had great influence, and can be read today with profit. It was written in the aftergloom of the great depression, during the early triumphs of Fascism and Nazism in 1940 and 1941, when the future of capitalism, socialism, and democracy all were in doubt. Schumpeter projected a future of declining capitalism, and rising socialism. He thought that democracy under socialism might be no more impaired and problematic than it was under capitalism.

He wrote a concluding chapter in

*Lecture presented at Seminar on the Market, sponsored by The Ford Foundation and the Research Institute on International Change of Columbia University, Moscow, October 29–November 2.

the second edition which appeared in 1946, and which took into account the political-economic situation at the end of the war, with the Soviet Union then astride a devastated Europe. In this last chapter he argues that we should not identify the future of socialism with that of the Soviet Union, that what we had observed and were observing in the first three decades of Soviet existence was not a necessary expression of socialism. There was a lot of Czarist Russia in the mix. If Schumpeter were writing today, I don't believe he would argue that socialism has a brighter future than capitalism. The relationship between the two has turned out to be a good deal more complex and intertwined than Schumpeter anticipated. But I am sure that he would still urge us to separate the future of socialism from that of Soviet and Eastern European Communism.

Unlike Schumpeter I do not include Socialism in my title, since its future as a distinct ideology and program of action is unclear at best. Western Marxism and the moderate socialist movements seem to have settled for social democratic solutions, for adaptations of both capitalism and democracy producing acceptable mixes of market competition, political pluralism, participation, and welfare. I deal with these modifications

of capitalism, as a consequence of the impact of democracy on capitalism in the last half century.

At the time that Adam Smith wrote *The Wealth of Nations,* the world of government, politics and the state that he knew—pre-Reform Act England, the French government of Louis XV and XVI—was riddled with special privileges, monopolies, interferences with trade. With my tongue only half way in my cheek I believe the discipline of economics may have been traumatized by this condition of political life at its birth. Typically, economists speak of the state and government instrumentally, as a kind of secondary service mechanism.

I do not believe that politics can be treated in this purely instrumental and reductive way without losing our analytic grip on the social and historical process. The economy and the polity are the main problem solving mechanisms of human society. They each have their distinctive means, and they each have their "goods" or ends. They necessarily interact with each other, and transform each other in the process. Democracy in particular generates goals and programs. You cannot give people the suffrage, and let them form organizations, run for office, and the like, without their developing all kinds of ideas as to

From *PS: Political Science and Politics,* September 1991, pp. 467–474. © 1991 by The American Political Science Association. Reprinted by permission.

how to improve things. And sometimes some of these ideas are adopted, implemented and are productive, and improve our lives, although many economists are reluctant to concede this much to the state.

My lecture deals with this interaction of politics and economics in the Western World in the course of the last couple of centuries, in the era during which capitalism and democracy emerged as the dominant problem solving institutions of modern civilization. I am going to discuss some of the theoretical and empirical literature dealing with the themes of the positive and negative interaction between capitalism and democracy. There are those who say that capitalism supports democracy, and those who say that capitalism subverts democracy. And there are those who say that democracy subverts capitalism, and those who say that it supports it.

The relation between capitalism and democracy dominates the political theory of the last two centuries. All the logically possible points of view are represented in a rich literature. It is this ambivalence and dialectic, this tension between the two major problem solving sectors of modern society—the political and the economic—that is the topic of my lecture.

Capitalism Supports Democracy

Let me begin with the argument that capitalism is positively linked with democracy, shares its values and culture, and facilitates its development. This case has been made in historical, logical, and statistical terms.

Albert Hirschman in his *Rival Views of Market Society* (1986) examines the values, manners and morals of capitalism, and their effects on the larger society and culture as these have been described by the philosophers of the 17th, 18th, and 19th centuries. He shows how the interpretation of the impact of capitalism has changed from the enlightenment view of Montesquieu, Condorcet, Adam Smith and others, who stressed the *douceur* of commerce, its "gentling," civilizing effect

on behavior and interpersonal relations, to that of the 19th and 20th century conservative and radical writers who described the culture of capitalism as crassly materialistic, destructively competitive, corrosive of morality, and hence self-destructive. This sharp almost 180-degree shift in point of view among political theorists is partly explained by the transformation from the commerce and small-scale industry of early capitalism, to the smoke blackened industrial districts, the demonic and exploitive entrepreneurs, and exploited laboring classes of the second half of the nineteenth century. Unfortunately for our purposes, Hirschman doesn't deal explicitly with the capitalism–democracy connection, but rather with culture and with manners. His argument, however, implies an early positive connection and a later negative one.

Joseph Schumpeter in *Capitalism, Socialism, and Democracy* (1942) states flatly, "History clearly confirms . . . [that] . . . modern democracy rose along with capitalism, and in causal connection with it . . . modern democracy is a product of the capitalist process." He has a whole chapter entitled "The Civilization of Capitalism," democracy being a part of that civilization. Schumpeter also makes the point that democracy was historically supportive of capitalism. He states, ". . . the bourgeoisie reshaped, and from its own point of view rationalized, the social and political structure that preceded its ascendancy. . ." (that is to say, feudalism). "The democratic method was the political tool of that reconstruction." According to Schumpeter capitalism and democracy were mutually causal historically, mutually supportive parts of a rising modern civilization, although as we shall show below, he also recognized their antagonisms.

Barrington Moore's historical investigation (1966) with its long title, *The Social Origins of Dictatorship and Democracy; Lord and Peasant in the Making of the Modern World,* argues that there have been three historical routes to industrial modernization. The first of these followed by Britain, France, and the United States, involved the subordination and transformation of the

agricultural sector by the rising commercial bourgeoisie, producing the democratic capitalism of the 19th and 20th centuries. The second route followed by Germany and Japan, where the landed aristocracy was able

---

The relation between capitalism and democracy dominates the political theory of the last two centuries.

---

to contain and dominate the rising commercial classes, produced an authoritarian and fascist version of industrial modernization, a system of capitalism encased in a feudal authoritarian framework, dominated by a military aristocracy, and an authoritarian monarchy. The third route, followed in Russia where the commercial bourgeoisie was too weak to give content and direction to the modernizing process, took the form of a revolutionary process drawing on the frustration and resources of the peasantry, and created a mobilized authoritarian Communist regime along with a state-controlled industrialized economy. Successful capitalism dominating and transforming the rural agricultural sector, according to Barrington Moore, is the creator and sustainer of the emerging democracies of the nineteenth century.

Robert A. Dahl, the leading American democratic theorist, in the new edition of his book (1990) *After the Revolution? Authority in a Good Society,* has included a new chapter entitled "Democracy and Markets." In the opening paragraph of that chapter, he says:

> It is an historical fact that modern democratic institutions . . . have existed only in countries with predominantly privately owned, market-oriented economies, or capitalism if you prefer that name. It is also a fact that all "socialist" countries with predominantly state-owned centrally directed economic orders—command economies—have not enjoyed democratic governments, but have in fact been ruled by authoritarian dictatorships. It is also an historical fact that

some "capitalist" countries have also been, and are, ruled by authoritarian dictatorships.

To put it more formally, it looks to be the case that market-oriented economies are necessary (in the logical sense) to democratic institutions, though they are certainly not sufficient. And it looks to be the case that state-owned centrally directed economic orders are strictly associated with authoritarian regimes, though authoritarianism definitely does not require them. We have something very much like an historical experiment, so it would appear, that leaves these conclusions in no great doubt. (Dahl 1990)

Peter Berger in his book *The Capitalist Revolution* (1986) presents four propositions on the relations between capitalism and democracy:

Capitalism is a necessary but not sufficient condition of democracy under modern conditions.

If a capitalist economy is subjected to increasing degrees of state control, a point (not precisely specifiable at this time) will be reached at which democratic governance becomes impossible.

If a socialist economy is opened up to increasing degrees of market forces, a point (not precisely specifiable at this time) will be reached at which democratic governance becomes a possibility.

If capitalist development is successful in generating economic growth from which a sizable proportion of the population benefits, pressures toward democracy are likely to appear.

This positive relationship between capitalism and democracy has also been sustained by statistical studies. The "Social Mobilization" theorists of the 1950s and 1960s which included Daniel Lerner (1958), Karl Deutsch (1961), S. M. Lipset (1959) among others, demonstrated a strong statistical association between GNP per capita and democratic political institutions. This is more than simple statistical association. There is a logic in the relation between level of economic development and democratic institutions. Level of economic development has been shown to be associated with education and literacy, exposure to mass media, and democratic psychological propensities such as subjective efficacy, participatory

aspirations and skills. In a major investigation of the social psychology of industrialization and modernization, a research team led by the sociologist Alex Inkeles (1974) interviewed several thousand workers in the modern industrial and the traditional economic sectors of six countries of differing culture. Inkeles found empathetic, efficacious, participatory and activist propensities much more frequently among the modern industrial workers, and to a much lesser extent in the traditional sector in each one of these countries regardless of cultural differences.

The historical, the logical, and the statistical evidence for this positive relation between capitalism and democracy is quite persuasive.

Capitalism Subverts Democracy

But the opposite case is also made, that capitalism subverts or undermines democracy. Already in John Stuart Mill (1848) we encounter a view of existing systems of private property as unjust, and of the free market as destructively competitive—aesthetically and morally repugnant. The case he was making was a normative rather than a political one. He wanted a less competitive society, ultimately socialist, which would still respect individuality. He advocated limitations on the inheritance of property and the improvement of the property system so that everyone shared in its benefits, the limitation of population growth, and the improvement of the quality of the labor force through the provision of high quality education for all by the state. On the eve of the emergence of the modern democratic capitalist order John Stuart Mill wanted to control the excesses of both the market economy and the majoritarian polity, by the education of consumers and producers, citizens and politicians, in the interest of producing morally improved free market and democratic orders. But in contrast to Marx, he did not thoroughly discount the possibilities of improving the capitalist and democratic order.

Marx argued that as long as capitalism and private property existed there could be no genuine democracy, that democracy under capitalism was bourgeois democracy,

which is to say not democracy at all. While it would be in the interest of the working classes to enter a coalition with the bourgeoisie in supporting this form of democracy in order

There is a logic in the relation between level of economic development and democratic institutions.

to eliminate feudalism, this would be a tactical maneuver. Capitalist democracy could only result in the increasing exploitation of the working classes. Only the elimination of capitalism and private property could result in the emancipation of the working classes and the attainment of true democracy. Once socialism was attained the basic political problems of humanity would have been solved through the elimination of classes. Under socialism there would be no distinctive democratic organization, no need for institutions to resolve conflicts, since there would be no conflicts. There is not much democratic or political theory to be found in Marx's writings. The basic reality is the mode of economic production and the consequent class structure from which other institutions follow.

For the followers of Marx up to the present day there continues to be a negative tension between capitalism, however reformed, and democracy. But the integral Marxist and Leninist rejection of the possibility of an autonomous, bourgeois democratic state has been left behind for most Western Marxists. In the thinking of Poulantzas, Offe, Bobbio, Habermas and others, the bourgeois democratic state is now viewed as a class struggle state, rather than an unambiguously bourgeois state. The working class has access to it; it can struggle for its interests, and can attain partial benefits from it. The state is now viewed as autonomous, or as relatively autonomous, and it can be reformed in a progressive direction by working class and other popular movements. The bourgeois democratic state can be moved in the direction of a socialist state by political action short of violence and institutional destruction.

Schumpeter (1942) appreciated the tension between capitalism and democracy. While he saw a causal connection between competition in the economic and the political order, he points out ". . . that there are some deviations from the principle of democracy which link up with the presence of organized capitalist interests. . . . [T]he statement is true both from the standpoint of the classical and from the standpoint of our own theory of democracy. From the first standpoint, the result reads that the means at the disposal of private interests are often used in order to thwart the will of the people. From the second standpoint, the result reads that those private means are often used in order to interfere with the working of the mechanism of competitive leadership." He refers to some countries and situations in which ". . . political life all but resolved itself into a struggle of pressure groups and in many cases practices that failed to conform to the spirit of the democratic method." But he rejects the notion that there cannot be political democracy in a capitalist society. For Schumpeter full democracy in the sense of the informed participation of all adults in the selection of political leaders and consequently the making of public policy, was an impossibility because of the number and complexity of the issues confronting modern electorates. The democracy which was realistically possible was one in which people could choose among competing leaders, and consequently exercise some direction over political decisions. This kind of democracy was possible in a capitalist society, though some of its propensities impaired its performance. Writing in the early years of World War II, when the future of democracy and of capitalism were uncertain, he leaves unresolved the questions of ". . . Whether or not democracy is one of those products of capitalism which are to die out with it. . ." or ". . . how well or ill capitalist society qualifies for the task of working the democratic method it evolved."

Non-Marxist political theorists

have contributed to this questioning of the reconcilability of capitalism and democracy. Robert A. Dahl, who makes the point that capitalism historically has been a necessary precondition of democracy, views contemporary democracy in the United States as seriously compromised, impaired by the inequality in resources among the citizens. But Dahl stresses the variety in distributive patterns, and in politico-economic relations among contemporary democracies. "The category of capitalist democracies" he writes, "includes an extraordinary variety . . . from nineteenth century, laissez faire, early industrial systems to twentieth century, highly regulated, social welfare, late or postindustrial systems. Even late twentieth century 'welfare state' orders vary all the way from the Scandinavian systems, which are redistributive, heavily taxed, comprehensive in their social security, and neocorporatist in their collective bargaining arrangements to the faintly redistributive, moderately taxed, limited social security, weak collective bargaining systems of the United States and Japan" (1989).

In *Democracy and Its Critics* (1989) Dahl argues that the normative growth of democracy to what he calls its "third transformation" (the first being the direct city-state democracy of classic times, and the second, the indirect, representative inegalitarian democracy of the contemporary world) will require democratization of the economic order. In other words, modern corporate capitalism needs to be transformed. Since government control and/or ownership of the economy would be destructive of the pluralism which is an essential requirement of democracy, his preferred solution to the problem of the mega-corporation is employee control of corporate industry. An economy so organized, according to Dahl, would improve the distribution of political resources without at the same time destroying the pluralism which democratic competition requires. To those who question the realism of Dahl's solution to the problem of inequality, he replies that history is full of surprises.

Charles E. Lindblom in his book, *Politics and Markets* (1977), concludes his comparative analysis of the

political economy of modern capitalism and socialism, with an essentially pessimistic conclusion about contemporary market-oriented democracy. He says

> We therefore come back to the corporation. It is possible that the rise of the corporation has offset or more than offset the decline of class as an instrument of indoctrination. . . . That it creates a new core of wealth and power for a newly constructed upper class, as well as an overpowering loud voice, is also reasonably clear. The executive of the large corporation is, on many counts, the contemporary counterpart to the landed gentry of an earlier era, his voice amplified by the technology of mass communication. . . . [T]he major institutional barrier to fuller democracy may therefore be the autonomy of the private corporation.

Lindblom concludes, "The large private corporation fits oddly into democratic theory and vision. Indeed it does not fit."

There is then a widely shared agreement, from the Marxists and neo-Marxists, to Schumpeter, Dahl, Lindblom, and other liberal political theorists, that modern capitalism with the dominance of the large corporation, produces a defective or an impaired form of democracy.

Democracy Subverts Capitalism

If we change our perspective now and look at the way democracy is said to affect capitalism, one of the dominant traditions of economics from Adam Smith until the present day stresses the importance for productivity and welfare of an economy that is relatively free of intervention by the state. In this doctrine of minimal government there is still a place for a framework of rules and services essential to the productive and efficient performance of the economy. In part the government has to protect the market from itself. Left to their own devices, according to Smith, businessmen were prone to corner the market in order to exact the highest possible price. And according to Smith businessmen were prone to bribe public officials in order to gain special privileges, and legal monopolies. For Smith good capitalism was competitive capitalism, and good government provided just those goods and services which the market needed to flourish, could not itself provide, or would not provide. A good government according to Adam Smith was a minimal government, providing for the national defense, and domestic order. Particularly important for the economy were the rules pertaining to commercial life such as the regulation of weights and measures, setting and enforcing building standards, providing for the protection of persons and property, and the like.

For Milton Friedman (1961, 1981), the leading contemporary advocate of the free market and free government, and of the interdependence of the two, the principal threat to the survival of capitalism and democracy is the assumption of the responsibility for welfare on the part of the modern democratic state. He lays down a set of functions appropriate to government in the positive inter-

---

. . . one of the dominant traditions of economics from Adam Smith until the present day stresses the importance for productivity and welfare of an economy that is relatively free of intervention by the state.

---

play between economy and polity, and then enumerates many of the ways in which the modern welfare, regulatory state has deviated from these criteria.

A good Friedmanesque, democratic government would be one ". . . which maintained law and order, defended property rights, served as a means whereby we could modify property rights and other rules of the economic game, adjudicated disputes about the interpretation of the rules, enforced contracts, promoted competition, provided a monetary framework, engaged in activities to counter technical monopolies and to overcome neighborhood

effects widely regarded as sufficiently important to justify government intervention, and which supplemented private charity and the private family in protecting the irresponsible, whether madman or child. . . ." Against this list of proper activities for a free government, Friedman pinpointed more than a dozen activities of contemporary democratic governments which might better be performed through the private sector, or not at all. These included setting and maintaining price supports, tariffs, import and export quotas and controls, rents, interest rates, wage rates, and the like, regulating industries and banking, radio and television, licensing professions and occupations, providing social security and medical care programs, providing public housing, national parks, guaranteeing mortgages, and much else.

Friedman concludes that this steady encroachment on the private sector has been slowly but surely converting our free government and market system into a collective monster, compromising both freedom and productivity in the outcome. The tax and expenditure revolts and regulatory rebellions of the 1980s have temporarily stemmed this trend, but the threat continues. "It is the internal threat coming from men of good intentions and good will who wish to reform us. Impatient with the slowness of persuasion and example to achieve the great social changes they envision, they are anxious to use the power of the state to achieve their ends, and confident of their own ability to do so." The threat to political and economic freedom, according to Milton Friedman and others who argue the same position, arises out of democratic politics. It may only be defeated by political action.

In the last decades a school, or rather several schools, of economists and political scientists have turned the theoretical models of economics to use in analyzing political processes. Variously called public choice theorists, rational choice theorists, or positive political theorists, and employing such models as market exchange and bargaining, rational self interest, game theory, and the like, these theorists have produced a substantial literature throwing new and often controversial light on dem-

ocratic political phenomena such as elections, decisions of political party leaders, interest group behavior, legislative and committee decisions, bureaucratic, and judicial behavior, lobbying activity, and substantive public policy areas such as constitutional arrangements, health and environment policy, regulatory policy, national security and foreign policy, and the like. Hardly a field of politics and public policy has been left untouched by this inventive and productive group of scholars.

The institutions and names with which this movement is associated in the United States include Virginia State University, the University of Virginia, the George Mason University, the University of Rochester, the University of Chicago, the California Institute of Technology, the Carnegie Mellon University, among others. And the most prominent names are those of the leaders of the two principal schools: James Buchanan, the Nobel Laureate leader of the Virginia "Public Choice" school, and William Riker, the leader of the Rochester "Positive Theory" school. Other prominent scholars associated with this work are Gary Becker of the University of Chicago, Kenneth Shepsle and Morris Fiorina of Harvard, John Ferejohn of Stanford, Charles Plott of the California Institute of Technology, and many others.

One writer summarizing the ideological bent of much of this work, but by no means all of it (William Mitchell of the University of Washington), describes it as fiscally conservative, sharing a conviction that the ". . . private economy is far more robust, efficient, and perhaps, equitable than other economies, and much more successful than political processes in efficiently allocating resources. . . ." Much of what has been produced ". . . by James Buchanan and the leaders of this school can best be described as contributions to a theory of the failure of political processes." These failures of political performance are said to be inherent properties of the democratic political process. "Inequity, inefficiency, and coercion are the most general results of democratic policy formation." In a democracy the demand for publicly provided services seems to be insatiable. It ultimately turns into a special interest, "rent seeking" society. Their remedies take the form of proposed constitutional limits on spending power and checks and balances to limit legislative majorities.

One of the most visible products of this pessimistic economic analysis of democratic politics is the book by Mancur Olson, *The Rise and Decline of Nations* (1982). He makes a strong argument for the negative democracy–capitalism connection. His thesis is that the behavior of individuals and firms in stable societies inevitably leads to the formation of dense networks of collusive, cartelistic, and lobbying organizations that make economies less efficient and dynamic and polities less governable. "The longer a society goes without an upheaval, the more powerful such organizations become and the more they slow down economic expansion. Societies in which these narrow interest groups have been destroyed, by war or revolution, for example, enjoy the greatest gains in growth." His prize cases are Britain on the one hand and Germany and Japan on the other.

> The logic of the argument implies that countries that have had democratic freedom of organization without upheaval or invasion the longest will suffer the most from growth-repressing organizations and combinations. This helps explain why Great Britain, the major nation with the longest immunity from dictatorship, invasion, and revolution, has had in this century a lower rate of growth than other large, developed democracies. Britain has precisely the powerful network of special interest organization that the argument developed here would lead us to expect in a country with its record of military security and democratic stability. The number and power of its trade unions need no description. The venerability and power of its professional associations is also striking. . . . In short, with age British society has acquired so many strong organizations and collusions that it suffers from an institutional sclerosis that slows its adaptation to changing circumstances and technologies. (Olson 1982)

By contrast, post-World War II Germany and Japan started organizationally from scratch. The organizations that led them to defeat were all

dissolved, and under the occupation inclusive organizations like the general trade union movement and general organizations of the industrial and commercial community were first formed. These inclusive organizations had more regard for the general national interest and exercised some discipline on the narrower interest organizations. And both countries in the post-war decades experienced "miracles" of economic growth under democratic conditions.

The Olson theory of the subversion of capitalism through the propensities of democratic societies to foster special interest groups has not gone without challenge. There can be little question that there is logic in his argument. But empirical research testing this pressure group hypothesis thus far has produced mixed findings. Olson has hopes that a public educated to the harmful consequences of special interests to economic growth, full employment, coherent government, equal opportunity, and social mobility will resist special interest behavior, and enact legislation imposing anti-trust, and anti-monopoly controls to mitigate and contain these threats. It is somewhat of an irony that the solution to this special interest disease of democracy, according to Olson, is a democratic state with sufficient regulatory authority to control the growth of special interest organizations.

Democracy Fosters Capitalism

My fourth theme, democracy as fostering and sustaining capitalism, is not as straightforward as the first three. Historically there can be little doubt that as the suffrage was extended in the last century, and as mass political parties developed, democratic development impinged significantly on capitalist institutions and practices. Since successful capitalism requires risk-taking entrepreneurs with access to investment capital, the democratic propensity for redistributive and regulative policy tends to reduce the incentives and the resources available for risk-taking and creativity. Thus it can be argued that propensities inevitably resulting from democratic politics, as Friedman, Olson and many others argue, tend to reduce productivity, and hence welfare.

But precisely the opposite argument can be made on the basis of the historical experience of literally all of the advanced capitalist democracies in existence. All of them without exception are now welfare states with some form and degree of social insurance, health and welfare nets, and regulatory frameworks designed to mitigate the harmful impacts and shortfalls of capitalism. Indeed, the welfare state is accepted all across the political spectrum. Controversy takes place around the edges. One might make the argument that had capitalism not been modified in this welfare direction, it is doubtful that it would have survived.

This history of the interplay between democracy and capitalism is clearly laid out in a major study involving European and American scholars, entitled *The Development of Welfare States in Western Europe and America* (Flora and Heidenheimer 1981). The book lays out the relationship between the development and spread of capitalist industry, democratization in the sense of an expanding suffrage and the emergence of trade unions and left-wing political parties, and the gradual introduction of the institutions and practices of the welfare state. The early adoption of the institutions of the welfare state in Bismarck Germany, Sweden, and Great Britain were all associated with the rise of trade unions and socialist parties in those countries. The decisions made by the upper and middle class leaders and political movements to introduce welfare measures such as accident, old age, and unemployment insurance, were strategic decisions. They were increasingly confronted by trade union movements with the capacity of bringing industrial production to a halt, and by political parties with growing parliamentary representation favoring fundamental modifications in, or the abolition of capitalism. As the calculations of the upper and middle class leaders led them to conclude that the costs of suppression exceeded the costs of concession, the various parts of the welfare state began to be put in place—accident, sickness, unemployment insurance, old age insurance, and the like. The problem of maintaining the loyalty of the working classes through two world wars resulted in additional concessions to working class demands: the filling out of the social security system, free public education to higher levels, family allowances, housing benefits, and the like.

Social conditions, historical factors, political processes and decisions produced different versions of the welfare state. In the United States, manhood suffrage came quite early, the later bargaining process emphasized free land and free education to the secondary level, an equality of opportunity version of the welfare state. The Disraeli bargain in Britain resulted in relatively early manhood suffrage and the full attainment of parliamentary government, while the Lloyd George bargain on the eve of World War I brought the beginnings of a welfare system to Britain. The Bismarck bargain in Germany produced an early welfare state, a postponement of electoral equality and parliamentary government. While there were all of these differences in historical encounters with democratization and "welfarization," the important outcome was that little more than a century after the process began all of the advanced capitalist democracies had similar versions of the welfare state, smaller in scale in the case of the United States and Japan, more substantial in Britain and the continental European countries.

We can consequently make out a strong case for the argument that democracy has been supportive of capitalism in this strategic sense. Without this welfare adaptation it is doubtful that capitalism would have survived, or rather, its survival, "unwelfarized," would have required a substantial repressive apparatus. The choice then would seem to have been between democratic welfare capitalism, and repressive undemocratic capitalism. I am inclined to believe that capitalism as such thrives more with the democratic welfare adaptation than with the repressive one. It is in that sense that we can argue that there is a clear positive impact of democracy on capitalism.

* * *

We have to recognize, in conclusion, that democracy and capitalism are both positively and negatively related, that they both support and subvert each other. My colleague, Moses Abramovitz, described this dialectic more surely than most in his presidential address to the American Economic Association in 1980, on the eve of the "Reagan Revolution." Noting the decline in productivity in the American economy during the latter 1960s and '70s, and recognizing that this decline might in part be attributable to the "tax, transfer, and regulatory" tendencies of the welfare state, he observes,

> The rationale supporting the development of our mixed economy sees it as a pragmatic compromise between the competing virtues and defects of decentralized market capitalism and encompassing socialism. Its goal is to obtain a measure of distributive justice, security, and social guidance of economic life without losing too much of the allocative efficiency and dynamism of private enterprise and market organization. And it is a pragmatic compromise in another sense. It seeks to retain for most people that measure of personal protection from the state which private property and a private job market confer, while obtaining for the disadvantaged minority of people through the state that measure of support without which their lack of property or personal endowment would amount to a denial of individual freedom and capacity to function as full members of the community. (Abramovitz, 1981)

Democratic welfare capitalism produces that reconciliation of opposing and complementary elements which makes possible the survival, even enhancement of both of these sets of institutions. It is not a static accommodation, but rather one which fluctuates over time, with capitalism being compromised by the tax-transfer-regulatory action of the state at one point, and then correcting in the direction of the reduction of the intervention of the state at another point, and with a learning process over time that may reduce the amplitude of the curves.

The case for this resolution of the capitalism-democracy quandary is made quite movingly by Jacob Viner who is quoted in the concluding paragraph of Abramovitz's paper, ". . . If . . . I nevertheless conclude that I believe that the welfare state, like old Siwash, is really worth fighting for and even dying for as compared to any rival system, it is because, despite its imperfection in theory and practice, in the aggregate it provides more promise of preserving and enlarging human freedoms, temporal prosperity, the extinction of mass misery, and the dignity of man and his moral improvement than any other social system which has previously prevailed, which prevails elsewhere today or which outside Utopia, the mind of man has been able to provide a blueprint for" (Abramovitz, 1981).

References

Abramovitz, Moses. 1981. "Welfare Quandaries and Productivity Concerns." *American Economic Review,* March.

Berger, Peter. 1986. *The Capitalist Revolution.* New York: Basic Books.

Dahl, Robert A. 1989. *Democracy and Its Critics.* New Haven: Yale University Press.

_____. 1990. *After the Revolution: Authority in a Good Society.* New Haven: Yale University Press.

Deutsch, Karl. 1961. "Social Mobilization and Political Development." *American Political Science Review,* 55 (Sept.).

Flora, Peter, and Arnold Heidenheimer. 1981. *The Development of Welfare States in Western Europe and America.* New Brunswick, NJ: Transaction Press.

Friedman, Milton. 1981. *Capitalism and Freedom.* Chicago: University of Chicago Press.

Hirschman, Albert. 1986. *Rival Views of Market Society.* New York: Viking.

Inkeles, Alex, and David Smith. 1974. *Becoming Modern: Individual Change in Six Developing Countries.* Cambridge, MA: Harvard University Press.

Lerner, Daniel. *The Passing of Traditional Society.* New York: Free Press.

Lindblom, Charles E. 1977. *Politics and Markets.* New York: Basic Books.

Lipset, Seymour M. 1959. "Some Social Requisites of Democracy." *American Political Science Review,* 53 (September).

Mill, John Stuart. 1848, 1965. *Principles of Political Economy,* 2 vols. Toronto: University of Toronto Press.

Mitchell, William. 1988. "Virginia, Rochester, and Bloomington: Twenty-Five Years of Public Choice and Political Science." *Public Choice,* 56: 101-119.

Moore, Barrington. 1966. *The Social Origins of Dictatorship and Democracy.* New York: Beacon Press.

Olson, Mancur. 1982. *The Rise and Decline of Nations.* New Haven: Yale University Press.

Schumpeter, Joseph. 1946. *Capitalism, Socialism, and Democracy.* New York: Harper.

The New Tribalism: Ethnic Strife Owes More to Present Than to History

Defending Human Rights in an Age of Ethnic Conflict

Robin Wright

Times Staff Writer

In Georgia, little Abkhazia and South Ossetia both seek secession, while Kurds want to carve a state out of Turkey. French Quebec edges toward separation from Canada, as deaths in Kashmir's Muslim insurgency against Hindu-dominated India pass the 6,000-mark. Kazakhstan's tongue-twisting face-off pits ethnic Kazakhs against Russian Cossacks, while Scots in Britain, Tutsis in Rwanda, Basques and Catalans in Spain and Tuaregs in Mali and Niger all seek varying degrees of self-rule or statehood.

The world's now dizzying array of ethnic hot spots—at least four dozen at last count—starkly illustrates how, of all the features of the post–Cold War world, the most consistently troubling are turning out to be the tribal hatreds that divide humankind by race, faith and nationality.

"The explosion of communal violence is the paramount issue facing the human rights movement today. And containing the abuses committed in the name of ethnic or religious groups will be our foremost challenge for years to come," said Kenneth Ross, acting executive director of Human Rights Watch, a global monitoring group based in New York.

Indeed, xenophobia, religious rivalry and general intolerance of anything different are often now more anguishing and cruel—not to mention costly in human lives and material destruction—than the ideological differences that until recently divided the world.

The reversion to some of the oldest organizational principles of humankind reflects an attraction seemingly more potent than the prevalent 20th-Century principle of assimilation either by choice or by force—concepts such as the U.S. "melting pot" or communism's "dictatorship of the proletariat."

Why is ethnicity so powerful? And why now, at the end of the 20th Century, in defiance of so much that the period has stood for?

Since Communist doctrine began unraveling in 1989, conventional wisdom has linked the psychology and politics of hatred to the end of totalitarian rule that repressed ancient rivalries.

Today's clashes between Serbs and Bosnian Muslims, for example, date back centuries to political and cultural hostility between the Ottoman and Austro-Hungarian empires. In Sudan, Africa's largest state, the war pitting Christian and animist black Africans in the south against the Arab Muslim north has roots in the 19th Century—even before the birth of the modern state.

"To a large extent, history is catching up with us. Most ethnic conflicts have a background of domination, injustice or oppression by one ethnic group or another," explained John Garang, the U.S.-educated chairman and guerrilla commander of the Sudan People's Liberation Movement in the south.

"In our case in the Sudan, it goes back centuries to the slave trade. The northern Sudanese were the slave traders selling people from the south," he said in an interview.

Yet the proliferation of hatreds is not simply history's legacy to the Post-Modern Era, a cruel trick that has made old differences seemingly emerge out of thin air after disappearing for decades. History provides only the context.

"Ethnicity is not enduring and unstinting; it's shaped and given form. And what we take to be historic and ancient is often modern and recent," said Augustus Richard Norton, a political scientist at the U.S. Military Academy at West Point.

The passions have instead been produced by a confluence of diverse factors, ranging from modernization and migration to democratization and limited resources, according to specialists. They flourish on fear and uncertainty.

FACTOR 1: MIGRATION

The most basic cause stems from the Modern Era, which opened the way for cultural standardization and mass migration, the latter capped in the 20th Century by the largest movement of humankind in history.

On the eve of the 21st Century, fewer than 10% of the world's 191 nations are still ethnically or racially homogeneous.

The impact of global migrations and intermixing is reflected in a stark fact: Depending on definition, there are now between 7,000 and 8,000 linguistic, ethnic or religious minorities in the world, according to Alan Phillips, director of Minority Rights Group, a human rights monitoring organization based in London. In fact, virtually every ethnic group has a minority branch living somewhere outside its own borders.

The sheer magnitude of migrations in an ever more crowded world makes clashes and conflict virtually unavoidable.

The amalgamation of the world's peoples has already resulted in a host of otherwise unlikely skirmishes—between descendants of Africans and Koreans in white-dominated Los Angeles, or between Asian Indians and blacks in South Africa ruled by descendants of Dutch and British settlers.

Ethnic and religious tensions have also risen due to anxieties that minority cultures will be eliminated—a not unjustified fear. In the 19th Century, South America boasted 1,000 Indian languages; in the late 20th, there are fewer than 200, according to the U.N. Development Program's 1993 Human Development Report, released last month.

Courtesy of communications and technology, modernization is also standardizing everything from dress to music, while industrialization and Westernization have challenged traditional skills and arts, especially in developing countries.

Even in Communist Tashkent, Islamic Tehran and island-nations like Taiwan, oral folklore is increasingly being replaced by Arnold Schwarzenegger videos, ethnic music by Madonna and Metallica tapes.

"The forces of modernization have given many people a sense that they don't belong anywhere, or that there's nothing permanent or stable in their lives," explained Allen Kassof, director of the Project on Ethnic Relations in Princeton, N.J.

"It's quite understandable that they then seek something that seems eternal and can't be taken away from them. One is membership in a group. Another is a belief system or religion."

Some cultures are already minorities in their own lands: Native Fijians are outnumbered by descendants of indentured Indian workers. Kazakhs are only 40% of Kazakhstan, about equal to descendants of Russian settlers in the large former Soviet republic. And throughout North and South America, Indian populations have dwindled to small percentages of the total.

"Cultures need to be respected and constantly asserted or they die. Hence the determination of many groups, particularly indigenous peoples, to participate actively to preserve and reassert their identity," the U.N. Development Program report added.

The proliferation of minorities in the 20th Century—and the consciousness accompanying it—has effectively created a new set of incentives for conflict. "The conflicts of the future are likely to be between people rather than states over issues related to culture, ethnicity or reli-gion," Mahbub ul Haq, a special U.N. Development Program adviser and former Pakistani minister of finance and planning, said in an interview.

FACTOR 2: POWER QUEST

The second factor is the deliberate manipulation of longstanding fears and passions by contemporary governments.

"[The year] 1992 has made clear that the roots of most of these conflicts lie less in eternal antagonisms than in particular governmental abuses that exacerbate communal tensions," according to Human Rights Watch's 1993 World Report.

In a variation of the old divide-and-rule tactic, a growing number of regimes have recently tried to build followings by exploiting ethnic, religious and other differences.

President Samuel K. Doe's heavy-handedness against all Liberian tribes except his own Krahn people and President Mohamed Siad Barre's manipulation of Somalia's diverse clans sparked two of Africa's nastiest civil wars. Both nations have since imploded.

In Sri Lanka, an estimated 20,000 have been killed and more than 1.5 million displaced since 1990 in a contemporary conflict sparked by age-old discrimination by predominantly Buddhist Sinhalese against minority Hindu Tamils.

Other governments claim that ethnic separatist or independence movements have forced responses that violate human rights.

On the grounds of fighting secessionists, the Indian government justifies torture, abductions and murder of Kashmiri Muslims and Punjabi Sikhs, and the Turkish government excuses abuses in handling minority Kurds, reports Human Rights Watch.

At the core of both tactics is a new breed of ethno-politicians "who see their future power base as lying in leading ethnic communities. They appeal to the basest human instinct by portraying a group as threatened from outside," Kassof said.

Among the most blatant examples have been former Communist leaders in Eastern Europe and the former Soviet republics—such as Serbian President Slobodan Milosevic and Uzbekistan President Islam Karimov—who are both trying to sustain their own careers by making fear and hate primary tools of politics.

In Sudan, Garang charged that civil war erupted largely because Hassan Turabi, the power behind Khartoum's government, wanted to impose Sharia, or Islamic law, throughout Sudan.

"Contemporary leaders use the accumulated historical animosity for their own political and economic gains. Turabi uses it to promote his Islamic agenda, which we consider a threat to our way of life and a violation of our human rights," he said. "And when those conditions reach a level of intolerance, then people go to war."

The rising ethnic tension over minority Hungarians in Romania, Slovakia and the rump Yugoslav nation—mostly remnants of the old Austro-Hungarian empire—is also less linked to the demise of communism than to post-Communist leaders who are exploiting the issue.

"The hatred is new, but it's built around traditional differences that, but for nationalist appeals of opportunistic leaders, would not have been transformed into hostility or warfare," explained Ross.

FACTOR 3: INSECURITY

The third major factor is related to ideology—both the current wave of democratization worldwide and the lack of alternatives.

Transitions to democracy, for example, can create uncertainty that fuels ethnic and religious passions, and eventually rivalries. "The problem is not democracy *per se,* but the turbulent transition to democracy," said Jack Snyder, a Columbia University political scientist.

As the former East Germans and Russians, South Africans and Jordanians have learned painfully, even political shock therapy does not produce overhauls overnight. Along the way, reforming governments have faced increasing unemployment, inflation, crime waves, public disillusionment and even resistance.

In South Africa, much of the black-on-black violence, now bloodier than black-white clashes during decades of apartheid, is a product of changing times. Zulus particularly have been reluctant to surrender their legendary identity, and the tacit power that went with it, in a new multiracial state.

"The tremendous psychological pressure on human populations from political change creates a sense of anxiety that frequently makes people seek refuge in belief systems that involve definitions of membership and belonging," Kassof said.

HUMAN RIGHTS HEROES
THE UNSUNG

RAJA SHEHADEH
Israeli-occupied territories
Shehadeh is a British-trained lawyer who co-founded Al Haq (Arabic for fairness, right, justice, law or truth), a Palestinian human rights organization that has gained an international reputation for its annual reports on human rights abuses in the occupied West Bank and Gaza Strip. Shehadeh is the author of "The Third Way," a widely read account of life under occupation.

"Peace can only come about after justice."

DR. BEKO RANSOME-KUTI
Nigeria
Ransome-Kuti is president of the Committee for the Defense of Human Rights, a Lagos-based organization founded in 1989, and chairman of the Campaign for Democracy, a coalition of human rights, student and labor groups formed in 1991 to pressure the military government to restore democracy to the country. He has been jailed numerous times for his pro-democracy activities. Nigeria's military rulers are scheduled to hand over power to a civilian government in August, but many Nigerians doubt the transition will take place.

"Our nation may be heading for an upheaval of unpredictable, but potentially calamitous, proportions."

WEI JINSHENG
China
Wei gained recognition during the Democracy Wall movement in the late 1970s with his vocal criticisms of the government. He launched Exploration, a magazine that published essays challenging the Beijing regime to move toward democracy. He was arrested in 1979 and sentenced to 15 years in prison for spreading "counterrevolutionary propaganda." He disappeared for more than a decade into China's secretive prison system until Asia Watch, a U.S.-based human rights organization, revealed in March of this year that he was being held at a labor camp near the Bo Hai Gulf.

"What is true democracy? It means the right of the people to choose their own representatives [who will] work according to their will and in their interests."

Ironically, the absence of an alternative to democracy also encourages ethnic and religious passions.

"Inter-communal strife is a product of the discrediting of alternative ideologies. The idea of Western democracy, while appealing to many, lacks an antithesis to those who do not want to adopt it was a way of life," Ross added. "So people fall back on their primordial identities, like religion and ethnicity, when there is no alternative available."

The most visible case is the explosion of political Islam in places like Algeria and Egypt. But as Islamists redefine identities and agendas, Algeria's ethnic Berbers and Egypt's Coptic Christians sense new threats—and are acting accordingly.

FACTOR 4: LIMITED RESOURCES

The final factor relates to resources and economics. At the simplest level, the struggle to survive can spawn or deepen ethnic or religious hatreds.

"The more limited the resources, the greater the danger of ethnic strife," said Garang. In Sudan, the multilayered hostility between northerners and southerners, Arabs and Africans, Muslims and Christians has been exacerbated by a hostile desert environment and the chronic recent cycle of drought and famine.

For a range of reasons not necessarily bad or intentionally devisive, ethnic groups are also often positioned differently in an economy. Again, change can accentuate differences, triggering hostility or drastic action.

Czechoslovakia was a prime example. Czechs were better positioned, due to their skills and economic activities in their republic, for radical market reforms. But the same plan hurt the Slovaks, because their economy centered on once-profitable but now outdated military and heavy industries difficult to adapt to free market conditions or the new European Community markets.

"This created very different incentives for the two republics and contributed significantly to Czechoslovakia's breakup," Snyder said.

For all the dangers unleashed by ethnicity, however, scholars and analysts all counsel against condemning or trying to block ethnic expression. "It's misguided to attack the politics of ethnicity as opposed to the intolerance of many ethnic politicians," Snyder warned.

"It's perfectly appropriate, for example, for black leaders to organize politically or to define their interests collectively along black lines, because neither suggests an intolerance of alternative ways of life or other races. It's their right."

Many also contend that there is no way to stop or reverse ethnicity. "Our tendencies toward separatism and tribalism seem to reflect something very deep in the human condition, which scholarship confirms," Kassof said.

Yet some hold out eventual hope that ethnicity will be less divisive. "At the end of the day, we will eventually have one human community," said Garang. "But that is still a long time away."

A Debate on Cultural Conflicts

The Coming Clash of Civilizations—Or, the West Against the Rest

Samuel P. Huntington

Samuel P. Huntington is professor of government and director of the Olin Institute for Strategic Studies at Harvard. This article is adapted from the lead essay in the summer issue of Foreign Affairs.

World politics is entering a new phase in which the fundamental source of conflict will be neither ideological or economic. The great divisions among mankind and the dominating source of conflict will be cultural. The principal conflicts of global politics will occur between nations and groups of different civilizations. The clash of civilizations will dominate global politics.

During the cold war, the world was divided into the first, second and third worlds. Those divisions are no longer relevant. It is far more meaningful to group countries not in terms of their political or economic systems or their level of economic development but in terms of their culture and civilization.

A civilization is the highest cultural grouping of people and the broadest level of cultural identity people have short of that which distinguishes humans from other species.

Civilizations obviously blend and overlap and may include sub-civilizations. Western civilization has two major variants, European and North American, and Islam has its Arab, Turkic and Malay subdivisions. But while the lines between them are seldom sharp, civilizations are real. They rise and fall; they divide and merge. And as any student of history knows, civilizations disappear.

Westerners tend to think of nation-states as the principal actors in global affairs. They have been that for only a few centuries. The broader reaches of history have been the history of civilizations. It is to this pattern that the world returns.

Global conflict will be cultural.

Civilization identity will be increasingly important and the world will be shaped in large measure by the interactions among seven or eight major civilizations. These include the Western, Confucian, Japanese, Islamic, Hindu, Slavic-Orthodox, Latin American and possibly African civilizations.

The most important and bloody conflicts will occur along the borders separating these cultures. The fault lines between civilizations will be the battle lines of the future.

Why? First, differences among civilizations are basic, involving history, language, culture, tradition and, most importantly, religion. Different civilizations have different views on the relations between God and man, the citizen and the state, parents and children, liberty and authority, equality and hierarchy. These differences are the product of centuries. They will not soon disappear.

Second, the world is becoming smaller. The interactions between peoples of different civilizations are increasing. These interactions intensify civilization consciousness: awareness of differences between civilizations and commonalities within civilizations. For example, Americans react far more negatively to Japanese investment than to larger investments from Canada and European countries.

Third, economic and social changes are separating people from longstanding local identities. In much of the world, religion has moved in to fill this gap, often in the form of movements labeled fundamentalist.

h movements are found in Western Christianity, Judaism, Buddhism, Hinduism and Islam. The "unsecularization of the world," . . . George Weigel has remarked, "is one of the dominant social facts of life in the late 20th century."

Fourth, the growth of civilization consciousness is enhanced by the fact that at the moment that the West is at the peak of its power a return-to-the-roots phenomenon is occurring among non-Western civilizations—the "Asianization" in Japan, the end of the Nehru legacy and the "Hinduization" of India, the failure of Western ideas of socialism and nationalism and, hence, the "re-Islamization" of the Middle East, and now a debate over Westernization versus Russianization in Boris Yeltsin's country.

More importantly, the efforts of the West to promote its values of democracy and liberalism as universal values, to maintain its military predominance and to advance its economic interests engender countering responses from other civilizations.

The central axis of world politics is likely to be the conflict between "the West and the rest" and the responses of non-Western civilizations to Western power and values. The most prominent example of anti-Western cooperation is the connection between Confucian and Islamic states that are challenging Western values and power.

Fifth, cultural characteristics and differences are less mutable and hence less easily compromised and resolved than political and economic ones. In the former Soviet Union, Communists can become democrats, the rich can become poor and the poor rich, but Russians cannot become Estonians. A person can be half-French and half-Arab and even a citizen of two countries. It is more difficult to be half Catholic and half Muslim.

Finally, economic regionalism is increasing. Successful economic regionalism will reinforce civilization consciousness. On the other hand, economic regionalism may succeed only when it is rooted in common

civilization. The European Community rests on the shared foundation of European culture and Western Christianity. Japan, in contrast, faces difficulties in creating a comparable economic entity in East Asia because it is a society and civilization unique to itself.

As the ideological division of Europe has disappeared, the cultural division of Europe between Western Christianity and Orthodox Christianity and Islam has re-emerged. Conflict along the fault line between Western and Islamic civilizations has been going on for 1,300 years. This centuries-old military interaction is unlikely to decline. Historically, the other great antagonistic interaction of Arab Islamic civilization has been with the pagan, animist and now, increasingly, Christian black peoples to the south. On the northern border of Islam, conflict has increasingly erupted between Orthodox and Muslim peoples, including the carnage of Bosnia and Sarajevo, the simmering violence between Serbs and Albanians, the tenuous relations between Bulgarians and their Turkish minority, the violence between Ossetians and Ingush, the unremitting slaughter of each other by Armenians and Azeris and the tense relations between Russians and Muslims in Central Asia.

The historic clash between Muslims and Hindus in the Subcontinent manifests itself not only in the rivalry between Pakistan and India but also in intensifying religious strife in India between increasingly militant Hindu groups and the substantial Muslim minority.

Groups or states belonging to one civilization that become involved in war with people from a different civilization naturally try to rally support from other members of their own civilization. Decreasingly able to mobilize support and form coalitions on the basis of ideology, governments and groups will increasingly attempt to mobilize support by appealing to common religion and civilization identity. As the

conflicts in the Persian Gulf, the Caucasus and Bosnia continued, the positions of nations and the cleavages between them increasingly were along civilizational lines. Populist politicians, religious leaders and the media have found it a potent means of arousing mass support and of pressuring hesitant governments. In the coming years, the local conflicts most likely to escalate into major wars will be those, as in Bosnia and the Caucasus, along the fault lines between civilizations. The next world war, if there is one, will be a war between civilizations.

Only Japan is non-Western and modern.

If these hypotheses are plausible, it is necessary to consider their implications for Western policy. These implications should be divided between short-term advantage and long-term accommodation. In the short term, it is clearly in the interest of the West to promote greater cooperation and unity in its own civilization, particularly between its European and North American components; to incorporate into the West those societies in Eastern Europe and Latin America whose cultures are close to those of the West; to maintain close relations with Russia and Japan; to support in other civilizations groups sympathetic to Western values and interests; and to strengthen international institutions that reflect and legitimate Western interests and values. The West must also limit the expansion of the military strength of potentially hostile civilizations, principally Confucian and Islamic civilizations, and exploit differences and conflicts among Confucian and Islamic states. This will require a moderation in the reduction of Western military capabilities, and, in particular, the maintenance of American military superiority in East and Southwest Asia.

In the longer term, other measures would be called for. Western civilization is modern. Non-Western civilizations have attempted to become modern without becoming Western. To date, only Japan has fully succeeded in this quest. Non-Western civilizations will continue to attempt to acquire the wealth, technology, skills, machines and weapons that are part of being modern. They will attempt to reconcile this modernity with their traditional culture and values. Their economic and military strength relative to the West will increase.

Hence, the West will increasingly have to accommodate to these non-Western modern civilizations, whose power approaches that of the West but whose values and interests differ significantly from those of the West. This will require the West to develop a much more profound understanding of the basic religious and philosophical assumptions underlying other civilizations and the ways in which people in those civilizations see their interests. It will require an effort to identify elements of commonality among Western and other civilizations. For the relevant future, there will be no universal civilization but instead a world of different civilizations, each of which will have to learn to co-exist with others.

Global debate on a controversial thesis

A Clash Between Civilizations —or Within Them?

Süddeutsche Zeitung

■ *A recent essay by Harvard professor Samuel P. Huntington in "Foreign Affairs" magazine—"The Clash of Civilizations?"—has attracted a good deal of attention not only in the U.S. but abroad, as well. Huntington is attempting to establish a new model for examining the post-cold-war world, a central theme around which events will turn, as the ideological clash of the cold war governed the past 40 years. He finds it in cultures. "Faith and family, blood and belief," he has written, "are what people identify with and what they will fight and die for." But in the following article, Josef Joffe, foreign-affairs specialist at the independent "Süddeutsche Zeitung" of Munich, argues that "kultur-kampf"—cultural warfare—is not a primary threat to world security. And in a more radical view, Malaysian political scientist Chandra Muzaffar writes for the Third World Network Features agency of Penang, Malaysia, that Western dominance—economic and otherwise—continues to be the overriding factor in world politics.*

A ghost is walking in the West: cultural warfare, total and international. Scarcely had we banished the 40-year-long cold war to history's shelves, scarcely had we begun to deal with the seductive phrase "the end of history," when violence broke out on all sides. But this time it was not nations that were behind the savagery but peoples and ethnic groups, religions and races—from the Serbs and Bosnians in the Balkans to the Tiv and Jukun in Nigeria.

Working from such observations, one of the best brains in America, Harvard professor Samuel Huntington, produced a prophecy, perhaps even a philosophy of history. His essay "The Clash of Civilizations?" has caused a furor. For centuries, it was the nations that made history; then, in the 20th century, it was the totalitarian ideologies. Today, at the threshold of the 21st century, "the clash of civilizations will dominate global politics." No longer will "Which side are you on?" be the fateful question but "What are you?" Identity will no longer be defined by passport or party membership card but by faith and history, language and customs—culture, in short. Huntington argues that "conflicts between cultures" will push the old disputes between nations and off center stage. Or put more apocalyptically: next world war, if there is one, will be a war between civilizations."

Between which? Huntington has made a list of more than half a dozen civilizations, including the West (the U.S. plus Europe), the Slavic-Orthodox, the Islamic, the Confucian (China), the Japanese, and the Hindu. At first glance, he seems to be right. Are not Catholic Croats fighting Orthodox Serbs—and both of them opposing Muslim Bosnians? And recently, the ruthless struggle between the Hindus and Muslims of India has re-erupted. Even such a darling of the West as King Hussein of Jordan announced during the Persian Gulf war: "This is a war against all Arabs and all Muslims and not against Iraq alone." The long trade conflict pitting Japan against the United States (and against Europe) has been called a "war"—and not only by the chauvinists. Russian Orthodox nationalists see themselves in a two-front struggle: against the Islamic Turkic peoples in the south and the soulless modernists of the West. And even worse: The future could mean "the West against the rest."

But this first look is deceptive; after a closer look, the apocalypse dissolves, to be replaced by a more complex tableau. This second look shows us a world that is neither new nor simple. First of all, conflicts between civilizations are as old as history itself. Look at the struggle of the Jews against Rome in the first century, or the revolt of the Greeks against the Turks in the 19th century. The Occident and Orient have been in conflict, off and on, for the last 1,300 years. Second, the disputes with China, Japan, or North Korea are not really nourished by conflicts among civilizations. They are the results of palpable national interests at work. Third, if we look only at the conflicts between cultures, we will miss the more important truth: Within each camp, divisions and rivalries are far more significant than unifying forces.

The idea of cultural war seems to work best when we examine Islam. The demonization of the West is a part of the standard rhetoric of Islamic fundamentalists. The Arab-Islamic world is one of the major sources of terrorism, and most armed conflicts since World War II have involved Western states against Muslim countries. But if we look more closely, the Islamic monolith fractures into many pieces that cannot be reassembled. There is the history of internecine conflicts, coups, and rebellions: a 15-year-long civil war of each against all in Lebanon (not simply Muslims against Maronite Christians), the Palestine Liberation Organization against Jordan, and Syria against the PLO. Then consider the wars among states in the Arab world: Egypt versus Yemen, Syria against Jordan, Egypt versus Libya, and finally Iraq versus Kuwait. Then the wars of ideologies and finally, the religiously tinted struggles for dominance within the faith—between Sunnis and Shiites, Iraq and Iran.

But most important: What does the term "Islam" really mean? What does a Malay Muslim have in common with a Bosnian? Or an Indonesian with a Saudi? And what are we to understand by "fundamentalism"? The Saudi variety is passive and inward-looking, while the expansive Iranian variety arouses fear. It is true that, from Gaza to Giza, fundamentalists are shedding innocent blood. But most of the Arab world sided with the West during the Gulf war. And, beyond this, only 10 percent of the trade of the Middle East takes place within the region; most of it flows westward. Economic interdependence, a good index of a common civilization, is virtually nonexistent in the Islamic world.

The real issue is not a cultural war but actually another twofold problem. Several Islamic nations are importing too many weapons, and some are exporting too many people. The first demands containment and denial, calling for continued military strength and readiness in the West. And what of the "human exports"? They are not just a product of the Islamic world but of the entire poor and overpopulated world—no matter what culture they are part of. Along with the spread of nuclear weapons and missiles, this is the major challenge of the coming century, because massive migrations of people will inevitably bring cultural, territorial, and political struggles in their wake. No one has an answer to this. But a narrow vision produced by the "West-against-the-rest" notion is surely the worst way to look for answers.

—*Josef Joffe*

The West's Hidden Agenda

Third World Network
FEATURES

Like Francis Fukuyama's essay "The End of History?" published in 1989, Samuel Huntington's "The Clash of Civilizations?" has received a lot of publicity in the mainstream Western media. The reason is not difficult to fathom. Both articles serve U.S. and Western foreign-policy goals. Huntington's thesis is simple enough: "The clash of civilizations will dominate global politics. The fault lines between civilizations will be the battle lines of the future."

The truth, however, is that cultural, religious, or other civilizational differences are only some of the many factors responsible for conflict. Territory and resources, wealth and property, power and status, and individual personalities and group interests are others. Indeed, religion, culture, and other elements and symbols of what Huntington would regard as "civilization identity" are sometimes manipulated to camouflage the naked pursuit of wealth or power—the real source of many conflicts.

 Reprinted with permission from *World Press Review*, February 1994, pp. 25-26. Originally from *Third World Network Features*.

But the problem is even more serious. By overplaying the "clash of civilizations" dimension, Huntington has ignored the creative, constructive interaction and engagement between civilizations. This is a much more constant feature of civilization than conflict per se. Islam, for instance, through centuries of exchange with the West, laid the foundation for the growth of mathematics, science, medicine, agriculture, industry, and architecture in medieval Europe. Today, some of the leading ideas and institutions that have gained currency within the Muslim world, whether in politics or in economics, are imports from the West.

That different civilizations are not inherently prone to conflict is borne out by another salient feature that Huntington fails to highlight. Civilizations embody many similar values and ideals. At the philosophical level at least, Buddhism, Christianity, Hinduism, Islam, Judaism, Sikhism, and Taoism, among other world religions, share certain common perspectives on the relationship between the human being and his environment, the integrity of the community, the importance of the family, the significance of moral leadership, and, indeed, the meaning and purpose of life. Civilizations, however different in certain respects, are quite capable of forging common interests and aspirations. For example, the Association of Southeast Asian Nations encompasses at least four "civilization identities," to use Huntington's term—Buddhist (Thailand), Confucian (Singapore), Christian (the Philippines), and Muslim (Brunei, Indonesia, and Malaysia). Yet it has been able to evolve an identity of its own through 25 years of trials.

It is U.S. and Western dominance, not the clash of civilizations, that is at the root of global conflict. By magnifying the so-called clash of civilizations, Huntington tries to divert attention from Western dominance and control even as he strives to preserve, protect, and perpetuate that dominance. He sees a compelling reason for embarking on this mission. Western dominance is under threat from a "Confucian-Islamic connection that has emerged to challenge Western interests, values, and power," he writes. This is the most mischievous—and most dangerous—implication of his "clash of civilizations."

By evoking this fear of a Confucian-Islamic connection, he hopes to persuade the Western public, buffeted by unemployment and recession, to acquiesce to huge military budgets in the post-cold-war era. He argues that China and some Islamic nations are acquiring weapons on a massive scale. Generally, it is the Islamic states that are buying weapons from China, which in turn "is rapidly increasing its military spending." Huntington observes that "a Confucian-Islamic military connection has thus come into being, designed to promote acquisition by its members of the weapons and weapons technologies needed to counter the military power of the West." This is why the West, and the U.S. in particular, should not, in Huntington's view, be "reducing its own military capabilities."

There are serious flaws in this argument. One, it is not true that the U.S. has reduced its military capability; in fact, it has enhanced its range of sophisticated weaponry. Two, though China is an important producer and exporter of arms, it is the only major power whose military expenditures consistently declined throughout the 1980s. Three, most Muslim countries buy their weapons not from China but from the U.S. Four, China has failed to endorse the Muslim position on many global issues. Therefore, the Confucian-Islamic connection is a myth propagated to justify increased U.S. military spending.

It is conceivable that Huntington has chosen to target the Confucian and Islamic civilizations for reasons that are not explicitly stated in his article. Like many other Western academics, commentators, and policy analysts, Huntington, it appears, is also concerned about the economic ascendancy of so-called Confucian communities such as China, Hong Kong, Taiwan, Singapore, and overseas Chinese communities in other Asian countries. He is of the view that "if cultural commonality is a prerequisite for economic integration, the principal East Asian economic bloc of the future is likely to be centered on China." The dynamism and future potential of these "Confucian" economies have already set alarm bells ringing in various Western capitals. Huntington's warning to the West about the threat that China poses should be seen in that context—as yet another attempt to curb the rise of yet another non-Western economic competitor.

> **"U.S. and Western dominance is at the root of global conflict."**

As far as the "Islamic threat" is concerned, it is something that Huntington and his kind have no difficulty selling in the West. Antagonism toward Islam and Muslims is deeply embedded in the psyche of mainstream Western society. The rise of Islamic movements has provoked a new, powerful wave of negative emotions against the religion and its practitioners. Most Western academics and journalists, in concert with Western policy makers, grant no legitimacy to the Muslim resistance to Western domination and control. When Huntington says, "Islam has bloody borders," the implication is that Islam and Muslims are responsible for the spilling of blood. Yet anyone who has an elementary knowledge of many current conflicts will readily admit that, more often than not, it is the Muslims who have been bullied, bludgeoned, and butchered.

The truth, however, means very little to Huntington. The title of his article "The Clash of Civilizations?" is quoted from [British educator] Bernard Lewis's "The Roots of Muslim Rage," an essay that depicts the Islamic resurgence as an irrational threat to Western heritage. Both Huntington and Lewis are "Islam baiters" whose role is to camouflage the suffering of and the injustice done to the victims of U.S. and Western domination by concocting theories about the conflict of cultures and the clash of civilizations. Huntington's "The Clash of Civilizations?" will not conceal the real nature of the conflict: The victims—or at least some of them—know the truth.

—*Chandra Muzaffar*

Jihad vs. McWorld

The two axial principles of our age—tribalism and globalism—clash at every point except one: they may both be threatening to democracy

Benjamin R. Barber

Benjamin R. Barber is the Whitman Professor of Political Science at Rutgers University. Barber's most recent books are Strong Democracy *(1984),* The Conquest of Politics *(1988), and* An Aristocracy of Everyone.

Just beyond the horizon of current events lie two possible political figures—both bleak, neither democratic. The first is a retribalization of large swaths of humankind by war and bloodshed: a threatened Lebanonization of national states in which culture is pitted against culture, people against people, tribe against tribe—a Jihad in the name of a hundred narrowly conceived faiths against every kind of interdependence, every kind of artificial social cooperation and civic mutuality. The second is being borne in on us by the onrush of economic and ecological forces that demand integration and uniformity and that mesmerize the world with fast music, fast computers, and fast food—with MTV, Macintosh, and McDonald's, pressing nations into one commercially homogenous global network: one McWorld tied together by technology, ecology, communications, and commerce. The planet is falling precipitantly apart and coming reluctantly together at the very same moment.

These two tendencies are sometimes visible in the same countries at the same instant: thus Yugoslavia, clamoring just recently to join the New Europe, is exploding into fragments; India is trying to live up to its reputation as the world's largest integral democracy while powerful new fundamentalist parties like the Hindu nationalist Bharatiya Janata Party, along with nationalist assassins, are im-

periling its hard-won unity. States are breaking up or joining up: the Soviet Union has disappeared almost overnight, its parts forming new unions with one another or with like-minded nationalities in neighboring states. The old interwar national state based on territory and political sovereignty looks to be a mere transitional development.

The tendencies of what I am here calling the forces of Jihad and the forces of McWorld operate with equal strength in opposite directions, the one driven by parochial hatreds, the other by universalizing markets, the one re-creating ancient subnational and ethnic borders from within, the other making national borders porous from without. They have one thing in common: neither offers much hope to citizens looking for practical ways to govern themselves democratically. If the global future is to put Jihad's centrifugal whirlwind against McWorld's centripetal black hole, the outcome is unlikely to be democratic—or so I will argue.

MCWORLD, OR THE GLOBALIZATION OF POLITICS

Four imperatives make up the dynamic of McWorld: a market imperative, a resource imperative, an information-technology imperative, and an ecological imperative. By shrinking the world and diminishing the salience of national borders, these imperatives have in combination achieved a considerable victory over factiousness and particularism, and not least of all over their most virulent traditional form—nationalism. It is the realists who are now Europeans, the utopians who dream nostalgically of a resurgent England or Germany, perhaps even a resurgent Wales or Saxony. Yesterday's

wishful cry for one world has yielded to the reality of McWorld.

The market imperative. Marxist and Leninist theories of imperialism assumed that the quest for ever-expanding markets would in time compel nation-based capitalist economies to push against national boundaries in search of an international economic imperium. Whatever else has happened to the scientist predictions of Marxism, in this domain they have proved farsighted. All national economies are now vulnerable to the inroads of larger, transnational markets within which trade is free, currencies are convertible, access to banking is open, and contracts are enforceable under law. In Europe, Asia, Africa, the South Pacific, and the Americas such markets are eroding national sovereignty and giving rise to entities—international banks, trade associations, transnational lobbies like OPEC and Greenpeace, world news services like CNN and the BBC, and multinational corporations that increasingly lack a meaningful national identity—that neither reflect nor respect nationhood as an organizing or regulative principle.

The market imperative has also reinforced the quest for international peace and stability, requisites of an efficient international economy. Markets are enemies of parochialism, isolation, fractiousness, war. Market psychology attenuates the psychology of ideological and religious cleavages and assumes a concord among producers and consumers—categories that ill fit narrowly conceived national or religious cultures. Shopping has little tolerance for blue laws, whether dictated by pub-closing British paternalism, Sabbath-observing Jewish Orthodox fundamentalism, or no-Sunday-liquor-sales Massachusetts puritanism. In the context of common markets, international law ceases to be a vision of justice and be-

 From *The Atlantic*, March 1992, pp. 53-55, 58-63. © 1992 by Benjamin R. Barber. Reprinted by permission of the author.

comes a workaday framework for getting things done—enforcing contracts, ensuring that governments abide by deals, regulating trade and currency relations, and so forth.

Common markets demand a common language, as well as a common currency, and they produce common behaviors of the kind bred by cosmopolitan city life everywhere. Commercial pilots, computer programmers, international bankers, media specialists, oil riggers, entertainment celebrities, ecology experts, demographers, accountants, professors, athletes—these compose a new breed of men and women for whom religion, culture, and nationality can seem only marginal elements in a working identity. Although sociologists of everyday life will no doubt continue to distinguish a Japanese from an American mode, shopping has a common signature throughout the world. Cynics might even say that some of the recent revolutions in Eastern Europe have had as their true goal not liberty and the right to vote but well-paying jobs and the right to shop (although the vote is proving easier to acquire than consumer goods). The market imperative is, then, plenty powerful; but, notwithstanding some of the claims made for "democratic capitalism," it is not identical with the democratic imperative.

The resource imperative. Democrats once dreamed of societies whose political autonomy rested firmly on economic independence. The Athenians idealized what they called autarky, and tried for a while to create a way of life simple and austere enough to make the polis genuinely self-sufficient. To be free meant to be independent of any other community or polis. Not even the Athenians were able to achieve autarky, however: human nature, it turns out, is dependency. By the time of Pericles, Athenian politics was inextricably bound up with a flowering empire held together by naval power and commerce—an empire that, even as it appeared to enhance Athenian might, ate away at Athenian independence and autarky. Master and slave, it turned out, were bound together by mutual insufficiency.

The dream of autarky briefly engrossed nineteenth-century America as well, for the underpopulated, endlessly bountiful land, the cornucopia of natural resources, and the natural barriers of a continent walled in by two great seas led many to believe that America could be a world unto itself. Given this past, it has been harder for Americans than for most to accept the inevitability of interdependence. But the rapid depletion of resources even in a country like ours, where they once seemed inexhaustible, and the maldistribution of arable soil and mineral resources on the planet, leave even the wealthiest societies ever more resource-dependent and many other nations in permanently desperate straits.

Every nation, it turns out, needs something another nation has; some nations have almost nothing they need.

The information-technology imperative. Enlightenment science and the technologies derived from it are inherently universalizing. They entail a quest for descriptive principles of general application, a search for universal solutions to particular problems, and an unswerving embrace of objectivity and impartiality.

Scientific progress embodies and depends on open communication, a common discourse rooted in rationality, collaboration, and an easy and regular flow and exchange of information. Such ideals can be hypocritical covers for power-mongering by elites, and they may be shown to be wanting in many other ways, but they are entailed by the very idea of science and they make science and globalization practical allies.

Business, banking, and commerce all depend on information flow and are facilitated by new communication technologies. The hardware of these technologies tends to be systemic and integrated—computer, television, cable, satellite, laser, fiber-optic, and microchip technologies combining to create a vast interactive communications and information network that can potentially give every person on earth access to every other person, and make every datum, every byte, available to every set of eyes. If the automobile was, as George Ball once said (when he gave his blessing to a Fiat factory in the Soviet Union during the Cold War), "an ideology on four wheels," then electronic telecommunication and information systems are an ideology at 186,000 miles per second—which makes for a very small planet in a very big hurry. Individual cultures speak particular languages; commerce and science increasingly speak English; the whole world speaks logarithms and binary mathematics.

Moreover, the pursuit of science and technology asks for, even compels, open societies. Satellite footprints do not respect national borders; telephone wires penetrate the most closed societies. With photocopying and then fax machines having infiltrated Soviet universities and *samizdat* literary circles in the eighties, and computer modems having multiplied like rabbits in communism's bureaucratic warrens thereafter, *glasnost* could not be far behind. In their social requisites, secrecy and science are enemies.

The new technology's software is perhaps even more globalizing than its hardware. The information arm of international commerce's sprawling body reaches out and touches distinct nations and parochial cultures, and gives them a common face chiseled in Hollywood, on Madison Avenue, and in Silicon Valley. Throughout the 1980s one of the most-watched television programs in South Africa was *The Cosby Show.* The demise of apartheid was already in production. Exhibitors at the 1991 Cannes film festival expressed growing anxiety over the "homogenization" and "Americanization" of the global film industry when, for the third year running, American films dominated the awards ceremonies. America has dominated the world's popular culture for much longer, and much more decisively. In November of 1991 Switzerland's once insular culture boasted best-seller lists featuring *Terminator 2* as the No. 1 movie, *Scarlett* as the No. 1 book, and Prince's *Diamonds and Pearls* as the No. 1 record album. No wonder the Japanese are buying Hollywood film studios even faster than Americans are buying Japanese television sets. This kind of software supremacy may in the long term be far more important than hardware superiority, because culture has become more potent than armaments. What is the power of the Pentagon compared with Disneyland? Can the Sixth Fleet keep up with CNN? McDonald's in Moscow and Coke in China will do more to create a global culture than military colonization ever could. It is less the goods than the brand names that do the work, for they convey life-style images that alter perception and challenge behavior. They make up the seductive software of McWorld's common (at times much too common) soul.

Yet in all this high-tech commercial world there is nothing that looks particularly democratic. It lends itself to surveillance as well as liberty, to new forms of manipulation and covert control as well as new kinds of participation, to skewed, unjust market outcomes as well as greater productivity. The consumer society and the open society are not quite synonymous. Capitalism and democracy

...elationship, but it is something than a marriage. An efficient free market after all requires that consumers be free to vote their dollars on competing goods, not that citizens be free to vote their values and beliefs on competing political candidates and programs. The free market flourished in junta-run Chile, in military-governed Taiwan and Korea, and, earlier, in a variety of autocratic European empires as well as their colonial possessions.

The ecological imperative. The impact of globalization on ecology is a cliché even to world leaders who ignore it. We know well enough that the German forests can be destroyed by Swiss and Italians driving gas-guzzlers fueled by leaded gas. We also know that the planet can be asphyxiated by greenhouse gases because Brazilian farmers want to be part of the twentieth century and are burning down tropical rain forests to clear a little land to plough, and because Indonesians make a living out of converting their lush jungle into toothpicks for fastidious Japanese diners, upsetting the delicate oxygen balance and in effect puncturing our global lungs. Yet this ecological consciousness has meant not only greater awareness but also greater inequality, as modernized nations try to slam the door behind them, saying to developing nations, "The world cannot afford *your* modernization; ours has wrung it dry!"

Each of the four imperatives just cited is transnational, transideological, and transcultural. Each applies impartially to Catholics, Jews, Muslims, Hindus, and Buddhists; to democrats and totalitarians; to capitalists and socialists. The Enlightenment dream of a universal rational society has to a remarkable degree been realized—but in a form that is commercialized, homogenized, depoliticized, bureaucratized, and, of course, radically incomplete, for the movement toward McWorld is in competition with forces of global breakdown, national dissolution, and centrifugal corruption. These forces, working in the opposite direction, are the essence of what I call Jihad.

JIHAD, OR THE LEBANONIZATION OF THE WORLD

OPEC, the World Bank, the United Nations, the International Red Cross, the multinational corporation . . . there are scores of institutions that reflect globalization. But they often appear as ineffective reactors to the world's real actors: national states and, to an ever greater degree, subnational factions in permanent rebellion against uniformity and integration—even the kind represented by universal law and justice. The headlines feature these players regularly: they are cultures, not countries; parts, not wholes; sects, not religions; rebellious factions and dissenting minorities at war not just with globalism but with the traditional nation-state. Kurds, Basques, Puerto Ricans, Ossetians, East Timoreans, Quebecois, the Catholics of Northern Ireland, Abkhasians, Kurile Islander Japanese, the Zulus of Inkatha, Catalonians, Tamils, and, of course, Palestinians—people without countries, inhabiting nations not their own, seeking smaller worlds within borders that will seal them off from modernity.

A powerful irony is at work here. Nationalism was once a force of integration and unification, a movement aimed at bringing together disparate clans, tribes, and cultural fragments under new, assimilationist flags. But as Ortega y Gasset noted more than sixty years ago, having won its victories, nationalism changed its strategy. In the 1920s, and again today, it is more often a reactionary and divisive force, pulverizing the very nations it once helped cement together. The force that creates nations is "inclusive," Ortega wrote in *The Revolt of the Masses.* "In periods of consolidation, nationalism has a positive value, and is a lofty standard. But in Europe everything is more than consolidated, and nationalism is nothing but a mania. . . ."

This mania has left the post-Cold War world smoldering with hot wars; the international scene is little more unified than it was at the end of the Great War, in Ortega's own time. There were more than thirty wars in progress last year, most of them ethnic, racial, tribal, or religious in character, and the list of unsafe regions doesn't seem to be getting any shorter. Some new world order!

The aim of many of these small-scale wars is to redraw boundaries, to implode states and resecure parochial identities: to escape McWorld's dully insistent imperatives. The mood is that of Jihad: war not as an instrument of policy but as an emblem of identity, an expression of community, an end in itself. Even where there is no shooting war, there is fractiousness, secession, and the quest for ever smaller communities. Add to the list of dangerous countries those at risk: In Switzerland and Spain, Jurassian and Basque separatists still argue the virtues of ancient identities, sometimes in the language of bombs. Hyperdisintegration in the former Soviet Union may well continue unabated—not just a Ukraine independent from the Soviet Union but a Bessarabian Ukraine independent from the Ukrainian republic; not just Russia severed from the defunct union but Tatarstan severed from Russia. Yugoslavia makes even the disunited, ex-Soviet, nonsocialist republics that were once the Soviet Union look integrated, its sectarian fatherlands springing up within factional motherlands like weeds within weeds within weeds. Kurdish independence would threaten the territorial integrity of four Middle Eastern nations. Well before the current cataclysm Soviet Georgia made a claim for autonomy from the Soviet Union, only to be faced with its Ossetians (164,000 in a republic of 5.5 million) demanding their own self-determination within Georgia. The Abkhasian minority in Georgia has followed suit. Even the good will established by Canada's once promising Meech Lake protocols is in danger, with Francophone Quebec again threatening the dissolution of the federation. In South Africa the emergence from apartheid was hardly achieved when friction between Inkatha's Zulus and the African National Congress's tribally identified members threatened to replace Europeans' racism with an indigenous tribal war after thirty years of attempted integration using the colonial language (English) as a unifier, Nigeria is now playing with the idea of linguistic multiculturalism—which could mean the cultural breakup of the nation into hundreds of tribal fragments. Even Saddam Hussein has benefited from the threat of internal Jihad, having used renewed tribal and religious warfare to turn last season's mortal enemies into reluctant allies of an Iraqi nationhood that he nearly destroyed.

The passing of communism has torn away the thin veneer of internationalism (workers of the world unite!) to reveal ethnic prejudices that are not only ugly and deep-seated but increasingly murderous. Europe's old scourge, anti-Semitism, is back with a vengeance, but it is only one of many antagonisms. It appears all too easy to throw the historical gears into reverse and pass from a Communist dictatorship back into a tribal state.

Among the tribes, religion is also a battlefield. ("Jihad" is a rich word whose generic meaning is "struggle"—usually the struggle of the soul to avert evil. Strictly applied to religious war, it is used only in reference to battles where the faith is under assault, or battles against a government that denies the practice of Islam. My use here is rhetorical, but does follow both journalistic practice and history.) Remember the Thirty Years War? Whatever forms of Enlightenment universalism might once have come to grace such historically related forms of monotheism as Judaism, Christianity, and Islam, in many of their modern incarnations they are parochial rather than cosmopolitan, angry rather than loving, proselytizing rather than ecumenical, zealous rather than rationalist, sectarian rather than deistic, ethnocentric rather than universalizing. As a result, like the new forms of hypernationalism, the new expressions of religious fundamentalism are fractious and pulverizing, never integrating. This is religion as the Crusaders knew it: a battle to the death for souls that if not saved will be forever lost.

The atmospherics of Jihad have resulted in a breakdown of civility in the name of identity, of comity in the name of community. International relations have sometimes taken on the aspect of gang war—cultural turf battles featuring tribal factions that were supposed to be sublimated as integral parts of large national, economic, postcolonial, and constitutional entities.

THE DARKENING FUTURE OF DEMOCRACY

These rather melodramatic tableaux vivants do not tell the whole story, however. For all their defects, Jihad and McWorld have their attractions. Yet, to repeat and insist, the attractions are unrelated to democracy. Neither McWorld nor Jihad is remotely democratic in impulse. Neither needs democracy; neither promotes democracy.

McWorld does manage to look pretty seductive in a world obsessed with Jihad. It delivers peace, prosperity, and relative unity—if at the cost of independence, community, and identity (which is generally based on difference). The primary political values required by the global market are order and tranquillity, and freedom—as in the phrases "free trade,"

"free press," and "free love." Human rights are needed to a degree, but not citizenship or participation—and no more social justice and equality than are necessary to promote efficient economic production and consumption. Multinational corporations sometimes seem to prefer doing business with local oligarchs, inasmuch as they can take confidence from dealing with the boss on all crucial matters. Despots who slaughter their own populations are no problem, so long as they leave markets in place and refrain from making war on their neighbors (Saddam Hussein's fatal mistake). In trading partners, predictability is of more value than justice.

The Eastern European revolutions that seemed to arise out of concern for global democratic values quickly deteriorated into a stampede in the general direction of free markets and their ubiquitous, television-promoted shopping malls. East Germany's Neues Forum, that courageous gathering of intellectuals, students, and workers which overturned the Stalinist regime in Berlin in 1989, lasted only six months in Germany's mini-version of McWorld. Then it gave way to money and markets and monopolies from the West. By the time of the first all-German elections, it could scarcely manage to secure three percent of the vote. Elsewhere there is growing evidence that *glasnost* will go and *perestroika*—defined as privatization and an opening of markets to Western bidders—will stay. So understandably anxious are the new rulers of Eastern Europe and whatever entities are forged from the residues of the Soviet Union to gain access to credit and markets and technology—McWorld's flourishing new currencies—that they have shown themselves willing to trade away democratic prospects in pursuit of them: not just old totalitarian ideologies and command-economy production models but some possible indigenous experiments with a third way between capitalism and socialism, such as economic cooperatives and employee stock-ownership plans, both of which have their ardent supporters in the East.

Jihad delivers a different set of virtues: a vibrant local identity, a sense of community, solidarity among kinsmen, neighbors, and countrymen, narrowly conceived. But it also guarantees parochialism and is grounded in exclusion. Solidarity is secured through war against outsiders. And solidarity often means obedience to a hierarchy in governance,

fanaticism in beliefs, and the obliteration of individual selves in the name of the group. Deference to leaders and intolerance toward outsiders (and toward "enemies within") are hallmarks of tribalism—hardly the attitudes required for the cultivation of new democratic women and men capable of governing themselves. Where new democratic experiments have been conducted in retribalizing societies, in both Europe and the Third World, the result has often been anarchy, repression, persecution, and the coming of new, noncommunist forms of very old kinds of despotism. During the past year, Havel's velvet revolution in Czechoslovakia was imperiled by partisans of "Czechland" and of Slovakia as independent entities. India seemed little less rent by Sikh, Hindu, Muslim, and Tamil infighting than it was immediately after the British pulled out, more than forty years ago.

To the extent that either McWorld or Jihad has a *natural* politics, it has turned out to be more of an antipolitics. For McWorld, it is the antipolitics of globalism: bureaucratic, technocratic, and meritocratic, focused (as Marx predicted it would be) on the administration of things—with people, however, among the chief things to be administered. In its politico-economic imperatives McWorld has been guided by laissez-faire market principles that privilege efficiency, productivity, and beneficence at the expense of civic liberty and self-government.

For Jihad, the antipolitics of tribalization has been explicitly antidemocratic: one-party dictatorship, government by military junta, theocratic fundamentalism—often associated with a version of the *Führerprinzip* that empowers an individual to rule on behalf of a people. Even the government of India, struggling for decades to model democracy for a people who will soon number a billion, longs for great leaders; and for every Mahatma Gandhi, Indira Gandhi, or Rajiv Gandhi taken from them by zealous assassins, the Indians appear to seek a replacement who will deliver them from the lengthy travail of their freedom.

THE CONFEDERAL OPTION

How can democracy be secured and spread in a world whose primary tendencies are at best indifferent to it (McWorld) and at worst deeply antithetical to it (Jihad)? My guess is that globalization will eventually vanquish retribalization.

...s of material "civilization" has yet encountered an obstacle it has been unable to thrust aside. Ortega may have grasped in the 1920s a clue to our own future in the coming millennium.

Everyone sees the need of a new principle of life. But as always happens in similar crises—some people attempt to save the situation by an artificial intensification of the very principle which has led to decay. This is the meaning of the "nationalist" outburst of recent years. . . . things have always gone that way. The last flare, the longest; the last sigh, the deepest. On the very eve of their disappearance there is an intensification of frontiers—military and economic.

Jihad may be a last deep sigh before the eternal yawn of McWorld. On the other hand, Ortega was not exactly prescient; his prophecy of peace and internationalism came just before blitzkrieg, world war, and the Holocaust tore the old order to bits. Yet democracy is how we remonstrate with reality, the rebuke our aspirations offer to history. And if retribalization is inhospitable to democracy, there is nonetheless a form of democratic government that can accommodate parochialism and communitarianism, one that can even save them from their defects and make them more tolerant and participatory: decentralized participatory democracy. And if McWorld is indifferent to democracy, there is nonetheless a form of democratic government that suits global markets passably well—representative government in its federal or, better still, confederal variation.

With its concern for accountability, the protection of minorities, and the universal rule of law, a confederalized representative system would serve the political needs of McWorld as well as oligarchic bureaucratism or meritocratic elitism is currently doing. As we are already beginning to see, many nations may survive in the long term only as confederations that afford local regions smaller than "nations" extensive jurisdiction. Recommended reading for democrats of the twenty-first century is not the U.S. Constitution or the French Declaration of Rights of Man and Citizen but the Articles of Confederation, that suddenly pertinent document that stitched together the thirteen American colonies into what then seemed a too loose confederation of

independent states but now appears a new form of political realism, as veterans of Yeltsin's new Russia and the new Europe created at Maastricht will attest.

By the same token, the participatory and direct form of democracy that engages citizens in civic activity and civic judgment and goes well beyond just voting and accountability—the system I have called "strong democracy"—suits the political needs of decentralized communities as well as theocratic and nationalist party dictatorships have done. Local neighborhoods need not be democratic, but they can be. Real democracy has flourished in diminutive settings: the spirit of liberty, Tocqueville said, is local. Participatory democracy, if not naturally apposite to tribalism, has an undeniable attractiveness under conditions of parochialism.

Democracy in any of these variations will, however, continue to be obstructed by the undemocratic and antidemocratic trends toward uniformitarian globalism and intolerant retribalization which I have portrayed here. For democracy to persist in our brave new McWorld, we will have to commit acts of conscious political will—a possibility, but hardly a probability, under these conditions. Political will requires much more than the quick fix of the transfer of institutions. Like technology transfer, institution transfer rests on foolish assumptions about a uniform world of the kind that once fired the imagination of colonial administrators. Spread English justice to the colonies by exporting wigs. Let an East Indian trading company act as the vanguard to Britain's free parliamentary institutions. Today's well-intentioned quick-fixers in the National Endowment for Democracy and the Kennedy School of Government, in the unions and foundations and universities zealously nurturing contacts in Eastern Europe and the Third World, are hoping to democratize by long distance. Post Bulgaria a parliament by first-class mail. Fed Ex the Bill of Rights to Sri Lanka. Cable Cambodia some common law.

Yet Eastern Europe has already demonstrated that importing free political parties, parliaments, and presses cannot establish a democratic civil society; imposing a free market may even have the opposite effect. Democracy grows from the bottom up and cannot be imposed

from the top down. Civil society has to be built from the inside out. The institutional superstructure comes last. Poland may become democratic, but then again it may heed the Pope, and prefer to found its politics on its Catholicism, with uncertain consequences for democracy. Bulgaria may become democratic, but it may prefer tribal war. The former Soviet Union may become a democratic confederation, or it may just grow into an anarchic and weak conglomeration of markets for other nations' goods and services.

Democrats need to seek out indigenous democratic impulses. There is always a desire for self-government, always some expression of participation, accountability, consent, and representation, even in traditional hierarchical societies. These need to be identified, tapped, modified, and incorporated into new democratic practices with an indigenous flavor. The tortoises among the democratizers may ultimately outlive or outpace the hares, for they will have the time and patience to explore conditions along the way, and to adapt their gait to changing circumstances. Tragically, democracy in a hurry often looks something like France in 1794 or China in 1989.

It certainly seems possible that the most attractive democratic ideal in the face of the brutal realities of Jihad and the dull realities of McWorld will be a confederal union of semi-autonomous communities smaller than nation-states, tied together into regional economic associations and markets larger than nation-states—participatory and self-determining in local matters at the bottom, representative and accountable at the top. The nation-state would play a diminished role, and sovereignty would lose some of its political potency. The Green movement adage "Think globally, act locally" would actually come to describe the conduct of politics.

This vision reflects only an ideal, however—one that is not terribly likely to be realized. Freedom, Jean-Jacques Rousseau once wrote, is a food easy to eat but hard to digest. Still, democracy has always played itself out against the odds. And democracy remains both a form of coherence as binding as McWorld and a secular faith potentially as inspiriting as Jihad.

Credits/ Acknowledgments

Cover design by Charles Vitelli

1. Country Overviews
Facing overview—British Tourist Authority photo.

2. Factors in the Political Process
Facing overview—United Nations photo.

3. Europe—West, Center, and East
Facing overview—United Nations photo.

4. The Third World
Facing overview—United Nations photo by T. Chen.

5. Comparative Politics
Facing overview—United Nations photo.

ANNUAL EDITIONS ARTICLE REVIEW FORM

■ NAME: _____ DATE: _____

■ TITLE AND NUMBER OF ARTICLE: _____

■ BRIEFLY STATE THE MAIN IDEA OF THIS ARTICLE: _____

_____

_____

_____

_____

■ LIST THREE IMPORTANT FACTS THAT THE AUTHOR USES TO SUPPORT THE MAIN IDEA:

_____

_____

_____

_____

_____

■ WHAT INFORMATION OR IDEAS DISCUSSED IN THIS ARTICLE ARE ALSO DISCUSSED IN YOUR
TEXTBOOK OR OTHER READING YOU HAVE DONE? LIST THE TEXTBOOK CHAPTERS AND PAGE
NUMBERS:

_____

_____

_____

_____

_____

■ LIST ANY EXAMPLES OF BIAS OR FAULTY REASONING THAT YOU FOUND IN THE ARTICLE:

_____

_____

_____

_____

■ LIST ANY NEW TERMS/CONCEPTS THAT WERE DISCUSSED IN THE ARTICLE AND WRITE A
SHORT DEFINITION:

_____

_____

_____

_____

*Your instructor may require you to use this Annual Editions Article Review Form in any number of ways:
for articles that are assigned, for extra credit, as a tool to assist in developing assigned papers, or simply
for your own reference. Even if it is not required, we encourage you to photocopy and use this page;
you'll find that reflecting on the articles will greatly enhance the information from your text.

ANNUAL EDITIONS:
COMPARATIVE POLITICS 94/95
Article Rating Form

Here is an opportunity for you to have direct input into the next revision of this volume. We would like you to rate each of the 61 articles listed below, using the following scale:

1. **Excellent: should definitely be retained**
2. **Above average: should probably be retained**
3. **Below average: should probably be deleted**
4. **Poor: should definitely be deleted**

Your ratings will play a vital part in the next revision. So please mail this prepaid form to us just as soon as you complete it.
Thanks for your help!

Annual Editions revisions depend on two major opinion sources: one is our Advisory Board, listed in the front of this volume, which works with us in scanning the thousands of articles published in the public press each year; the other is you—the person actually using the book. Please help us and the users of the next edition by completing the prepaid article rating form on this page and returning it to us. Thank you.

Rating	Article	Rating	Article
	1. Europeans Fear That Leaders Are Not Equal to Their Task		34. The Maths of Post-Maastricht Europe
	2. Has the Sun Set on Britain?		35. European Union: Now What?
	3. Britain's Constitutional Question		36. Goodbye to a United Europe?
	4. Should John Major Go?		37. Reinventing the Politics of Europe
	5. Parties in Question		38. Diagnosis: Healthier in Europe
	6. An Ireland Undivided?		39. Europe's Recession Prompts New Look at Welfare Costs
	7. The Invisible Wall		40. And Now the Hard Part
	8. The Dark Winter of Helmut Kohl		41. Nationalism Redux: Through the Glass of the Post-Communist States Darkly
	9. Germany and Its European Environment		42. Looking at the Past: The Unraveling of the Soviet Union
	10. Germans Turn Their Backs on Politics		
	11. A Long Year in German Politics		43. The Hangover
	12. The "Old" and the "New" Federalism in Germany		44. The Russian Elections: Weimar on the Volga
	13. The French Funk		45. The Road to Ruin
	14. France: The Right Triumphs		46. Let's Abolish the Third World
	15. Mr. French		47. Mexico's Efforts at 'Salinastroika' Omit Needed Political Reforms
	16. Thoughts on the French Nation Today		
	17. Political Renewal Italian Style		48. The Revolution Continues
	18. The Godmother		49. Africa: Falling Off the Map?
	19. Political Revenge in Italy		50. South African Parliament Adopts New Constitution
	20. Old Sake in New Bottles		
	21. A Prince of Politics Ascends		51. In China, Communist Ideology Is Dead, but Party Shell Lives On
	22. Japan: The End of One-Party Dominance		
	23. The End of Politics		52. The Long March from Mao: China's De-Communization
	24. Identity Crisis on the Left		
	25. Western Europe Is Ending Its Welcome to Immigrants		53. India: Charting a New Course?
			54. Miracles Beyond the Free Market
	26. Frenchwomen Say It's Time to Be 'a Bit Utopian'		55. The Visible Hand: The State and East Asia's Economic Growth
	27. Women, Power, and Politics: The Norwegian Experience		56. A New Era in Democracy: Democracy's Third Wave
	28. We the Peoples: A Checklist for New Constitution Writers		57. The 'Missing Middle' of Democracy
			58. Capitalism and Democracy
	29. What Democracy Is . . . and Is Not		59. The New Tribalism: Ethnic Strife Owes More to Present Than to History
	30. Parliament and Congress: Is the Grass Greener on the Other Side?		
			60. A Debate on Cultural Conflicts
	31. Electoral Reform: Good Government? Fairness? Or Vice Versa. Or Both		61. Jihad vs. McWorld
	32. Presidents and Prime Ministers		
	33. As the World Turns Democratic, Federalism Finds Favor		

(Continued on next page)

OUT YOU

Name_____ Date_____

Are you a teacher? ☐ Or student? ☐

Your School Name _____

Department _____

Address _____

City _____ State _____ Zip _____

School Telephone # _____

YOUR COMMENTS ARE IMPORTANT TO US!

Please fill in the following information:

For which course did you use this book? _____

Did you use a text with this Annual Edition? ☐ yes ☐ no

The title of the text? _____

What are your general reactions to the Annual Editions concept?

Have you read any particular articles recently that you think should be included in the next edition?

Are there any articles you feel should be replaced in the next edition? Why?

Are there other areas that you feel would utilize an Annual Edition?

May we contact you for editorial input?

May we quote you from above?

ANNUAL EDITIONS: COMPARATIVE POLITICS 94/95

BUSINESS REPLY MAIL

First Class   Permit No. 84   Guilford, CT

Postage will be paid by addressee

The Dushkin Publishing Group, Inc.
Sluice Dock
DPG **Guilford, Connecticut 06437**